MIDDLE AGE AND AGING

MIDDLE AGE AND AGING

A Reader in Social Psychology

Edited by BERNICE L. NEUGARTEN

The University of Chicago Press · Chicago and London

The University of Chicago Press, Chicago 60637
The University of Chicago Press, Ltd., London

©1968 by The University of Chicago. All rights reserved
Published 1968. Printed in the United States of America

94 93 92 91 90 89 88 87 86   12 11 10 9 8

ISBN: 0-226-57381-8 (clothbound)
*   0-226-57382-6 (paperbound)*

Library of Congress Catalog Card Number: 68-55150

To the memory of

RAYMOND G. KUHLEN

PREFACE

Increasing numbers of social scientists are focusing attention upon the second half of the life span. In several research centers in the United States, groups of subjects studied since birth are now in their mid-forties, and the developmental psychologists who have been following their progress find themselves studying middle age. Clinical psychologists, whether in hospitals, clinics, or community mental health centers, are spending an increasing proportion of their time with aged clients. Sociologists, as they study new patterns of work and leisure, the effects of increasing numbers of older persons upon the social structure, and the growth of age-segregated communities, are perforce turning attention to the field of aging.

At the same time it is becoming evident also that research in aging is beginning to contribute to the mainstream of the two disciplines. On the part of psychologists, the study of aging is leading to revised theories of personality development and theories of psychological adaptation; and on the part of sociologists, to increased understanding of processes of social accommodation, socialization, and social change.

These are only a few of the reasons that departments of psychology and sociology are inaugurating courses in aging and are increasing their programs of research and research training in this area.

There is presently a dearth of textbook and teaching materials available, a fact that is all too apparent to the instructors in colleges and universities who are organizing new courses in this field. The present volume is an attempt to provide assistance in that regard. It is shaped to a considerable degree by the experience of the editor, who for some fifteen years has been teaching a course in adulthood and old age to graduate students in social sciences at the University of Chicago. When this course was first introduced in the Committee on Human Development in the early 1940's, it represented something of a pioneer effort in an area that is now coming to be called the developmental behavior sciences. In the first years of that curricular effort, the lack of published materials was a major handicap. Today the situation has drastically altered, for a wealth of studies has appeared, many being of considerable sophistication. The problem is now mainly one of organization, for the studies are scattered throughout a wide range of psychological and sociological books and journals. It is hoped that the present book may make easier the tasks of both the student and the instructor who are faced with a rapidly growing literature from which to choose.

Presumably anyone who elects to edit a book of readings regards the problem of selection as formidable. In the present instance the problem has seemed even more difficult because the processes and problems of aging are inherently multidisciplinary. Biological, psychological, social, economic, and political factors are intricately interwoven in influencing the course of aging. The editor has been uncomfortably aware of this fact in narrowing the range of topics to be included.

As is evident from the title, the emphasis in this volume is upon social and psychological processes as individuals move from middle age to old age. The selections represent some of the major topics that lie closest to the question, What social and psychological adaptations are required as individuals move through the second half of their lives? In the attempt to steer a course between breadth and depth of coverage, and as a glance at the contents will indicate, the decision has been made to select relatively few topics, but to include at least five or more papers on each topic. Thus, major attention is given to age status and age-sex roles; to psychological changes in the life cycle; to social-psychological theories of aging; to attitudes toward health; to changing family roles; to work, retirement, and leisure; to certain other dimensions of the immediate social environment such as friendships, neighboring patterns, and living arrangements; to differences in cultural settings; and to perspectives of time and death.

The book makes no pretext, therefore, of presenting a comprehensive or well-rounded view of aging. The most regrettable omission, perhaps, has to do with biology, for it is particularly true of the older person that biological and health factors must be taken into account in understanding psychological and social behavior. Also omitted from this book is any systematic attention to abilities—intelligence, learning, language, psychomotor skills—that whole area which constitutes so large a part of psychology. Neither is there room in this book for studies of particular problem groups or deviant groups —the indigent, the ill, the psychiatrically disabled—except as a particular author may refer to such a group in pointing up a finding or a principle that has relevance for the wider population of "normal" middle-aged and older people.

Because the book is addressed primarily to the graduate student, priority has been given to empirical studies and, wherever possible, to studies in which the research methods are clearly described. At the same time, in the hope of encouraging research in yet unexplored areas, the editor has sometimes passed over an investigation of elegant research design in favor of one that presents an innovative method or a provocative conceptual approach. In this same connection, selections have been made also with the intent of illustrating a relatively wide range of research methods: questionnaires, surveys, depth interviews, projective tests, participant observation, and content analyses of magazine fiction.

Finally, another problem of balance has been kept in mind. Because many readers are likely to be new to the field of aging, at least some of the major issues and points of view in the field need to be presented. Accordingly a number of papers have been included which are not reports of single investigations, but which are discussional or theoretical in nature, or which summarize a set of related issues around a particular research question. The last section of the book includes four papers that pose various problems of research strategy in studying change over time and in generalizing from given samples of middle-aged and older people.

Each section of the book has a brief introduction intended to orient the reader to the major issues being addressed by the respective authors and to indicate the logic of the grouping. All references cited in the book appear in the bibliography at the end. To make the bibliography of maximum value, we have placed in parentheses after each reference the page numbers in this book where that reference has been cited.

I am indebted to Mrs. Elizabeth Garber for her outstanding editorial assistance and to Mrs. Bernice Spivek for her many forms of aid in preparing the manuscript for publication.

BERNICE L. NEUGARTEN

Committee on Human Development
University of Chicago

CONTENTS

PART I

AGE STATUS AND AGE-SEX ROLES

Age is an underlying dimension of social organization, for in all societies the relations between individuals and between groups are regulated by age differences. Thus far, however, little systematic attention has been paid by sociologists or social psychologists to the ways in which age groups relate to each other in modern complex societies, to age-grading, to relations between generations, or to systems of norms which govern age-appropriate behavior. Because the socially regulated system of age status provides a context for studies of the social psychology of aging, a group of six papers dealing with age status and age roles has been placed first in this book.

The first of these papers is an analysis of some of the plural systems of age status that characterize modern American society. It shows how social definitions of age are changing within the family and within our economic, political, and legal systems. The paper includes a brief discussion of the increased delineation of age groups that has occurred in recent decades and the question of whether or not our society is becoming a gerontocracy. This paper provides a background for those that follow and points up some of the research areas that need to be developed in establishing what might be called a sociology of age.

The second paper illustrates how some of the concepts regarding age norms may be elaborated by empirical research. Based upon the questionnaire method, the study indicates something of the consensus that exists regarding age-appropriate behavior in adults; indicates that different age groups perceive more and less age constraint operating in the society; and illustrates some of the differences between

personal attitudes and attitudes ascribed to the generalized other.

The two papers that follow are focused upon another aspect of the age-status system, namely, the delineation of the aged as a special group within the society and the extent to which they may be said to form a subcultural group (in some ways parallel, perhaps, to the so-called adolescent subculture). Two contrasting views are juxtaposed: Rose points to the social and economic forces which are leading to the development of an aging subculture and argues that there is a growing group-consciousness and group-identification among the aged in modern America. Streib, on the other hand, marshals the arguments against the view of the aged either as a minority group or as a separate subcultural group. He argues that the aged are to be seen as a statistical aggregate or a social category, but not as a genuine social or cultural group.

The last two papers move from concepts of social organization to the consideration of specific age-sex roles in adulthood, and in so doing provide a bridge from the sociology to the psychology of aging. These two papers are of interest not only because of their substantive findings, but also because they illustrate research techniques which are useful in dealing with complex data (techniques which have thus far been infrequently utilized by social psychologists).

The paper by Martel is based upon content analyses of magazine fiction that appeared in America from 1890 to 1955. To the extent that such stories are accurate reflections of social reality, the analyses point to some of the historical changes in values and in role perceptions which presumably affect persons who

3

grow old in different social climates and who are socialized to different concepts of appropriate age-sex role behavior.

The paper by Neugarten and Gutmann is based upon the Thematic-Apperception Test and demonstrates how analyses of projective responses may be applied to group data. Middle-aged and older persons are shown to have different perceptions of male-female roles in the family and to perceive a reversal in authority and dominance patterns between the sexes. These differences in perceptions are interpreted by the authors as reflections not only of social reality but of personality differences in the two age groups of respondents. In the latter connection this paper might be read in conjunction with those on personality that constitute Part III of this book.

BERNICE L. NEUGARTEN and JOAN W. MOORE

THE CHANGING AGE-STATUS SYSTEM

In all societies, age is one of the important factors in determining the ways people behave toward each other. Certain biological and social events come to be regarded as significant punctuation marks in the life line and to signify the transition points from one age status to the next. Thus, to take a well-worn example, puberty is regarded in some societies as the event which marks entry into adulthood, and elaborate *rites de passage* mark its importance. In other societies, like our own, puberty carries little significance with regard to age status, and there are no social rituals to mark its occurrence. A second example relates to the end of life. In societies in which biological death is viewed as a transition from the mundane to the sacred level of existence, there are long and elaborate preparations for the event. In societies in which biological demise is viewed as putting an end to the individual, death becomes a taboo subject, to be discussed not even with the aged.

In all societies age-status systems emerge, in which duties, rights, and rewards are differentially distributed to age groups which themselves have been socially defined. In societies where the division of labor is simple and the rate of social change is slow, an all-embracing system becomes formalized; and family, work, religious, and political roles are allocated and regulated accordingly.

A modern complex society, by contrast, is characterized by plural systems of age status that become differentiated in relation to particular social institutions. These age-status systems make use of the common index of chronological age, but they vary in the extent to which they are explicit and formal. Age-grading in a typical American school, for example, is much more formal than in the typical American family. Social age definitions may be inconsistent from one institution to the next, as in the case when the male is defined as "adult" at eighteen and is eligible for military service, and when the female is "adult" at eighteen and may marry without the consent of parents; but when neither is "adult" enough to vote until 21.

As the American society has changed from the agrarian to the industrialized, from small town to metropolis, so also have there been changes in the social definitions of age groups, in age norms, and in relations between age groups in the society.

A comprehensive analysis of social change in regard to age patterns lies outside the scope of this paper, but in the sections to follow we have chosen illustrations of change within certain of our social institutions: the family, the economic system, and the political and legal systems. These changes, not all of them in the same direction, are viewed as the accompaniment of underlying biological, social, and economic developments in the changing society. There has been, first of all, the growth and redistribution of the population, with the present high proportions of the very young and the very old, and the striking increase in longevity that has produced a new rhythm of life-timing and aging. Superimposed upon this changing biological base, and reflecting other dramatic changes in technology and urbanization, far-reaching alterations have occurred in the economic system and in the family system, alterations which have led in turn to changing relationships between age groups.

THE FAMILY

Concepts of social age and age status are readily illustrated within the institution of the family. The points along the life-line at which the individual moves from "child" to "adolescent" to "adult" are socially defined, although they are timed in close relation to biological development. After physical maturity is been dramatic changes over the past decades as age at marriage has dropped, as children are born earlier in the marriage, and, with increased longevity, as the duration of marriage has increased.

Marriage implies maturity within the family cycle. With the lowering of age at marriage it may be said that adulthood is occurring earlier than before within the family. The earlier timing of adulthood is reinforced also by the fact that parenthood is occurring earlier; and to the extent that parenthood means financial and legal responsibility for offspring, parenthood is becoming shorter, for children

TABLE 1

MEDIAN AGE OF HUSBAND AND WIFE AT SELECTED STAGES OF THE LIFE
CYCLE OF THE FAMILY, FOR THE UNITED STATES: 1890 TO 1980

Stage	1890	1940	1950	1959	1980
Median age of wife at:					
First marriage...............	22.0	21.5	20.1	20.2	19.5–20.4
Birth of last child............	31.9	27.1	26.1	25.8	27–28
Marriage of last child........	55.3	50.0	47.6	47.1	48–49
Death of husband............	53.3	60.9	61.4	63.6	65–66
Median age of husband at:					
First marriage...............	26.1	24.3	22.8	22.3	22–23
Birth of last child............	36.0	29.9	28.8	27.9	29–30
Marriage of last child........	59.4	52.8	50.3	49.2	51–52
Death of wife...............	57.4	63.6	64.1	65.7	68–69

SOURCE: Sussman, 1963, p. 37. The figures in this table for 1890, 1940, and 1950 were previously published in Glick, Feb. 1955, Table 1. Those for 1959 and 1980 were estimated by methods similar to those used for earlier dates. (Editor's note: Although the projections for 1980 as shown in the last column indicate otherwise, a *rise* in age at first marriage for females has been occurring since the late 1950's. See Parke and Glick, 1967.)

reached, social age continues to be marked off by relatively clearcut biological or social events in the family cycle. Thus marriage marks the end of one social age period and the beginning of another; as does the appearance of the first child, the departure of children from the home, and the birth of the children's children. At each stage, the individual takes on new roles, and his prestige is altered in relation to other family members.

THE QUICKENING FAMILY CYCLE

Changes in timing of the events of the family cycle have been well documented, as shown in Table 1 where analyses have been based upon census data. There have are being born increasingly soon after marriage, are being spaced more closely together, and are then leaving home at an earlier age. It follows that grandparenthood also comes at an earlier chronological age than in preceding generations.

Historically, then, the family cycle may be said to have quickened, as marriage, parenthood, empty nest, and grandparenthood all occur earlier now than in 1900. At the same time, widowhood tends to occur later than before. The trend is toward a more rapid rhythm of events through most of the family cycle, then an extended interval (now some 15 to 17 years) in which husband and wife are the remaining members of the household, a period which is sometimes called the period of the gerontic family.

SOCIAL CLASS DIFFERENCES

The timing of the family cycle is not the same at all socioeconomic or social class levels. The general pattern of historical change we have described has affected people at all levels; but the family cycle begins, then runs its course, a few

reached: leaving the parental home, marriage, birth of first child, birth of last child. Figure 1 illustrates the regularity of these differences for women. (For men, although there was somewhat more variability, the pattern was generally the same. For example, men at the lowest

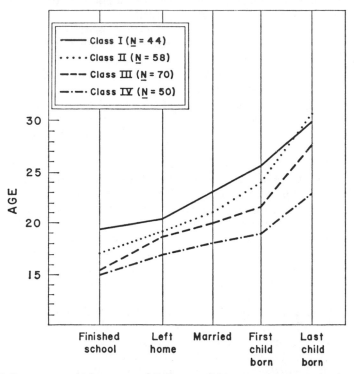

FIG. 1.—Median ages at which women of different social status reach successive events in the family cycle.

NOTE.—Women classified according to husband's occupation: Class I, business executives and professional persons; Class II, white-collar workers; Class III, blue-collar workers; Class IV, itinerant and unskilled workers.

years later in life for men and women at higher social levels. In a study, for instance, of the life histories of adults presently aged forty to seventy who reside in a midwestern city, a high correlation has been established between social class and age at successive points in the family cycle.[1] For both men and women, the higher the social class, the later in life each of the following events had been

class-level had been 22 on the average when their first child was born; men at blue-collar occupational levels, 25; men in white-collar occupations, 27; and business executives and professionals, 29.)

The timing of this sequence of events hinged primarily upon age at leaving

[1] The studies drawn upon here have been described more fully in a paper by Olsen and Neugarten, 1959.

school; that is, the older a man or woman had been upon the completion of formal education, the older he was when he married, when he became a parent, and so on. This is not a startling finding, given the well-established relationship between social class level and amount of formal education, to say nothing of the inevitable ordering in time between marriage, childbearing, and subsequent events in the family cycle. What is significant, however, is the clear implication that the timing of the family cycle is not only biologically regulated, but socially regulated; that social expectations become differentiated among different socioeconomic groups; and that these expectations are reflected in behavior—in this case, in the overall regularity of time intervals between family events.

ECONOMIC FACTORS

Definitions of social age within the institution of the family may thus be said to be intimately intertwined with the system of social status in our society. The relationship between the age-status system and the social class system is mediated through the economic institutions of the society, a fact that is well illustrated by census data regarding age at marriage. Since 1890, as we have seen, age at marriage has dropped. The decline has not been a steady one, however. Economic obstacles to marriage became obvious during the Great Depression, as witnessed in the proportion of the total population who were marrying, as well as in the age at marriage. Although over the past century an increasingly large proportion of the American population has been marrying, this increase almost stopped in the 1930's. It was the marriage rates for men under 20 and for women under 18 that declined most drastically, indicating that "demand" for marriage is more elastic in the younger age groups than in older; i.e., marriage rates are affected by economic factors, but particularly at younger ages. In the decade of the 1940's, with its economic prosperity,

particularly during the years of World War II, a precipitous rise occurred in the proportion of the population that was married, the so-called "marriage boom." Also in this decade a sharp drop in age at marriage occurred for both men and women. That age norms in the family respond directly to economic changes in the society at large is clear in this case, although many social and psychological factors, in addition to economic, were involved.

Getting married, although it defines maturity within the family, is no longer synchronous with the attainment of maturity in the economic sphere. No longer does marriage signify that the legal head of the household is ready to be the breadwinner, nor even that the period of his formal education and occupational training has ended. With the needs of the American economy for larger numbers of technical and professional workers, the length of time being devoted to education is correspondingly increased for more and more young people. There is not, however, an accompanying delay with regard to marriage, as was true in preceding generations (and as was demonstrated in the life-history data described above). In 1966, for example, of all males enrolled in colleges and graduate schools, nearly one out of four were married; of all females, nearly one in seven. Although the proportion of married college men under age 21 was small, this proportion was almost 40 percent for those aged 22 to 24, and almost 72 percent for those aged 25 to 29.

The accompanying phenomenon is the young wife who works to support her husband through school (although there is also an increasing proportion of parental couples who continue to provide financial support for married children in college). The changing roles of women, but particularly the changing sex-role patterns with regard to the timing of economic maturity, are reflected in the rising proportion of young married women who are in the labor force. In 1890, only 6 percent of married women aged 14 to 24 were working outside the home; by 1950, this proportion had climbed to 26 per cent; and by 1960, to 31 per cent. While these percentages reflect marriages in which husbands are working as well as those in which husbands are still in school, they reveal in both instances not only that young wives are increasingly sharing the economic burdens of new households, but also that young women are doing so at younger and younger ages. The social age of economic maturity is being more frequently deferred for males; but not for females.

We shall comment again in the subsequent section on changing sex-role patterns with regard to the timing of maturity, but at this point in the discussion, the facts that contribute to the lowered age at marriage are these: that as economic changes proceed in the society, there are changes in expectations with regard to age-appropriate behavior; it has become socially acceptable now for young men to reverse the traditional sequences of events and for family maturity to precede rather than follow economic maturity. There are obviously other factors that affect age at marriage and, in doing so, affect the timing of age-status changes in the family; but these are perhaps sufficient to illustrate the complex relationships between age norms and underlying social and economic factors.

The new rhythms of social maturity impinge also upon other aspects of family life. Parent-child relationships are influenced in many subtle ways by the fact that half of all new fathers in the early 1960's were under 23 and half of all new mothers, under 21. Changes in parental behavior, with fathers reportedly becoming less authoritarian and with both parents sharing more equally in tasks of homemaking and child-rearing, may reflect in part this increased youthfulness. It is the relative youth of both parents and grandparents, furthermore, that may be contributing to the complex patterns of help between generations that are now

becoming evident, including the widespread financial help that flows from parents downward to their adult children.[2] Similarly, with more grandparents surviving per child, and with an extended family system that encompasses several generations, new patterns of child-rearing are emerging in which child-grandparent relations take on new significance.

THE ECONOMIC SYSTEM

Concepts of social age and age status apply also to economic institutions, where the period of economic productivity may be regarded as "maturity" and where the period of economic dependency in the first part of the life line is regarded as "immaturity." Dependency in this sense occurs also in the last part of the life line; and the point at which the individual enters the period of economic "old age" becomes defined as his age at retirement.

Still other stages can be distinguished. Within the first period of dependency, there is a period of preparation and training for the economic role. These are the years of education and apprenticeship, when the individual is still partly a learner and only partly a producer. Then come the various stages of the productive period: the rise, peak, and decline that are typical of certain work careers; the four or five peaks, requiring retraining for new jobs, that are typical of certain other careers. At each stage, the individual takes on new roles and his status changes in relation to work colleagues, so that he may be said to occupy a new position within the age-status system that characterizes his occupational group. These various career stages can be translated into

[2] Very little research has been carried out regarding the variable of age as it relates to patterns of family interaction. Investigators, for example, have not yet considered age-of-parent a central variable in studying child-rearing techniques; nor even in studying relations between generations. An exception to this statement is the study by Haber (1962).

social ages, but their number and timing vary greatly from one occupation to another, as becomes immediately apparent when the career patterns of teachers, say, are compared with those of business executives.

Two major points, entry into and exit from the labor market, are the events that mark off economic "maturity." Since the patterns of labor force participation are so different for the two sexes, they should be looked at separately.

SEX DIFFERENCES

For men, the period of economic maturity has been shortened over the past labor force as a whole was only 3 percent. The increasing degree to which young males are excluded from the labor market means, in the framework of the present discussion, that their economic maturity is being increasingly delayed.

Paralleling the decline in labor force participation for young men is the equally striking decline for men over 65. As shown in Table 2, the proportion of men in this age group in the labor force in 1966 had dropped to approximately one out of four and the majority of these are in the 65–69 age interval. Of those who worked, the proportion who worked full time had declined markedly. These trends result in

TABLE 2

LABOR FORCE PARTICIPATION RATES FOR
YOUNG AND OLD MALES, 1947–1966

| | PERCENTAGES | | | |
	Age 16–17	Age 18–19	Age 65 and over	Total (all men 16 and over)
1947..........	52	81	48	87
1957..........	51	78	38	86
1966..........	47	69	27	81

SOURCE; *1967 Manpower Report*, U.S. Department of Labor, p. 202, Table A-2

decades by the prolonging of economic dependency at one end, and by the truncation of economic productivity at the other end. For the youngest groups, aged 10 to 15, labor force participation had virtually disappeared by 1940, and by 1967 the lower age limit for official statistics on persons in the labor force was raised from 14 to 16 years. For older boys, the proportion in the labor market has fallen, as shown in Table 2; and of those who work, the proportion who work full time has decreased sharply. In recent years, furthermore, those teen-aged boys who are categorized as being full time in the labor force have suffered severely from unemployment. In 1966 a full 10 percent of the 18-to-19-year-olds were unemployed, while the rate for the a shortened period of economic maturity and an earlier onset of "economic old age."[3]

[3] At the same time, it is true that the average length of working life for American males has increased by more than one-third since 1900, from about 31 to 42 years, largely as the result of improved health and longevity. Thus, while men are retiring from the labor market at earlier ages, this trend is nevertheless superimposed upon the long-term trend of an increased number of men living beyond 65, and the generally increased number of years men of today spend in the labor market.

Something of the same point must be made with regard to women workers. For women the gains in longevity have been even more striking. Although there are special sets of factors involved in the proportion of women in the labor market at one or another period in the life line, increased longevity and improved health also

This, together with increasing age restrictions in employment, has had widespread social consequences for the age-status system in America. As with teen-agers, one effect has been to delineate the group over 65 as a special age group, one with special economic and social needs. The effects have not all been in the direction of lowering the status of the aged, however. Despite the fact that a higher proportion of the aged suffer economic deprivation than of other age groups, and despite the evidence that the aged are assigned a position of low status in this society, the aged now constitute a leisured class, and the effects are not uniformly detrimental to their prestige in the society. We shall return to this point later in commenting upon age groups as sub-cultures.

The pattern of labor force participation is a very different one for women than for men. In the past fifty years changes in the patterns for the two sexes have gone in somewhat opposite directions. Not only has the proportion of women in the labor market risen dramatically, but the characteristics of women who work have changed even more strikingly. In 1890, 13 per cent of the women who worked were married; in 1959, 55 per cent. As recently as 1940 only one out of ten female workers had children at home under 18; by 1961, it was one out of three.

The change in age distribution is of special interest. As can be seen from Figure 2, where the proportions of women workers at successive ages are shown in relation to the events of the family cycle, the proportion of very young women in the labor force has increased, rather than decreased, since 1890. This is contrary to the trend for young men. It is in the middle years, however, that the change is most striking. For women aged 35 to 44 the proportion working had jumped by 1966 from 12 to 47 percent; and for

women aged 45 to 54, from 11 to 52 percent.

These data illustrate the differences between the sexes with regard to the whole pattern of the work life. For men the trend is to shorten the total number of years spent in the labor force, for men to be older when they start to work and younger when they retire. For most women, the trend is in the opposite direction, to extend the total number of years spent in the labor force.

In the present context, the implication is not that many women become economic producers and are therefore defined as economic "adults" for the first time in their middle years (although this is indeed the perception of themselves that many women hold).[4] The implication is, rather, with regard to the age-status system. For large numbers of American women, but particularly for those at higher levels of education, the return to the labor force brings with it an increase in status that affects the relationships, not only between the sexes but between the generations within the family. It is not only the mother who works now, but also the grandmother.

The timing, then, of immaturity, maturity, and postmaturity in economic terms has clearly altered over the past decades. Indeed, changes in these respects are so fundamental that they have led, along with related changes of social age within the family, to the broad redefinitions of age groups that may be said to have emerged in America over the past fifty years as adolescents, on the one hand,

[4] A discussion of what might be called the social psychology of aging—attitudes of age groups toward each other, self perceptions with regard to age, and perceptions of the life line—lies outside the scope of the present discussion. It is probable, however, that the sex differences mentioned here with regard to status in the family and the economy are contributing to major differences between the sexes in patterns of aging.

operate in the case of women to produce longer potential periods in the labor force.

and the aged, on the other, have been set apart as special groups in the society.

There has also been increasing differentiation of the sexes with regard to social age. For males, the coming of age in the family is hastened with earlier marriage and earlier fatherhood, but this earlier maturity is accompanied by a delay in economic maturity. This inconsistency in the timing of social maturity does not occur, by and large, for females who are taking on adult roles earlier than before in both the family and in the economic system. For women, the transition into adulthood may therefore be said to be more synchronous than for men.

The differences in social aging become apparent again in middle age. Lightened family responsibilities, and the taking on of new economic and civic roles now tend

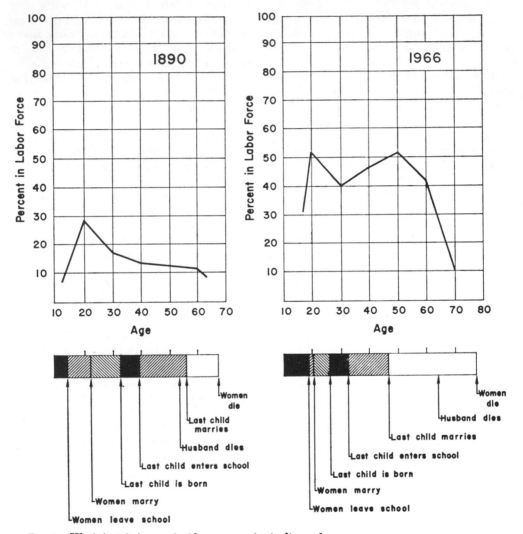

Fig. 2.—Work in relation to significant stages in the lives of women.

Sources: National Manpower Council, *Womanpower*. New York: Columbia University Press, 1957, p. 307. Right-hand portion of figure has been revised based on labor-force data taken from *1967 Manpower Report*, U.S. Department of Labor, Table A-2, p. 202, and on family cycle data taken from Glick, Heer, and Beresford, 1963, p. 12.

to coincide with the biological changes of the climacterium, producing an increasingly accentuated transition period in the lives of women. Figure 2 shows that a few generations ago, with larger families and with children spaced further apart, the last child married and the nest emptied, as it were, when women were 55 years old. Today, this event occurs at 47 (on the average), the age frequently mentioned in medical literature as the average age at menopause. This is the age also when the proportion of women on the labor market is at its highest. The significance of this new transition period is reflected, perhaps, in the increasing frequency with which the phrase, "the middle-aged woman" is being used to delineate a special age-sex group.

The social definition of old age, on the other hand, is more clearly delineated for men than for women. It is true that women also retire from the labor market, but as yet retirement produces a significant change in the lives of fewer women than men.

OCCUPATIONAL DIFFERENCES

The rhythms of the life line that we have been describing hold true for the population as a whole, but there is great variability at different occupational levels. Many social as well as economic and technological factors are at work in creating differences from one occupation to another in the timing of career stages, in the rewards that may be expected at each stage, and in the relationships between age groups. Some of these factors can be illustrated, first, by comparing traditional with newly-emerging professions.

Career timing in the traditional professions of law and medicine probably responds more slowly to technological changes than in the new professions. Yet even within law and medicine there has been notable lengthening of the time required for training and, accordingly, lengthening of the period of economic immaturity. Few lawyers, for example, ever started practice before they reached

the age of 25, but now even that small percentage is declining. The major change in legal training since 1920 is in the increased years of college required before entering law school. In 1921 the American Bar Association recommended two years of college before law school; by 1955, three; and by 1961, four state bar associations were requiring college degrees, or the equivalent of four years.

In medicine, the major changes are related, not to the number of years in school so much as to the number of apprenticeship years spent in clinical training. Thus, although today's graduates of medical schools are no older than those of 1915, an increasing proportion of practicing doctors are specialists; and specialization requires two to five years of hospital residency in addition to a year of internship.

In both law and medicine the extension of training, as well as specialization, reflects the attempt to cope with the increased complexity of knowledge required of the practicing professional. Perhaps even more significant for the relations between the age groups is the accompanying problem of obsolescence of skills and technical knowledge, a problem that characterizes all occupational groups. Age lines tend to become blurred and age-deference systems weakened in instances where the younger man's up-to-date knowledge has the advantage over the older man's experience.

In medical meetings the problems of bringing new knowledge and new techniques to practicing physicians have been emphasized for many years; and by 1962 more than a dozen state bar associations were sponsoring programs in continuing education for lawyers. As "going back to school" becomes an increasingly common phenomenon for the mature man, younger and older men find themselves students in the same local seminars and conferences. This produces another blurring of age differences.

Not only is the early period of the professional career being prolonged, but traditional patterns of relationships between neophytes and the experienced are disappearing in even the traditional professions.

In new professions, age patterns have responded even more quickly to scientific and technological change, as shown by sharp decreases in average age even in a single decade. Thus in 1940, thirty percent of electrical and mechanical engineers were under age 35; by 1950, it was 43 and 41 percent respectively. In the same year, in an even more recently developed field, 62 percent of all aeronautical and chemical engineers were below age 35. To take still another example, geologists who specialized in newer fields like economic geology were several years younger, on the average, than those who specialized in more traditional fields like mineralogy and geomorphology.

It is not only, then, that younger men enjoy increasing prestige within the traditional professions, but that many of the new professions which themselves are growing in prestige are heavily loaded with younger men. Although the definitive data are lacking, it is likely that in such new professions, not only are traditional patterns of age-deference absent, but also that economic rewards come early in the career line as compared with other occupations. The shortage of engineers in the 1960's, for example, brought full-page newspaper advertisements offering premium salaries to new graduates of engineering schools.

The career pattern is quite different for business leaders and for professionals. Several studies show that the average age of the business elite has risen steadily since 1870. In that year their average age was 45; now it is approximately 54. The same pattern is shown in a comparison of business elites over the shorter interval between 1928 and 1952, where minimum age had increased from 4 to 6 years. Only one year of this total was the result of increased pre-business training, for age at entry had increased only from 20 to 21. The lengthened pre-leadership period had taken place largely within the business world proper, from point of entry to point of top job.[5] The increase in size, complexity, and bureaucratization that characterizes big business today is accompanied, then, by a lengthening of the early phases of the career line. It takes longer now than in earlier generations for a man to rise to the top of the administrative ladder.

THE INDUSTRIAL HIERARCHY

If we consider, next, the skill hierarchy in industry, important changes are evident in the age composition of the three basic levels of the hierarchy. Gross census data show, for instance, that skilled workers (craftsmen and foremen) are getting older. From 1930 to 1960, there was a drop in the proportions under 35, but a rise in the proportion aged 45 to 64. There is a similar aging trend among the semiskilled. At the level of the unskilled, however, the trend in age composition is different. Here, in the same thirty-year period, the proportions of young and old increased at about the same low rate.

These data are useful in indicating, although indirectly, some of the changes occurring with regard to the rewards expected at successive social ages in the work life, and with regard to the relations between age groups. These implications will be clearer, perhaps, if we refer to the economic and sociological history of the shoe industry, which has been said to epitomize American industrial history.

In shoemaking, the economic life line of the skilled worker was once clearly divided into apprentice, journeyman, and master. A man advanced through this skill hierarchy as he grew older, and each advance brought with it increased wages, increased security, and increased prestige.

[5] The studies of business leaders mentioned in the preceding paragraphs are these: Gregory and Neu, 1952; and Warner and Abegglen, 1955.

Gradually this situation changed, as the use of machines brought the growth of the factory system. Distinctions between workers were no longer related to age, for the skill hierarchy ceased to exist. Without the advantage of added skill, the older worker became the less efficient worker; and by the time of the Depression in 1930, he had become the expendable worker. The total irrelevance of traditional expectations was made plain. Advanced age no longer brought any assurance of increased economic rewards.

The solution for the worker became collective action; and seniority became a major objective in union organization and union bargaining. Seniority now functions with regard to age much as skill functioned earlier. Increased age still means increased money and security. The major difference is that age no longer means prestige. No longer is a deference between age groups inherent in the industrial system.

Although the changes in age composition at the three levels of the skill hierarchy are produced by many sets of factors, one set of factors are those we have been discussing. With seniority rather than skill operating, the young worker can enter the labor force at the unskilled level as before, but, remaining there, he can soon obtain some of the rewards of increasing wages and increasing security. The incentive is diminished for young men to undertake a relatively deprived period of apprenticeship and then to work at semi-skilled or skilled levels. In turn, this means that many of the rewards of work come at relatively younger ages to a larger proportion of workers than in earlier times in our history.

With the growth of automation the age-reward hierarchy is likely to change even more in the direction we have been describing, that is, to destroy the old age-preferential system. If, as is predicted, automation reduces the employer's needs for a stable work force, seniority will no longer operate to bring increased economic rewards with age.

These are illustrations, then, of the complexity of social change with regard to age-status. Not only do transitions in career lines occur at different chronological ages than before, but there are marked changes in the relations between age groups and in the expectations of economic reward at successive social ages in the work life. Still other dimensions of a changing age-status system become salient when we move from the economic to other institutions of our society.

POLITICAL INSTITUTIONS

When we turn to political institutions, our interest is only secondarily upon social age definitions and patterns of timing. There is but one formal differentiation that is made with regard to age and political participation, that between the immature and the mature. Eligibility to vote is the sign of political maturity; and it is determined now, just as in earlier periods of American history, by the single index of chronological age.

No change has occurred in the timing of political maturity. There have been surges of political interest in recent decades in lowering the voting age, particularly at the time of World War II and with the Vietnam war, when many persons considered it a social injustice that men were considered mature enough to enter military service before they were 21 but not mature enough to vote. Nevertheless, despite a lowered voting age in several states, political age-of-maturity has undergone no change at the national level.

An examination of political institutions is relevant however with regard to certain other issues that relate to age-status: the ways in which increased longevity may be affecting the political system of the society; and whether or not there is growing self-awareness in different age groups that might have a divisive effect upon the society. We shall look first at

15

patterns of political participation and political leadership where there are certain empirical data that bear directly upon these issues.

POLITICAL PARTICIPATION

Participation in political life is a complex phenomenon, only partly measurable by empirical indices. One such index, however, is voting behavior.

The proportion who vote in national elections increases from young adulthood up through middle age. Data from 1952 and 1956 nationwide samples, for example, showed an increase in these proportions up to age 62, then a decrease. Another indicator of political participation, although a somewhat ambiguous one, is identification with a political party. Studies of party identification show an age pattern somewhat similar to that for voting, with a steady increase in the proportion of the strongly identified as age increases. In this instance, however, the increase continues up to age 75.

These indices of increased political participation with age have sometimes been interpreted as due primarily to historical change or generational differences: for instance, that, as an indirect reflection of the growth in size and complexity of the society, groups coming to maturity in the 1940's and 1950's had less sense of political efficacy and thus participated less in political life than groups who came to maturity in the 1920's and 1930's. The same findings have also been interpreted, however, as due primarily to aging itself. For example, in a cohort analysis carried out on survey data gathered in 1946, 1950, 1954, and 1958, increases with age in regard both to frequency of voting and extent of party identification were attributed to changes in the life-cycle rather than to the effects of historical events (Crittenden, 1963).

A marked increase in political awareness in the young is occurring in the late 1960's, given the highly-publicized political protest movements on college campuses and the involvement of college students in civil rights and anti-war demonstrations, an increase which would seem to add weight to the historical interpretation. Despite the vocal minorities of student activists of the right and of the left, it is not altogether clear, however, what proportion of the total college population is involved in political action or what proportion of the young people of the nation feels committed on national or international issues. It is too soon, also, to know whether the perceived increased political participation will reflect itself in larger proportions of young people exercising the vote than in the 1950's; and if so, whether or not those who are young in the late 1960's will continue to vote in higher proportions than their 1950 counterparts at later stages of their lives.

Differences in political participation are one of the many ways in which age groups in our society are differentiated in life style, or, in one sense of the term, one of the ways in which age subcultures are evident. The extent to which this differentiation is increasing is, however, not easily determined. There has been a great deal written, pro and con, on whether there is a politics of age developing in the United States.

The picture is confused at both ends of the political life-cycle. Most political sociologists tend to agree that for groups under 65 other factors (geographical, ethnic, religious, educational) override the factor of age in influencing political and voting behavior; but there is a rising controversy over the extent to which age-related considerations are beginning to dominate the political views of groups over 65. Some suggest that, with increased numbers of retired persons living on fixed incomes and with a host of other economic and social changes that lead to increasing visibility of the aged as a group, a social movement is being created in which consciousness of age is the dominant feature (Rose, 1962). This movement is predicted ultimately to partake of political overtones in which age will override the other influences which now have centripetal effects upon the aged as a political group.

The opposite point of view is put forth with equal conviction. There are political analysts who point to the short-lived character of political movements among the aged in the Depression years (EPIC, Ham-and-Eggs, the Townsend movements); who regard the growth of the McLain movement in California in the late 1950's as due to a set of special circumstances; who point out that no political movements of the aged seem to develop in areas where the aged form a large proportion of the population but are not migrants; and who believe that, now the battle for Medicare has been won, the political effectiveness of the National Council of Senior Citizens will become dissipated. Older people seem thus far to be inclined to "vote their age" only on issues such as full employment, medical care, and increased Social Security benefits; and even on these issues there is little evidence by the late 1960's that the aged are voting as a bloc.

It remains to be established whether a politics of old age will emerge on the American scene or if the aged will in the long run continue, as now, to be integrated into existing political parties.[6]

POLITICAL LEADERSHIP

Despite the popular notion that America is a young country, the trend has been that the age of political leaders, like economic leaders, grows greater from decade to decade.[7]

In general, and despite some striking exceptions to which we shall return presently, the more recently elected the official and the more his responsibility, the older he is upon entering office. On the state level, contemporary studies show that state representatives are younger than

state senators and that both are younger than governors. As is true in business, the increase in average age from one level of leadership to the next reflects not only the underlying increase in longevity and the factor of seniority, but also the fact that persons at high political levels may be serving increasingly longer "apprenticeships" at lower levels. All but a few governors, for instance, were active in public life previous to their election as governors. If it is true that political issues are becoming more complex from decade to decade, it may also be true that it takes a longer time for most political leaders to work their way up through lower levels.

At the Congressional level, Senators have long been a relatively senior group, and, as a group, have not aged much since 1900. The average age of Senators in 1899 was 56.8; and in 1962, it was 58. The average age of Representatives, however, had risen from 48 to 53 in the same period of time. Cabinet members have also tended to become older in successive decades: the median age of all cabinet members was 55 in the period from 1900 to 1924; it rose to 60 in the next 25 years.

The overall aging trend is most notable in the judiciary, and particularly at the state Supreme Court level. To take but one example, a century ago (in the period from 1838 to 1868) Justices of the Iowa Supreme Court were 37 years old on the average at time of taking oath. In the period from 1933 to 1961, the average was 58.

For federal Supreme Court Justices, the average age at taking oath of office reached a high of 59 during the period

[6] The data on political participation and the various interpretations of age differences are taken from Angus Campbell, "Social and Psychological Determinants of Voting Behavior," in Donahue and Tibbitts, 1962; Campbell, 1960; Lane, 1959; Lipset, 1960.

[7] These data on age of state representatives, governors, congressmen, cabinet members, and judges have been culled from a variety of sources, including: Wahlke, Eulau, Buchanan, and Ferguson, 1962; Gurwell, 1941, p. 157; Lehman, 1947, p. 342; "Aging in General," 1962, pp. 104–5; and Schmidhauser, in Donahue and Tibbitts, 1962.

from 1920 to 1932; then declined to 54 during the period from 1933 to 1961. This reversal probably reflects an important political issue that arose in the 1930's when President Roosevelt's proposals for enlarging the Supreme Court as a means of overcoming its political conservatism (the so-called "court-packing" proposals) became an attack upon "nine tired old men."

Any reversal in age trend based on so few cases as the number involved in Supreme Court appointments must obviously be interpreted with great caution. Yet there is no doubt of the significance of Roosevelt's attack on the aging Court, even though the attempt to "pack" the Court failed. In what may be the first national public opinion poll concerning gerontocracy, a Gallup poll conducted in 1937 showed that 64 percent of the nation's voters favored a constitutional amendment that would force retirement of the Justices between the ages of 70 and 75. In 1939, even after the political saliency of the issue was somewhat reduced, a similar poll showed that 58 percent still favored arbitrary retirement of Supreme Court and other federal judges at age 70.

Although it is seldom that the age of political leaders becomes so controversial, age became a source of anxiety several times in the past two decades: at the death of President Roosevelt and with the illnesses of President Eisenhower and President Johnson. It may be that public attention was focused more upon the health of presidential candidates and incumbents than upon their age per se. Nevertheless, there are observers who perceive a reversal of the long-term trend toward gerontocracy at various places in government.

Within the framework of the present discussion the significant fact is that expectations with regard to age are shifting in the political as well as in other areas of the American society. "Maturity" with regard to political leadership seems to be increasingly independent of chronological age. Perhaps this is but a reflection of the fact that the significance of age is not readily measurable, given the complexity of factors that influence political decision-making. This complexity of factors operates both on the part of electors in going to the polls, and on the part of political leaders who, once in office, formulate national and international policies; and it is difficult to assess the importance of age in either setting.

AWARENESS OF AGE GROUPS

As we have been illustrating, social age definitions, age norms, and age-appropriate behavior are responsive to social and economic changes. At the same time, age norms become formalized through the legal institutions of the society. The laws come to reflect, both directly and indirectly, the extent to which age differentiations are regarded as important, and the points in the life line at which these differentiations are made.

One dramatic example has been the federal social security legislation enacted in 1935, in which age 65 was specified as the age at which men were eligible to draw retirement benefits. Although this legislation was in direct response to economic changes in the society, it provides an instance in which a legal definition has itself had important influence upon the definition of a particular age group. Although 65 was established as the age of retirement largely because of the particular economic and demographic conditions that prevailed in the middle 1930's, age 65 has come to signify the transition point into old age in many other areas of life. In many public and private programs of services, in the mass media, and in many other informal ways, 65 has come to be the reference point by which to distinguish the old from the middle-aged.

It may be said that, with the growing differentiation that characterizes modern society, there has been increasing awareness on the part of the American public of age differences and of the special needs of various age groups. Historically, it has been children, then adolescents, and now

the aged that have been singled out for attention. This fact is evidenced, for example, in the official platforms of political parties, where references to special legislation on behalf of children are to be found well before 1900 (Cain, 1963). From 1900 to the Depression of the 1930's, references to the aged also appear, but only in the platforms of the splinter political parties, as when, for example, the Social Democrats asked for old age insurance in 1900, and the Progressives did the same in 1912.

By 1932 the aged had taken their place alongside children as an age group widely recognized as having special needs and as creating special problems for the society at large. Thus the Democratic platform in 1932 included a statement on old age insurance; and in 1936, there was a special section on Old Age and Social Security in addition to a section on youth. By 1940, the platform included reminders not only that child labor had finally been outlawed, but also that young people had been aided by the National Youth Administration and Civilian Conservation Corps programs of the New Deal. The Republican Party platforms also showed awareness of special age groups during this period, although with proposals that differed from those of the Democratic Party. Since 1944, both major parties have continued to speak out about children, youth, and the aged.

Another index of this increasing public awareness is the emergence of special occupations and agencies which serve special age groups. Teaching to children was an early specialty, of course; but through the years requirements for teaching various age groups have tended to become increasingly differentiated. In most states, for instance, specialized training is required for teachers at primary, elementary, and high school levels; and training with regard to the special characteristics of the students being served is now becoming desirable in adult education as well.

Other traditional professions have de-

veloped specialties dealing with clientele of specified age ranges. In medicine, pediatrics was certified as a specialty in 1933. Although there are present differences of opinion in medical circles regarding the wisdom of certifying a specialty in geriatrics, the trend in practice is in that direction, with some physicians referring to themselves as geriatricians. Similarly, with the development of juvenile court laws, the legal profession has developed specialists in the problems of children and youth.

Perhaps nowhere has age specialization been so notable as in the social services, where specialists in dealing with children were identifiable by the mid-nineteenth century when the respective merits of institutional and foster-home care for children was one of the major controversies in the developing social work profession. The efforts of social welfare specialists have been reflected also in increasing activity within state and federal agencies. At the state level, early efforts were to eradicate abuses in the use of child labor, the first such law appearing in Pennsylvania in 1848. By 1930 all states had child labor or child welfare laws. At the federal level, the first White House Conference on the Care of Dependent Children was called in 1909 and the establishment of the Children's Bureau followed in 1912. There have been White House conferences on children and youth at successive ten-year intervals, involving professional and lay people from all segments of the society.

It was not until the Depression that there was any marked public attention paid to services for adolescents. Again, government as well as private groups became involved, with the Civilian Conservation Corps and the National Youth Administration representing massive efforts to cope with the problems of unemployed young people; and with the growth of youth centers, called by one authority a

"spontaneous nationwide movement for teenagers," being founded in many communities. Services to adolescents became a significant specialty in social work in World War II, when the Associated Youth Serving Organizations were formed in 1943 in an effort to improve and extend services to adolescents who were remote from the conventional agencies. The "hard-to-reach" became an interesting target of youth specialists among social workers.

The aged have only very recently become a specially-served group. Social clubs, such as the Golden Age Clubs, senior centers, and other recreational provisions for the aged have been developing very rapidly since the end of World War II under various private and public auspices. Industrial and union groups are becoming increasingly involved. State governments have even more recently begun to take an active part in providing services for the aged, with the first permanent state commission to deal with problems of the aged established in Connecticut in 1945. The first National Conference on Aging, held in 1950, provided the impetus for establishing state commissions; and within a year after the 1961 White House Conference on Aging, all fifty states had established one or more agencies on aging.

AGE SUBCULTURES

The recent attention being given to two so-called age subcultures, one of youth and one of old age, may illustrate best how such age-group awareness stems from the nature of the changing society.

We have dealt earlier with the departure of the adolescent from the labor market. Perhaps more important for the development of a youth subculture is the fact that adolescents stay in school, where they remain relatively segregated from other age groups and where they develop a set of shared values and tastes that are different in some ways from those of the general society. The subculture of the teen-aged is usually described as one based upon leisure, at least in the sense that the emphasis is upon consumption rather than production of goods and services, and as one in which high value is placed upon clothes, automobiles, the paraphernalia of sports and recreation, and upon fun and popularity. The distinctiveness of this teen subculture is debatable, even though some authors have made extreme claims for its separation, even for its alienation from the adult culture (see Coleman, 1961; Daedalus, 1962; Annals of American Academy, 1961). In the 1960's adult culture may also be said to be characterized by an orientation to consumption, by high value upon clothes, automobiles, recreation, fun, and popularity.

Whether or not "subculture" is an accurate term, there seems little doubt that in recent years this age group has been increasingly delineated in the public view. The very term "teen-age" has become colloquial only since 1930. The teen consumption market has been developed within recent years, and the fact, for instance, that girls are buying clothes, cosmetics, and magazines designed exclusively to meet their tastes, argues a degree of self-consciousness as an age group. Since the Depression, teen-agers have been viewed also as a problem group. The rise in juvenile crime, the more recent appearance of hippie culture, and the use of psychedelic drugs have added but other dimensions to this view. The anxiety about teen-agers' irresponsibility and irrationality is reflected even in recent scientific writing.

The emergence of a subculture of the aged is similarly a debatable phenomenon. The increase in the proportion of those who are retired has made this age group socially visible and, as noted above, it has become the focus of both social-service and political action in recent decades. As yet, however, evidence of a developing subculture of the aged is equivocal at best. For example, there is no clear analog among the aged to the teen-agers' daily congregation in the school. There are, to be sure, some tendencies toward residential segregation. First, the aged are left

behind when younger people move to new communities, so that they are disproportionately to be found in rural counties, chiefly in the middle west, in the older neighborhoods of large cities, and in older suburbs. Second, there are a growing number, although still a very small proportion, of the more well-to-do retired who take the initiative and migrate to "retirement communities" in Florida, California, and other southwestern states. In such retirement communities, a subculture of the aged may be developing, one oriented to the use of leisure. That retirement communities are indeed producing a subculture of the aged has been suggested by some observers who point to the fact that social class, sex, and ethnic considerations play less role in the social relationships of the inhabitants than would be the case if these communities reflected the cultural patterns characteristic of other American communities (Rose, 1962).

It is too soon, then, to speak of a subculture of the aged, given the fact that so small a proportion is represented in retirement communities, and the fact that on the whole the aged in the late 1960's are still a relatively poor, ill-educated, heavily ethnic, and rural population. The next generation of pensioners will be different from the present one insofar as they will be less differentiated from other age groups in respect to income, education, and ethnicity. Whether or not they will become more segregated, by choice or by assignation, cannot be determined. At the same time, higher incomes, better health, and more years of retirement may well stimulate the further development of a subculture of leisure for the aged—a development which may, by making old age a less unattractive period of life, raise the prestige of this age group.

The foregoing analysis of changes in the American age-status system refers to the period through the mid-1960's. This picture is likely to change more within the next decade because, due to the birth rates of the 1940's, there will be dramatic shifts in the age distribution of persons on the labor market. In the 1950's there were approximately 2 million boys and girls reaching age 18 each year, and in the early 1960's, about $2\frac{3}{4}$ million. In a single year, however, 1965, the number jumped to $3\frac{3}{4}$ million, and this flood of young people will continue at the same level through the decade of the 1970's. Although increased proportions of these young people went at least part way through college in the 1960's, nevertheless larger and larger numbers entered the labor market. It is expected that 26 million new young workers will begin their careers in the 1960's as compared with 19 million in the 1950's (Clague, 1962).

At the same time, the number of the aged will increase in the decade of the 1970's with increases in longevity, even though their proportion of the total population will decrease. (Within the total population of adults aged 21 and over, the proportion of those 65 and over will remain about the same.)

Without reference to the state of the economy, nor to the various other factors of social change which will influence the general picture, these alterations in the age distribution of the society will lead to new relationships between the young, the middle-aged, and the old, and, in turn, to new changes in the age-status systems of American society.

2

BERNICE L. NEUGARTEN, JOAN W. MOORE,
and JOHN C. LOWE

AGE NORMS, AGE CONSTRAINTS, AND ADULT SOCIALIZATION

In all societies, age is one of the bases for the ascription of status and one of the underlying dimensions by which social interaction is regulated. Anthropologists have studied age-grading in simple societies, and sociologists in the tradition of Mannheim have been interested in the relations between generations; but little systematic attention has been given to the ways in which age groups relate to each other in complex societies or to systems of norms which refer to age-appropriate behavior. A promising group of theoretical papers which appeared twenty or more years ago have now become classics (Benedict, 1938; Davis, 1940; Linton, 1936; Lowie, 1920; Mannheim, 1952; Parsons, 1942; Prins, 1953; Van Gennep, 1908), but with the exceptions of a major contribution by Eisenstadt (1956) and a provocative paper by Berger (1960), little theoretical or empirical work has been done in this area in the two decades that have intervened, and there has been little development of what might be called a sociology of age.

The present paper deals with two related issues: first, with the degree of constraint perceived with regard to age norms that operate in American society;

Reprinted from The *American Journal of Sociology*, vol. 70, no. 6 (May, 1965), by permission of the authors and The University of Chicago Press. © 1965 by The University of Chicago.

This study was financed by research grant no. 4200 from the National Institute of Mental Health.

second, with adult socialization to those norms.[1] Preliminary to presenting the data that bear upon these issues, however, a few comments regarding the age-norm system and certain illustrative observations gathered earlier may help to provide context for this study.

BACKGROUND CONCEPTS AND OBSERVATIONS

Expectations regarding age-appropriate behavior form an elaborated and pervasive system of norms governing behavior and interaction, a network of expectations that is imbedded throughout the cultural fabric of adult life. There exists what might be called a prescriptive timetable for the ordering of major life events: a time in the life span when men and women are expected to marry, a time to raise children, a time to retire. This normative pattern is adhered to, more or less consistently, by most persons in the society. Although the actual occurrences of major life events for both men and women are influenced by a variety of life contingencies, and although the norms themselves vary somewhat from one group of persons to another, it can easily be demonstrated that norms and actual occurrences are closely related. Age norms and age expectations operate as prods and brakes upon behavior, in some instances hastening an event, in others de-

[1] With some exceptions, such as the work of Merton (1957), sociologists have as yet given little attention to the broader problem of adult socialization.

laying it. Men and women are aware not only of the social clocks that operate in various areas of their lives, but they are aware also of their own timing and readily describe themselves as "early," "late," or "on time" with regard to family and occupational events.

Age norms operate also in many less clear-cut ways and in more peripheral areas of adult life as illustrated in such phrases as "He's too old to be working so hard" or "She's too young to wear that style of clothing" or "That's a strange thing for a man of his age to say." The concern over age-appropriate behavior is further illustrated by colloquialisms such as "Act your age!"—an exhortation made to the adult as well as to the child in this society.

Such norms, implicit or explicit, are supported by a wide variety of sanctions ranging from those, on the one hand, that relate directly to the physical health of the transgressor to those, on the other hand, that stress the deleterious effects of the transgression on other persons. For example, the fifty-year-old man who insists on a strenuous athletic life is chastised for inviting an impairment of his own health; a middle-aged woman who dresses like an adolescent brings into question her husband's good judgment as well as her own; a middle-aged couple who decide to have another child are criticized because of the presumed embarrassment to their adolescent or married children. Whether affecting the self or others, age norms and accompanying sanctions are relevant to a great variety of adult behaviors; they are both systematic and pervasive in American society.

Despite the diversity of value patterns, life styles, and reference groups that influence attitudes, a high degree of consensus can be demonstrated with regard to age-appropriate and age-linked behaviors as illustrated by data shown in Table 1. The table shows how responses were distributed when a representative sample of middle-class men and women aged forty to seventy[2] were asked such questions as:

"What do you think is the best age for a man to marry? . . . to finish school?" "What age comes to your mind when you think of a 'young' man? . . . an 'old' man?" "At what age do you think a man has the most responsibilities . . . accomplishes the most?"[3]

The consensus indicated in the table is not limited to persons residing in a particular region of the United States or to middle-aged persons. Responses to the same set of questions were obtained from other middle-class groups: one group of fifty men and women aged twenty to thirty residing in a second midwestern city, a group of sixty Negro men and women aged forty to sixty in a third midwestern city, and a group of forty persons aged seventy to eighty in a New

[2] The sample was drawn by area-probability methods (a 2 per cent listing of households in randomly selected census tracts) with the resulting pool of cases then stratified by age, sex, and socioeconomic status. Using the indexes of occupation, level of education, house type, and area of residence, these respondents were all middle class. The data were gathered in connection with the Kansas City Studies of Adult Life, a research program carried out over a period of years under the direction of Robert J. Havighurst, William E. Henry, Bernice L. Neugarten, and other members of the Committee on Human Development, University of Chicago.

[3] For each item in the table, the percentages that appear in the third and fourth columns obviously vary directly with the breadth of the age span shown for that item. The age span shown was, in turn, the one selected by the investigators to produce the most accurate reflection of the consensus that existed in the data. The way in which degree of consensus was calculated can be illustrated on "Best age for a man to marry." Individuals usually responded to this item in terms of specific years, such as "20" or "22" or in terms of narrow ranges, such as "from 20 to 23." These responses were counted as consensus within the five-year age range shown in Table 1, on the grounds that the respondents were concurring that the best age was somewhere between twenty and twenty-five. A response such as "18 to 20" or "any time in the 20's" was outside the range regarded as consensus and was therefore excluded.

England community. Essentially the same patterns emerged in each set of data.

THE PROBLEM AND THE METHOD

Based upon various sets of data such as those illustrated in Table 1, the present investigation proceeded on the assumption that age norms and age expectations operate in this society as a system of social control. For a great variety of be-

generalized other? Finally, using this congruence as an index of socialization, can adult socialization to age norms be shown to occur as respondents themselves increase in age?

The instrument.—A questionnaire was constructed in which the respondent was asked on each of a series of items which of three ages he would regard as appropriate or inappropriate, or which he would approve or disapprove. As seen in

TABLE 1

Consensus in a Middle-Class Middle-Aged Sample Regarding Various Age-related Characteristics

	Age Range Designated as Appropriate or Expected	Percent Who Concur	
		Men (N=50)	Women (N=43)
Best age for a man to marry...........................	20–25	80	90
Best age for a woman to marry........................	19–24	85	90
When most people should become grandparents...........	45–50	84	79
Best age for most people to finish school and go to work...	20–22	86	82
When most men should be settled on a career...........	24–26	74	64
When most men hold their top jobs.....................	45–50	71	58
When most people should be ready to retire.............	60–65	83	86
A young man...	18–22	84	83
A middle-aged man...................................	40–50	86	75
An old man..	65–75	75	57
A young woman......................................	18–24	89	88
A middle-aged woman................................	40–50	87	77
An old woman.......................................	60–75	83	87
When a man has the most responsibilities...............	35–50	79	75
When a man accomplishes most........................	40–50	82	71
The prime of life for a man...........................	35–50	86	80
When a woman has the most responsibilities.............	25–40	93	91
When a woman accomplishes most.....................	30–45	94	92
A good-looking woman...............................	20–35	92	82

haviors, there is a span of years within which the occurrence of a given behavior is regarded as appropriate. When the behavior occurs outside that span of years, it is regarded as inappropriate and is negatively sanctioned.

The specific questions of this study were these: How do members of the society vary in their perception of the strictures involved in age norms, or in the degree of constraint they perceive with regard to age-appropriate behaviors? To what extent are personal attitudes congruent with the attitudes ascribed to the

the illustrations below, the age spans being proposed were intended to be psychologically rather than chronologically equal in the sense that for some events a broad age span is appropriate, for others, a narrow one.

A woman who feels it's all right at her age to wear a two-piece bathing suit to the beach:
When she's 45 (approve or disapprove)
When she's 30 (approve or disapprove)
When she's 18 (approve or disapprove).

Other illustrative items were:

A woman who decides to have another child (when she's 45, 37, 30).

A man who's willing to move his family from one town to another to get ahead in his company (when he's 45, 35, 25).

A couple who like to do the "Twist" (when they're 55, 30, 20).

A man who still prefers living with his parents rather than getting his own apartment (when he's 30, 25, 21).

A couple who move across country so they can live near their married children (when they're 40, 55, 70).

The thirty-nine items finally selected after careful pretesting are divided equally into three types: those that relate to occupational career; those that relate to the family cycle; and a broader grouping that refer to recreation, appearance. and consumption behaviors. In addition, the items were varied systematically with regard to their applicability to three periods: young adulthood, middle age, and old age.

In general, then, the questionnaire presents the respondent with a relatively balanced selection of adult behaviors which were known from pretesting to be successful in evoking age discriminations. A means of scoring was devised whereby the score reflects the degree of refinement with which the respondent makes age discriminations. For instance, the respondent who approves of a couple dancing the "Twist" if they are twenty, but who disapproves if they are thirty, is placing relative age constraint upon this item of behavior as compared to another respondent who approves the "Twist" both at age twenty and at age thirty, but not at age fifty-five. The higher the score, the more the respondent regards age as a salient dimension across a wide variety of behaviors and the more constraint he accepts in the operation of age norms.[4]

The sample.—A quota sample of middle-class respondents was obtained in which level of education, occupation, and area of residence were used to determine social class. The sample is divided into six age-sex cells: fifty men and fifty women aged twenty to thirty, one hundred men and one hundred women aged thirty to fifty-five, and fifty men and fifty women aged sixty-five and over. Of the four hundred respondents, all but a few in the older group were or had been married. The great majority were parents of one or more children.

The only known bias in the sample occurs in the older group (median age for men is sixty-nine; for women seventy-two) where most individuals were members of Senior Citizens clubs and where, as a result, the subsample is biased in the direction of better health and greater community involvement than can be expected for the universe of persons in this age range. While Senior Citizens is a highly age-conscious and highly age-graded association from the perspective of the wider society, there is no evidence that the seventy-year-old who joins is any more or any less aware of age discriminations than is the seventy-year-old who

[4] For each item of behavior, one of the ages being proposed is scored as the "appropriate" age; another, the "marginal"; and the third, the "inappropriate" (the age at which the behavior is usually proscribed on the basis of its transgression of an age norm). A response which expresses disapproval of only the "inappropriate" age is scored 1, while a response which expresses disapproval of not only the "inappropriate" but also the "marginal" age receives a score of 3. The total possible score is 117, a score that could result only if the respondent were perceiving maximum age constraint with regard to every one of the thirty-nine items. A response which expresses approval or disapproval of all three ages for a given behavior is scored zero, since for that respondent the item is not age-related, at least not within the age range being proposed.

The "appropriate" age for each item had previously been designated by the investigators on the basis of previous findings such as those illustrated on Table 1 of this report. That the designations were generally accurate was corroborated by the fact that when the present instrument was administered to the four hundred respondents described here, more than 90 percent of respondents on successive test items checked "approve" for the "appropriate" one of the three proposed ages.

does not join.[5] The older group was no more or less homogeneous with regard to religious affiliation, ethnic background, or indexes of social class than were the other two age groups in this sample.

Administration.—To investigate the similarity between personal attitudes and attitudes ascribed to the generalized other, the questionnaire was first administered with instructions to give "your personal opinions" about each of the items; then the respondent was given a

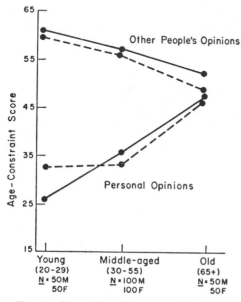

Fig. 1.—Perception of age constraints in adulthood, by age and sex. An analysis of variance for the data on "personal opinions" showed that age was a highly significant variable (F is statistically reliable beyond the .001 level); and the interaction between age and sex was significant (F is reliable at the .05 level). For the data on "other people's opinions," age alone is a significant variable (F is reliable beyond the .001 level). Dotted line, women; solid line, men.

second copy of the questionnaire and asked to respond in the way he believed "most people" would respond.[6]

In about half the cases, both forms of the instrument were administered consecutively in personal interviews. In the remainder of the cases, responses on the first form were gathered in group sessions (in one instance, a parents' meeting in a

school), and the second form was completed later and returned by mail to the investigator.

The two types of administration were utilized about evenly within each age-sex group. No significant differences in responses were found to be due to this difference in procedure of data-gathering.

FINDINGS

The findings of this study can be read from Figure 1. The figure shows a striking convergence with age between the two sets of attitudes.

1. Age trends within each set of data are opposite in direction. With regard to personal opinions, there is a highly significant increase in scores with age—that is, an increase in the extent to which respondents ascribe importance to age norms and place constraints upon adult behavior in terms of age appropriateness.

[5] On the other hand, members of Senior Citizens are more likely to be activists and to regard themselves as younger in outlook than persons who do not join such groups. If this is true, the age differences to be described in the following sections of this paper might be expected to be even more marked in future studies in which samples are more representative.

[6] The problem being studied here relates to problems of conformity, deviation, and personal versus public attitudes. As is true of other empirical research in these areas, the terms used here are not altogether satisfactory, in part because of the lack of uniform terminology in this field. For example, while age norms are in some respects related to "attitudinal" and "doctrinal" conformity as posed by Merton (1959), these data do not fit that analytical framework because age norms are less clear-cut than the norms Merton discusses, and the realms of attitudinal and doctrinal conformity are less prescribed. Similarly, the projection of personal attitudes upon the generalized other has been studied by Getzels and Walsh (1958) but their theoretical model is not altogether applicable because in the present research the phenomenon of projection cannot be demonstrated. The same lack of fit exists with the concepts used by Rokeach (1960); and with the concepts of social norms, norms of common consent, and personal norms as used by Bott (1957). The *self, generalized other* terminology is therefore regarded as the most appropriate for describing the present data.

2. With regard to "most people's opinions" there is a significant decrease in scores with age—that is, a decrease in the extent to which age constraints are perceived in the society and attributed to a generalized other.

3. Sex differences are minimal with the exception that young women stand somewhat outside the general trend on "personal opinions," with scores that differentiate them from young men but not from middle-aged women.

DISCUSSION

The difference shown in these data between personal attitudes and attitudes attributed to the generalized other (a finding that holds true for all but the oldest respondents) implies that age norms operate like other types of norms insofar as there is some lack of congruence between that which is acknowledged to be operating in the society and that which is personally accepted as valid. It is noteworthy, on the one hand, that age norms are uniformly acknowledged to exist in the minds of "most people." While the data are not shown here, on each one of the thirty-nine behavioral items some 80 percent or more of all respondents made age discriminations when asked for "most people's opinions." In other words, general consensus exists that behaviors described in the test instrument are age-related. On the other hand, respondents uniformly attributed greater stricture to age norms in the minds of other people than in their own minds. This difference was reflected in the scores for every respondent as well as in the mean scores.

These findings indicate that there is an overriding norm of "liberal-mindedness" regarding age, whereby men and women consistently maintain that they hold more liberal views than do others. In many ways this situation is reminiscent of the phenomenon of pluralistic ignorance, in which no respondent's personal view of the attitudes of others is altogether correct (Allport, 1924). In other ways, however, this may be a situation in which re-

spondents tend to exaggerate, rather than to misconstrue, the opinions of others. A young person who says, in effect, "I am not strict about age norms, but other people are," is indeed correct that other people are stricter than he is (as shown in these data on "personal opinions"); but he exaggerates, for other people are not so strict as he thinks. Similarly, when an old person says, in effect, "I think this is the norm, and other people think so, too," he is also partly correct that other old people agree with him, but he ignores what *young* people think.

These partial misconceptions have at least two implications: first, when a person's own opinions differ from the norms he encounters, he may exaggerate the differences and place the norms even further away from his own opinions than is warranted. Second, it may be that in considering age norms the individual gives undue weight to the opinion of persons who are older or stricter than himself and ignores the opinions of others who are younger or less strict. In both instances, the norm image is not the average of all opinions encountered but the image of the "ideal" norm. In the case of age norms, the "ideal" norms may well be those held by older persons.

The findings of this study are also of interest when viewed within the context of adult socialization. Cross-sectional data of this type must be interpreted with caution since the differences between age groups may reflect historical changes in values and attitudes as much as changes that accompany increased age itself. Still, the findings seem congruent with a theory of adult socialization: that personal belief in the relevance and validity of social norms increases through the adult life span and that, in this instance, as the individual ages he becomes increasingly aware of age discriminations in adult behavior and of the system of social sanctions that operate with regard to age appropriateness. The middle-aged and the old seem to have learned that age is a reasonable criterion by which to evaluate behavior, that to be "off-time" with regard to life events or to show other age-deviant behavior brings with it social and psychological sequelae that cannot be disregarded. In the young, especially the young male, this view is only partially accepted; and there seems to be a certain denial of age as a valid dimension by which to judge behavior.

This age-related difference in point of view is perhaps well illustrated by the response of a twenty-year-old who, when asked what he thought of marriage between seventeen-year-olds, said, "I suppose it would be all right if the boy got a good job, and if they loved each other. Why not? It isn't age that's the important thing." A forty-five-year-old, by contrast, said, "At that age, they'd be foolish. Neither one of them is settled enough. A boy on his own, at seventeen, couldn't support a wife, and he certainly couldn't support children. Kids who marry that young will suffer for it later."

Along with increased personal conviction regarding the validity of age norms goes a decreased tendency to perceive the generalized other as restrictive. The overall convergence in the data, a convergence which we have interpreted in terms of adult socialization, may reflect status and deference relationships between age groups in American society, where high status is afforded the middle-aged and where social enforcement of norms may generally be said to be vested in the mature rather than the young. The young person, having only recently graduated from the age-segregated world of adolescents, and incompletely socialized to adult values, seems to perceive a psychological distance between himself and "most people" and to feel only partially identified with the adult world. This is evi-

denced by the fact that when asked, "Whom do you have in mind when you think of 'most people'?" young adults tended to answer, "Older people."

Only for old people is there a high degree of congruence between personal opinions and the opinions ascribed to others. This may reflect not only the accumulated effects of adult socialization and the internalization of age norms, but also a certain crystallization of attitudes in the aged. Older respondents volunteered the most vehement and the most opinionated comments as they moved from item to item, as if to underscore the fact that their attitudes with regard to age and age-related behaviors are highly charged emotionally. Under these circumstances, there is likely to be a blurring of distinctions between what the respondent himself regards as right and what he thinks other people would "naturally" regard as right.

With regard to sex differences, the fact that young women perceive greater constraints regarding age-appropriate behavior than do young men is generally congruent with other evidence of differences in socialization for women and men in our society. Young women are probably more highly sensitized to the imperatives of age norms than are young men, given the relatively more stringent expectations regarding age at marriage for women.

It should be recalled that the present study is based upon quota samples of middle-class respondents and that accordingly the findings cannot be readily generalized to other samples. Nevertheless, the findings support the interpretation that age norms are salient over a wide variety of adult behaviors and support the view that adult socialization produces increasingly clear perception of these norms as well as an increasing awareness that the norms provide constraints upon adult behavior.

3

ARNOLD M. ROSE

THE SUBCULTURE OF THE AGING: A TOPIC FOR SOCIOLOGICAL RESEARCH

This paper presents a number of related hypotheses and logical deductions. It offers no data except for an illustrative example here and there, but looks forward to empirical testing.

A subculture may be expected to develop within any category of the population of a society when its members interact with each other more than they interact with persons in other categories. This occurs under two possible sets of circumstances. (1) the members have a positive affinity for each other on some basis (e.g., gains to be had from each other, long-standing friendship, common background and interests); (2) the members are excluded from interaction with other groups in the population to some significant extent. In American society, both sets of circumstances occur for most older people, although for some (who thereby become isolates) only the second develops with age and they never come to express an affinity with other older people.

The positive affinity which many older people feel for each other is based partly on their physical limitations, and hence common interests in a physically easy and calm existence, partly on their common role changes, and partly on having had common generational experiences in a rapidly changing society. The rejection by younger age groups is based partly on the same factors, but also partly on the unspoken contempt for inefficacy in our

Reprinted from *The Gerontologist*, 2 (1962): 123–27.

general culture. Retired people—who can no longer earn a living, whose physical abilities to get around and engage in sports are limited, and whose prospects for new achievements and success in competition are slim—experience a sharply diminished status. This is abetted by the absence of special marks of prestige attached to aging which are found in other societies, such as the attribution of special wisdom, the automatic accession to a higher political position, or the use of titles of respect (such as the title "U" in Burma, applied to all persons over 40 years of age). Thus the elderly tend to interact with each other increasingly as they get older, and with younger persons decreasingly, and hence develop a subculture. The greater the separation of older people from other age categories, both as individuals and as a social group, the greater the extent and depth of subcultural development.

Not all of the distinctive behavior of the elderly can be attributed to the aging subculture; the following may also be involved: (1) biological and personal idiosyncrasies associated with physical aging; (2) generational changes which cause older people to act out a "general culture" appropriate for an earlier period but which has become "old-fashioned" for contemporaries; (3) general cultural norms for the behavior of the elderly held by all in the society (for example, conservative styles of clothing which are favored for the elderly by all age levels).

Since a person only gradually becomes old and must continue to play some role in the general society, the elderly retain a good deal of the general culture and some even carry on roles typical of younger age groups. The extent of isolation from the larger society (for example, through congregate living) varies from one older person to the next. Thus, different old people have different degrees of involvement in the aging subculture.

There may even be categorical differences, such as the possible tendency for the wealthy and educated aging to retain more contact with the larger society than do the poorer and ill-educated and hence acquire less of a distinctive aging subculture. In one sense, we hypothesize, older people may be more involved in a general culture than are middle-aged persons: this is in that older people lose some of the other subcultural variations—based on class, region, sex, and possibly even ethnic identification—characteristic of the middle aged population (Aldridge, 1959). They are somewhat more likely to unite on the basis of age than on the basis of these other divisions, relatively speaking, and thus the aging subculture is a more general one than are the subcultures found among the rest of adult society. On the other hand, for some of the elderly, perhaps for those who had been socially mobile, there may be regression to earlier ethnic and class characteristics.

Influences which keep the elderly in contact with the larger society, and thus tend to minimize the development of an aging subculture, include: (1) the contacts with the family, which are not reduced by the parents getting older and in some respects may increase as the adult children "settle down" after marriage and as the older man after retirement has more time for association with his family; (2) the mass media, which seem to play an increasing role in contemporary society and which have a tendency to cut across all subcultural variations; (3) continued employment, even on a part-time basis, which keeps the older person in contact with a work group, an occupational association, and the economic standards of

the general society; (4) an attitude of active resistance toward aging and toward participation in the aging subculture. This might result from unusually good physical and mental health, so that the person is biologically younger than his chronological years would indicate, from an opportunity to have a special identification with some younger group in the society, or from a negative rejection of the aging and the aging subculture. The latter alone, if not associated with some opportunity to have contacts with the general society beyond those afforded to most older people, will often result in isolation and group self-hatred. By "group self-hatred" I mean a strongly negative attitude toward the self because one has a negative attitude toward the group or category which nature and society combine to place one in. The concept grew up in dealing with certain social and psychological phenomena in minority groups (see, for example, Rose, 1949).

Let us turn from a consideration of the general factors creating and influencing an aging subculture in our society to a consideration of some of the specific content of that subculture. The areas of life chosen for analysis represent some of the variation in the aging subculture; they do not present a comprehensive picture.

First, the status system of the elderly is only partially a carry-over of that of the general society (Aldridge, 1959; Hoyt, 1954). Two kinds of status must be recognized for the retired elderly—that which is accorded them by the general society (and which is generally markedly lower than that for a younger person of like wealth, education, and earlier achievement) and that which is developed out of the distinctive values of the aging subculture. Certainly wealth carries over from the general culture as an important factor in status, with some significant exceptions: (1) with income from occupation gone, the variations in incomes from investments, pensions, and social security tend to be significantly less than previous incomes from occupations; (2) some of the attitudes toward wealth must develop of the type "you can't take it with you," and yet expenditures for night life, travel, and other expensive amusements must be curtailed for reasons of health, so that wealth must have somewhat less importance than it did at any earlier age. Occupational prestige probably carries over into old age also, but its effect is also probably less when the occupation is no longer practiced and the occupation itself is changing.

The same is true of the prestige arising from the former holding of power. As previous holding of power and earlier achievement fade into the past, they are of diminishing influence in conferring prestige. General education probably carries over more since it is of current utility to the aging, but it too must have something of a dated quality. In preceding generations, youngsters were much less likely to be kept in school to the levels they are now likely to, and the education they did receive is, in some respects at least, regarded as old-fashioned today. These sources of status which carry over from the earlier years are probably of maximum influence for the elderly when they continue to live in the same community. If they have changed communities, occupational prestige after retirement must go down markedly, and the other factors must be of reduced importance. If the aged individual is socially isolated, as sometimes happens, these factors in former status carry current prestige only as a sort of legend.

Two related factors may be hypothesized as having special value in conferring status within the subculture of the elderly. One is physical and mental health. This is not a highly significant value for most younger people (except for the relatively small percentage who do not have it, and they react as individuals, not as members of a group with a subculture).[1] Good health, however, is sufficiently rare, and becoming rarer with advancing age, so that old people make much of it and exhibit a special admiration for those who

remain healthy. A sickly old man who cannot take care of himself has little status among the elderly (or among any in the society, except perhaps his family) even if he is wealthy, whereas a vigorous old man with keen senses will be accorded high status among his compeers even though he lives exclusively on a modest pension.

The second distinctive factor in the status system of the aging is social activity. This is, of course, partly based on physical and mental health, but it includes much more. Especially in recent years, many of the aging accord high status to those of their number who are willing and able to assume leadership in various social influence and expressive associations composed primarily of the aging. We shall give more extended consideration to this in our later discussion of aging self-consciousness. Here we may simply note that, because social activity among some of the elderly is based partly on physical and mental health, some of those who rise to prominence among the aging are persons of little previous eminence or skill and experience in group leadership.

There may be other distinctive factors in the status system in the aging subculture which deeper observation would reveal. One approach would be through an examination of the social participations and communications of the elderly. Little is known about this among social gerontologists, but there must be stores of data in the commercial studies of audiences for the mass media and in other types of public opinion polls.

Another important social value toward which the attitudes of the aging must differ markedly from those of the rest of the

[1] Cultural values have at least one characteristic in common with economic values: to have high value they must be relatively scarce. Thus, younger people do not gain much status merely by being healthy (because most of them are) unless they are prize specimens of good health.

31

population is sex. While recent studies (Kinsey, Pomeroy, & Martin, 1948; Kinsey, Pomeroy, Martin, *et al.*, 1953) suggest that older people are more capable of having sex relations, and actually do have them, than was formerly supposed, it seems likely that interest in sex declines with the years. Many older people in the United States today were raised in an era of sexual puritanism and the double-standard, in which it was assumed to be natural that men had strong sex drives until they grew impotent in old age, while women naturally did not have significant sexual drives and they lost what they did have when they became old. This generational factor helps to keep interest in sex low. There are, of course, a few sexual radicals among older people, who keep up a high level of sexual interest and activity.

After retirement, when men spend as much time around the house as house-wives, and there is much less of a clear-cut difference of economic role, the social and sexual distinctions between men and women are diminished. Many older men and women, particularly in the lower income groups, seem to seek sex differentiation in their social life. The unbalanced sex ratio among older people (121 women past 65 for every 100 men) must have some effect on their attitudes toward sex and sex differentiation. Perhaps it is simply that men are pampered and fussed over by their female associates; perhaps it is a woman-dominated social relationship in which men's wishes and interests are ignored because they are so greatly outnumbered.

There are many other areas of the aging subculture that could be analyzed and speculated about. Their self-conceptions, their attitudes toward death, marriage (Kleemeier, 1954), their interpersonal relationships and leisure (Hoyt, 1954), their argot, their distinctive rituals, and scores of other significant factors in their behavior and outlook must be significantly affected by their age. There is perhaps less basis for speculation about these topics, in the almost complete absence of empirical data, than about the topics we have already considered. There is one topic, however, for which there is some empirical evidence available, and it is one that is of growing significance for the aging. This is what I call "aging group-consciousness," and to define it effectively I must first talk about the "aging self-conception." These concepts, as aspects of the aging subculture, will take up the remainder of this paper.

The age of 65 has more or less come to be considered as the age of entering old age in American society. It seems likely that the Social Security Act of 1935 did more to define this limit than any other single event. Probably most private pension schemes adopted or proposed since that date have taken the age of 65 as the date of retirement. Compulsory retirement requirements have become much more frequent since 1935, and they often adopted 65 years as the age of effectuation. The double exemption on the income tax for those past the age of 65 did not become highly significant until the great increase of tax rates during the Second World War, when they served to accentuate the importance of turning 65. Thus a legal definition helped to differentiate more sharply a social category. Even today, however, not all persons past the age of 65 are considered elderly: the exceptions are mainly those who are not retired, mainly among the self-employed, who are generally in the upper status occupations. Among non-gainfully employed women, for whom there is no definite age of retirement or who have in effect retired much earlier when their youngest child left home, entrance into the social category of "the elderly" is not so clear-cut.

Regardless of precisely what age they enter into the ranks, most Americans come to think of themselves as elderly. There tends to be a marked change in self-conception, which includes a shift in thinking of oneself as progressively physically and mentally handicapped, from independent to dependent, and from aspiring to declining (Rose, 1961; Rosow, 1961). Because most of the changes associated with the acquisition of the role and self-conception of being elderly are negatively evaluated in Aemrican culture, and because there is no compensatory attribution of prestige, as in other societies, the first reaction of most older people is some kind of disengagement and depression. The disengagement is by no means completely voluntary: the older person is *pushed* out of his occupation, and even out of leadership roles in many kinds of non-occupational associations. It is a matter mainly of social fact, not so much of natural inevitability, that the American reaching the age of 65 shifts into a social role of disengagement (Cumming, Dean, Newell, & McCaffrey, 1960; Cumming & Henry, 1961). The actual physical and mental decline is not generally very great in today's conditions of advanced medical science and social welfare, and in any case usually develops gradually rather than suddenly. The culture, however, defines the past-65 persons as elderly and manifests this definition in a variety of ways. Some, of course, resist the shift to the new role and the negative self-conception, and try, whether successful or not, to hold onto the pre-65 role and self-conception.

During the past decade in the United States, we have been witnessing the growth of a new phenomenon which is greatly expanding the scope of the aging subculture. This is what may be called aging group-consciousness or aging group-identification. Some people have begun to think of themselves as members of an aging *group;* in their eyes the elderly are being transformed from a category into a group. Probably only a minority of the elderly have so far taken this social psychological step, but their number is growing. One of the early manifestations is to join some kind of a recreational or other expressive association in which they can interact almost exclusively with persons of similar age. Then they begin to take some pride in this association, as evidenced, for example, by the title of the organization—Golden Age Club, Senior Citizen Club, or Live Long and Like It Club. A social worker may have helped to get the club started, but the elderly take it over and the social psychological transformation toward group pride is theirs.

The next phase occurs when they begin to talk over their common problems in a constructive way. Probably elderly people have been complaining for some time about their reduced income, their inadequate housing, the difficulty of paying for medical care if they should be struck with a chronic illness, their reduced prestige, and general social neglect. Recently, however, they have come to talk about such not only with reference to themselves as individuals but with awareness that these things occur to them as a social group. Further, they have begun to talk in terms of taking social action, not merely individual action, to correct the situation. Thus far, this advanced minority has supported certain government actions, both legislative and executive. Their current support of Congressional bills for financing health care is to be seen in this context. It is all the more significant that they are radical supporters of this legislation for the benefit of the elderly when the majority of them are political conservatives on most other issues (Campbell, 1962). The elderly seem to be on their way to becoming a voting bloc, with a leadership that acts as a political pressure group. It remains to be seen whether the future political activities of the aging are integrated into the existing political parties or whether they become segregated as in the McLain movement in California (Pinner, Jacobs, & Selznick, 1959).

There have been some objective trends creating changed conditions that increase the likelihood that older people would develop group self-consciousness. First, there has been the growing number of persons past 65, from 5% in 1900 to 9% in 1960. Second, there has been the afore-mentioned increase of compulsory and voluntary retirement, with the loss of integration into the general society that having an occupation entails. Third, for various reasons associated with a changing economy and increasing migration, there has been less of a tendency for adult children to live in the homes of their parents, who retained their position as heads of the household, and more of a tendency for intergenerational dwelling-together to take the form of the elderly parents living as dependents in the homes of their adult offspring. Fourth, because of the advances in medical science greatly reducing the age at which most women stop bearing children, there has been a tendency for a much larger proportion of the population to reach the age of 65 in physical vigor and health. Fifth, the same causes have resulted in a larger proportion of older people getting the chronic illnesses with greatly increased costs of medical care and hence greater likelihood of financial and physical dependency. All of these trends have combined to create new problems for the older population at the same time as it has given them a new, distinctive position in the society, set apart more from those under the age of 65. These are the conditions which enhance the likelihood that the elderly would develop a sense of group-consciousness.

For the growing minority that has reacted against the negative self-conception characteristic of the aging in our society and has seen the problems of aging in a group context, there are all the signs of group identification. There is a desire to associate with fellow-agers, especially in formal associations, and to exclude younger adults from these associations. There are expressions of group pride and corollary expressions of dismay concerning the evidence of deterioration in the outgroup —the younger generations. With this group pride has come a self-acceptance as a member of an esteemed group and the showing off of prowess as an elderly person (for example, in "life begins at 80" types of activities). There are manifestations of a sense of resentment at "the way elderly people are being mistreated," and of taking of social action to remove the sources of their resentment. These are the signs of group identification that previous sociological studies have found in ethnic minority groups. Perhaps the first to note the minority group aspects of the aging was Barron (1953). I do not mean to exaggerate this parallel, nor to state that most older people today show most of these signs, but the evidence of the growing group identification among older people in the United States today is available to even the casual observer.

Sociologists now need to go beyond casual observation and engage in systematic studies of this formation of group identification, of this transformation of a social category into a social group. The whole area of the subculture of the aging needs objective investigation, in the same manner in which sociologists have already studied ethnic, regional, and occupational subcultures. The opportunity to study these things in birth and in development should not be missed. One reason they have been neglected by sociological researchers thus far is that the aging have been a low prestige segment of the population, and only the "social reform" element has been willing to study them. The objective trends, however, seem to point to a higher status for the aging in the future, so we can anticipate that even the sociologist will find it respectable to conduct research in this field.

4

GORDON F. STREIB

ARE THE AGED A MINORITY GROUP?

Sociologists face the perennial problem of semantics. Often their words have both a professional and an everyday meaning. This creates confusion not only in the minds of laymen but of sociologists themselves. An example of this confusion over terminology is found in terms "aging" and "aged." By applying the concept of "minority group" to the aged in American society, sociologists have used the image-producing meaning of the term as if it were a technical term.

THE CONCEPT, MINORITY GROUP, IN SOCIETY

The literal meaning of minority is "the smaller number." In this sense most societies have many minority groups. In a complex society such as the United States the number of these groups is limitless. If less than 50 per cent of the population have a particular trait, that trait characterizes them as a "minority group." Less than 10 per cent of the total population are over age 65. In the statistical sense, therefore, the aged may be considered a minority group. If this were the only

Reprinted with permission of the Macmillan Company from *Applied Sociology*, ed. Alvin W. Gouldner and S. M. Miller, chap. 24. Copyright The Free Press of Glencoe, 1965.

This paper is part of a current program of research on aging and retirement conducted by the Department of Sociology of Cornell University. The research was initially supported by a grant from the Lilly Endowment, Inc. The work has also received financial assistance from the National Institute of Mental Health, United States Public Health Service under grant M-1196 and from a research grant of the Social Security Administration, Department of Health, Education, and Welfare, Washington, D.C.

criterion, or even the principal one, we would also view as minority groups collectors of antique dolls, persons with incomes over $35,000 per year, or sociologists interested in problems of aging. This numerical or statistical approach to the aged as a minority group cannot yield analytic clarification, for it focuses attention on the frequency or incidence of a characteristic, rather than on its functional social meaning.

Sociologists define "minority group" not only in terms of frequency of characteristics, but also of the objective and subjective features of a group, and of its way of fitting into the social setting. Wirth, for example, stresses the reciprocal dominance-submission patterns between groups, the sense of identification, actual deprivation or exclusion from privileges, and frustrated expectations. In the case of the aged, the dominant group is a constantly changing one, for as people grow older, they presumably move from the dominant-young category to the old-submissive category. Wirth has defined a minority as ". . . a group of people who, because of physical or cultural characteristics, are singled out from the others in the society in which they live for differential and unequal treatment, and who therefore regard themselves as objects of collective discrimination. The existence of a minority in a society implies the existence of a corresponding dominant group with higher social status and greater privileges. Minority status carries with it the exclusion from full participation in the life of the society" (Wirth, 1945, p. 347). It can be noted that this definition does not even mention frequency of incidence.

Sociologists who have viewed the aged as a minority group rarely test their assumption by referring to all the elements of Wirth's definition. Breen, for example, makes a plausible case when he writes: "In many respects the aged show characteristics of a minority group. They are subject to categorical discrimination, they have relatively high visibility, and, in many parts of our society, they constitute a functioning subgroup. Stereotypes are held about the group, and individuals are judged thereby. Prejudice is not uncommon, especially in industry, where persons over age 40 are discriminated against in employment practices. Thus, the ingredients necessary to the development of minority group status are present for the aged. The characteristics commonly attributed to minority groups as a result of such categorization may be expected to develop among older persons" (Breen, 1960, p. 157).[1]

And yet it can be argued just as plausibly that the aged are not a group in a true sociological sense. They have little feeling of solidarity, consciousness of kind, or group spirit. Moreover, the aged do not have any distinct cultural traits, and usually do not operate as a distinct group. *In a strict sociological sense the aged are a statistical aggregate or a social category, not a genuine group.* Age is a biologically determined status of the life cycle which every member of society can expect to achieve if he lives long enough. Minority group members, on the contrary, are so defined through all stages of the life cycle. Membership is exclusive and permanent.

It has been claimed that the aged are similar to women as a minority group.[2] The work of Helen M. Hacker has been cited to support this contention, but a careful reading of her work indicates that she is cautious in drawing the analogy. Hacker writes: ". . . Few women believe themselves to be members of a minority group in the way in which some Negroes, Jews, Italians, etc., may so conceive themselves" (Hacker, 1951, p. 61).[3] At another point, she is careful to point out: "It has been indicated that women fail to present in full force the subjective attributes commonly associated with minority groups. That is, they lack a sense of group identification and do not harbor feelings of being treated unfairly because of their sex membership" (Hacker, 1951, p. 62).[4]

Simone de Beauvoir, denying that women constitute a minority group in society, makes similar points. Indeed, her comments on women can be neatly paraphrased: The aged are not a minority group for they have no past, no history, no religion of their own, and unlike the proletariat, they have no solidarity of work and interest. They are not herded together in the way that creates community feeling among the American Negroes, the ghetto Jews, the workers of Saint-Denis, or the factory hands of Renault. They usually live dispersed among the young, attached through residence, housework, economic conditions and social standing to other people—husbands, wives, children, friends—more to family than to other old people. If they belong to the bourgeoisie, they feel solidarity with the old of that class, not with proletarian old people; if they are white, their allegiance is to white men, not to Negro old people (Beauvoir, 1953, p. xix).

[3] Myrdal preceded Hacker in discussing women as a minority group. In Appendix 5, "A Parallel to the Negro Problem," he writes, "in every society there are at least two groups of people, besides the Negroes, who are characterized by high social visibility expressed in physical appearance, dress, and patterns of behavior, and who have been 'suppressed.' We refer to women and children." (Myrdal, 1944, vol. 2, p. 1073.)

[4] The low degree of group identification by women is not to be confused with feelings of personal and sexual identity as women.

[1] Barron was among the first to use the term in this manner. See Barron, 1961, pp. 55–68. See also Barron 1954, pp. 56–8.

[2] From the statistical standpoint, women are, of course, not a minority group.

In considering the aged as a minority group it is useful to spell out the dimensions of the concept. We have pointed out that the everyday statistical meaning does not apply to the aged; nor does the traditional concept of minority group which emphasizes a dominant majority, because the dominant group is a constantly changing one. The present paper tests the evidence for considering the aged as a minority group. First, we specify the criteria for defining a minority group and then examine the evidence relevant to each criterion.

Let us turn to the criteria for specifying minority group characteristics.

1. Members of the group possess identifying characteristics with accompanying status-role expectations throughout the life cycle.

2. There is a prevailing sentiment that this status characteristic makes group members less deserving of respect and consideration (as Negroes, Jews, ethnic groups, etc.). This is often discernible in current stereotypes and clichés about (*a*) work performance and (*b*) appropriate activities.

3. Possession of the status characteristics is associated with a sense of group identity.

a. There is intragroup identity, or a sense of consciousness-of-kind.

b. There is intergroup identity in that the status provides others with an absolute criterion for group identification.

4. There is a readiness to organize as a political pressure group.

5. The possession of the status characteristic leads to differential access to power, privileges and rights.

a. Civil rights are sometimes denied.

b. Group members may not be found among the elite and influential members in the society.

c. There may be restrictions on political roles and activities.

6. Possession of the status characteristic may lead to: *a.* less economic and social security; *b.* unequal access to work; *c.* residential segregation; *d.* social isolation.

With the above criteria in mind, we shall examine a variety of empirical data to determine the degree of correspondence between the aged in the United States and the concept of minority groups.

1. DOES THE CHARACTERISTIC IDENTIFY ALL WHO POSSESS IT THROUGHOUT THE LIFE CYCLE?

Clearly this is not so for the aged. It would be equally justifiable to study children as a minority group. They too are a statistical minority. They possess distinct physical traits, their age defines their cultural role; they would consider themselves (if they could articulate their feelings) deprived by adults, and objects of adult prejudice and discrimination. They are a source of social conflict. Yet to analyze "the young" as a minority group would only hinder understanding their social role.

2. DOES THE MAJORITY GROUP HOLD STEREOTYPES AND CLICHÉS ABOUT THE AGED?

(*a*) *Work performance.*—One way to test whether the aged constitute a minority group is to ascertain whether other categories of persons in the community think they deserve less respect and privilege than others. Let us begin with attitudes to their work. Do people relate the fact of age (like the fact of race) to less adequate work performance?

Recently, Breen and his associates at Purdue conducted an interview study of attitudes and opinions about older persons. They chose a random sample of over 700 persons from age 20 to 80 in a county in Indiana. These investigators report that all age categories are more likely to say that the old are better workers than younger persons. However, the Pur-

37

due investigators found some differences of attitude between the two groups. For example, there is a tendency for older persons to maintain that the old are better workers than the young. But the younger persons in the study were more likely to say that there are only individual differences in the quantity and quality of work produced by various age groups. Perhaps what is of greatest interest, when we consider the aged as a minority group, is that only 7 per cent of the respondents from age 20 to 40 display any negative attitude toward older workers. This Indiana study shows clearly that older workers are not held in low esteem[5] by younger age categories in the community (Breen *et al.*, 1951, p. J15).

On the other hand, in an Iowa study of self-appraisal of working ability, an overwhelming majority of men sixty and over stated that they could not do their regular work as well as when they were in their 30's and 40's (Martel and Morris, 1961, pp. 33–34). Unfortunately, the investi-

[5] That older workers are not held in lower esteem should not be confused with the unemployment of many older persons. About one man in five between ages 60 to 64 was not working according to a study conducted by the National Opinion Research Center; a random sample of all older persons not in institutions was interviewed. The same survey reports that among men 65 and over about six in every ten were not in the labor force (i.e., retired). This cannot, however, be considered evidence of "under-employment" and discrimination without determining how many of these older people withdrew voluntarily from the labor force, or were retired because of a realistic handicap. There is evidence that employers do discriminate against older workers. See Slavick and Wolfbein, 1960, pp. 306–10; Shanas, No. 17, 1960, pp. 1–3. Shanas reports that her findings are comparable to those of the Census Bureau. The findings on the employment or lack of employment of older persons should also not be confused with the sources of income of older persons. We note, for example, a report which lumps all older persons together and shows that employment constitutes a source of income for only 24 per cent of all persons over age 65. See United States, 87th Congress, 1961, p. 14. In terms of employment and income, a substantial number of older persons are deprived, but this does not mean that they constitute a minority group.

gators limited their questioning on this point to men who had already changed from their regular job to some other kind of employment. Thus, a crucial category of employed older persons was excluded.

Studies conducted at the University of Illinois in which supervisors rated the effectiveness of older workers suggest a need to reappraise the effectiveness of older workers in a variety of jobs. The general conclusion, based upon studies of 3,000 workers, is that they are useful and productive workers. However, caution is required in interpreting the findings, and the author's conclusions are instructive: "While the findings of this study are highly favorable to older personnel we must avoid the tendency to infer more than is actually indicated. There is a suggestion, for example, that older people tend to become more efficient by virtue of their age alone. This, of course, is not true because it fails to consider that the older personnel in this survey represent a selective group in several senses: only those with motivation have continued to work, only those with the best apparent capabilities were selected for employment, and only the fittest have survived dismissal" (Peterson, BMA 15, p. 8. See also Peterson, 1953 and Peterson, 1954.)

Thus, when we examine the evidence on work performance we find varying judgments by younger workers, older workers, and by supervisors. As might be expected, persons in each of these categories view work performance from different perspectives; but the over-all rating tends to be favorable.

(b) *Appropriate activities.*—The Purdue study offers additional evidence that younger people do not hold more stereotyped notions about appropriate activities for the old than the old themselves. Respondents were asked to indicate which social activities they thought "improper or unfitting" for older persons (if the respondent was over 60, the interviewers were instructed to insert an age decade ten years older than that of the respondent). While all age groups agree that

"Sedentary-Social" activities are appropriate for persons over 65, persons in the younger age categories were *more likely* to suggest activities for older persons which are socially more vigorous than the older respondents believed appropriate for their age group (Breen *et al.*, 1951, p. E6).

3. GROUP IDENTITY

(*a*) *Self-Image.*—Another important way to distinguish a minority group is the group's own sense of identification. To what extent do the aged view themselves as a separate and distinct group possessing its own sociological identity?

Do older persons look upon themselves as elderly, middle aged, or old? In four different surveys of persons over sixty years of age, conducted over a period of years at Cornell University, we found that the majority of persons considered themselves to be "middle-aged." Only among those over 65 is there any noticeable tendency to identify themselves as "old" or "elderly." The crucial age break is somewhere between 65 and 70. We found, for example, that among a large population of persons approximately 64 years old, and gainfully employed, about two-thirds classified themselves as "middle-aged" and another 20 percent as "late middle-aged."[6] Only 10 percent identified themselves as elderly, and about 3 percent as old. These survey data tend to support the claim that older persons do not think of themselves as members of an "old" or "elderly" subgroup.

(*b*) *Absolute criteria for group identification employed by others.*—The Indiana study conducted by the Purdue group

[6] The tendency to rate oneself or one's group or social category in a more favorable manner has been observed in other contexts. When a person ranks his own or a similar occupation, his own evaluation is always considerably *higher* than the average appraisal of the position. See National Opinion Research Center, 1953, p. 415. See also the work of Landsberger and Hulin in which they report that labor leaders are more likely to rate officials higher than members (Landsberger and Hulin, 1961).

reports that people in all age categories identify "middle age" and "old age" not by an absolute criterion, but by a relative one. Most respondents said, "It depends upon the individual" (Breen *et al.*, 1951, p. D7).[7]

Researchers have had difficulty establishing absolute criteria for identifying the aged as a group. Some investigators have chosen sixty as the beginning of old age and others sixty-five, because it is a common retirement age. The question is this: does chronological age determine when a person is old? Cumming and Henry, for example, state, "The most important criterion was age. . . . Thus, in order to follow a panel, people whose youngest members were entering middle age and whose oldest were entering old age, we decided upon a twenty-year range, from fifty to seventy" (Cumming and Henry, 1961, p. 27). It is pertinent to add that these same investigators found it necessary to undertake a special analysis of "The Very Old," those persons in their eighties whom the researchers considered to be members of "a biological, and possibly psychological, elite" (Cumming and Henry, 1961, p. 201).

4. READINESS TO ORGANIZE AS AN IDENTIFIABLE PRESSURE GROUP

Among minority groups (e.g., Negroes, Puerto Ricans) in American society, this internal sense of identity, or self image, reinforced by the external definition of separateness that society applies to the subgroup, is often translated into attempts at political action as a pressure group.

Since the time of the Townsend Movement, there have been appeals to the aged to act as a cohesive pressure group. A

[7] Tuckman and Lorge have reported that when one examines the responses by age category, there is a slight tendency for older persons to specify the beginning of old age at a higher age than younger persons. See Tuckman and Lorge, 1953, pp. 483–488.

study of the California Institute of Social Welfare (the McLain movement) reveals how the weak sense of group identity among the aged inhibits such efforts (Pinner, Jacobs, and Selznick, 1959).

In recent years, the McLain movement has been one of the most effective in organizing older persons. The most radical proposal of the McLain organization was to eliminate the means test in the Old Age Assistance Law. McLain and his organization purported to advance the interest of approximately 273,000 Californians over 65 who were recipients of Old Age Assistance. These people constituted 30 percent of those 65 and over. In 1952, about 23 percent of the persons on OAA were on the membership roster of the California Institute of Social Welfare. At the peak of their activity, the membership of the CISW constituted about 7 percent of the population over age 65 in the state of California.

McLain achieved his greatest political success in 1948 when the voters of the state passed a proposition changing the administration of the Old Age Assistance law and raising the amount of money for the recipients. The victory was due to a slim majority of 1 percent of the total vote cast. The following year in a special election the proposition was repealed; the margin of loss in this second election was 13 percent of the total vote. Although the political climate of California is somewhat idiosyncratic, it is relevant to note that even at the peak of the success of the McLain movement this group never constituted a cohesive political unit. This was due mainly to the lack of group identification among the aged. Pinner and his associates stress this point in their analysis of the organization. They report that pensioners hesitated to identify themselves as aged or pensioners, and preferred to be called "citizens." Moreover, open-ended interviews of a subgroup of McLain followers revealed no evidence of "we-feeling" (sense of group identification).

A large majority of the respondents in the survey favored organizations to protect the needs and "rights" of the aged because they cannot take care of themselves. *But a small number (12 percent) thought the aged should defend themselves against a hostile world.* Pinner and his associates report the the older persons felt that the need for a group stemmed from their bewilderment about the problems of dependency. "In their view, organizations will either do for them what they cannot do for themselves, or enable them to manage their own affairs more actively. *It is not identification with older persons, or a general desire for political action that impels participation in organizations*" (Pinner, Jacobs, and Selznick, 1959, p. 90. Italics added.)

That the aged lack a sense of identification as a minority group is also illustrated in the California study. Questions were designed to determine who the pensioners thought should be included in the organization. Members of the Institute are more likely than nonmembers to express a preference for mixed groups. The authors emphasize that older persons regard organizations like the McLain Institute as "groups *useful to* the aged, not as groups *of* the aged" (Pinner, Jacobs, and Selznick, 1959. Italics by Pinner *et al.*).

5. DIFFERENTIAL ACCESS TO
POWER, PRIVILEGES AND RIGHTS

(*a*) *Civil rights.*—Are the property rights of the aged restricted? No. Are the aged denied equal protection of the law? No. Are they deprived of suffrage? No. Excluded from public office? No. If these people are deprived of such rights, it is because they are members of ethnic, racial, or religious minorities, not because they are old.

Readiness to organize as an identifiable pressure group is related to the realization that their group characteristic denies them equal access to power, privileges, and rights.[8] The Pinner study indicates that

[8] It would be instructive to ascertain the special privileges for the aged in the form of tax exemptions, lower or nonexistent admission

the aged supported the McLain movement more because of their bewilderment about the privileges due them than because of their interest in a political demand for privileges denied them.

There is no evidence that older people are denied civil rights because of their age. Indeed, the evidence suggests that the aged are more likely to exercise their right to vote than younger people.[9] Schmidhauser has made an interesting analysis of voting patterns in Iowa. He found in that state, as in a number of others, that the rural areas have a larger proportion of representatives in the state legislature than their numbers warrant. "Because they constitute so great a proportion of the population of the over-represented rural areas, the aged have the strategic political advantage of being concentrated where their numbers are most effective in state legislative election" (Schmidhauser, 1958, p. 116–17).[10] Moreover, since the long-range national trend is for the aged to settle in rural areas, they will continue to have a disproportionate voice in state legislative bodies.

(b) Elites and influentials.—Possession of the group characteristics "justifies" denial of equal access to economic, social, and political opportunities to minority groups. They are, therefore, over-represented among the less-privileged, and under-represented among the elites.

Studies of local elite systems suggest that the aged are over-represented among elites. In Hunter's study of Regional City, a financial and industrial city of 500,000 population in the Southeast, the men of power in the community tend to be the wealthy businessmen and bankers.[11] This seems to hold for other communities which have been studied. Although the top power group in Regional City is divided into the older and younger group, the *older* group ultimately exercises the most influence in the community. As Hunter says, "In most instances decision-making tended to be channeled through the older men at some point in the process of formulation . . ." (Hunter, 1953, p. 80. See also pp. 29–30; 40–41.) Because the chief power wielders are older persons in Regional City, I suspect that power policies there and elsewhere are dictated by the economic interests of the power groups. *Older men may exercise a pivotal function in decision-making even though they do not operate as a gerontocracy.*[12]

Although we find greater complexities in the national power structure than in the local scene, the evidence suggests that older persons exercise considerable influence.[13] Harvey Lehman conducted an

charges, etc. Mohawk Airlines, for example, has recently inaugurated a Golden Age Club with one third reduction in fare.

[9] John R. Schmidhauser has summarized some of the pertinent literature in his article, "The Political Behavior of Older Persons, A Discussion of Some Frontiers in Research," 1958, p. 115. He is careful to point out that a number of political studies employ age 55 for the older age group, rather than age 65, the common age used in private retirement programs and for the male eligibility for benefit under OASI. This discrepancy in definition does not detract from the pertinence of the findings on the voting patterns of the aged.

[10] Some minorities, such as Jews and Negroes, may have strategic voting power when they live in concentrated areas in a city.

[11] More recent investigations question Hunter's generalizations about the power structure. See Janowitz, 1961.

[12] West reports that the older members of the small community he studied had a "stranglehold" on most of the wealth in the county (West, 1945, pp. 110–11). He also noted that older women exerted considerable social control in a small town. He writes: "Certainly through the dread and fear of them which exists, *old women* exert a great restraining influence against deviation from stricter and older moral patterns." *Ibid.*, p. 105, italics added.

[13] For example, in 1961 16 United States Senators were between 60 and 64 years of age and 31 were 65 or older. Also, only two members of the United States Supreme Court were under 60. Yet no one claims that older Senators or Justices act as representatives of the old. It shows, how-

exhaustive study of the relation of age to achievement and leadership.[14] His work indicates that the elderly acquire positions of leadership more frequently in contemporary society than was true in earlier periods in our history. He offers evidence that U.S. Senators and Representatives, U.S. Supreme Court Justices, Secretaries of State, heads of federal bureaus and services tend to be older when one compares periods like 1900–1940 and 1789–1874. Donald Matthews reaches a similar conclusion in his study of political decisionmakers (Matthews, 1954, p. 33). It was an old man–G. Stanley Hall–the eminent psychologist and retired president of Clark University, who at age 75 noted in his book, *Senescence: The Last Half of Life:* "Perhaps the world is a little too much in the hands of people who are a little too old. but this is being rapidly remedied" (Hall, 1923, p. 135). Hall made this provocative assertion in 1923, but the ensuing years have not borne out his prediction.[15]

(*c*) *The political role of the aged.*—The political role of the aged is related in a complex manner to many other factors. The aged, for example, have a high sense of political duty as is evidenced by their voting behavior, but other age groups rate higher in their belief that individual political action can affect the political process. On the other hand, the investigators who conducted a detailed study of voting behavior and political processes in one urban community (Elmira, New York), reported that younger adults tended to show respect for the political opinions of their elders. Moreover, the authors of this study stated that over a tenth of the workers of both major par-

ties were from the retired or widowed categories (Berelson, Lazarsfeld, and McPhee, pp. 104, 164).[16]

Weighing the various elements in the political process, it appears that the aged are not viewed as a minority group in political affairs nor do they act as one. Schmidhauser summarized his review of the literature by saying: "Virtually all of the foregoing discussions of the growing population proportions of older people—their strategic location for state legislative politics in certain states, their high voting record in presidential elections and probable high participation record in nonpresidential general and primary elections, their higher motivation toward political participation, their possible roles as public affairs leaders—all these underscore the real as well as potential influence oldsters have in American politics" (Schmidhauser, 1958, p. 120).

6. DEPRIVATION

(*a*) *Economic and social security.*—Many of the aged, like many of the minority groups, are underprivileged. This is the principal reason for the minority group analogy. Consider health, for example: The aged are sicker, spend more time in hospitals, and are less likely to recover from chronic illnesses than younger persons. But the fact of neediness does not warrant viewing the aged as a minority group. Nor does focusing attention on providing for their medical and health needs as if they were a homogeneously sick group.[17] Shanas has pointed out, "The current public discussion of the health needs of the older people, which tends to classify all persons

---

ever, that older persons occupy positions of power and influence in a youth-oriented society.

[14] See Lehman, *Age and Achievement*, 1953, pp. 269–88. Lehman's statistical series varies from one occupational category to the other. The interested reader should consult Lehman's work for the pertinent details and qualifications.

[15] The election of President John F. Kennedy confirmed Hall's prediction.

[16] The local leadership of the minority party in Elmira (Democratic) was held by six men, all over seventy years of age (Berelson, Lazarsfeld, and McPhee, 1954, pp. 160–2).

[17] If we consider only those older persons living in the general community, and exclude the estimated 3 to 5 percent in institutions, we find that only 10 percent of a nation-wide probability sample of persons 60 and over are classified as "very sick." See Shanas (May, 1960), pp. 752–3.

65 and over as a homogeneous group, has obscured rather than clarified the differing requirements for medical care of various groups of the aged." (Shanas, No. 16, 1960, p. 29).

There are many aged people who are economically underprivileged. But these people, for the most part have been underprivileged throughout their life cycle. The neediness of the aged is concentrated among Negroes, the lower educated persons, the foreign-born, etc.—in short, the groups who generally suffer the greatest economic pressures. Old age compounds these pressures for them. One of the major subgroups of the aged whose economic security is lowest, is the widowed female over 75 years of age.[18] Many of the aged are underprivileged in several ways and suffer deprivation. But that is not the problem for this paper. Age, as a status characteristic, compounds multiple deprivations for many groups, including minority groups. But a "deprived group" is not synonymous with a "minority group."[19]

Economists who study the economic status of the aged tend to concentrate on the objective or financial aspects of the problem. Sociologists have looked at the economic needs of the aged, not only in objective terms, but also in the subjective terms of the older persons themselves. In the Iowa survey, for example, the investigators asked questions about satisfaction with standard of living and adequacy of income. The results indicate that most of the respondents were reluctant to complain about their economic situation. The authors conclude: "From the various statements made by the interviewees concerning income adequacy, it appears that more than a third were well-satisfied financially, perhaps another 50 to 60 percent saw their position as adequate, and one out of ten was seriously dissatisfied. Considering the income levels reported by the survey population, (annual average of $2,400 for the men and $1,500 for the women), it appears that a good many were fairly well-adjusted to living on incomes that would rate very low by the standards of younger American adults" (Martel and Morris, 1961, p. 41).[20]

(b) *Equal access to jobs.*—Workers are often denied jobs solely because of their advancing age. Here is the first genuine equivalent between "the aged" and other minority groups, indeed, evidence that such practices are widespread is found in the laws in seven states which forbid discrimination in employment on the basis of age (Barron, 1961, pp. 63–66).

Yet even here the analogy breaks down. The age range covered in these laws varies from state to state, but, in general, they refer to persons of 40 to 65.[21] Thus it is the rights of the middle-aged, and not of the old, that are being legally protected against discriminatory practices.[22] If this

[18] The complexity of the economic situation of the aged has been cogently discussed by Steiner and Dorfman, 1957. There have been changes in the income status of the aged since the Steiner and Dorfman study was published. Gordon states: "There is considerable evidence that both the money and the real income status of the aged have improved. . . ." Gordon, 1960, p. 225.

[19] If home ownership is considered a mark of privilege and affluence, the aged are more privileged than other segments of the population. However, home ownership presents financial disadvantages as well as advantages. For a discussion of the subject, see Corson and McConnell, 1956, pp. 89–91.

[20] Another study supporting the point of view of the Iowa study is Thompson and Streib, 1958, pp. 18–34. The Iowa investigators, it should be noted, believed that their findings tended to underestimate feelings of economic deprivation.

[21] For details on these laws see *The Aged and Aging in the United States—A National Problem*, Report No. 1121, U.S. Senate, 86th Congress, Second Session. Subcommittee on the Problems of the Aged and Aging, Washington: U.S. Government Printing Office, 1960. See inserts between pages 50–1.

[22] The effect of these anti-discrimination laws has not been thoroughly studied. However, one piece of research made before New York had such a law, showed that New York placed a

criterion justifies the minority group concept, it is the middle-aged, not the old, who constitute the minority group.

(*c*) *Residential segregation.*—Does being aged result in residential segregation as it does sometimes for ethnic and racial minorities? One might cite the segregation of the ages in institutions; but fewer than 5 percent of older persons are in institutions. Many older persons live alone, but they are not ghettoized. Most surveys have found, moreover, that older persons would rather live by themselves than with children or other relatives.[23] This kind of residential segregation is clearly of a different type than the kind imposed upon Negroes, Puerto Ricans, and other ethnic minorities.

(*d*) *Social isolation.*—Even if advanced age does not in fact lead to spatial segregation, one might argue that it results in segregation in a psychological sense: that the aged are not necessarily ecologically isolated, but are socially isolated from personal and community contacts.

This claim, however, would be difficult to support. Studies both in the United States and in Great Britain have shown that the aged have a high degree of social contact with their children and other relatives.[24] The data from the Iowa survey are illustrative. The investigators report, for example, that less than ten percent of the men and less than five percent of the women say, "I wish my family would pay more attention to me." Moreover, almost forty percent of both sexes report that they have more friends now than ever before (Martel and Morris, 1961, p. 52).

Writers who argue that the aged are a minority group claim that the old are lonely, isolated, unhappy people.[25] Our point is not to deny that there are isolated older persons; (indeed it is quite likely that the proportion of the lonely and unhappy is greatest among the old: but it does not follow that because some aged face these social circumstances, they therefore constitute a minority group. In a study of two small upstate New York communities, Taietz and Larsen (unpublished) found that their data do not support the notion that the aged are less integrated in the community than other age categories. The older heads of households participated less in employment activities because some were retired. However, in three general areas used to index community integration (behavioral factors,

higher percentage of older workers than Massachusetts, which had a law at the time. See *Good News for Later Life*, Legal document #8, New York State Joint Legislative Committee on Problems of the Aging, 1958, p. 23. Barron reports that during the first year of the law's operation in New York, 148 complaints were initiated and 54 were settled; nine cases were sustained on the basis of discrimination (Barron, 1961, p. 66).

[23] The careful survey conducted in Iowa is informative on this point. The investigators asked: "Which of the following living arrangements would be acceptable to you, if circumstances led you to seriously consider them?" Six alternative arrangements were mentioned and about two-thirds of the respondents said that living alone was the most acceptable. The next alternative selected by almost a third was living in a project for elderly people (with separate apartments or cottages for each where you had to do your own cooking) (Martel and Morris, 1961, p. 46).

[24] For data on the British urban, working class see Townsend, 1957, pp. 31–40. For a summary of American data see Streib and Thompson, "The Older Person in a Family Context," 1960, pp. 476 ff. The Iowa survey can be cited in this connection: ". . . most parents in the sample did maintain regular contacts with at least some of their children and grandchildren, and derived important satisfactions from these relations. Well over half said they had visited with a son or daughter during the week preceding the survey, and more than 40 percent had spent time with a grandchild. Nearly 75 percent saw one or more of their children at least once a month, and about 38 percent said they visited with all their children at least that often." These investigators added that about 5 percent of the parents in the study "complained of neglect by their families" (Martel and Morris, 1961, p. 52).

[25] Again the Iowa study offers interesting evidence on this point. It was reported that 73 percent of the men and 83 percent of the women state that their lives are still busy and useful. There is, however, a sharp decline in this feeling after age 75 (Martel and Morris, 1961, p. 86).

attitudes, and situational) the aged did not display the characteristics of a minority group.[26]

A report on an urban area (Kansas City) by Havighurst, which employed different indices of community integration, offers evidence which supports the findings of the New York study. He found that for men "role performance goes down consistently but slightly with age . . ." and for women he found that "there is no relationship between age and role performance" (Havighurst, 1957, p. 321).[27] The analysis of what Havighurst defined as role patterns (role performance scores characteristic of eight or more persons in the study) showed little or no relationship to age. Another study conducted in an urban setting (San Francisco) offers corroboration that age is a less important variable than economic level as a correlate of community integration and participation in formal associations. Bell and Force found: "In the high economic status neighborhoods the percentage of frequent attenders increases with increasing age, but in the low economic status neighborhoods no such trend exists" (Bell and Force, 1956, p. 34).

THE CONCEPT OF "DISENGAGEMENT" OF THE AGED

We might ask whether the aged are denied access to educational opportunities or admission to voluntary clubs and associations. The evidence indicates that the aged use both types of facilities infrequently. But this is not due to denial of access (Tibbitts, 1961, p. 8–9) but rather, to older people's definition of such activities as inappropriate or undesirable. (Older people say that they think members of their families and friends would consider

them unusual if, for example, they return to school (Breen *et al.*, 1951, p. H-6).

The data on these points lend more support to the concept of disengagement as a social psychological accompaniment of advancing age than to the concept of the aged as a minority group (Cumming, Dean, Newell, McCaffrey, 1960, pp. 23–35).

In brief, the idea of disengagement suggests that the aged individual may be described "as participating with others in his social systems in a process of mutual withdrawal, rather than being deserted by others in the structure" (Cumming *et al.*, 1960, p. 35). Usually, the disengagement process begins in the sixth decade of life and is marked by a reduction in interaction. This results in a more self-centered style of behavior among the aged who are ambulatory. The authors of the theory of disengagement have called it a tentative theory (Cumming and Henry, 1961, pp. 232–33).[28] However it suggests new insights and a reasonable explanation for some kinds of behavior and interactions, previously represented as minority group reactions. The theory suggests, for example, that what some writers have described as stereotyping of the old by the young and social isolation of the old may result from individual and societal withdrawal and changes in the expectations of both young and old.

SUMMARY

In summary, viewing the aged as a minority group does not clarify their social role in our society. The aged do not share a distinct and separate culture; membership in the group defined as

---

[26] The study included only male heads of households, and the age categories were under 45, 45 to 65, and over 65 years of age. There were 215 males over 65 who were interviewed.

[27] In the Kansas City study 234 persons were in the age range 40 to 70. It might be argued that this was not a study of the aged. Indeed the author refers to his study as one of the middle-aged.

[28] In conducting the study of disengagement, the investigators included only the middle strata of the class structure. The highest and lowest strata were excluded. Hence, the theory and the data may have a class bias. See Cumming and Henry, 1961, pp. 232–3.

"aged" is not exclusive and permanent, but awaits all members of our society who live long enough. As a result, age is a less distinguishing group characteristic than others such as sex, occupation, social class, and the like. True, many aged persons possess distinctive physical characteristics. But even here there is a broad spectrum, and these "stigmata" do not normally justify differential and discriminatory treatment by others. The aged have little feeling of identification with their age group: they have a low degree of collective consciousness; hostility towards a depriving out-group is exceptional. The aged are not organized to advance their own interests and are not particularly attracted to such organizations. Nor are they systematically deprived of power and privileges. They are not herded in ghettos, deprived of civil rights, excluded from public facilities, or from jobs they are qualified to perform. That they are often underprivileged economically and have more frequent health problems is more the result of handicaps that often accompany aging, than of social organization or group structure.

From the standpoint of conceptual clarity and empirical fact, the notion of the aged as a minority group does not increase understanding. It obscures it.

5

MARTIN U. MARTEL

AGE-SEX ROLES IN AMERICAN MAGAZINE FICTION (1890–1955)

"In studying trends in discussion and opinion, the volumes of leading periodicals may well be regarded in much the way in which a geologist looks at the strata of the earth's crust. Here are precipitated layers of evidence about the intellectual and emotional life of past years. . . . To build and hold circulation, editors of successful publications must discover and express attitudes acceptable to their readers . . . [Magazine fiction stories] have peculiar advantages in throwing light upon the values which at various periods have commanded the enthusiasm of the great reading public. . . . Just as illustrators draw their characters in the styles of the day, so the authors dress the personalities of their stories in the attitudes of the day. . . . The problem is to approach these strata of opinion sediment in the impartial and systematic spirit of science."

—HORNELL HART, 1933

One of the hardest problems in social research is that of obtaining comparable, longitudinal information about broad social changes that work themselves out over a period of generations Generally, the difficulties are more acute the further into the past one seeks to go, and the more one is concerned with ordinary patterns of life in society rather than larger scale events (and those involving elites) which are more likely to become matters of public record.

The present study has been concerned with changes in family, work, community and leisure roles associated with urban-industrialization. Since these changes have been occurring now over a period of several centuries, we wanted to obtain comparative information, going back as far as possible, before the main impetus of the

Revised version of a paper presented at the 1963 annual meetings of the American Sociological Association in Los Angeles. The reported investigation (known as the "Storyville Study") has been carried out in the closest collaboration with George J. McCall.

industrialization process had developed. Due to a paucity of more direct information sources, an explanatory study was made of the possibility of using background portrayals of community life in the more "realistic" magazine fiction-stories as indicators of role changes in various subgroups of the society. In this. we were following in the footsteps of Hornell Hart, Hans Gerth and several others who have made use of periodical fiction-sources in the study of social change.[1]

For analysis purposes, samples of fiction were drawn from the *American, Cosmopolitan, Ladies' Home Journal*, and the *Saturday Evening Post*, in selected vol-

[1] Hart's pioneering work is summarized in "Changing Attitudes and Interests" (1933). While historians and others often made use of periodical materials before this time, Hart is the first we know who began to systemize problems of sampling and analysis. Subsequent studies in this vein include Ruth Inglis, (1938); Berelson and Salter (1946); and Johns-Heine and Gerth (1949). Also valuable is England (1960).

umes published since the 1880's (see Figure 1). Volume-years were chosen so as to include times of extreme national crisis (the two World Wars and the depression of the 1930's), as well as periods of relative normalcy. Within each sampled volume, story selections were limited to those presented in settled American community locations at times contemporaneous with the publication year.

Our content-analysis of the sampled stories posed unusual problems, since we wanted to include a large number of

to be made in analyzing each selected story. In many ways our approach was modeled after the structured interview survey, where each person interviewed is presented with the same questions in the same order; and our Codebook might be likened to a structured Interview Guide. As in many structured surveys, however, we also systematically included a number of "open-ended" questions in the hope of finding valuable clues and insights on changing social roles from our author informants.

FIG. 1.—COMPARISON OF TWO "STORYVILLE" SAMPLES*

CHARACTERISTICS	PRIME SAMPLE	STUDENT SAMPLE
Magazines	*American Cosmopolitan Ladies' Home Journal Saturday Evening Post*	*American* .... *Ladies' Home Journal Saturday Evening Post*
Volume Years	1890; 1925; 1955	1890; 1905; 1910; 1917; 1925; 1933; 1937; 1942–3; 1955
Short Stories	1st 10 "realistic" stories per volume (in settled, contemporary locales).	1st 10 per volume (as in Prime Sample), plus all others in quota issues.
Story Totals	40 per sample year	45 per year (average)
Content Analysis	*1960 Storyville Codebook.* Structured analysis of all Codebook variables & open-ended study of values, goals and story themes.	*1960 Student Schedule.* An abbreviated analysis of role patterns and conflicts using a structured list, carried out by sociology seniors as a course assignment.

* All Prime Sample stories were read and analyzed by George J. McCall and by the writer. Student Sample materials received at least two independent analyses, and only those which were corroborative have been included. The 1885 *Post* volume substitutes for the 1890 volume since a national search failed to locate a complete set of issues for any closer year. Codebooks for both samples are available on request.

characteristics of the social roles portrayed, in order to be able to examine their interrelations and the sequences of change they exhibited. The large number of variables made it difficult to analyze many different stories from disparate historical eras while maintaining adequate standards of comparability.

As a result, we developed a more structured procedure of content-analysis than those employed in previous researches of this type. Our method centered around the preparation of a standardized Codebook, indicating in some detail the nature and sequence of classificatory judgments

The core analysis of our sampled stories consisted of a character-by-character examination of the social roles and relationships portrayed, a "sociometric" analysis if you will. For each story character, we examined (1) the role-activities the character performed, (2) the norms and expectations upheld for each character by his associates (in the stories), and (3) the extent to which the character's activities were encouraged or discouraged by the other characters. We also recorded pertinent expressions of moral values in terms of which the accepted and rejected role-patterns were justified in Storyville.

Perhaps it should be said that our analysis approach largely ignored the story-narratives as such: the story plots, the dramatic emphasis given to the incidents portrayed, and the plot resolution. Our focus was on the ethnographic backdrops against which the stories were presented, and on the values attributed by the authors to characters of various types.

With our large number of variables, our content analysis became a quite laborious and time-consuming undertaking, a factor that has severely limited the size of the sample we have been able to encompass so far. For example, the "complete" analysis by our method of a short story of average length takes five or six hours, just for two basic readings and the recording of the classifications made. (One reason we limited ourselves to short stories.)

The rewarding side of having included many variables is that we have netted a rich and intriguing harvest of findings on changing social roles and values in Storyville. What follows is in the nature of a sampler of some of the more important changes, bearing upon the life-cycle organization of family, work and community roles of adults—selected partly to indicate something of the range of content-patterns contained in the archives of magazine fiction.

By way of qualification, it must be emphasized that one cannot simply assume that fictional ethnographics correspond to social facts in a uniform manner. Several previous studies (Martel, 1964; Albrecht, 1956) have demonstrated that the correspondence between the world of fiction and of social reality is a fickle one, even in the more realistic fictional works.

We have attempted with partial success to deal with the problem of variable correspondence by formulating and testing out a set of discriminative criteria for distinguishing the more-or-less valid ethnographic portrayals in different sorts of fictional works. It has at least proven possible to specify some of the grosser patterns of distortion that are found quite

prevalently in our American magazine samples and to formulate a number of eliminative criteria as guidepoints for interpretation. For example, we have found that valid descriptions tend to be restricted to fictional in-groups corresponding to the model readership in their basic social statuses; portrayals of other groups excluded from the readership tend to reflect in-group stereotypes more than out-realities. Since our sampled magazines have been highly selective in their readership appeals, catering mainly to the adult, literate, English-reading public in the broad middle-classes (outside of the South), whatever validity our trend findings possess must be attributed to this sub-population of the society. It further appears that the in-group portrayals over-emphasize those commonalities of the readership that most distinguish the readers from others in the society; and that they are likely to reflect values and ideals more than social practices, particularly where the practices fail to live up to the ideals upheld. These qualifications also must be taken into account.

CHANGING ROLE-PATTERNS IN STORYVILLE

Two basic changes are shown in the organization and location of community life which—in the "socio-logic" of the stories—seem to underlie a large number of more specific trends during the period.

The first is urbanization. In 1890, our first sample year, most of the stories are presented in rural settings or in smaller towns. The actual proportion of rural-town settings is 75%—a figure substantially higher than that for the readership at the time.

Social life in 1890 is neighborhood-centered, with the neighborhoods consisting of interacting family groups. This portrayal, interestingly, even tends to appear in those stories that are presented in the larger cities.

In both the rural and urban stories, the middle-class neighborhoods are described as socially encompassing, "multi-bonded" groups whose members enact almost all of their important roles and relationships within the neighborhood milieu. The neighborhoods, moreover, are homogeneous in terms of race, religion and nationality for the most part. Little personal contact is described between persons of diverse social origins, and quite often the "villain" of the early stories is a stranger whose background and social identities fall outside of the Storyville-readership in-group.

Over the period, the story locations follow the urbanward relocation of the American population (and, incidentally, its Westward expansion). By 1917 a drastic "resettlement" has occurred in the cities, and from that point on the issue is decided.[2]

A related change occurs in what may be called urban generationality. In the 1920's most of the stories are presented in cities but most of the characters are portrayed as being close to rural backgrounds. In fact, a near majority of the city characters are identified as the children of farmers, a pattern that as best I can tell is demographically correct. We might say then, by analogy to the distinctions made for immigrants between 1st-generation, 2nd-generation, and so forth, that the characters are predominantly 1st-generation urban in the 1920's, and many of the dramatic plots center around conflicts between the newly urbanizing

younger characters and their town-or-rural parents. (In the height of the flapper era, incidentally, the stories split between the rural vs. urban side, in "who wins" in the plot resolutions.)

By 1955 the striking thing is that the characters overwhelmingly are city people, and there are few indications that they ever were anything else. In fact, farmers, who are very much at the center of the sociometric circle in 1890, have dropped out entirely from that circle by 1955. We find no instances of close relations of any kind described between characters in the urban majority and the few farmers who make their way into the stories. There is something of a continuation of the long-standing fictional theme of the town-boy-or-girl who goes to the big city in our 1955 sample, but the "town" in question now is likely to be Baltimore, Cleveland, or Cincinnati.

Most important, with the disappearance of rural life there also is a marked decline in the local neighborhood as a social center (previously reported by England, 1960). A role-segmentation process is portrayed over the period that has received much comment in the sociological literature; individuals carry out their different social roles primarily with different associates. This change is accompanied by profound alterations in the life-cycle organizations of adult social roles in the family, marriage, work, and the community.

Some of the main changes indicated, very briefly, are as follows.

1. DECLINE IN FAMILY OF ORIENTATION

There is a shift away (by young adults) from close involvement with and dependency upon their family-of-orientation—that is, their parents, brothers and sisters. (Table 1, based on character-by-character ratings of "closeness-of-attachment" to each of the other characters.)

In 1890 parents and siblings are very important associates to young adults in their twenties, the attachment both by

[2] The "urbanization" trend in Storyville does not evenly correspond to that in the population or the readership. In the period of transition from 1890 to 1925, the "urbanization rate" in the stories greatly exceeds that in the population, settling down surprisingly close to the actual proportions from that point on. It may be, considering that in many ways this is the "turning point" in the actual society for rural-urban predominance, that the exaggerated urbanization shift in Storyville validly reflects a phenomenological change during this period, in the public consciousness.

50

young men and women being closest to mothers. From the 1920's on, the prevalence of such close attachments becomes much less, with increasing emphasis instead on associations with friends, the opposite sex, marriage and parenthood.

Interestingly, there is a correlative trend that came as a complete surprise to us, for which we have been unable to find any previous substantiation or clear ex-

most frequently between mother-son, father-daughter, brother-sister and even uncles and nieces. By 1955, however, the shoe is on the other foot, sex combinations with mother-daughter, father-son, and sister-sister now receiving greatest emphasis. (No tendency toward "Momism"

TABLE 1

FAMILY ATTACHMENTS OF ADULT CHARACTERS IN SELECTED YEARS,
BY SEX, AGE, AND RELATIONSHIP

(%-Distributions)*

| RELATION TO CHARACTER | MALE CHARACTERS (AGES) | | | | | | | | | FEMALE CHARACTERS (AGES) | | | | | | | | |
| | 18–24 | | | 25–39 | | | 40–60 | | | 18–24 | | | 25–39 | | | 40–60 | | |
Volume year†	1	2	3	1	2	3	1	2	3	1	2	3	1	2	3	1	2	3
Father......	14	22	25	15	6	12	0	0	0	67	60	12	24	37	15	0	0	0
Mother.....	43	33	16	28	6	6	0	0	0	56	45	41	27	24	27	0	0	0
Brother.....	14	0	0	16	15	6	0	4	4	15	20	6	19	8	9	11	5	7
Sister.......	28	11	0	10	15	4	15	7	9	26	30	19	12	23	21	7	15	7
Son.........	0	0	0	4	0	14	15	9	30	4	0	12	8	0	16	39	15	20
Daughter....	0	0	0	10	0	6	45	20	22	7	0	18	2	4	24	39	21	67
Spouse......	14	22	16	26	35	33	40	33	26	30	10	47	42	48	60	46	50	47
Other relative(s)....	30	0	0	12	16	6	40	11	17	37	10	12	19	18	6	36	20	47
No family associates...	36	44	50	48	59	67	35	50	30	30	25	24	46	41	44	36	35	27
Number of characters.	14	9	12	54	34	51	20	46	23	27	20	17	26	27	32	28	20	15

* PRIME SAMPLE: (Storyville "In-Groups" only). Percentages of major characters portrayed as having some attachments to various members of their families. Ambivalent orientations are included here but those of enmity are not.
† VOLUME YEARS: (1) 1890; (2) 1925; (3) 1955.

planation. That is—a shift away from a cross-sex emphasis within the family, to increasing emphasis on same-sex attachments. The finding is supported by several independent methods used in analyzing the stories, the crucial independence of which is that we were totally unaware of such a possibility during the reading. The finding appeared only after a detailed, summary, statistical analysis was made. (Tables 1 & 2.)

In 1890 close attachments are portrayed

is indicated at all. In fact, quite the opposite.)

For parent-child relations (with adult children, that is) it further appears that (1) sons gain in satisfaction for their fathers, while daughters become more the object of frustration; and (2) something of the reverse is indicated for mothers, with daughters becoming more satisfying associates. (Table 3.)

Perhaps those who are more psycho-analytically astute among us can help us

TABLE 2

FRIENDSHIPS OF ADULT STORY CHARACTERS IN SELECTED YEARS, BY SEX AND GENERATION

(%-Distributions)*

STATUSES OF FRIENDS	MALE CHARACTERS (AGES)									FEMALE CHARACTERS (AGES)								
	18–24			25–39			40–60			18–24			25–39			40–60		
Volume year†	1	2	3	1	2	3	1	2	3	1	2	3	1	2	3	1	2	3
Same sex:																		
Older.....	36	0	25	10	0	4	0	0	0	44	10	12	23	0	6	0	0	0
Peer......	33	22	56	42	6	14	30	4	4	22	30	6	31	7	28	29	0	5
Younger..	0	0	8	0	0	0	25	2	10	0	0	0	0	0	0	45	10	10
Opposite sex:																		
Older.....	14	0	16	6	0	3	0	0	0	19	0	18	5	7	24	14	0	0
Peer......	7	67	58	19	52	42	5	7	17	55	72	65	27	60	44	14	0	10
Younger..	0	0	0	0	0	0	20	11	10	0	0	0	0	0	0	15	10	5
Number of characters.	14	9	12	54	34	51	20	46	23	27	20	17	26	27	32	28	20	15

* PRIME SAMPLE: (Storyville "In-Groups" only.) Percentages of major characters portrayed as having close or moderate friendships in various characters. Classifications are based on the same "Closeness-of Attachment" scale as in Table 1 for family relations with the same inclusion criteria.

† VOLUME YEARS: (1) 1890; (2) 1925; (3) 1955.

TABLE 3

SATISFACTION- AND FRUSTRATION-SOURCES OF STORY CHARACTERS AGES 40 YEARS OR OLDER (1890 AND 1955), BY SEX

(Percent of All Satisfaction and Frustration Sources)

Satisfaction	1890	1955	% Dif.	Frustration	1890	1955	% Dif.
Men				*Men*			
Work..........	18	34	+16	Work..........	27	57	+30
Children.......	22	22	0	Children........	14	30	+16
Son(s)........	5	15	+10	Son(s).........	3	6	+ 3
Daughter(s)...	19	11	− 8	Daughter(s)...	13	24	+11
Marriage.......	14	14	0	Marriage........	20	21	0
Religion or church	10	0	−10	Religion or church	1	0	0
Neighbors.......	8	2	− 6	Neighbor	3	1	0
Retirement......	0	0	....	Retirement......	0	4	+ 4
Women...........				*Women*			
Children........	22	36	+14	Children........	27	21	− 6
Son(s).........	10	15	+ 5	Son(s).........	12	7	− 5
Daughter(s)...	12	20	+ 8	Daughter(s)....	15	14	0
Marriage.......	18	18	0	Marriage........	17	32	+15
Work..........	5	21	+16	Work..........	4	13	+ 9
Religion....	11	0	−11	Religion.........	1	0	0
Giving help......	8	1	− 7				

to puzzle out the hidden meanings here, which may, of course, be purely literary artifacts having no actual correspondence in the society. But then again, there may be something to it.

As the emphasis within the family is increasingly focused on same-sex pairs (excluding marriage), a compensatory shift appears in relations outside, where same-sex friendships become less frequent in favor of cross-sex relations.

2. LOSS OF PARENTAL AUTHORITY

Corresponding to the above, there is a loss of authority by parents over their adult (and adolescent) children that will come as no surprise—concerning decisions to date, court, marry, choose career and so forth.

In 1890, family authority tends to follow the age-hierarchy. Parents are in command, particularly in relation to their daughters. Filial disobedience is rare, and where it occurs it is a serious matter.

By 1955, a notable shift in the burden-of-proof occurs. The norm changes from one of filial obedience to one of parental non-interference in their grown children's decisions. And, where disagreements arise they are more serious because the parent "interferes" than because the offspring disobeys.

More generally, an ideal of inter-generational autonomy is upheld both for parents and their grown-up children. Along with this, less social distance appears accompanied by easier affectuality between fathers and sons and mothers and daughters. (This may be related to the cross-sex to same-sex shift that has been mentioned, which may reflect the operation of a number of partly independent causes.) On the increase of affectuality, it must be said that this increase is mainly shown on the parents' side and more often than not is not reciprocated.

3. DECLINE IN FAMILY OBLIGATIONS GENERALLY AND IN EXTENDED FAMILY ATTACHMENTS

Contrary to expectations, we did not find strong indications of a 3-generation

family system in 1890, of the type that frequently has been assumed in much of the family sociology literature. We are speaking here not only of 3-generation residence within the same household, which hardly is essential to the pattern, but of the broader possibility that adult children upon marrying will settle within the same neighborhood as their parents, within range for regular association and the carrying out of mutual help obligations. Few cases appear where any adult children reside in the same local community as their parents after marriage, and there are many portrayals of family dispersions—e.g., where relatives come "visiting" from a distance, at irregular intervals. Also interesting to us was the suggestion in several stories that the dispersion pattern may have been fairly "new" in 1890 and not solidly accepted.

Instead of the traditional extended family structure centering around the obligation for children to settle with or near their parents, we find typically a neighborhood congeries of nuclear families, closely related and fulfilling many of the help-functions often attributed to kinship without the bond of formal kinship ties. It may well be, if our ethnography is valid, that the traditional extended-family patterns apparently found in the European antecedents of Americans were more disrupted in migration and transplantation than has been recognized.

But there *are* frequent mentions of relatives, and various significant associations are described. A fair number of the characters have cousins, uncles and aunts, and we have several instances of levirate as well as sororate patterns (i.e., orphaned children taken in by parents' sisters and brothers). Over the period, these more distant kinship relations become less frequent and important, although a few cases still appear in 1955. (The greatest decrease, again, is found in cross-sex relationships.)

4. EMERGENCE OF THE "PEER GROUP"

Outside of the family, there is increasing emphasis on peer relations and most of all with the opposite sex. (Same-sex friendships increase for very young adults but decrease among men aged twenty-five or older and among women past age eighteen.)

In part, there seems to be a trend toward increasing segregation by generation relating crucially to changes in the neighborhood structure. (The trend also appears within the family.) The development is partly supported by Census and other figures on residential areas during the latter part of our period.

The greatest decline is in the incidence of friendships between young women and middle-aged neighbors, a trend seemingly related to the attrition of neighborhood family ties. In the early period, such relations are quite frequent, taking on something of an "auntly" character between a young girl and a mature woman-friend of her mother's. In the later period, while "opportunities" are portrayed for such associations through work or other contacts, closer friendships across the age-lines hardly appear.

5. MARRIAGE

Several important changes in marriage are indicated, most of which are in accordance with previous claims. Perhaps the major change indicated is a shift away from a partnership conception in the late nineteenth century, to growing emphasis on romance, affectuality. companionship and young parenthood.

As our stories have it, there was to be sure some decided value placed upon romance and courtship in the 1890's, but the honeymoon was short-lived. Most important, affectual satisfaction and compatibility were neither the major criteria of desirability in a mate nor of judging marital success. A man was valued most for being a steady, dependable, "good provider," and an effective disciplinarian of the chil-

dren. For the woman, virtue, "character," emotional strength and her skill at household management seem to have been most important. Note that these values could only be fully realized and expressed over many years of a lifetime, and the value of a satisfactory spouse tends to be portrayed as increasing over the lifespan, reaching its zenith in later middle-age.

By 1955, as partnership values are displaced, the locus of expression and fulfillment also changes, viewed in lifetime perspective. Increasingly, value is placed on the early years of marriage and parenthood, when the values emphasized, such as "fun," "charm," physical vitality, and allure, are relatively at their height. Correspondingly, there is something approaching a deterioration of marriage-values portrayed by middle-age, after the children are grown and independent. We might say that with the value changes, marriage after age 40 declines in "market-value," a loss that is greater by far for the woman than the man. In the sociologic of the stories, the deflation of wifehood relates to the loss of functions as parent and as household manager (technological unemployment, we might say in part, through the advent of labor-saving devices).

In our story sample, there are no clear compensations for the older women to take the place of her earlier marital and parental roles. The loss of role and status is fairly total. (It may be worth noting that the growth of "women's organizations" in our society among women in this age group receives hardly a mention—even in the *Ladies' Home Journal*.)

6. WORK ROLES AND VALUES

A highly complex change is indicated in the "meaning of work" for men at different stages of adult life. In several ways, this change for men partly parallels those concerning the marital and family roles of women that have been mentioned.

Too simply, we might say that in 1890 work is primarily a matter of "necessity" for the man. That is, while the ability of a man to make a dependable living greatly affects his social standing in his family and neighborhood, within broad limits a man's social standing is not crucially dependent upon his wealth, achievement, or occupational success. This finding seems partly interpretable in terms of the fairly rigid stratification system depicted for the time, with little prospect, encouragement, or orientation to mobility. The crucial standing of the individual is within the locality group (rather than the broader community or occupational situs); and within this group a man's social standing is based upon his personal characteristics and neighborhood participation in their totality. Over the period, increasing value is placed on wealth and occupational success as criteria of a man's position in the social hierarchy. This trend (again in the sociologic of Storyville) is meaningfully related to the emergence of secondary society and urban social life. There is a corresponding segmentation of "reference groups" whose status judgments count most for the individual. In 1890 the locality group appears to be the principal determiner of an individual's standing; from the 1920's on this group is replaced by a plurality of groups corresponding to major social roles. Each group is likely to judge the individual on the basis of limited spheres of contacts with him (i.e., coworker by his work, neighbors by his neighborly relations with them). While "personality" clearly still counts for much, it is often the selective personality attached to a role that is significant. One may be a quite different "person" at home, at work, in the lodge, and so forth, with little necessary carryover from one sphere to the other.

The trend mentioned toward increasing value on wealth and achievement is far from uniform over the period, and differs significantly for young men and for the middle-aged. For men under 40 the trend is simplest. There is a fairly steady increase in achievement emphasis, becoming most pronounced in the 1950's. We might say the process is one toward an "afflu-

ence" of aspirations. In 1890 the main concern in the "middle-class" was with making a secure living; as the period unfolds it becomes more necessary to have income sufficient for luxuries for one to be satisfied with his position. And the aspiration-level in this respect (leaving aside periods of economic depression) becomes higher through time. By contrast, for the middle-aged there is something of an up-and-down, cyclical trend in achievement emphasis. The emphasis rises notably from 1890 to 1925, but then declines to a lower point still in 1955. Most striking is the fact that, while in 1925 the economically well-to-do are portrayed as being reasonably satisfied, in 1955 it is precisely the middle-aged professionals and others of wealth who are portrayed as being most restless and unfulfilled. (We might say that where monetary success "succeeds" in 1925, there is a partial "failure of success" by 1955.) The decrease in achievement values for middle-aged men in Storyville does not mean a rejection of these values. Rather, there seems to be increasing desire for success-plus-something-more, without a definite indication of what the "something more" might be.

Taking the two different trends together, for the young and the middle-aged, our findings suggest a relocation in the period of life during which occupational striving is valued and strongly encouraged for the American man. There is a growing contraction of the time for hard work to the young-adult period, with a search for other values during middle-age and afterwards.

7. CHANGE IN SOCIOLOGICAL
PRIME-OF-LIFE

The various trends indicated in family, work, marriage and other roles seem to partly sum up to a fundamental change in the life-cycle organization of adult social roles for men and women if we can believe the stories. We might say there has been a shift in the sociological prime-of-life from mature middle age (in 1890) to young adulthood (in 1955). This change appears more drastic for women but also is of enormous consequence for men. For both it involves basic redefinitions of functional roles and values, with major implications for personal identity and security.

In the 1890's the standing of the middle-aged is generally high in Storyville, based upon a variety of valued social roles they perform as parents, spouses, relatives, neighbors, friends, and (for some men) as employers. The standing of the middle-aged woman in many ways is higher than that of the man. Her standing derives crucially from her position in the family. While the families at this time are portrayed as moderately patriarchal in character, the wife has a great deal of autonomy and authority as the "in-plant manager," the person inside the premises who is in charge, especially of her daughters and of household organization. From an emotional standpoint, she is the pivotal member, the "social-emotional leader" (in Robert F. Bales's sense) who is expected to be a reservoir of emotional strength and fortitude. She also is a highly skilled "craftsman" in her varied capacities as chef, preparer-of-food (starting, let's recall, with a live chicken, etc.), housekeeper and maternal guardian, the possessor of a complex body of knowledge and skills brought to fruition over many years of experience. While her life is far from an easy one, it is highly significant by prevailing social values and (under favorable conditions) socially secure.

For both men and women, the middle-age period is the time of greatest independence, respect, esteem, prestige and social involvement. It is, moreover, a time of active involvement in the affairs of the young, through association with children, neighbors, relatives, and of course with grandchildren. In fact, characters at every stage of life are described as being involved, both directly and indirectly, in the affairs of others at every other life stage.

Middle-age is a central phase of life in another important sense. The main goals relating to marriage, work, family, and community participation are goals the successful realization of which can only be found during the mature adult years. The goals described take on the character of "life-tasks," involving a gradual unfolding over the course of the adult life-span.

By 1955 the main goals and social values reach their climax between ages 20 to 40; life-after-forty tends to be defined as "anti-climactic." For men, the change applies most of all to work roles, where age progressively becomes a negative factor in open-competition with youth. For the woman, it applies most of all to marriage and parenthood, where age becomes associated with loss of glamor and function. In general, the mature adult retires into the background as youth comes to the fore; the change is most extreme for women who are described as being largely without recourse.

Age changes its meaning, from the connotations of "experience," "wisdom" and "seasoning" to those of "past the prime," partly "out of it," and perhaps to some degree of being "not with it."

It must be emphasized that the changes mentioned are relative, and there are important continuities as well. Most of the values receiving emphasis in our 1955 sample have some currency in the earliest period, and the older values do not totally disappear. By the standards of the 1890's, the middle-aged in 1955 are quite well off in a number of significant respects. The most important of these ways that we have been able to discern relate to ease-of-living (freedom from fatigue), health, and economic well-being, which might be juxtaposed against the losses of valued social participation and social standing. In the context of our stories, if we imagine somehow bringing our characters to life and informing them of the contrasts between the periods so as to elicit their preferences, our impression is that most would elect for the world of 1890 given only these two choices.

The social changes in life organization fall hardest on the aged, who suffer a virtual "symbolic abandonment" in the stories, relegated to less prominent roles and excluded from membership in the main adult Storyville in-group. In 1890, the aged characters have a fair number of close associations with younger adults. In 1955, not a single character over age 60 is described as having a close reciprocal attachment with a middle-aged or young adult. Their only significant associations are with peers or children. Their destiny seems to be one of banishment—to the "senior citizen" magazines.

CONCLUDING REMARKS

We cannot, of course, assume that changing role-patterns in magazine stories provide authentic indicators of actual changes in the society without the greatest caution. Our method crucially involves the assumption that the role-portrayals common to many different stories during a period (by many different writers, and subject to varied editorial control) have some correspondence to social reality. However, the assumption requires a great many qualifications, and we do not claim to know what many of these should be. Common portrayals may reflect widely held, distortive stereotypes, idealized misrepresentations, or patterns of very limited subgroups in the society.

Confidence in the conclusions of any study of this type can only be obtained through comparative study, drawing upon the widest range of corroborative sources for substantiation. At present, we only can offer limited corroboration for the trend-findings presented, and for some we have no ready witnesses to summon forth. We personally find some of our findings puzzling—for example, the pervasive shift indicated within families from cross-sex to same-sex emphasis. However, there are other findings which have a "ring of plausibility" about them which lead us to take them seriously even where we cannot yet subject them to rigorous consistency checks.

It seems plausible that the age-related shift in work-achievement values, with greater achievement emphasis for men during the early years of occupational participation, may represent a genuine trend in the subpopulations from which our magazines' readers were drawn. The judgment of "plausibility" may in fact be based upon "informal" consistency-checks with other documentary sources, or it may merely indicate that the findings fit our own preconceptions. All we ask at the moment is that our wares be considered with an open mind, while awaiting more conclusive evidence.

6

BERNICE L. NEUGARTEN and DAVID L. GUTMANN

AGE-SEX ROLES AND PERSONALITY IN MIDDLE AGE:
A THEMATIC APPERCEPTION STUDY

The original purpose of this investigation was to explore the use of projective techniques in studying adult age-sex roles in the family. At least two considerations prompted the choice of the Thematic Apperception Test technique. The first was that the responses would be relatively uncensored, more closely related to the respondent's personal values and experiences than those he might feel constrained to give in answer to more direct questions. Second, fantasy material, although presenting certain difficulties of analysis as compared with questionnaire data, would have a decided advantage for exploratory research. The richness and unstructured nature of projective data enable the investigator to follow an inductive process; he can follow up clues as they appear in the data rather than check dimensions and hypotheses defined in advance.

The primary concern of the study was with the collective role images of husbands, wives, sons, and daughters, as those images emerged from the projections of different respondents. After the role images had been delineated, the investigators turned to implications in the data regarding the personalities of the respondents. Thus, this investigation broadened in scope as the research progressed, and, as will become clearer in following

Abridged from *Psychological Monographs,* vol. 72, no. 17, 1958 (whole no. 470). Copyright 1958 by the American Psychological Association and reproduced by permission. A different version of this material is reprinted as chapter 3 of *Personality in Middle and Late Life,* ed. Bernice L. Neugarten (New York: Atherton Press, 1964).

sections, this report deals not only with familial roles but also with the relations between role image and personality in middle age.

THE SAMPLE

The study population consisted of 131 men and women, distributed by age, sex, and social class, as shown in Table 1. The

TABLE 1

THE SAMPLE

	40–54		55–70	
	Men	Women	Men	Women
Middle class....	18	22	14	13
Working class...	21	12	15	16
Total = 131 ...				

middle-class men were well-to-do business executives and professionals, none of whom were retired. The working-class men were stable blue-collar workers, of whom three had retired. Of both groups of women, the large majority were married housewives, only a few of whom held part-time or full-time jobs outside the home. With only a few exceptions, all the people in the study population were native-born of north European ethnic backgrounds. The large majority grew up in Kansas, Missouri, or neighboring Midwest states. Almost all were Protestant. With regard to family status, of the total 131 cases, only four women had never married; only eight of the men and six of

Fig. 1

the women were childless. One-half of the women and one-third of the men were grandparents.

THE DATA AND METHODS OF ANALYSIS

A specially drawn picture was used, one designed specifically to evoke the sentiments and preoccupations of middle-aged respondents in relation to family roles (Fig. 1).

Three levels of inquiry were employed in using the picture. The person was asked, first, to tell a story about the picture—a story with a beginning, a middle, and an end. Then the interviewer, moving clockwise around the picture and beginning with the figure of the young man, asked the respondent to assign an age and to give a general description of each of the four figures. Again moving clockwise, the respondent was finally asked to describe what he thought each figure in the picture was feeling about the others.

STIMULUS VALUE OF THE PICTURE

Almost without exception, all respondents saw the picture as representing a two-generation family. One of the younger figures, most often the young man, was frequently seen as being outside the primary group, usually in the role of suitor or fiancée, son-in-law or daughter-in-law. Although always structured as a family situation, the stories varied widely. It might be a story of a young man coming to ask for the daughter's hand in marriage and being opposed by the older woman; it might be a mother, father, daughter, and son-in-law having a casual conversation before dinner; it might be a young couple asking for financial help from parents; or it might be an older couple coming to visit the younger.

It is within the setting of the two-generation family, then, that the role images of the young man, young woman, old man, and old woman emerged.

GENERAL APPROACH TO ROLE ANALYSIS

Having used the three levels of inquiry, the data for each figure can be regarded as a set of expectations as to how that category of person (YM, YW, OM, OW) relates to the social environment and to other categories of persons in the family in terms of action and affect. It is this set of expectations which were regarded operationally as the role description. The following assumption was made: granted that the different attributes ascribed by the respondent to the four figures in the picture have their roots in intrapsychic determinants, the respondent's expectations, based on his experiences with real people, will still have a highly determining effect on which aspects of the self he chooses to ascribe to each figure in the picture. In other words, the investigators took the respondent's perceptions as projections, mindful of the fact that what was given was intrapsychically determined, but trusting that the interactional social reality had called out and directed the projection.

ILLUSTRATION OF THE METHOD

The first step in the analysis was to see what was the preoccupation around which the respondent had built his story, for the role descriptions took on greater meaning once the basic theme, or preoccupation, was understood.

For example, a woman tells the following story:

"I think the boy is going away to the service. He's telling the mother and father. That's his wife with him. The father is pretty downhearted about it. He has a downcast look on his face. His wife doesn't feel too good about it, but she's trying to pacify the older couple. They've just been married. I can't tell how it'll end up. If he has to go overseas to fight, there's always the possibility he won't come back.

(General description of the YM) Sort of

a boy who has always been close to his parents. Looks like a nice kind of boy.

(General description of the YW) Looks very sympathetic. She's a real nice girl. She's trying to sympathize with the old people.

(General description of the OM) Looks like a nice homebody. Nice fellow.

(General description of the OW) I can't see enough of her face. I couldn't say any more, because there's no face to go by. Sort of refined, from her stature.

(YM's feelings) He thinks they're all right, or he wouldn't have sat down. . . . Well, some boys wouldn't care how their folks felt, but he seems to realize that they're hurt.

(YW's feelings) She thinks her husband is a pretty fine fellow, or she wouldn't be trying to sympathize with his folks.

(OM's feelings) He's pleased with the young folks. He's interested in what his son's going to do.

(OW's feelings) She's in a bad place—can't see enough of her. I really couldn't say."

The theme which underlies this story is the theme of family dispersion, the "empty nest." The respondent tells us, in effect, that the children are leaving home and that they "won't come back."

Looking first at the description of the young man, in the story proper we are told what his action is: to leave home, presumably for some dangerous and rigorous extrafamilial environment. His action has emotional consequences for the parents, consequences which he does not seek to mitigate. His face is set beyond the boundaries of the primary group, and his only action in the group is the rather formal one of making this position clear to his parents. "He's telling the mother and father."

We are next told about the young man that he has always been close to his parents. The implication is that an earlier relationship of the son to the parents is now ending. It is of interest that the respondent speaks of the YM's affiliation to the parents only when she discusses him in the general, nonsituational context. When she is asked to consider him in relation to the immediate situation and to the

actors in it, the theme of remoteness infuses the portrayal. This point is made clear when the respondent is again asked to put the young man back into the interactive context and to discuss his feelings there. Now he emerges as one who, although essentially detached, still adheres to minimal social forms. The respondent has difficulty in ascribing any but the most qualified feeling to him: "thinks they're all right," and "seems to realize that they're hurt." The YM's reaction to the parents' feelings is a relatively intellectualized one: he "realizes" or recognizes their existence, while it is his wife who "sympathizes" with them. Even this modest affective gesture on the part of the YM is doubted, for the respondent goes out of her way to assure us that the YM is not like other boys who "wouldn't care how their parents felt." In the respondent's whole recital, then, she attributes to the YM only minimal and grudging affiliation to the parents.

We can now make this general statement about the perception of the young man's familial role—his basic orientation is to rigorous and compelling nonaffective extrafamilial concerns, and intimacy for him is to be found with peers of the opposite sex. Although not too long ago (in terms of subjective time) the primary, parental group was a major focus of his interest, his present role there is governed by moral directives (superego demands) rather than by spontaneous warmth. These directives, coming into conflict with his more compelling extrafamilial interests, result in a posture of grudging punctiliousness, of bare attention to formal, socially defined demands. Himself barely participant in the family—although at the same time, a source of concern to the parents—he leaves to his wife the mediation of the emotional issues between himself and his parents. He is generally governed by outside demands, as though those demands were more congenial to his energies and motivations than are the demands made by the parental group.

Turning to the YW, we are given a

different image. In the story proper she, too, appears as one whose actions are directed toward the parents, but, whereas the YM's action toward the parents—telling them that he is leaving—begins and ends his contact with them, her action—"trying to pacify them"—implies a continuing and multifaceted relationship with the older group. The young man only tells them about himself and at the most can only "recognize" the effects of his announcement on the parents. The young woman, although she "doesn't feel too good about it," does not deal with her own reaction but attempts to alleviate the parents' grief. The word "pacify" implies maternal behavior, as does the pattern of dealing with the woes of others rather than with her own.

Our interpretation of the young woman's strong, maternal concern with intimate human relations is strengthened when we look at the general description given of her. Here, the respondent persists in seeing the YW in relation to the current crisis. Again she is seen as a person whose actions are nurturant and consoling, but at this point an element of emotional distance enters into the description. The young woman is "trying" to sympathize with the older group. Here is an implication of some barrier against emotional rapport between the old group and the YW, a barrier which she feels impelled to overcome. The description of the YW's feelings give us a clue as to why she attempts to overcome the barrier. It is because of her regard for her husband that she feels a responsibility to his parents. We are told that her primary affiliation is to her husband and that responsibility to the parents is secondary, stemming from her marital tie. She takes form now as a person who must deal nurturantly with various aspects of the interpersonal universe, although institutional and generational barriers may exist between her and certain others. If formal ties exist between her and other people, she seeks to enrich the formal ties with empathic bonds.

Taking the role description as a whole and seeing it against the theme of "empty nest," we see the young woman's role as one of emotional liaison, operating in the widening breach between the parental and filial generations. Her husband moves off into what are viewed as distant and threatening events while she, though drawn after him, bridges the gap and maintains some version of the lost emotional ties between parents and children. Against the background of traumatic family dispersion, her role has a maternal quality: although her primary tie is to her husband, her immediate concern is for those who have been injured by the course of events, and she attempts in maternal fashion to compensate the injured through her nurturance. In sum, her role is complementary to her husband's in that, while he moves off to "do battle," she tarries behind to handle the human consequences of his actions and decisions.

Turning to the figure of the old man, we first see him as feeling sad at the news of his son's leaving. No actions are ascribed to him. He reacts to traumatic situations with feeling, but he is not seen as acting out his feelings or doing anything to alter the situation which made him sad.

At the level of general description, we are told that he is "a nice homebody," positively regarded. His major cathexis or emotional investment is to the family, and it is there that he is gratified. Values relevant to his role are those of comfort and ease in an affiliative setting.

Moving to the feelings ascribed to the old man, we notice a shift away from the initial description given of him. Where he was initially saddened, he is now "pleased" with the young people, and he will maintain a meaningful, although somewhat intellectualized interest in his son's future activity. There is still no intimation that he will act to change the course of his son's affairs—the son will "do," and the father will be interested—but a note of equanimity has entered the description. If we examine this shift in light of the theme of family dissolution, we conclude that it represents a concept of defensive adjustment, adjustment to the inescapable reality of the young man's maturity through defensive denial of strong personal feeling. After some initial depression, the old man resigns himself to the fact of the breach and returns to the emotional *status quo*. Although the young group, especially the YM, is no longer reciprocally affiliative, the old man's outward feelings toward them remain basically unchanged.

The old man's role, then, somewhat like the young woman's, is an adjustive one. He buffers the shocks of transition. Accepting the reality of change, he acts to minimize the consequent feelings and to find new bases for intimacy in the new situation. It is of particular interest that the old man attempts to maintain the *status quo* by changing himself and hiding his own feelings. At no point in the protocol does he act to change anything outside himself.

This interpretation of the old man's role gains support when we turn to the old woman. In the story proper we are told nothing about her; her presence is merely noted. At the general level of description, perception of her is again denied. In effect, we are told that she has no emotionally expressive surface ("there's no face to go by"). She is associated only with "refinement," a description which implies that she has no contact with a freely affective, spontaneous environment. (By contrast, the old man is the "homebody.") The word "refined" suggests the values of restraint, pride, and possibly a defensive rigidity.

As to the old woman's feelings, the respondent tells us, in effect, that she cannot imagine any feeling states which might pertain, because the OW is "in a bad place." Although there is a relative paucity of data about the OW, we nevertheless obtain the strong impression of

rigidity and withdrawal in the figure. Viewed against the thematic background, this rigidity and withdrawal takes on meaning as a possible mode of coping with crisis, but a mode which is quite different from the one defined for the old man. Faced with the trauma of family breakdown, the old man's role is to adjust to the inevitable by minimizing his own reactions. The adjustive mode ascribed to the old woman seems to stress denial of the trauma and its emotional consequences, strict control, and magical defenses against her vulnerability. The old man's adjustment, although a defensive one, still is oriented toward a social universe and untroubled contact with others in future situations. The old woman's role has a more primitive, egocentric quality, as if the vulnerability of the self were the only concern and as if this concern justifies the use of archaic defenses—such as complete denial of a painful situation.

Granted that both the old man's and old woman's roles may represent possible solutions of the respondent's own problem—her defenses against the problem she has proposed—the investigators' primary interest is with the content of the roles as they emerge from the respondent's fantasy and to which figure in the picture each role is ascribed.

TREATMENT OF THE DATA

Using the method illustrated above, each protocol was analyzed for role descriptions of each of the four stimulus figures. Interpretations were recorded separately for each figure. The protocols were divided according to the sex of the respondent but were analyzed without knowledge of the respondent's age or social class.

RELIABILITY OF INTERPRETATIONS

The question of reliability of interpretations was dealt with at an early stage in the research. Using nine protocols selected at random, two judges rated each of the four figures on a five-point scale for each of twelve personality characteristics, and the ratings were then corre- lated. The average coefficients of correla- tion were .81 for the YM, .88 for the YW, .83 for the OM, and .88 for the OW.

This procedure proved to be a some- what oblique test of reliability, since it was later decided not to deal with the role descriptions on the basis of such ratings, but rather to continue to draw summary descriptions of the figure and then to categorize the descriptions ac- cording to similarity. At the same time, this test of reliability was a relatively stringent one for this type of data.

QUANTIFYING THE DATA

Once all the protocols had been ana- lyzed and decoded, the data for each figure were treated separately. The pro- cedures with reference to the data on the old man will be described here since these were the first to be dealt with and since findings regarding the OM influenced in some ways the organization of the other sets of data.

All the descriptions were grouped on the basis of similarity into mutually ex- clusive categories, attempting always to judge similarity in terms of the most salient features ascribed to the OM by the respondent. This was a lengthy process since the attempt was to establish cate- gories that would produce the least dis- tortion of the original data. At the same time, having become aware that there were age differences in the perceptions of the OM, the investigators attempted to structure the categories in such fashion as to highlight the age differences.

Six major categories were finally de- lineated and arranged along a continuum termed "dominance-submission." At one end were those categories in which, what- ever other characteristics were ascribed to the OM, he was always a dominant figure within the family. At the other end were those categories in which he was seen as a passive or submissive figure. Dominance or submission was judged in terms of the OM's impact on the situa-

tion; the extent to which others deferred to him; the extent to which resolutions of family issues depended upon his wishes, his judgments, or his decisions.

Dealing next with one after another subsample of respondents (middle-class men, middle-class women, working-class men, working-class women), frequency distributions were made in which the role descriptions were plotted by category and by age of respondent. The distribu- tions were then tested for statistical sig- nificance by applying the chi-square method.

For each subsample of respondents there was a shift with age in the percep- tions of the OM. The role descriptions given by younger respondents (aged forty to fifty-four) more often fell in those categories in which the OM is de- scribed as dominant; the descriptions given by older respondents (aged fifty- five to seventy) most often fell in those categories in which the OM is passive. The number of cases in each subsample was too small to establish reliable chi- square values, but the trend was present in every group. Cases were then com- bined into larger groupings—all male, all female, all middle class, all working class. The age trends were now even more pro- nounced (P values were between .05 and .01). Finally, when all respondents were grouped together, the age shift was un- questionably reliable (P was .001).

At this point, whereas age of respond- ent consistently produced variation in the data, it was not clear which of the original variables—age, sex, or social status—was the most important in producing the over-all variation. A further step was therefore taken. Ratings on dominance- submission were assigned to each cate- gory of role description; these ratings were then submitted to an analysis of variance. It was found that of all the vari- ables—age, sex, social status, and the inter- actions thereof—only age was significant

(*P* was beyond .001). The data on the OW were also subjected to analysis of variance, with the same result emerging.[1]

THE OLD MAN

The figure of the OM seems to symbolize for respondents the ego qualities of the personality: the rational rather than the impulsive approach to problems, concern over the needs of others, reconciliation between opposing interests, cerebral competence.

The descriptions of the OM fall into six major categories that can be ordered along a continuum from dominance to submission.

1. "Altruistic authority." In this category the OM is seen in a position of authority in the family, and he uses his authority to benefit the young people or the family as a whole. He is the benevolent monarch, the nurturant wise man, whose actions are altruistically motivated and lead only to benevolent outcomes. He operates effortlessly and easily in this role.

2. "Assertive, but guilty." These descriptions are those in which the OM attempts to further his own ends, but is restrained by inner reluctances, doubts, or guilt. He occupies a position of strength and asserts himself in the family, and, although he is not opposed by others, he nevertheless cannot easily and single-mindedly press for his announced goals. There is always some quality of inner doubt about the justice of his claims. He is conflicted, unsure, the insecure autocrat. "He thinks it's about time those kids left home and earned their own living—he hates to tell them, though."

3. "Formal authority." Here the father is the authority, but by default. His authority is challenged as the story progresses, or other individuals take action to decide outcomes while he acts only to approve those outcomes. He is described here not so much in terms of service to others (as in Category 1), but in terms of pliability to the wishes of others. He merely approves decisions which have already been thrashed out among more active figures.

4. "Surrendered authority." It is indicated here that the OM could be the authority

if he desired—he possesses the requisite qualities—but he refuses and/or abandons the role. In some instances, he is initially described as dominant, but, as the story unfolds, he is relegated to a more submissive position. In other instances, he is ascribed the qualities associated with leadership, but these qualities are split away from action—they have no impact on the events of the story, they do not impinge on outcomes, they find no overt behavioral expression. He is inwardly "tough" but overtly passive, or he has "executive qualities" but leaves the decision up to his wife. In no instance is there an intrusion of the OM as a dominant force on the family scene.

5. "Passive, affiliative." Here the OM is described in terms of what might be called maternal qualities. He is unflaggingly and uncritically affiliative toward the others. He "loves everybody." He accepts, resignedly, outcomes which he may not approve. He is dominated by his wife, but seems to feel no discomfort or resentment in the situation. In stories where the OW is opposing some action proposed by the young people, such as marriage, the OM's attitude is one of affiliating with both sides—of saying affectionately to the OW, "Why fight the inevitable?"

6. "Passive, cerebral." Grouped here are those descriptions which present the OM as passive and withdrawn. He lacks any announced affiliative attachments to others. The issue of authority does not even arise. His wife rules the family, and he remains remote, both in terms of action and affect, from the family drama. As this drama swirls about him, he "thinks." (The content of his thought or its relevance to the situation is rarely specified.) The OM controls events from behind the forehead, as it were, and takes a certain satisfaction in the freedom this provides him. As one male respondent put it, "He's made up his mind about the thing. He's waiting for the old woman to tell them what to do."

AGE DIFFERENCES

As shown in Table 2, there is a consistent shift, with increasing age of respondent, from seeing the OM in situations of power in the family toward seeing him as passive and submissive. (This

[1] Findings *re* the YM and YW are omitted from the present version of this paper.—ED.

64

age shift is statistically significant beyond the .005 level.)

The stimulus figure of the OM confronts the majority of younger respondents with the issue of familial authority. (If Category 4 is included, then approximately 75 percent of all younger respondents see the OM either as an authority figure or as one who possesses the potential for authority.)

Each of the first four categories in Table 2 represents a different resolution of the issue of male dominance. The first two represent active resolutions. If the issue is met head on—if, that is, the OM defines self-gratifying goals and uses his

position of authority to achieve them (Category 2)—then ambivalence and guilt are the necessary results. If, on the other hand, the OM uses his authority nurturantly for the benefit of others, he can act easily and comfortably in his position (Category 1). The more passive solutions involve either the OM's sanctioning of the wishes of others and attempting no intervention in the family scene (Category 3) or the more outright abandonment of the authoritative status altogether (Category 4).

TABLE 2

ROLE DESCRIPTIONS OF THE OLD MAN

Category	40–54		55–70	
	Men	Women	Men	Women
1. Altruistic authority:				
Middle class	5	9	2	1
Working class	3	3	1	3
Total	20*		7	
2. Assertive, but guilty:				
Middle class	2	0	2	2
Working class	6	1	1	1
Total	9		6	
3. Formal authority:				
Middle class	5	5	0	0
Working class	2	3	1	0
Total	15		1	
4. Surrendered authority:				
Middle class	2	3	4	3
Working class	6	1	3	2
Total	12		12	
5. Passive, affiliative:				
Middle class	0	4	2	6
Working class	3	4	3	8
Total	11		19	
6. Passive, cerebral:				
Middle class	4	1	4	1
Working class	1	0	6	2
Total	6		13	

* The chi-square test was applied to these category totals. The probability that the distribution occurred by chance is less than .001.

For our forty–fifty-four group, the issue being dealt with around the role of the OM is not only that of male dominance, however, but also that of male aggression in the family. The problem seems to be how the OM can be an authority without being arbitrarily, and perhaps harmfully, self-assertive. How can the cultural demand—that the father is head of the family—be met without exposing the family to male aggression? The solution seems to involve the stressing of the moral function of authority: the OM must be either an active force for good, or, by "letting things happen," he passively cooperates with the others in arriving at positive outcomes.

For older respondents, the OM no longer presents the issue of masculine authority. The stories are now those in which the OM has no impact upon family events, and he presents only one or another image of passivity. (Of all respondents aged fifty-five–seventy, 55 percent are found in the last two categories. If Category 4 is included—the OM abandoning or surrendering authority—then 80 percent of all older respondents see the OM among the categories of submission and denial of authority.)

The age shift in the image of the OM from dominance to submission is elaborated in several ways. The forty-year-old respondent sees the OM as being in doubt about his own assertive tendencies; the sixty-year-old sees him as being the passive object of others' assertion. In the forties, the OM is seen as attempting to control events. In the sixties, he attempts only to control and order the cognitive environment, the symbolic traces of objects and events. In the forties, it is proposed that the OM is aware of the pressures from an impulsive and willful woman, but that he can allow the OW full expression and still wisely control the course of events. In the sixties, it is proposed that impulse, in the form of the OW, is left in charge of the field, that the OM's wisdom can control events only behind the forehead. The OM has moved from a stance of intrafamilial autonomy to "intracranial" autonomy.

In regard to the implications for personality differences in respondents, it has been said that the figure of the OM symbolizes ego qualities of the personality. With increased age of respondent, the ego, as personified by the OM, seems to contract. On the one hand, it is no longer in contact with impulse life, controlling and channeling it (the OM no longer controls the OW's impulsivity). On the other hand, the ego is no longer in a position of mastery relative to the outer world (the OM is not successful in the extrafamilial world). Ego functions are turned inward, as it were, and, although rational thought processes are still important in the personality, thought is no longer relevant to action.

THE OLD WOMAN

The old woman, by comparison to the other figures in the picture, is the key figure in the family. The family is her arena, and within it she emerges in full scope and complexity. There are, for instance, a number of stories that might be labeled "Oedipal" in theme—stories in which the YW is being claimed by the YM or vice versa and in which there is conflict between the young and the old. In these stories, it is always the OW, but not the OM, who is seen as the protagonist in the struggle.

For the OW, the major issue is around retentiveness of the young—what the extent and the nature of the tie between herself and her children is to be. This issue always has strong emotional components for her.

In contrast to the young woman, the OW is seen as standing on her own feet, a person in her own right. The psychological distance between her and the old man is much greater than that between the two young figures. Whereas the YW and YM are seen in a close, collaborative relationship, the OW and OM stand separate and apart. They are often described in polar terms—if one is dominant, the other is submissive; if one is nurturant, the other is narcissistic.

The OW is not always seen as comfortable in her role, and she is the only figure who is as often described by respondents in negative as in positive terms.

Descriptions of the old woman were grouped into six major categories. Al-

though the categories are ordered in Table 3 along the general continuum from submission to dominance, there are really two major themes which, in one or another combination, form the basis for

TABLE 3

ROLE DESCRIPTIONS OF THE OLD WOMAN

CATEGORY	40-54		55-70	
	Men	Women	Men	Women
1. Submissive, nurturant:				
Middle class:	10	6	1	3
Working class.....	4	2	2	3
Total...........	24*		9	
2. Controlled by OM:				
Middle class.......	1	9	1	0
Working class.....	5	5	1	2
Total...........	20		4	
3. Limited by children:				
Middle class.......	2	3	1	1
Working class.....	3	2	2	4
Total...........	10		8	
4. The good mother:				
Middle class.......	2	0	7	2
Working class.....	7	0	3	2
Total...........	9		14	
5. The matriarch:				
Middle class.......	1	3	0	3
Working class.....	1	0	1	1
Total...........	5		5	
6. Hostile self-assertion:				
Middle class.......	2	1	4	3
Working class.....	1	1	5	4
Total...........	5		16	

* The chi-square test was applied to these category totals. The probability that the distribution occurred by chance is less than .001.

the differentiation. The first is the theme of control over others—whether the OW is seen as submissive and controlled (categories 1, 2, 3) or as dominant and the controller (categories 4, 5, 6). The second theme is that of the nature of impulsivity—whether the OW is viewed as benign and nurturant (categories 1, 4, 5) or self-assertive and aggressive (categories 2, 3, 6).

1. "Submissive, nurturant." Here the OW is viewed as passive relative to the determination of outcomes. She is affiliative, nurturant, benevolent, but never self-assertive. She takes a position of deference to a wise, authoritative old man. She is the fluttery, "little-woman" type and never intrudes on the masculine prerogatives of thought and decision. She is dependent on her husband for guidance and for control. To the extent that she takes action at all, the action is nurturant, promoting the best interests of others, especially the young.

2. "Controlled by OM." Here the OW is seen as aggressive and impulsive, but she is controlled by the OM. Although she is something of a "battle-ax," she is more the family nuisance than the family menace. Her rages do not intimidate; they merely annoy. The wise and tolerant husband allows her free expression of her feelings, but deftly controls her. He determines outcomes and guarantees nurturant solutions to the autonomy-seeking young, often in the face of the OW's active opposition.

3. "Limited by children." Here, as in the preceding category, an aggressive, domineering OW tries to extend her control over a resistant environment. While she now dominates her husband, she is successfully opposed and limited by the YW and/or the YM. The OM cannot provide a buffer between the intrusive OW and the young, but the young take up the cudgels for themselves and win out against the OW.

4. "The good mother." Here the issue of dominance-submission is not specifically introduced, though the OW is implicitly given the decisive role in the disposition of affairs. The OW is the good, nurturant mother who guides and supports her gratified husband and children. She is mild, benign, maternal. Though she has the most effective role in the family, there is no tension between her and the others. The view is rather of harmonious interaction, where it is only right and "natural" that the mother holds the most important place in the family.

5. "The matriarch." In this category the OW is seen as a forceful and aggressive authority. While, however, she has complete sway over the others, this leads only to benign results. The family, rather than opposing her, bask contentedly in their dependent and submissive positions. Everyone benefits from her rule.

6. "Hostile self-assertion." Here the OW is a stereotyped figure, one who exercises a harsh, arbitrary, and unopposed control. Her dominance is not tempered by any redeeming strain or affiliation or nurturance, nor does she have any concern for others. The OW is either pictured as the embodiment of amoral id—all impulse and wrath—or the punitive superego who harshly judges others and rigidly defines the moral code—a superego armed, as it were, with the energies of the id.

AGE DIFFERENCES

As shown in Table 3, role definitions of the old woman, like those of the other three figures, vary consistently with age of respondent. Whereas the age shift in the perception of the old man's role is in the direction of increasing submissiveness, the OW moves from a subordinate to an authoritative family role. (The age shift is statistically stable at the .001 level.)[2]

Younger respondents view the OW as sensitive to, or checked by, outer demands and pressures. Older respondents propose

[2] In a subsequent study of forty-seven older men in which the same TAT card was used, Margaret Thaler Singer found essentially the same perceptions of the OM and OW (Singer, 1963, pp. 230–31).

that the OW has come to be the embodiment of controls, strictures, limits. She has taken over the moral and directive qualities which, for younger respondents, were seen as operating outside herself.

In general, with increasing age of respondent, the OW emerges more and more as the most feeling, demanding, and aggressive figure, as the other figures tend toward greater passivity, colorlessness, and conformity. In stories told by older respondents, the point at which the OW is described tends frequently to signal the breakthrough of impulsivity, as if the OW represents unchecked impulse in a scene otherwise populated by more constricted, conforming, or affiliative figures.[3]

As regards respondents themselves, the old woman symbolizes the impulsive, self-centered qualities of the personality (in contrast to the OM, who symbolizes ego qualities of the personality). The age shift in perception of the OW implies, therefore, increasing pressures from the impulse life in the face of decreasing ego controls.

FANTASY DATA IN RELATION TO SEX-ROLE BEHAVIOR

Since these findings have been derived from projective data, what are their implications for role behavior?

The individual, in filling real-life roles, resolves tensions between personal needs and social expectations. The task of the ego is to organize the various affective components of the personality into a personally expressive, though socially acceptable, pattern of behavior. When presented with the picture, however, a different demand is made of the respondent. He is asked not to act in the real family setting, but to breathe vitality into a representation of family life. The task of the

[3] Perhaps the projection of impulsive elements of personality on the figure of the OW is partially stimulated by her facelessness in the picture. If impulsivity is regarded by respondents as ego-alien, it might well be ascribed to that figure in the picture which provides fewest cues regarding social interaction.

ego is not one of integrating various aspects of the self into a coherent pattern of behavior, but the opposite—in effect, to distribute various components of the self among the various figures in the picture.

This fractionating of the components of personality makes the thematic apperception technique a valuable clinical instrument, but it also imposes qualifications on its use in the study of social roles. In the latter case, the respondent describes a living complexity (the role of OM or OW) in terms of only one or a few facets of the self. The projected aspect of the self, temporarily winnowed out of the total personality, tends to be expressed in exaggerated form. The result is a certain stereotypy and a certain overemphasis in the role descriptions. The task of the role analyst is thus made correspondingly difficult. The role patterns he wishes to describe may have been distorted into nonviable extremes as they have become the focuses for conflicting elements in the respondents' personalities. Rather than objective role descriptions, his data are the affective connotations of role behavior, those which people limit and modify in real life.

The findings presented here must be interpreted with caution, then, in applying them to actual role behavior. It should be kept in mind that, if the respondent speaks of the old man as weak and passive and the old woman as dominant and manipulative, he is describing not only two polar forms of behavior but also two aspects of himself and that both aspects will find some (though not equal) expression in his own behavior. If the respondent is an older man, he cannot be described merely on the basis of his description of the old man as passive and weak, for the respondent is a person who also has needs for strength and dominance. It is the nature of the task—responding to the picture—which allows him to describe the old man in more unitary ways than are actually true of himself.

These considerations apply equally with regard to collective role images that emerge from groups of respondents. For example, many older respondents seem to agree that older men are passive, affectless, and isolated from the stream of family events. They are described as "smoking their pipes" and "thinking." It cannot be assumed, however, that the only role of older men in the family is to stand in the corner, thinking and smoking. People who live in the family setting, young or old, do interact with others and do impinge on the environments of other family members. What can be justifiably assumed from this image is not that older men never interact or relate, but that the very activities through which they express the outward forms of intimacy also tend to highlight their desire for passivity and isolated contemplation. The image does not report the daily reality of the older man's role; rather, it is a sharply drawn, condensed expression of the affective mode which underlies his activities. The sharpness of the image is derived from the condensed expression of what is seen as being central to the figure of the old man and from the affective components of the respondents' personalities identified with this central tendency.

What we have in these data, then, is centrality rather than experienced complexity of role behavior.

To take another example, in many stories, especially in those told by men, the description of the old woman provides a point at which unchecked impulse breaks into a scene otherwise peopled by more restrained or affiliative figures. She is a figure of primal omnipotence and wrath —"a devil. Very strict. Must run everything and everybody." In one sense the description functions to bring the aggressive impulse life of the respondent into the story.[4] What emerges is not an unbiased account of the old woman, but a picture of the old woman as it is filled out

by aggressive energy that has its locus in the respondent himself. (It is the respondent's own denied rage, projected on to the figure of the old woman, that he calls a "devil.") Women who live in a social environment cannot act purely from unmediated primitive impulse. They would soon be hospitalized, institutionalized, or dead. What we are being told in such accounts is that older women's behavior in the family expresses, for those respondents preoccupied with such issues, a central quality of free aggression.

Bearing such considerations in mind, these findings can nevertheless be related to actual role behavior. This relationship is posited on the grounds that the affective complexes energizing the perception of the stimulus figures are indeed cued by the respondents' expectations of such figures in real life. Granted that various components of the respondent's own personality migrate toward one or another stimulus figure, the impressive fact is the consistency with which the same personality components migrate to the same figure in the picture. For instance, for both men and women respondents, it is almost always the old woman, not the old man, to whom impulsivity, aggressivity, and hostile dominance are ascribed. This consistency cannot be explained by chance. The assumption seems warranted that there is something common to the actual role behaviors of older women that elicits this consistency in respondents' fantasies.

To sum up, projective data do not yield descriptions of the total and complex role of the older woman in the family as that role is expressed in everyday, overt behavior (similarly for other figures). What is obtained instead is a central aspect of

[4] In real life the respondent's wife may function so as to express elements of the respondent's impulse life that are denied expression in his own behavior. Our findings hint at the possibility that males often handle their aggression in the family by proposing that they are the passive object of attack from a woman, rather than by proposing that aggression stems from themselves.

the role, an aspect that, in one translated form of behavior or another, is being recognized by both men and women.

The role images of all four figures varied consistently with age and sex of respondent, but not with social class. Most striking was the fact that, with increasing age of respondents, the old man and old woman reversed roles in regard to authority in the family. For younger men and women (aged forty–fifty-four) the old man was seen as the authority figure. For older men and women (aged fifty-five–seventy) the old woman was in the dominant role, and the old man, no matter what other qualities were ascribed to him, was seen as submissive.

The different images of all four figures presented by men and women at the two age levels imply personality changes in the years from forty to seventy. For example, women, as they age, seem to become more tolerant of their own aggressive, egocentric impulses; whereas men, as they age, of their own nurturant and affiliative impulses. To take another example, with increasing age in both men and women, ego qualities in the personality seem to become more constricted—more detached from the mastery of affairs and less in control of impulse life.

PART II

THE PSYCHOLOGY OF THE LIFE CYCLE

A psychology of the life cycle has been slow to develop, in part because we have no psychology of adulthood in the sense in which we have a child psychology; in part because of the enormous difficulties of conceptualization involved when the life-history becomes the unit of investigation and when the most fruitful dimensions by which to deal with such complex units still elude us; and in part because systematic longitudinal data do not yet exist sufficient to these purposes.

(In sociology, we are in something of a parallel position. Much is known about the social behavior of adults, but we have little that can be called a sociology of age, a sociology in which the age-status system is studied as one of the social contexts for examining life-cycle phenomena and in which age norms and age-appropriate behaviors have been investigated as essential elements of social reality.)

The group of papers included here are steps in this direction. In building a psychology of the life cycle, the influence of Dr. Charlotte Buhler has been great. It is exemplified here in the paper by Else Frenkel-Brunswik, one of Buhler's students in Vienna in the 1930's. The paper is based upon data gathered by Buhler and her co-workers. It describes five biological phases of the life cycle and relates the biological curve of life to the biographical (that is, to external events, internal reactions, and accomplishments and productions). The paper is accompanied by an earlier introductory note written by the late Professor Raymond G. Kuhlen, who himself contributed much to the study of the life cycle, as evidenced in the book, *Psychological Development through the Life Span* (Pressey and Kuhlen, 1957).

Next represented is Erikson's theory of ego development, one of the few theories that specifically encompasses the total life cycle. The paper is a short excerpt from Erikson's discussion of what he calls the "Eight Stages of Man," and presents his concepts of the two crises in ego development that characterize middle and late adulthood: generativity (in middle adulthood, the expansion of ego interests and the accompanying sense of having contributed to the future); and ego integrity (in old age, the basic acceptance of one's life as having been inevitable, appropriate, and meaningful).

Peck's paper that follows is also addressed to the periods of middle age and old age. He identifies several crisis stages that occur in the second half of life, saying that these stages and the tasks presented at each stage are as worthy of close attention as the stages of early life. He then describes the particular adaptive capacities that become salient as the adult attempts to resolve the successive psychological crises.

Neugarten's .paper is focused upon middle age as a major turning period in the life cycle. Based on depth interviews with 100 highly successful men and women aged 45 to 55, the paper presents some of the psychological issues that preoccupy this group. One major finding is the extent to which middle-aged people are aware of a changing time-perspective and their shift to restructure life in terms of time left to live, rather than time since birth.

The next two papers deal with creativity and productivity, and with the question of when in the life cycle creative persons make their contributions. In the first of these two papers, Lehman carries forward the work on age and achievement that he first published in book form in 1953, and shows that both past and present generation scientists produced a disproportionate share of their discoveries not later than ages 30 to 39. This set of findings fits generally his earlier findings that peak creativity in a wide array of occupations and professions is evidenced relatively early in the life span (although there are differences among the fields of the arts, sciences, government, athletics, business, and so on). In the second of these two papers, Dennis presents data to show that the highest rate of output in various groups of creative persons comes later, in the 40's or soon thereafter, and that productivity remains relatively high for many of his groups into the 60's. It should be noted that although both investigators studied creative persons, they have been concerned with different measures: Lehman, with outstanding works; Dennis, with total output. (The reader should note, also, that the two investigators used somewhat different methods of sampling and of dealing with the problem of longevity.) Both papers include discussions of the complexity of factors involved in productivity and of the difficulty of disentangling cause-and-effect relationships.

The paper by Kuhlen is organized around a different dimension of the life cycle, motivation, and is an overview of changing needs and motivations that characterize people as they move through adulthood. The discussion is focused first upon growth-expansion motives, and second upon anxiety and threat as a source of motivation. The author deals with concepts of critical periods, life goals, engagement-disengagement, the self-concept; and he stresses individual differences, particularly with regard to sex and social class.

The last two papers in this section are written from a different perspective from those that precede. They are concerned primarily with questions of theoretical frameworks that may be more or less appropriate in studying adulthood. Neugarten's paper is written from the point of view of a developmental psychologist (although the term "development" is regarded as awkward in considering middle-aged and older adults). The paper is concerned with the problems of delineating orderly and sequential changes that occur with the passage of time as individuals move from adolescence through old age, and with antecedent-consequent relationships. The discussion is addressed principally to conceptual problems in relating childhood to adulthood and in relating biological to social pacemakers of change in personality. The last part of the paper proposes that the age-status system be viewed as one of the social contexts for understanding time-related change and draws attention to the importance of social as well as biological time clocks.

The last paper, by Becker, is written from the point of view of a symbolic-interactionist and suggests that social scientists should look primarily to the effects of social structure on experience in attempting to understand change and stability in personality. He proposes that the process of situational adjustment is the explanation of change; and the process of commitment, an explanation of stability. Although, in the view of this editor, Becker sets up something of a straw man in accusing psychologists of taking for granted unchanging components in the self or personality, and while his explanation of commitment as a psychological process is not fully developed, the paper is valuable in presenting a view of the life cycle from a sociological framework, and in reminding the reader of the need to integrate social as well as psychological dimensions into a theory of adult personality. Some of the concepts in these last two papers may prove useful in establishing what might be called a "developmental behavioral science."

7

ELSE FRENKEL-BRUNSWIK

ADJUSTMENTS AND REORIENTATION IN THE COURSE OF THE LIFE SPAN

When the life span is studied in its entirety it is possible to discern certain significant shifts in motivations and needs and in frustrations and problems. New strivings may result or new orientations may evolve. The present research is notable not only for the broad developmental period studied, but also for its method—the study of biographies and autobiographies. The paper presents an insightful interpretation of what happens psychologically as age increases, as the life span is negotiated. It is suggested that some five major phases can be identified, and that a psychological curve of life paralleling the biological curve, but somewhat retarded as compared with the biological curve, can be discerned. However, it should be kept in mind that these studies were conducted in Austria, and thus the ages at which these investigators put the divisions of the life span are based on data from a culture which in many respects (e.g., age of retirement) differs from what is found in the United States. Nonetheless, the present paper is rich in hypotheses relating to the psychological trends and problems during maturity and old age.

—RAYMOND KUHLEN

Within the past few years there has been developed in Vienna, under the leadership of Professor Charlotte Buhler, a type of empirical research to determine what general principles hold for the human life span.[1] The aim of the investigation here reported was to describe the psychologi-cal development of human beings and to attempt to determine the regularity with which the various phases of life succeed one another in this development.

In order to study our problem it was necessary to become closely acquainted with a great number of life-stories and to compare these lives with one another. In the past few years in Vienna around four hundred biographies of individuals from various nations, social classes, and vocations have been critically studied. Wherever it was possible, letters, diaries, and other documents were also utilized for the purpose of control and also to secure additional information. Furthermore, in order to secure data on living people, of whom no biographies were obtainable, a method of direct questioning, similar to

Reprinted from *Psychological Studies of Human Development*, rev. ed., ed. Raymond G. Kuhlen and George G. Thompson (New York: Appleton-Century-Crofts, 1963), pp. 161–71.

[1] The results to be described in this article are reported and discussed in detail in Charlotte Buhler's comprehensive book, *Der menschliche Lebenslauf als psychologisches Problem* (Leipzig, 1933), and in the more special investigations made before and after the book was published, under the direction of Charlotte Buhler and Else Frenkel at the Psychological Institute of the University of Vienna. The present article was translated from the German by Annette Herzman.

that used in clinical interviews, was introduced. With the help of this method, it became possible to obtain data also on the lives of the working classes, since interviewers went to old peoples' homes, to the poor, and out into the country.

Through these methods, the research material was able to cover the lives of engineers and physicians, politicians and actors, businessmen and industrial magnates, artists and scientists, lawyers and journalists, priests and nuns, officers and soldiers, pilots and mountain climbers, teachers, workers, waiters, farmers, clerks, servants, janitors, etc. The material includes both men and women, and also persons without vocation or employment.

The life-stories were individually analyzed and compared with one another with the help of statistics. In this way an *inventory* was obtained of everything that happened to the individuals concerned, or was experienced inwardly, or accomplished in the various periods of life.

There are three groups of data which were collected in as exact and detailed a manner as possible.

1. The first type is the *external events* of life, everything that a person does, his behavior. Among them, the different fields of activity in which the individual takes an active part are called the *dimensions* of behavior. For instance, practical dimensions would be such as one's study, profession or creations; social dimensions: one's family, friends, or help for others, but also playing cards, etc.; furthermore, sport, travel, hobbies, religious activity, etc., constitute other dimensions. It was possible through our material to set up an approximately complete list of the important activities. We distinguished, in all, ninety-seven such dimensions. We were particularly interested in dividing these activities according to age.

2. The second group of data collected was the *internal reactions* to these events. It is important to know what the individual thinks about his own life. We tried to gather material therefore from letters, diaries, and autobiographical notes, or through direct questioning about these "subjective data." For instance, do the individuals write or tell us that their fate is a happy or an unhappy one (that they have already found the right vocation, their goal in life), or do they mention what they believe to be their wishes and their duties, etc.? All such utterances were also systematically collected and their distribution over the whole course of life was studied.

3. Besides observing the objective behavior and the subjective experiences, we can also study, thirdly, the relation of the course of life to its objective results: namely, the *accomplishments and productions* of man.[2] We gathered material therefore on creative work, its effect on others, and its success, in the individual cases.

THE GENERAL BIOLOGICAL CURVE OF LIFE

In presenting the results obtained, we will begin with a description of biological development because a consideration of these facts was instrumental in giving rise to this study, and because these facts through their exactness and clarity are particularly well suited to serve as a basis for the psychological material.

Many biologists divide the life span into three *growth* phases, the first (lasting until perhaps 25) of progressive growth, the second (lasting until almost 45) of stability of growth, and a third phase of decline or regressive growth. Other biologists divide biological development on the basis of reproductive capacity, designating also three periods marked by the acquisition, the possession, and the loss of reproductive ability.

Let us combine both of these points of view in our consideration of the biological development. The period of progressive growth is divided into two parts through the acquisition of the ability to reproduce around the fifteenth year of

[2] The analysis of the material on creativity has been omitted from this abbreviated paper.

78

life. In the same way the period of restriction or regressive growth is cut in two, through the loss of the reproductive ability at fifty-five (which is the average for men and women). Thus *five biological periods* are formed, all of them marked off by a principal change in direction, such as an important acquisition or loss. The third and middle period, lasting roughly from twenty-five to forty-five, could be represented schematically by a horizontal line, surrounded symmetrically by the periods of ascent (first and second phase) and descent (fourth

which would allow us to survey the whole behavior of the individual during the course of his life. Since a great deal happened in a person's life we had to summarize in a graphic presentation all the facts about one person, as it is seen in the following sketch, Figure 1.

The diagram shows the life of the mother of Goethe. Up to a certain point we can observe that new spheres and new fields of activity are added. In all fields of

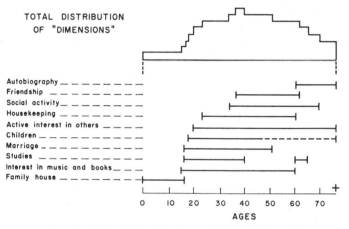

FIG. 1.—Life of Elizabeth Textor-Goethe (1731–1808)

and fifth phase) of the "biological curve" of life.

THE BEHAVIOR PATTERN DURING THE DIFFERENT PHASES OF LIFE

Biologically, it is possible to speak of the process of life in terms of rise and decline, ascent and descent. Can we also observe in the distribution of the psychological data a regularity, certain characteristics common to all? Can we find a parallel here to the biological structure? The results show that the changes in the abundance of activity (dimensions) and its distribution are phenomena corresponding to growth and decay. In order to show this it was necessary to use a method of presentation of the material

life, expansion, ascent and increase, can be noticed. The period in the middle of life, called the culmination period, includes the largest and most complete number of dimensions. In this period we find stability also, since losses are replaced by new acquisitions. Beginning with a certain age (around the fiftieth year), certain activities are given up and external losses, such as a case of death, are not compensated for any more. One can observe a decline, a form of retirement from life. If we at first only take those data which relate to the behavior of the individual and present them graphically, we will find here also the ascent and descent in the curve, as it is clearly shown in the upper part of Figure 1. It should be emphasized that other lives, even those of simple working men, would show a very similar general distribution.

Furthermore, we are again able to differentiate *five periods*. The first period is the one in which the child lives at home, and in which his life centers around a narrow group of interests, school and family.

A second period begins between the sixteenth and twentieth year (the average for the cases studied is around seventeen years). The turning point (most of the time quite sharply defined) is characterized by the entrance into a self-chosen and independent activity (in 78.5 percent of our 140 cases) and by the first independently acquired personal relations (32 percent). Frequently the turning point can be placed at the time when the youth leaves the home of his family. We find in this period a building up of new activities, an "expansion" of the dimensions. But all the activities in this period (which lasts until the twenty-eighth year of age on the average) are of *preparatory character*. In only 21.5 percent of the 140 cases is an activity chosen at the beginning of the second period definitive for life. Certain "unspecific" activities are chosen, such as literary, philosophical, artistic, and religious interests, further study, and also the tendency toward loneliness and daydreaming. The motor activities which are expressed in wanderlust and sport are also very strongly represented. Many personal relations are acquired at this time, but they are usually only temporary. Within the limits of our material, sexual relations begun by men before their twenty-eighth year last considerably less time (9.8 years on the average) than those begun after the twenty-eighth year (29.8 years on the average).

The third period begins between the twenty-sixth and the thirtieth years of life (the mean is 28.6 years). Paralleling the corresponding biological period, this sector of life includes the *largest number of dimensions*. A great deal happens at the beginning of the third phase, just as was noted at the beginning of the second, so that its entrance is clearly defined. It begins in most cases with the final and *definite choice* of vocation (in 69 percent of our 140 cases studied) and, furthermore, with the choice of a definite personal tie together with the establishment of a home (52.5 percent). This phase (which lasts until approximately fifty years of age) is the *culmination period* of life. It is representative as the most fruitful period in professional and creative work. The social activities reach their high point also, since this is the time of the most numerous personal relations, and the greatest amount of social intercourse. Motor dimensions are represented in the form of travel for professional and personal reasons.

The average beginning of the fourth phase is 48.5 years. The criteria which were decisive in characterizing the first three phases were those which applied to the building up of life, whereas a decrease in the amount of activities and the appearance of "negative dimensions" (such as sickness, loss of associates, etc.) ushers in the fourth and fifth phases, and are the characteristic signs which announce the turning point toward the new period. Cases of death (of relatives and friends) which had less effect in the earlier periods because they were compensated through new acquisitions, acquire now a great deal of importance for the individual (in 34.5 percent of our cases). Individuals are also strongly affected by other losses of personal or economic nature, or damage to their bodily strength (in 41.1 percent of our cases such losses were decisive). Furthermore, at this time a change in the type of work is noted, especially in those cases where vital activities (sport, physical labor, etc.) are concerned. The actor becomes a director, the athlete becomes a trainer, the sailor a writer, and so on. In 21.5 percent of the 140 cases studied we find a complete retirement from work around fifty years of age.

The transition to the fourth phase is marked by psychological crises, just as in the biological development crises also appear at this time (menopause). This will be clearly shown in the treatment of the data on subjective experience. But we can also see here the tendency to change, discontent, and complete negation, as shown objectively through certain events. We find, for instance, the most frequent occurrence of trips taken for rest or recuperation between the ages of forty-five and forty-eight, with a decrease lasting until the age of sixty. This can be looked upon as renewal of unrest, showing itself in an intensified wanderlust, and a frequent change of residence. In the short time between the forty-fifth and forty-eighth years there is further a transitory inclination toward daydreaming and loneliness to be found. Unspecific activities, such as literary interests, a tendency toward retrospection, which otherwise first appear at sixty years, are also to be noticed here as a transitory condition. A high point in the destruction of one's own creative work (according to S. Fischer in about 40 percent of her fifty cases of creative individuals) is to be found at the beginning of this period. These objective data show us the crisis which takes place at this time, and which we will mention again later. This phase brings with it also a decrease in the number of dimensions, a restriction. However, the factual dimensions, such as the specific activity in one's profession or creative work, are still comparatively numerous. In particular, everything which is related to independent creative work very often first reaches its culmination point in this period. The social activities are shifted somewhat into a new field, since, although the general sociability lessens, the more philanthropic activities begin first at this time. In respect to the motor dimensions, a decrease in participation in sport and an increase in country life are noted.

The decline which we noted in the fourth phase, mostly in connection with the vital processes, becomes much more evident with the beginning of the fifth phase. The average age at which this phase starts is 63.8 years, based again upon

the 140 cases studied by Frenkel and Kral. The fifth phase is often introduced by complete retirement from one's profession and from any sort of work in 64.5 percent of our cases. Sickness constitutes the turning point in 44.5 percent of the cases, death among close associates in 33 percent of the cases. Very obvious in this phase is the great decrease in the factual and social dimensions, whereas hobbies, such as collecting stamps, love of animals and flowers, etc., increase in frequency. Retrospection, the writing of memoirs, and the death cult are all very characteristic of this period. Furthermore, the occupation with politics, studying a subject out of interest, and other unspecific activities, as well as the making of various plans, can again be observed. This seems to show a certain similarity to the second phase, a repetition of certain youthful traits. The social dimensions which one finds in this period are various types of active helpfulness, advice, consolation, etc. A strong preference for country life can also be observed. Analogous to the first phase, which seems to stand on the periphery of life but not yet taking place in it, the fifth phase finds the individual more or less "after" life, in that he has loosened the ties, has given up the plan of life which he had built up for himself.

Our results have shown that, just as in the biological structure, the psychological structure of the course of life can be divided into phases which are clearly marked off from one another through certain turning points in life. These turning points usher in, in very short time, parallel and permanent changes in many fields of life, all of which allow us to imply that a basic transposition takes place. During the course of each phase one finds in general only a further development of that which was laid out at the beginning of the given phase.

THE BEHAVIORAL PATTERN AS RELATED TO THE BIOLOGICAL CURVE

If we notice the ages at which the respective phases begin, we will see that the phases of the biographical curve *are retarded in comparison to the biological.* We are therefore forced to suppose that some factor is present in the psychological development which influences this deviation and which is independent of the biological function in the narrowest sense of the term. The ability to give the most capable performance in athletics culminates at the same time as the corresponding biological high point, whereas in the manual worker the culmination point is retarded ten years, and in the mental worker still another ten years. We find, therefore, that there are a number of functions—we may call them the vital functions—which are correlated with the biological curve, and, furthermore, a number of psychological functions, such as knowledge, experience, training, which, because they help toward a rise in capability, counteract the biological decline.

The psychological functions are subject to another set of laws, and are therefore responsible for the deviation of the biographical curve from the biological. These factors will be analyzed still better when we bring the subjective data, the inner experiences, under consideration.

As has been done through the study of biographies and through interviews, we are able to differentiate two groups of experiences. The one is closely dependent upon and runs parallel to biological expansion and restriction. We find in the inner life of man, at first, the wish to learn to know a great deal, to try out a number of things, to expand; then, finally, mostly after much struggling, he finds it necessary to give up a great deal. His inner experiences are then of the sort which correspond to his weakened bodily condition, and which point to resignation and restriction.

We also find, however, a second group of experiences, which appear for the first time during adolescence. The young person asks himself for the first time, although in a quite theoretical form, for what purpose he should live at all, or what his design or calling or "objective" in life should be. Actually every person does not only wish to live and exist, but he wishes to have some reason for existing. This reason can be another person, a thing (e.g., money or position), or an idea (e.g., religion or science).

Since the question is first raised during adolescence, we can call this the first step out into life, because in connection with this question the young person begins making decisions about his vocation and his future life. Still, that does not mean that the "purpose" in life is conclusively found at this time. The young person has been given a preliminary answer to his question and he has for the first time made an independent decision about what he wishes to do or study, but we know that he will remain irresolute for a long time, and will make a definite decision as to his vocation and his partner in life only after a lapse of time. And, even if he has made his decisions sooner, these decisions are very often confirmed and accepted through inward conviction much later. Soon the individual is not satisfied simply to know definitely how and for what purpose he is living. He desires now to turn out to "be" someone. This question as to what the results of one's life will be, now becomes very important.

When we now ask how these two groups of experience, the one corresponding to the vital functions, which we call "needs," and the other made up of our aims in life and their realization, are distributed over life, we observe an interesting alternation. In the first half of life, our subjective experience is determined primarily by our needs, in the sense of the expansion of the individual. On the contrary, in the second half of life, the individual regards as more important certain tasks which he has set for himself, or which have been set for him by society, or which have come from some code of values such as religion or science.

In general, we can say that around forty-five years of age a change takes place in that the "needs," which come from the biological nature of man, become less important, and the duties directed by our ideals and our conscience, or laid down by authority and practical demands, play a more dominant role. In connection with this we find at the same time a change in the objects which are of relevancy in life. At first the individual himself plays the important role in his wishes and duties. Later, other more objective interests are placed in the foreground.

Deviations from this general law of development were found only in those subjects who were diagnosed by physicians as *neurotics*. In these cases the wishes strongly outweighed the duties, even in the third and fourth phase. Another type of neurotic personality, the person with a compulsion neurosis, seems to be made up exclusively of duties. The character of these duties, however, corresponds to that of a much earlier phase of development of the individual, since they are of a very general nature out of which no concrete tasks are developed. Another outstanding characteristic of these neurotic personalities is that the subject-matter about which they talk falls into other spheres than does that of the normal person. For instance, some compulsion neurotics, whose emotional life is disturbed, place sexuality in the sphere of duties and not in the field of wishes, as a healthy person does. In this way the sphere of duty has taken over all those individual and social demands which otherwise are guaranteed their realization through the normal biological needs.

We may call the transference from the field of need to the field of duties, which is dictated by society and inner developmental factors, *transference in dominance*. In such changes in dominance a developmental step in early childhood is now repeated, but on a higher level. When we say a child is ripe for school we mean he is capable of giving up the arbitrariness which a four-year-old still evinces, and he is willing to subordinate himself to the group and to accept and perform his tasks.

Still another developmental process which we have observed in the course of life is to be found in early childhood. During the school age the child acquires a maturity in the performance of his tasks; he can now utilize material in a "specific" way. For instance, when the small child is given some blocks, he hits them against his bed. He first begins to build things with these blocks in a later stage of development. We then can say that he uses the material in an adequate way or in the manner for which it was "specified."

This development toward *specification* in the use of materials repeats itself again in the course of life. Namely, in the second phase we find a functional period of activity in mental as well as physical work. This activity is without a goal, being done only for the pleasure in doing it. It is only later that the transition is made to organized, practical, and planned work. Suitable interests are rarely found by the individual during the second phase of his life.

Summarizing, we can say that in the transference of dominance (i.e., a change in stress from needs to duties) and in the gradual specification of interests, the finding of one's calling or objective in life, we have found two important developmental laws.

If, looking back, we consider the inner experiences of man and their arrangement in the course of life, we find that according to our material they are also divided into five phases.

The young person just passed through childhood—the first phase of life—makes the first plans about his life and his first decisions in adolescence or shortly afterwards. Here begins the second phase of experience. It is characterized first through the fact that the young person wishes to acquire contact with reality. He experiments with people and professions. An "expansion" of his person takes place. Also characteristic for him is the temporary nature of his attitudes as to what his life calling will be.

A study, carried out by E. Dichter with fifty-three subjects, dealing with self-criticism of the individual's abilities, which we should like to mention here, showed that the experimental subjects in the second phase of life still were not clear about a great many of their abilities. The average was fourteen abilities in the second phase, about which the individual was subjectively undecided, and in the fourth phase only five abilities. These facts show the tendency toward expansion, and also the uncertainty of this second phase. One does not know which traits can be, and which should be, trained. Chiefly those traits pertaining to character, the body, or social abilities, occupy the mind of the youth of this period.

First, at the end of the second phase (around the twenty-eighth year) the utterances show that the individuals have become clear as to their definite attitude toward life. As has been seen, during the third phase, vitality is still at its high point, while direction and specification are now also present, so that very often this time is found to be the culmination period for subjective experiences.

The transition to the fourth phase very often is introduced by a crisis, since at this point the unfolding of the individual powers has come to a standstill, and much has to be given up which depends upon physical aptitude or was connected with the biological needs. Contrary to the descent of the biological curve and the experiences which are connected with that, we find here an ascending scale by virtue of new interest in the results and productivity of life. If one asks a person in this phase to relate his abilities, he names very few of them and mostly those which are connected with his profession.

Finally, in the fifth phase we find more strongly mentioned age, premonitions of death, complaints of loneliness, and often those persons in this phase are occupied with religious questions. This last period contains experiences of a retrospective nature and considerations about the future, that is, about oncoming death and one's past life. The balance-sheet of life is drawn up, so to speak. This is expressed often through the writing of memoirs and autobiographies. This last phase of life has a certain parallelism queerly enough with the age of adolescence; on the one hand, the adolescent leaves the life of childhood; on the other, he must make the transposition to his future life. The diary is used as a means of helping him clear up his problems in this period of transition.

However, not all types of experience are found to be present in every individual. For instance, in a few cases, only the vital functions have had an influence upon their lives, and therefore only one group of experiences is found. We are thinking in particular of Casanova, or of many women whose life has a short blooming period, and then is completely extinguished. Lives in which sexual experiences play the chief role and in which very little compensatory effects through more sublimated interests are present, and also no productions of any sort, work or children, show an unquestionable subjective decline in the second half of their lives. Physical efficiency is taken as the only measure for the building up or breaking down of their lives. Casanova said in his thirty-eighth year, "The beginning of my end began on this day." Still in most lives, the reduction in vitality is not experienced as a negative affair, since a change from a more physical to a more mental life takes place and the second half of life takes on a more positive form. The ability to transpose oneself, to take on another attitude toward life is a character trait which is almost a necessity for success in life. For the psychology of development it is important that the individual both in personal and in practical fields not only satisfies his needs but that he also at some time accepts certainties and tasks, and works for them.

8

ERIK H. ERIKSON

GENERATIVITY AND EGO INTEGRITY

EDITOR'S NOTE:

As background for Peck's formulation of psychological stages in the second half of life, the student should be familiar with Erik Erikson's theory of ego development, one of the few examples of a developmental theory of personality that specifically encompasses adulthood as well as childhood and adolescence. Erikson formulated eight stages of ego development from infancy to old age, each stage representing a choice or a crisis for the expanding ego. The effects of maturation, experience, and social institutions on the growing individual are encompassed in the theory; and the resolutions of ego crises are seen as determining the future development of the personality, the individual's success in adapting to both inner- and outer-world demands, and his evaluation of self.

The eight stages are: (1) in early infancy, development of a sense of basic *trust* versus a sense of distrust; (2) in later infancy, when anal-muscular maturation has occurred, a growing sense of *autonomy* versus a sense of shame and doubt; (3) in early childhood, the period of greatest locomotor development, a developing sense of *initiative* versus a sense of guilt; (4) in the middle years of childhood, a sense of *industry* versus a sense of inferiority; (5) in adolescence, a sense of *ego identity* (certainty of self, and a sense of continuity and belonging regarding career, sex role, and a system of values) versus role confusion; (6) in early adulthood, the development of *intimacy* (mutuality with a loved partner of the opposite sex with whom the individual is able to regulate the cycles of work, procreation, and recreation) versus a sense of ego isolation; (7) in middle adulthood, the development of *generativity* (expansion of ego interests and a sense of having contributed to the future) versus a sense of ego stagnation; and (8) in late adulthood, a sense of *ego integrity* (a basic acceptance of one's life as having been inevitable, appropriate, and meaningful) versus a sense of despair (fear of death).

In Erikson's theory, a different psychological issue constitutes the nuclear conflict or crisis for the ego at each developmental stage, but the same issue is also present in preceding and later stages. For example, while the problem of ego identity is predominant in adolescence, it is also present in adulthood and old age, although in a form modified by the individual's life history, and by the degree of his success in meeting the

Reprinted from Erik H. Erikson, *Childhood and Society*, 2d rev. ed. By permission of W. W. Norton & Company, Inc. Copyright 1950, © 1963 by W. W. Norton & Company, Inc. New York. London: Hogarth Press.

earlier crises. A solution at any stage of ego development has its effects on all subsequent stages; and an individual cannot successfully resolve issues, say, of ego integrity if he has not successfully resolved issues of intimacy and generativity.

Because Erikson's publications are readily available (Erikson, 1950, 1953, 1956, 1959, 1963) the full statement of the theory is not included in this book. Only his descriptions of generativity and ego integrity are reproduced here because they are immediately relevant to Peck's exposition that follows.

GENERATIVITY VS. STAGNATION

In this book (Erikson, 1963) the emphasis is on the childhood stages, otherwise the section on generativity would of necessity be the central one, for this term encompasses the evolutionary development which has made man the teaching and instituting as well as the learning animal. The fashionable insistence on dramatizing the dependence of children on adults often blinds us to the dependence of the older generation on the younger one. Mature man needs to be needed, and maturity needs guidance as well as encouragement from what has been produced and must be taken care of.

Generativity, then, is primarily the concern in establishing and guiding the next generation, although there are individuals who, through misfortune or because of special and genuine gifts in other directions, do not apply this drive to their own offspring. And indeed, the concept generativity is meant to include such more popular synonyms as *productivity* and *creativity*, which, however, cannot replace it.

It has taken psychoanalysis some time to realize that the ability to lose oneself in the meeting of bodies and minds leads to a gradual expansion of ego-interests and to a libidinal investment in that which is being generated. Generativity thus is an essential stage on the psychosexual as well as on the psychosocial schedule. Where such enrichment fails altogether, regression to an obsessive need for pseudo-intimacy takes place, often with a pervading sense of stagnation and personal impover-

ishment. Individuals, then, often begin to indulge themselves as if they were their own—or one another's—one and only child; and where conditions favor it, early invalidism, physical or psychological, becomes the vehicle of self-concern. The mere fact of having or even wanting children, however, does not "achieve" generativity. In fact, some young parents suffer, it seems, from the retardation of the ability to develop this stage. The reasons are often to be found in early childhood impressions; in excessive self-love based on a too strenuously self-made personality; and finally (and here we return to the beginnings) in the lack of some faith, some "belief in the species," which would make a child appear to be a welcome trust of the community.

As to the institutions which safeguard and reinforce generativity, one can only say that all institutions codify the ethics of generative succession. Even where philosophical and spiritual tradition suggests the renunciation of the right to procreate or to produce, such early turn to "ultimate concerns," wherever instituted in monastic movements, strives to settle at the same time the matter of its relationship to the Care for the creatures of this world and to the Charity which is felt to transcend it.

If this were a book on adulthood, it would be indispensable and profitable at this point to compare economic and psychological theories (beginning with the strange convergencies and divergencies of Marx and Freud) and to proceed to a discussion of man's relationship to his production as well as to his progeny.

Only in him who in some way has taken care of things and people and has adapted himself to the triumphs and disappointments adherent to being, the originator of others or the generator of products and ideas—only in him may gradually ripen the fruit of these seven stages. I know no better word for it than ego integrity. Lacking a clear definition, I shall point to a few constituents of this state of mind. It is the ego's accrued assurance of its proclivity for order and meaning. It is a post-narcissistic love of the human ego —not of the self—as an experience which conveys some world order and spiritual sense, no matter how dearly paid for. It is the acceptance of one's one and only life cycle as something that had to be and that, by necessity, permitted of no substitutions: it thus means a new, a different love of one's parents. It is a comradeship with the ordering ways of distant times and different pursuits, as expressed in the simple products and sayings of such times and pursuits. Although aware of the relativity of all the various life styles which have given meaning to human striving, the possessor of integrity is ready to defend the dignity of his own life style against all physical and economic threats. For he knows that an individual life is the accidental coincidence of but one life cycle with but one segment of history; and that for him all human integrity stands or falls with the one style of integrity of which he partakes. The style of integrity developed by his culture or civilization thus becomes the "patrimony of his soul," the seal of his moral paternity of himself (". . . pero el honor / Es patrimonio del alma": Calderón). In such final consolidation, death loses its sting.

The lack or loss of this accrued ego integration is signified by fear of death: the one and only life cycle is not accepted as the ultimate of life. Despair expresses the feeling that the time is now short, too

short for the attempt to start another life and to try out alternate roads to integrity. Disgust hides despair, if often only in the form of "a thousand little disgusts" which do not add up to one big remorse: *"mille petits dégôuts de soi, dont le total ne fait pas un remords, mais un gêne obscure"* (Rostand).

Each individual, to become a mature adult, must to a sufficient degree develop all the ego qualities mentioned, so that a wise Indian, a true gentleman, and a mature peasant share and recognize in one another the final stage of integrity. But each cultural entity, to develop the particular style of integrity suggested by its historical place, utilizes a particular combination of these conflicts, along with specific provocations and prohibitions of infantile sexuality. Infantile conflicts become creative only if sustained by the firm support of cultural institutions and of the special leader classes representing them. In order to approach or experience integrity, the individual must know how to be a follower of image bearers in religion and in politics, in the economic order and in technology, in aristocratic living and in the arts and sciences. Ego integrity, therefore, implies an emotional integration which permits participation by followership as well as acceptance of the responsibility of leadership.

Webster's Dictionary is kind enough to help us complete this outline in a circular fashion. Trust (the first of our ego values) is here defined as "the assured reliance on another's integrity," the last of our values. I suspect that Webster had business in mind rather than babies, credit rather than faith. But the formulation stands. And it seems possible to further paraphrase the relation of adult integrity and infantile trust by saying that healthy children will not fear life if their elders have integrity enough not to fear death.

9

ROBERT C. PECK

*PSYCHOLOGICAL DEVELOPMENTS IN THE
SECOND HALF OF LIFE*

STAGES IN PSYCHOLOGICAL DEVELOPMENT IN THE SECOND HALF OF LIFE

Erikson, like Freud before him, conceived his "stages" of early life by considering the psychological problems that must be universally met and mastered at specific developmental (age) periods. Thus, his first four stages are defined as "psychic developmental tasks" which must be faced in infancy and childhood. The fifth, Identity, seems to be defined as it is because adolescence (at least, in our society) uniquely poses the problem of developing a new kind and sense of identity. That is, this problem does not ordinarily arise acutely during middle childhood; and it can not be perfectly resolved if deferred to the adult years. The sixth and seventh stages are defined and located as they are, it seems, because they describe tasks which are uniquely crucial issues in young adulthood. That is, they do not arise until adolescent problems are behind, and they probably can not be successfully deferred much beyond the age of thirty.

Erikson's eighth stage, however, Ego-Integrity vs. Despair, seems to be intended to represent in a global, nonspecific way all of the psychological crises and crisis-solutions of the last forty or fifty years of life. Clearly, his phrasing of

Adapted from *Psychological Aspects of Aging*, Proceedings of a Conference on Planning Research, Bethesda, Maryland, April 24–27, 1955, ed. John E. Anderson (Washington, D.C.: American Psychological Association, 1956), pp. 44–49. Reproduced by permission.

it states a major issue of life after thirty. A closer look at the second half of life, however, suggests that it might be accurate and useful to divide it into several quite different kinds of psychological learnings and adjustments, at different stages in the latter half of life. If this is true, these stages and the tasks they present may be as worthy of distinct definition and study as Erikson has devoted to the stages of early life. For reasons which will be discussed later, the chief chronological division which seems sound is between a Middle Age period and an Old Age period. Within these periods, the stages may occur in different time sequence, for different individuals.

MIDDLE AGE

1. *Valuing Wisdom vs. Valuing Physical Powers.*—One of the inescapable consequences of aging, after the late twenties, is a decrease in physical strength, stamina, and attractiveness (if, as in America, "attractiveness" is usually defined as "young-looking"). On the other hand, the sheer experience which longer living brings can, if it is used, make the middle aged person able to accomplish a good deal more than younger people, *though by a different means.*

"Wisdom" seems to be a widely used word which may sum up this increment in judgmental powers that aging makes possible.

Wisdom is to be distinguished from intellectual capacity. It might be defined as the ability to make the most effective choices among the alternatives which intellectual perception and imagination present for one's decision. Such choice-making is affected by one's emotional stability, and one's unconflicted or conflicted motivation-set, as well as by intellectual ability. Sheer life experience seems to be essential in giving one a chance to encounter a wide range of emotional relationships, as a corrective to the over-generalized perceptual-attitudinal set derived from one's necessarily limited experience in one family, and one subculture, during childhood and adolescence.

Judging from personality analysis of some thousands of business people in the middle range of life—mostly men—it is my impression that most reach a critical transition point somewhere between the late thirties and the late forties. Some people cling to physical powers, both as their chief "tool" for coping with life, and as the most important element in their value-hierarchy, especially in their self-definition. Since physical powers inevitably decline, such people tend to grow increasingly depressed, bitter, or otherwise unhappy as they grow older. Moreover, they may become increasingly ineffective in their work roles and social roles, if they try to rely on physical powers which they no longer possess. (This appears to be a major etiological element in the "middle age depression," particularly in men.)

Conversely, it has been my impression that those people who age most "successfully" in this stage, with little psychic discomfort and with no less effectiveness, are those who calmly invert their previous value hierarchy, now putting the use of their "heads" above the use of their "hands," both as their standard for self-evaluation and as their chief resource for solving life problems.

Thus, it might be conceived that the optimum course for people who reach this first stage of physical decline is to switch from physique-based values to wisdom-based—or mental-based—values, in their self-definition and in their behavior.

2. *Socializing vs. Sexualizing in Human Relationships.*—Allied to general physical decline, but partially separate from it, is the sexual climacteric. The opportunity the climacteric presents might be this: that people can take on a new kind of value for one—or to a much more dominant degree—as individual personalities, rather than primarily as sex-objects.

If a person takes positive action at this point, redefining men and women as individuals and as companions, with the sexual element decreasingly significant, it would at least be understandable that interpersonal living *could* take on a depth of understanding which the earlier, perhaps inevitably more egocentric, sex-drive would have tended to prevent to some degree.

3. *Cathectic Flexibility vs. Cathectic Impoverishment.*—The phenomenon for which this label is intended might equally well be described as "emotional flexibility": the capacity to shift emotional investments from one person to another, and from one activity to another. In some ways, this cross-cuts any and all adjustive shifts that are made throughout life. The reason for considering it as a distinct function, perhaps more crucial in middle age than at earlier ages, rests in the fact that this is the period, for most people, when their parents die, their children grow up and leave home, and their circle of friends and relatives of similar age begins to be broken by death.

On the other hand, for many people this is the time of life when they have the greatest range of potential cathexis-objects. They have the widest circle of acquaintances in their community and vocational worlds. They have achieved informal and formal status as "mature" or "experienced" people, to whom others actively turn. In fact, this may give them contacts with people over the widest age-range, from young to old, which they will ever encounter. Further, by contrast with younger ages, it may be that experience with a greater variety of people, of roles, of relationships, can lead to a more complex set of more varied, differentiated relationships than is possible at younger ages.

Some people suffer an increasingly impoverished emotional life through the years, because as their cathexis-objects disappear they are unable to reinvest their emotions in other people, other pursuits, or other life settings. Hence this too looks like a crisis-stage where positive adaptation requires new learning—not only of specific new cathexis, but of a generalized set toward *making* new cathexes (or redefining existing cathectic relationships, as in the case of grown-up children).

4. *Mental Flexibility vs. Mental Rigidity.*—One of the major issues in human growth and living seems to be the question, which will dictate one's life—oneself, or the events and experiences one undergoes? Some people learn to master their experiences, achieve a degree of detached perspective on them, and make use of them as *provisional* guides to the solution of new issues. There are other people who seem to become dominated by their experiences. They take the patterns of events and actions which they happen to have encountered, as a set of fixed inflexible rules which almost automatically govern their subsequent behavior.

In any case, there appears to be a widespread feeling by a great many people that "too many" tend to grow increasingly set in their ways, inflexible in their opinions and actions, and closed-minded to new ideas, as they go through the middle years. This is often said of elderly people; but it seems that the *first* time when it becomes a critical issue for most people may well be during middle age, when they have peak status, have worked out a set of "answers" to life, and may be tempted to forego further mental effort to envision new or different "answers."

Like Cathectic Flexibility, this function cross-cuts all adaptive learning behavior. It is no doubt particularly related to stage one, Wisdom vs. Physique; but insofar as

it may be a generalized phenomenon, including that first choice-point as a special case, it may be worthy of separate study.

OLD AGE

1. *Ego Differentiation vs. Work-Role Preoccupation.*—The specific issue, here, particularly for most men in our society, is created by the impact of vocational retirement, usually in the sixties. What this phrase is intended to represent is a general, crucial shift in the value system by which the retiring individual can reappraise and redefine his worth, and can take satisfaction in a broader range of role activities than just his long-time specific work role. The chief issue might be put this way: "Am I a worthwhile person only insofar as I can do a full time job; or can I be worthwhile in other, different ways—as a performer of several other roles, and also because of the kind of person I am?"

The process of ego-differentiation into a complex, varied set of self-identifications begins in early childhood. There are reasons, however, for considering it a centrally important issue at the time of vocational retirement. For most men, the ability to find a sense of self-worth in activities beyond the "job" seems to make the most difference between a despairing loss of meaning in life, and a continued, vital interest in living. (For many women, this stage may arrive when their "vocational" role as mother is removed by the departure of the grown children. In that case, this crisis-stage might well come in middle age, for many women.)

Thus, one critical requisite for successful adaptation to old age may be the establishment of a varied set of valued activities and valued self-attributes, so that any one of several alternatives can be pursued with a sense of satisfaction and worthwhileness. This, at any rate, is what the term ego-differentiation is here intended to represent.

2. *Body Transcendence vs. Body Preoccupation.*—Old age brings to almost everyone a marked decline in resistance

to illness, a decline in recuperative powers, and increasing experience with bodily aches and pains. For people to whom pleasure and comfort mean predominantly physical well-being, this may be the gravest, most mortal of insults. There are many such people whose elder years seem to move in a decreasing spiral, centered around their growing preoccupation with the state of their bodies.

There are other people, however, who suffer just as painful physical unease, yet who enjoy life greatly. It may be that these are people who have learned to define "happiness" and "comfort" more in terms of satisfying human relationships, or creative activities of a mental nature, which only sheer physical destruction could seriously interfere with. In their value system, social and mental sources of pleasure and self-respect may transcend physical comfort, alone.

This is the hypothesis underlying the selection of this issue as a critical decision-point of old age. While such an orientation must almost certainly be developed in its initial form by early adulthood, if it is to be achieved at all, old age may bring the most critical test of whether this kind of value system has been achieved. In the form in which this issue occurs in late life, it may thus be viewed as one of the goals of human development. It recognizes that physical decline occurs, but it also takes account of mental and social powers which may actually increase with age, for many people.

3. *Ego Transcendence vs. Ego Preoccupation.*—One of the new and crucial facts of old age is the appearance of the certain prospect of personal death. In earlier years death comes unexpectedly, as it were; but elderly people know it must come. Chinese and Hindu philosophers, as well as Western thinkers, have suggested that a positive adaptation is possible even to this most unwelcome of prospects. The constructive way of living the late years might be defined in this way: To live so generously and unselfishly that the prospect of personal death—

the night of the ego, it might be called—looks and feels less important than the secure knowledge that one has built for a broader, longer future than any one ego ever could encompass. Through children, through contributions to the culture, through friendships—these are ways in which human beings can achieve enduring significance for their actions which goes beyond the limit of their own skins and their own lives. It may, indeed, be the only *knowable* kind of self-perpetuation after death.

Such an adaptation would not be a stage of passive resignation or of ego-denial. On the contrary, it requires deep, active effort to make life more secure, more meaningful, or happier for the people who will go on after one dies. Since death is the one absolute certainty for all people, this kind of adaptation to its prospect may well be the most crucial achievement of the elder years. Success in this respect would probably be measureable, both in terms of the individual's inner state of contentment or stress, and in terms of his constructive or stress-inducing impact on those around him. It seems reasonable to suppose that one could find objective evidence that there are destructive effects from a narrowly ego-centered clinging to one's private, separate identity, at the expense of contributing to others' welfare or happiness. The "successful ager" at this final stage would be the person who is purposefully active as an ego-transcending perpetuation of that culture which, more than anything else, differentiates human living from animal living. Such a person would be experiencing a vital, gratifying absorption in the future. He would be doing all he could to make it a good world for his familial or cultural descendants. While in a sense, this might be considered a vicarious source of satisfaction, actually as long as one lives this is a direct, active, emotionally significant involvement in the daily life around one. It might almost be seen as the most complete kind of ego-realization, even while it is focused on people and on issues which go far beyond immediate self-gratification in the narrow sense.

USE OF DEVELOPMENTAL CRITERIA RATHER THAN AGE CRITERIA FOR STUDYING STAGES IN LATER LIFE

If stages in later life are to be defined, certain special problems must be faced which do not pertain, or not as much, to the study of early life. For one thing, there is far greater variability in the chronological age at which a given psychic crisis arises in later life, than is true of the crisis-points of youth. For instance, one critical test of Cathectic Vitality occurs when one's children grow up and leave home for good. In one family, this may occur in the parents' late thirties. In another family, the parents may be close to sixty before this happens. Thus, if one practical criterion of mastery of a later-life psychological task is the person's handling of certain critical experiences, then older people who are equated for the *stage* they are "working on" may differ very widely in chronological *age*.

An even more complex situation exists, moreover. In studying children who are at the pre-pubertal stage, we can almost take it for granted that they are almost all working on the same *total set* of developmental tasks. With adults, the pattern of developmental tasks can vary more greatly, from one individual to another. For example, the man whose children are grown when he is forty, may not yet have experienced the male climacteric; he may still be working "uphill" to master his vocational role; and he may just be entering a widened circle of social, political or other activities, and a widened circle of friends. This makes "the departure of children" a much different thing for this man, than for a man of sixty whose youngest child is just leaving home; who is nearing vocational retirement; whose family and friendship circle has been broken by several deaths; and whose interest or potency in sexual activity may be markedly less than in his earlier years.

One practical conclusion might be drawn from such reflections, with regard to the conceptualizing of stages in later life: they may have to be much more divorced from chronological age than is true of the childhood stages. There probably are still certain broadly delimitable periods, such as "middle age" and "old age" but these are apt to be statistical artifacts, describing "the average person" of 40–60, or some such span. There are bound to be some people of 65 who act, think and feel like the "middle age" group, while other 65-year-olds act, think and feel very elderly. At least, observation indicates that this is likely to be found.

This leads to one conclusion about the design of future researches on aging: it may be that the best way to get samples which are homogeneous with respect to their "stage in life," will be to use some "stage" criterion and disregard chronological age, except as it proves to be similar for the members of a sample which is defined by a nonchronological criterion. To illustrate, it may be that most can be learned about the principles of psychological development and learning in later life if samples are drawn of women who are at the climacteric, regardless of age; of men who are at the point of retiring (probably less independent of age, for reasons of social policy); of parents whose youngest child has just left home; *et al.*

10

BERNICE L. NEUGARTEN

THE AWARENESS OF MIDDLE AGE

In a recent issue of *Time*, that widely-read magazine of news and editorial opinion that appears each week in the United States, there appeared on the front cover a picture of Lauren Bacall, the movie actress, and the caption, "The Command Generation." The cover story turned out to be a journalist's description of middle age and of the position of the 40-to-60-year-old group in the current American scene. After the rueful recognition that, unhappily, Lauren Bacall is not an altogether typical representative of the age group—not, at least, on the basis of our own studies—the next appraisal was that the caption was not an inept one and that it reflected the same evaluation of middle age that has emerged in most of our own interviews with adults of various ages.[1]

Middle-aged men and women, while

they by no means regard themselves as being in command of all they survey, nevertheless recognize that they constitute the powerful age-group vis-à-vis other age groups; that they are the norm-bearers and the decision-makers; and they live in a society which, while it may be oriented towards youth, is controlled by the middle-aged. In this sense, the *Time* editors have a view that is consonant with our own, even if theirs has been less laboriously derived and more colorfully stated.

There is space here to describe only a few of the psychological issues of middle age as they have emerged from our studies; and to draw primarily from only one of our investigations, one in which 100 well-placed men and women were interviewed at length concerning the salient characteristics of middle adulthood. These people were selected randomly from a pool of names originally drawn from University alumni lists, various business and professional directories, with some drawn also from *American Men of Science* and *Who's Who in America*.

The enthusiasm manifested by these persons as the interviews progressed was only one of many confirmations that middle age is a period of heightened sensitivity to one's position within a complex social environment; and that reassessment of the self is a prevailing theme. Most of this group, as anticipated, were highly introspective and highly verbal persons who evidenced considerable insight into the changes that had taken place in their careers, their families, their status, and in the ways in which they dealt with both their inner and outer worlds. Generally

---

Reprinted by permission of the British Broadcasting Corporation from their publication *Middle Age*, ed. Roger Owen (London: British Broadcasting Corporation, 1967).

This study was carried out in collaboration with Dr. Ruth J. Kraines, Lecturer in Human Development, University of Chicago, and Dr. James E. Birren, Professor of Psychology, University of Southern California.

[1] An extensive set of studies has been carried out in the Committee on Human Development at the University of Chicago over the past decade: studies of personality, of adaptational patterns, of career lines, of age-norms and age-appropriate behaviour in adults, and of attitudes and values across social-class and generational lines. The total number of men and women who have participated now totals something over 2,000. Each study in the series has been based upon a relatively large sample of normal people, none of them volunteers, and all of them residing in one or another metropolitan community in the middle west.

the higher the individual's career position the greater was his willingness to explore the various issues and themes of middle age. In a sense these persons were employing their talents in mapping out for us the dimensions of their lives and in acting as highly-qualified informants about themselves and others whom they had observed.[2]

THE DELINEATION OF MIDDLE AGE

There is ample evidence in our data that middle age is perceived as a distinctive period in the life cycle, one which is qualitatively different from other age periods. Chronological age is no longer the positive marker that it was earlier in life, when to become older means to become bigger, more attractive, or more important; neither is it the positive marker that it becomes again in advanced old age, when each additional year lived increases one's distinction. Middle-aged people look to their positions within different life contexts—body, career, family—rather than to chronological age for their primary cues in clocking themselves. Often there is a differential rhythm in the timing of events within these various contexts so that the cues utilized for placing oneself in this period of the life cycle are not always synchronous. For example, one business executive regards himself as being on top in his occupation and assumes all the prerogatives that go with seniority in that context, yet, because his children are still young, he feels he has a long way to go before completing his major goals within the family.

[2] The description of this sample is worth stressing, since all too often the attention of the psychologist has been focused upon the problem cases or upon the clinical populations that present themselves for study, to the neglect of the normal or the highly successful. As yet we have no developmental psychology of adulthood; and psychology as a science has just begun to study the five or six decades that constitute the adult portion of the life span with something of the fascination that it has been studying the first two decades that constitute childhood and adolescence.

DISTANCE FROM THE YOUNG

Generally the middle-ager sees himself as the bridge between the generations, both within the family and within the wider contexts of work and community. At the same time he has a clear sense of differentiation from both the younger and older generations. In his view, young people cannot understand nor relate to the middle-aged because they have not accumulated the prerequisite life experiences. Both the particular historical events and the general accumulation of experience create generational identification and mark the boundaries between generations. One 48-year-old says,

"I graduated from college in the middle of the Great Depression. A degree in Sociology didn't prepare you for jobs that didn't exist, so I became a social worker because there were openings in that field . . . Everybody was having trouble eking out an existence, and it took all your time and energy . . . Today's young people are different. They've grown up in an age of affluence. When I was my son's age, I was much more worldly, what with the problems I had to face. I was supporting my father's family at his age. But my son can never understand all this . . . he's of a different generation altogether . . ."

The middle-ager becomes increasingly aware of the distance—emotionally, socially, and culturally—between himself and the young. Sometimes the awareness comes as a sudden revelation:

"I used to think that all of us in the office were contemporaries, for we all had similar career interests. But one day we were talking about old movies and we realized that the younger ones had never seen a Shirley Temple film or an Our Gang comedy . . . Then it struck me with a blow that I was older than they. I had never been so conscious of it before . . ."

Similarly, another man remarked:

"When I see a pretty girl on the stage or in the movies—we used to say 'a cute chick'—and when I realize, 'My God, she's about the age of my son', it's a real shock. It makes me realize that I'm middle-aged."

An often-expressed preoccupation is how one should relate to both younger and older persons and how to act one's age. Most of our respondents are acutely aware of their responsibility to the younger generation and with what we called 'the creation of social as well as biological heirs.' One corporation executive says,

"I worry lest I no longer have the rapport with young people that I had some years back. I think the reason I'm becoming uncomfortable with them is that they're so uncomfortable with me. They treat me like I treated my own employer when I was 25. I was frightened of him . . . But one of my main problems now is to encourage young people to develop so that they'll be able to carry on after us . . ."

And a 50-year-old woman says,

"You always have younger people looking to you and asking questions . . . You don't want them to think you're a blubbering fool . . . You try to be adequate as a model . . ."

A newspaper writer, not himself one of our respondents, summarized the feelings of many of these men and women in the following words:

". . . the realization suddenly struck me that I had become, perhaps not an old fogy but surely a middle-aged fogy . . . For the train was filled with college boys returning from vacation . . . They cruised up and down the aisles, pretending to be tipsy . . . boisterous, but not obnoxious; looking for fun, but not for trouble . . . Yet most of the adult passengers were annoyed with them, including myself. I sat there, feeling a little like Eliot's Prufrock, 'so meticulously composed, buttoned-up bespectacled, mouth thinly set' . . . Squaresville."[3]

The awareness that one's parents' generation is now quite old does not lead to the same feeling of distance from the parental generation as from the younger generation.

[3] Sidney J. Harris, "Strictly Personal," *Chicago Daily News*, Chicago, May 11, 1965.

"I sympathize with old people, now, in a way that is new. I watch my parents, for instance, and I wonder if I will age in the same way."

The sense of proximity and identification with the old is enhanced by the feeling that those who are older are in a position to understand and appreciate the responsibilities and commitments to which the middle-aged have fallen heir.

"My parents, even though they are much older, can understand what we are going through; just as I now understand what they went through . . ."

Although the idiosyncrasies of the aged may be annoying to the middle-aged, an effort is usually made to keep such feelings under control. There is greater projection of the self in one's behavior with older people, sometimes to the extent of blurring the differences between the two generations. One of our women recounted an incident that betrayed her apparent lack of awareness (or denial) of her mother's aging:

"I was shopping with mother. She had left something behind on the counter and the clerk called out to tell me that the 'old lady' had forgotten her package. I was amazed. Of course the clerk was a young man and she must have seemed old to him. But the interesting thing is that I myself don't think of her as old . . . She doesn't seem old to me . . ."

DIFFERENCES BETWEEN MEN AND WOMEN

Women, but not men, tend to define their age status in terms of timing of events within the family cycle. For married women, middle age is closely tied to the launching of children into the adult world, and even unmarried career women often discuss middle age in terms of the family they might have had. One single woman said,

"Well, fifteen years ago I didn't consider myself middle-aged. Before I was thirty-five, the future just stretched forth, far away . . . I think I am doing now what I want. In fact, the things that troubled me in my thirties about marriage and children don't bother me now because I'm at the age where many women have already lost their husbands. . . . I have two nieces and three nephews, and I enjoy them very much without having any of the worries and burdens that go with it."

Men, on the other hand, perceive the onset of middle age by cues presented outside the family context, often from the deferential behavior accorded them in the work setting. One man described the first time a younger associate held open a door for him; another, being called by his official title by a newcomer in the company; another, the first time he was ceremoniously asked for advice by a younger man.

Men perceive a close relationship between life-line and career-line. Middle age is the time to take stock. Any disparity noted between career-expectations and career achievements—that is, whether one is 'on time' or 'late' in reaching career goals—adds to the heightened awareness of age. One 47-year-old lawyer said,

"I moved at age forty-five from a large corporation to a law firm. I got out at the last possible moment, because after forty-five it is too difficult to find the job you want. If you haven't made it by then, you had better make it fast, or you are stuck."

The most dramatic cues for the male, however, are often biological. The increased attention centered upon his health; the decrease in the efficiency of the body; the death of friends of the same age—these are the signs that prompt many men to describe bodily changes as the most salient characteristic of middle age.

"Mentally I still feel young, but suddenly one day my son beat me at tennis . . ."

Or,

"It was the sudden heart attack in a friend that made the difference. I realized that I could no longer count on my body as I used to do . . ."

Health changes are more of an age marker for men than for women. Despite the menopause and other manifestations of the climacterium—an event, incidentally, to which very few of these women attach psychological significance—women refer much less frequently to biological changes and to concern over health. "Body-monitoring" is the term we used to describe the large variety of protective strategies for maintaining the middle-aged body at given levels of performance and appearance; but while these issues take the form of a new sense of physical vulnerability in men, they take the form of "rehearsal for widowhood" in women. Women are more concerned over the body-monitoring of their husbands than of themselves.

Another difference between the sexes is marked. Most of the women interviewed feel that the most conspicuous characteristic of middle age is the sense of increased freedom. Not only is there increased time and energy now available for the self, but also a satisfying change in self-concept. Whether married or single, the typical theme is that middle age marks the beginning of a period in which latent talents and capacities can be put to use in new directions.

Some of these women describe this sense of freedom coming at the same time that their husbands are reporting increased job pressures or—something equally troublesome—job boredom. Contrast this typical statement of a woman,

"I discovered these last few years that I was old enough to admit to myself the things I could do well and to start doing them. I didn't think like this before . . . It's a great new feeling . . ."

with the statement of one man,

"You're thankful your health is such that you can continue working up to this point. It's a matter of concern to me right now because I'm forty-seven, and I have two children in college to support . . ."

96

or with the statement of another man, this one a history professor,

"I'm afraid I'm a bit envious of my wife. She went to work a few years ago, when our children no longer needed her attention, and a whole new world has opened to her. But myself? I just look forward to writing another volume, and then another volume . . ."

THE CHANGING TIME-PERSPECTIVE

Both sexes, although men more than women, talked of the new difference in the way time is perceived. Life is restructured in terms of time-left-to-live rather than time-since-birth. Not only the reversal in directionality but the awareness that time is finite is a particularly conspicuous feature of middle age. Thus,

"You hear so much about deaths that seem premature. That's one of the changes that comes over you over the years. Young fellows never give it a thought . . ."

The recognition that there is "only so much time left" was a frequent theme in the interviews. In referring to the death of a contemporary, one man said,

"There is now the realization that death is very real. Those things don't quite penetrate when you're in your twenties and you think that life is all ahead of you. Now you know that death will come to you, too."

Another said,

"Time is now a two-edged sword. To some of my friends, it acts as a prod; to others, a brake. It adds a certain anxiety, but I must also say it adds a certain zest in seeing how much pleasure can still be obtained, how many good years one can still arrange, how many new activities can be undertaken . . ."

THE PRIME OF LIFE

Despite the new realization of the finiteness of time, one of the most prevailing themes expressed by these middle-aged respondents is that middle adulthood is the period of maximum capacity and ability to handle a highly complex environment and a highly differentiated

self. Very few express a wish to be young again. As one of them said,

"There is a difference between wanting to *feel* young and wanting to *be* young. Of course it would be pleasant to maintain the vigour and appearance of youth; but I would not trade those things for the authority or the autonomy I feel—no, nor the ease of interpersonal relationships nor the self-confidence that comes from experience."

The middle-aged individual, having learned to cope with the many contingencies of childhood, adolescence and young adulthood, now has available to him a substantial repertoire of strategies for dealing with life. One woman put it,

"I know what will work in most situations, and what will not. I am well beyond the trial and error stage of youth. I now have a set of guidelines . . . And I am practised . . ."

Whether or not they are correct in their assessments, most of our respondents perceive striking improvement in their exercise of judgment. For both men and women, the perception of greater maturity and a better grasp of realities is one of the most reassuring aspects of being middle-aged.

"You feel you have lived long enough to have learned a few things that nobody can learn earlier. That's the reward . . . and also the excitement. I now see things in books, in people, in music that I couldn't see when I was younger . . . It's a form of ripening that I attribute largely to my present age . . ."

A vice-president of a large publishing company said,

"When I think back over the errors I made when I was 28 or 30 or 35, I am amazed at the young men today who think they can take over their companies at 28. They can't possibly have the maturity required . . . True maturity doesn't come until around 45 . . . And while some of the young men are excellently educated, we middle-aged men are no longer learning from a book. We've learned from past experience . . ."

There are a number of manifestations of this sense of competence. There is, for instance, the 45-year-old's sensitivity to the self as the instrument by which to reach his goals; what we have called a preoccupation with self-utilization (as contrasted to the self-consciousness of the adolescent):

"I know now exactly what I can do best, and how to make the best use of my time ... I know how to delegate authority, but also what decisions to make myself ... I know how to buffer myself from troublesome people ... one well-placed telephone call will get me what I need. It takes time to learn how to cut through the red tape and how to get the organization to work for me ... All this is what makes the difference between me and a young man, and it's all this that gives me the advantage ..."

There is the heightened self-understanding that provides gratification. One perceptive woman described it in these terms:

"It is as if there are two mirrors before me, each held at a partial angle. I see part of myself in my mother who is growing old, and part of her in me. In the other mirror, I see part of myself in my daughter. I have had some dramatic insights, just from looking in those mirrors ... It is a set of revelations that I suppose can only come when you are in the middle of three generations."

There is also the keen sense of expertise. One man said,

"I believe in making decisions ... They may appear to others to be snap decisions, for I make them quickly and I don't look back and worry about what might have been if it had been done another way. I've had enough experience ... I've been through it fifty times, so when I make decisions that seem to come out of the clear blue sky, they just represent a big lot of experience. I've been over the same ground before and I have the ready answer ..."

In pondering the data on these men and women, we have been impressed with the central importance of what might be called the executive processes of personality in middle age: self-awareness, selectivity, manipulation and control of the environment, mastery, competence, the wide array of cognitive strategies.

We are impressed, too, with reflection as a striking characteristic of the mental life of middle-aged persons: the stocktaking, the heightened introspection, and above all, the structuring and restructuring of experience—that is, the conscious processing of new information in the light of what one has already learned; and turning one's proficiency to the achievement of desired ends.

These people feel that they effectively manipulate their social environments on the basis of prestige and expertise; and that they create many of their own rules and norms. There is a sense of increased control over impulse life. The successful middle-aged person often describes himself as no longer "driven," but as now the "driver"—in short, "in command."

11

HARVEY C. LEHMAN

THE CREATIVE PRODUCTION RATES OF PRESENT VERSUS PAST GENERATIONS OF SCIENTISTS

In this study the words "present generation" refer to scientists who were still living at the time when the source book which cited their contributions was published, even though some of the contributors may have died since then. And the words "past generation" refer to scientists born subsequent to the year 1774, and who were known to be deceased at the time when the history which cited their contributions was published. To permit concise expression and to avoid monotonous repetition, the expressions "still-living" and "present generation" will be employed interchangeably hereinafter and similarly the word "deceased" will be employed as a synonym for the expression "past generation."

Although the total performance of the still-living contributors cannot now be fully known because many of them will probably add to their distinguished already-published output, it is true also that while this is occurring other oncoming young workers will also start making their contributions. This raises the question of whether the relative production rates of the several age groups will change appreciably in the years that lie directly ahead.

BACKGROUND

One day in the fall of 1928 I came across a journal article which discussed the prime years of man's life (Nelson,

Abridged from the *Journal of Gerontology*, vol. 17, no. 4 (October, 1962). The unabridged version of this article contains a valuable bibliography on this topic.

1928). In it the author vigorously pooh-poohed Robert S. Woodworth's assertion that the period from 20 to 40 is the most favorable one for doing creative work of the highest order (Woodworth, 1921). The author then proceeded to list a number of eminent individuals who did top-notch work up to the age of 80. By selecting some exceptional cases and disregarding all others it is possible, of course, to obtain spurious evidence which will seem to support almost any wishful thinking whatsoever. However, in the aforementioned article the writer obviously was grasping at exceptional cases to prove his *a priori* belief.

A sounder method for study of the correlation between age and achievement would be to canvass authoritative histories of science, noting the dates on which important discoveries have either been made or first reported, and then ascertaining the ages of the various scientists when they first announced their outstanding work. Starting with this assumption, some 25 years later I published my book, *Age and Achievement* (1953).

In that book, I tried to set forth data from authoritative sources which revealed the age levels at which man's most creative work has been done in the sciences and mathematics and also in medicine, music composition, philosophy, various types of literature, paintings in oil, sculpture, practical inventions, and other areas. Because anyone who is still living may yet produce his masterpiece, my book covered mainly dead "greats," and in selecting great achievements for study, to avoid any bias on my part, I employed lists of foremost achievements that had been compiled by experts within each specific field. The findings were presented in the form of tables and graphs, and adequate allowance was always made for the fact that young workers are more numerous than are older ones.

Meanwhile my interest had broadened and before long I was studying not only outstanding creative achievements but also the ages at which champion performances had been exhibited by athletes, chess players, noted orators, and others. Since leaders do not admit of such study be-

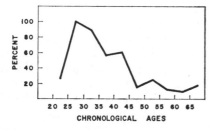

Fig. 1.—Age versus contributions to progress in atomic physics, representing 154 superior contributions by 138 "still-living" contributors (or 1.12 works each).

cause objective data on the quality of their performance is unobtainable, for the following I ascertained merely the ages at which they had occupied their prominent posts, namely, statesmen, college presidents, foreign diplomats, heads of large corporations, and judges on the United States Supreme Court. I also studied the ages at which business men, movie actors, movie actresses, and movie directors were near the top of the earning-power scale, as well as the ages at which annual incomes of $1,000,000 or more were received.

I tried similarly to find the ages at which best performances were displayed by the following: makers of the world's rare violins, leading contract bridge players, checker players, rodeo winners, horseshoe pitchers, champion typists, and authors of notable church sermons.

The interested reader can find my col-

lective findings summarized briefly in the final chapter of my book (1953). Since publishing my book I have tried both to supplement my earlier findings and also to find such flaws as I can find in my earlier published results. This study is the first that I have made of the production rates of still-living groups.

PROCEDURE

The meaning of the words "creative production rate" is illustrated by Figure 1, which presents information regarding chronological age versus contributions to the progress of atomic physics. Data for the construction of this figure were obtained from a book by Wehr and Richards (1960) entitled *Physics of the Atom*. In the appendix of this book the authors have inserted a chronology entitled, The Atomic View of Nature, in which they attempt to pinpoint specific discoveries and other creative accomplishments which have an important bearing on atomic physics.

Because atomic physics is a recent development, to complete their chronology, Wehr and Richards included the contributions of many still-living contributors. Thus, of 345 contributions cited by them, 154 (or 45%) were made by contributors who were still among the living at the time their chronology was published.

Figure 1 reveals by 5-year intervals the chronological ages at which 138 contributors, who were alive in 1958, made a total of 154 contributions to atomic physics, or a life-long average of 1.12 contributions per contributor. In study of Figure 1, it should be understood that it sets forth the *average* number of contributions per 5-year interval. Adequate allowance is thus made for the larger number of youthful workers. This statement applies to all age curves presented herein.

Although the Wehr-Richards chronology was published in 1960, it includes no contributions made subsequent to 1958. Therefore, in order to obtain sound arithmetical averages, I assumed that each of the then-living contributors died in 1958.

That is to say, regardless of when it was published, insofar as my present study is concerned, any book that includes no contributions made subsequent to, let us say, year X, has a terminal year of X.

Employment of the year of publication, 1960, rather than the terminal date of 1958, would have been unsound for my present purpose because such a procedure would have counted as unproductive several years during which production may have occurred but which could not have received due recognition in the Wehr-Richards chronology.

AGES AT WHICH THE MAXIMUM PRODUCTION RATES WERE ATTAINED

Figure 1 shows that, for the 5-year interval from 25 to 29, inclusive, the contributors listed in the Wehr-Richards chronology who were still among the living in 1958, but who to suit my present purpose died (statistically) during that year, made a total of 0.0617 contributions. But at ages 60 to 64 the then-living contributors made an average of only 0.00633 contributions. In Figure 1 the curve is so drawn as to be only 0.00633/0.0617 as high at 60 to 64 as at 25 to 29. The curve is drawn in this manner in order to show graphically that the average number of contributions per individual was only 0.00633/0.0617 as great at 60 to 64 as it was at 25 to 29.

If, regardless of the number of workers that remained alive, the 60 to 64-year-old workers had contributed at the same average rate as did the 25 to 29-year-old workers, the curve in Figure 1 would remain as high at the 60 to 64-year-old age level as it is at the 25 to 29-year-old level. Actually, it exhibits a very noticeable and consistent decrement at the uppermost age levels, thus indicating that the contributors became progressively less productive at those ages.

It is true, of course, that all or almost all of the individuals whose production rate is shown in Figure 1 are still living and producing and therefore that Figure 1

does not take into account their entire life-work. It is also true, however, that in the years directly ahead, other contributors who were too young to have started making their contributions prior to 1958 will also be producing scientific contributions. Hence, it is not necessarily true that the *relative production rates* of the successive age groups as revealed in Figure 1 will change very greatly.

In addition to the Wehr-Richards chronology, age data were obtained from several other source-books. For example,

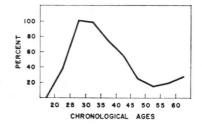

Fig. 2.—Age versus contributions to progress in atomic energy, representing 412 superior contributions by 269 "still-living" contributors (or 1.53 works each).

data for the construction of Figure 2 were obtained from the second edition of Glasstone's *Sourcebook on Atomic Energy*, which was published in 1958 with a terminal date of 1957.

EDITOR'S NOTE: Professor Lehman shows similar curves for still-living astronomers, mathematicians, and botanists, data which are omitted here because of space limitations.

PRESENT VERSUS PAST GENERATIONS

Because many of the earlier workers were reluctant to publish (Cavendish, Newton, *et al.*), age data for contributors born prior to about the year 1775 may be less trustworthy than age data for those born more recently. Therefore, in this study I shall present data only for deceased contributors born subsequent to 1774.

Data for both curves of Figure 3 were obtained from Kelly's *Encyclopedia of Medical Sources* (1948). Since this present study concerns itself only with creative achievement of the very highest order, rather than with whatever may get itself into print, a studied effort was made to locate sources that contain only the most select, and hence of necessity, small numbers of accomplishments.

In Figure 3 the broken line sets forth age data for 2,374 deceased contributors born subsequent to 1774, who made 5,128 contributions to medicine. The solid line reveals, on the other hand, comparable in-

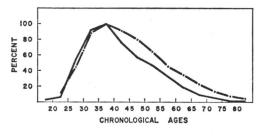

Fig. 3.—Age versus contributions to progress in medicine. *Solid* line, 3911 superior contributions by 2051 "still-living" contributors (an average of 1.91 works each). *Broken* line, 5128 contributions by 2374 deceased contributors born subsequent to 1774 (an average of 2.16 works each).

formation regarding 2,051 contributors who made 3,911 contributions and who were still among the living during the terminal year (1947) of Kelly's *Encyclopedia*.

Notice in Figure 3 that, although the maximum production rates for both the still-living and for the deceased workers occur at ages 35 to 39, the production rate for the present generation contributors rises very slightly more abruptly and also wanes somewhat more precipitously than does the production rate for the past generation contributors.

EDITOR'S NOTE: Professor Lehman shows similar data for still-living compared to past generations of chemists, physicists, mathematicians, and other scientists, data which are omitted here because of space limitations.

POTENTIAL VERSUS REALIZED PRODUCTION RATES

Since these curves represent only the production rates that have been realized at successive age levels and not potential production rates, they certainly do not imply that there is a decrement in the *potential* of these gifted individuals that corresponds to the decrements in the curves. Most psychologists believe that few persons ever actually reach the very peak of performance of which they are capable, and, if we can assume that most *individuals* fail to attain their potential peak performance, it is inconceivable that any entire *age group* has ever done so. Since most individuals and *all* age groups are probably content to come to rest at some point below their maximal potential performance, the decrements in these curves probably do not parallel a decrement in the *ability* to achieve at the older age levels.

ASSUMPTIONS UNDERLYING THIS STUDY

In making this study it is not assumed that when a contribution to science is first published any mortal can say precisely just how important that contribution is destined to be, or that the historian of science is able to identify each and every outstanding contribution to his field. It is assumed only that whether or not a contribution to, say chemistry for example, is an important one can best be judged by those who have written our standard histories of chemistry and that, collectively, the historians can, with a fair degree of accuracy and with no bias toward any one age group, make lists of contributions to their fields that possess high merit.

It is assumed also that the present generation chemists whose published findings are now being cited and discussed in our histories of chemistry are our most likely present-day candidates for professional immortality. Granted that, in the days to come, some of the work of present generation contributors (now cited and discussed in histories of chemistry) may be overvalued, and granted also that the work of others whose findings are now ignored by historians will make their future entry into histories of science, it nevertheless seems probable that these changes will occur on a random basis *insofar as the ages of the contributors at time of making their contributions is concerned.* Since it is individual contributions and not the collective work of entire age groups that chroniclers choose for inclusion in their histories of science, it seems probable that at least a rough proportionality will be maintained between the way in which our present-day historians evaluate the production of the successive age groups and the way in which future historians will do so.

THE PROBLEM OF CAUSATION

Although I would be happy to be able to state the specific causes for the age differences in production rates, the mere fact that I have assembled some statistics is no indication that I know any more with reference to the cause-and-effect relationships than does the reader. The causes of such complex behaviors as those I have studied are probably multiple, complex, interrelated, and they doubtless vary from individual to individual. To attack the problem of even the most general causative factors effectively it will be necessary for generations of entire teams of workers from divers fields of endeavor to make cooperative efforts in that direction. Certainly, no one individual, alone and unaided, could hope to accomplish much along that line.

As has been emphasized by Fraser (Anon., 1946), clinical research on aging as an isolated variable is practically impossible at the present time. This results from the fact that there are always many uncontrolled variables to consider. Because in old age pathological conditions are so generally present, in addition to old age itself, and because these pathological conditions are often obscure and illusive, Fraser suggested that it would be better for clinicians to concentrate on studying the pathological conditions themselves rather than to attempt clinical study of the age factor alone. The age factor of itself could hardly be regarded as *causing* anything at all. It is the *concomitants* of advancing age that need to be examined.

Since it is self-evident that further research on creative production and how to make the most of it is greatly needed, here are some not particularly subtle speculations regarding conceivable causes (but unmeasured and perhaps unmeasurable by use of the principle of the single variable) for the rapid rise of the curves in early maturity and their decline after attaining an earlier maximum. With advance in chronological age beyond the early twenties there is likely to be found: a decrement in physical vigor and sensory capacity, more illness, glandular changes, more preoccupation with practical concerns, less favorable conditions for concentration, weakened intellectual curiosity, more mental disorders, and an accumulation of unfavorable habits. For example, some elderly tend to be set in their ways, a poor condition for bold discovery. Moreover, the individual who already has achieved prestige and recognition may try less hard thereafter to achieve further success.

FACTS VERSUS ARTIFACTS

Statistics can be tricky. What they reveal depends on our ability to interpret them. Our problem here is to examine possible reasons for the different decrements in the production rates of the present and the past generations of scientists. To ascertain whether this apparent difference is a genuine or a spurious one, it is first necessary to answer the following questions.

1. Are the contributions of the present and of the past generations of scientists of

reasonably equal average merit? As has been shown elsewhere (Lehman, 1953), the production rate for creative contributions of superior average merit tends to wane more rapidly than does the production rate for contributions of lesser average merit. Therefore, really to prove that the decrements at the older ages have changed within recent times, it would first be necessary to make sure that the production rates under consideration are based upon output of equal or nearly equal merit. Needless to say, this would be a difficult if not an impossible undertaking.

If, because of the difficulty of evaluating recent research findings, the historians whose books I studied were more hesitant about citing and discussing the contributions of present generation workers than those of past generation workers, it may well be that the contributions of the present generation contributors that were chosen by the historians for citation are on the average somewhat superior to those that they selected from the total output of the past generation workers. If this is what the historians did, it alone could account for the differential decrements.

2. With the passage of time has there been any significant change as regards the eagerness of scientists to publish their findings? It is asserted in a recent publication (Caplow, 1958) that in many major universities, the evaluation of the faculty member's job performance is based almost exclusively on publication and that, as one result of this, it has become the ambitious academician's goal in many instances to accumulate a long list of published titles as early as is practicable. If this alleged trend be a fact, and if this tendency has influenced our most gifted, as well as our run-of-the-mine scientists, it could have lessened the time lag that inevitably occurs between the making of a scientific discovery and the announcement thereof. This obviously would have produced the more rapid decrement in the age curves for the more recently-born scientists.

3. Is increasingly strong competition responsible for the results reported herein? As is well known, within recent times the contributor to almost every field of science has had a lot more competition for honors in his field than did his predecessors. Therefore, with far more contributions from which to choose, the modern historian of science may perhaps have been able to cite recent contributions that possess somewhat greater average excellence than do the contributions they cited and that were made by past generation workers. That is to say, it is conceivable that my finding reflects no actual change in production rate for contributions of equal merit but merely the fact that the more recent research output has had to measure up to a higher standard of excellence.

SUMMARY AND CONCLUSIONS

From 11 histories of chemistry, 11 histories of physics, and 15 histories of other fields of research, 37 pairs of statistical distributions were made, each member of each pair having been made with data obtained from the same book. Of each of the 37 pairs of distributions one member included age data for the deceased and the other member data for still-living contributors. When, by use of median percentage values, separate age curves were drawn which showed production rates for the chemists, for the physicists, and for the 15 groups of other scientists, the curves for each of these three still-living were found to decline somewhat more abruptly and to terminate earlier than did the curves for the deceased. But for the reasons already mentioned this difference is probably not significant. I speak here not of statistical significance but of *meaningful* significance.

On the whole it seems clear that both past and present generation scientists have produced more than their proportionate share of high-quality research *not later than* at ages 30 to 39 and it is as useless to bemoan this fact as to deny it. It might have been supposed that, as scientific knowledge accumulates, the time when the first important research is done would be pushed to older and older ages. Never-

theless, my data provide no support for that supposition, inasmuch as the curves for the past and for the present generation contributors ascend at almost identical rates.

12

WAYNE DENNIS

CREATIVE PRODUCTIVITY BETWEEN THE AGES OF 20 AND 80 YEARS

Any developmental psychologist is likely to agree that ideally the Ss of a longitudinal study should be followed from birth to death, but he is probably not willing himself to undertake an investigation of such length. His reasoning is easy to understand.

Unless he can be given in advance an assurance of exceptional longevity, or of a posthumous corps of research assistants, he cannot be sure that his project will be completed.

Like most psychologists, he assumes that all data which he is to treat must be recorded by himself. In this respect he differs from scholars and the historians who expect to deal primarily with materials which have been recorded by others.

One of the purposes of this paper is to demonstrate that psychologists can make use of data which have been recorded by others. But the paper has primarily a substantive interest. It attempts to examine age changes in productivity. In pursuing this aim it finds documentary evidence most useful.

MATERIALS AND METHODS

The plan of the study.—The paper presents data on the life curve of productivity of 738 persons, all of whom lived to age 79 or beyond. It is concerned primarily with the following two questions: What are the differences among various fields of effort with respect to age curves of productivity? What are the probable causes of these differences?

Reprinted from the *Journal of Gerontology*, vol. 21, no. 1 (January, 1966).

The Ss of the study were persons engaged in scholarship, the sciences, and the arts. In studying only persons interested in these areas, it is obvious that at the moment we are neglecting most of mankind. But no single study can encompass the world's population, and the investigator has the acknowledged right to undertake a limited task. He must, of course, be cautious in drawing general conclusions. Nevertheless, the possibility exists that the principles discovered in the study of particular groups may have a wider applicability.

Selection of subjects.—There were two general criteria for the selection of each person included in the study. First, both the year of his birth and the year of his death must be known and must be separated by 80 or more years. In most instances this requirement insures that the S lived to age 80 or beyond. However, since month and day of birth and death are not taken into consideration and often are not available, by subtracting year of birth from year of death to obtain ages, we have included among our Ss persons born in a certain month who died in earlier months of their 80th year without reaching age 80. However, in the interest of economy of expression, we shall frequently refer to all of our Ss as having reached age 80, and undoubtedly most of them did. (Productivity before age 20 and after age 80 will not be included in our data.)

A second requirement for the inclusion of each S was that there must be available a relatively complete dated record of his works. This requirement, in most cases, limited us to persons born after 1600, since dated records of productivity are seldom available for earlier centuries. In some fields, which will be noted later, the *Ss* were even more limited with respect to the historical periods from which they were selected.

Sources of data on productivity.—Table

The category of scholars includes English historians, English philosophers, and English scholars of Biblical, classical, and oriental literature. All scholars were British, since we used as a sourcebook the *Cambridge Bibliography of English Liter-*

TABLE 1

PERCENTAGE OF TOTAL WORKS BETWEEN AGES 20–80
WHICH WERE DONE IN EACH DECADE

	N		AGE DECADE					
	Men	Works	20's	30's	40's	50's	60's	70's
Scholarship:								
Historians............	46	615	3	19	19	22	*24*	20
Philosophers.........	42	225	3	17	20	18	*22*	20
Scholars.............	43	326	6	17	*21*	*21*	16	19
		Means	4	18	20	20	*21*	20
Sciences:								
Biologists............	32	3456	5	22	*24*	19	17	13
Botanists............	49	1889	4	15	*22*	*22*	*22*	15
Chemists............	24	2420	11	21	*24*	19	12	13
Geologists...........	40	2672	3	13	22	*28*	19	14
Inventors...........	44	646	2	10	17	18	*32*	21
Mathematicians.......	36	3104	8	*20*	*20*	18	19	15
		Means	6	17	*22*	21	20	15
Arts:								
Architects...........	44	1148	7	24	*29*	25	10	4
Chamber musicians....	35	109	15	*21*	17	20	18	9
Dramatists..........	25	803	10	27	*29*	21	9	3
Librettists..........	38	164	8	21	*30*	22	15	4
Novelists...........	32	494	5	19	18	*28*	23	7
Opera composers......	176	476	8	30	*31*	16	10	5
Poets...............	46	402	11	21	*25*	16	16	10
		Means	9	23	*26*	21	14	6

Note: Maximum values are shown in italics.

1 lists for each group of *Ss* its designation, the number of persons in it, and the total number of works produced by members of the group in each decade of life between ages 20 and 80.

The composition of these groups will now be described.

For the most part, in forming groups of *Ss* and in obtaining data on output we have made use only of sourcebooks available in English. As a consequence, in several groups our subjects are entirely American or British.

ature, Vol. II, 1660–1800 and *Vol. III, 1800–1900.* For these scholars, the output for each person refers to the number of books produced, since other publications are seldom listed in the *Cambridge Bibliography.* Because the period covered by the sourcebooks ends at 1900, we could include in this group only scholars who reached age 80 before 1900.

The scientists chosen for study were as follows: eminent biologists chosen from histories of biology (Locy, 1925; Nordenskiöld, 1935); eminent chemists, chosen from a history of chemistry (Hilditch, 1911); British and Irish botanists who were not among the eminent biologists but are listed in Britten and Boulger (1931), and geologists mostly American listed in Nickles (1923). In addition to these men we also placed in the science group inventors listed in the *Dictionary of American Biography* and eminent mathematicians whose names were obtained from histories of mathematics (Bell, 1937; Cajori, 1937; Smith, 1929).

The data on the productivity of biologists, botanists, chemists, and mathematicians were obtained from the *Royal Society of London's Catalog of Scientific Literature, 1800–1900*. Because the sourcebook was limited to a particular century, the Ss were necessarily limited to those whose lives from age 20 to age 80 fell within the century. Since the Royal Society's Catalog contains only scientific papers, other material such as popular articles, books, and monographs were necessarily excluded from the indices of scientific output. The records of output for inventors were obtained by searching the U.S. List of Patents.

As is shown by Table 1, persons listed as belonging to "the arts" included architects, composers of chamber music, dramatists, librettists, novelists, opera composers, and poets. The source of names and of data on productivity of architects was provided by Colvin (1954). Whenever possible, an architect's age with respect to one of his works was recorded as his age at the beginning of construction of this work. If this date was not known, the next subsequent known date, such as date of completion or of partial completion, was substituted.

For chamber music composers, our source of data was Cobbett (1929). This catalog is international with respect to its coverage.

The dramatists were English playwrights. The source was Nicoll (1952–1959). In determining a dramatist's age with regard to each of his works, we used either his age at the first printing of the work or at its first production, whichever was the earlier.

The New York Public Library has prepared a card index of librettists, which gives for each librettist dates of his birth and death and the operas for which he wrote librettos. His age at the first production of each opera was obtained by consulting Loewenberg (1955).

Data on opera composers were also obtained from Loewenberg (1955). This work, which is international in scope, covers all operas produced between 1600 and 1924. The composer's age with respect to each of his works refers to his age at the time of its first production.

Information concerning British novelists was obtained, from the *Cambridge Bibliography 1600–1900*. The author's age with respect to a novel was recorded as his age at the date of publication.

Our final group consisted of minor British poets, whose volumes of poetry are listed in the *Cambridge Bibliography*. Only books of original poetry were included in our data; i.e., translations, selected works, etc., were excluded.

Limitations in the data.—It will be noted that our different groups of Ss are not uniform with regard to their degree of eminence. Some sources, such as histories of science, are highly selective. On the other hand, Loewenberg attempts to include every person who ever composed an opera which was produced.

The units of productivity employed for the different groups also are unequal. Certainly the composition of an opera ordinarily requires greater effort than does the writing of a one-page scientific note, yet within its group each is counted as one unit of output. However, in no treatment of our data do we directly compare such unlike data. Despite differences with respect to selectivity of subjects and in size of unit of measurement, we believe it will be shown that certain trends in output were consistent.

Age changes in productivity.—Our results are presented in two ways. Table 1 shows the percentage of the total output of each group between ages 20 and 80 which was produced in each of these six decades. This method of presentation makes it possible in the case of each group to compare decades with each other and also to make intergroup comparisons of the distribution of productivity regardless

less than the output of the 30's. In most groups the productivity of the 20's was only half as great, or less than half as great as the output of the 30's. In each field these differences were statistically significant. (In this paper this term will be used to indicate a *P* of 0.01 or less.)

The number of contributions made in

TABLE 2

OUTPUT OF EACH DECADE STATED AS A PERCENTAGE OF THE
OUTPUT OF THE MOST PRODUCTIVE DECADE

	N		AGE DECADE					
	Men	Works	20's	30's	40's	50's	60's	70's
Scholarship:								
Historians	46	615	11	50	76	89	100	84
Philosophers	42	225	14	76	90	82	100	88
Scholars	43	326	26	78	100	100	73	90
Sciences:								
Biologists	32	3456	22	90	100	81	69	55
Botanists	49	1889	17	67	100	98	100	70
Chemists	24	2420	45	87	100	80	49	53
Geologists	40	2672	12	47	81	100	70	53
Inventors	44	646	11	35	51	55	100	65
Mathematicians	36	3104	43	100	100	95	100	75
Arts:								
Architects	44	1148	24	82	100	84	36	12
Chamber musicians	35	109	70	100	78	96	87	43
Dramatists	25	803	31	93	100	73	29	9
Librettists	28	164	26	70	100	72	48	12
Novelists	32	494	20	69	64	100	80	24
Opera composers	176	476	26	97	100	50	30	16
Poets	46	402	46	87	100	65	65	40

of differences in total output and in units of measurement.

Table 2 presents the same data in a different way. In this table, for each group the decade in which absolute output was the highest was given the value of 100% and the records of all other decades were stated proportionately. This method again makes it possible to observe readily the rise and fall of productivity regardless of the absolute number of contributions made in any field or in any decade.

Productivity in the 20's.—In each group the output of the 20's was considerably

the 20's was a small part of the total output. In some groups it was as little as 2% of the total and in no group did it exceed 15% of the total. Among the scholars and scientists, age 20 to 29 was the least productive period. For these persons this decade was exceeded in output even by the 70's. Only in some of the arts were the 20's more productive than the 70's.

Output before age 20 was omitted from our study because pilot studies showed that very little creative work was produced in the teens.

Productivity in middle age.—For almost

all groups, the period 40–49 was either the most productive decade or else its record was only slightly below that of the peak decade. In only one field (chamber music) were the 30's higher in output than the 40's. In all other cases in which the 40's were not the most productive years, this honor went to a later period.

Productivity in the 70's.—For scholars as a whole, the 70's were as productive as the 40's. The scientists, on the other hand, showed a significant decline in the 70's. The output of that decade was only 75% to 53% of the peak rate. Among our groups of scientists, the biologists, chemists, and geologists declined most with age, mathematicians and botanists least.

The decline in productivity in the arts was considerably greater than in science. Dramatists, architects, and librettists, respectively, produced in their last decade only 9%, 12%, and 12% as much as in their peak years. Persons in the arts who held up best were composers of chamber music and poets. They produced in their 70's 43% and 40% as much, respectively, as in their most productive periods. These percentages were below the lowest percentages recorded for any science. The contrast between the steady output of the scholars and the steep decline in arts is sharp.

To what extent did the decade of the 70's enable men to add to the output which they had achieved prior to age 70? Between 70 to 79, scholars increased their preceding number of books by 25%. Scientists in their 70's increased their number of earlier articles by 18%. However, this decade enabled persons in the arts to add to their previous output by only 6%.

DISCUSSION

We have noted that artists in general "hit their stride" in output earlier than the other groups under consideration.

What are the causes of these differences in early productivity? An obvious possibility is that persons in arts need not undergo a long formal education before they begin to produce, whereas scholars and scientists are required to have a protracted preparation before productivity begins.

Another difference between the groups lies in the time required to produce a unit of work. The musician and the poet, by intense effort, may sometimes complete a contribution within a very short period of time, but a history of Rome or a record of the voyage of the Beagle cannot be dashed off in a week. Extensive gathering and evaluation of data usually must precede scholarly and scientific contributions. It may be significant that chemists and mathematicians were relatively more productive in their 20's than were other groups of scientists. Perhaps creative work in mathematics and in chemistry does not require the long period of study and of data gathering which characterizes other kinds of scientific work. Obviously further studies are needed to elucidate these points.

While our interpretation of the differences in the relative amount of work done in the early decades is not proposed as final, at present we are inclined to believe that the explanation lies primarily in the requirements for different kinds of contributions. Some careers require much more preparatory study and gathering of data than do others. This principle may prove to apply not only to differences between major fields, such as arts, scholarship, and sciences, but also to differences within fields, such as the apparent difference between chemists on the one hand and botanists and geologists on the other with respect to their early output.

We turn now to a discussion of the causes of the differences between the sharp decline in output in the later years which occurred in the arts, the moderate decline among scientists, and the almost steady maintenance of productivity among the scholars.

When one attempts to explain these differences, the possibility suggests itself that biological aging occurs earlier among artists than among scientists and earlier among scientists than among scholars. However, data on longevity do not support this hypothesis, nor do we know of any other data which would tend to confirm it.

A second possibility is that the groups may differ in the extent to which emotional problems in the later years may interfere with productivity. Pathological disorders increase sharply in the later decades. Raskin (1936) has shown that literary persons are more prone to psychological incapacitation than are scientists. This difference may be slight in the early decades, because mental disorders are rare in all groups at these ages, but they may loom large in later life; i.e., the differences in productivity between persons in the arts and persons in scholarship and science in later years may increase with age as psychological difficulties become more prevalent among artists. At present few data indicate whether or not this interpretation is correct. In our opinion it deserves further study.

A third hypothesis is that group differences in age decrement in productivity may be related to the amount of effort required to create a unit of work. With increasing age the individual declines in the number of hours he can work, the energy he can expend, and the speed with which he can recover from fatigue. It can be argued that if in an area of creativity the traditional unit of output is characteristically small, if no prolonged expenditure of energy is required, and if no great fatigue is generated, there may be little reduction in output with age. Conversely, fields of activity which inherently require intense, prolonged, and fatiguing effort may be more susceptible to the effects of age.

This hypothesis does not seem to be supported by our results. It is assumed that the composition of an opera and the composition of an historical work each requires continued effort over a considerable period of time. Yet the output of composers declined markedly with age and the works of historians did not. Mere differences in energy requirements do not

appear to explain this difference in decrement.

Finally, we come to those factors which, in our opinion, contribute most to the differences in age decrements. These are the contrasting ways in which productivity is achieved in the three fields of endeavor with which we are here concerned. The contrasts are various. For one thing, in some fields it is proper and customary for a person to have collaborators or assistants; in other fields, contributions must be primarily personal and individual. Second, in some kinds of work, a contribution requires the use of data or materials which must be collected, stored, and classified; in other areas, no contributions can be derived by such processes. Third, in some fields a person receives credit for modifying, or amplifying, or restating his previous views; in other areas, a contribution must consist of new work, not the revision of an earlier one.

With respect to each of these pairs of possibilities, it seems that the first alternative describes the situation which faces the scholar, while the second alternative describes what is expected in the arts. The scientist occupies an intermediate position.

Let us expand this point. In the first place, the utilization of assistants in collecting materials, in arranging them, and in assessing them is considered proper on the part of scholars and scientists, but is usually not considered appropriate in the arts.

To illustrate: Bancroft (1800–1891) (Nye, 1944), a famous American historian with considerable personal financial means, employed men to find and copy documents which he needed in connection with preparing his history of America. In addition to his paid assistants, diplomats and friends in foreign posts also supplied him with materials. For an historian this is entirely proper. In contrast, one can hardly envisage an opera composer or a poet paying for or requesting comparable assistance in the composition of an opera or a poem.

Pavlov (1849–1936) (Babkin, 1951), the famous Russian physiologist, exemplifies in the field of science the extent to which productivity may be enhanced and continued through aid from others. A review of Pavlov's work shows that the enormously time-consuming task of gathering data was done largely by others working under his supervision. Babkin, who worked with Pavlov for 10 years and knew him well during the last 35 years of his life, gives a revealing picture of some aspects of Pavlov's productivity.

When Pavlov was director of the Institute of Experimental Medicine, and later when he was director of the School of Experimental Physiology, graduates of Russian medical schools came to his laboratory to complete the research thesis required for the M.D. degree.

"Each doctor, on joining the laboratory, was allotted a subject, which was usually the continuation of a problem worked on by his immediate predecessor . . . Pavlov personally supervised the majority of the experiments . . . With the help of these graduate students Pavlov, as it were, multiplied the results that could be produced by his own two hands." [Babkin, pp. 70–71.]

"After the Revolution of 1917, there were about 40 people working with Pavlov. When he was 74 he wrote, 'My work progresses on a large scale. A great many workers have gathered, and I cannot accept all who want to come. . . .' Pavlov now resembled a chess player, playing several boards at once. The data obtained by one worker could be confirmed and carried a step further by the research of another worker." [Babkin, pp. 113–114.] "Pavlov's research could not have been carried out on so large a scale without the assistance of so many co-workers." [P. 123.]

Such facilities rendered it possible for Pavlov to remain highly productive to the end of his life.

On the other hand, if the Russian government had offered to provide a dramatist or a novelist with a comparable staff of assistants in order that his output of plays or novels should not diminish, it is not likely that he could have made effective use of these helpers, or that the world would have given him credit for works produced in this fashion. The scholar and the scientist can utilize systematically stored information in ways which are not characteristic of persons in the "beaux arts."

The methods of Bancroft, the historian, again serve to illustrate this point. Bancroft rose at five or six in the morning to copy facts from his sources into his "daybooks," one book for every year to be covered. In another notebook, called a topic-book, he copied materials relative to topics such as The Army, Washington, Foreign Affairs, etc. As Nye (1944) says (p. 289),

"If he wished, for example, to write five pages on national finance in 1784, the proper page gave him all the facts in chronological order, cross-indexed and supported by reference to the original sources."

While Bancroft had an excellent memory, with such work-habits memory was scarcely necessary.

In six years of this routine, between ages 76 and 82, Bancroft produced a completely new work, *The History of the Formation of the Federal Constitution*. At age 89 he completed a life of Van Buren which was based upon notes made 40 years earlier. It is no wonder his productivity in his 80's seemed to be as high as in any earlier decade.

If Wordsworth had attempted to write in his later years a poem on the French Revolution, using methods comparable to those of Bancroft, he would have referred to his revolutionary diary, written at ages 19–26, consulted all poems on the Revolution written by others, placed on his desk a rhyming dictionary, and started to work. Naturally Wordsworth did not work in this way, but if he had done so, his later poetry would not have been improved.

A successful instance of the methodical use of accumulated information is provided by Noah Webster (1758–1843) (Scudder, 1895) who first described the differences between the British and the American usages of the English language. He listened to Britons and Americans, he read newspapers, he read books, he took voluminous notes. Making use of these materials, between the ages of 48 and 68 he produced his *American Dictionary of the English Language*. A revision was completed at age 82, and he was at work on another revision at his death at age 85. Neither a novelist nor a dramatist can proceed in quite the same way. They cannot create a novel or a play by compilation, nor do they usually find it feasible to revise a previously published work. In general, architects, music composers, and creative writers, if they are to be recorded as being productive in their later years, must produce genuinely new works on an individual basis, whereas the requirements for continued productivity on the part of the scholar and scientist are different.

Comparisons of our productivity data with those of Lehman.—While Lehman in *Age and Achievement* (1953) was concerned primarily with the ages at which *outstanding* works were done, he has several tables which bear titles such as "Percentage of total contributions during each decade of life." If the reader compares these with our tables, he will find differences which are striking. For example, Lehman's Table 38 in Chapter 15 entitled "Percentage of total contributions to philosophy during each decade of the philosophers' lives" indicates that the contributions made in the 70's by philosophers constituted only 2% of their total, whereas the comparable value in our data is 22%. In Lehman's table the output of philosophers was highest in the 30's. A considerable decline occurred subsequently. Our data shows no such decline. Many other apparent discrepancies could be pointed out.

The explanation is simple. In his Chapter 15, Lehman was dealing with the number of contributions which were made in each decade of life without regard to the number of contributors who were surviving in each decade. Thus the fact that philosophers, according to Lehman, have produced more work in the 30's than in any other decade is primarily due to the fact that in the 30's more philosophers were still alive. In this respect Chapter 15 in *Age and Achievement* differs from most of Lehman's other chapters.

When we attempt to make comparisons between Lehman's findings and ours with regard to productivity, we encounter other difficulties. Lehman's data on output *per decade per survivor* ordinarily refer only to superior works, not to total output. But in a few tables he does refer to total output per decade per survivor. Thus his Figure 29 shows the mean productivity of philosophers living in each decade of life. The data represented in this figure show a decline with age which is greater than we have found. Again the differences in findings are probably due to differences in methodology. In our tables, the men whose later records were examined are the same men whose early records were examined. In Lehman's data, however, only some of the persons represented in the 30's are represented in the 70's, since many were deceased by age 70. So far as we can determine, Lehman has no tables which are made up in the same way as ours; i.e., based on the unselected output of persons all of whom lived to be 80. He has some data on men, all of whom reached 80, but these data refer only to "notable" contributions, not to total productivity. In other words, no findings of Lehman's relative to productivity contradict our data, since his were not gathered in the same manner as ours. It is our view that no valid statements can be made concerning age and productivity except from

113

longitudinal data involving no drop-outs due to death.

In the present paper we have not been concerned with the frequency of "outstanding" contributions at different ages, the subject which engages most of Lehman's attention. At this point we feel obliged to indicate whether or not our data may have some bearing on that topic.

On another occasion we have argued (Dennis, 1956) that the apparent superiority of certain decades with respect to the output of outstanding works may be in part the result of defects in methodology. Our views on this topic have not changed, but we have no desire to repeat our former arguments at this time.

It is relevant here to indicate that in each field in which there is a sharp decrease with age in *total* output there is also an age decline in *superior* works. For example, since, as of 1924, the date of Loewenberg's publication, only 24 operas had been written by men in their 70's, it is obvious that not many *great* operas can be found which have been composed in this decade of life. Our data tend to show that in the arts the age decline in productivity is sufficient to account for a considerable part of the decrement in "outstanding" contributions. However, lessened productivity cannot be a major factor in any decrement in superior works observed among scholars, since scholars continue to be productive. But a full consideration of the factors which may produce data showing a decline with age in works of high quality is beyond the scope of the present paper.

SUMMARY

Data have been presented from documentary sources showing trends with age in the productivity of 738 persons, each of whom lived to age 79 or beyond. These men were engaged in 16 areas of work which were classified in three major groups as scholarship, the sciences, and the arts.

It was found that, in many groups, the decade of the 20's was the least productive period. However, persons in the arts produced a larger part of their life-time output in this decade than did scholars and scientists. Relatively speaking, persons in the fine arts and in literature were more productive in the 20's and the 30's than were the scholars and scientists. The highest rate of output, in the case of nearly all groups, was reached in the 40's or soon thereafter. From age 40 onwards the output of scholars suffered little decrement. After age 60 the productivity of scientists decreased appreciably and the output of persons in art, music, and literature dropped even more than did that of scientists. This brief summary, however, does not do justice to the differences which occur within each major category.

The interpretation proposed is that the output curve of the arts rises earlier and declines earlier and more severely because productivity in the arts depends primarily upon individual creativity. Scholars and scientists require a greater period of training and a greater accumulation of experience and of data than do artists. The use of accumulated data and the possibility of receiving assistance from others permit the scholar and scientist to make more contributions in their later years than do those in art, music, and literature.

13

RAYMOND G. KUHLEN

DEVELOPMENTAL CHANGES IN MOTIVATION DURING THE ADULT YEARS

Whatever the specific role assigned to motivation by psychologists interested in learning and performance, there is little disagreement that it is an important variable, especially in more complex types of learning and "real life" situations. The psychological needs of individuals determine in part those aspects of the environment to which they attend and respond, the direction in which efforts are expended, and the amount of energy thrown into a task. But in addition, motivational concepts have proved extremely useful in understanding the behavior of individuals and groups at any one point in time, and define some of the more important variables determining the course of development as the years pass.

After consideration of some of the circumstances that result in developmental changes in motivation, the bulk of the present discussion will focus, first, upon growth-expansion motives, and second, upon anxiety and threat as a source of motivation. As one views the course of human life, growth-expansion motives seem to dominate the first half of the adult years, with needs stemming from insecurity and threat becoming important in the later years. While this is obviously an oversimplification of the picture, and circumstances will vary greatly from individual to individual and from group to group, these contrasting trends appear to emerge from various studies of the adult life span.

Reprinted from James E. Birren, ed., *Relations of Development and Aging* (1964), chap. 13, pp. 209–46. Courtesy of Charles C. Thomas, Publisher, Springfield, Illinois.

FACTORS INFLUENCING DEVELOPMENTAL CHANGES IN ADULT MOTIVATION

At the outset, it may be worthwhile to examine some of the factors that are likely to result in important differences between people of various ages in their motivational patterns. Whether a need is aroused and influential or quiescent and latent in particular phases of adult life will likely be a function of a number of the variables to be discussed below.

CHANGES IN AROUSAL CUES, ENVIRONMENTAL STIMULATION AND EXPECTATIONS

It is a matter of common observation, as well as a conclusion from psychological research, that even relatively satiated human desires can be aroused given the proper environmental stimulation, that motives may be weakened to the point of near disappearance if long periods of years are encountered with little opportunity for gratification of reinforcement, and that new motivational tendencies may appear if new types of stimulation or expectation (and reinforcement) are encountered. A society or culture decrees in many subtle ways, and in some not so subtle, that certain types of stimulation will be brought to bear on certain age groups and largely withheld from those of other ages. One of the problems that has plagued investigators of adult learning, for example, is the fact that once he has mastered his job, the typical adult is neither stimulated nor required to master new skills or understandings. The sameness of stimulation—whether on the job, in recreation, in marriage and sex—may be an important factor in the apparent decline of certain motivational tendencies, such as curiosity. An important, though unanswered, question concerns the nature of age trends under circumstances which permit or require that older individuals be subjected to new types of stimulation. Does a middle-aged person who changes jobs or spouses find career or sex drives rekindled, for example?

Moreover, since the motivational tendencies of people are very largely learned as a result of the reward and punishment systems to which they are exposed during the course of early development, it is reasonable to expect that motives may be *changed* during adulthood if the individual is exposed to a new set of punishment and reward patterns. Thus, as an individual moves into a new role, e.g., is perceived by others as being middle-aged or old, he may be subjected to a new pattern of expectations, a new set of approvals and disapprovals, with the result that in due course new motives may appear.

SATISFACTION OF NEEDS AND CHANGING MOTIVATION

It is helpful in understanding some of the motivational changes that occur during the adult years to assume that human beings have a number of "needs" which vary in importance. In a sense they are arranged in a hierarchy with the influence of higher level needs being to a considerable extent dependent upon the state of affairs with respect to lower level needs. Maslow (1943), among others, has argued that, generally speaking, more basic needs must be satisfied before higher level needs become operative. This particular conception of the relationship among psychological needs is useful in explaining some of the changes in motivation that come with adult years.

Among middle-class Americans, for example, career drives are likely to take precedence over many other psychological needs, and dominate the years of young adulthood, perhaps even to the point of resulting in minimal contact with family. If by forty or forty-five, the career-oriented individual has achieved economic security and success, the need to "get ahead" (the achievement need) may be much less in evidence, and the former career-oriented individual may turn more frequently to family or to community activities as sources of gratification. "Affiliation" or "service" needs then may be more important. A similar change in the importance of sex as a drive may occur with the passage of years, and in part for the same reasons. In addition to having a strong sex drive in sheer biological terms, the adolescent or young adult is likely to be frustrated in his free expression and satisfaction of this drive. With marriage and more ready satisfaction of sex needs other motivations may emerge as important. One may speculate that Maslow's conception may partially account for the fact that sex needs may take precedence over convention in adolescence whereas the reverse may be true of the parents of adolescents.

In sum, needs that are important in one phase of life may fade out and give way to others simply because they have become relatively satisfied. However, if circumstances should again arise which result in the frustration of a need previously satisfied that need may again become active. For example, autonomy needs may be strong in youth, but become submerged as the individual becomes independent and self-directing. But if a situation should later arise where his autonomy is threatened, by a domineering employer or even by the protective cloak of kindness with which we sometimes envelop old people, then the need to be self-directive and independent may reassert itself.

AGE-RELATED FRUSTRATION OF NEEDS

It was suggested above that the lower level of more basic needs may become inoperative and thus give way to higher level needs *when they are satisfied*. It is also not unlikely that chronic frustration will tend similarly to make need inoperative. Lewin and his students pointed out some years ago that when children were unable to obtain an attractive goal object, such as toys within their vision but out of reach, they soon behaved as though the toys were no longer a part of their psychological field. Similarly, long and chronic frustration of some need may result in the individual turning to other sources of satisfaction. His behavior seems subsequently to reflect other motivations. Thus, while a person may experience a reduction in achievement need and career drive because he has been successful, by like token he may experience a similar decrease because he has been chronically unsuccessful.

Because frustration may play a pervasive role in motivational changes, as suggested in the preceding paragraphs as well as in the preceding pages, it may be worthwhile to specify some of the age-related factors that may prove frustrating and hence influence the motivational complex of the adult. Five sources of frustration merit comment.

First is the degree of status accorded people of different ages in the particular society in which they live out their lives. There seems to be general agreement that the American society tends to be geared to and to idealize youth, with the result that older individuals not only are frustrated somewhat with respect to status needs, but are very likely to encounter reduced opportunities for gratification of other rather important needs.

In the second place, people of different ages are likely to experience limitations and pressures of time and money. Man is a time-bound organism, in the sense that he has only twenty-four hours a day at his disposal.[1] This fact forces people, especially those in certain age ranges, to make choices, to push aside certain in-

[1] Man also has a relatively finite life span. Time perspectives, in this sense, will be mentioned later.

terests and activities which they previously enjoyed. Unpracticed and unreinforced, often for many years, certain motivational tendencies may essentially disappear. As in the case of time, unavailability of money can result in certain "needs" dropping out of the picture, because of lack of practice and lack of reinforcement, whereas increasing availability of funds may result in their reappearance and the development and cultivation of new needs.

Whereas time is relatively absolute and can be stretched only a little by efficiencies, money can be made to increase by appropriate expenditure of effort. Some data suggest that economic demands are greater in the thirty to forty decade (Johnson, 1951). At such a point in life, the economic drives can be highly motivating forces. Economic pressure, coupled and merged with career advancement desires, probably accounts for a large share of the young adults enrolled in adult education programs. The force of the economic drive is apparent even in the history of geniuses whose productivity often bears a striking relationship to their need for money.

A third frustrating or limiting circumstance influencing motivation at different ages involves physical change and decline. The decline in physical energy, resiliency, strength and reaction time—the general slowing down of the organism—has a pervasive effect upon behavior, perhaps as evident as anywhere in the recreational pursuits which people of different ages engage in. While it is generally assumed that physiological drives are important motivators in infancy and early childhood, to be replaced gradually by the socially derived motives which soon come to dominate the behavioral scene, the question may well be raised as to whether physiological pressures and tensions may not again become important motivators in the later years. One may argue that such

117

would be the case due to the fact that as frustrating agents they demand attention. In some cases there does seem to be general concern and preoccupation with physiological functioning, but how general this may be is uncertain. But if physiological pressures again become important, they become so in a different psychological context. In early infancy social needs have not yet developed. In old age the difficulties of physiological function, of digestion and elimination, for example, and greater susceptibility to fatigue and illness may make satisfaction of derived needs more difficult or impossible and require greater attention to diet and general regimen. A re-emergence of physiological pressures as a motivating force may result.

Fourth, a middle-aged or older person may feel threatened and insecure because of skill deficits generated by rapid technological advance that has left him outdated. It should be noted that gains on vocabulary and information subtests of general ability tests may obscure this fact suggesting, as they do, increasing cognitive resources as experience accumulates.

Fifth, and finally, is the greater threat and frustration that people may encounter because of their inability to do anything about some of the disturbing circumstances and sources of unhappiness which they experience. A person tends to get "locked in" particular circumstances as he marries, has children, invests in property, accumulates training and seniority, and may find himself unable to move out of a frustrating situation from which the younger uncommitted individual could easily free himself. Threats, such as of loss of job, are thus more serious for the committed, and older, individual than for the younger.

CRITICAL PERIODS AND MOTIVATIONAL CHANGES

The foregoing discussion has suggested that certain motives may be stronger at some periods of life than at others because of the degree to which special stimulation, special frustration, or satisfaction is encountered at those ages. Are there to be found any particularly critical periods in the life span? Do, for example, changes such as those associated with the menopause result in a reorganization of the motivational structure of the individual? While the evidence seems to be essentially negative with respect to the menopause period, it does seem probable that various factors combine to concentrate satisfactions and threats at particular periods of life. Scott and others (1951) have advanced the hypothesis that "critical periods" may be found at various points throughout the life span, particularly at those points when important changes in the social relationships of individuals occur. If this hypothesis has merit, it may be expected that such events as marriage, becoming a parent or grandparent, or loss of spouse or job would influence in important ways the motivational pattern of an individual. Sometimes the effects may be dramatic, as in the instance of an elderly spinster who became quite a different person subsequent to the death of the domineering sister with whom she had lived her entire adult life.

Changing time perspectives represent another factor causing critical periods in the motivational history of the individual. The point in life, perhaps the late thirties or early forties, when one comes to the realization that time and life is not infinite probably has quite a significant effect upon one's orientation and motivation. The here and now becomes much more important; if goals are to be achieved, they must be achieved soon. One is almost forced to structure his psychological present and future on a "real" rather than an "unreal" level. Biology and culture combine to set particular sublimits within the total span of life. Thus, thirty seems to be a critical time for the single woman hoping for marriage; the forties for the individual striving for success in career but not yet achieving it; the late forties for the woman who has married late and wants children; retirement age for the

118

professor who wants to finish a book before leaving the university.

Depending upon the circumstances in
individual cases, critical points introduced
by changing time perspectives may very
well result in reorientations of such magnitude that one can in a very real sense
think of an important change, not simple
in goal object but in motivation pattern,
or one might anticipate heightened motivation as time begins to run out. For
others there may be a building up of unhappiness and anxiety, which in themselves represent strong motivating forces.
And at any and all of these points there
may be periods of serious self-appraisal.

GROWTH-EXPANSION
MOTIVES

In the introductory paragraphs to this
paper it was pointed out that discussion
would focus upon (a) growth-expansion
motives and (b) anxiety and threat as a
source of motivation. We turn to the first
of these now, to an array of needs which
can be considered together since they
tend to have in common the promotion
of growth and expansion. These needs include those commonly assigned such labels as *achievement, power, creativity* and
self-actualization, as well as broader orientation, suggested by such phrases as
need to attain and maintain a significant
role, need for expansion and ongoingness,
generative needs. Buhler (1951, 1957)
who has written extensively on changing
needs as major explanatory variables in
the life cycle, tends to subsume such motives as just listed under the general category of *expansion,* and to urge that
there is a continuing need for expansion
throughout the life span. Though this is
likely true, as will be suggested below, it
is also probably true that such needs dominate behavior more obviously in the
years up to middle age.

ACHIEVEMENT AND SOCIAL NEEDS

A number of studies have demonstrated
the greater importance of achievement
needs in early adult years, especially for

men (Kuhlen and Johnson, 1952; Mc-
Clelland, 1953), and a recent study by
means of projective pictures of a nationwide sample of adults showed high points
in young adulthood and middle age followed by a decrease in need achievement,
but an increase in need power (Veroff,
Atkinson, Feld, and Gurin, 1960).

In another study by Neugarten and
Gutmann (1958), young men were described as actively striving toward goals,
as self-propelled, achievement oriented.
In contrast the older men were inactive,
submissive and introspective. Interestingly
enough, while the female subjects did not
give responses that could be categorized
in the same way, they did portray the
older female in the picture as characterized by a marked increase in dominance
and assertion.

The data are not entirely consistent,
however. Reissman (1953) for example,
has reported that older high achievers
were more willing than young high
achievers to undergo the inconvenience
of moving to a new city and to accept
limitations upon freedom of religious and
political expression for the sake of a better
position.

Affiliation needs and social interests
play a prominent role in life, and are here
classified under growth and "expansion"
needs since it is through expanding social
relationships with individuals and groups
that many people are able to achieve a
sense of significance. Although it is difficult to infer whether there are marked
changes in strength of affiliation and related social needs with age (the data of
Veroff *et al.,* 1960, suggest a decline in
the case of women), certainly there are
important shifts in ways in which such
needs are satisfied. There is, as is well
known, an upsurge of social interest during the course of adolescence and into the
early twenties. But from that point on
there seems to be less interest in extensive
social interaction with large numbers of

individuals, and a shift to a greater liking for closer relationships with fewer people. Studies by Strong (1943) and by Bendig (1960) are consistent with this observation.

CHANGES IN GOAL.

The postulation of a need or set of needs for continuing growth and expansion serves to relate in a meaningful way the goals and interests of people of different ages. As Buhler points out, family and work constitute major avenues of expansion, until these no longer offer possibility of continued satisfaction, whereupon interests shift to other kinds of activity. This shift from one orientation to another as a result of continued frustration of the possibility of "expanding" along the lines of marriage and family on

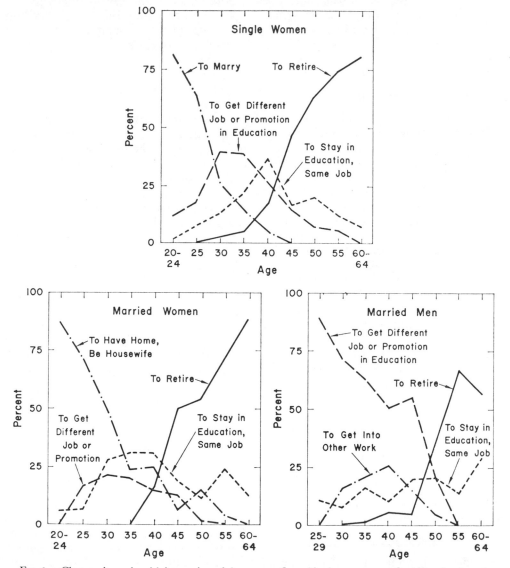

FIG. 1.—Changes in goals with increasing adult age as reflected in the responses of public school teachers to the question, "What would you most like to be doing ten years from now?" (From R. G. Kuhlen and G. H. Johnson, Change in goals with increasing adult age, *J. Consult. Psychol.*, *16* [1952]:1–4.)

the part of single women is illustrated in a study by the present writer (Kuhlen and Johnson, 1952). The basic data are presented in Figure 1. When asked what they most wanted to be doing ten years hence, the vast majority of young single women gave marriage and family as a goal. This response dropped off rapidly by thirty or thirty-five and was suceeded by desire to get a new or better job, a

activities, and orientations with increasing years reveal a shift from active direct gratifications of needs to gratifications obtained in more indirect and vicarious fashion. An illustration of this trend is found in a study by the present writer (Kuhlen, 1948) in which an age sequence

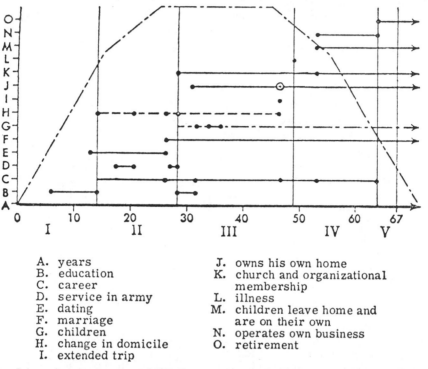

A. years
B. education
C. career
D. service in army
E. dating
F. marriage
G. children
H. change in domicile
I. extended trip
J. owns his own home
K. church and organizational membership
L. illness
M. children leave home and are on their own
N. operates own business
O. retirement

FIG. 2.—Schematic representation of Bill Robert's course of life. (From Ch. Buhler, "Meaningful Living in the Mature Years," chap. 12. pp. 345–87 in *Aging and Leisure*, ed., R. W. Kleemeier, New York, Oxford University Press, 1961.)

shift not apparent among married women. Other studies suggest that this process of forced reorientation in major goals is likely to be accompanied by considerable stress. The increasing participation of married women in organizational activities at around fifty years of age, as shown in another study done at Syracuse (Kuhlen 1951), may be interpreted as an effort to achieve a sense of significance in a new setting now that children have left home.

In total, analysis of changes in interests,

emerged in reasons given for major happy episodes in life. Starting with the late teens or early twenties, the following sequence was evident: romance, marriage, birth of children, satisfaction with children's success. Presumably, through identification with one's own children, one achieves a sense of continuing expansion when one's own life becomes stagnant. It is of further interest, though not well documented in research, that people of older ages seem to evidence a greater interest in genealogy and in religion, particularly in a belief in immortality. These orientations may well represent efforts, albeit unconscious, to maintain a sense of ongoingness even when it is recognized that one's own years are short.

EXPANSION, CONSTRICTION, AND DEGREE OF "INVESTMENT" IN LIFE

Presumably, if Buhler is correct that needs for expansion are continuing, such shifts as just noted may reflect not so much a decrease in need strength (at least

with increasing age has already been suggested by the less direct, more vicarious methods of achieving gratification characterizing the later years. In total, there seems to be a reduction in "drive level," a decrease in ego-involvement in life. The latter is reflected in analyses of Thematic Apperception Test stories obtained in the Kansas City study of middle and old age. Older people told less complex stories, introduced less conflict and peopled their stories with fewer inhabitants. Also a reduction in ego energy seems to occur, as reflected in a count of the number of

TABLE 1

MEAN EGO-INVOLVEMENT AND EGO ENERGY SCORES OF MEN AND WOMEN COMBINED, DERIVED FROM TAT DATA

(Adapted from Rosen and Neugarten, 1960)

AGE	NUMBER INTERVIEWED	EGO-INVOLVEMENT		EGO ENERGY	
		Introduced Figures	Introduced Conflict	Assertive	Emotional Intensity
40–49	48	2.23[a]	3.02[a]	13.19[a]	5.75
50–59	48	1.67[b]	2.38	12.27[b]	5.17[b]
64–71	48	.94[c]	2.35[c]	11.54[c]	4.08[c]

[a] Applying Tukey's test to the Studentized Range, the difference between means for the youngest and middle age groups is significant at or beyond the .05 level.

[b] The difference between means for the middle and oldest age groups is significant at or beyond the .05 level.

[c] The difference between means for the youngest and oldest age groups is significant at or beyond the .01 level.

over a wide range of years) as a change in method of gratification necessitated by decreasing capacity or opportunity to obtain the gratifications as actively and directly as was possible at an earlier age. Figure 2 illustrates, nonetheless, that life tends to be characterized by a curve of expansion and constriction. Partly, constriction is forced upon the individual by extraneous circumstances. Retirement age is reached, spouse and friends die, opportunities are withdrawn. But partly, too, the typical middle-aged or older person has less energy to invest, has less new experience to relish, and has less reason to exert himself. For such reasons, possibly, he "invests" less in life.

This decreased investment in living

assertive rather than passive activities described and in ratings of the emotional intensity of stories. The relevant data, reported in a paper by Rosen and Neugarten (1960), are summarized in Table 1. Gurin et al. (1960) reported older people worry less than younger individuals, a finding which they also interpret as reflecting less investment in life.

Paralleling the shifts described in Figure 2 for an individual, is a general pattern of expansion and restriction in a whole array of life activities. This is evident in age curves relating to income, family size, participation in organizations (Kuhlen, 1951), and in the social life space as reflected in the relative number of psychological settings penetrated in the community (Barker, 1961). Similar to these patterns of expansion restriction, are the curves obtained by Schaie (1959) for scores on a social responsibility test. These scores increased until the mid-fifties and then decreased among a sample of 500 subjects ranging in age from twenty to seventy.

DISENGAGEMENT

Presumably data such as the foregoing, but more especially data from the Kansas City study of middle and old age, led to the recent proposal of a theory of aging to which was given the label "disengagement," an interpretation first presented in 1960 by Cumming and her associates, and later given more formal form and elaboration in a book (Cumming and Henry, 1961). In a sense, this hypothesis asserts a reversal of a need for expansion, i.e., in later years the individual is motivated to disengagement. Though the point is not made as explicitly as might be wished, the implication is that the disengaged state of affairs is something *desired for its own sake* and not a second-best role adopted as a means of avoiding the threat developing in more significant participation or as a result of societal rejection from more significant roles.

This "theory" has not yet been subjected to extensive independent test, but some data are beginning to appear. Thus a recent study bears on the hypothesis implied by those proposing the disengagement theory that in old age psychological equilibrium accompanies passivity whereas at younger ages active participation is necessary for equilibrium. The data recently reported by Tobin and Neugarten (1961) do not support this view. They found that an index of life satisfaction was correlated *more* highly with participation in older years than in middle age. Although the supporters of the disengagement theory hypothesize that there would be no loss in morale with increased age or with retirement, available data suggest much loss does occur. Kutner and his associates (1956)

have shown morale decrease with age, and Phillips (1957) has reported more maladjustment among old people who have moved into less favored roles. Another study, by Filer and O'Connell (1962), is especially noteworthy in that it involved an *experimental* manipulation of environmental conditions. A special attempt was made to modify for an experimental group the environmental conditions. A special attempt was made to modify for an experimental group the environmental demands and expectancies in a veterans' domiciliary so as to provide a "useful-contribution" climate. Care was taken to avoid the appearance of a "special project" and the participants were probably not aware of the group they were in. Nor was the rater who evaluated their later adjustment. Significant gains in adjustment characterized the experimental group.

A recent report by Dean (1960), one of the collaborators in an early statement of the disengagement theory, has presented data on the decline of "instrumentality" in support of the theory. The present writer is inclined to place an opposite interpretation upon these findings, concluding that the data show oldsters to be quite unhappy about their lot because of their loss in instrumentality. The basic data in this study involved responses to the questions "What are the best things about being the age you are now?" and "What are the worst things about being the age you are now?" The responses were classified in several ways, but we focus our attention here on two categories: (1) "*Output:* responses emphasize active engagement in the social environment, with focus on achievement, responsibility, power and influence, utility, knowledge, experience." (2) "*Frustrated output:* The obverse of the above. Responses emphasize loss of ability to do, to achieve, to assume responsibility; loss of respect from others. This category in-

123

cludes responses about physical weakening, if this weakening is seen primarily as interfering with 'doing.' " It is significant that in response to the question concerning "best things" the "output" responses decline from 37 percent in the fifties to 3 percent in the eighties. This decline, in and of itself, does not indicate *purposeful* disengagement. Indeed, that people increasingly (with age) *resent* the loss of opportunity to achieve and assume responsibility is implied in the *increasing* frequency of responses to the "worst things" question, which fell in the "frustrated output" category. The percentages for four successive age groups (50's, 60's, 70's, 80's) were 22, 31, 53, and 48. In the two oldest age groups, 70–79, 80+, this response was the *most frequent* category, suggesting very real unhappiness at their inability to remain "engaged."[2]

One more example of inconsistency of data bearing on the disengagement hypothesis, that of religious interest, is appropriate inasmuch as there is no formalized pressure for a person to become "disengaged" from religious institutions as there is in the case of work. It will be recalled, also, that increased interest in religion in old age, particularly belief in immortality, was cited earlier as reflecting a need for continued "expansion." Cumming and Henry (1961, p. 91) are explicit on this point: "It is a common belief that religious piety and practice increase with age . . . On the other hand, disengagement theory would predict a decrease in the interest in religion as normative control is lessened." Not only do the data reported by these authors seem to this writer inconsistent within themselves, and inconsistent with their own hypothesis, but other studies have indicated an increasing belief in immortality throughout the adult years (Barron, 1961) with unanimous or near unanimous belief in the very old age groups, e.g., over ninety

(Cavan *et al.*, 1949). Although extensive participation in church programs drops off with age, attendance holds up remarkably well in view of the general decline with age in out-of-home activities. And almost all evidence that has come to the writer's attention bearing on "sedentary" participation—radio listening, reading,— shows an increasing interest in religion with age. Moreover, as Lehman (1953) has pointed out, more than any other organizations, religious organizations qualify as gerontocracies. It is not unlikely that the source of the differences of opinion regarding the importance of religion in old age lies in the fact that there are several possible indices of religiousness. It is probable that indices based on different definitions will show differing, in fact, contrasting trends with age.

Despite the contradictory lines of evidence summarized in the foregoing paragraphs, it is probable that the disengagement concept will have considerable heuristic value. Already it appears to have stimulated a variety of studies which have added to the store of empirical data on aging, and may well provide an appropriate explanation of aging trends in an, as yet undefined, segment of the population even though not applicable to the generality.

ANXIETY AND THREAT AS A SOURCE OF MOTIVATION

We turn now to another source of motivation, namely anxiety, which for reasons earlier noted, seems to increase and become more generalized as people move into the middle and later years of life. This anxiety may not only generate constructive efforts to reduce it, sometimes through education or therapy, but is especially important as a generator of defensive and handicapping behavior patterns. As will be recalled, it was suggested in earlier pages of this chapter, as well as in the immediately preceding paragraphs, that there is reason to believe that social and physical losses, coupled with

[2] One may also interpret an older study by Simmons (1946), Kutner *et al.* (1956) and Philip (1957) as contradictory to the disengagement hypothesis.

increasing responsibilities and commitments, may well generate increasing anxiety with age. It is probable that the tendency to become anxious and susceptible to threat constitute an increasingly important motivating force in late middle-age and the older years of life. Indeed, a number of writers (e.g., Kaufman, 1940; Atkin, 1940) who have attempted theoretical explanations of the aging process, have seized upon anxiety generated by social and physical losses as the primary age-related independent variable. Various personality changes, such as conservatism, intolerance of ambiguity, and rigidity are construed as ego defenses, or maneuvers, utilized to control the anxiety so generated.

It should come as no surprise to the reader that this particular interpretation of aging is not well accepted by people in the middle-aged or older categories. Indeed, when the writer presented these views at an adult education conference some years ago, it was denounced as "a theory of decay." While, to be sure, there is much that is virtuous in an emphasis upon positive achievement and "expansion," a realistic approach requires that we take into account the "negative" side of the motivational picture as well. To this we turn next, and with sufficient reference to data to demonstrate the probability that such trends do indeed occur.

Anxiety is one among a number of symptoms of maladjustment. A recent factor analysis by Veroff, Feld, and Gurin (1962) of the symptoms of subjective "adjustment" and maladjustment has identified several dimensions that warrant our attention. Five factors were identified in the analysis of the data for males: (1) felt psychological disturbance, (2) unhappiness, (3) social inadequacy, (4) lack of identity, and (5) physical distress. All but the last of these factors were also apparent in the analysis for women. The data described below relate to age trends in a number of these variables.

CHANGES IN SUBJECTIVE "HAPPINESS"

It is fairly axiomatic that a person is not well adjusted unless he is reasonably happy and contented. And about the only way one can discover whether this is so is to ask him. Subjective though the data are, they nonetheless have important implications for the issue at hand. Although the trends to be reported are for "happiness," it seems reasonable to assume that the trends for "unhappiness"—which are more directly suggestive of anxiety—would be essentially the mirror image of the curves for happiness, though a neutral group (neither happy nor unhappy) might vary in size from age to age and thus make the reflection less than exact.

One would anticipate that happiness would increase with age as important previously frustrated needs are satisfied. Thus, in young adulthood, in contrast to adolescence, sex needs and needs for autonomy are more likely to be satisfied, and important life developments in the area of family and work probably bring a sense of achievement and security, and presumably happiness. Later, as losses and limitations are encountered, these would presumably be given opportunities for direct need satisfaction, and happiness would be reduced. An unpublished study by Kuhlen (1948) shows this curvilinear relationship and studies by Morgan (1937), by Landis (1942), by Gurin and his associates (1960), and Cavan and others (1949) show losses in middle and later years.

We have, then, in one important symptom of adjustment, an indication that as people get older, at least beyond middle-age, their reported happiness decreases on the average, and presumably the incidence of unhappiness increases.

CHANGES IN "SELF-CONCEPT"

It is apparent that the well-adjusted individual will have positive self-regarding attitudes, whereas the individual who is maladjusted and insecure—and hence more susceptible to anxiety and threat—will tend to have a low regard of himself and be lacking in self-confidence. Again, one would anticipate that the character of the self-concept would vary curvilinearly with age, becoming more favorable during the periods of gains and increased status, and less favorable in the years beyond when losses are being experienced. Although there have been some interesting theoretical considerations of developmental changes in self-concept during the adult year (see particularly Erikson, 1959, and Buhler, 1962), there are relatively few developmental *data* available. One of the few arrays of data with which this writer is acquainted that shows a curvilinear relationship of self-concept to age was assembled by Lehner and Gunderson (1953), utilizing a draw-a-person test. It was found that men tended to draw larger figures the older they got up to about age thirty and thereafter they draw smaller pictures, whereas women draw larger pictures up to age forty and then smaller pictures. Since it is often assumed that in such picture drawing the individual projects his self-image, it possibly may be inferred that these trends reflect trends in self-evaluation, and that the picture is drawn larger until the individual senses that he has passed the prime of life.

Some of the data bearing on the self-concept in later years are on the amusing side, though nonetheless revealing. For example, when taking intelligence tests in the course of an experiment, older college professors made twice as many self-belittling comments as did those younger (Sward, 1945). And older women,[3] particularly older single women, have a strong tendency to omit their ages from autobiographical sketches in such places as *Who's Who* and *American Men of Science* (Norman, 1949). Presumably this is done because such admission is

[3] Age, incidentally, was estimated by facts they gave regarding year of graduation from college.

painful to themselves, or viewed as self-damaging in the eyes of others. More systematic is the study by Mason (1954) who administered a number of measures of self-concept to several groups from different backgrounds. A group of institutionalized indigent old people had more negative self-concepts than did a group of independent, middle-class oldsters, and both, in turn, had more negative self-concepts than did a more youthful low economic group. However, individual differences among the old groups were greater then among the young, suggesting that reactions to the aging process vary substantially among individuals.

Still a further line of evidence is of interest here, particularly since it is often said that a person is as young—or as old—as he feels. Thus, how one classifies one's self age-wise may be construed as reflecting his self-concept. The surprising finding from several studies (Tuckman and Lorge, 1952; Phillips, 1957; Kutner *et al.*, 1956) is that many people of quite advanced years often describe themselves as "middle-aged"—half of over 300 individuals over seventy years of age in one of the studies and about a third of those over seventy-five in another. That one's subjective age has significant implications is suggested by the fact that, with actual age controlled, those oldsters who rated themselves as middle-aged in one study (Havighurst, 1953) were better adjusted on other measures, and that in another study (Kogan and Wallach, 1961) a relationship was found between subjective age and indices of caution, when chronological age was held constant. Curiously, however, this latter relationship was attributable almost entirely to a rather high relationship to subjective age and caution in that portion of the group that was low in measured anxiety. The investigators considered the lack of relationship between subjective age and "decision caution" in the high anxiety group to stem from the greater heterogeneity of this group, a circumstance they thought due to the different possible meanings of high anxiety for older people. For the low anxiety subjects, the theoretical interpretation stressed the importance of "image maintenance" in bringing about behavioral consistency.

This relationship between self-concept or self-image and "decision confidence" brings us to another major line of evidence relating to self-concept, namely, that bearing on the self-confidence of individuals of different ages. As suggested above, one would expect that individuals with positive self-concepts would be more self-confident, whereas those with

basic facts are presented in Table 2 where it is also shown that a reliable relationship between caution and age exists among the older group of women, but not among the men. These data suggest that aging experiences in the American culture affect the sexes differentially with respect to decline of confidence and caution, both with respect to timing and degree.

Another, possibly very significant, finding was the fact that the odd-even reli-

TABLE 2

AGE DIFFERENCES IN SELF-CONFIDENCE AND CAUTION

(Adapted from Wallach and Kogan, 1961)

	Young	Old	p	r* (Older Group)
Confidence index (Low scores indicate confidence):				
Men....................	2.83	3.19	< .01	....
Women.................	3.11	3.08	NS	....
p....................	< .01	NS	....	....
Deterrence of failure (caution) (High scores indicate caution):				
Men....................	5.82	6.38	< .01	.05 (NS)
Women.................	5.88	6.36	< .02	.33 (p < .01)
p....................	NS	NS	....	....

* Correlation is between age and "Deterrence of failure" score and age in the older group. "Older men" averaged 70.2 years (SD ± 7.3); women 69.5 years (SD ± 7.7). Number of subjects: 132 young women, 89 older women; 225 younger men, 65 older men. Young people were college students.

negative self-concepts would be less self-confident. Following our expectation that self-concept would improve during those phases of the life span where there are pronounced gains and evidences of accomplishment, Brozek (1952) has shown that men around fifty were more self-confident on a questionnaire than those younger. Wallach and Kogan (1961) have compared younger adults (college age) and a group of older adults (between 47 and 85 years of age) on a number of measures of caution and self-confidence. They found a number of interesting relationships one of which involved the fact that the older group was more cautious than the younger group, and, in the case of men, less self-confident. The

ability of the test involving degree of caution (a dozen verbally described situations with respect to which the subjects were asked to recommend action) was higher for the older group (*r:* males, .80; females, .80) than for the younger group (*r:* males, .53; females, .63). This finding may be interpreted as indicating a greater *generality* of caution, i.e., less dependence upon specific situational factors, among the old than among the young. This particular finding, if confirmed, has substantial theoretical significance. The fruitfulness of a theoretical interpretation of aging in terms of anxiety and threat depends in part upon the degree to which anxiety is shown to be generalized and not highly situational in origin.

127

Still another study (Kogan and Wallach, 1961) is of interest here, partly because of the fact that it utilized a different technique, but also because it compared the values placed upon different phases of the life span by a younger and older group of subjects. With respect to "self-concept," the concepts "myself" and "ideal person" were included among those studied by means of the semantic differential, with special reference to the evaluative factor score. Here again a decline in the favorability of the self-concept in old age appeared. The difference between the old and young was especially

were reliably less negative toward old age and death than were the younger. Thus, while older people place a negative valuation upon their phase of life, they seem to achieve a certain adaptation to old age, and do not view it nearly as negatively as do young adults.

CHANGES IN INCIDENCE OF ANXIETY SYMPTOMS

Evidence presented thus far in this section indicates rather clearly that as people get older, they are less happy, have more negative self-concepts, and have experienced a loss of self-confidence. One

TABLE 3

AGE DIFFERENCES IN MEAN EVALUATIVE SCORES (SEMANTIC DIFFERENTIAL) FOR SEVERAL LIFE STAGE CONCEPTS

(Adapted from Kogan and Wallach, 1961)

| | CONCEPT | | | | | |
	Baby	Youth	Middle-Age	Elderly	Old-Age	Death
Men:						
Young	2.24	.99	.61	− .77	− .97	−3.02
Old	1.75	1.05	.29	− .69	− .11	−2.25
p	NS	NS	NS	NS	.02	NS
Women:						
Young	2.32	1.17	.22	−1.02	−1.79	−4.28
Old	2.09	1.35	.20	−1.14	− .30	−2.33
p	NS	NS	NS	NS	.001	.001

significant in the case of the "ideal person." This was interpreted by the authors as suggesting "that older individuals are either more willing to admit unfavorable elements into their image of the ideal or that the very connotation of the concept evokes a more negative reaction in an older person whose age status renders unrealistic any aspirations toward an unrealized ideal self. . . . However, such devaluation may have ego defensive properties for both old and young individuals."

Table 3 contains scores on the "evaluative factor" for those concepts relating to developmental stages in life. It will be noted that both young and old age groups of both sexes assign negative valuations to such concepts as elderly, old age, and death. However, the older individuals

would expect increases in anxiety symptoms to parallel these changes. Trends should be examined under two conditions: first, under what might be considered "normal" circumstances of living, and second, under stressful or threatening conditions. Study in these two settings is desirable because, as is the case of physiological functioning, the effects of aging are not likely to be so noticeable under normal conditions as under conditions of stress. Thus, we might anticipate that people would not show much in the way of trends in anxiety symptoms with age under normal conditions of living, but would under conditions of environmental or organic stress.

The bulk of the data obtained under ordinary conditions of living, seem to be consistent with this expectation. Despite the common expectation that "nervousness" would increase with age or be particularly noticeable at certain points, such as menopause, no particular age trends appear (Hamilton, 1942). Nor was an increase with age in the frequency of nervous symptoms evident among a large number of individuals taking health examinations in another study (Britten, 1931). No age trends or a trend toward decreased anxiety might well be expected, in view of the fact that people tend to

with some twenty symptoms of psychological distress. A factor analysis suggested four factors which were labeled "psychological anxiety," "physical health," "immobilization," and "physical anxiety," Table 4 carries the percentage of subjects in various age groups who evidenced high scores in three of these factors. It will be noted that there is a substantially greater incidence of anxiety

TABLE 4

PERCENTAGE OF SUBJECTS OF VARIOUS AGES WHO RECEIVED
HIGH SCORES (6, 7, OR 8) ON "PSYCHOLOGICAL ANXIETY,"
"IMMOBILIZATION," AND "PHYSICAL ANXIETY"

(Adapted from Gurin, Veroff, and Feld, 1960)

	AGE					
	21–24	25–34	35–44	45–54	55–64	65–plus
Psychological anxiety:						
Men	5	6	8	11	14	17
Women	10	14	17	20	29	34
Immobilization:						
Men	22	10	10	3	1	2
Women	14	15	12	6	5	4
Physical anxiety:						
Men	3	4	4	8	13	17
Women	8	9	10	14	17	28
No. of subjects:						
Men	65	252	241	209	146	161
Women	98	344	307	250	183	191

seek out those circumstances in life which are positively rewarding and non-threatening. To the degree that one is successful in this, as he is likely to be as time (age) passes, and so long as this state of affairs is maintained, no increase with age in anxiety would be anticipated. This seems to be the finding of a number of *early* studies.

However, certain facts emanating from a recent national mental health survey appear to be contrary to the earlier findings and warrant particular attention because of the size and representativeness of the sample. The interview schedule utilized in this survey contained questions dealing

symptoms among older people than among younger except in the instance of the factor dealing with immobilization.

These investigators offer the following interpretation of the greater incidence among young adults of anxiety symptoms classified under the tentative label of immobilization:

"Immobilization, ennui, and lack of energy are all psychological states that suggest lack of integration, rather than insurmountable, immediate psychological difficulty. In a life situation, where one is caught among different pressures for integration of the self—pressures that may operate at cross-purposes (such as the 'achievement versus housewife' conflict for some women) or pressures that are so varied that they are not all attainable at the same time—one may frequently experience a lack of integration. Such pressures are more likely to occur early in life and then gradually diminish as patterns of integration are chosen. Until such integration occurs, however, one might expect that a common reaction to these cross-pressures which are too divergent or too numerous to handle would be withdrawal, with its concomitant restlessness and disruption. Since this problem is more often encountered by the young adults, perhaps this is one reason that young people are prone to symptoms of the immobilization type." [Gurin, Veroff, and Feld, 1960, pages 191–192][4]

Adequate explanations of the contrast between this recent study and earlier findings are not readily apparent. Differences in methodology or in sample may be responsible, or it may be that current times are confused and stressful compared to the social-political context of earlier research. As will be developed next, older individuals seem particularly susceptible to stress, and thus it is possible that under current "normal" conditions they may reflect more anxiety.

For more definitive evidence regarding reactions of people of different ages to stressful situations, one may cite reports of observations in "naturalistic settings" and studies which were specifically designed to check this phenomenon. Welford (1951), among others, offers as one explanation of the reluctance of older individuals to cooperate in experiments is their unwillingness to expose themselves to the threat of the new situation. Another study of younger adult years, done by the present writer (Kuhlen, 1951) during World War II, revealed a greater relationship between age and anxiety symptoms among enlisted naval personnel who were presumably in a more stressful situation than were others.

Two other studies, utilizing different

procedures, suggest an increase in anxiety with age. In these studies, reaction time to stimulus words was utilized as a measure of threat or stress. While data bearing on words representing different areas of life will be considered below, relevant to the current discussion is the reaction time to words such as *worry, afraid, unhappy, restless, anxious.* Such words may be considered generalized anxiety "stimuli" in contrast to a word like "church" which represents the religious area of life. Powell and Ferraro (1960) in one study and Olsen and Elder (1958) in another found reaction time to these words to increase with adult age. Since these generalized anxiety words were interspersed with words from potentially stressful areas of living, it is not clear whether the results should be construed as bearing on changes under "normal" circumstances of living or under "stressful" circumstances.

Although the data are by no means as extensive as one might wish, either with respect to the range of symptoms sampled or the range of ages, the evidence does suggest that increasing age brings increasing susceptibility to stress and threat. Presumably this threat is engendered by cultural and physical losses that are experienced with increasing age and by various and sundry commitments which are more binding as age increases and which make threats more serious. Certainly more careful studies should be undertaken of this variable, not only for the purpose of marking out the age relationships under different conditions, but also with respect to determining the degree to which increasing age brings with it a generalized type of anxiety which might be reflected in an array of behaviors, in contrast to anxiety which is fairly specific to certain situational changes that occur with age. In view of the theoretical importance of anxiety as a variable influencing personality and performance changes with age such studies assume great importance.

[4] This interpretation of the nature of the psychological task facing young adults is not unlike that suggested by Erikson (1959).

The foregoing discussion has given some indication of age changes in the gross amount of anxiety present at different ages as this is reflected in the incidence of general anxiety symptoms. Data indicating particular sources of worry and anxiety are likely to be especially useful to those concerned with human betterment.

That there can be striking age differences in the source of anxiety and tension during the young adult years and middle age is shown in the data presented in Figure 3. In this study, instead of using a verbal questionnaire, subjects were presented with words, taken one at a time, which were chosen to represent different areas of living. Since it is well known that people tend to block up, and thus to react more slowly to stimuli which are disturbing to them, comparison of their reactions to these critical words with their reactions to a list of neutral words can be taken as some indication of the degree to which particular area of life sampled by the critical words represents a source of anxiety or tension.

The subjects in this study were all white female public school elementary teachers, half of whom were married and half of whom were single, twenty-five of each group in each of the age categories shown in the chart. It is to be noted that there are important differences between those who are married and single, i.e., between those who occupy different roles in life and hence are exposed to different threats and have different opportunities for need satisfaction. Particularly striking is the anxiety evoked by heterosexual words among single women in the younger adult years and the rapid drop-off as age increases to sixty. Married women, who have greater opportunity for satisfaction of sex needs, show relatively little anxiety and relatively slight change with age. Single women, for whom career begins to become a primary source of satisfaction by around thirty, show a peak of concern with this area in the thirties, whereas married women show little age trend. Similar striking differences are found between the married and unmarried groups with respect to social acceptability, but in the instance of religion, physical health, and teacher-supervisor relationship the trends are similar, increasing with age in each instance. It is of some significance, that in each of the seven areas, with the exception of teacher-supervisor relationships, single women show more anxiety and concern than do married women. Whether this is due to selection, the more maladjusted being those who do not marry, or due to a generalized anxiety resulting from a "minority group" status is not clear.

Other data (Dykman, Heiman, and Kerr, 1952) confirm the fact that different ages in young adulthood and middle age are characterized by different problems, and suggest that changes in problems continue into old age. Morgan (1937) and Havighurst and Albrecht (1953), among others, have presented data describing specific worries of very old people.

INDIVIDUAL DIFFERENCES

It has been argued in this paper that the changing motivational picture of the adult years can be painted in two broad strokes, one emphasizing growth-expansion motives which are translated into a succession of goals, the other emphasizing anxiety, generated by physical and social losses, which constitutes the motivational source for various handicapping, but nonetheless protective, defense maneuvers. Although both motivational patterns are important throughout life, it has been suggested that the first more clearly dominates the young adult years, the latter the later years of life. Whatever merit such a conceptualization may have as far as the generality is concerned, it is obvious that there will be important differ-

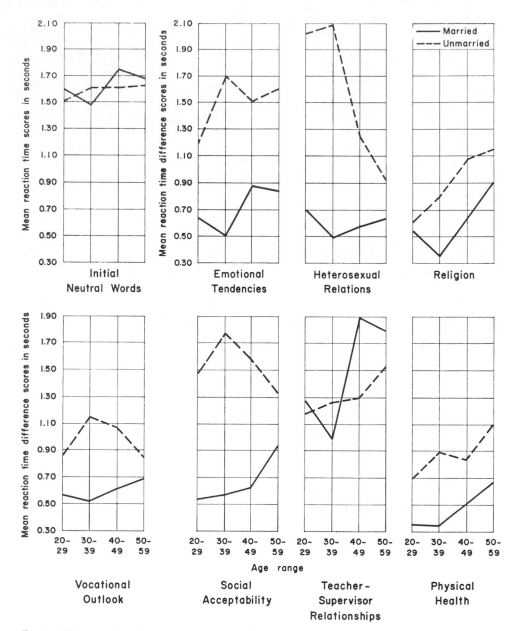

Fig. 3.—Mean reaction time scores in seconds of married and unmarried teachers at various age ranges to initial neutral words, and mean reaction time difference scores in seconds of married and unmarried teachers at various age ranges to "critical" words taken from various psychological adjustment areas. (From Powell and Ferraro, 1960.)

ences among individuals as to how and the degree to which these tendencies are translated into specific goals or specific maneuvers, and the ages at which one tends to outweigh the other. As illustrative of differences among individuals, it will be instructive to examine certain contrasts between meaningful subgroups of the population where data are available.

DIFFERENCES IN THE ONSET OF
THE THREAT OF AGE

It may be hypothesized that a critical point, motivationally, in the life history

cultures, the point can be made by selected sample data. Incidence of suicide varies greatly between the sexes and between Negroes and white groups. Whereas the rate constantly climbs for white males with age, for females it is a relatively level smoothly rounded curve, with an actual decline in the advanced years. These differences may be interpreted as reflecting the more stressful environment in which males live, and the fact that with increasing age it is more difficult for them

TABLE 5

DIFFERENCES AMONG SOCIAL GROUPS IN THEIR PERCEPTION OF AGING

(From p. 4a of *Aging and the Aged*, The University of Chicago Reports, vol. 12, no. 2, November 1961)

	Upper Middle	Lower Middle	Working	Lower
Men Look at Aging:				
When is a man . . . ?				
"Mature," "at the prime of life,"				
"most confident".............	40	35	30	25
"Middle-aged"................	47	45	40	40
"Old".......................	70	70	60	60
Women Look at Aging:				
When is a woman . . . ?				
"Good looking"...............	35	30	27	25
"Most confident".............	38	35	30	35
"In her prime"................	40	40	38	35
"Old".......................	70	70	67	65

of the individual is that point at which he senses that the process of expansion is concluding and begins to become sensitive to certain irreversible losses. Such a point would presumably be somewhat delayed in an oriental culture where age is venerated as compared to a typical western culture where an unfriendly attitude toward old age is probably more characteristic. Generally speaking, in those subcultures (or in those individuals) where age brings continuing success and status, there presumably would be less threat associated with the process than in a subculture (or in an individual) where losses are experienced relatively early.

While data are not available for all sub-

to maintain their role. Geared as men are to the work life, career frustrations and inability to find useful employment presumably would be a serious blow to self-concept and the generator of unhappiness and anxiety.

Two lines of evidence are presented with respect to social economic and social class differences. The first involves social class differences in the way people perceive the prime of life and aging. In Table 5 which summarizes answers given by men and women with respect to certain matters, the most striking difference relates to answers to the question of when is a man "mature," "at the prime of life," "most confident." The lower-lower class individuals gave twenty-five years of age and those in successively higher social classes regularly raised the age until those in the upper middle class gave a mean age of forty. Similarly upper middle class individuals defined "middle age" and "old" as notably older than did those in lower-lower class groups. When women were asked what age a woman was most "good looking," "most confident,", "in her prime'," or "old," again the lower-lower class groups gave younger ages than did those in the upper middle classes.

age. These people, even under stressful economic conditions, seemed not particularly threatened by loss of employment regardless of age.

Other significant subgroups of the population can very readily be identified. Buhler (1933) for example, has contrasted a "psychological curve" of life with the "biological" curve of life, and has pointed out that those individuals who are most dependent upon physical status—e.g., strength or attractiveness—have psychological curves closely approximating the

PROPORTION EMPLOYED, ACCORDING TO AGE, FOR FOUR OCCUPATIONAL CLASSES, UNITED STATES, 1940

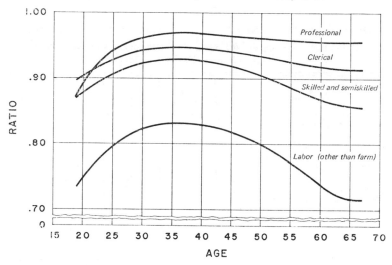

FIG. 4.—The differential threat of aging for various economic groups as reflected in age trends in the percentage employed in different categories at different ages. Data are for 1940, a time when cultural discrimination would likely be better reflected than in times of peak employment. (From L. I. Dublin and A. J. Lotka, *The Money Value of a Man*, rev. ed., New York: Ronald Press. 1946.)

But perhaps more critical than such perceptions is the age at which economic threat is experienced by members of different occupational categories. We go back to 1940, depression years, for a good example of this phenomenon, since it would be under conditions of economic stress that such threats would be most clearly revealed. The data in Figure 4 show clearly that it is the laboring group who experiences earliest and in most pronounced fashion the threat of loss of employment. In the upper professional group, very little change occurred with

biological curve of life, whereas those engaged in mental pursuits have a psychological curve lagging the physical curve. One would expect, for example, a narcissistic person, a chorus girl, or a prize fighter to feel the threat of age much earlier than a non-narcissistic person, a university professor, or a physician.

DIFFERENCES IN DEGREE OF FUTURE ORIENTATION AND MEANING OF LIFE

A number of writers have commented on the fact that certain lives seem to have "unity," that certain individuals seem well

134

integrated and "inner-directed." In contrast, other individuals seem responsive to the many different situations in which they find themselves. Some people seem "future-oriented" and work toward deferred gratifications; others live essentially for the present. Such differences are likely to be especially, but not exclusively, evident in the different meanings that work and career have for different individuals.

Differences of this nature assume importance in evaluating the generality of "expansion" needs in human lives, and in assessing the overall character of motivational changes during the adult years. Filer and O'Connell (1962), for example, have noted that despite a mean gain among a group of oldsters under conditions of a useful contributing climate (a finding which, as noted earlier, was interpreted as failing to substantiate the "disengagement" hypothesis), some individuals made no gain and some lost. Quite properly these authors have noted that any theory of aging must encompass such contrasting trends among individuals. What seems "disengagement" may not really be this if the individual were not "engaged" psychologically to begin with. And, for others, "disengagement" may actually mean "re-engagement," in the sense of retiring "to" rather than "from." Investigations into the personal meanings with which different people invest their goals and their varied behaviors, and the relationship of the specifics of their lives, singly and in patterns to their more fundamental motivations are very much needed.

Of those psychologists interested in aging, Charlotte Buhler has probably been most interested in fathoming the meaning and unity of the course of human life, and of describing this meaning in terms of changing motivations, sequences of goals and self-conceptions. In her most recent papers (1957, 1962), she has given especial emphasis to the meaningfulness of life, self-realization, and fulfillment. For many people, she argues, life is a meaningful project involving self-deter-

mination toward goals, with various episodes of self-assessment along the way, and ending in fulfillment or failure. Something of the range of individual differences is suggested by her categorization of those individuals interviewed (Buhler, 1961). Four groups were identified:

1. Those who felt they had done their lives' work and wanted to rest and relax and were content to do so.
2. Those who felt that their active life was never finished and who continued striving to the end.
3. Those who, though not satisfied with their lives and accomplishments, but lacking strength, ability or will-power to go on struggling, find an unhappy sort of resignation.
4. Those who led thoughtless and meaningless lives, and who are now not only frustrated but bothered by guilt and regret.

In her overall evaluation, Buhler concluded that more critical in old age maladjustment than functional decline and insecurity is the individual's self-assessment as to whether he did or did not reach fulfillment. This she felt was true of the person who had hoped for accomplishments, but often, as well, for the person who did not think of his life as a whole at the outset but who later became aware of a pattern.

Although Buhler's generalizations reflect clinical impressions and are not so well-supported by empirical data as many psychologists might wish, her points seem well taken and square sufficiently with subjective observations and experiences to suggest an important area of research as well as hypotheses to give that research direction. The suggested focus is upon basic motivational tendencies, sequences of goals, meaningfulness and fulfillment—with attention to differences among individuals and the kinds of antecedent and concurrent conditions that have brought them about.

SUMMARY

It has been suggested in this paper that hypothesizing two broad motivational patterns—one of growth and expansion, the other of anxiety and threat—will serve to integrate a wide variety of data reflecting developmental changes during the adult life span. The major points made in the development of this notion are as follows:

1. It was suggested first that a number of factors interact to cause age changes in adult motivation. These include age-related differences in cultural stimulation and expectation, the degree to which satisfaction or chronic frustration of certain major motives over time paves the way for the emergence of other motives, and the degree to which people experience social and physical losses in highly valued areas. Becoming "locked" into a situation (as is likely to occur as age increases) tends to make frustrations keener, and changing time perspectives seem to create critical points in the motivational history of individuals.

2. The postulation of a need for "growth-expansion" serves to integrate in a meaningful way the commonly observed goals and interests of people. One notes shifts in goals and interests from career and family, to community interests, to identification with children's success, to religious and philosophical interests. In general, although "growth-expansion" motives seem important throughout life, their satisfaction is by less direct and more vicarious means in older years. As age increases, there appears to be less personal investment (ego-involvement, energy) in life and in the satisfaction of needs.

3. The recently advanced "theory of disengagement," which suggests that people seek a disengaged state as something valued in its own right, seems not particularly supported by the data, though this view is having a stimulating effect upon research.

4. The evidence seems particularly clear that anxiety and susceptibility to threat increase with the passage of time, and that this circumstance tends to be the motivational source for many of the behavioral (personality) changes that occur with age. This particular trend has important implications for adult educational methodology.

5. Individual differences are, of course, great, and important differences have been demonstrated with respect to sex and social-economic class. Among the important differences are the ages at which irreversible losses become evident, the degree to which one's life is seen as a meaningful pattern, and the ways in which various subgroups of the population translate their "needs" into specific goals or adapt particular patterns of defense against losses.

14

BERNICE L. NEUGARTEN

ADULT PERSONALITY: TOWARD A PSYCHOLOGY
OF THE LIFE CYCLE

A psychology of the human life cycle has been slow in making its appearance. From one point of view, biological and sociological perspectives have not yet been integrated into an overarching theory of human behavior, nor have they been combined even in describing a meaningful context against which to view psychological change over the life cycle. From a different point of view, the primary problem is that we lack a developmental psychology of adulthood in the sense that we have a developmental psychology of childhood. Because the term "development" has been used with such a wide variety of philosophical as well as scientific meanings, it will be strategic for purposes of the present discussion to avoid the awkward juxtaposition of the terms, "adult" and "development" and to speak of the need for a psychology of adulthood in which investigators are concerned with the orderly and sequential changes that occur with the passage of time as individuals move from adolescence through adulthood and old age, with issues of consistency and change in personality over relatively long intervals of time, and with issues of antecedent-consequent relationships.

Using this definition, the field of adult psychology and adult personality remains an underpopulated one among psychologists. The effect has been, to speak metaphorically, that as psychologists seated

An adapted version of this paper appears in *Readings in General Psychology*, ed. Edgar Vinacke (New York: American Book Company, 1968).

under the same circus tent, some of us who are child psychologists remain seated too close to the entrance and are missing much of the action that is going on in the main ring. Others of us who are gerontologists remain seated too close to the exit. Both groups are missing a view of the whole show.

One of our problems lies in the fact that we are as yet without sufficient systematic data on adults. A few sets of data have been reported in which individuals have been studied from childhood into adulthood (Havighurst *et al.*, 1962; Hess, 1962; Honzik, 1966; Kagan and Moss, 1962); but these studies are few in number, and despite the growing recognition of the importance of longitudinal research, there have been as yet no major longitudinal studies of men and women as they move from youth to middle age, or from middle age to old age. There have been even fewer carefully designed and well-controlled cross-sectional studies of adult personality in which age differences, to say nothing of age *changes*, have constituted a central axis of investigation (Kuhlen, 1964).

Not only is there a paucity of data, but more important we are without a useful theory. Personality theorists have not for the most part faced the questions of stability and change over the entire life cycle. Attention has been focused primarily upon the first two but not on the last five sevenths of life. Although Erikson's formulation of the stages of ego development is a notable exception (Erikson 1963); and although Jung (1933),

Buhler (1933, 1935, 1962), Fromm (1941), Maslow (1954), Peck (1955) and White (1963) have made important contributions, there is no integrated body of theory that encompasses the total life span.

At the same time we are aware that changes in personality occur in adulthood and that the personality is by no means fixed once the organism becomes biologically mature (Worchel and Byrne, 1964). There is evidence on all sides: the changes that occur in adults undergoing psychotherapy or religious conversions or brain-washings, or who live in concentration camps or prisons or ghettos or institutions for the aged. Nor need we look to such extreme situations. We are impressed with—although so far as I know, no one has yet systematically studied—the changes in personality that accompany motherhood in young women, for example, or that accompany career success in middle-aged men.

To the psychologist, of course, as to any other scientist, much more is known than can be easily demonstrated. Confronted with the need to produce systematic evidence, the investigator who turns his attention to the study of adult personality is faced, first, with the problem of delineating those personality processes that are the most salient at successive periods in adulthood; then with the problem of describing those processes in terms that are appropriate; then to distinguish those changes that relate to increasing age from those that relate, say, to illness on the one hand or to social and cultural change, on the other; then—and only then—to interpret his findings in light of the question, Which of these processes and changes are orderly and sequential, and which are not? At the same time, because theory and observation must proceed simultaneously, he must always be concerned with the construction of a body of theory that will help account for his findings.

The present paper is addressed primarily to conceptual problems in relating childhood to adulthood, and in relating biological and social pacemakers of change in personality. In this connection we shall turn attention, first, to the delineation of salient issues in adult personality and the types of personality change that are measurable in middle-aged and old adults, mainly to illustrate some of the conceptual problems involved in predicating continuity or discontinuity over the life cycle. Second, in describing an age-status system as one of the social contexts for viewing time-related changes, we shall comment upon the presence of social as well as biological time clocks.

THE SALIENT ISSUES IN ADULTHOOD

First, with regard to the delineation of the salient issues: The criticism is sometimes made that psychologists focus on different phenomena and make use of different explanatory concepts for studying different age levels; and that they sometimes seem to regard children, adolescents, adults, and old people as members of different species. One implication is that if we were fortunate enough to have longitudinal data, the life span could be seen in more continuous and more meaningful terms and antecedent-consequent relations could more readily be investigated.

While this may be true, it is also true that longitudinal studies have thus far had a child-centered or what might be called a "childomorphic" orientation. The variables selected for study have been those particularly salient in childhood; or else those measured retrospectively from the data gathered when the subjects were children. In either instance, the investigator is confined to data and to concepts which may be only of secondary relevance when he attempts to explain the varieties or sequences in adult behavior. In this respect there are countless studies in the child-development literature that deal with dependence, aggression, cognition, the fate of the Oedipal-personality, issues which, when projected into adulthood, lose much of their compelling quality.[1]

What, then, are the salient issues of adulthood? At one level of generality, it might be said that they are issues which relate to the individual's use of experience; his structuring of the social world in which he lives; his perspectives of time; the ways in which he deals with the major themes of work, love, time, and death; the changes in self-concept and changes in identity as he faces the successive contingencies of marriage, parenthood, career advancement and decline, retirement, widowhood, illness, and personal death.

These issues take different form at dif-

[1] Perhaps this point can be made more clearly if we move outside the area usually delineated as personality. A recent review of research on the relationship between college grades and adult achievement is summarized by the author's statement that "present evidence strongly suggests that college grades bear little or no relationship to any measures of adult accomplishment." (Hoyt, 1965)

It is widely acknowledged that school grades are a salient issue to the child or adolescent himself; and at the same time, they are important to the psychologist as an index of the child's intellectual progress and of his success in relating to the adult world. It is known also that school grades are excellent predictors of later school and college grades; furthermore, that there is a close relationship between grades and measures of intelligence in children. Finally, knowledge of the distribution of intelligence test scores and of school grades in large populations of children has led to constant modifications, in our theories of the nature and growth of intelligence.

Yet when we move to adulthood, these relationships and the interpretations to be drawn from them become relatively useless. We cannot predict from school to later achievement; indeed, we have no well-established criterion of adult achievement. Next, lacking a criterion by which to standardize a test, we have no test of intelligence that will help us—except in the grossest sense—to predict adult accomplishment. Finally, of course, we have no theory of adult intelligence that is useful, in this sense, beyond the very first steps in the work career, namely *selection* of occupation.

We are even worse off when we come back to the field of personality and when we attempt to apply what we think we know about children to what we would like to know about adults.

ferent age periods in adulthood. Some of these issues as they apply to middle age are described earlier in this book, in the paper entitled "Awareness of Middle Age," where the data have been obtained from lengthy interviews with 100 men and women aged 45 to 55, selected because they have been visibly successful in career or in civic pursuits. In pondering the descriptions these people gave of the issues which preoccupy them, we have been impressed (as with the findings from some of the earlier studies in this series) with the central importance of what might be called the executive processes of personality: self-awareness, selectivity, manipulation and control of the environment, mastery, competence, the wide array of cognitive strategies.

We are impressed, too, with the heightened importance of introspection in the mental life of middle-aged persons: the stock-taking, the increased reflection, and above all, the structuring and restructuring of experience—that is, the processing of new information in the light of experience; the use of this knowledge and expertise for the achievement of desired ends; the handing over to others or guarding for oneself the fruits of one's experience.[2]

It is perhaps evident that these psychological issues are ones to which the investigator comes unprepared, as it were, from his studies of children and adolescents. It is perhaps evident also why it is

[2] If confronted with the question of whether or not there are any "inherent' or "inevitable" changes in personality that accompany adulthood, there is at least one that would come at once to mind: the conscious awareness of past experience in shaping one's behavior. Psychologists are accustomed to the idea that experience is registered in the living organism over time and that behavior is affected accordingly. But in the case of the human organism, it is not merely that experience is recorded; it is that the *awareness* of that experience becomes increasingly dominant.

that to psychologists of adulthood, most of the existing personality theories seem inadequate. Neither psychoanalytic theory nor learning theory nor social-role theory are sufficiently embracing of the data. Where, except perhaps to certain ego-psychologists who use terms such as "competence," "self," and "effectance," can we look for concepts to describe the incredible complexity shown in the behavior of a business executive, age 50, who makes a thousand decisions in the course of a day? What terms shall we use to describe the strategies with which such a person manages his time, buffers himself from certain stimuli, makes elaborate plans and schedules, sheds some of his "load" by delegating some tasks to other people over whom he has certain forms of control, accepts other tasks as being singularly appropriate to his own competencies and responsibilities, and, in the same 24-hour period, succeeds in satisfying his emotional and sexual and aesthetic needs?

It is the incongruity between existing psychological concepts and theories, on the one hand, and the transactions that constitute everyday adult behavior, on the other, to which I am drawing attention.

CHANGES IN PERSONALITY IN THE SECOND HALF OF LIFE

Although change and consistency in adult personality is a problem area which has thus far attracted relatively few psychologists, evidence is nevertheless beginning to accumulate that systematic and measurable changes occur in the second half of life. While the series of studies carried out at Chicago have not been longitudinal, we have begun to delineate processes of change that are characteristic of individuals as they move from middle to old age (Neugarten et al. 1964).

The middle years of life—probably the decade of the fifties for most persons—represent an important turning point, with the restructuring of time and the formulation of new perceptions of self, time, and death. It is in this period of the life line that introspection seems to increase noticeably and contemplation and reflection and self-evaluation become characteristic forms of mental life. The reflection of middle-age is not the same as the reminiscence of old age; but perhaps it is its forerunner.

Significant and consistent age differences are found in both working class and middle class people in the perceptions of the self vis-à-vis the external environment and in coping with impulse life. Forty-year-olds, for example, seem to see the environment as one that rewards boldness and risk-taking and to see themselves as possessing energy congruent with the opportunities perceived in the outer world. Sixty-year-olds, however, perceive the world as complex and dangerous, no longer to be reformed in line with one's wishes, and the individual as conforming and accommodating to outer-world demands.

Important differences exist between men and and women as they age. Men seem to become more receptive to affiliative and nurturant promptings; women, more responsive toward and less guilty about aggressive and egocentric impulses. Men appear to cope with the environment in increasingly abstract and cognitive terms; women, in increasingly affective and expressive terms. In both sexes older people move toward more egocentric, self-preoccupied positions and attend increasingly to the control and satisfaction of personal needs.

With increasing old age, ego functions are turned inward, as it were. With the change from active to passive modes of mastering the environment, there is also a movement of energy away from an outer-world to an inner-world orientation.[3]

[3] To this increased "interiority" of personality, we once gave the term psychological "disengagement," a term that accurately reflects the quality of some of these processes. The term has since become associated in the field of ger-

Whether or not this increased "interiority" has inherent as well as reactive qualities cannot yet be established. It may be that in advanced old age, biologically-based factors become the pacemakers of personality changes; but this is a question which awaits further disentangling of the effects of illness from the effects of aging, effects which are presently confounded in most older persons who are the subjects of psychological research.

Another important finding in this series of studies is that, in the age-range 50 to 80, and in relatively healthy individuals, age does not emerge as a major variable in the goal-directed, purposive qualities of personality. In other words, while consistent age differences occur in covert processes (those not readily available to awareness or to conscious control and which have no direct expression in overt social behavior), they do *not* appear on those variables which reflect attempted control of the self and of the life situation.[4] Age-related changes appear earlier and more consistently, then, in the internal than in the external aspects of personality.

Nor is this all the evidence that exists of dynamic changes in personality in the second half of the life span. Lieberman, for instance, following a somewhat different line of inquiry, has found measurable changes in psychological functioning at the very end of life; changes which seem to be independent of illness and which seem to be timed, not by chronological age or distance from birth, but by dis-

Bernice L. Neugarten
Adult Personality

tance from death (Lieberman, 1965). Similarly, Butler posits the universal occurrence in old people of an inner experience that he calls the life review; a process that perhaps accounts for the increased reminiscence of the aged and which often leads to dramatic changes in personality (Butler, 1963).

It might be pointed out, parenthetically, that awareness of approaching death should perhaps not be viewed as a signal for the dissolution of the personality structure, but instead as the impetus for a new and final restructuring: an event that calls for a major readaptation, and which leads in some individuals to constructive, in others, to destructive reorientations.

There is at least some evidence, then, that personality change can occur all along the life span; and that any personality theory which is to be useful to us in comprehending the life-cycle must take account of changes in advanced old age as well as in other periods of life.

RELATIONS BETWEEN BIOLOGICAL AND PSYCHOLOGICAL CHANGE

This leads us back to questions of theory. Sometimes the very theories of developmental psychology hinder us in constructing a psychology of the life cycle. In this respect, the changes observable in behavior with the passage of short intervals of time—a month, six months, a year—are dramatic when one regards a young biological organism, and no less compelling are the overall regularities of biological change. It has been tempting for students of behavior to draw parallels between biological phenomena and psychological, and on this basis to establish a developmental psychology of childhood and adolescence. It has been relatively easy, if not always accurate, first to assume, then to look for ways of describing sequential and orderly progressions in psychological and social behavior. It has

ontology, with issues of social role behavior, optimum patterns of aging, and even with the value systems of investigators as well as social policy makers who are concerned with the position of the aged in American society. Because the word has now taken on such a wide variety of meanings I prefer now to substitute the phrase "increased interiority of the personality."

[4] This differentiation reminds us of Brewster Smith's two personality "sub-systems"—one which he has called the adaptive or "external"; the other, the internal (Smith, 1959).

been easy to take growth as the model, to borrow from the biologist the concepts of increasing differentiation and integration, and the concept of an end-point toward which change is necessarily directed. It has been understandable, therefore, that we have used the biological clock as a frame of reference, looking to biological changes as the pacemakers of psychological and taking for granted the intimate relationship between these two classes of phenomena.

The difficulty with this approach, however, can be illustrated from one of our investigations in which we proposed to study the psychological correlates of the biologic climacterium in middle-aged women. Along with other psychologists, we have been impressed with the changes in behavior that accompany puberty and with the interpretation that the personality differences that are measurable in adolescents relate to major *developmental* components of biological change. We reasoned by analogy that there should also be biologically-based developmental components in the personality differences observable in middle-aged women—in short, that if puberty is an important developmental event in the psychology of females, so, probably, is the climacterium.

Accordingly we selected a sample of 100 normal women aged 43 to 53 from working-class and middle-class backgrounds, and obtained data on a large number of psychological and social variables. Using menopausal status as the index of climacteric status (presence or absence of observed changes in menstrual rhythm, or cessation of menses), we found climacteric status to be unrelated to our wide array of personality measures. Furthermore, there were very few significant relationships between severity of somatic and psychosomatic symptoms attributed to climacteric changes and these variables.

Granted that the question would be better pursued by a longitudinal rather than a cross-sectional method, nevertheless the negative findings were more largely due, we believe, to the fact that we were pursuing a certain parallelism between childhood and adulthood, a parallelism that probably does not exist.

This is not to say that the menopause is a meaningless phenomenon in the lives of women; nor that biological factors are of no importance in adult personality. Instead these comments are intended to point out: (1) that the menopause is not necessarily the important event in understanding the psychology of middle-aged women that we might have assumed it to be from a biological model or from psychoanalytic theory—not as important, seemingly, as illness; or worry over possible illness; nor, even, as worry over possible illness that might occur in one's husband rather than in oneself; (2) that the timing of the biological event, the climacterium—at least to the extent that we could perceive it—did not produce order in our data; and (3) above all, that psychologists should proceed cautiously in assuming the same intimate relationships between biological and psychological phenomena in adulthood that hold true in childhood.

THE AGE-STATUS SYSTEM

As already suggested, the biological components of human development take a certain precedence in viewing personality change in childhood and early adolescence, and perhaps also in the very last part of the life span when biological decrement may overwhelm other components in the personality. There remains, however, the span of the adult years—a period of now approximately 50 years, beginning when the organism reaches biological maturity around age 20 and extending to approximately 70. In this long part of the life span the biological model is obviously insufficient, and we need a social framework for understanding the timing patterns that occur.

Psychologists have, of course, already looked at personality in one after another social context—the family, the school, the community, as well as in relation to social-structural variables in the society at large. Thus, social class groups, ethnic and religious groups, and now again, racial groups are studied with regard to the ways in which these groups create different subcultures and, through processes of socialization, the ways they produce both similarities and differences in personalities. One major context has been neglected, however: the age structure of the society, the network of age-norms and age-expectations that govern behavior, and the ways in which age groups relate to each other.[5]

Expectations regarding age-appropriate behavior form an elaborated and pervasive system of norms governing behavior and interaction, a network of expectations that is imbedded throughout the cultural fabric of life for the adult as much as for the child. There is a prescriptive time-table for the ordering of life events: a

[5] An analogy is appropriate: in sociology social stratification is a well-delineated field of study, and social class is recognized as one of the basic dimensions of social organization. Social classes, in turn, have been described as subcultures; and a tradition has developed of studying the behavior of both children and adults in relation to the social class to which they belong and in the context of the social-status structure of the community in which they live.

In similar fashion, some of us began several years ago to focus attention on the factor of age as another of the basic dimensions of social organization and the ways age groups relate to each other in the context of different social institutions. By a dimension of social organization, I refer to the fact that in all societies an age-status system exists, a system of implicit and explicit rules and expectations that govern the relations between persons of different ages. Certain behaviors come to be regarded as appropriate or inappropriate for each age group; and the relations between age groups are based upon dimensions of prestige, power, and deference. Older children have prestige in the eyes of younger; adolescents, in at least many ways, recognize the power of adults; and both children and adults, in at least some ways, show deference to the old. Each age group occupies a given status; and the system as a whole undergoes alterations in line with other social, economic, and political changes in the society. (See, in this book, Part I, the paper entitled "The Changing Age-Status System" by the present author.)

time when men and women are expected to marry, a time to raise children, a time to retire. This pattern is adhered to, more or less consistently, by most persons in the society, and even though the actual occurrences of these events are influenced by various life contingencies, it can easily be demonstrated that norms and actual occurrences are closely related.

Age norms and age expectations operate as prods and brakes upon behavior, in some instances hastening an event, in others, delaying it. Men and women are not only aware of the social clocks that operate in various areas of their lives, but they are also aware of their own timing and readily describe themselves as "early," "late," or "on time" with regard to family and occupational events.

Whether we identify ourselves as developmental psychologists or as social psychologists or as personality psychologists, we have perhaps taken the social dimension of age status so for granted that, like the air we breathe, we pay it no attention. As soon as it is pointed out we agree, of course, that the society is organized by age—rights, duties and obligations are differentially distributed according to age; and the relations between age-groups change with historical time, as is so evident now, for instance, with the growth of political protest among college-age youth and with the changing age-base for political and social responsibility in our society.

Every encounter between individuals is governed, at least to some extent, by their respective ages. When we meet a stranger—indeed, when we first glance at any person—we think first in categories based on age and sex. We notice, first, "this is a male child," or "a young female," or "an old man"; and we pattern our behavior accordingly—according, that is, to our own age and sex in relation to the other person's. So automatic and so immediate is this regulation of behavior that only when the cues are ambiguous do we give it full awareness—as, for instance, when we face an adult of indeterminate age and when we fumble about in discomfort lest we make a blunder. Age, then, provides one of the basic guidelines to social interaction.

At the same time that psychologists have neglected the age status dimension of social behavior, we have also neglected its relevance for providing various phenomena of personality internal to the individual. For example, although we always report the ages of the children whom we are studying, we seldom investigate directly the way in which the child himself thinks of his age or the way his perception of age colors his relations to other people. We have talked at length about sex-role identity, but not about changing age-role identity. We have given very little systematic study to the way in which children, let alone adults, internalize age-norms and age-expectations. Nor have we even attended to the ages of the adults who deal with the child. In most of the studies of child-rearing no mention at all is to be found of the age of the parent, to say nothing of the way parental age might regularly be built into research designs as an important variable.

The saliency of age and age-norms in influencing the behavior of adults is no less than in influencing the behavior of children. The fact that the social sanctions related to age-norms take on psychological reality can be readily granted. One has only to think of the young woman who, in 1940, was not yet married by age 25; or who, in 1966, is not yet married by 21; and who, if present trends continue over another few decades, will soon lie awake nights worrying over spinsterhood by the time she is 18. The timing of life events provides some of the most powerful cues to adult personality.

In our recent investigations we have perceived age norms and the age-status system as forming a backdrop or cultural context against which the behavioral and personality differences of adults should be

viewed. Early in this line of inquiry, we began to study the outlines of the age-status system and the extent to which there was consensus in the minds of adults. We began with questions of middle-aged men and women in the belief that by virtue of their age, they would have relatively accurate perceptions of an age-status system (if such perceptions could be elicited at all); and we asked them a series of questions such as,

"What would you call the periods of life that people go through after they are grown up?" For instance, we usually refer to people first as babies, then as children, then as teen-agers.

"After a person is grown up, what periods does he go through?"

"At what age does each period begin, for most people?"

"What are the important changes from one period to the next?" [Neugarten and Peterson, 1957.]

We discovered a commonly-held set of perceptions with regard to adult age periods, each with a distinguishing set of transition points and a distinguishing set of psychological and social themes. Thus, our respondents seemed to share a view that adulthood can be divided into periods of young adulthood, maturity, middle age, and old age, each with its distinctive characteristics and each with its own psychological flavor.

At the same time there were sex differences in these perceptions, and differences between members of different social classes. The timing of middle age and old age occurs earlier to working-class than to middle-class men and women.

For instance, the typical upper-middle-class man, a business executive or a professional, tended to divide the lifeline at 30, at 40, and at 65. He considered a man "mature" at 40; at the "prime of life" at 40; and as "having the greatest confidence in himself" at 40. A man is not "middle-aged" until almost 50; nor is he "old" until 70.

The unskilled worker, on the other hand, saw the life line as being paced

144

more rapidly. For him, the major dividing points were placed at 25, 35, and 50. In his view a man is "middle-aged" by 40; "old" by 60.

In the eyes of upper-middle-class people, the period of young adulthood—up until about 30—is a time of exploration and groping: a period of "feeling one's way," of trying out and getting adjusted to jobs and careers, to marriage, to one's adult roles; a period of experimentation. By contrast, to our working-class man young adulthood is the period, not when issues are explored, but when issues are settled. They may be settled by giving up a certain type of autonomy—"when responsibility is *hung* on you," and where the undertone is one of regret; or the issues may be settled by establishing one's independence—the "now you are a man" refrain—but in either case, young adulthood to the working man is the time when one gives up youth with a note of finality and takes over the serious business of life—job, marriage, children, responsibilities.

In these first several studies, the gross outlines of an age-status structure that seems to crosscut various areas of adult life were delineated. While their view of the life span was more implicit than explicit in the minds of many respondents, it seemed nevertheless to provide a frame of reference by which the experiences of adult life were seen as orderly and rhythmical. More important, progression from one age-level to the next was conceived primarily in terms of psychological and social changes rather than in terms of biological changes.

We also asked questions regarding age-appropriate and age-linked behaviors: "What do you think is the best age for a man to marry. . . . to finish school . . . to hold his top job . . . to retire?"

"What age comes to your mind when you think of a young man? . . . an old man? . . ."

There was widespread consensus on such items. Among the middle-class middle-aged, for instance, 90 percent said the

best age for a man to marry was from 20 to 25. Nor was the consensus limited to middle-aged persons or to persons residing in a particular region of the U.S. When responses to the same set of questions were obtained from other middle-class groups, essentially the same patterns emerged in each set of data.

When we looked at life history data with regard to the ages at which major events had actually occurred, we found striking regularities within social-class groups, with the actual occurrences following the same patterns described above. The higher the social class, the later each of the following events was reported by our respondent: age at leaving school, age at first job, age at marriage, age at parenthood, age at top job, grandparenthood—even, in women, their reported age of menopause.

The perceptions, the expectations, and the actual occurrences of life events, then, are closely related, and the regularities within social class groups indicate that these are *socially* regulated.

Given this view that age norms and age expectations operate in the society as a system of social control, we undertook still another study of their psychological correlates, asking, How do members of the society vary in their perception of the strictures involved in age norms, or in the degree of *constraint* they perceive with regard to age-appropriate behaviors?[6] We devised a questionnaire using items that relate to occupational career, some that relate to the family cycle, and some that refer to recreation, appearance, and consumption behaviors. For instance:

"Would you approve a couple who likes to dance the 'Twist' when they are age 20? Would you approve if they are age 30? If they are age 55?

[6] See the paper by Neugarten, Moore, and Lowe, in Part I, entitled "Age Norms, Age Constraints, and Adult Socialization," for a fuller description of this study.

"What about a woman who decides to have another child when she is 45? When she is 37? When she is 30?

"A man who is willing to move his family from one town to another to get ahead in his company when he's 45? when he's 35? 25?

"A couple who move across country so they can live near their married children when they are 40? 55? 70?"

We devised a score which reflected the degree of refinement with which the respondent makes age discriminations, then used this instrument with a group of 400 middle-class men and women divided into young (20–29), middle-aged (35–55), and old (65+). (Neugarten, Moore, Lowe, 1965.) We found a significant increase in scores with age—that is, increase in the extent to which respondents ascribe importance to age norms and place constraints upon adult behavior in terms of age appropriateness. The middle-aged and the old seem to have learned that age is a reasonable criterion by which to evaluate behavior; that to be "off-time" with regard to life events or to show other age-deviant behavior brings with it social and psychological sequelae that cannot be disregarded. In the young, especially the young male, this view is only partially accepted; and there seems to be a certain denial of age as a valid dimension by which to judge behavior.

This age-related difference in point of view is reflected in the response of a 20-year-old who, when asked what he thought of marriage between 17-year-olds, said, "It would be OK if the boy got a job and if they loved each other. Why not?" While a 45-year-old said, "At that age, they'd be foolish. He couldn't support a wife and children. Kids who marry that young will suffer for it later."

We have begun also to study the correlates in personality and behavior of being "on time" or "off time." Persons who regard themselves as early or late with regard to a major life event describe ways in which the off-timeness has other psychological and social accompaniments.

We are pursuing this line of inquiry now with regard to career timing. Thus, in a study of Army officers (the Army is one of the most clearly age-graded occupations available for study) the men who recognize themselves as being too long in grade—or late in career achievement—are also distinguishable on an array of social and psychological attitudes toward work, family, community participation, and personal adjustment.

These studies have relevance for a theory of the psychology of the life-cycle in two ways: First, in indicating that the age structure of a society, the internalization of age-norms, and age-group indentifications are important dimensions of the social and cultural *context* in which the course of the individual life line must be viewed;

Second, because these concepts point to at least one additional way of structuring the passage of time in the life span of the individual, *providing a time clock* that can be superimposed over the biological clock, together they help us to comprehend the life cycle. The major punctuation marks in the adult life line tend (those, that is, which are orderly and sequential) to be more often social than biological—or, if biologically based, they are often biological events that occur to significant others rather than to oneself, like grandparenthood or widowhood.

If psychologists are to discover order in the events of adulthood, and if they are to discover order in the personality changes that occur in all individuals as they age, we should look to the social as well as to the biological clock, and certainly to social definitions of age and age-appropriate behavior.

CONCLUSION

In conclusion I would like to return once again to the problem of a personality theory that will encompass the life cycle.

In commenting upon the salient issues of adulthood and in illustrating in particular from middle age, I have tried to illustrate the need for a theory which will emphasize the ego or executive functions of the personality; one which will help account for the growth and maintenance of cognitive competence and creativity, one that will help explain the conscious use of past experience.

In illustrating from our findings regarding differences between intrapsychic and adaptive aspects of personality as persons move from middle- to old-age, and from our findings with regard to biological climacterium in woman, I have tried to illustrate some of the problems involved in any theory of personality that is based primarily upon a biological model of the life span.

Finally, in describing some of our studies regarding the age-status system and the pervasive quality of age-norms in influencing the psychology of adulthood, I have suggested at least one of the sociological components that, in addition to the biological, provides a view of the orderliness of change that underlies the total life cycle.

15

HOWARD S. BECKER

PERSONAL CHANGE IN ADULT LIFE

Personal change in adult life is an important phenomenon deserving more research. In undertaking such research, we should be aware that the kind of change that takes place depends on who is categorizing and evaluating it, and beware of the biases introduced by a too easy acceptance of conventional categories. Instead of seeking explanations of change and stability in elements of personality or in peoples' values, we should look to the effects of social structure on experience. The process of situational adjustment suggests an explanation of change; the process of commitment suggests an explanation of stability.

People often exhibit marked change—in their attitudes, beliefs, behavior and style of interaction—as they move through youth and adulthood. Many social scientists, and others interested in explaining human behavior, think that human beings are governed by deep and relatively unchanging components of the personality or self, so that important changes at late stages in the life cycle are viewed as anomalies that need to be explained away. They may trace the roots of behavior to personality components formed in early childhood—needs, defenses, identifications, and the like—and interpret change in adulthood as simply a variation on an already established theme. Or they may, more sociologically, see the sources of everyday behavior in values established in the society, inculcated in the young during childhood, and maintained thereafter by constraints built into major communal institutions. Like the personality theorists, those who use values as a major explanatory variable see change in adulthood as essentially superficial, a new expression of an unchanging underlying system of values. In either case, the scientist wishes to concern himself with basic processes that will explain lasting trends in individual behavior.

Both these approaches err by taking for granted that the only way we can arrive at generalized explanations of human behavior is by finding some unchanging components in the self or personality. They err as well in making the prior assumption that human beings are essentially unchanging, that changes which affect only such "superficial" phenomena as behavior without affecting deeper components of the person are trivial and unimportant.

There are good reasons to deny these assumptions. Brim, for instance, has persuasively argued that there are no "deep" personality characteristics, traits of character which persist across any and all situations and social roles (Brim, 1960). In any case, it is clearly a useful strategy to explore the theoretical possibilities opened up by considering what might be true if we look in other directions for generalizable explanations of human behavior.

A good many studies are now available which suggest that an appropriate area in which further explanations might be

Abridged from *Sociometry*, 27 (1964): 40–53, by permission of the American Sociological Association.

sought is that of social structure and its patterned effects on human experience. Two of these seem of special importance, and I devote most of what I have to say to them. The process of *situational* adjustment, in which individuals take on the characteristics required by the situations they participate in, providing an entering wedge into the problem of change. It shows us one example of an explanation which can deal with superficial and immediate changes in behavior and at the same time allow us to make generalized theories about the processes involved. The process of *commitment*, in which externally unrelated interests of the person become linked in such a way as to constrain future behavior, suggests an approach to the problem of personal stability in the face of changing situations. Before dealing with these processes, however, I will consider a problem of definition which reveals a further influence of social structure, this time an influence on the very terms in which problems of socialization are cast.

THE EYE OF THE BEHOLDER

Many of the changes alleged to take place in adults do not take place at all. Or rather, a change occurs but an optical illusion causes the outside observer to see it as a change quite different in kind and magnitude from what it really is. The observer (a layman or a social scientist looking at the phenomenon from a layman's point of view), through a semantic transformation, turns an observable change into something quite different.

Take, for example, the commonly asserted proposition that the professional education of physicians stifles their native idealism and turns it into a profound professional cynicism. Educated laymen believe this, and scientific studies have been carried out to test the proposition (Eron, 1955; Christie and Merton, 1958). Observed changes in the behavior of fledgling physicians attest to its truth. Doctors are in fact inclined to speak with

little reverence of the human body; they appear to be and probably are to a large extent unmoved in the emotional way a layman would be by human death; their standards are not as high as the layman thinks they ought to be, their desire for wealth stronger than it ought to be.

People describe these changes with reference to an unanalyzed conception of idealism and cynicism. It would not be unfair to describe the conception as the perspective of a disgruntled patient, who feels that the doctor he has to deal with is thinking about other things than the patient's welfare. The perspective of the disgruntled patient itself draws on some very general lay conceptions which suggest that those who deal with the unpleasant and the unclean—in this case, with death and disease—must of necessity be cynical, since "normal people" prefer what is pleasant and clean and find the unclean repulsive.

But why should we assess and evaluate the change that takes place in the doctor as he goes through professional school from the point of view of his patient? Suppose we look at it instead from the characteristic perspective of the medical profession. If we do this, we find (as we would find if we studied the views of almost any occupation toward the institutions which train people for entrance into them) that medical schools are typically regarded as too idealistic. They train students to practice in ways that are not "practical," suited to an ideal world but not to the world we live in. They teach students to order more laboratory tests than patients will pay for, to ignore the patient's requests for "new" drugs or "popular" treatments (Freidson, 1961, pp. 200–202), but do not teach students what to do when the waiting room holds more patients than can be seen during one's office hours.

It is a paradox. In one view, professional training makes physicians less idealistic, in the other, more idealistic. Where does the truth lie? I have already noted that many of the changes seen as signs of increasing cynicism in the young physician do in fact take place. It can equally be demonstrated that the changes which make him seem too idealistic also take place. The medical students we studied at the University of Kansas, expected, when they graduated, to practice in ways that would be regarded as hopelessly idealistic by many, if not most, medical practitioners. They proposed to see no more than 20 patients a day; they proposed never to treat a disease without having first made a firm diagnosis. These beliefs, inculcated by a demanding faculty, are just the opposite of the cynicism supposed to afflict the new physician (Becker *et al.*, 1961, pp. 426–28).

The lesson we should learn from this is that personality changes are often present only in the eye of the beholder. Changes do take place in people, but the uninformed outsider interprets the change wrongly. Just as doctors acquire new perspectives and ideas as a result of their medical training, any adult may acquire new perspectives and ideas. But it would be a mistake to assume that these changes represent the kind of fundamental changes suggested by such polar terms as "idealism" and "cynicism." We learn less by studying the students who are alleged to have lost their idealism than we do by studying those who claim to have become cynical.

Even so, adults do change. But we must make sure, not only by our own observation but also by careful analysis of the terms we use to describe what we see, that the changes we try to explain do in fact take place.

SITUATIONAL ADJUSTMENT

One of the most common mechanisms in the development of the person in adulthood is the process of situational adjustment. This is a very gross conception, which requires analytic elaboration it has not yet received. But the major outlines are clear. The person, as he moves in and out of a variety of social situations, learns the requirements of continuing in each situation and of success in it. If he has a strong desire to continue, the ability to assess accurately what is required, and can deliver the required performance, the individual turns himself into the kind of person the situation demands.

Broadly considered, this is much the same as Brim's notion of learning adult roles. One learns to be a doctor or a policeman, learns the definitions of the statuses involved and the appropriate behavior with respect to them. But the notion of situational adjustment is more flexible than that of adult role learning. It allows us to deal with smaller units and make a finer analysis. We construct the process of learning an adult role by analyzing sequences of smaller and more numerous situational adjustments. We should have in our minds the picture of a person trying to meet the expectations he encounters in immediate face-to-face situations; doing well in today's chemistry class, managing to be poised and mature on tonight's date, surmounting the small crises of the moment. Sequences and combinations of small units of adjustment produce the larger units of role learning.

If we view situational adjustment as a major process of personal development, we must look to the character of the situation for the explanation of why people change as they do. We ask what there is in the situation that requires the person to act in a certain way or to hold certain beliefs. We do not ask what there is in him that requires the action or belief. All we need to know of the person is that for some reason or another he desires to continue his participation in the situation or to do well in it. From this we can deduce that he will do what he can to do what is necessary in that situation. Our further analysis must adjust itself to the character of the situation.

Thus, for example, in our present study

of college undergraduates,[1] we find that they typically share a strong desire to get high grades. Students work very hard to get grades and consider them very important, both for their immediate consequences and as indicators of their own personal ability and worth. We need not look very deeply into the student to see the reason for his emphasis on grades. The social structure of the campus coerces students to believe that grades are important because, in fact, they are important. You cannot join a fraternity or sorority if your grades do not meet a certain minimum standard. You cannot compete for high office in important campus organizations if your grades are not high enough. As many as one-fourth of the students may not be able to remain in school if they do not raise their grades in the next semester. For those who are failing, low grades do not simply mean blocked access to the highest campus honors. Low grades, for these unfortunates, mean that every available moment must be spent studying, that the time the average student spends dating, playing, drinking beer or generally goofing off must be given over to the constant effort to stay in school. Grades are the currency with which the economy of campus social life operates. Only the well-to-do can afford the luxuries; the poor work as hard as they can to eke out a marginal existence.

The perspectives a person acquires as a result of situation adjustments are no more stable than the situation itself or his participation in it. Situations occur in institutions: stable institutions provide stable situations in which little change takes place. When the institutions themselves change, the situations they provide for their participants shift and necessitate

[1] Statements about college students are based on preliminary analysis of the data collected in a study of undergraduates at the University of Kansas, in which I collaborated with Blanche Geer and Everett C. Hughes. A monograph reporting our findings is in preparation. The study was supported by the Carnegie Corporation of New York.

development of new patterns of belief and action. When, for instance, a university decides to up-grade its academic program and begins to require more and different kinds of work from its students, they must adjust to the new contingencies with which the change confronts them.

Similarly, if an individual moves in and out of given situations, is a transient rather than a long-term participant, his perspectives will shift with his movement. Wheeler has shown that prisoners become more "prisonized" the longer they are in prison; they are more likely to make decisions on the basis of criminal than of law-abiding values. But he has also shown that if you analyze prisoners' responses by time still to be served, they become more law-abiding the nearer they approach release (Wheeler, 1961). This may be interpreted as a situational shift. The prisoner is frequently sorry that he has been caught and is in a mood to give up crime; he tends to respect law-abiding values. But when he enters prison he enters an institution which, in its lower reaches, is dominated by men wedded to criminal values. Studies of prisons have shown that the most influential prisoners tend to have stable criminal orientations and that inmate society is dominated by these perspectives (Cressey, 1961; Cloward, *et al.*, 1960). In order to "make out" in the prison, the new inmate discovers that he must make his peace with this criminally oriented social structure, and he does. As he approaches release, however, he realizes that he is going back into a world dominated by people who respect the law and that the criminal values which stand him in such good stead in prison society will not work as well outside. He thereupon begins to shed the criminal values appropriate to the prison and renews his attachment to the law-abiding values of the outside world.

Situational adjustment is very frequent-

151

ly not an individual process at all, but a collective one. That is, we are not confronted with one person undergoing change, but with an entire cohort, a "class" of people, who enter the institution and go through its socializing program together. This is most clearly the case in those institutions which typically deal with "batches" of people (Goffman, 1961, p. 6 ff.). Schools are perhaps the best example, taking in a class of students each year or semester who typically go through the entire training program as a unit, leaving together at the end of their training.

But situational adjustment may have a collective character even where people are not processed in groups. The individual enters the institution alone, or with a small group, but joins a larger group there already, who stand ready to tell him how it is and what he should do, and he will be followed by others for whom he will perform the same good turn (Strauss, 1959; Becker and Strauss, 1956). In institutions where people are acted upon in groups by socializing agents, much of the change that takes place—the motivation for it and the perceived desirability of different modes of change—cannot be traced to the predilections of the individual. It is, instead, a function of the interpretive response made by the entire group, the consensus the group reaches with respect to its problems.

The guidelines for our analysis can be found in Sumner's analysis of the development of folkways (Sumner, 1907; Cohen, 1955; Cloward and Ohlin, 1960). A group finds itself sharing a common situation and common problems. Various members of the group experiment with possible solutions to those problems and report their experiences to their fellows. In the course of their collective discussion, the members of the group arrive at a definition of the situation, its problems and possibilities and develop consensus as to the most appropriate and efficient ways of behaving. This consensus thenceforth constrains the activities of individual members of the group, who will probably act on it, given the opportunity.

The collective character of socialization processes has a profound effect on their consequences. Because the solutions the group reaches have, for the individual being socialized, the character of "what everyone knows to be true," he tends to accept them. Random variation in responses that might arise from differences in prior experiences is drastically reduced. Medical students, for instance, began their training with a variety of perspectives on how one ought to approach academic assignments. The pressure generated by their inability to handle the tremendous amount of work given them in the first year anatomy course forced them to adopt collectively one of the many possible solutions to the problem, that of orienting their studying to learning what the faculty was likely to ask about on examinations. (Where the situation does not coerce a completely collective response, variation due to differences in background and experience remains. Irwin and Cressey [1962; see also Becker and Geer, 1960] argue that the behavior of prisoners, both in prison and after release, varies depending on whether the convict was previously a member of the criminal underworld.)

In addition, where the response to problematic situations is collective, members of the group involved develop group loyalties that become part of the environment they must adjust to. Industrial workers are taught by their colleagues to restrict production in order that an entire work group may not be held to the higher production standard one or two people might be able to manage (Roy, 1952). Medical students, similarly, find that they will only make it harder for others, and eventually for themselves, if they work too hard and "produce" too much (Becker et al., 1961).

One major consequence of the collective character of situational adjustment, a result of the factors just mentioned, is that the group being socialized is able to deviate much more from the standards set by those doing the socializing than would be possible for an individual. Where an individual might feel that his deviant response was idiosyncratic, and thus be open to persuasion to change it, the member of a group knows that there are many who think and act just as he does and is therefore more resistant to pressure and propaganda. A person being socialized alone, likewise, is freer to change his ways than one who is constrained by his loyalties to fellow trainees.

If we use situational adjustment as an explanation for changes in persons during adulthood, the most interesting cases for analysis are the negative cases, those instances in which people do not adjust appropriately to the norms implicit or explicit in the situation. For not everyone adjusts to the kind of major situational forces I have been discussing. Some prison inmates never take on criminal values; some college students fail to adapt campus values and therefore do not put forth their full effort in the pursuit of grades. In large part, cases in which it appears that people are not adjusting to situational pressures are cases in which closer analysis reveals that the situation is actually not the same for everyone involved in the institution. A job in the library may effectively remove the prisoner from the control of more criminally oriented prisoners; *his* situation does not constrain him to adopt criminal values.

More generally, it is often the case that subgroups in an institution will often have somewhat different life situations. College, for instance, is clearly one thing for men, another for women; one thing for members of fraternities and sororities, another for independents. We only rarely find an institution as monolithic as the medical school, in which the environment is, especially during the first two years, exactly alike for everyone. So we must make sure that we have discovered the effective environment of those whose personal development we want to understand.

Even after removing the variation in personal change due to variation in the situation, we will find a few cases in which people sturdily resist situational pressures. Here we can expect to find a corresponding weakness in the desire to remain in the situation or to do well in it, or a determination to remain in the situation only on one's terms or as long as one can get what one wants out of it. Many institutions have enough leeway built into them for a clever and determined operator to survive without much adjustment.

COMMITMENT

The process of situational adjustment allows us to account for the changes people undergo as they move through various situations in their adult life. But we also know that people exhibit some consistency as they move from situation to situation. Their behavior is not infinitely mutable, they are not flexible. How can we account for the consistency we observe?

Social scientists have increasingly turned to the concept of commitment for an explanation of personal consistency in situations which offer conflicting directives. The term has been used to describe a great variety of social-psychological mechanisms, such a variety that it has no stable meaning. Nevertheless, I think we can isolate at least one process referred to by the term commitment, a process which will help explain a great deal of behavioral consistency (Becker, 1960).

Briefly, we say a person is committed when we observe him pursuing a consistent line of activity in a sequence of varied situations. Consistent activity persists over time. Further, even though the actor may engage in a variety of disparate acts, he sees them as essentially consistent; from his point of view they serve him in pursuit of the same goal. Finally, it is a distinguishing mark of commitment that the actor rejects other situationally feasible alternatives, choosing from among the available courses of action that which best suits his purpose. In so doing, he often ignores the principle of situational adjustment, pursuing his consistent line of activity in the face of a short-term loss.

The process of commitment consists in the linking of previously extraneous and irrelevant lines of action and sets of rewards to a particular line of action under study. If, for instance, a person refuses to change jobs, even though the new job would offer him a higher salary and better working conditions, we should suspect that his decision is a result of commitment, that other sets of rewards than income and working conditions have become attached to his present job so that it would be too painful for him to change. He may have a large pension at stake, which he will lose if he moves; he may dread the cost of making new friends and learning to get along with new working associates; he may feel that he will get a reputation for being flighty and erratic if he leaves his present job. In each instance, formerly extraneous interests have become linked to keeping his present job. I have elsewhere described this process metaphorically as the making of side-bets. "The committed person has acted in such a way as to involve other interests of his, originally extraneous to the action he is engaged in, directly in that action. By his own actions . . . he has staked something of value to him, something originally unrelated to his present line of action, on being consistent in his present behavior. The consequences of inconsistency will be so expensive that inconsistency . . . is no longer a feasible alternative (Becker, 1960, p. 35)."

A person may make side-bets producing commitments consciously and deliberately or he may acquire them or have them made for him almost without his knowledge, becoming aware that he is committed only when he faces a difficult decision. Side-bets and commitments of the later type, made by default, arise from the operation of generalized cultural expectations, from the operation of impersonal bureaucratic arrangements, from the process of individual adjustment to social positions, and through the need to save face.

One way of looking at the process of becoming an adult is to view it as a process of gradually acquiring, through the operation of all these mechanisms, a variety of commitments which constrains one to follow a consistent pattern of behavior in many areas of life. Choosing an occupation, getting a job, starting a family—all these may be seen as events which produce lasting commitments and constrain the person's behavior. Careful study might show that the operation of the process of commitment accounts for the well-known fact that juvenile delinquents seldom become adult criminals, but rather turn into respectable, conventional, law-abiding lower-class citizens. It may be that the erratic behavior of the juvenile delinquent is erratic precisely because the boy has not yet taken any actions which commit him more or less permanently to a given line of endeavor.

Viewing commitment as a set of side-bets encourages us to inquire into the kind of currency with which bets are made in the situation under analysis. What things are valuable enough to make side-bets that matter? What kinds of counters are used in the game under analysis? Very little research has been done on this problem, but I suspect that erratic behavior and "random" change in adult life result from situations which do not permit people to become committed because they deny to them the means, the chips, with which to make side-bets of any importance.

Members of medical faculties complain, for instance, that students' behavior toward patients is erratic. They do not exhibit the continued interest in or devotion to the patient's welfare supposed to characterize the practicing physician. They leave the hospital at five o'clock, even though a patient assigned to them is in critical condition. Their interest in a surgical patient disappears when the academic schedule sends them to a medical ward and a new set of student duties. The reason for students' lack of interest and devotion becomes clear when we consider their frequent complaint that they are not allowed to exercise medical responsibility, to make crucial decisions or carry out important procedures. Their behavior toward patients can be less constrained than that of a practicing physician precisely because they are never allowed to be in a position where they can make a mistake that matters. No patient's life or welfare depends on them; they need not persist in any particular pattern of activity since deviation costs nothing (Becker *et al*, 1961, pp. 254–73).

The condition of being unable to make important side-bets and thus commit oneself may be more widespread than we think. Indeed, it may well be that the age at which it becomes possible to make lasting and important side-bets is gradually inching up. People cannot become committed to a consistent line of activity until later in life. As divorce becomes more frequent, for instance, the ability to make a lasting commitment by getting married becomes increasingly rare. In studying the possibilties of commitment afforded by social structures, we discover some of the limits to consistent behavior in adult life.

(It might be useful to apply similar concepts in studies of child socialization. It is likely, for instance,that children can seldom commit themselves. Our society, particularly, does not give them the means with which to make substantial side-bets, nor does it think it appropriate for children to make committing side-bets. We view childhood and youth as a time when a person can make mistakes that do not count. Therefore, we would expect children's behavior to be flexible and changeable, as in fact it seems to be.)

Situational adjustment and commitment are closely related, but by no means identical, processes. Situational adjust-ment produces change; the person shifts his behavior with each shift in the situation. Commitment produces stability; the person subordinates immediate situational interests to goals that lie outside the situation. But a stable situation can evoke a well-adjusted pattern of behavior which itself becomes valuable to the person, one of the counters that has meaning in the game he is playing. He can become committed to preserving the adjustment.

We find another such complementary relationship between the two when we consider the length of time one is conventionally expected to spend in a situation, either by oneself or by others, and the degree to which the present situation is seen as having definite connections to important situations anticipated at some later stage of development. If one sees that his present situation is temporary and that later situations will demand something different, the process of adjustment will promote change. If one thinks of the present situation as likely to go on for a long time, he may resist what appear to him temporary situational changes because the strength of the adjustment has committed him to maintaining it. This relationship requires a fuller analysis that I have given it here.

CONCLUSION

The processes we have considered indicate that social structure creates the conditions for both change and stability in adult life. The structural characteristics of institutions and organizations provide the framework of the situations in which experience dictates the expediency of change. Similarly, they provide the counters with which side-bets can be made and the links between lines of activity out of which commitment grows. Together, they enable us to arrive at general explanations of personal development in adult life without requiring us to posit unvarying characteristics of the person, either elements of personality or of "value structure."

A structural explanation of personal change has important implications for attempts to deliberately mold human behavior. In particular, it suggests that we need not try to develop deep and lasting interests, be they values or personality traits, in order to produce the behavior we want. It is enough to create situations which will coerce people into behaving as we want them to and then to create the conditions under which other rewards will become linked to continue this behavior. A final medical example will make the point. We can agree, perhaps, that surgeons ought not to operate unless there is a real need to do so; the problem of "unnecessary surgery" has received a great deal of attention both within and outside the medical profession. We might achieve our end by inculcating this rule as a basic value during medical training; or we might use personality tests to select as surgeons only those men whose own needs would lead them to exercise caution. In fact, this problem is approaching solution through a structural innovation: the hospital tissue committee, which examines all tissues removed at surgery and disciplines those surgeons who too frequently remove healthy tissue. Surgeons, whatever their values or personalities, soon learn to be careful when faced with the alternative of exposure or discipline.

PART III

SOCIAL-PSYCHOLOGICAL THEORIES OF AGING

The disengagement theory may be said to have been the first explicitly stated social-psychological theory of aging to appear in the literature of social gerontology. First described by Cumming, Dean, Newell and McCaffrey in 1960, then elaborated by Cumming and Henry in 1961 in the book *Growing Old*, the theory set off a lively controversy among both American and European investigators that has as yet shown few signs of abating. The theory has been widely quoted, often misinterpreted, and often refuted— in the latter instance, sometimes on the basis of empirical evidence, sometimes not.

Unfortunately there is no brief paper written by its authors that does justice to their exposition of disengagement. The 1960 paper was an early approximation of the theory, much modified in the book that followed; and subsequent papers by Cumming (1963) and by Henry (1963), while indicating alterations in their original position, do not include an exposition of the original statement that is sufficient to communicate the issues to the uninitiated reader. As a consequence, the student is referred to the book *Growing Old* for a full statement of the theory and the evidence on which it was based; and, for brief summaries of the theory, to the introductory sections of the paper to follow by Havighurst, Neugarten and Tobin and the paper by Arnold Rose.

The disengagement theory emerged from analyses of the first sets of data gathered in connection with a large community study of middle-aged and older people known as the Kansas City Studies of Adult Life. When all the field work was completed and the full data analyzed by other members of the research team, it became evident that the theory needed revision. The first two papers to follow describe successive steps in analyzing the Kansas City data. In the first, Havighurst, Neugarten and Tobin distinguish conceptually between disengagement as a *process* and disengagement as a theory of *optimum aging*, and present the evidence that supports the first but that negates the second. The authors show that both social and psychological changes that occur with aging are aptly described by the term disengagement; but they show also, contrary to the implications of the Cumming-Henry book, that social engagement, not disengagement, is generally related to psychological well-being.

This relationship does not hold, however, for all persons; and in the second paper, the same authors go further in explaining the complex relationships between levels of engagement and psychological well-being by focusing on differences in personality. They describe the diverse patterns of aging that characterize Kansas City 70-year-olds, patterns based on three sets of data: personality type, social role activity, and life-satisfaction. Personality is regarded as the pivotal dimension in predicting relationships between social engagement and psychological well-being, and the authors conclude that the disengagement theory is not adequate to account for the findings.

The brief paper that follows has been taken from the book by Reichard, Livson and Petersen, *Aging and Personality* (1962). It presents a short description of the personality types that emerged from a study of 87 older men, a study based upon Frenkel-Brunswik's psychoanalytic model of personality. The five personality types described are similar in many ways to those described in the preceding paper;

and the relations between personality type and adjustment to aging, while based on less systematic data than are present for the Kansas City sample, are generally congruent.

Of the last two papers in this Part, one is a brief report by Maddox of a longitudinal study in which the same older persons were re-evaluated at two-year intervals, and in which persistence rather than change in life-styles characterized most of the subjects. The author interprets these data as being contrary to the disengagement theory, saying that if the theory had been supported, levels of social engagement would have shown decrease rather than consistency over time.

In the last paper, Rose argues that disengagement theory is inadequate on theoretical grounds. He calls the theory a landmark in sociological functionalism, then criticizes the functionalist approach, maintaining that the facts of aging are better interpreted in a historical-cultural context or in a symbolic-interactionist framework.

16

ROBERT J. HAVIGHURST, BERNICE L. NEUGARTEN,
and SHELDON S. TOBIN

DISENGAGEMENT AND PATTERNS OF AGING

In the social-psychological literature of gerontology there are two general points of view with regard to optimum patterns of aging. Both are based on the observed facts that as people grow older their behavior changes, the activities that characterized them in middle age become curtailed, and the extent of their social interaction decreases. The two theories then diverge.

The first view, one that might be called the "activity" theory, implies that, except for the inevitable changes in biology and in health, older people are the same as middle-aged people, with essentially the same psychological and social needs. In this view, the decreased social interaction that characterizes old age results from the withdrawal by society from the aging person; and the decrease in interaction proceeds against the desires of most aging men and women. The older person who ages optimally is the person who stays active and who manages to resist the shrinkage of his social world. He maintains the activities of middle age as long as possible and then finds substitutes for those activities he is forced to relinquish: substitutes for work when he is forced to retire; substitutes for friends and loved ones whom he loses by death.

In the disengagement theory, on the other hand, as originally described by our colleagues, Cumming and Henry (1961), the decreased social interaction is interpreted as a process characterized by mu-

Unpublished paper presented at the International Association of Gerontology, Copenhagen, August, 1963. Abridged.

tuality; one in which both society and the aging person withdraw, with the aging individual acceptant, perhaps even desirous of the decreased interaction. It is suggested that the individual's withdrawal has intrinsic, or developmental, qualities as well as responsive ones; that social withdrawal is accompanied by, or preceded by, increased preoccupation with the self and decreased emotional investment in persons and objects in the environment; and that, in this sense, disengagement is a natural rather than an imposed process. In this view, the older person who has a sense of psychological well-being will usually be the person who has reached a new equilibrium characterized by a greater psychological distance, altered types of relationships, and decreased social interaction with the persons around him.

It is to be noted that, implicitly or explicitly, both theories involve value judgments. In the first, the presumption seems to be that, at least in modern Western societies, it is better to be active than to be inactive; to maintain the patterns characteristic of middle age rather than to move to new patterns of old age. In the second theory, it is presumably better to be in a state of equilibrium than in a state of disequilibrium; and better to acquiesce in what is a "natural," not an imposed, process of change. Furthermore, many investigators, including the present authors, in their concern with issues of "successful" aging, have introduced still another set of values in implying that it is better to be happy than unhappy, and that the aging individual himself rather than an observer is the best judge of his success.

Given the difficulties of value-free observations, the focus in the present report will be upon measures of social and psychological interaction, measures of the individual's satisfaction with life, and the relationships between these measures. In an effort to increase objectivity, a distinction is being drawn between disengagement as a *process*—a process which has both its outer and inner, its social and its psychological manifestations—and disengagement as a *theory of optimum aging*.

Presented first is the evidence concerning the process of disengagement; evidence that underlies the conclusion of the present authors that disengagement is, indeed, an accurate term for describing the social and psychological changes characteristic of aging in modern American society. Presented second are the relationships between measures of disengagement and measures of affect and satisfaction with life; evidence that underlies our conclusions that both the activity theory and the disengagement theory of optimal aging need major modifications; and that neither theory is adequate or sufficiently complex to account for the present findings.

Third we shall propose that personality is the pivotal dimension in the various patterns of aging that have emerged from our data and suggest ways of exploring the area of personality difference.

THE SAMPLES AND
THE DATA

In order to study the relations between engagement and life satisfaction, it is necessary to establish reliable measures of engagement; then to measure engagement in persons who represent some definite population group. These steps have now been completed in the Kansas City Study of Adult Life, using two samples of men and women who have been studied over a period of six years.

The first sample, referred to as the panel group, were persons aged 50 to 70 at the time they were first interviewed in 1956. The panel represents a stratified probability sample of middle and working class white persons of this age range residing in the metropolitan area of Kansas City. Excluded were the chronically ill and the physically impaired. The method by which the panel was selected resulted in a group that is biased toward middle class—in other words, a group that is better educated, wealthier, and of higher occupational and residential prestige than is true of the universe of 50-to-70-year-olds.

The second group, referred to as the quasi-panel, were persons aged 70–90 who joined the Kansas City Study two years after field work had begun. This older group was built up on the basis of quota sampling rather than probability sampling. The group consists of middle- and working-class persons, none of them financially deprived and none of them bedridden or senile.

While the panel probably has a greater middle-class bias than the quasi-panel, it is likely that the second sample, the older members of the study population, are less representative of their universe than is true of the panel members. Not only are these older persons better off financially, but they are in better health than most 70- to 90-year-olds; thus they represent an advantaged rather than a typical group.

Of the original panel, 62 percent are included in the present study. These persons remained as cooperating respondents at the end of seven rounds of interviews. Of the original quasi-panel, 49 percent remained at the end, after five rounds of interviews. Thus, in addition to the various biases operating in the original selection of the two groups (for instance, 16 percent of those on the initial sample list refused to join the panel), there is an unmeasurable effect on the present study due to sample attrition. Of the attrition, 27 percent has been due to deaths; 12 percent, to geographical moves; and the rest, to refusals to be interviewed at some time during the series of interviews, usually because of reported poor health. There is evidence also that persons who were relatively socially isolated constituted a disproportionate number of the dropouts. (The present sample is that which remains of the one described at greater length in Cumming and Henry (1961). The population being reported here, by contrast, is aproximately 55% of the original group, and accordingly has become increasingly less representative of the universe from which it was drawn.)

A total of 159 men and women serve as

of the respondent's life pattern, his attitudes, and his values. Included was information on the daily round of activities and the usual week-end round; on other household members, relatives, friends, and neighbors; on income, work, and retirement; religion; voluntary organizations; estimates of the amount of social interaction as compared with the amount at age 45; attitudes toward old age, illness, death, and immortality; questions about loneli-

TABLE 1

THE STUDY POPULATION: BY SEX, SOCIAL CLASS, AND AGE IN 1962

SOCIAL CLASS	AGE GROUP						
	54–59	60–64	65–69	70–74	75–79	80–94	Total
Upper middle:							
Men.............	7	4	4	2	4	1	22
Women..........	3	2	3	4	7	4	23
Lower middle:							
Men.............	2	4	3	1	4	4	18
Women..........	4	6	5	7	6	6	34
Working:							
Men.............	5	7	5	6	5	4	32
Women..........	4	6	3	5	8	4	30
Total:							
Men.............	14	15	12	9	13	9	72
Women..........	11	14	11	16	21	14	87
	25	29	23	25	34	23	159

the study group for the present report. Table 1 shows the distribution by age, sex, and social class in 1962, when the final round of interviews was completed. The upper-middle class is composed of business and professional occupations; the lower-middle includes the lower white-collar occupations and a few skilled manual workers; and the working class represents blue-collar workers who are above the lowest 15 percent of the American population in income. Since many of the sample were retired or widowed, the principal occupation of the subject or spouse at the time of his best job was taken as the major index of social status.

The data consisted of lengthy and repeated interviews covering many aspects

ness, boredom, anger; and questions regarding the respondent's role models and his self-image. There were also thematic apperception tests included in some of the interviews. A special long interview was carried out with 88 of the sample by a clinical psychologist.

THE MEASURES OF ENGAGEMENT

It is well to begin with a distinction between *social* engagement and *psychological* engagement. The first refers to the interactions that occur between the aging individual and the persons he meets face to face in the course of everyday living; and refers, therefore, to interactions which would be directly visible to an ob-

163

server (although they are assessed here on the basis of the respondent's own report).

The second refers to behavior that may not be directly observable, that reflects the extent to which the aging individual is preoccupied with, and/or emotionally invested in, persons and events in the external world. The respondent may or may not be aware of changes in quantity or quality of his psychological involvements.

The two types of engagement are usually, but not always, related. The individual whose work, family, and recreational activities bring him into interaction with a great many people in the course of the day is usually the individual who is highly invested in other persons, objects, and events in the environment; while the individual who is socially withdrawn tends also to be psychologically withdrawn. On the other hand, there are many persons for whom this relationship does not hold true: persons who become relatively isolated but who try unsuccessfully to maintain a high level of social participation; and persons whose work, family, and other social commitments remain high in the face of their own preference for increased privacy and what might be termed a growing indifference to many of the persons around them.

With increasing age, the two types of disengagement might be found to proceed independently of each other. It is a matter of major importance whether or not they do, indeed, occur at different rates; and whether one usually precedes the other. In the activity theory for instance, it is presumed that social disengagement occurs in the absence of psychological disengagement; and to the extent that the older person shows psychological withdrawal it is in response to the changed social climate in which he finds himself. In the disengagement theory, however, it is presumed that psychological disengagement accompanies, or even precedes the social; and that disengagement is, accordingly, a developmental phenomenon, inherent within the individual.

Because the question of order and timing of change along these two dimensions is of such theoretical significance, we have attempted to differentiate measures of social from measures of psychological engagement. If psychological disengagement is shown to precede social, this would provide evidence (though not proof) that we are dealing with a developmental phenomenon.

SOCIAL ENGAGEMENT

Social engagement was measured in two ways. The first, called the *Interaction Index*, is a judgment made by the investigator of the amount of each day R spends in the kind of social interaction with other persons in which the hints, cues, and sanctions which govern and control behavior can be exchanged. Scoring was based on verbatim reports of R's daily round of activities. The score does not relate directly to the variety of roles or the number of people interacted with. An aged man who spends all day at home with his wife may receive as high a score as a person who works at a job with others, who has an active social and recreational life, but who lives alone.

The second approach to social engagement involved a set of three measures, all three related to performance in eleven life-roles: worker, spouse, parent, grandparent, kin-group member, home-maker, friend, neighbor, citizen, club-member, and church-member. The first of these is *Present Role Activity*, a summation of subscores based on ratings of extent and intensity of activity in each of the eleven roles. For example, a man who lives with his wife, but who shares with her few activities other than perfunctory routines such as eating his meals in her company, is rated low in the role of spouse. By contrast, a man who plans and carries out most of his day's activities in the company of his wife is rated high in the role of spouse. A widowed man is scored zero on spouse, thus diminishing his total score on Present Role Activity.

A related measure is that of *Ego-Invest-*

ment in Present Roles—the extent to which the individual is ego-involved in his various life-roles. For example, the man who prides himself on being a good husband and who gives evidence of this as he talks about his relationship with his wife, is rated high on investment in the role of spouse. Although ego-investment stands somewhere between social and psychological engagement as we have defined the two, the measure used here correlated .87 with role-activity for this sam-

Each S was rated on all three of these measures with regard to each of the eleven roles. Two independent judges rated each case, and the ratings were averaged. Reliability of ratings was high. For instance, for all ratings on the first 30 cases, and using consecutive pairs from among 10 judges, there were 50 percent exact agreements, and 95 percent agree-

TABLE 2

AGE DIFFERENCES IN INTERACTION INDEX, ROLE BEHAVIOR,
AFFECT, AND LIFE SATISFACTION

| AGE IN 1962 | NUMBER | | INTERACTION INDEX | | MEASURES OF ROLE-BEHAVIOR | | | | | |
| | | | | | Present Role Activity | | Ego Investment in Present Roles | | Changes in Role Activity since Age 60 | |
	M	F	M	F	M	F	M	F	M	F
54–59......	14	11	2.6	2.8	43.7	49.1	34.6	42.0	− 1.5††	− 1.3††
60–64......	15	14	2.5	2.8	45.9	42.7	35.3	34.0	− 1.0	− 2.2
65–69......	12	11	2.6	2.7	44.1	47.9†	32.5	37.5	− 3.1	− 3.4
70–74......	9	16	2.4	2.5	44.6	38.4	30.1	29.2	− 3.1	− 5.8
75–79......	13	21	2.2	2.4	42.0	37.3	29.0	28.5	− 6.4	− 7.3
80–94......	9	14	2.0	2.1	28.9	31.5	19.2	27.1	−10.0	−10.5
54–69.....	41	36	2.6	2.8	44.6	46.5	34.2	37.9	− 1.8	− 2.2
70–94.....	31	51	2.2	2.4*	38.9*	36.1**	26.5**	28.4**	− 6.6**	− 7.7**

* The difference on the measures between the below-70- and over-70-year-olds is significant at the .05 level.

** These differences are significant beyond the .01 level.

† The sharp upward turn in Role Activity for the 65–69 age women is due in part to the fact that this group included an unusually low proportion of widows and never-married women, and therefore had an unusually high proportion of women with positive scores in the "spouse" role.

†† For this group, the questions referred to change over the past 10 years.

ple. It seemed better, accordingly, to treat it as a measure of social engagement rather than as a measure of psychological engagement.

The third measure is *Change in Role Activity since Age 60* (or, for those under 70, change in the past 10 years.) For example, a man who had fully retired from a full-time job would be rated as having had the maximum negative change in that role. Another man who had become a grandfather but who spent only a few days a year with his grandchildren would be rated as having a small positive change in that role.

ments within one step on a five-step scale.

The fact that social disengagement takes place with increasing age is documented in Table 2, which shows the relations between age and each of the social interaction measures.

Although there is a statistically reliable decrease on these measures between the under-70 and the over-70 groups, the numbers in each age-group are too small to permit conclusions about changes from one five-year age group to the next. Involved also is the fact that given an almost 50 percent attrition in the total sample over the six years of data gathering, and the fact that the groups are based upon age in 1962 rather than in 1956, the age-groups are by no means to be regarded as equally representative.

For example, the 65- to 69-year-old group that remained in the study in 1962 was different in many ways from the other age groups. It included an unusually low proportion of widows and never-married women (widows and never-married women were 50, 18, and 75 percent, respectively, in the age groups 60–64, 65–69, and 70–74.) There had also been an

TABLE 3

CHANGE IN EGO ENERGY OVER
A 5-YEAR INTERVAL

Age in 1962	N	Mean Score in 1957	Mean Score in 1962
55–59........	24	16.6	14.6
60–64........	28	16.1	14.3
65–69*.......	16	19.1	18.3
70–76........	25	14.2	13.9
Total.......	93	16.3	15.0**

* The 65–69 group was only a part of the total 65–69 group who were studied in 1957. By 1962 there had been more losses in this group than in others owing to deaths and geographica moves.

** The difference between means for the total group is significant at the .01 level.

NOTE. Because of the small numbers in each age group; and because the subgroups are not equally representative, age differences should not be read from either column 2 or column 3, but from the differences between the two columns—that is, from the test-retest differences.

unusually high attrition rate in this group due to deaths and to geographical moves.

For reasons such as these, the overall age trends, but not the differences between adjacent age-groups, provide the reliable indices of change in Table 2 as well as in successive tables. (In the authors' judgment, it is primarily the uncontrollable losses and uneven attrition rates in the subsamples that are reflected in the irregularities in the data shown in the tables.)

PSYCHOLOGICAL ENGAGEMENT

Two measures of psychological engagement are reported here, both based on the Thematic Apperception Test, and both reflecting "inner" or covert processes.

Ego energy is the name applied to certain dimensions of ego functions: (1) the ability to integrate wide ranges of stimuli; (2) the readiness to perceive or to deal with complicated, challenging, or conflictual situations; (3) the tendency to perceive or to be concerned with feelings and affects as these play a part in life situations; and (4) the tendency to perceive vigorous and assertive activity in the self and in others.

Methods of measuring these dimensions on the TAT have been reported in an earlier study, where it was suggested that there is an intrinsic decrease of ego energy in the latter part of life (Rosen and Neugarten, 1960). This decrease may be due to aging of the central nervous system; to a welling up of unacceptable impulses in the later years which require the use of ego energy for their repression; and/or to the decline in visual and auditory acuity and in physical energy which may place an added burden on the ego when it must act in complex situations. These latter conditions would interfere with the use of ego energy in meeting the demands of everyday life and thus reduce the amount of ego energy available for dealing with the outer world.

The TAT was given to respondents in the second round of interviews, in 1957; and again, in the seventh round, in 1962. When protocols were analyzed without knowledge of age of respondent or date of testing, the data showed consistent drop in ego energy for each of the age-groups, as shown in Table 3. This drop in scores is interpreted as indirect evidence of psychological disengagement.

The second index of psychological engagement relates to what may be called *ego-style*, as inferred from TAT stories. Without knowledge of age of respondents, TAT protocols for the 135 people for whom these data were available were grouped into three major categories. The categories differ according to the manner in which the respondent perceives psychological issues represented in the pictures and the manner in which he attempts to resolve or to master those issues (Gutmann, 1964).

The category called *Active* included those stories in which issues are perceived as originating primarily in the external world, and in which the approach is assertive and active. In the *Passive* category there is a tendency to withdraw from active engagement with the external world in favor of more passive positions. Aggression and self-assertion are alien to the ego. The self, rather than the world, is the focus of control. In the *Magical* category, stories often contain misinterpretations and distortions of stimuli so gross as to suggest that primitive motivations are interfering with the respondent's accurate perception of the world. Ego functions have undergone regression, and attempts at resolutions are more often magical than realistic.

When the protocols were decoded for age of respondent, the age distribution of ego-styles that emerged is shown in Table 4. The increased frequency of Passive and Magical styles in the older age groups —styles in which the self or the inner impulse life pose more salient issues than do stimuli from the external world—is interpreted as evidence of psychological disengagement.

THE RELATIONSHIP BETWEEN SOCIAL AND PSYCHOLOGICAL DISENGAGEMENT[1]

There is substantial evidence in Tables 2, 3, and 4 for decline in both social and psychological engagement: there is demonstrable change with age in the degree and quality of activity in the various life-roles; and a withdrawal of psychological investment from the external environment.

[1] Although both show a decline with age, there is a relatively low degree of correlation between our measures of psychological and social engagement—that is, the individual who is low on one is not necessarily low on the other. In addition to the fact that psychological dis-

There is clearer decline in psychological than in social engagement in the 50's, possibly a foreshadowing of the social disengagement that appears in the 60's and 70's. The evidence that the psychological seems to precede the social implies that disengagement may be, in some respects,

TABLE 4*

EGO STYLES: BY AGE

EGO-STYLE	AGE		
	50–56	57–60	61–70
Active:			
Male..............	11	7	5
Female...........	10	9	5
Total**.........	21	16	10
Passive:			
Male..............	7	13	11
Female...........	8	4	11
Total**.........	15	17	22
Magical:			
Male..............	6	3	10
Female...........	2	3	12
Total**.........	8	6	22

* This analysis was carried by David L. Gutmann and has been described in greater detail elsewhere (Gutmann, 1964).

** The distribution of age subtotals is significantly different from chance at the .01 level, by the Chi-Square test.

engagement seems to precede social disengagement, there are probably three other factors involved: (1) In many important ways, the individual cannot control nor manipulate the environment in ways to suit his needs. He cannot, for instance, choose to become widowed or to become a grandparent; and in this sense he cannot choose, except within limits, a pattern of life that will yield a high score or a low score on role activity. (2) It is not known how much psychological disengagement may occur before this process manifests itself in social behavior; or, conversely, how much of the quality we have called ego-energy is required to sustain a high level of role activity. Perhaps the psychological changes occurring within this sample are all below the threshold, in this regard. (3) In a larger and more representative sample, one in which relatively disadvantaged as well as advantaged 70- and 80-year-olds were included, it might be expected that psychological and social engagement would show a greater degree of correlation.

a developmental phenomenon—a process that has intrinsic, as well as responsive, elements. It is true that the present evidence is insufficient to establish this point. Psychological disengagement might represent an anticipatory response process, rather than a developmental one, a process in which the individual anticipates shrinkage in his social world and undergoes adaptive (or defensive) preparatory maneuvers by withdrawing cathexis from the external world. It appears to us more likely, however, given the nature of our psychological measures, that the disengagement process has at least certain developmental elements. At any rate, this is a testable hypothesis which merits further investigation.[2]

MEASURES OF AFFECT AND SATISFACTION

With this evidence for disengagement as a *process* of aging, we turn next to the relations between measures of engagement on the one hand and measures of affect and life satisfaction on the other hand.

LIFE SATISFACTION

The concept of "life satisfaction" as a measure of psychological well-being has been defined in an earlier publication. Rating scales were devised for five components of life satisfaction: Zest (vs. apathy); Resolution and Fortitude; Congruence between desired and achieved goals; Positive self-concept; and Mood tone (Neugarten *et al.* 1961). In brief, an individual was regarded as being at the positive end of the continuum of psychological well-being to the extent that he: (A) takes pleasure from whatever the round of activities that constitutes his everyday life; (B) regards his life as meaningful and accepts resolutely that which life has been; (C) feels he has succeeded in achieving his major goals; (D)

[2] See the paper by Gutmann in Part VIII of this book, "Aging among the Highland Maya." Gutmann reports substantially the same findings for Mayan man as for Kansas City man.

holds a positive image of self; and (E) maintains happy and optimistic attitudes and mood.

Each of these five components was rated on a five-point scale; and the ratings were summed to obtain an overall rating with a possible range from 5 (low) to 25 (high). In making the Life Satisfaction Ratings, all the interview data on each respondent were utilized. Thus the ratings are based, not on *R*'s direct self report of satisfaction (although some questions of this type were included in the interviews), but on the inferences drawn by the raters from all the information available on *R*, including his interpersonal relationships and the way in which others reacted toward him.

The ratings were made on seven rounds of interviews covering a period of six years in the lives of the respondents. In every case the ratings of two judges working independently were combined. The coefficient of correlation between ratings of two judges for 177 cases was .78 (becoming .87 when the Spearman-Brown coefficient of attenuation is used). For the 159 cases in the present study, LSR scores ranged from 8.5 to 25, with a mean of 17.8 and a standard deviation of 3.3.

It should be noted that the LSR is not limited to feelings of satisfaction with one's present situation. Two of the five components—Resolution or Fortitude, and Congruence between desired and achieved goals—are based upon a person's attitude toward his life as a whole. *R* might be depressed or apathetic at the time of the interview and still be given fairly high LSR ratings if he accepts resolutely and positively that which life has been for him and if he feels that he has achieved his personal goals in life.

AFFECT REGARDING PRESENT ROLE ACTIVITY

Another measure of psychological well-being was a rating on affect regarding present level of activity in the life-roles. This rating differed from the LSR in being related only to the respondent's feelings about his present activities. (The correlation coefficient between LSR and Affect-*re*-Present-Role-Activity was .46.) A separate rating was made for each of the life-roles, and the ratings were added to give the total "affect" score. A person who was not working, or who was widowed, or who was not a grandparent, was scored zero in these roles, which lowered his total score. Ratings were based on the seventh interview (1962) with such additional evidence as could be obtained from the earlier interviews. The

AFFECT *re* CHANGE IN ROLE ACTIVITY

A third measure, as the name itself implies, relates to change rather than to present activity patterns. This was a rating made by judges on the basis of responses to numerous questions asking about changes in role patterns and how the respondent felt about these changes.

The relation of age to each of these three measures of affect and/or satisfaction are shown in Table 5.

TABLE 5

AGE DIFFERENCES IN AFFECT AND IN LIFE SATISFACTION

AGE	NUMBER		LIFE SATISFACTION RATING		AFFECT *re* PRESENT ROLE ACTIVITY		AFFECT *re* CHANGE IN ROLE ACTIVITY	
	M	F	M	F	M	F	M	F
54–59.......	14	11	17.9	17.8	37.5	42.3	− .37	.33
60–64.......	15	14	17.2	18.5	38.3	35.4	− .47	− .50
65–69.......	12	11	19.0	17.2	33.4	35.1	.25	2.30
70–74.......	9	16	18.9	16.7	38.0	34.5	−1.00	−1.30
75–79.......	13	21	17.8	18.9	33.1	34.5	.31	−1.05
80–94.......	9	14	16.9	16.6	27.9	32.4	−5.11	−4.36
54–69.....	41	36	18.0	17.9	36.6	37.7	− .19	.62
70–94.....	31	51	17.9	17.6	33.0*	33.9*	−1.64	−2.02*

* The overall age trend, but not the differences between adjacent age-groups, provides the reliable index of decline with age. The differences between the under-70 and over-70 groups are statistically reliable at the .05 level or beyond.

ratings of two judges were averaged for each case. (These ratings were of the same level of reliability as those of LSR.)

Affect-*re*-Present-Activity was not necessarily correlated with level of activity in a role. For example, a man who was still working but wished to retire was rated average or low with regard to affect *re* role of worker. To take another example, a woman who seldom saw her grandchildren and who was therefore rated low in activity as grandmother would be rated high on affect in the grandmother role if she was content with this state of affairs. Another woman who saw her married daughter every day, but complained that her children neglected her, was rated low in affect for the mother role.

RELATIONS BETWEEN ENGAGEMENT AND SATISFACTION

The general question that concerns us first is whether people become more or less content with their level of activity as they grow older. We wanted to know how the sense of psychological well-being varies in relation to role activity and to change of role activity, as persons move from middle age through old age.

There are two ways of approaching this question. The first is to examine the age trends on the various measures.

AGE TRENDS

For this purpose we need to look again at Tables 2 and 5. Examination of these two tables shows that there are decreases in role-activity and in ego-investment with age; and at the same time, Affect-*re*-Role-Activity decreases. Furthermore, there is increasingly more negative Affect-*re*-Change as people grow older.

Thus, in general, as activity decreases, the sense of well-being associated with it decreases during the years after 60. Most respondents regret the losses in activity, and increasingly so at the oldest ages.

On the other hand the Life Satisfaction Rating does not decrease appreciably with age. People are generally able to accept a loss in role activity as they move through their 70's. They regret the loss,

sons who show the opposite combinations —persons who are content though they are relatively inactive; and persons who are discontent even though they are relatively active.

Next, the correlation is − .60 between *change* in role activity (change is usually, though not always, in the direction of decrease) and affect regarding the change. In other words, the greater the loss of activity, the greater are the negative feelings attached thereto.

Let us turn next to the correlation between role-activity and LSR. Since LSR reflects the subject's evaluation of himself and his life as a whole, both past and pres-

TABLE 6

CORRELATIONS BETWEEN MEASURES OF ENGAGEMENT AND
MEASURES OF SATISFACTION

(N = 159)

	B	C	D	E	F	G
A Present Role Activity..............	.87	.73	− .51	.40	.46	.53
B Ego Investment in Present Roles....	....	.79	− .44	.41	.51	.54
C Affect *re* Present Role Activity......	....	....	− .41	.43	.46	.38
D Change in Role Activity Since Age 60*	....	....	....	− .60	− .27	− .30
E Affect *re* Change in Role Activity...	....	....	....	....	.35	.22
F Life Satisfaction Rating............	....	....	....	....	....	.43
G Interaction Index.................	....	....	....	....	....	X

* The change in role activity is usually, but not always, a decrease. The more the decrease, the less positive the affect. It is this relationship that is expressed in the negative sign of the correlations.

and regard it with negative affect; yet, at the same time, they maintain a positive evaluation of themselves and satisfaction with past and present life as a whole.

CORRELATIONS BETWEEN MEASURES

The second approach to the relations between activity and satisfaction is to consider the statistical intercorrelations between our various measures, as shown in Table 6.

The correlation between role-activity and Affect-*re*-Role-Activity is .73 for the total group. This suggests that the usual patterns to be found in this sample are high activity together with positive affect, and low activity together with negative affect. At the same time, given the size of the correlation coefficient, there are per-

ent, it might be expected that this measure would have a lower correlation with present role-activity than do the Affect measures. This proves to be the case, since the correlation between activity and LSR is .46.[3]

Both these approaches to the data—age trends on separate measures, and correlations between measures—thus yield the same general findings: that those older persons who continue the greatest amounts of activity generally have greater psychological well-being than those

[3] This correlation obscures sex differences: the correlation for men under 70 is .65 and for women under 70 it is .20. For men over 70 the correlation is .44 and for women over 70 it is .52. The correlation drops with increasing age for men, but goes up for women.

who have lower levels of activity. At the same time, this relationship is far from consistent, and all four combinations of activity and satisfaction exist—that is, high-high and low-low are the most frequent; but there are also high-low and low-high patterns.

Neither the "activity" theory nor the disengagement theory accounts satisfactorily for this diversity.[4]

CHANGES WITH AGE IN CORRELATIONS BETWEEN MEASURES

If the decrease of role activity is easily tolerated or even welcomed by people as they grow older—as is implied by the disengagement theory—then the correlation coefficients between role activity, affect, and LSR should become smaller in size with advancing age.

To test this hypothesis, the respondents were divided into two groups, those above 70 and those below 70; and the correlations between measures were computed separately for each group. The two sets of intercorrelations are not reproduced here, but they are very similar, which negates the hypothesis. Furthermore, the correlations between activity, ego-investment, and affect-*re*-activity are even higher for those persons over 70 than for those under 70. This indicates that there is no dropping off of concern regarding activity as people move beyond age 70; and, again, that the hypothesis is not substantiated.

With the varied patterns of activity,

[4] In a crossnational study now being completed groups of 70-75-year-old retired teachers and retired steelworkers were drawn from each of six cities: Bonn (West Germany), Vienna, Nijmegen (Holland), Milan, Warsaw, and Chicago. In group after group the correlations were positive between social role activity and a measure of psychological well-being similar to the LSR; and for all 300 cases pooled, the correlation turned out to be .45, almost exactly the same correlation as found here in the Kansas City data. Findings from the crossnational study are expected to appear soon in a monograph to be entitled *Adjustment to Retirement: A Crossnational Study*, edited by R. J. Havighurst, B. L. Neugarten, H. Thomae, and J. M. A. Munnichs.

affect, and life satisfaction before us, we plan to turn next in our analyses of the Kansas City data to a consideration of the ways in which differences in personality are related to these patterns. Meanwhile, to summarize our findings thus far:

1. Our data provide convincing evidence of decline in both social and psychological engagement with increasing age. Disengagement seems to us to be a useful term by which to describe these processes of change.

2. In some ways our data support the activity theory of optimal aging: as level of activity decreases, so also does the individual's feeling of contentment regarding his present activity.

3. At the same time, the data in some ways support the disengagement theory of optimal aging. The relationship between life satisfaction and present activity while positive, is only moderate, thus providing all four combinations of activity and life-satisfaction: high-high and low-low, but also high-low and low-high.

4. We conclude that neither the activity theory nor the disengagement theory of optimal aging is itself sufficient to account for what we regard as the more inclusive description of these findings: that as men and women move beyond age 70 in a modern, industrialized community like Kansas City, they regret the drop in role activity that occurs in their lives. At the same time, most older persons accept this drop as an inevitable accompaniment of growing old; and they succeed in maintaining a sense of self-worth and a sense of satisfaction with past and present life as a whole. Other older persons are less successful in resolving these conflicting elements—not only do they have strong negative affect regarding losses in activity; but the present losses weigh heavily, and are accompanied by a dissatisfaction with past and present life.

5. There appear to be two sets of values operating simultaneously, if not

within the same individual then within the group we have been studying: on the one hand, the desire to stay active in order to maintain a sense of self-worth; on the other hand, the desire to withdraw from social commitments and to pursue a more leisurely and a more contemplative way of life. Neither the activity theory nor the disengagement theory of optimum aging takes sufficient account of this duality in value patterns.[5]

6. The relations between levels of activity and life satisfaction are probably influenced also by personality type, particularly by the extent to which the individual remains able to integrate emotional and rational elements of the personality. It is for this reason, also, that neither the activity nor the disengagement theory is satisfactory, since neither deals, except peripherally, with the issue of personality differences. This topic requires further exploration in these data.

[5] The late Dr. Yonina Talmon-Garber, in discussing these findings with us, suggested that the activity theory and the disengagement theory of optimal aging might themselves reflect historical changes in value patterns. As the American society becomes more leisure- than work-oriented, there may be an effect upon the theories put forth by social scientists regarding the sources of satisfaction with life.

A final comment may be warranted in relating disengagement to patterns of aging. The increased freedom of the aged implied in the disengagement theory lies, perhaps, in the freedom from role obligations; the man who is retired and whose family and community responsibilities are diminished is more free to pursue those activities and those ideas that he regards as important. To one individual this may mean freedom to indulge in material comforts, to indulge passive and succorant needs, and to take on a more hedonistic or carefree life. For another this may mean freedom to pursue what he regards as the important social values and to devote more time to the examination of philosophical and religious concepts. For still another, this may mean freedom to choose the work and community roles that symbolize his sense of worth and to remain highly engaged.

From this perspective, the aging individual may or may not disengage from the pattern of role activities that characterized him in middle age. It is highly doubtful, however, that he ever disengages from the values of the society which he has so long internalized. It is even more doubtful that the aging individual ever disengages from the personality pattern that has so long been the self.

17

BERNICE L. NEUGARTEN, ROBERT J. HAVIGHURST,
and SHELDON S. TOBIN

PERSONALITY AND PATTERNS OF AGING

In a report prepared for the International Congress of Gerontology in 1963, my colleagues and I presented a summary of the data obtained in a large-scale study of aging that has been in progress over the past several years in the United States, a study known as the Kansas City Study of Adult Life. (See preceding article, Disengagement and Patterns of Aging.) We said that, in the light of our findings, neither the "activity" nor the "disengagement" theory seemed adequate. Having followed several hundred persons aged 50 to 80 over a six-year interval, we found a positive correlation between the extent of social interaction and psychological well-being, a correlation that is even higher in persons aged 70 and over than persons aged 50 to 70. In other words, those older persons who are highly engaged in various social roles generally have greater life satisfaction than those who have lower

Reprinted from *Gawein: Tijdschrift van de Psychologische Kring aan de Nijmessgse Universitiet*, Jrg. 13, Afl. (May, 1965), pp. 249–56.
This paper, with a brief introduction describing the activity and the disengagement theories (the same introduction given in the preceding paper in this volume) was first presented by the first-named author at a meeting of the Dutch Gerontological Society in March 1964 and was published in the Dutch Journal, *Gawein*, in May 1965. The same data were reported by the second-named author to an American audience at a research conference in St. Louis in March 1967 and subsequently republished in *The Gerontologist* in March 1968. The disengagement theory was first set forth by our colleagues in the book *Growing Old* (Cumming and Henry, 1961). It has since been modified as in a paper by Cumming (1963) and in a paper by Henry (1963).

levels of engagement. At the same time the relationship is not a consistent one. There are some older persons who are low in social role activity and who have high life satisfaction; and vice-versa, there are others who are high in activity, but low in satisfaction.

On the basis of these findings, we have moved on to studying differences in personality. Presumably there are certain personality types who, as they age, disengage with relative comfort and who remain highly contented with life. Others disengage with great discomfort and show a drop in life satisfaction. Still others will long have shown low levels of role activity accompanied by high satisfaction and these latter persons will show relatively little change as they age. In this view, then, personality becomes the important variable—the fulcrum around which the other variables are organized.

We have attempted to order our data in such a way as to describe the *patterns of aging* that characterize the men and women in our study. To do so, we have used three sets of data: (1) personality type; (2) extent of social role activity; and (3) degree of life-satisfaction.

1. Our personality types are based on an ego-psychology model, in which individuals were rated on 45 different personality variables reflecting both cognitive and affective personality attributes. The types were established empirically, by methods of factor analysis (Neugarten and Associates, 1964).

2. Role-activity measures are made up of ratings of the extent and intensity of

activity in eleven different social roles: parent, spouse, grandparent, kin-group member, worker, homemaker, citizen, friend, neighbor, club-and-association member, and church member. For example, with regard to the role of spouse, a man who lives with his wife, but who shares with her few activities other than perfunctory routines such as eating his meals in her company, is rated low in the role of spouse; while a man who plans and carries out most of his day's activities in the company of his wife is rated high in this role. The role-activity score is a sum of ratings in the 11 different-roles.

3. The life-satisfaction measure is a sum of ratings on five different components. An individual is regarded as high in psychological well-being to the extent that he (a) takes pleasure from whatever the round of activities that constitutes his everyday life; (b) regards his life as meaningful and accepts resolutely that which life has been; (c) feels he has succeeded in achieving his major goals; (d) holds a positive image of self; and (e) maintains happy and optimistic attitudes and moods (Neugarten et al., 1961).

These three sets of measures and the assessments of our subjects were carried out by independent teams of investigators.

In describing the patterns based on these three variables, personality type, role activity, and life-satisfaction, we shall report here only those patterns found in our 70- to 79-year-old men and women. In this age-group almost all the

TABLE 1

PERSONALITY TYPE IN RELATION TO ACTIVITY
AND LIFE SATISFACTION (AGE 70–79)
(N = 59)

PERSONALITY TYPE	ROLE ACTIVITY	LIFE SATISFACTION		
		High	Medium	Low
Integrated	High	9 A	2	
	Medium	5 B		
	Low	3 C		
Armored-Defended	High	5 D		
	Medium	6	1 E	
	Low	2	1	1
Passive-Dependent	High		1 F	
	Medium	1	4	
	Low	2	3	2 G
Unintegrated	High		2	1
	Medium	1		
	Low		2	5 H
	Total	34	16	9

NAME OF PATTERN

A—Re-organizer   E—Constricted
B—Focused   F—Succorance-Seeker
C—Disengaged   G—Apathetic
D—Holding On   H—Disorganized

men had retired, and this is the group in which the transition from middle age to old age has presumably been accomplished.

A few words about this sample: Of the larger group who formed the original population in the Kansas City Study of Adult Life, about 60 percent remained after six years. The loss of cases is an important factor; and the overall effect has been to produce a relatively select group over time. Thus the patterns described here do not, by any means, encompass all types of older persons to be found in a community, but only those relatively advantaged 70-year-olds who have better-than-average health, cooperativeness, and general well-being. There are 59 persons in this age group, 50 of whom fell into one or another of eight patterns of aging.

To help keep the patterns in mind, we shall describe them primarily in terms of the four major personality types. As shown in Table 1, these are the "integrated," the "defended," the "passive-dependent," and the "disintegrated" personalities. These four groups are then further divided according to role activity score and according to life-satisfaction ratings, to yield eight patterns.

First, there are 17 in this group of 70-year-olds who are "integrated" personalities: well-functioning persons who have a complex inner life and at the same time, intact cognitive abilities and competent egos. These persons are acceptant of impulse life, over which they maintain a comfortable degree of control; they are flexible, open to new stimuli; mellow, mature. All these individuals, it happens, were high in life satisfaction. At the same time, they were divided with regard to amount of role activity:

There is one pattern we called the *reorganizers*, who are the competent people engaged in a wide variety of activities. (These are marked A in Table 1.) They are the optimum agers in some respects—at least in the American culture, where there is high value placed on "staying

young, staying active, and refusing to grow old." These are persons who substitute new activities for lost ones; who, when they retire from work, give time to community affairs or to church or to other associations. They reorganize their patterns of activity.

There is a second pattern which we called the *focused* (Group B in Table 1). These are integrated personalities, with high life satisfaction, but who show medium levels of activity. They have become selective in their activities, with time, and they now devote energy to and gain their major satisfaction from one or two role areas. One such case, for instance, was a retired man who was now preoccupied with the roles of homemaker, parent, and husband. He had withdrawn from work and from club-memberships and welcomed the opportunity to live a happy and full life with his family, seeing his children and grandchildren, gardening, and helping his wife with homemaking which he had never done before.

The next pattern we called the *disengaged* (Group C in Table 1). These are also integrated personalities with high life satisfaction, but with low activity; persons who have voluntarily moved away from role commitments, not in response to external losses or physical deficits, but because of preference. These are self-directed persons, not shallow, with an interest in the world, but an interest that is not imbedded in a network of social interactions. They have high feelings of self-regard, just as do the first two groups mentioned, but they have chosen what might be called a "rocking-chair" approach to old age—a calm, withdrawn, but contented pattern.

Next we come to the men and women whose personality type was the "armored" or the "defended." These are the striving, ambitious, achievement-oriented personalities, with high defenses against anxiety and with the need to maintain tight controls over impulse life. This personality group provided two patterns of aging:

One we called the *holding-on* pattern (Group D in Table 1). This is the group to whom aging constitutes a threat, and who respond by holding on, as long as possible, to the patterns of their middle age. They are quite successful in their attempts, and thus maintain high life satisfaction with medium-or-high activity levels. These are persons who say, "I'll work until I drop," or "So long as you keep busy, you will get along all right."

The other group of "defended" personalities we called the *constricted* pattern of aging (Group E in Table 1). These are persons busily defending themselves against aging; preoccupied with losses and deficits; dealing with these threats by constricting their social interactions and their energies and by closing themselves off from experience. They seem to structure their worlds to keep off what they regard as imminent collapse; and while this constriction results in low role activity, it works fairly well, given their personality pattern, to keep them high or medium in life satisfaction.

The third group of personalities are the passive-dependent types, among whom there are two patterns of aging:

The *succorance-seeking* (Group F) are those who have strong dependency needs and who seek responsiveness from others. These persons maintain medium levels of activity and medium levels of life satisfaction, and seem to maintain themselves fairly well so long as they have at least one or two other persons whom they can lean on and who meet their emotional needs.

The *apathetic* pattern (Group G) represents those persons in whom passivity is a striking feature of personality and where there is low role activity and medium or low life satisfaction. These are also "rocking-chair" people, but with very different personality structures from those we have called the disengaged. This apathetic pattern seems to occur in persons in whom aging has probably reinforced long-standing patterns of passivity and apathy. Here, for instance, was a man who, in the interviews, was content to let his wife do his talking for him; and there was a woman whose activities were limited entirely to those of maintaining her physical needs.

Finally there was a group of unintegrated personalities (Group H) who showed a *disorganized* pattern of aging. These were persons who had gross defects in psychological functions, loss of control over emotions and deterioration in thought processes. They were maintaining themselves in the community, but they were low both in role activity and in life satisfaction.

These eight patterns, in accounting for 50 of the 59 cases, provide considerable coherence in our data on 70- to 79-year-olds. If our original sample had been more representative of the universe of 70-year-olds, perhaps we might have a greater number of discrete patterns, some of them, for example, centered around low physical vitality and poor health. (A larger number of patterns would not necessarily be the case, however, since it may be that persons who survive into the 70's are already a select group, in whom only certain patterns of aging are to be found.)

In any case, it is clear, from this brief description of patterns, that neither the "activity" nor the "disengagement" theory of successful aging accounts for the empirical findings. A "personality-continuity" or "developmental" theory of aging needs to be more formally set forth.

People, as they grow old, seem to be neither at the mercy of the social environment nor at the mercy of some set of intrinsic processes—in either instance, inexorable changes that they cannot influence. On the contrary, the individual seems to continue to make his own "impress" upon the wide range of social and biological changes. He continues to exercise choice and to select from the environment in accordance with his own

176

long-established needs. He ages according to a pattern that has a long history and that maintains itself, with adaptation, to the end of life.

In summary, then, we regard personality as the pivotal dimension in describing patterns of aging and in predicting relationships between level of social role activity and life satisfaction. There is considerable evidence that, in normal men and women, there is no sharp discontinuity of personality with age, but instead an increasing consistency. Those character-

istics that have been central to the personality seem to become even more clearly delineated, and those values the individual has been cherishing become even more salient. In the personality that remains integrated—and in an environment that permits—patterns of overt behavior are likely to become increasingly consonant with the individual's underlying personality needs and his desires.

18

SUZANNE REICHARD, FLORINE LIVSON, and PAUL G. PETERSEN

ADJUSTMENT TO RETIREMENT

Successful adjustment to retirement appears to depend less on how active a man is than on whether his activities develop out of lifelong needs and interests. For some, retirement is tolerable only if they are able to carry on activities that use job skills or that otherwise preserve their occupational identity. Others welcome the opportunity to turn to interests outside their jobs. Some find security in social isolation after retirement, or in freedom from pressure and responsibility. Others find isolation lonely and leisure demoralizing. Those in our study group who adjusted well to retirement were able to develop a life style that provided continuity with the past and met long-term needs. When activities fail to meet such needs, retirement can lead to an abrupt break in life pattern and a sense of alienation. Developing hobbies, often recommended for the retired, seems most useful when these hobbies arise naturally out of earlier interests.

Thus, there are a number of different patterns of adjustment to aging and retirement—some successful and some unsuccessful. The way that a man grows old depends to a degree on his personality—on what his psychological drives are and his ability to satisfy them in old age. Personality has an important effect on whether a man grows old successfully, and on how he goes about it.

We were able to identify three personality types among men who adjusted well to aging and two among those who ad-

Reprinted from Suzanne Reichard, Florine Livson, and Paul G. Petersen, *Aging and Personality* (New York: John Wiley and Sons, 1962), pp. 170–72.

justed poorly. The three well-adjusted types of men adapted to aging differently but equally successfully. Similarly, the two poorly adjusted types responded to old age in different ways.

The largest group identified among the well adjusted we called the "mature." These men moved easily into old age. Relatively free of neurotic conflict, they were able to accept themselves realistically and to find genuine satisfaction in activities and personal relationships. Feeling their lives had been rewarding, they were able to grow old without regret for the past or loss in the present. They took old age for granted and made the best of it. A second group, whom we labeled the "rocking-chair men" because of their general passivity, welcomed the opportunity to be free of responsibility and to indulge their passive needs in old age. For these men, old age brought satisfactions that compensated for its disadvantages. A third well-adjusted group consisted of persons who maintained a highly developed but smoothly functioning system of defenses against anxiety. Unable to face passivity or helplessness in old age, they warded off their dread of physical decline by keeping active. Their strong defenses protected them from their fear of growing old. We called them the "armored."

Among those who were poorly adjusted to aging, the largest group of individuals we called the "angry men." Bitter over having failed to achieve their goals earlier in life, they blamed others for their disappointments and were unable to reconcile themselves to growing old. A second group of maladjusted men also looked back on their past lives with a sense of disappointment and failure, but unlike the angry men they turned their resentment inward, blaming themselves for their misfortunes. These men tended to be depressed as they approached old age. Growing old underscored their feelings of inadequacy and worthlessness. We called this group the "self-haters."

With the exception of the mature group, many of whom had had difficulties in personal adjustment when they were younger, these personality types appeared to have been relatively stable throughout life. Poor adjustment to aging among the angry men and the self-haters seemed to stem from lifelong personality problems. Similarly, the histories of the armored and rocking-chair groups suggest that their personalities had changed very little throughout their lives.

The prevailing American view has been that those old people are happiest who continue to participate actively in the life of the community. Sharply differing from this predominant view is the so-called theory of disengagement, which has appeared in some of the recent literature; this theory holds that persons who age successfully find orderly ways to withdraw from social roles. The behavior patterns of our three types of well-adjusted men show both types of adjustment. In other words, both activity and disengagement can occur among those well adjusted to aging. As our findings suggest, there are different but equally successful patterns of good adjustment to aging.

Two of the well-adjusted groups, the mature and the armored, functioned equally well at work, and were actively interested in hobbies, in social activities, and organizations. However, the mature men continued to participate actively even after retirement because they enjoyed what they were doing, while the armored continued active because of a compulsive need to "keep busy" as a defense against aging. Patterns of behavior that are externally similar may satisfy dissimilar needs. On the other hand, the rocking-chair group show that disengage-

ment is a satisfactory mode of adjustment for some aged persons.

Some writers believe that successful aging depends on the degree to which one has freed himself of inner conflicts and realized his potential earlier in life. Of the three successful patterns of aging we identified, the mature came closest to achieving this goal. Our findings, however, suggest that others, either through strong defenses or new opportunities for satisfaction, may nevertheless enjoy a happy old age.

How general are our five patterns of adjustment to aging? Since our study group was not drawn from a cross section of the aged population, we cannot say. Moreover, we looked for patterns only among men who adjusted well or poorly to aging, omitting one-fifth of the sample who fell in the middle range. There is a need to extend this type of research to a larger spectrum of the aged population in order to shed additional light on modes of adjustment to aging. It may be possible to identify, in larger samples of the male population, patterns of adjustment which were not revealed in our study.

There is also a need to extend this type of research to female samples. Since growing old presents somewhat different problems to women, particularly those who have spent the greater part of their lives as housewives, we should expect to uncover some differing patterns of adjustment among women, although there would also be reason to expect that some of the personality types identified in this study would also show up in a female sample.

The identification of personality types that adjust in differing ways to the problems of aging and retirement should not, of course, be interpreted to suggest that differences in attitudes toward aging and retirement are to be explained solely, or even largely, on the basis of personality variations. Other studies have indicated clearly that differences in income status, occupation, and cultural background have an important influence on attitudes toward the problems of growing older and leaving the labor force. Yet, as we pointed out in the introduction, substantial differences in attitudes are found within occupation and income groups—differences that might be expected to be associated with variations in personality. Because of limitations of sample size, however, we were not in a position to analyze the interaction between such factors as income and occupation, on the one hand, and personality differences on the other. It remains for other studies to explore these relationships more fully.

19

GEORGE L. MADDOX

PERSISTENCE OF LIFE STYLE AMONG THE ELDERLY: A LONGITUDINAL STUDY OF PATTERNS OF SOCIAL ACTIVITY IN RELATION TO LIFE SATISFACTION

In the analysis of behavioral or attitudinal phenomena among the elderly, change rather than persistence is more often the focus. Concentration on change, usually decremental, within some aggregate of elderly individuals in the typical case results in attention being given neither to distinguishing *changers* from *non-changers* nor to the establishing base lines against which individual change may be measured in a meaningful way. This state of affairs is in part the result of the use of cross sectional, in contrast to longitudinal, design. Both theoretical and methodological considerations suggest, however, the relevance of studying persistence as well as change in the patterns of behavior and attitudes among elderly longitudinally. Data from the Duke Geriatrics Project support this contention.

Consider, for example, the patterns of activity and life satisfaction reported by a panel of 148 non-institutionalized volunteer subjects 60 years of age and older. These panelists have been continually under observation over the past seven years and are the survivors of an initial panel of 250. The details of their selection and the explanation of panel attrition has been discussed elsewhere (Maddox, 1963). In brief, initially the panelists were demonstrably a social, psychological, and physical elite among the elderly and became more so through time. The panel data,

First published by Verlag der Wiener Medizinische Akademie, Wien 1966, in the *Proceedings of the Seventh International Congress of Gerontology*, 6:309–11, Vienna 1966.

therefore, can be used to illustrate aspects of aging processes but not to describe the probable state of affairs among elderly persons generally.

With few exceptions, research in the United States has consistently supported the hypothesis that, among the elderly, maintenance of contact with the social environment is a condition of maintaining a sense of life satisfaction. The principal exception is, of course, the work of Cumming and Henry on disengagement (1961) which draws exactly the opposite conclusion; that is, reduction of interaction with the environment among the elderly is eventually a condition of the maintenance of life satisfaction. Although the evidence against disengagement theory as a general explanation of aging process cannot be reviewed here (see Maddox, 1965), one issue raised by the critics of Cumming and Henry is especially relevant to the concern of this paper. This is the suggestion that the disengaged state is most likely to be observed primarily among the very old whose declining health reduces their capacity to play any social roles successfully and among those for whom disengagement is a life style antedating old age. The evidence presented below reinforces these probable explanations.

Elsewhere it has been shown that among the Duke panelists activity, on the average, does tend to decrease with age (Maddox, 1963). Decrease in contact with the environment, however, must be interpreted in relation to an individual's own baseline. Gradual decrease in activity through time for an elderly person with a history of active contact with his environment when, even with the experienced decrease he is relatively more active than his peers, must be distinguished from more consequential modifications in activity. The persistence of a life style involving a relatively high level of involvement with the environment is as much a possibility as its opposite as indicated by the report of the panelists under consideration.

sion is reinforced by other data about panelists variously categorized in Table 1.

Consider, for example, the categories "predominantly above," "predominantly below," and "other." Is there a tendency for the last observation in these non-uniform series to indicate a disengaged state? Of the 68 subjects of the three relevant categories, only four displayed a pattern of low activity and high life satisfaction at the time of the third observation. Clearly there is not a tendency for this pattern

TABLE 1

PATTERNS OF ACTIVITY AND LIFE SATISFACTION* AMONG SELECTED
PANELISTS, THREE REPORTS AVAILABLE

PATTERN	MALE		FEMALE		TOTAL	
	N	%	N	%	N	%
Activity and satisfaction:						
Consistently above mean†...........	14	21.9	24	28.5	38	25.7
Predominantly above mean**........	13	20.3	13	15.4	26	17.6
Consistently below mean............	12	18.7	9	11.0	21	14.2
Predominantly below mean..........	6	9.5	5	5.9	11	7.4
Activity below, satisfaction above mean:						
Consistently.....................	4	6.2	3	3.6	7	4.7
Predominantly...................	7	10.9	7	8.3	14	9.4
Other patterns......................	8	12.5	23	27.3	31	21.0
Totals........................	64	100.0	84	100.0	148	100.0

* Based on the Cavan activity and attitude inventories (Maddox, 1963).
† Consistent refers to all 3 reports.
** Predominant refers to 2 of the 3 reports.

eration. For example, individuals who ranked high or low in activity initially tended to maintain their ranking in the panel through time (see Table 1). This was also true of reported life satisfaction. In fact, such persistence was characteristic of a large majority of the panelists (79%). Fourteen percent of the panelists did display persistently what might be called the disengaged pattern in which life satisfaction is maintained in spite of a low level of activity. But, these data suggest that a pattern of disengagement is more adequately viewed as the continuing life style of particular individuals than as a likely culmination of a process characteristic of all aging individuals. This conclu-

to emerge among individuals who at the initial observation did not display it.

Four characteristics did differentiate somewhat the panelists who displayed one or another pattern of activity in relation to life satisfaction. The pattern of high activity/high life satisfaction was associated with being younger, with better health, with higher socioeconomic status, and with above average intelligence (WAIS); the pattern of low activity/low life satisfaction was associated with the absence of these characteristics. The differences are not, however, particularly remarkable. The difference in age, e.g., is only about two years. This means that at the third round of observations the average age of the former category would be approximately 74, and the latter, 76. Relatively more importance is attached to factors of social status, health and intelligence. The individuals displaying the disengaged patterns are in fact the oldest in the panel (average age 80) at the third observation; but there is a considerable range of ages in each category. This would argue again for the conclusion that the disengaged pattern is not simply a function of age. Moreover, individuals at an advanced age who eventually display the disengaged pattern may have arrived there by very different routes, some as a result of a persistent life style and other as a result of the gradual modification in advanced age of a life-time pattern of high activity and high life satisfaction.

This research reinforces the hypothesized importance of assessing persistence in individual life styles which reflect differences in the degree of contact with the environment and the relevance of this contact for the maintenance of life satisfaction. If life style is, as it appears to be, such an important variable, then longitudinal study of individual careers is crucial in the understanding of social processes of aging.

20

ARNOLD M. ROSE

A CURRENT THEORETICAL ISSUE IN SOCIAL GERONTOLOGY

A new field of research, especially one dealing with a social problem, is likely to emerge without using any explicit theory, and then gradually to adapt general theoretical formulations already in use in kindred fields. Thus, the earliest research in social gerontology was descriptive in character, but soon concepts like "adjustment," "role changes," "loss of roles," "changing self-concept" were borrowed from symbolic-interactionist theory in social psychology—a theoretical position to which many of the early social gerontologists adhered. Burgess, who probably can be considered to be the father of social gerontology, was also the source of the symbolic-interactionist concepts in some of the early research in the field. It was not until 1961, however, that systematic statements of symbolic-interactionist theory applied to the problems of social gerontology appeared. There were two such papers written independently (Cavan, 1962; Rose, 1961).

Much of the research in social gerontology today is explicitly or implicitly guided by interactionist theory, broadly conceived. The utility of this theory is thus constantly being tested in empirical research work. Research in social gerontology not guided by interactionist theory has tended to be descriptive or to interpret the facts of aging in an historical-cultural context.

There has been one major exception which has received considerable attention in recent years. This is the work of Cumming and her collaborators (Cumming,

Reprinted from *The Gerontologist*, vol. 4, no. 1 (March, 1964).

Dean, Newell, & McCaffrey, 1960; Cumming & Henry, 1961). The book, *Growing Old* (Cumming & Henry, 1961), is a major study in the framework of functionalist theory, a theory which has guided much empirical research in anthropology but very little in sociology; hence Cumming's work is a landmark in sociological functionalism. It is the purpose of the present essay to evaluate the Cumming and Henry book as a statement of theory and as a test of a specific theory. We are not here concerned with the research method or its manner of utilization in that book. We shall also be concerned with theoretical essays written by Cumming (1963), Henry (1963), and Parsons (1963) two years after the publication of *Growing Old*.

There has been such widespread misinterpretation of the theory of disengagement, as expressed in the Cumming and Henry book, that it is essential to state what it is before it be evaluated. It is *not* an hypothesis which states that, as people get older, they are gradually separated from their associations and their social functions. Such a hypothesis had been stated many times before Cumming and Henry and was generally assumed to be a fact. After all, this is what was meant by Burgess (1950) in his discussion of the "roleless role." Nor does the theory of disengagement state that, as people become physically feebler or chronically ill, they are thereby forced to abandon their associations and social functions. This is a matter of logic and also long been assumed to be a fact.

Cumming and Henry (1961) wisely

excluded from their sample any person who was in poor physical or mental health and explicitly denied that their conception of disengagement rests on ill health. Finally, the theory of disengagement does *not* say that because older people tend to have a reduced income in our society, they can no longer afford to participate in many things. That also would be a matter of logic and has long been known to be a fact. Cumming and Henry wisely excluded from their sample anyone who did not have the minimum of money needed for independence. To test *their* hypothesis, as distinguished from the popular misinterpretations of their hypothesis, Cumming and Henry must have made these exclusions.

The Cumming and Henry theory of disengagement is that the society and the individual prepare *in advance* for the ultimate "disengagement" of incurable, incapacitating disease and death by an *inevitable, gradual and mutually satisfying process of disengagement from society.* Each of these terms must be understood before the theory can be understood. Disengagement is inevitable, because death is inevitable, and according to a basic principle of functionalism, society and the individual always accommodate themselves to the solid facts of existence. Society and the individual always seek to maintain themselves in equilibrium and avoid disruption according to the functionalist. Since death must soon come to an older person, both society and the older person himself prepare for it sociologically and psychologically, so that when it comes the individual has divested himself of life's functions and associations and is ready for it. In this way, the death of an older person is not disruptive to the equilibrium of a society. The death of a young person, by accident or acute disease, *is* disruptive, and the society has a harder time accommodating to it.

Cumming and Henry compare the disengagement of an older person to the gradual and inevitable withering of a leaf or a fruit long before frost totally kills it.

This total process must be gradual, in the sense that it involves a period of preparation for death, although disengagement from some *specific* association or function may come suddenly. It is mutually satisfying; society is pleased when the death of one of its members does not disrupt its ongoing functions (such as child-bearing, carrying on economic production, or the work of one of its voluntary associations). And the individual can face death with relative equanimity because he no longer has any social ties; he has said all his "goodbyes" and has nothing more to do, so he might as well "leave."

Because death is a universal fact, the social and psychological disengagement of the elderly must be a universal fact, according to the theory. It is thus not bound to any one culture, even though Cumming and Henry take all of their cases from Kansas City, Missouri. Of course, there are different degrees and speeds of disengagement among different societies, and within any one society some people resist disengagement while others start on its course even before they become elderly. Cumming and Henry say that the values in American culture of competitive achievement and of future orientation make this society especially negative toward aging and hence encourage disengagement. But the process itself must be understood to be inevitable and universal, according to the theory, and not limited to any one group in a society or any one society.

In her 1963 essay, Cumming expressed the need to recognize some of the complexities of aging as modifiers of the theory, but adhered to the "main outlines" of the earlier theory. She pointed out that the original study "did not take into account such non-modal cases as widowhood before the marriage of the last child or of work protracted past the modal age of retirement" (p. 378). She recognized that there are individual differences in disengagement, and even "typologies of withdrawal and retreat" based on deeply-rooted differences in character and in biological temperament. She went so far as to recognize that as lively oldsters were disengaged from their more important social roles, they might temporarily *increase* their recreational activities. She pointed out several other causes of disengagement besides the anticipation of death, such as rapid social change making obsolete some of the roles of older people, the gulf between generations in a future-oriented society, and the drastic shift in roles for men when they retire. While these latter points permit the distinctive characteristics of American society to modify the universal character of the theory, Cumming essentially has adhered quite closely to the basic outlines of the functionalist theory of disengagement.

Parsons (1963), the outstanding contemporary exponent of functional theory in sociology, accepted the Cumming theory of disengagement, while adding to it the idea that old age is the consummatory phase of life, a "period of 'harvest', when the fruits of his (the older person's) previous instrumental commitments are primarily gathered in."

Henry, however, in his 1963 discussion, deviated considerably from the theory. He started from the commonly observed *fact* of disengagement, rather than from the theoretical functional necessity of disengagement. In fact, he avoided functional theory altogether. His interest was primarily in the psychological rather than the sociological characteristics of disengagement, stating that, "engagement and disengagement become a general form of personality dynamic, and the disengagement of the aged, a special case" (p. 14). Further, he retreated from the notion that disengagement is inevitable (although he used the word "intrinsic") and he allocated a major role to the "culture's definition of the good and the bad." He agreed with certain critics of the theory of disengagement that "several styles of aging are possible" (p. 15). In general, one might say that Henry in 1963 was closer to certain critics of the theory of disengagement than he was to Cumming.

There have been three lines of criticism of the Cumming-Henry book. One questions the process of disengagement and holds that not only is it not inevitable but that non-engagement in the later years is simply a continuation of a *life-long* social psychological characteristic of *some* people. One finds this idea even in Henry's 1963 paper, and it has received empirical foundation in the researches of Reichard, Livson, and Petersen (1962), of Williams and Wirths (1963), and of Videbeck and Knox (1965). The latter authors, for example, show that 90% of those non-participant after 65 years of age were also non-participant 5 years earlier, while 90% of those participant after 65 were also participant 5 years earlier. Further, at each earlier period of life (since their research was not limited to the elderly but traced patterns of participation for a 5-year period among samples of people at all age levels), there is a comparably high correlation between degree of participation at the beginning and end of each 5-year period. For these authors, there is a type of person who throughout his life had limited or few social involvements, and they do not think of disengagement as a process characteristic of old age.

A second line of criticism of the Cumming-Henry book challenges their value judgment that disengagement is desirable for older people. Havighurst, Neugarten, and Tobin (1963) have stated this criticism most clearly and have provided empirical evidence that the engaged elderly, rather than the disengaged, are the ones who generally, although not always, are happiest and have the greatest expressed life satisfaction.

The third line of criticism of the Cumming-Henry book analyzes disengagement in a context of the social structure and social trends and finds the theory a poor interpretation of the facts. This point of view in which I am mainly interested and to which I shall devote the remainder of this paper, acknowledges that a large proportion of the older people in the United States tend to lose many of their adult roles. But it considers this fact to be a function of American culture in this phase of its organization, not a universal for all time. American culture accords a low status to the elderly; we have a youth-centered society. Many other societies accord special prestige and power to the elderly, do not disengage them from adult roles, or create new age-graded roles of importance for them. The situation of the elderly in the United States has been especially unfavorable in the last 50 years, with the decline of the self-employed occupations and the rise of compulsory retirement. These trends have meant that the major social role for men in the society is not open to most elderly persons. Forced disengagement in the occupational role has tended to cause disengagement in auxiliary roles, for example, in the occupational associations (trade union, businessmen's association, professional organization) and the "service clubs" which have a membership based on economic activity. Thus cultural values and economic structure have combined to create a condition in which a large proportion of the elderly people are non-participant.

Those men who remain economically active past 65 years do not disengage, even in the unfavorable cultural value system of the United States. The politician, the employer, the self-employed professional, do not disengage until they become physically or mentally feeble. In fact, they often take on additional membership and leadership roles after they pass 65 years.

The great bulk of the American people, however, are required to retire from remunerative occupations at about 65 years of age, and this situation is not likely to change. There are certain new trends, however, which are counteracting the forces which make for disengagement of the elderly. Most of these trends are not "inevitable," in the functionalist's sense;

some are a product of deliberate organizational effort; others emanate from conditions that have nothing to do with the elderly but their influence will touch the elderly. We have arrived at the following list of such trends by examining the major changes now occurring in American society and forecasting their effects on the aging.

1. Modern medical science and health are allowing an ever-increasing proportion of those reaching 65 to remain in good health and physical vigor. It is doubtful that vigorous people will be as content to disengage as are those of the present generation of the elderly who have been weakened by earlier disease and by overly strenuous work. Loss of vigor may well be a factor in preventing many old people today from participating and, if that should be overcome, at least the motivation to disengage may diminish.

2. Social security legislation and private pension plans and annuities are slowly increasing the economic security of the retired. If older people have more money to spare from the bare necessities of life, which is true of only a small minority today, they may, like that well-to-do minority today, be more able and willing to continue their costlier participations.

3. I have elsewhere shown how older people in the United States are beginning to form a social movement to raise their status and privileges and that this movement is likely to gain an increasing number of adherents (Rose, 1962, 1965). Such a trend will influence the participation of the elderly in several ways: (a) It will provide a new engagement especially for older people; (b) It will inform the younger generations of the plight of the elderly, and may possibly make society less insistent that older people disengage (already we see, for example, a tendency of younger people to volunteer to transport older neighbors to meetings, church services, polling places, etc.); (c) It may

raise the prestige and dignity of age, that is, reversing the negative cultural value mentioned earlier, and such a change would remove the major cause of present disengagement. If the elderly had high prestige, society would not force them to disengage, and the elderly themselves, like the few prestigious elderly today, would be less likely to disengage.

4. The trend toward earlier retirement from chief life role (occupation for men and child-rearing for women), while now a factor causing disengagement, may eventually become an influence for re-engagement. Studies of the family life cycle (Glick, 1955) show that the average young woman today is having her *last* child at the age of 26, which means that her last child is ceasing to be dependent on her at the age of 40 to 45. Most women at this young age are just not going to be willing to disengage, even though they have lost their chief life role, and are going to have strong motivations to re-engage. The same will be true of men if the age of retirement creeps downward, as some economists tell us it will, significantly below 65 years. The new re-engagements have not yet emerged clearly, although for many middle-class women they seem to include voluntary associations and gainful employment. But it does seem probable that many of the new re-engagements will be able to continue past the age of 65 years and not necessitate a second disengagement as old age is reached.

5. The types of engagements for which older people would be eligible have increased in number and openness. There are ever-new types of voluntary activities available in American society. There are many hobbies that have recently taken on an occupational aspect—such as stamp trading (Christ, 1965)—which provides satisfying and even prestigious roles for elderly men. There has also been an expansion in the cultural definition of the male role, so that men may today participate in artistic activities and hobbies that formerly were defined as feminine (in-

cluding knitting, weaving, painting, etc.). Further, there has been a cultural redefinition of leisure-time activities as good in themselves, so that retired men do not necessarily feel a loss of status simply because they are no longer engaged in remunerative employment.

The disengagement theorists are completely oblivious to such trends and assume that a given cultural-social system, that of the United States today, is "inevitable" and more or less universal in the position it accords the elderly. Their ethnocentrism is pointed up more sharply, by evidence quite different from our own, by Talmon (1963). Talmon shows how, in the different cultural system of the Israeli Kibbutz, there is little disengagement of the elderly but rather "a restructuring of roles and relationships and a shift in their relative importance rather than mere decline" (p. 10).

I believe it is no accident that the disengagement theorists, although they are sophisticated sociologists and may be skilled researchers, are ethnocentric and ignore major social trends. I believe that it is due to the general functionalist theory which underlies Cumming's work. With this approach, one largely ignores history, with its pointing up of trends from past to present and from present to future, and even minimizes cross-cultural variations by emphasizing the universal "functional prerequisites of culture" which Cumming extends to include the necessity of society to pre-adjust to death. The approach of the functionalist is to start with a certain observation about social life, in this case disengagement, exaggerate it so it seems to be characteristic of *all* persons in the category observed and then seek to demonstrate why it inevitably "must be" and cannot be changed.[1] The function-

[1] A comparable sequence can be found in Parsons' (1942) taking up the observation that the nuclear family has tended to replace the extended family in American society. This observation had been made earlier by Simmel and Park, but Parsons exaggerated it, ignored countertrends, and sought to show why the trend

188

alists' assumption that "whatever is, must be" merely ruins an initially valid observation by exaggerating it and denying any possibility of countertrends by declaring its inevitability.

Two approaches have dominated research in social gerontology. One seeks to interpret the facts of aging in a historical-cultural context; the basic fact and factual trends of American society are considered to be the matrix for the social processes of aging. The second theoretical orientation is the interactionist, which seeks to interpret the facts of aging in terms of the interactions among the aging themselves

was inevitable. Since then, a spate of research articles have demonstrated factually that the trend never existed or has been reversed.

and between the aging and others in the society. Cultural values and meanings are the most important elements in these interactions, and these are never assumed to be universal or unchanging. The neat, integrated "systems" of the functionalists may appeal to the esthetic sense of readers, but it seems to us that the facts of social life, in this case of the aging, are too complicated and varied to be encompassed in any notion of equilibrium. Cultural history and human interactions, organizing concepts which have thus far dominated research in gerontology, are better guideposts.

PART IV
THE SOCIAL PSYCHOLOGY OF HEALTH

The social psychology of health is not only a topic of major interest to social scientists generally, but it poses a particularly salient group of problems with regard to middle-aged and older people, of whom a high proportion suffer from one or more chronic health conditions. While the topic cannot be done justice in the present volume, this group of papers illustrates some of the complex issues involved.

The first paper on attitudes toward menopause is based on interviews and questionnaire data gathered from several hundred women aged 21 to 65. Consistent differences appeared between younger and older subgroups (between those women who had and those who had not yet experienced the changes of the climacterium), with the older groups having generally more favorable attitudes than the younger and with the older attributing less significance to the menopause than did the younger.

In the paper by Rosen and Bibring, an analysis of the psychological reactions of male patients to a heart attack, the authors show that age is a significant variable; 50-year-olds react typically with overt depression, while 30-year-olds are "overly cheerful" and 60-year-olds show constrained cheerful affect. Social class differences are also systematically related to the ways in which men rationalize about and adapt to illness, especially to a subsequent rather than a first heart attack. The authors draw on other studies of personality change in discussing how a heart attack may have differing implications for men at different stages of the life cycle.

The data reported in the next paper by Shanas *et al.* are based on national samples of persons aged 65 and over in each of three countries, United States, Britain, and Denmark. In highlighting cultural differences in attitudes, the paper shows the importance of social and psychological factors in self-evaluation of health. The proportion of health optimists, realists, and pessimists is shown to vary from one country to the next; and not only is there a relationship between self-evaluation of health and degree of functional incapacity, but also between evaluations of health and other subjective attitudes such as loneliness and alienation.

(Health factors and attitudes toward health are treated also in the paper by Masters and Johnson on sexual behavior, in Part V; and in the paper, "Awareness of Middle Age," in Part II.)

In the paper by Lowenthal the focus is upon mental rather than physical health. The author presents carefully-analyzed data on a large sample of old people hospitalized for mental illness compared with a community sample, and assesses the prevalent assumption that social isolation is an important correlate (if not cause) of mental illness. She differentiates four different patterns of isolation, and concludes that lifelong extreme isolation (or alienation) is not necessarily conducive to the development of the kinds of mental disorder that bring persons to the psychiatric ward in their old age. Late-developing isolation may be more of a consequence than a cause of mental illness. The author suggests also that physical illness may be the critical antecedent to both the isolation and the mental illness. (Other papers in this book which bear upon the relations of social participation and mental health include the two papers by Havighurst, Neugarten and Tobin in Part III; that by Reichard, Livson and Petersen also in

Part III; and the other paper by Lowenthal in Part VII.

The paper by Butler introduces a different issue regarding the relations of age, health, and social-psychological factors. The author first summarizes the findings from one of the major multidisciplinary studies of aging thus far undertaken, a study aimed at the fundamental problem of differentiating the effects of disease from the effects of aging, and reported at greater length in the book, *Human Aging* (Birren, Butler, Perlin, Yarrow and Greenhouse, 1963). That study provided carefully-analyzed data in support of the view that aging and disease represent separable phenomena, and that much of what has been attributed to the first should more properly be attributed to the second; or, in other words, that health is more significant in determining a wide variety of functions than is chronological age. In the present paper, Butler discusses briefly the relations of age and health to personality variables and to sociocultural variables. The paper indirectly raises the same question (although from a different perspective) that is posed in the paper by Schaie in the Appendix and in the paper by Lieberman in Part IX; namely, whether or not chronological age should be used as an index of aging, a question which is obviously of great import in the consideration of research strategies in this field.

21

BERNICE L. NEUGARTEN, VIVIAN WOOD, RUTH J. KRAINES,
and BARBARA LOOMIS

WOMEN'S ATTITUDES TOWARD THE MENOPAUSE

The menopause, like puberty or pregnancy, is generally regarded as a significant event in a woman's life; one that is known to reflect profound endocrine and somatic changes; and one that presumably involves psychological and social concomitants as well. Although there is a large medical and biological literature regarding the climacterium[1], there are few psychological studies available, except those reporting symptomology or those based on observations of women who were receiving medical or psychiatric treatment. Even the theories regarding the psychological effects of the climacterium are based largely upon observations of clinicians—psychoanalytic case studies, psychiatric investigations of climacteric psychoses, and observations of their middle-aged patients made by gynecologists and other physicians (*August*, 1956; *Barnacle*, 1949; *Deutsch*, 1945; *Fessler*, 1950; *Hoskins*, 1944; *Ross*, 1951; *Sicher*, 1949).

Unlike the case with puberty or pregnancy, developmental psychologists have not yet turned their attention to the

Abridged from *Vita Humana*, 6 (1963): 140–51, with the permission of the publisher, S. Karger, Basel/New York.

This research was facilitated by USPHS Grant no. M-3972.

[1] *Menopause* and *climacterium* (as well as the more popular term, *the change of life*) are often used interchangeably in the literature. In more accurate terms, *menopause* refers to the cessation of the menses; and *climacterium* to the involution of the ovary and the various processes, including menopause, associated with this involution.

menopause, and to the possible relationships, whether antecedent or consequent, between biological, psychological, and social variables. [A paper by the psychoanalyst *Therese Benedek* (1952) is a notable exception.] Neither is there a body of anthropological or sociological literature that describes the prevailing cultural or social attitudes to be found in America or other Western societies regarding the menopause.

As preliminary to a larger study of adjustment patterns in middle age, a number of exploratory interviews were gathered in which each woman was asked to assess her own menopausal status (whether she regarded herself as pre-, "in", or postclimacteric). She was then asked the basis of this assessment; what, if any, symptoms she had experienced; what her anticipations of menopause had been, and why; what she regarded as the worst and what the best aspects; and what, if any, changes in her life she attributed to the menopause.

It was soon apparent that women varied greatly in their attitudes and experiences. Some, particularly at upper-middle-class levels, vehemently assured the interviewer that the menopause was without any social or psychological import; that, indeed, the enlightened woman does not fear, nor—even if she suffers considerable physical discomfort—does she complain about the menopause.

"Why make any fuss about it?"

"I just made up my mind I'd walk right through it, and I did . . ."

"I saw women complaining, and I thought I would never be so ridiculous. I would just sit there and perspire, if I had to. At times you do feel terribly warm. I would sit and feel the water on my head, and wonder how red I looked. But I wouldn't worry about it, because it is a natural thing, and why get worried about it? I remember one time, in the kitchen, I had a terrific hot flush . . . I went to look at myself in the mirror. I didn't even look red, so I thought, 'All right . . . the next time I'll just sit there, and who will notice? And if someone notices, I won't even care . . .' "

Others confessed to considerable fear:

"I would think of my mother and the trouble she went through; and I wondered if I would come through it whole or in pieces . . ."

"I knew two women who had nervous breakdowns, and I worried about losing my mind . . ."

"I thought menopause would be the beginning of the end . . . gradual senility closing over, like the darkness . . ."

"I was afraid we couldn't have sexual relations after the menopause—and my husband thought so, too . . ."

"When I think of how I used to worry! You wish someone would tell you—but you're too embarrassed to ask anyone . . ."

Other women seemed to be repeating the advice found in women's magazines and in newspaper columns:

"I just think if a woman looks for trouble, she'll find it . . ."

"If you fill your thinking and your day with constructive things—like trying to help other people—then it seems to me nothing can enter a mind already filled . . ."

"If you keep busy, you won't think about it, and you'll be all right . . ."

Underlying this variety of attitudes were two common phenomena: first, whether they made much or made little of its importance, middle-aged women were willing, even eager, to talk about the menopause. Many volunteered the comment that they seldom talked about it with other women; that they wished for more information and more communication. Second, although many professed not to believe what they termed "old wives' tales", most women had nevertheless heard many such tales of the dangers of menopause, and could recite them easily: that menopause often results in mental breakdown; that it marks the end of a woman's sexual attractiveness as well as her sexual desires; and so on. Many women said, in this connection, that while they themselves had had neither fears nor major discomforts, they indeed knew other women who held many such irrational fears or who had suffered greatly. (The investigators interpreted such responses as indicative, at least in part, of the psychological mechanism of projection.)

THE INSTRUMENT

Following a round of preliminary interviews, a more systematic measurement of attitudes toward the menopause was undertaken. A checklist was drawn up containing statements culled from the exploratory interviews and from the literature on the subject. For example, the statement, "Women generally feel better after the menopause than they have for years," appears in a pamphlet about menopause for sale by the U.S. Government Printing Office (*U.S. Public Health Service*, 1959). "Women who have trouble with the menopause are usually those who have nothing to do with their time," is a statement made by a number of interviewees. "A woman in menopause is likely to do crazy things she herself does not understand" is a statement made by a woman describing her own behavior. Respondents were asked to check, for each statement, 1. agree strongly; 2. agree to some extent; 3. disagree somewhat; or 4. disagree strongly. Because of the projective phenomenon already mentioned, the statements were worded in terms of "other women", or "women in general" rather than "self" (see Table 2).

The checklist was then pre-tested on a sample of 50 women aged 40 to 50. Following the analysis of those responses, the instrument was revised and the number of items reduced to 35. Certain statements were eliminated because they drew stereotyped responses; others, because of overlap.

THE SAMPLES

The revised Attitudes-Toward-Menopause Checklist, hereafter referred to as the ATM, was administered as part of a lengthy interview to a sample of 100 women aged 45 to 55 on whom a variety of other data were being gathered. These 100 women, referred to here as the C or

varied from group to group, with an average of about 75% responses. From this larger pool, Groups A, B, and D were drawn.

The composition of the four samples, by age and level of education, is shown in Table 1. All the women in all four groups were married, all were mothers of one or more children and, with the exception of a few in Groups B and D, all were living with their husbands. None of these women reported major physical illness or disability.

These groups of women, although by

TABLE 1

THE SAMPLES: BY AGE AND LEVEL OF EDUCATION

Group	Number	Age	High School Graduation or Less	Percents One or More Years of College	No Information
A........	50	21–30	8	90	2
B........	52	31–44	33	50	17
C........	100	45–55	65	35	0
D........	65	56–65	54	46	0

Criterion group, had been drawn from lists of mothers or graduates from two public high schools in the Chicago metropolitan area. None of these women had had surgical or artificial menopause, and all were in relatively good health.

Once the data on the ATM had been analyzed for the Criterion group the question arose, how do women of different ages view the menopause? Accordingly, the instrument was administered to other groups of women contacted through business firms and women's clubs. Directions for filling out the ATM were usually given in group situations, and the respondents were asked to mail back the forms to the investigators along with certain identifying information (age, level of education, marital status, number and ages of children, and health status). The proportion responding

no means constituting representative samples, are biased in only one known direction: compared with the general population of American women, they are higher on level of education, for they include higher proportions of the college-educated. This is especially true of Group A and Group D.

FINDINGS

Level of Education.—When responses to the ATM were analyzed for differences between the women in each age group who had and those who had not attended college, only a few scattered differences appeared, a number attributable to chance.

As already indicated, however, the four samples of women represent relatively advantaged groups with regard to educational level. It is likely that in more heterogeneous samples educational level would emerge as a significant variable in women's attitudes toward menopause.

Age Differences.—As shown in Table 2 consistent age differences were found. Illustrated statements are ordered in the table according to the pattern that emerged from a factor analysis carried out on the responses of Group C.[2] That

analysis, although serving a purpose extraneous to the present report, provided groupings of the statements that are

[2] Responses were scored from 1 to 4; and on the matrix of intercorrelations, the principal component method of factor extraction by Jacoby and the Varimax program for rotation were used. Seven factors, accounting for 85% of the variance, emerged from that analysis, fac-

TABLE 2

ATTITUDES TOWARD MENOPAUSE: BY AGE

ILLUSTRATIVE ITEMS	PERCENTAGE WHO AGREE,[a] IN AGE GROUPS			
	A 21–30 (N = 50)	B 31–44 (N = 52)	C 45–55 (N = 100)	D 56–65 (N = 65)
I. *"Negative Affect"*:				
28. Menopause is an unpleasant experience for a woman	56	44	58	55
34. Women should expect some trouble during the menopause	60	46	59	58
33. In truth, just about every woman is depressed about the change of life	48	29	40	28
II. *"Post-Menopausal Recovery"*:				
24. Women generally feel better after the menopause then they have for years	32*	20*	68	67
27. A woman gets more confidence in herself after the change of life	12*	21*	52	42
17. After the change of life, a woman feels freer to do things for herself	16*	24*	74	65
35. Many women think menopause is the best thing that ever happened to them	14*	31	46	40
III. *"Extent of Continuity"*:				
12. Going through the menopause really does not change a woman in any important way	58*	55*	74	83
IV: *"Control of Symptoms"*:				
4. Women who have trouble with the menopause are usually those who have nothing to do with their time	58	50*	71	70
7. Women who have trouble in the menopause are those who are expecting it	48*	56*	76	63
V. *"Psychological Losses"*:				
18. Women worry about losing their minds during the menopause	28*	35	51	24*
11. A woman is concerned about how her husband will feel toward her after the menopause	58*	44	41	21*
VI. *"Unpredictability"*:				
6. A woman in menopause is apt to do crazy things she herself does not understand	40	56	53	40
10. Menopause is a mysterious thing which most women don't understand	46	46	59	46
VII. *"Sexuality"*:				
3. If the truth were really known, most women would like to have themselves a fling at this time in their lives	8*	33	32	24
19. After the menopause, a woman is more interested in sex than she was before	14*	27	35	21

[a] Subjects who checked "agree strongly" or "agree to some extent" are grouped together.

* The difference between this percentage and the percentage of Group C is significant at the 05 level or above.

meaningful also for studying age differences.

Overall inspection of the data (only partly shown in Table 2) shows first that, as anticipated, young women's patterns of attitudes toward the menopause are different from those of middle-aged women. When each group is compared with the Criterion group, the largest number of significant differences are found between Groups A and C; then between B and C.

At the same time, it appears that it is not age alone, but age and experience-with-menopause that are probably operating together. There are very few differences between Groups C and D; and relatively few between A and B. The major differences lie between the first two and the last groups—in other words, between women who have and those who have not yet experienced the changes of the climacterium. Although there is not a one-to-one correlation between chronological age and age-at-menopause, approximately 75% of the women in Group C, as well as all those in D, reported that they were presently experiencing or had already completed the "change of life". Only a few of Group B had yet entered "the period of the change".

Age differences follow a particular pattern from one cluster of statements to the next. Thus, on the first cluster, "negative affect", there are no significant differences between age groups nor between statements. In each instance, about half the women agree that the menopause is a disagreeable, depressing, troublesome, unpleasant, disturbing event; and about half the women disagree.

On the second cluster of statements, however, there are sharp age differences,

---

tors which have been named "negative affect," "post-menopausal recovery," and so on, as indicated in Table 2. Within each group of statements, the order is that of their loadings on the respective factor. It should be kept in mind that a somewhat different factor pattern might have emerged from the responses of Groups A, B, or D.

and in general, all in the same direction: middle-aged women recognize a "recovery", even some marked gains occurring once the menopause is past. The postmenopausal woman is seen as feeling better, more confident, calmer, freer than before. The majority of younger women, by contrast, are in disagreement with this view.

On the third and fourth clusters age differences, while not so sharp as on the second cluster, are numerous and are again consistent in direction: namely, middle-aged women take what may be interpreted as the more positive view, with higher proportions agreeing that the menopause creates no major discontinuity in life, and agreeing that, except for the underlying biological changes, women have a relative degree of control over their symptoms and need not inevitably have difficulties. This is essentially the view that one woman expressed by saying, "If women look for trouble, of course they find it."

Of the remainder of the statements, those that form the fifth, sixth, and seventh clusters as well as those that fit none of the clusters, age differences are scattered and inconsistent in direction, depending evidently upon the particular content and wording of each statement. It is interesting to note, for instance, that on No. 18, "Women worry about losing their minds", it is the Criterion group, Group C, which shows the highest proportion who agree.

It is also of interest that on Nos. 3 and 19, it is the youngest group who disagree most with the view that menopausal women may experience an upsurge of sexual impulse. In this connection, the interviews with Group C women, many of whom had not completed the change of life, showed a wide range of ideas about a woman's interest in sex relations after the menopause. The comments ranged from, "I would expect her to be less interested in sex, because that is something that belongs more or less to the childbearing period," to, "She might become more interested because the fear of pregnancy is gone." Many women expressed considerable uncertainty about the effects of the menopause on sexuality.

DISCUSSION

That there should be generally different views of menopause in younger and in middle-aged women is hardly a surprise. Any event is likely to have quite different significance for persons who are at different points in the life line.

One reason why fewer middle-aged as compared to younger women in this study viewed menopause as a significant event may be that loss of reproductive capacity is not an important concern of middle-aged women at either a conscious or unconscious level. In the psychological and psychiatric literature it is often stated that the end of the reproductive period —the "closing of the gates", as it has been described (Deutsch, 1945, p. 457)—evokes in most women a desire for another child. If so, women might be expected to view menopause as most significant at that time in life when the loss of reproductive capacity is imminent. Yet this was not the case in these data.

There is additional evidence on the same point from our interview data. Of the 100 women in the Criterion group, only 4, in responding to a multiple-choice question, chose, "Not being able to have more children" as the worst thing in general about the menopause. (At the same time, 26 said the worst thing was, "Not knowing what to expect"; 19 said, "The discomfort and pain"; 18 said, "It's a sign you are getting old"; 4 said, "Loss of enjoyment in sex relations"; 22 said, "None of these things"; and 7 could not answer the question.) It is true, of course, that all these women had borne children; but the same was true of all the younger women in Groups A and B. Many Group C women said, in interview, that they had raised their children and were now happy to have done, not only with menstruation and its attendant annoyances, but also with the mothering of small children.

The fact that middle-aged as frequently as younger women view the menopause as unpleasant and disturbing is not irreconcilable with their view of the menopause as an unimportant event. As one woman put it, "Yes, the change of life is an unpleasant time. No one enjoys the hot flushes, the headaches, or the nervous tension. Sometimes it's even a little frightening. But I've gone through changes before, and I can weather another one. Besides, it only a temporary condition."

Another woman joked, "It's not the pause that refreshes, it's true; but it's just a pause that depresses."

The middle-aged woman's view of the postmenopausal period as a time when she will be happier and healthier underscores the belief in the temporary nature of the unpleasant period, a belief that is reinforced perhaps by hearing postmenopausal women say, as two said to our interviewer:

"My experience has been that I've been healthier and in much better spirits since the change of life. I've been relieved of a lot of aches and pains."

"Since I have had my menopause, I have felt like a teen-ager again. I can remember my mother saying that after her menopause she really got her vigor, and I can say the same thing about myself. I'm just never tired now."

The fact that most younger women have generally more negative views is perhaps because the menopause is not only relatively far removed, and therefore relatively vague; but because, being vague, it becomes blended into the whole process of growing old, a process that is both dim and unpleasant. Perhaps it is only the middle-aged or older woman who can take a differentiated view of the menopause; and who, on the basis of experience, can, as one woman said, "separate the old wives' tales from that which is true of old wives."

22

JACQUELINE L. ROSEN and GRETE L. BIBRING

*PSYCHOLOGICAL REACTIONS OF HOSPITALIZED
MALE PATIENTS TO A HEART ATTACK: AGE
AND SOCIAL-CLASS DIFFERENCES*

Fifty male patients, 35–67 years of age, hospitalized because of heart attack, showed striking differences in their overt psychological responses to their illness. Responses ranged from frank depression to cheerfulness, from extreme anxiety to casualness, and from scrupulous cooperation with the medical regimen to active defiance. Ratings on these variables were based on systematic interview data obtained from attending nurses. Additional data were obtained through series of interviews with 20 patients and physicians. Analysis of the data suggested the importance of age and social class factors in the observed differences. The findings are discussed with reference to research on normal personality changes with age, and to reports on social class differences.

The active man who is suddenly hospitalized with a heart attack must face, besides the threat of death or the possibility of a painful or crippling chronic disease, immediate drastic changes in his pattern of living. As soon as the diagnosis of acute myocardial infarction is suspected, he is placed on a medical regimen of complete bed rest. This means that for two weeks or longer, until the greatest danger of extending damage to his heart has passed, he must remain almost immobile, allowing others to fulfill even his smallest physical needs. And yet he may feel "well" and able to do things for himself. This stringent regimen may dramatize to the patient the precariousness of his physical condition. Moreover, for many patients who are accustomed to and highly invested in being active and independent, the sudden shift to a role of helpless, passive dependency may, in itself, constitute a serious emotional threat.

The major issues that confront the hospitalized coronary patient appear to be similar, though extreme and telescoped, to the tasks that a man faces as he ages (Berezin, 1963; Cumming and Henry, 1961). It was reasoned, therefore, that the older patient, who, theoretically, has coped with increasing passivity, dependence, and bodily decline, might differ significantly in his response to the illness from either the younger patient, who has not yet faced these tasks, or the middle-aged man, who is actively struggling to master them. Moreover, it is widely known that the risk of heart disease increases with age and is the "No. 1 killer" in this country. The notion thus prevails that a "coronary" is an old man's affliction, signaling the end of the road—a stigma that might have varying implications for men at different stages of their lives. For these reasons, in the present study of the psychological responses of a group of male patients with heart disease to the acute phases of their illness, primary con-

Reprinted from *Psychosomatic Medicine*, vol. 28, no. 6 (November-December 1966). Abridged. Hoeber Medical Division of Harper & Row, Publishers. © 1966 by American Psychosomatic Society, Inc.

sideration was given to possible age-related differences.

That a patient's emotional responses to the diagnosis of heart disease are important in his treatment and prognosis is widely accepted. His reactions may limit his ability to comply with the prescribed medical regimen (Bibring, 1956). There is much evidence, also, that emotional stress, like physical exertion, may adversely affect the clinical course of the disease (Reiser *et al.*, 1954; Reiser and Bakst, 1959).

Observations made during the preliminary phase of this research revealed marked differences in patients' overt reactions to their illness and treatment, particularly in the display of depression, anxiety, and resistance to the medical regimen. These, then, were the three major variables examined in this study.

REPORTS ON PSYCHOLOGICAL REACTIONS TO HEART DISEASE

Most reports on patients' psychological reactions to heart disease are speculative or based on clinical impressions from medical or psychiatric practice, though a few recent studies stem from more systematic investigations. There is, nevertheless, wide agreement that the most frequent reactions are anxiety, depression, and denial of the illness (Bellak, 1952; Cleveland and Johnson, 1962; Dovenmuehle and Verwoerdt, 1962; Friedberg, 1956; Reiser and Bakst, 1959; Stieglitz, 1954; Weiss *et al.*, 1957). Commonly mentioned in connection with these reactions are the failure of some patients to comply with the prescribed regimen and a tendency of others, during the chronic phases of the illness, to limit themselves to the point of semi-invalidism.

Among the factors generally cited as *determining* a patient's response to his impairment are his premorbid personality structure, the severity of his illness, his relationships with his physician and family, what the illness means to him, his financial position, and whether he is able to return to work without loss of status or income (Bellak and Haselkorn, 1956; Fox *et al.*, 1954; Kaplan, 1956; Reiser, 1951; Reiser and Bakst, 1959; Stine, 1958). Although strong agreement exists, more definitive studies may refine knowledge of these issues. The work of Dovenmuehle and Verwoerdt (Dovenmuehle and Verwoerdt, 1963), for instance, brought into question the general assumption of an unqualified close relationship between depression and severity of illness, suggesting that only after the first three years is a mild cardiac condition less likely than a severe one to provoke serious depressive symptoms. Depression in their sample was also associated with lowered self-esteem, but not with other frequent concomitants of depression in psychiatric patients, such as death wishes and irritability (Dovenmuehle and Verwoerdt, 1962).

Only a few discussions in the studies have been concerned with the patient's age at onset as a potentially meaningful factor. Reiser and Bakst (1959) found that a frequent problem in "middle-aged men" is the use of previously adaptive ego defenses, such as denial, which in the context of cardiac illness may lead to open, rebellious unwillingness to adhere to a prescribed medical regimen. Dovenmuehle and Verwoerdt (1962) did compare young and old patients on the incidence of depression and found no difference, but omitted from consideration patients in their 50's, who proved to be a significant age group in the present research.

METHOD

THE SAMPLE

The sample consisted of 50 employed male patients, under 70 years of age and without known brain pathology, who were admitted to the hospital with a confirmed diagnosis of acute myocardial infarction. Thirty-three of them had had no previous diagnosis of a heart ailment; the remaining 17 had suffered prior heart attacks or had a clinical history of coronary artery disease. Thirty of the 50 consisted of all patients meeting the above criteria who were hospitalized during a 2-month period. This group was studied only indirectly, through observations of nursing personnel. The remaining 20 subjects, selected earlier as part of an intensive, longitudinal study, differed from the larger group by their active participation in research interviews, which necessitated not only their cooperation but that of their physicians as well. Refusals by physicians were minimal, however, and all patients approached for the study co-operated at least through the initial interviews. While the effects of the research itself on this group cannot be assessed, these subjects did not differ from those in the larger group on the variables studied, or on significant sample characteristics.

The age range of the over-all sample was from 35 to 67 years. All subjects, with the exception of two who held part-time jobs, were fully employed prior to their present heart attack. Twenty-nine were categorized as white-collar and 21 as blue-collar workers. (Occupation was the only index of social class available on all subjects.) All were urban dwellers. Another bias was in favor of Jewish patients—35 in all—the remainder being of Catholic or Protestant faiths. Caution is necessary, therefore, in generalizing from the results of the study prior to verification of findings in hospitals serving different ethnic groups.

Most of the subjects were in the care of private physicians, a reflection of their membership in health-insurance plans, not necessarily their financial status. Finally, 6 of the 9 patients who were separated, divorced, or widowed were past 60.

SOURCES OF DATA

The Nurses' Interviews.—The data on which the statistical part of the study was based were obtained through semistructured interviews with nurses most actively engaged in the patients' daily care. Twenty-nine nurses were interviewed, and 3 more participated in a reliability study.

The nurse's interview usually took place toward the end of the third week of the patient's hospitalization, allowing time for an ample sampling of behavior and yet preceding the usual point of hospital discharge, 3–4 weeks after the acute onset. Both open-ended and forced-choice questions were included. First, the nurse was asked for a description of the patient's personality and behavior. Then she was questioned about his symptoms, reaction to pain and to medical procedures; his moods, worries, interests, and relationship with others; how he spent his time and how he felt about going home; his sleeping habits, appetite, response to bed rest and physical care; and how he reacted to permission to increase his activities. Other questions covered the degree of the patient's emotional dependency and demandingness, special requests he made, and the most difficult aspects of caring for him. At one point the nurse was asked whether her patient had been predominantly cheerful or sad and depressed; at another, whether he had appeared to be more on the tense, anxious side, or more relaxed; in both cases the nurse was requested to explain her answer. She was also questioned as to whether he had resisted any of the limitations placed on him, and to elaborate.

Additional Interviews.—In addition to the nurses' interviews, which provided comparable data on all 50 subjects, 20 patients were interviewed in the hospital at least twice by research psychiatrists, and most of them 4 or 5 times. With few exceptions, concurrent interviews were conducted with the patients' wives or other close relatives by a psychiatrist, psychologist, or social worker. Over half of this group of subjects and their relatives were again interviewed one or more times after hospital discharge, as were the participating physicians. These interviews, most of them tape-recorded and transcribed, focused on various aspects of the patient's reactions to his illness as well as on his general personality and life circumstances, past and present.

Medical Charts.—Medical charts on all 50 patients provided information on their medical history, present illness and treatment, and basic identifying data on age, marital status, residence, religious affiliation, and occupation.

TREATMENT OF THE DATA

Two judges, using only the nurses' interview data, assigned each subject to one of two categories on three dimensions, as described below. The ratings were made independently, and one judge had no knowledge of identifying characteristics such as the subject's age or occupation. The ratings were based on overt behavior and verbalizations as described by the nurses, not on the nurses' inferences about what the patient's "real" or underlying feelings might be.

Overt Signs of Depression.—Each subject was classified either as showing "overt signs of depression" or as being "always cheerful." The first category was used for patients whose observed behavior indicated feelings of sadness, gloomy preoccupations, a sense of hopelessness, self-devaluation, self-accusation, apathy, emotional withdrawal, etc. The following are specific examples: the patient cried and wanted someone with him at all times; he talked about his father's death from a heart attack and spoke pessimistically about the future; he didn't smile or talk much but just lay there; he seemed to have no energy and wore a sad expression on his face; he said once he was ashamed and felt he no longer was the man he had thought he was; mostly he was pretty cheerful and friendly, but sometimes you saw tears in his eyes and he didn't want to talk.

Thus, the "depressed" category included not only those few patients who were consistently and deeply depressed

but, for statistical reasons, also those who displayed this affect only at times.

The "always cheerful" category was reserved for patients whose overt behavior ranged from "pleasantly outgoing" to euphoric, but excluded any patients who, though rated by the nurse as "predominantly cheerful," were described anywhere in the interview as displaying periods of overt depression.

Representative statements from the nurses for this second category were: he amused you and tried to make you laugh; he was friendly and always complimentary to the staff; he was considerate of his roommate and really seemed to like people; he was friendly, outgoing, and interested in what was going on outside himself; he was jovial and cheerful all the time, but he must have been depressed underneath, even though he never showed it.

Overt Signs of Anxiety.—Unlike the category of depression, classifications of anxiety were based on the patient's *predominant* state, since even the most "relaxed" patient became anxious during periods of pain or on the rare introduction of a cardiac monitor with its audible recording of the heartbeat.

The following kinds of statements were judged as substantiating a nurse's assessment of her patient as "predominantly tense and anxious": he constantly asked questions about his illness and was afraid to move; he needed a lot of reassurance, was extremely fidgety, and talked incessantly; he called for the nurses frequently and talked about his fears of having a recurrence and his worries about going home; he seemed nervous all the time, his hands quivered when his pulse was taken, his speech was rapid, and his eye movements were quick and darting.

Typical descriptions considered as valid evidence for a nurse's evaluation of her patient as "predominantly relaxed" were: he never got excited, always seemed to accept things; he never rushed the nurses or got annoyed with them, and seemed to enjoy hospital routine; he had a relaxed, kidding attitude and never questioned medical procedures; he liked to nap and read and watch television and play cards; he was easygoing and nothing seemed to bother him except that first day he came in when he was having a lot of pain.

Cooperation with the Medical Regimen.—Since complete bed rest was required of all subjects, patients who got out of bed before permission was granted were classified "uncooperative." In addition, any patient who remained in bed but carried out activities which he knew were specifically against orders at that time (for example, shaving himself) was also categorized as uncooperative. Examples of such behavior were: he used to get up and go to the bathroom when he wasn't supposed to; he resisted all limitations—bed rest, feeding, hospital routine, etc.; he sneaked down to the coffee shop, refused to take off his suit and tie, and had wild drinking sprees; he would feed or shave himself if not watched.

All patients who cooperated fully with their prescribed regimens constituted the second category on this dimension.

Reliability of Measures.—The reliability of the nurses' interviews was checked by administering the form to a second nurse who had participated in the care of each of 7 subjects. There was perfect agreement between the two sets of ratings on each subject. With respect to the total sample of 50 subjects, the agreement between judges on each of the three major variables was .94 or greater.

Course of Medical Recovery.—Finally, each patient was rated on the course of his recovery. On the basis of medical records, nurses' interviews, and conferences with physicians, the patient was grossly classified as having either a relatively uneventful course or a difficult one. He was classified as having a "difficult course" in the presence of factors such as the following, an "uneventful" one in their absence: periodic occurrence of severe pain following the acute episode; symptoms or complications necessitating the extended use of oxygen, the introduc-

tion of a cardiac monitor or other nonroutine procedures observable to the patient; a medical setback requiring the withdrawal of permission for increased activity or significant delays in scheduled activities or hospital discharge date.

It is important to note that all subjects received varying amounts of sedatives or tranquilizers during hospitalization. Because of individual differences in response to drugs, however, the possible effects of

TABLE 1

PATIENT'S AGE AT ONSET OF PRESENT HEART ATTACK AND OVERT SIGNS OF DEPRESSION DURING HOSPITALIZATION

(N = 50)*

Age at Onset	Overtly Depressed	Always Cheerful
39 and under....	0	7
40–49..........	3	3
50–59..........	15	7
60 and over.....	3	12

* The two groups under 50 years of age were combined for purposes of statistical analysis. $\chi^2 = 11.24$; df 2; $p < .01$.

this variable on the emotional and behavioral ratings could not be measured. Moreover, since dosage was increased in the presence of pain, the extent to which the drug variable might blur an association between "course of medical recovery" and the behavioral variables is also unknown.

RESULTS

AGE-RELATED DIFFERENCES

Depression.—Table 1 shows that the incidence of overt depression was significantly higher in the 50-year-olds than in younger and older subjects. Actually, the incidence was highest in the 50- to 55-year range, in which 13 of 15 subjects were rated "depressed."

None of the background factors other than age accounted for the observed differences.

Cooperation with the Medical Regimen.—Only the age factor differentiated reliability between cooperative and uncooperative subjects, the latter predominating among those under 60 years of age, as shown in Table 2.

Manifest Anxiety.—In contrast to the above, no significant association was found between age and manifest anxiety (Table 3).

TABLE 2

PATIENT'S AGE AT ONSET OF PRESENT HEART ATTACK AND CO-OPERATION WITH MEDICAL REGIMEN DURING HOSPITALIZATION

(N = 50)*

Age at Onset	Unco-operative	Co-operative
39 and under....	4	3
40–49..........	2	4
50–59..........	9	13
60 and over.....	2	13

* The three groups under 60 years of age were combined for purposes of statistical analysis. $\chi^2 = 4.14$; df 1; $P < .05$.

Qualitative Differences.—The *30-year-olds* were consistently described by the nurses as being "overly cheerful" or "very jovial" and even "manic." They were seen as flirtatious and seductive and liking to joke around with the personnel. Those who resisted the medical regimen did so in a lighthearted manner. Whether verbal or motor, their communications centered on their masculine strength, independence, and sexual attractiveness.

The small group of *40-year-olds* was characterized by no specific pattern and thus will be omitted from the discussion on age-related findings.

The *50-year-olds*, in contrast to other age groups, were characterized by the nurses as "hard to get to know" because they were "hostile" or "withdrawn." Within this age range, those patients in their *middle* 50's were described as the most depressed, "agitated," "rude," and flagrantly defiant of their regimens.

Finally, the *60-year-olds* were predominantly "sweet and fatherly," "kind and easy-going," and "always with something nice to say." Even the two patients who resisted their regimens did so in minor ways.

SOCIAL CLASS AND PRIOR CARDIAC STATUS

A preliminary analysis of the relationship between anxiety and prior cardiac status suggested that patients suffering a second or subsequent cardiac episode were more frequently classified as anxious than those with a first attack. It was found, however, that the difference between the two "prior cardiac status" groups could be

TABLE 3

PATIENT'S AGE AT ONSET OF PRESENT HEART ATTACK AND MANIFEST ANXIETY DURING HOSPITALIZATION

(N = 50)*

Age at Onset	Anxious and Tense	Predominantly Relaxed
39 and under....	4	3
40–49..........	3	3
50–59..........	14	8
60 and over.....	7	8

* The two groups under 50 years of age were combined for purposes of statistical analysis. $\chi^2 = .93$; df 2; P = N.S.

accounted for by the relative absence of overt anxiety in blue-collar workers with a first heart attack, as shown in Table 4. As with the factor of age, neither religious affiliation nor course of medical recovery was significantly related to manifest anxiety.

RELATIONSHIPS AMONG THE BEHAVIORAL VARIABLES

What first appeared to be a positive relationship between manifest anxiety and depression was accounted for chiefly by the coincidence of these affects in the 50-year-olds with a clinical history of heart disease and did not hold for the first heart attack group. Nor was "co-operation with the medical regimen" significantly linked with either of these variables.

DISCUSSION

AGE-RELATED DIFFERENCES

The over-all hypothesis that age is an important variable in the psychological reactions of male patients to the acute phases of coronary artery disease gains support from the findings on depression and cooperation with the medical regimen. However, that men in their 50's would respond with more overt depression than younger or older patients was not specifically predicted. Clues to the variations that were observed are provided by psychological studies of the normal aging process in our society.

To oversimplify greatly, such studies (Cumming and Henry, 1961; Gurin *et al.*, 1960; Gutmann, 1964; Gutmann *et al.*, 1959; Lubin, 1964; Neugarten and Gutmann, 1958; Rosen and Neugarten, 1960) indicate that young men are highly invested in being active and autonomous, stressing their virility and external achievement. Men past 60, on the other hand, seem to have moved to a passive, dependent, compliant position, and to have resolved, at least partially, their conflicts about doing so, emphasizing instead the importance of being kind and moral. Hence the older man may most readily accept the limitations imposed by his illness, perhaps even having anticipated such illness as a part of aging. But so alien to the young patient is the helpless, dependent role, and so unusual is the diagnosis for his stage in life that he may take the longest time to accept and integrate the seriousness of his illness, the first step being adamant denial.

On the other hand, men in their 50's appear to encounter a period of crisis (Peck and Berkowitz, 1964), reminiscent of adolescence (Josselyn, 1952), in which there is open conflict over the shift from the active orientation of youth to the passive position of later years (Gutmann *et al.*, 1959). These men still cling to achievement-autonomy goals, feeling they must

push on; yet they have begun to doubt their ability to reach these goals, and while some are no longer certain that the rewards of striving are so desirable, they are reluctant to retreat from the struggle. There is evidence that the critical turning point may come at mid-decade, when the involutional melancholias characteristically occur in males (Ewalt *et al.*, 1957), and

TABLE 4

INCIDENCE OF MANIFEST ANXIETY IN HOSPITALIZED WHITE-COLLAR AND BLUE-COLLAR PATIENTS WITH FIRST AND WITH SUBSEQUENT HEART ATTACKS*

	Anxious and Tense	Predominantly Relaxed
First attack		
White-collar.......	12	7
Blue-collar.........	8	11
Subsequent attack		
White-collar.......	9	2
Blue-collar.........	4	2

* Statistical analyses of the data in this table yield the following:
1. Total first-attack and total subsequent-attack groups: $\chi^2 = 4.45$; df 1; $P < .05$; ($N = 50$).
2. First-attack white-collar and first-attack blue-collar groups: $\chi^2 = 5.78$; df 1; $P < .02$; ($N = 33$).
3. Subsequent-attack white-collar and subsequent-attack blue-collar groups (Fisher exact probability test [Siegel, 1956]): $P = N.S.$; ($N = 17$).
4. First-attack white-collar and total subsequent-attack groups: $\chi^2 = .76$; df 1; $P = N.S.$; ($N = 36$).
5. First-attack blue-collar and total subsequent-attack groups: $\chi^2 = 9.11$; df 1; $P < .01$. ($N = 31$).

after which (according to the published tabular data of Gutmann *et al.*, 1959 [Cumming and Henry, 1961]) there appears to be wider acceptance of passive wishes.

Since the heart attack theoretically accentuates the very issues with which he has been actively struggling, the 50-year-old must be especially vulnerable to its psychological impact. With self-doubts having already developed, this patient cannot easily deny that his illness may preclude fulfillment of his goals, and in fact his doubts may be confirmed. Moreover, the immediate demands for passivity and dependence concretely represent the position toward which advancing age has begun to propel him, but which he is not yet prepared to accept. Thus the heart attack may assault most drastically the self-esteem of the man in his 50's and render him depressed (Bibring, 1953). At the same time, perhaps especially if he is at the critical turning point just described, he may rebel against his loss of autonomy by belligerent defiance of the medical regimen. But his very act of defiance, in its self-destructiveness, may betray, like depression itself, a loss of hope.

SOCIAL CLASS AND PRIOR CARDIAC STATUS

Statistical analysis revealed that in patients with a first heart attack, the display of anxiety was more frequent in white-collar than in blue-collar workers. Do other sources of data from the present study offer support of these unexpected statistical relationships? Is there corroborating evidence from other investigations? What is the rationale for the blurring of such differences at the point of a second heart attack? It is with these questions that the remaining discussion is concerned.

Anxiety is the individual's response to perceived danger (Bibring, 1953; Freud, 1959; Fromm-Reichman, 1960; Riezler, 1960). His assessment of the danger and of his ability to overcome the threat determines the degree of anxiety. When the nature of the threat is uncertain and the ways of conquering it are unknown, anxiety is greatest.

Uncertainty is the hallmark of coronary artery disease. How the patients subjectively coped with this uncertainty was a major focus of investigation of the subsample of 20 men interviewed by research psychiatrists. The patients were asked, for instance, about their theories of causation in heart disease and what factors they thought were responsible for their own heart attacks. They were also asked what they thought could be done to prevent subsequent episodes and whether this was possible for them as individuals.

Striking variations with socioeconomic background appeared both in response to these questions and in the patients' appraisals of and overt reactions to their medical management.

First Heart Attack: the White-Collar Workers.—A central concern of the white-collar workers was that the future course of the disease might be beyond human control.

A young businessman expressed this doubt in regard to a second attack as follows: "I've thought about it, and the answer depends on whether this is really something which is within one's control. If it isn't then these things are liable to happen again."

These patients, familiar with the extensive reports on heart disease in lay publications, had become aware of the possible role of emotions in the etiology of the illness. Consistently they stated that their emotions might have contributed in important ways to their heart attack and expressed doubt about their ability to change. The following remarks exemplify these concerns: "I've been the kind of person to let profits ride, you know, and not to cash them. I won't do this any more. I mean, I'll try. It's difficult for me to sit here and say for sure exactly what will turn out." At least four of them were so concerned that they sought psychiatric help.

These patients knew also about contradictory theories of prevention and treatment, and were especially sensitive to and worried about the meaning of the differences between their medical regimen and that of other coronary patients. They were suspicious, too, of reassurances about their physical condition that appeared inconsistent with the strict limitations placed on their activity.

A physician said of one of the patients in this group, for instance: "He read a good deal about heart attacks while he was in the hospital. He asked everyone under the sun who had had a heart attack what medicines they were taking, and questioned me, 'Why aren't I getting the same those people are?'"

A professional man said that his cousin had been allowed to sit up in bed ten days after his heart attack and in a chair on the fifteenth day: "I'm on my seventeenth day now and am not allowed to sit up yet. I get suspicious. . . . Perhaps I had it harder than he had it."

A businessman concerned that he was not allowed to resume activities at the same rate as other coronary patients said of his physician: "Well, he told me that I haven't really seriously hurt my heart. There is really no damage. But he doesn't even allow me to feed myself. Well, that's his orders. He goes by the book. Other doctors may be different."

Their anxiety was magnified when these patients perceived differences in physicians' opinions regarding their condition. A salesman, for instance, had the impression that the house staff thought his doctor was sending him home too soon. Laughing half-heartedly, he concluded, "Perhaps my doctor is more competent and feels he knows more about it."

Many expressed directly their opinion that their physicians were not "squaring" with them. One patient remarked, "He turns his back on his patients; he doesn't seem to want to talk to them." Another simply said, "They never tell you anything, you know."

Some felt infantilized and expressed their resentment and anxiety in childlike ways, as in the case of another professional man who had read that his medication was used in experiments to kill rats by bleeding them to death. One day, he reported, he frightened his doctor by pretending to have extracted his own tooth.

But even when the physician is fully trusted and goes out of his way to demonstrate to a patient that he is making excellent progress, the white-collar worker's doubts may persist.

This was the case with a patient in a profession allied to medicine, who had a strong family history of coronary artery disease. His physician not only showed him the promising daily laboratory reports and explained his choice of medical regimen in detail, but brought him scientific studies to disprove the patient's conviction that because of hereditary factors he was doomed. Even so, the patient remained in dread of complications and frequently rang for the nurses to test how long it would take them to reach him in case of crisis. Once when they were delayed by an emergency down the hall, his anxiety mounted to panic: "What if there were two emergencies at once!"

For the white-collar worker, then, denial of the essential uncertainty of coronary artery disease is almost impossible. As one patient put it: "Even the doctor doesn't know when a person is going to have a heart attack. It's been proven where a patient has gone to his physician and had an electrocardiogram, and examined perfectly well. Then he goes home and drops dead."

This relatively knowledgeable and skeptical group of patients may constitute a special source of frustration and anxiety for hospital personnel. The white-collar worker constantly confronts them with their own uncertainties about coronary artery disease, taxing their ingenuity, to provide reassurance in the face of their own doubts. Especially in younger personnel, this patient may generate a conflict between the wish to offer support and the fear of being dishonest. Thus perplexed, the inexperienced doctor or nurse may evade questions, offer abundant stock reassurance, or divulge his knowledge with untimely, pessimistic frankness.

Hence the white-collar worker, by the very ways in which he attempts to diminish his anxieties, unwittingly creates an atmosphere in which uncertainties are fostered.

First Heart Attack: the Blue-Collar Workers.—In contrast to the white-collar patients, the blue-collar patients tended to give concrete and definitive theories of causation and prevention. Consistently, these patients implicated one or two physical factors (never emotional) which they did not seem eager to question. Whatever their underlying fears may have been, they expressed confidence that they could avoid another heart attack.

One patient, for instance, when told by his doctor to lose weight, concluded that obesity had caused his heart attack and another one could be avoided by dieting. Another patient, upon learning that he was receiving medication to thin his blood, said that his attack occurred because his blood had been too thick and had clotted. He further stated that the anticoagulant drug had dissolved the clot, leaving no residual damage, and that it would not only prevent another attack but add 20 years to his life. His doctor told him that he would be as good as new, and, in fact, he saw himself as rejuvenated.

A third member of this group, whose heart attack occurred while he was working in intense heat, discovered a newspaper article linking high temperatures with heart attacks. Accordingly, he requested and obtained a job transfer within his company which would remove him from the pathogenic conditions, and he felt that his major problem was over.

The blue-collar worker focused his major concern on his work. If he was assured that he would still have a job of equal status and pay, his anxiety receded. He appeared to accept the authority of his physician and did not ask for the rationale of his treatment. Hence, these patients did not create in the hospital staff the kinds of conflicts that the white-collar workers did by their anxious and watchful curiosity. In fact, they appeared to gain support from the environment for their attempts to deny the uncertainties surrounding them.

Studies on Social Class Differences.— Although there have been no published studies directly comparable to the present one, other investigators using various indexes of social class have described characteristic differences that are consistent with the present findings. These include contrasts between middle-class (roughly comparable to the white-collar workers) and lower-class persons. The former are described as: accustomed to thinking and classifying abstractly rather than in concrete and particularistic terms (Schatzman and Strauss, 1955); employed in occupations requiring more self-direction rather than acceptance of authoritarian rules (Kohn, 1964); more sensitive to communications from others and thinking more in terms of motivation for behavior (Schatzman and Strauss, 1955); more susceptible to psychological anxiety (Gurin et al., 1960) in comparison to the denial of psychic pain which appears to be a mechanism linked with lower-class status (Hollingshead and Redlich, 1958).

These studies support the conclusion that the variations in overt anxiety found in the present sample could reasonably be linked with social-class differences. However, it should be emphasized that the use of occupational status as the sole indicator of a patient's position in the social-class structure in the present study was dictated by lack of consistent information on other relevant variables. In view of the differences observed between the white-collar and blue-collar patients and the strong relationship that exists between occupation and educational level (Kahl, 1957), it is likely that the latter variable may prove the more powerful single predictor of anxiety in this area of inquiry. The higher levels of education enjoyed by middle-class people make possible a degree of internal scrutiny that is difficult to achieve in the absence of skills in dealing with the abstract that college training sometimes provides (Kohn, 1964). Moreover, the ideology of higher education, which emphasizes openness to knowledge and search for complicated cause-effect relationships, appeared potent in the development and persistence of anxiety in those white-collar subjects in this research who were known to have advanced academic degrees.

The Second Heart Attack.—At the

point of a second attack, the blue-collar worker seems to join the white-collar patient in his anxiety and sense of uncertainty. No longer can he deny the possibility of a recurrence. It *can* happen again because it has now happened twice. In one dramatic case, a blue-collar worker who had cracked jokes and seemed totally unworried during his first stay was described by his nurse as returning after a second attack, some two months later, silent and paralyzed with fear.

The sudden crumbling of a patient's defense against anxiety when stricken for a second time appears to reflect not only a loss of faith in preventive measures but an emotional investment in the heart itself, developed since his first attack. If he followed his medical regimen after leaving the hospital, he found that his heart almost literally directed his life, especially if he was placed on anticoagulants, with the necessity for frequent laboratory tests, changes in dosages, and warnings to avoid minor cuts and bruises. With knowledge of this continuing medical concern, even the patient who initially most denies impairment must begin to question his recovery, though his worry may be disguised.

In follow-up studies 2–3 months after the first attack, some patients described twinges in the chest—which they hastened to attribute to "a little indigestion." Even those who ignored restrictions seem relieved when they suffered no ill effects. For example, the patient who pre-viously maintained that anticoagulants had rejuvenated him, proudly announced that he had made it safely up seven flights of stairs when an elevator broke down. In effect, the victim of a heart attack gradually becomes "educated" in the uncertainties of his illness, and hence more vulnerable to anxiety in a subsequent episode.

QUESTIONS FOR FURTHER RESEARCH

Are the trends suggested by the present study, assuming replication, specific to a heart attack, or do similar differences occur in other major illnesses? Do the observed age-related responses persist in the chronic phases of heart disease? Are there, on the other hand, uniform, age-related shifts in affect and behavior? Or are the age-related issues at their sharpest at point of acute onset and later blurred by the passage of time and the patient's return to a more active life in the community, so that other factors—medical, situational, and personal—become more important in his response to the illness?

Research in these directions might extend and refine current psychological theories of illness and of aging as well, clarifying how the aging process both affects and is affected by the patient's psychological responses to this major disease of the middle and later years.

23

ETHEL SHANAS, PETER TOWNSEND, DOROTHY WEDDERBURN,
HENNIG FRIIS, POUL MILHØJ, and JAN STEHOUWER

THE PSYCHOLOGY OF HEALTH

Health has its subjective as well as its objective aspects. The physician makes an assessment of the health of a patient based on the presence of pathology; the patient, however, evaluates his health in his own way. The two evaluations, that of the doctor and that of the patient, sometimes agree; sometimes they do not. An individual's assessment of his health in old age, as in youth and in middle age, is based upon various factors, some of which may be quite separate from medically verified conditions. Some old people with major or minor impairments think that they are well; other old people with similar complaints think that they are sick.

This idiosyncratic self-assessment of health can be illustrated by the cases of three old people in the United States. Mrs. Robinson, Mrs. Slayton, and Mrs. Igoe are all widows in their 80's. Mrs. Robinson and Mrs. Slayton are both quite feeble, yet Mrs. Robinson says her health is poor and Mrs. Slayton says her health is good. Mrs. Igoe, on the contrary, seems physically well, yet she says her health is poor.

Mrs. Robinson is 81 years old. She

Abridged and adapted from Ethel Shanas *et al.*, *Old People in Three Industrial Societies* (London and New York: Atherton Press, 1968). Reprinted by permission of the publishers. Copyright 1968, Atherton Press, New York. All rights reserved.

The material in this paper comes from a cross-national study based on national samples of persons aged 65 and over in the United States, Britain, and Denmark. An earlier study particularly relevant to this topic is reported in Ethel Shanas, *The Health of Older People* (Cambridge, Mass.: Harvard University Press, 1962).

shares a home with two divorced daughters, both in their 50's. She reports difficulty with each of the tasks that make up the index of capacity. She says she often feels as though she is going to fall "flat on my face;" she has difficulty in seeing; she has gall bladder trouble and arthritis. Mrs. Robinson was ill in bed during the last year, and saw the doctor during the last month. Although Mrs. Robinson says that her health is "poor," on the whole she considers her health to be about the same as the health of other people her age.

Mrs. Slayton is also an 80-year-old widow. She lives alone. She is hard of hearing, badly crippled by arthritis, and reports that she has difficulty in going out of doors, washing and bathing, dressing, and putting on her shoes. She often feels as though she is about to fall. Mrs. Slayton says that she cannot walk stairs at all and that a neighbour has to help her dress. The housework is done by her daughters, who live about ten minutes' distance. Despite her impairments, Mrs. Slayton says that her health is good for her age. She spent no time in bed during the past year and has not seen the doctor for several months. In fact, Mrs. Slayton says that her health is better than the health of most people her age.

Mrs. Igoe is 82 years old, a widow, and like Mrs. Slayton she lives alone. Mrs. Igoe can get about indoors and out. She reports some difficulty in walking stairs, but otherwise reports no physical impairments. She says that she can and does do heavy household tasks like washing windows and cleaning floors. Mrs. Igoe was ill in bed during the past year, and her daughter who lives nearby came in to take care of her. Mrs. Igoe sees the doctor every month. She considers her health to be poor, but about the same as the health of other people her age.

Mrs. Robinson is a health realist; Mrs. Slayton, a health optimist; and Mrs. Igoe, a health pessimist.[1]

The problems inherent in interpreta-

health. In a summary report, the investigator states:

"Fewer people . . . regarded themselves as strong than were given the evaluation 'almost well.' On the other hand, the doctors classed as 'ill' and 'very ill' more people than placed themselves in these cat-

TABLE 1

SELF-EVALUATION OF HEALTH OF PERSONS AGED 65 AND OVER, BY AGE AND SEX

(Percentage Distribution)

SELF-EVALUATION OF HEALTH	MEN						WOMEN						ALL					
	65–66	67–69	70–74	75–79	80 and Over	All	65–66	67–69	70–74	75–79	80 and Over	All	65–66	67–69	70–74	75–79	80 and Over	All
Denmark:																		
Good.....	52	55	56	55	62	56	55	50	48	46	47	49	53	52	52	51	54	52
Fair......	30	31	29	31	22	29	35	33	35	36	33	35	33	32	32	34	28	32
Poor.....	18	14	15	13	16	15	10	17	17	18	20	16	14	15	16	15	18	16
Total...	100	100	100	100	100	100	100	100	100	100	100	100	100	100	100	100	100	100
N=[a]....	184	262	316	225	156	1,143	218	269	396	251	166	1,300	402	531	712	476	322	2,443
Britain:																		
Good.....	61	62	59	61	62	61	57	58	53	48	55	54	59	60	55	54	58	57
Fair......	26	30	27	26	25	27	28	29	31	37	30	31	27	29	29	32	28	29
Poor.....	13	8	14	12	13	12	15	13	16	15	15	15	14	11	16	14	14	14
Total...	100	100	100	100	100	100	100	100	100	100	100	100	100	100	100	100	100	100
N=[a]....	164	226	286	201	123	1,000	211	285	436	291	265	1,488	375	511	722	492	388	2,488
United States:																		
Good.....	54	56	59	47	51	55	58	48	51	44	52	51	56	51	54	46	52	52
Fair......	28	24	26	34	32	28	27	34	31	34	27	31	28	30	29	34	29	30
Poor....	17	20	15	19	17	17	15	18	18	22	21	18	16	19	17	21	19	18
Total...	100	100	100	100	100	100	100	100	100	100	100	100	100	100	100	100	100	100
N=[a]....	176	229	346	182	146	1,079	205	303	423	226	191	1,361[b]	381	532	769	408	337	2,440[b]

[a] Detailed information on non-response is not given in this or subsequent tables if 98 percent or more of all eligible respondents have answered the question.

[b] Thirteen women of unknown age are included in this distribution.

tion or evaluation of the health status of old people and of the self-assessment that old people make of their health are emphasized in a Soviet study of some 18,000 persons aged 80 and over. In this study old people were examined by physicians who then made an assessment of their health status. At the same time, each old person was asked to describe his own

[1] These terms are adapted from the studies of self-assessment of health made by George L. Maddox and others at Duke University. See Maddox, 1964.

egories. Some of the old people did not know they were suffering from serious diseases" (Sachuk, 1963, p. 2).

SELF-EVALUATION OF HEALTH

The majority of old people in Denmark, Britain, and the United States say that they are in good health for their age. There is no clear-cut relationship among old people in any of the three countries between advances in age and either an increase or a decline in the proportion of old persons who feel that their health is good. In each country, more old men than old women are likely to be optimistic about their health. And, finally, old people in Britain, both men and women, are more likely than old people in either Denmark or the United States to say that their health is good.

There is no marked decline with age in the proportion of old people who feel that their health is good. About the same proportion of persons in every age category say their health is good. Indeed, persons over 80 still living at home tend to make more optimistic evaluations of their health than those in the immediately younger age group, that is, those aged 75 to 79.

Men are more likely than women to say their health is good.[2] This finding was expected, since men report less incapacity than women. This difference in health attitudes is consistent for all age groups in both Denmark and Britain, except for the years immediately following retirement. In Denmark, as in the United States (but not in Britain, however), in the years just after 65 men are more likely than women to say their health is poor. Once the age of 70 is reached, however, the general pattern reasserts itself. Men in Denmark and in the United States (as in Britain) are more likely than women to say their health is good, and less likely than women to say their health is poor.

Whether or not an old person says his

[2] Peter Townsend reports a number of extremely frail institutionalized old people who continued to describe their health as good. This may be a function of the reference group they were using for self-comparison, or it may simply be a clinging to another status, that of the "well." Self-assessment or evaluation of health seems to have a major role in determining the behavior of the elderly. In a study of mentally disturbed old people the single item most clearly related to the eventual psychiatric diagnosis was the answer to the question "How is your health?" See Kay and Roth, 1961, p. 306.

health is good or poor is related to his degree of incapacity. This will be demonstrated shortly. It is also related to the culture or style of life of the country in which he lives. Let us illustrate: in each country old men report less incapacity than old women and they are more likely than women to say their health is good. It is doubtful whether old men are actually in better health than old women. Statistics on length of life indicate that women outlive men. In Denmark, Britain, and the United States, however, men are the dominant sex. They are expected to be stronger than women, hardier, and less complaining. This cultural pattern is followed through the life span and into old age. Consequently, old men in comparison with old women are more likely to say their health is good.

The differences in national style among the three countries are evident in the self-evaluations that old people make of their health. Old people in Britain, both men and women, are generally more optimistic about their health status than old people in either Denmark or the United States. These findings were not anticipated, since the highest scores on the index of incapacity were reported from Britain, and the lowest from the United States. The British character, with its emphasis on "making do" and "keeping a stiff upper lip," is nowhere better illustrated than among the elderly. The physical changes associated with aging are accepted by the British with fewer complaints than are expressed in comparable situations by either the Danes or the Americans.

The American aged, on the other hand, are more likely than either the Danes or the British to report that their health is poor. Americans in the older age groups (those 75 and over) report substantially less incapacity than the British and somewhat less incapacity than the Danes on almost every question on the incapacity scale. Yet, compared to the Europeans the Americans appear unwilling to accept the physical limitations of age.

The self-evaluation that old people make of their health is highly correlated with their reports of restrictions on mobility, their sensory impairments, and their overall incapacity scores. In general, if an old person says his health is poor, he has some physical basis for this self-judgment.

In each country, the more mobile the old person is, the more likely he is to say his health is good. The highest proportion of persons who say their health is good is found among those who can go outdoors without restrictions; the highest proportion of persons who say their health is poor is found among the housebound.

In each country, old people with sensory impairments are more likely than other old people to say their health is poor. The two indices of sensory impairments investigated in the survey were vertigo (giddiness) and blindness. What is of special interest is the extent to which reports of vertigo, rather than blindness, are associated with a self-evaluation of "poor" health. In both the United States and Denmark, the blind person is more than twice as likely as his sighted counterpart to say that his health is poor; however, in all three countries the person who reports that he has spells of vertigo is from three to four times as likely as his less handicapped counterpart to say his health is poor.

The old person's self-rating of his health is a guide to his degree of incapacity as measured by our index.

The index of incapacity in the present survey is primarily derived from the work of Peter Townsend in Great Britain. It focuses on the ability of the old person to perform those minimal tasks which make him independent of others for personal care. (The tasks are: go outdoors, walk up and downstairs, get about the house, wash and bathe, dress and put on shoes, cut toenails.) The inability to perform any one of the six tasks in the

index without assistance from another person is an incapacitating handicap to an old person. Being unable to cut one's own toenails and the resulting foot problems may be just as great a handicap to the elderly person's daily functioning as a sensory impairment or the symptoms of a chronic disease. Scores on the index of incapacity may range from zero to 12. A score as high as 7 or more means that a person can do all of the six listed tasks only with difficulty and at least one task not at all, or that he can do some of these tasks with difficulty, and some, not at all.

For each country and for both sexes, the higher the incapacity score, the greater the proportion of old people who feel their health is poor. Interestingly enough, in all three countries there are a group of health optimists, persons with incapacity scores of 7 or more who think their health is good. The proportion of health optimists ranges from 12 percent in Denmark to 27 percent in Britain. Some proportion of those with only minimal impairments (scores of zero to two on our scale) considered themselves to be in poor health and undoubtedly should be classified as health pessimists. In each country, however, optimism about health among the elderly is more usual than pessimism.

A country-by-country comparison of the relationships of self-ratings of health and reported mobility and incapacity emphasizes once more the cultural differences between the three countries. The majority of people will not say they think their health good when they are housebound or unable to go about alone. Similarly, persons with high incapacity scores, as has been indicated, usually do not say their health is good. On the other hand, we have already remarked on the health optimism of old people in Britain: these old people, when housebound or restricted in their mobility, are almost twice as likely as either the Danes or the Americans to say their health is good. Further, a substantial proportion of old people in Britain continue to describe their health as "good" in the presence of high incapacity scores. One-fourth of the British with the highest scores on the incapacity scale, twice as great a proportion as either the Danes or the Americans, continue to rate their health as "good."

The greatest contrasts in their self-assessment of health appear between the British and the American aged. Unlike the British, who continue to describe their health as good for their age despite their ailments, the Americans, once they admit to ailments, also begin to complain about their health. Those Americans who have only minimal incapacity (scores of 2 or less) are only slightly more likely than either the British or the Danes to say their health is poor. Once the Americans have incapacity scores as high as three, however, the proportion who rate their health as poor jumps to 51 percent, compared to 29 percent for the Danes and 24 percent for the British. Old people in the United States apparently set such high standards of "wellness" for themselves that any restriction on functioning is interpreted as a sign of poor health.

The American aged, more than either the Danes or the British, tend to equate sensory impairments with poor health. Such impairments, like limitations on mobility or the inability to perform the simple physical tasks on the index of incapacity, constitute flaws in the image that old people in the United States have of themselves. The great clue of this self-image is physical independence and activity. Old people in the United States, like other Americans, want to be independent, to be able to take care of themselves. Such independence is equated with activity. Once American old people believe that their capacity for physical independence and activity is threatened, they begin to feel that their health is poor. [This] is in keeping with the analysis that Stanley King (1963) has made of illness in American society:

"One might say that illness, is, therefore, a kind of alienation in American society, alienation from a set of expectations that puts particular stress upon independent achievement. The passivity and dependence involved in illness are also characteristics of behavior which are counter to the activism of American society" (p. 112).

The sociologist Talcott Parsons has considered the role of illness in both Britain and the United States. Our reports of the health assessment of the aged verify his theoretical analysis. In the United States, with its stress on activism, to be ill is "inherently undesirable" (Parsons, 1958, p. 176). The sick person has an obligation to recover, to put himself in the care of those who are qualified to help him. He must continue to be able to achieve, or in the instance of the aged, to remain active. If the old person is not active, he feels he is in "poor health." In Britain, on the contrary, somatic illness is considered to be beyond the responsibility of the individual. It is self-control which is stressed (Parsons, 1958, pp. 184–87). The elderly in Britain, then, respond to their physical limitations by acceptance and continue to report that their health is good.

OTHER SUBJECTIVE ATTITUDES

In this survey we have asked only a few questions about subjective attitudes. We ask people whether they are lonely, whether time passes slowly for them, and how their health compares with the health of other people their age. The first two questions—those on loneliness and the passage of time—are interrelated, since both deal with the old person's feelings of alienation. Loneliness in the aged individual has been defined as ". . . a vague sense of being alone and . . . dissatisfied about the nature of his actual contacts" (Munnichs, 1964, p. 2). Like self-reports of loneliness, the conception of time as moving slowly, as hanging heavy on one's hands, the report of days being endless, also reflect the aged person's sense of detachment from other persons.[3]

In each country, those persons who say their health is poor are more likely than persons who say their health is good to report that they are often lonely. Time passes much more slowly for those in poor health than it does for those who say their health is good.

The question may be raised whether living alone, with its effect on reducing the number of social contacts of old people, is more important than illness in producing reports of loneliness or alienation. Or does self-conception of illness reshape the social environment of the old person more than actual separation from others? (Yarrow, 1963.)

Our data show that those who live alone are more likely than those who live with others to report they are often lonely. Yet in each country, when living arrangements are held constant and those in good health living alone are compared with those in fair and poor health living alone, a higher proportion of those in fair and poor health say that they are often lonely. The same finding emerges when those in good health and those in poor health living with others are compared: a substantially higher proportion of those in fair and poor health say that they are often lonely.

It is apparent that irrespective of the old person's living arrangements, self-assessment of health affects feelings of loneliness. The same pattern is demonstrated in the respondents' replies to the question "Does time pass slowly for you?" Old people living alone are more likely than other old people to say that time passes slowly for them. When living arrangements are held constant, however, those in fair or poor health are significantly more likely than those in good health to say that time is passing slowly.

Our findings on the strong relationship

*Editor's note: See the Wallach and Green article in Part IX of the present volume; they indicate that time moves more quickly for old people than for young in a "well" sample.

Ethel Shanas and others
The Psychology of Health

between health assessment and feelings of loneliness and alienation on the part of old people confirm in some measure the report of Kay and Roth investigating the psychiatric disorders of old age. They found that living arrangements were less important in association with mental illness than the actual physical disability of the old person. Kay and Roth (1961) state:

"Physical disability, including sensory loss, comes out strongly as the most important major associated factor, followed by reduction in number of personal contacts, poverty, and deviating personality traits. These factors appear to be at least as important among mentally disturbed subjects living at home as among those admitted to mental hospitals" (p. 307).[4]

To recapitulate, in all three countries, people who think they are sick are more lonely and alienated than those who think they are well. The strong relationship between self-judgment of health and the index of incapacity suggests that perhaps, over-all, it may be the feeling of poor health that brings with it feelings of loneliness.

THE PSYCHOLOGY OF HEALTH

Old people in Denmark, Britain, and the United States share certain common attitudes about their health; they also exhibit differences in health attitudes which may be attributed to national style or character.

Old age is accompanied by a decline in physical fitness and an increasing experience with body aches and pains. Each person makes his own accommodation to his changing body. Some people become preoccupied with their bodily state, and each ache and pain is magnified. It is these persons who become health pessimists and

*A comparable result is reported in an American study by Lowenthal, 1964. See also Schwartz and Kleemeier, 1965.

report their health as poor when objective indices suggest their health is fairly good. Other people seem to ignore physical discomfort. It is these persons who are the health optimists, who insist they are well in the face of appalling physical distress or who overemphasize their physical fitness and the extent to which their health is better than the health of other people.

Robert Peck has given one of his best statements of the importance of health in later life. In considering the major developmental tasks that face old people, Peck argues that one of these is the choice between what he calls "body transcendence" and "body preoccupation." The old person must decide whether he is to dominate his body or whether his body is to dominate him. Peck says:

"For people to whom pleasure and comfort mean predominantly physical well-being, this [declining health] may be the gravest, most mortal of insults. There are many such people whose elder years seem to move in a decreasing spiral, centered around their growing preoccupation with the state of their bodies.

"There are other people, however, who suffer just as painful physical unease, yet who enjoy life greatly. . . . In their value system, social and mental sources of pleasure and self-respect may transcend physical comfort, alone" (Peck, 1956, p. 47).

The health attitudes of old people are influenced by the way each comes to regard his body. The majority of old people seem to have a conception of how well or how sick they are which is consistent; that is, their health attitudes and their answers to questions on physical functioning are in agreement. For some old people, however, their self-evaluations of health do not necessarily correlate with these objective indices of their health status. It is these persons in all three countries who, in their behavior, best represent the theoretical types suggested by Peck's analysis—namely, the "body-transcendent" and the "body-preoccupied."

In all three countries, men are more op-timistic than women about their state of health. The old man's optimistic self-evaluation of his health, as has been indicated, is undoubtedly related to psychological rather than physical factors. There is some evidence, however, that in the years immediately after retirement, a time when men are seeking a meaningful new role for themselves, men are less optimistic about their health than women of the same age.

Persons over 80 still living in the community tend to be optimistic about their health. These very old people are a selected population. The most deteriorated among those over 80 are no longer in the community. Although many people over 80 in the community are quite frail, others are active and mobile. Our findings reinforce those of Cumming and Parlegreco (1961) in their study of very old people in Kansas City. These investigators say:

"There is some evidence that living to be over 80 . . . is associated with being a member of a biological, and possibly psychological elite. Furthermore, very old people often have a surprisingly high level of social competence and seem able to maintain high spirits" (p. 201).

Like Cumming and Parlegreco, we find a marked difference between persons in their 70's and those 80 or over. Old people in their middle 70's appear to be depressed about their health; those over 80 are optimists.

"Through the interviews of the seventies there runs a thread of pessimism which sometimes borders into irritability and self-pity. . . . Among the eighties there is less complaining and more chirpiness, sometimes a mood of using up the last days of life in tranquility and sometimes a genuine carefree quality" (p. 202).

In all three countries most old people think their health is at least as good or perhaps even better than the health of their contemporaries. Only a small group of people think their health is poor, and worse than the health of others. Those persons who feel their health is poor are far more likely than other persons to express feelings of loneliness and alienation. Whether poor health is responsible for these feelings of alienation and for spontaneous reports of unhappiness cannot be directly determined from the survey data. A possible interpretation of the relationship between reports of poor health and reports of alienation can be found in psychiatric studies of old people. Psychiatrists familiar with the elderly agree that psychic depression is widespread in this age group, even among those living in the community. Overconcern with one's body and associated depressive feelings are common manifestations of such depression (Busse, 1961). Old people who exhibit the extreme type of body-preoccupation, whether or not they also have physical complaints, may indeed be suffering from psychic depression.

Certain differences in health attitudes among old people in the three countries apparently are the result of differences in national style or mode of behavior. Observers have described the Danes as essentially middle class; the British as patient, polite, and non-complaining; the Americans as active and gregarious. These overall descriptions obviously do not apply to all Danes without exception, or to all British, or to all Americans. Yet, there is enough truth in them so that they appear likely explanations of certain differences in health attitudes among old people.

Danish old people in good health are more likely to think they resemble their fellows than either the British or the Americans, to say that their health is better than that of other old people, and more likely to say it is about the same as the health of others. Danes in poor health, however, are equally as likely as the British to say their health is worse than the health of other people.[5]

The elderly in Britain compared to the Danes or the Americans put the most optimistic interpretation on their impairments and incapacities. Despite the fact that they report more incapacity than old people in either Denmark or the United States, old people in Britain are the most likely of all old people to say their health is good. Furthermore, along with the Americans, but perhaps for different reasons, the majority of old people in Britain report that their health is better than the health of other people.

The American aged are the most likely of all old people to respond to even minimum impairment by saying that their health is poor. Americans of all ages are active people, and any restriction on activity seems to evoke a maximum response from them. Irrespective of health status, the American aged are more likely than either the British or the Danes to say that they are lonely. The majority of Americans, however, like the majority of the British, think their health is better than the health of other people. We may say that the Americans think their health is better than the health of others because they are optimists, the British because it is unbecoming to complain.

The similarities and the differences from country to country in the health attitudes of the aged reinforce the beliefs with which we began this analysis. First, the general response of old people in Western societies to the physical changes of aging are similar: some old people are health realists; others, pessimists; still others, optimists. Second, within each country, national styles of behavior affect the manner and the degree of each such response.

[5] This finding with its suggestion of psychic depression among the elderly in poor health is consistent with other studies of the Danish temperament. Denmark has one of the highest suicide rates in the western world, 22.4 per 100,000 persons in 1956, compared to 10.8 per 100,000 for the United States (1960 data). See Rudfeld, 1962, p. 207. United States data from U.S. Bureau of the Census, *Statistical Abstract of the United States* (Washington, D.C.: U.S. Government Printing Office, 1962), p. 66. See also Hendin, 1964.

24

MARJORIE FISKE LOWENTHAL

SOCIAL ISOLATION AND MENTAL ILLNESS IN OLD AGE

Alienation and isolation have been crucial concepts in studies of mental and emotional disorders ever since Durkheim's pioneering work on suicide (1960). Forty years later, Faris and Dunham (1960) showed that rates and types of treated mental disorders were related to the socioeconomic characteristics of urban census tracts, finding that schizophrenia was more frequent in the central districts of cities, while manic-depressive psychoses and the organic psychoses of old age did not reveal such patterns. The organic psychoses of old age, however, did appear to increase with an increase in poverty. These authors hypothesized that persons in the central districts are more likely to be alienated or isolated, and that these social factors are thus related to a high rate of schizophrenia. More recently, the Hollingshead and Redlich (1958) study in New Haven showed that the proportion of treated psychoses was highest among the members of the most underprivileged classes, and Meyers and Roberts (1959), studying intensively a subsample of the same population, related these differences in part to alienation and isolation from the rest of the community and to unsatisfactory interpersonal relations.

Meanwhile, social theorists have gone on to refine and elaborate the concepts of alienation, anomie, and isolation. One of Merton's five modes of individual adapta-

Abridged from the *American Sociological Review*, vol. 29 (1964), no. 1.

The program on which this study is based is supported by National Institute of Mental Health Grant 3M-9145 and has also received supplementary support from the California Department of Mental Hygiene.

tion was retreatism. He characterized persons adopting this mode as, sociologically speaking, the true "aliens," and Charlie Chaplin's bum was his prototype for this kind of alien (Merton, 1949, p. 144). Recently, Seeman has postulated five components of alienation, namely, powerlessness, normlessness, social isolation, meaninglessness and self-estrangement (Seeman, 1959), and Dean has focused on the first three (Dean, 1961).

Empirical sociological studies have explored the role of social isolation in the etiology of specific mental disorders, especially schizophrenia (Kohn and Clausen, 1955; Jaco, 1954; Weinberg, 1955). Just as the concepts of alienation and anomie have been refined for theoretical and empirical purposes, so these and other authors have encountered the need for further elaboration of the idea of social isolation apart from the context of objective social deprivation. Peter Townsend, in his study of elderly people in a London district, has underscored the necessity of distinguishing between objective circumstances and subjective states—between isolation and loneliness (Townsend, 1957). Friis and Manniche, in a Copenhagen survey, also point out that being alone is not necessarily correlated with loneliness (Friis and Manniche, 1961), and Pagani reports similar findings from a survey in Milan (Pagani, 1962).

Psychiatrists and psychoanalysts have analyzed the role of isolation as defense mechanism and symptom (Eissler, 1959). Frieda Fromm-Reichmann, in one of her last works, explored various subjective states of loneliness, distinguishing between "real loneliness," which she considered disintegrative and incommunicable, and creative isolation. She suggested that more careful study may indicate that loneliness plays an important part in the genesis of mental disorder (Fromm-Reichmann, 1959).

Social isolation has also been specifically postulated as a crucial aspect of the aging process itself. Parsons (1942) singles out isolation as a characteristic of the elderly in middle- and upper-middle-class urban society. Changes in social roles, involving fewer contacts or a decrease in their intensity, have been explored in a number of empirical studies of aging (Blau, 1961; Bellin, 1961; Phillips, 1957, 1961). In the work of Cumming and Henry, a theory of social disengagement is the major framework for analyzing the aging process, and the authors postulate that the relation between interaction and morale decreases with advancing age (Cumming and Henry, 1961).

On the face of it, the relation between isolation and mental illness assumed or demonstrated in many of these works, and the well-established fact that social contacts decrease with advancing age, together might account for the higher rates of first admissions to mental hospitals among the elderly that have been reported in recent studies (Locke *et al.*, 1960; Malzberg, 1956). Studies conducted by clinicians have given rise to conjecture about a causal relation between isolation and the incidence of physical and mental disorder (Chalke, 1957; Connolly, 1962; Gruenberg, 1954), and, more specifically, between isolation or lack of social integration and the development of the senile psychoses and the late schizophrenias (Williams, *et al.*, 1942; Kay and Roth, 1961). But, just as the studies of increasing isolation in relation to aging have pretty much left open the question of voluntary versus involuntary disengagement, so have these left open the question of age-linked (or illness-linked) versus long-standing isolation. At this stage of our knowledge, one is inclined to agree

with Hunt that "all things considered . . . it would seem wisest, pending the outcome of further research, to consider the social isolation hypothesis as unconfirmed (though by no means discredited)" (Hunt, 1959).

Early in the research program of which this present exploratory study is a part, it was apparent that the elderly persons in the psychiatric wards of San Francisco General Hospital had lived far more isolated lives just prior to admission than had their peers who remained in the community. The original purpose of this present study was to analyze three degree-of-isolation groups in the hospital sample and an isolated group in the community sample in order to gain further insight into the relation between what had been assumed to be age-linked isolation and mental illness in old age. Some unexpected results of this analysis prompted a re-examination of the isolates on a case-by-case basis which led in turn to the finding that we were dealing with differences in kind as well as degree. We hope that the resulting typology will constitute a small contribution to the study of isolation which, as Wilensky has pointed out, has remained underdeveloped, "a casualty of the cost not only to society but to the researcher of reaching the isolate" (Wilensky, 1961). The immediate practical objective is to develop hypotheses to be tested in ongoing research in geriatric mental illness.

INDICATORS OF ISOLATION

The parent samples from which the subgroups to be analyzed here were drawn consist of (a) a population of 534 persons 60 years of age and older admitted to the psychiatric screening wards of the San Francisco General Hospital in the calendar year 1959 (total admissions in this age group numbered 774, but 240 persons were excluded from the sample because they had had psychiatric admissions prior to age 60 or because they did not meet San Francisco County residence requirements) and (b) a sample of 600 community residents 60 years of age and older, drawn on a stratified random basis from 18 census tracts in San Francisco. The data reported here were gathered during the "baseline" year of 1959, though all surviving and locatable people in both samples were also interviewed twice more, at approximately annual intervals.

The initial screening criteria used for the selection of the subgroups were, for the hospital sample, level of social activity in the two weeks prior to admission, presence or absence of personal others (friends or relatives) in the decision-making process that eventuated in admission to the psychiatric ward, and the availability of personal others as informants after admission. For the community sample, only the social interaction question was used as an initial screening criterion. Because of the more elaborate criteria available for the hospital sample, it was possible to delineate a group of extreme isolates, whom we shall call "pure" isolates, as well as a group of semi-isolates whose social deprivation was somewhat less extreme. For the community sample, due to the more structured nature of the data, no semi-isolates could definitely be discerned. Groups of social interactors, however, were drawn from both samples.

The 52 *"pure" isolates* located among the hospitalized are people who had no friends or relatives involved in the decision-making process that led to hospitalization, and for whom no such persons could be located after they had been admitted to the psychiatric ward. On the social activity question, these patients reported no contact with a friend or relative in the two weeks prior to admission. In addition, a careful reading of detailed interview transcripts, which include material on current and past social relationships, revealed that they had had no contact of any kind with a friend or a relative for approximately three years. All of them were, not surprisingly, living alone, except for five from a county old age home and 11 who had been living alone but had briefly occupied institutional way-stations (such as jail or a medical ward) en route to the psychiatric screening wards.

Seventy-seven year old Mr. E. is not untypical of those in circumstances of extreme isolation at the time of admission. He has worked mainly as an itinerant laborer and has lived in nearly every state in the union, retiring in 1948 when he became eligible for Social Security. Since that time he has lived in several rooms or small apartments in San Francisco. He has two siblings but does not know where they are, and says he did not marry because he "wanted to be alone." He is a periodic drinker whose landlady found him otherwise "quite normal" (although he was hallucinating at the time of admission). He had arrived on the psychiatric ward from the county jail where he had been sent for breaking some car windows "because I'd had too much beer." His diagnoses were chronic brain syndrome and alcohol addiction. He appeared not at all unhappy about the prospect of state hospitalization. "It doesn't matter where I am because I keep to myself." He was still in the state hospital at the second and third contacts, and had had no visitors except one from his former landlady. Asked whether he corresponded with anyone, his reply was: "I never liked people to mix with. I am just reticent."

The 56 *semi-isolates* were persons who had no friends or relatives involved in the decision-making process and for whom no personal others could be located after hospitalization. They reported some social contacts in the period prior to admission, but a review of their protocols indicated that these were, by and large, both casual and infrequent.

Mrs. C. is a 66 year old retired nurse who has been a widow for 30 years. She went to the psychiatric ward voluntarily because she was "terribly nervous" and feared that she was developing an addiction to barbiturates she had taken since having a partial gastrectomy. Her diagnosis was psychogenic (affective disorder). She said she had no contact with relatives and that "all of my friends are gone." At another point in the interview she said she had seen no one since her gastrectomy a year earlier. Still later, she remarked that she did not want her friends to know she is ill. At any rate, she refused to name friends, and at the second interview a year later, in a state hospital, she said she had spread the word that she was visiting her brother in British Columbia.

The 30 *community isolates* were screened out first on the basis of their having reported only casual contacts or no contacts at all within the two weeks prior to the interview. Their protocols were then reviewed, and only persons who gave no evidence of having any recent contact (i.e., within about three years) with a friend or relative were retained for the final sample. The following brief vignettes provide a glimpse of the living styles of these community isolates.

"Bill" (he refused to give his last name and may not know what it is) is an 83 year old single man who still runs his own tobacco-news-candy stand and has no intention of retiring. He is not eligible for Social Security because "I can't prove my birth, I never knew my parents, I don't think I had any brothers or sisters. Tried to find out for years." He talks with his customers, sometimes strikes up conversations in parks or cafeterias, but otherwise has no social contacts. "I'm either working or in my room or having lunch," he explains. He formerly worked as a door-to-door salesman "all over the country" and enjoys living alone. He considers himself very healthy and says he has no problems. His chief pleasure is fishing.

Mr. C. is a 72 year old retired Navy watertender who apparently retired because of tuberculosis, but the disease is no longer active. He does not know whether he has any relatives or not, and has no social contacts except "I see the manager once a month about the rent." He is very

happy not to be working, and spends his time watching television and reading newspapers and magazines. The interviewer notes that "he seemed pleased with his living arrangement and pretty contented all around."

Social interactors in both samples include all people who had attended a social function or visited friends in the two-week period prior to the interview. There were only 39 such persons among the hospitalized and all but two of them also had relatives or friends involved in the decision-making process or as collaterals (or both).

The remainder of the hospital sample mustered personal others, mainly relatives at the time of crisis, but had no social contacts with friends in the two weeks just prior to admission. They therefore fall between the semi-isolates and the interactors, and will consequently be useful for comparison purposes.

Utilizing these same criteria, 417 persons in the community sample were identified as social interactors. Perusal of the protocols of the 39 hospital interactors and of a random 10 percent subsample of the community interactors satisfied the analyst that these persons were in fact functioning on a high level of social interaction. There was, however, some indication that the community interactors had broader and more numerous social contacts than the hospitalized.

The "remainder" group in the community sample comprises 144 persons who fall between the isolates and the interactors. An indeterminate number of these 144 persons would presumably resemble the hospital semi-isolates in a time of crisis, but as yet no criteria have been developed for pinpointing them. While a column for them appears in the tables, for the sake of completeness in presentation of the data, they have not been included in this analysis.

ISOLATION AND OLD AGE

If the extreme isolation manifest in these subgroups were largely a consequence of the aging process, one would expect to find the hospitalized isolates older than the interactors. Furthermore, since women live longer than men, and since there are more very old women than very old men among the hospitalized, one would also expect to find more women among the isolates. Actually, however, the pure isolates and the interactors within the hospital sample closely resemble each other in respect to age, and both groups are somewhat younger than the remainder of the hospital sample. Nor does sex composition bear out an assumption that extreme isolation is necessarily age-linked. Despite the preponderance of very old women among the hospitalized, about three-fourths of the isolates are men while about three-fourths of the interactors are women. (Whether our screening devices excluded extremely isolated women, or whether such women simply do not exist is an open question. One possibility, supported by some hospitalized cases, is that female isolates tend to form symbiotic relationships, usually with a sister, the two constituting an isolated pair.) Among the community iso-

TABLE 1

SUBGROUP BY AGE AND SEX

	HOSPITAL SAMPLE				COMMUNITY SAMPLE		
	Pure Isolates	Semi-Isolates	Inter-actors	Re-mainder	Isolates	Inter-actors	Re-mainder
	%	%	%	%	%	%	%
Men:							
60–69..........	29	20	5	18	30	28	20
70–79..........	35	20	16	19	33	15	15
80+..........	8	16	5	8	23	5	14
Women:							
60–69..........	11	14	33	12	7	30	17
70–79..........	6	12	28	23	7	16	17
80+..........	11	18	13	20	....	6	17
Total..........	100	100	100	100	100	100	100
(N)..............	(52)	(56)	(39)	((387)	(30)	(417)	(144)

TABLE 2

SUBGROUP BY MARITAL STATUS

	HOSPITAL SAMPLE				COMMUNITY SAMPLE		
	Pure Isolates	Semi-Isolates	Inter-actors	Re-mainder	Isolates	Inter-actors	Re-mainder
	%	%	%	%	%	%	%
Single..............	47	29	10	13	63	19	18
Divorced or separated	24	25	18	21	17	13	11
Widowed..........	29	44	46	38	20	34	44
Married..........	....	2	26	28	....	34	27
Total..........	100	100	100	100	100	100	100
(N)*..............	(49)	(55)	(39)	(381)	(30)	(417)	(143)

* Totals differ from those in Table 1 because persons whose marital status was unknown were omitted.

lates, too, the majority (86 percent) are men.

If extreme isolation were largely the result of a decrease in social interaction with advancing years, one would expect more age-linked changes, such as widowhood, among the isolates. Again, however, the data do not support the assumption. There are proportionately more widows and widowers among the interactors than there are among the isolates in both the hospitalized and the nonhospitalized samples. Conversely, more than four times as many hospitalized isolates as in-

sample fall into the lowest quartile.[1] Conversely, nearly a third of the hospitalized interactors and well over half of the community interactors are in the upper two quartiles. The socioeconomic status of the hospitalized semi-isolates, however, is only slightly higher than that of the extreme isolates. More than two-fifths of both the community and hospital isolates lived in the "south of Market" area which includes San Francisco's Skid Row.

TABLE 3

SUBGROUP BY SOCIOECONOMIC STATUS

QUARTILE	HOSPITAL SAMPLE				COMMUNITY SAMPLE		
	Pure Isolates	Semi-Isolates	Inter-actors	Re-mainder	Isolates	Inter-actors	Re-mainder
	%	%	%	%	%	%	%
1 (High)............	....	8	10	9	7	38	20
2.................	3	4	21	18	7	24	33
3.................	18	11	38	31	16	19	25
4 (Low)............	79	77	31	42	70	19	22
Total..........	100	100	100	100	100	100	100
(N)*.............	(38)	(48)	(39)	(351)	(30)	(409)	(143)

* Totals differ from those in Table 1 because persons who could not be scored on at least two of the three components of socioeconomic status were omitted.

teractors are single, and the ratio for the community sample is more than three to one.

The age distribution of the community isolates closely resembles that of the hospital isolates, though they are older than the community interactors. In part because they are older, they are also more likely to be retired than the community interactors. Otherwise, being predominantly male and predominantly single, they closely resemble the hospitalized pure isolates.

The frequently imputed relation between low socioeconomic status and isolation is amply supported in both samples. As shown in Table 3, 79 percent of the extreme isolates in the hospital sample and 70 percent of those in the community

ISOLATION AND MENTAL ILLNESS IN OLD AGE

If extreme isolation were a causative factor in mental illness among the elderly, one would expect to find more pure isolates among the hospitalized than in the community. And indeed, about 10 percent of the hospitalized are extreme isolates, compared with 5 percent of the community sample. This difference is misleading, however, because of the high correlation between extreme isolation and very low socioeconomic status. In comparison with the elderly in San Francisco as a whole, the hospital sample consider-

[1] The index of current economic position is based on a combination of monthly rent, annual income, and the Tryon Index of San Francisco census tracts.

ably over-represents and the community sample moderately under-represents the very lowest socioeconomic groups. If the two samples had identical socioeconomic distributions, they might well include almost identical proportions of pure isolates.

Furthermore, if extreme isolation were correlated with mental disorder in old age, more persons rated disturbed psychiatrically should be found among the community isolates than among the community interactors. This is true, but again, we know that, quite apart from the level of social interaction, low socioeconomic status is linked to a higher incidence of interactors in the hospital sample. Once more, the assumption is not borne out as shown in Table 4. Forty-four percent of the interactors have a diagnosis of psychogenic disorder alone or in combination with an organic disorder, compared with 25 percent of the semi-isolates and 22 percent of the pure isolates. (Inspection of cases indicates also that affective outnumber paranoid disorders in all three groups: interactors, semi-isolates, and isolates.)

All three subgroups have fewer organic disorders than the remainder of the sample. Alcoholism, alone or in combination with acute or chronic brain syndrome, is somewhat more frequent among

TABLE 4

SUBGROUP BY SOCIOECONOMIC STATUS AND DEGREE OF PSYCHIATRIC IMPAIRMENT, COMMUNITY SAMPLE ONLY

PSYCHIATRIC RATING	ISOLATES		INTERACTORS		REMAINDER		TOTAL SAMPLE	
	High SES	Low SES	High SES	Low SES	High SES	Low SES	High SES	Low SES
High............	% (100)	% 77	% 95	% 80	% 68	% 75	% 89	% 78
Low................	....	23	5	20	32	25	11	22
Total........	(100)	100	100	100	100	100	100	100
(N)*.............	(4)	(26)	(253)	(156)	(75)	(68)	(332)	(250)

* Totals differ from those in Table 1 because persons who were not scored on socioeconomic status were omitted.

psychiatric disorder (Berkman, 1964). In the community sample as a whole, and as shown in Table 4 over one-fifth of those coming from the lowest socioeconomic strata were rated psychiatrically disturbed, the same as the proportion of isolates who were so rated. These ratings were made by psychiatrists on the basis of a review of the protocols. For a description of rating procedures, see Lowenthal and Berkman (1962).

The development of schizophrenia has been linked to isolation for older as well as for younger age groups (Kohn and Clausen, 1955; Kay and Roth, 1961). If it were linked to the extreme isolation manifested by our subgroups, more psychogenics (particularly paranoids) should appear among the isolates than among the the isolates and semi-isolates than it is among interactors.

In general, the isolates and the interactors differ more in physical than in psychiatric terms. The pure isolates ranked much lower than the rest of the hospital sample on the physician's rating of physical condition at time of admission, and the interactors considerably higher (elderly persons with psychogenic disorders are in general physically healthier than those suffering from organic brain disease). On ratings of degree-of-psychiatric impairment, on the other hand, the three subgroups did not differ greatly from each other nor from the rest of the hospital sample. Similarly, on two Guttman scales measuring, roughly, physical and social self-maintenance, the interactors ranked far higher on physical self-maintenance.

Community sample subjects were not examined physically or psychiatrically. On the crude measure of physical disability used in the community, however, isolates and interactors do not differ appreciably. (Components of this health scale are: days in bed past year, medical care past month, hospitalization past 10 years, and serious physical illness past 10 years.)

A NOTE ON ISOLATION AND MORALE

That low morale may be an intervening factor between isolation and the development of deviant behavior, including men-

change, and the feelings of loneliness. On none of these items do the hospitalized pure isolates and the interactors represent polar extremes. In fact, on only one of them—energy—do the isolates and interactors differ by more than 12 percentage points from each other. Only on the depression and sleep items do the hospitalized differ dramatically from the non-hospitalized—the majority of both isolates and interactors in the community were not depressed and had no sleep problems.

The question of loneliness was not ap-

TABLE 5

SUBGROUP BY DIAGNOSIS, HOSPITAL SAMPLE ONLY

Diagnosis	Pure Isolates	Semi-Isolates	Inter-actors	Re-mainder
	%	%	%	%
Psychogenic disorder, alone or in combination with organic disorder..............	22	25	44	23
Alcohol addiction, alone or in combination with organic disorder..................	20	21	15	15
Organic disorders only..................	58	54	41	62
Total...........................	100	100	100	100
(N)*.................................	(50)	(52)	(39)	(384)

* Totals differ from those in Table 1 because persons not diagnosed were omitted.

tal illness, is an at least implicit assumption in much of the literature. In fact, the concept of alienation has been variously elaborated as including two or all three of these components (i.e., isolation, low morale, and deviant behavior) (Merton, 1949; Seeman, 1959; Dean, 1961). If this were true of the extreme isolation among older people in our samples, the three hospitalized groups should form a continuum on various subjective states of morale, and the community isolates should differ from community interactors in the same direction.

Five questions indirectly relating to morale were asked in the baseline interview: opinion of own age, presence or absence of depression, sleep patterns, energy

proached directly in the baseline interview, but there were two checklist questions where it could appear—"main current problems" and "inconveniences in living arrangements." When loneliness was not checked it did not necessarily mean that the person was not lonely, but only that some other problem took priority. In both the hospital and the community samples, reports of loneliness were somewhat *less* frequent among the isolates. And in the interview protocols, spontaneous remarks about being lonely were far more likely to be made by the interactors than by the pure isolates, who often went out of their way to protest that they were *not* lonely.

Throughout our analysis we have found

less evidence of an even progression from extreme to semi-isolation to interaction than would be expected if we were dealing with a continuum. These apparent inconsistencies suggest that the pure isolates and the semi-isolates may be different in kind.

A. THE "PURE" ISOLATES (HOSPITAL SAMPLE)

On the basis of their life style patterns and their own remarks, two patterns are discernible among the pure isolates: a lifelong pattern of isolation just as extreme as that noted at the time of admission, and a pattern of social adjustment which is best described as marginal. These two patterns could perhaps both be subsumed under the mode of adjustment that Merton designated as retreatism (Merton, 1949, pp. 142–44) but one group seems to have been completely alienated from the start, while the other, having tried and failed, is more aptly described as defeated.

The Alienated (lifelong extreme isolation).—The 25 lifelong pure isolates are predominantly men (80 percent) and predominantly single (84 percent), the remainder having been divorced or separated very early in life after a short marriage. Three-fifths had had occupations involving either geographic mobility, a predominantly masculine setting, or both, such as seaman, logger, longshoreman, or itinerant laborer. No persons of white-collar status or above were in this group. Three of them had sustained head injuries early in life and nearly half had severe visual or hearing defects at the time of the first interview (it was generally not possible to determine the duration of these defects). A disproportionately high number (one-fifth) had a history of tuberculosis. Only seven of the 25 did not have either a history of tuberculosis, an early head injury, or a sensory defect. More than half were born abroad, over two-thirds had a history of alcoholism or a diagnosis of alcohol addiction, and the majority lived on Skid Row or in its environs. They frequently said that they

had been lone wolves all their lives and that they liked being alone, and they rarely mentioned loneliness as a problem of their past or current lives. If they did mention an acquaintance, they did not know his last name nor where he lived. Three sociopaths with histories of shoplifting, drug addiction, and sex offenses are in this group; several had been arrested for drinking. Those who were still hospitalized at the first year follow-up were generally observed to be belligerent and hostile on the wards.

The Defeated (lifelong marginal social adjustment).—The remaining 22 pure isolates about whom information is available present a different picture. About two-thirds of them are men, and nearly half have had white-collar or skilled blue-collar occupations. Somewhat fewer, though still nearly half, have a diagnosis of alcohol addiction or a history of problem drinking. They are more likely than the alienated to mention loneliness as a problem, and only one of them said that he likes to be alone. For several men and one woman, the development of alcoholism may have constituted a disruptive factor leading to divorce or separation and a consequent withdrawal from society (or their marital problems may have caused an increase in their drinking). For women, early widowhood or divorce often constituted a turning point. Two had abrupt downward shifts in occupation (one without a history of alcoholism). Compared with the alienated, the defeated had initial advantages in terms of education, being born in the United States, and not having any early physical disorders or traumas. In contrast to the alienated, who tended to remain single, these people often had more than one marriage and divorce. Problems having to do with personal losses figure frequently in their protocols, the death of a parent (usually the mother) or a sibling more often than a spouse, but they tend to blame themselves for their poor adjustment. While none of the alienated isolates had ever attempted suicide, three of these people had. Those who went to state hospitals were often observed to be withdrawn on the wards, though they would respond if spoken to.

Rather typical of this group is the following 62 year old man: Mr. S. was admitted to the psychiatric screening wards because he had tried to commit suicide with chloroform. He was somewhat reticent about his life history, but one is able to piece together the facts that he was trained as a lawyer at an Eastern university, became a career Naval officer, and sometime in middle life, for obscure reasons, was asked to resign from the Navy. At this point, he married a waitress and went to Europe with all of his life savings, some $50,000. The money disappeared quickly and the marriage soon ended in divorce. Since that time he has had innumerable jobs in travel agencies and small businesses. He currently has been trying, without much success, to give language and piano lessons. The only money he has left is $160 a month from a trust fund. Mr. S. reports that the most difficult thing he ever had to face in his life was when the doctor told him that his mother would only live for four months (he had lived with his mother until she died when he was 43, and says he has been depressed ever since).

Unlike the first group, who seem deliberately to have chosen a nonconformist way of life, the majority of these people, somewhere along the line, made attempts at a conventional social adjustment but failed. For most, the extreme isolation apparent at the time of admission seems to be the end-result of the very low level of social interaction that had persisted throughout their adult lives. The few who sustained an apparently intimate relationship for some time seem to have lived otherwise socially marginal lives, so that the loss of one person resulted in pure isolation. These losses had usually taken place at least three or four years before admission.

B. THE SEMI-ISOLATES (HOSPITAL SAMPLE)

These semi-isolates sometimes resembled the pure isolates and sometimes the interactors or the remainder of the hospitalized sample. Closer inspection suggests that they are composed primarily of two rather distinct groups (13 are unclassifiable due to paucity of data).

The Blamers (lifelong marginal social adjustment).—The 18 people in this group, like the defeated among the pure isolates, give evidence of having made a marginal social adjustment all their lives. If there was a friend or relative somewhere, the relationship was described in instrumental terms: a brother 2,000 miles away who handled finances, a friend who brought in groceries. Like the alienated, this group is largely male (16 of the 18). Like the defeated, about half have a history of alcoholism or problem drinking, and they include more skilled and white-collar workers than the alienated. Half are single, and most of the rest were separated or divorced early in life. Like the defeated, too, they mentioned losses or hurts involving others, usually but not always, far in the past. Closer reading, however, reveals that while they felt sorry for themselves as did the defeated, they tended to blame others or circumstances for their suffering. This mechanism may well produce somewhat less withdrawal than does the tendency to blame oneself, thus accounting for the less extreme degree of isolation we find in this group at the time of admission.

Sixty-seven year old Mr. N., a single man who was for nine years an Army private and later an itinerant laborer, has a sister in Monterey and a brother in Chicago, but "never" sees them. He had a diagnosis of alcoholism, but his landlord said he had never seen him drunk. The patient describes himself as "a rover" who was "never a mixer," and "I feel fine about it." He blames it all on his mother who was a tiny woman and "who had a strap around her neck and if you did not obey, you get it, whack, and that is why I wanted to get away from people."

These "blamers," then, like the defeated, differ from the alienated in being likely to have made some attempt at an intimate relationship. They differ from each other mainly in mode of reaction to their isolation and in the degree of their isolation at the time of admission: the defeated had no contacts, the blamers had a few casual ones.

The Late Isolates.—The second category of semi-isolates is different in kind, comprising 25 persons whose extreme isolation apparently developed later in life. They are older than the groups whose isolation was lifelong or almost lifelong, half being over 80, whereas among the other groups, between two-fifths and one-half were under 70. There are more women than men among them, they rarely have a history of alcoholism or problem drinking, two-thirds are widowed (they are often childless), and nearly half have had white-collar jobs or better. Some had out-of-town relatives who appeared after their stay on the screening ward. While the state of isolation apparent at the time of admission had usually persisted for a few years, there was no suggestion in their protocols that large stretches of their lives had been solitary. They were much more likely to be diagnosed as having acute brain syndrome than the lifelong isolated groups, possibly because they were not as tough as the lifelong isolates nor as accustomed to looking out for themselves. Most also had underlying chronic brain syndromes of long standing, and a review of their protocols suggests that their isolation may well have developed only after deterioration began. More often than not, there is also a fairly recent history of injury, physical illness, or severe sensory impairment.

The landlord of a 74 year old widow with diagnosis of acute and chronic brain syndromes, and with no friends or relatives except a brother in the Midwest, reports that after her eyesight began to fail two years prior to admission she did not eat properly. Since that time, she had also lost contact socially, and at the time of admission was very concerned about "who's going to take care of me after I'm dead and gone."

Apart from sensory defects and severe injuries, such as broken hips, several of these patients had suffered from heart disease, cancer, or "small strokes."

Omitting the unclassifiable, we now have four instead of two patterns of isolation among the hospitalized:

	Percent
A. The *totally isolated* at time of admission, including:	
1. The lifelong alienated (lifelong "extreme" isolation)	28
2. The defeated (lifelong marginal isolation)	24
B. The *semi-isolated* at time of admission, including:	
3. The chronic blamers (lifelong marginal isolation)	20
4. The late isolates	28
	——
	100
	(90)

(While some of the 39 *interactors* among the hospitalized showed signs, at the time of hospitalization, of having defeatist or blaming tendencies, nothing in their reports of themselves or in their collaterals' reports about them indicates a lifelong pattern of this order. Most of them, however, reveal some social withdrawal in comparison with earlier periods of life, thus differing in degree but not necessarily in kind from the late isolates.)

THE COMMUNITY ISOLATES

The research question appropriate to the three long-isolated groups would be: "How does lifelong isolation bear on the development of mental illness in old age?" And, for the fourth group: "What does an increase in social isolation, or social deprivation, relative to earlier periods of life, have to do with the development of mental illness in old age?"

Pertinent to exploration of the first question is the pattern of isolation found among the extreme isolates in the community.

In several ways the community isolates and the pure isolates among the hospitalized closely resemble each other: they are predominantly male, predominantly single, and come from the lowest socioeconomic groups. The community isolates are somewhat older, somewhat less likely to be foreign born, and there are fewer to whom a history of alcoholism can be definitely attributed (though some clearly have a drinking problem). No specific life history data were collected for them, but on the basis of spontaneous comments and answers to open-ended questions, such as those having to do with major problems, self-image, and stressful and pleasant periods, it is possible to roughly categorize the community sample into probable lifelong isolates and others whose extreme isolation apparently developed later.

Over two-thirds of the 30 community pure isolates have, according to their own statements or by implication, quite clearly been extremely isolated all their lives. Six appear not to have become extreme isolates until middle or later life. These changes usually resulted from loss of spouse through death or separation, and one suspects that for such people (predominantly men) the spouse had been the main, if not the only, social contact. Like the blamers and the defeated among the hospitalized, they seem to have made, and to have ostensibly preferred, marginal social adjustments all or most of their lives. None offers any evidence of changes in social contact that might be attributed to the aging process. (Two of the 30 community isolates are unclassifiable.)

Occupationally, though not in terms of socioeconomic status, the community isolates differ somewhat from the alienated in the hospital sample. The geographically mobile type of occupation (longshore-man, logger, itinerant laborer) is less conspicuous, though a fifth of them spent most of their working lives in the armed forces. Phrases such as "I'm a lone wolf and always have been" abound. More than a fourth were in jobs involving continual contact with the public, such as hotel and transport workers. Especially conspicuous among the latter were news or tobacco vendors, some of whom were still working when interviewed. Those who were retired said they missed contact with "the public," and those who were working said they would miss it when they did retire.

As a whole, then, the community isolates appear for the most part to be composed, like the alienated, of the "lifelong extremes," with a fifth of them probably representing a "lifelong marginal" social adjustment like the defeated or the blamers. Differences in work history, however, suggest that retreatism is somewhat less common: the hospitalized alienated found a work milieu made up of marginal persons like themselves, whereas the community isolates tended to relate to a "normal," if anonymous, public. Paucity of data makes it difficult to classify them further. They do not appear to be as hostile as many of the alienated among the hospitalized, but this difference may be due to the fact that many of the hospitalized suffered from organic brain diseases which may have triggered release of a hostility the community group represses. And more authoritarian occupational structures, clearly defined daily goals as provided in the armed services, or continual contact with the public, may have protected them against their own impulses. In any case, on the surface, community lifelong extreme isolates look more like unemotional "avoiders" than like the hostile alienated, the defeated, or the blamers among the hospitalized. Matter-of-factness characterizes their comments:

231

An 80 year old retired city transport driver, single:

"I'm a lone wolf. I strictly mind my own business, quiet—that covers it."

A 64 year old news vendor who is still working:

"I like to be independent, I'm not too friendly—usually by myself. Always been the same."

SUMMARY AND IMPLICATIONS

If these new subgroups were larger, we could now re-run our tables, distinguishing between the lifelong extreme, the lifelong marginal, and the late isolates. As it is, this analysis must rest with the finding that most of the extreme isolates among the aged in the community, as among the hospitalized, have always been that way. Bearing this in mind, as well as the division of the hospitalized semi-isolates into two groups (the lifelong and the late), we are now in a position to suggest a hypothesis about the relation between lifelong extreme isolation and mental illness, and to refine the research questions bearing on the problem of age-linked isolation.

Lifelong Isolation and Mental Illness.— On the basis of screening criteria applied to the time of the interview and a period of a few years before it, groups of extreme or pure isolates were found in both the community and hospital samples. We conjectured that, if economic factors were held constant, the proportions in the hospital sample would be no greater than those found in the community. A more detailed analysis of these two groups showed that among the 52 hospitalized persons characterized as pure isolates at the time of admission, slightly less than half gave evidence of having maintained such a state all or nearly all of their lives. We have called these people the "alienated." Four-fifths of the community group gave similar though not such complete evidence of lifelong extreme isolation, and while they do not appear as hos-

tile as the hospitalized, they too seem to warrant the description "alienated."

Again, if economic factors were held constant, there would doubtless have been as many lifelong alienated in the community at large as among the hospitalized. Furthermore, the community "alienated" were rated (by reviewing psychiatrists) at least as robust psychiatrically as persons of similar socioeconomic status in the rest of the community sample. The conclusion seems justified, then, that this type of lifelong extreme isolation is not necessarily conducive to mental illness in old age. Nor does it seem to be conducive to a particular kind of mental illness in old age, for there were no more paranoid (or other affective) disorders among the hospitalized alienated than among the rest of the sample. While such an alienated life style might in itself be culturally defined as a form of mental illness, lack of interpersonal relationships, which is one of its main characteristics, may help to prevent the development of overt psychogenic disorder (or to prevent its detection if it does develop).

Two additional groups of persons who have led marginal rather than totally isolated existences all or most of their lives also emerged from among the hospitalized. One of these groups, which we have called the defeated, comprised some of those showing extreme or "pure" isolation at the time of admission. These individuals attempted social adjustment, usually in early adulthood, but retreated, often rather quickly. Their tendency was to blame themselves for their "failure" and to feel sorry for themselves. Only a few of the isolates in the community sample revealed this pattern.

The other hospitalized group whose histories gave evidence of lifelong marginal social existences was found among those who were semi-isolated at the time of admission. They resembled the defeated in many ways, but they did not withdraw quite so completely from interpersonal relationships, and their most characteristic tendency was to blame other persons or circumstances, rather than themselves, for their isolation. While one or two of the community isolates gave some hints of this "blaming" pattern, no semi-isolated group of community subjects was definable for this study, and the question must be left open as to whether such a life style does indeed exist, and to the same degree, among the community as among the hospitalized aged. Further research may well indicate that it is among those who have led marginal social existences, who have tried but failed, so to speak, that a higher incidence of mental illness in old age is found.

The alienated, the defeated, and the blamers differ in kind from the age-linked isolates found among the hospitalized semi-isolates, while the latter appear to differ only in degree from the remainder of the hospitalized sample. This leads us back to the problem that prompted our interest before we encountered the life-long isolates: namely, isolation relative to earlier periods of life, developed as a result of the death of friends or relatives, of voluntary or involuntary disengagement, or of other changes linked to the aging process. Is there any evidence that such relative social isolation is causally linked with the development of mental illness in old age, and if so, with any particular type of disorder?

Age-Linked Isolation and Mental Illness.—The data suggest that there may be no relation between age-linked isolation and types of mental disorder in old age, considering as "types," for the time being, simply the distinction between psychogenic and organic. As we have seen, those who suffered the greatest relative isolation (the 25 late isolates) include far fewer persons with psychogenic disorders than the interactors; conversely, the interactors include proportionately twice as many persons diagnosed as suffering from psychogenic disorders as the more isolated remainder of the sample. Findings of other studies which have linked schizophrenia to isolation for both old and young had, in the beginning, led us to

suspect that the interactors would have a predominance of affective disorders whereas the paranoids would be left in the more isolated remainder of the sample. This does not appear to be the case, however, since the interactors include about equal proportions of paranoids and affectives.

Since the late isolates resemble the remainder of the hospital sample both in comparatively greater incidence of organic disorder and in greater isolation than is found among the interactors, one might postulate that relative social isolation is linked to the development of organic rather than psychogenic psychoses in old age. While there certainly are many more organic than psychogenic disorders among these elderly first admissions (12 percent psychogenic only, 58 percent organic only, the remainder having both types of diagnosis), this possibility is no more supported by the data than the hypothesized correlation between isolation and psychogenic, particularly paranoid, disorders. The pure organics in the hospital sample as a whole report no more social change (death of a spouse or another close relative, illness of an important other, change in social living arrangement, retirement) than do those with a psychogenic diagnosis, nor are there any appreciable differences between the "pure" psychogenics and the "mixed" (those who also have a diagnosis of organic brain disorder).

This leaves us with the rather obvious conclusion that the interactors' superior physical condition and lack of intellectual deterioration permits them to maintain their comparatively high degree of interaction, and that the generally poor physical condition and greater intellectual deterioration of the organics who constitute the majority of the remainder of the sample has resulted in their greater isolation. Relative isolation, then, may be more of a consequence than a cause of

mental illness in old age, and the consequences for psychogenics may be less
severe than for organics because of their
generally superior physical condition.

Since we know from a companion study
now under way that the hospital sample
is considerably sicker physically than
older people in the community, a corollary hypothesis is that a physical change
preceded and may be causally related to
both the relative social isolation and the
development of mental disorder. Tentative support for this hypothesis is provided by the following findings.[2]

1. An earlier decision-making analysis
   of this sample of aged people has
   shown that, for the majority of the
   hospitalized, physical factors were
   among the reasons for admission
   given by collaterals.
2. In answer to the question on major
   life-changes since age 50, serious
   physical illness was reported for
   about three-fourths of the sample
   (such illness, incidentally, was just
   as likely to be found among the pure
   psychogenics as among the organics).
3. The social interactors differ from
   the late isolates mainly in respect to
   their superior physical condition,
   ranking much higher both in terms
   of the physician's rating of general
   health and on the physical self-
   maintenance scale, and these physical differences far outweigh differences in psychiatric disability.

To summarize briefly, then: lifelong
extreme isolation (or alienation) is not
necessarily conducive to the development
of the kinds of mental disorder that bring
persons to the psychiatric ward in their
old age; lifelong marginal social adjustment may be conducive to the development of such disorder; late-developing
isolation is apparently linked with mental disorder but it is of no greater significance among those with psychogenic disorders than among those with organic
disorders, and may be more of a consequence than a cause of mental illness in
the elderly; finally, physical illness may
be the critical antecedent to both the isolation and the mental illness.

[2] Indirect support for such an hypothesis, linking physical illness with isolation and both with
low morale, is also to be found in the work of
Kutner and his colleagues in a survey of community aged in New York. Their relative isolates
(by no means as extreme as the isolates we have
dealt with here) are in poorer health than their
nonisolates, and also of poorer means. They
postulate that among persons of very low socioeconomic status, isolation is more likely to accompany declining health, and "from illness and
isolation arises a sense of futility, cynicism or
resignation that expresses itself in a variety of
ways." Bernard Kutner *et al.*, 1956, p. 157.

25

ROBERT N. BUTLER

THE FAÇADE OF CHRONOLOGICAL AGE:
AN INTERPRETATIVE SUMMARY

To look anew at some of the prevailing ideas and previously reported findings concerning both the processes of human aging and the nature of aged persons, we undertook a series of collaborative studies involving 21 investigators representing a number of separate academic disciplines and medical specialties in a pilot project beginning in December 1955. We had two basic research strategies in mind: first, the selection of the medically healthy, community-dwelling aged, so that we might maximize the opportunity of studying the effects of *time*, or chronological aging, itself and minimize the effects of sickness, institutionalization, and social adversity; second, the introduction of the collaborative, multidisciplinary approach to enhance the opportunity for a more comprehensive evaluation of the many factors known, or believed, to determine the façade of chronological aging.

Such an approach seemed particularly appropriate in view of the fact that so much of the literature concerning the aged and aging had heretofore derived principally from studies of the sick and institutionalized. The dominant theme had been upon *decline*. Little appeared to be known about healthy and socially autonomous aging. We knew that certain cultural stereotypes affected the contemporary picture of the aged and the process of aging.

We conceived aging to be a process of change involving all aspects of the organ-

Abridged from the *American Journal of Psychiatry*, vol. 119, no. 8 (February, 1963).

ism but not necessarily occurring in an interrelated or synchronous manner. In order to examine a broad range of physical, physiological, psychological, psychodynamic, and social processes to gain some understanding of the changes occurring with advancing age, we therefore undertook an intensive study of "normal" men above the age of 65 years. How might we disentangle the contributions of disease, social losses, preexisting personality, and the like from changes that might more properly be regarded as age-specific? This was the broad screening question.

Illustrative of some specific questions which investigators held in mind were: (1) Are the changes in cerebral blood flow and cerebral metabolic rate previously described in the literature the result of aging of the nervous system or the result of disease? (2) To what extent is the postulated slowing in speed of psychomotor skills the result of a general process of change in the CNS? (3) What personality factors contribute to adaptation and maladaptation of the community-dwelling older individual to the crises of late life? (4) How do environmental factors, of cultural background and of immediate circumstances, contribute to adaptation (maladaptation) of the aged?

The term "aging" may be used to denote characteristic patterns of late life changes, which are eventually shown by all persons though differing in rate and degree. Models of aging may vary and different antecedents of biological, environmental, social or random nature have been advanced. Models will continue to be introduced so long as the phenomenon remains the mystery that it is to us today.

Although the purpose of the report is to emphasize findings and interpretations likely to be *of particular interest to the psychiatrist*, this multidisciplinary project on human aging as a whole is our subject.[1]

SAMPLE

Males were chosen as subjects for several reasons. The likelihood of profound endocrinological changes in the female suggested the advantage of male subjects in our pilot study. The predominant use of male subjects in the research literature on aging provided opportunities for comparison. Limiting the study to one sex also simplified research administration.

Screening for medical health was stringent and a final sample of 47 male volunteers with a mean age of 71 and range of 65 to 91 was obtained. The sample is not offered as representative and, in fact, certain features raise issues as to the general applicability of the findings. However, we believe that careful specification of the population makes possible comparisons with other groups. We also believe that wherein relationships were found (as opposed to descriptive characterization), the likelihood of general applicability, or at least its further testing, is possible.

The social and cultural data should be of particular interest to the growing field of social psychiatry. These subjects lived

in urban environments at the time of the study and in most cases had done so for long periods. Twenty had been born in foreign countries, having migrated in childhood or early youth. The religious breakdown was not representative of the American population as a whole. There was a wide range of educational background—men with college degrees, men with almost no formal education. (The actual educational level of any aging group is extremely difficult to estimate in terms of our present educational structure.) The estimated median years of formal education of the 47 men was 9.5 years, which is somewhat higher than the median indicated by the 1950 census for the same age group in the general urban population of the United States (8.3 years).

Many occupations were involved, over-representing the higher status white-collar occupations and under-representing the lower status manual occupations, *e.g.*, 23% had been professional persons during their work careers. Of the 47 men, 32 were fully retired at the time of the study and had been so for an average of 7 years. The annual average income received between 40 and 60 years of age was $4,300 with a range of $1,200 to $10,000. At the time of study, the median income was $3,100 with a range of $500 to $14,000. (Because of certain internal discrepancies within the data there was reason to wonder at the reliability of income figures.) The later years of life had brought fairly severe income reductions for almost half the men. The majority were living in intact families, 31 in their own households with their wives and 6 in the households of relatives.[2]

In summary, it may be seen that the men in this sample appeared to be in somewhat more fortunate circumstances than the general aged population of the United States. Not only did they have

[1] Dr. Seymour Perlin, now Chief, Division of Psychiatry, Montefiore Hospital, New York, N.Y., and I were the psychiatrists participating in this project. Dr. James E. Birren acted as coordinator. A volume, *Human Aging: A Biological and Behavioral Study* (1) reporting the methods, findings and interpretations of the entire project, was edited with Drs. James E. Birren, Samuel W. Greenhouse, Louis Sokoloff and Marian Yarrow, representing psychology, statistics, neurophysiology and social psychology respectively. Dr. Walter Obrist, presently of Duke University, conducted the EEG studies. Drs. Mark Lane and Thomas Vates, and later Dr. Leslie Libow, served as the medical internists in this project.

[2] According to the 1950 census. 3.1% of the population 65 and over were in institutions, including mental hospitals, but not general hospitals.

236

generally excellent health, one of the basic reasons for their selection, but they had better than average educational backgrounds and better than average incomes; they tended to retire with fair economic comfort and to continue to exist in private households with their wives in urban environments.

Except for the fact of community residence, selection did not depend upon other social and cultural characteristics. Since there were variations within social and cultural categories, however, it was possible to examine for any effects.

MEDICAL CHARACTERIZATION

On the basis of extensive medical examinations, the sample was further divided into two groups: Group 1, with 27 subjects, was of optimal health without apparent disease; Group 2, with 20 subjects, was also of good health, but evidence for asymptomatic or subclinical disease was found. Of these volunteers 10 showed signs of minimal, essentially extracerebral, arteriosclerosis, such as elongation and tortuosity of the aorta, EKG abnormalities, absent peripheral pulses, x-ray evidence of calcification in the aorta or carotid siphon, or retinal arteriosclerosis.

The clinical diagnosis of arteriosclerosis is limited by current methods of detection. Group 1 had no detectable evidence of arteriosclerosis; the 10 in Group 2 did. The remaining 10 members of Group 2 were so classified because of such findings as minimal to moderate rheumatoid arthritis, asymptomatic elevation of the level of blood uric acid, and diet-controlled diabetes.

That arteriosclerotic changes may be present in the vascular system of Group 1 is more than possible. Nonetheless, it seemed appropriate to classify our subjects on the bases for detection available. In view of our significant findings, we consider our classification to have been useful.

Moreover, in our 5-year follow-up, it was found that arteriosclerosis, as classi-

fied here, statistically significantly related to mortality.

METHODS

Two broad research strategies have already been described: a third major tool was that of statistical control and analysis of the data. All data collected by individual investigators were maintained by the statisticians and the findings of each discipline were not made known to other investigators to minimize the possibilities of bias. In addition to the application of customary statistical analytical techniques, the data of individual disciplines were reduced and various principal component and regression analyses undertaken.

Each of the 47 men were brought to the Clinical Center at Bethesda, Md. where they remained for two weeks and proceeded through the series of investigations following a routine schedule.[3] They resided in a unit for experimental subjects normal controls) where nursing observation as well as customary research nursing care was conducted.

METHODS OF INDIVIDUAL DISCIPLINES

The nitrous oxide procedure of Kety-Schmidt was utilized in the study of cerebral blood flow and metabolism.

EEG's were recorded on an 8-channel Grass electroencephalograph, using both bipolar and monopolar techniques. Frequency analysis was used as well as clinical reading of the tracings.

Twenty-three tests for measuring cognition and psychomotor responses were done, ranging from traditional procedures such as the Wechsler Adult Intelligence Scale to special techniques such as Perception of Line Difference Test (developed by Birren and Botwinick, 1955). Hotelling's Principal Component method was employed in an attempt to determine

[3] The study period began Dec. 1955 and ended June 1957.

the minimum number of factors necessary to account for the common variance in a wide range of psychological measurements in older men, and for purposes of interdisciplinary correlation. (Rorschach, TAT and other projective tests were administered, but the results will not be discussed here.)

Three psychiatric interviews (2 to 3 hours in length) were conducted under standard conditions; these were observed through a one-way vision mirror by an observer-psychiatrist, and were recorded and audited in an adjoining room. Systematic rotation of the roles of interviewer and observer was introduced to minimize systematic bias. In addition to traditional psychiatric evaluation, exploration of topics believed to be of particular significance to the aged was undertaken (*e.g.*, experience of changes, attitudes toward the future and toward death). Attempts were made to objectify and quantify observations and interview material, through the use of rating scales, content analyses, and independent judges.

Detailed interview guides were used in the social psychological studies which involved a significant family member as well as the volunteer; the resulting data were coded independently by two of the investigators. Eighty percent was set arbitrarily as the necessary level of coder agreement. Like other social psychological studies of the aged, the primary data source was the self-reports of the aged, but unlike them, the accounts of intimate informants and observations of the volunteers during their residence were additional sources of data, providing a check on validity.

FINDINGS[4]

This sample of aged volunteers was quite different from and superior to other samples of aged persons that have been

[4] Since more than 600 variables were measured or observed, the results of this project cannot be reported here in full. To Drs. Samuel W. Greenhouse and Donald Morrison, we are indebted for contributions to design and for statistical analysis.

previously described. This might have been expected from the selection for medical health and social competence. Broadly speaking, our men were vigorous, candid, interesting and deeply involved in everyday living. In marked contradiction to the usual stereotype of "rigidity" of the aged, these individuals generally demonstrated mental flexibility and alertness. They continued to be constructive in their living; they were resourceful and optimistic.

The internists were also very impressed by the over-all excellence of health and physical vigor of the sample. Comparatively few differences were demonstrated in the many functions tested in the medical survey between the aged and the young (Birren, *et al.*, 1963).

In contrast to the previous literature and expectations, the studies of cerebral circulation and metabolism revealed no significant difference in cerebral blood flow and oxygen consumption between a group of normal young subjects (mean age 21 years) and the elderly men (mean age 71 years), selected as described (Dastur, *et al.*, 1963). Where reductions in cerebral blood flow did occur it was found to be a function of those subjects with evidence of arteriosclerosis (Group 2).

COGNITIVE PROCESSES

Intellectual performance in this sample was superior to the young normal controls who were also tested and with the previously studied aged samples; however the psychologists did find evidence of some slowing in speed which they attributed to aging (Botwinick and Birren, 1963).

Group 1 (optimally healthy subjects) scored better than Group 2 when the 23 psychological tests were taken as a whole (less than .01), suggesting the sensitivity of cognition to health. Five principal components were derived from analysis undertaken, the first and fourth of which were interpreted as a general intellective factor and a speed factor, respectively.

Functional psychiatric disorders occur in the medically healthy, community-resident elderly which are not a function of either cerebrovascular disease, so far as present methods can detect it, nor of chronological age itself. The healthy aged are subject to disorders which appear similar to those affecting the young and these disorders, including depression, do not correlate with cerebral physiological variables (Perlin and Butler, 1963).

The prevalence of functional psychopathology in our elderly sample was similar to that which has been reported in various studies of younger volunteer populations (Lasagna, 1954; Perlin *et al.*, 1958). Mild reactive depression constituted the most common single diagnostic class (19% of the entire sample).

Searching for early prodromal signs of senility, it was found that among the individuals who were evaluated as exhibiting "senile qualities," common characteristics were observed involving intellectual functions and feelings: namely, decreased comprehension, memory, attention, and set, as well as reduced emotional responsiveness. It should be emphasized that "senile quality," perhaps in retrospect a poor term, means mild, early mental decline. Chronological age did not differ between the senile and the normal aging or senescent individuals, suggesting that senility is not an inevitable consequence of aging itself. Indeed, the importance of chronological age as an over-riding factor in the psychiatric disorders of the aging appears questionable as a result of this study; the significance of other factors including personality, psychosocial disruptions and losses, diseases and the like was recognized.

Efforts were directed toward further defining the aging experience of an individual in terms of intrinsic and environmental changes and reactions to them (Werner *et al.*, 1961). All volunteers described changes, the mean number of which was 15. The greatest number of changes reported were physical, followed by personality-affective, socio-psychological and cognitive changes. However, changes were not uniformly viewed as deficit in character by the aged subject as they are so frequently described in the literature pertaining to old age. Changes were often reported as positive and constructive. Nor were changes uniformly viewed as unalterable. Although acceptance was the most frequently reported reaction to physical decreases, compensations were reported to social psychological decreases.

Importance of personality in response to losses and disruptions (we have grouped such events under the term crises) was apparent. The effective use of insight involving accurate perception of the changed circumstances of old age and appropriate behavioral modifications was a common occurrence. Other adaptive patterns included the use of activity to extreme counter-phobic maneuvers, in which the aged person undertakes excessive, at times personally dangerous, activities to demonstrate his youth, his prowess and his fearlessness before aging and death. Denial of aging changes was found to be a useful reparative measure against depression (Butler and Perlin, 1957). The adaptive use of life long psychopathology (*e.g.*, schizoid and obsessive mechanisms), maladaptive prior to the aging period, was observed. Maintenance of a functional sense of identity seemed to be crucial to successful adaptation. An apparent alternative to the shattering of functional identity was the acceptance of a stereotype identity of an aging person. In addition to age crises in identity, severe psychological isolation and depression were especially frequent maladaptive clinical patterns.

In contrast to other age groups where diagnosis is reasonably predictive of adaptation, in the aged the discrepancy between diagnosis and adaptation seemed to be much greater, suggesting a need for revision of diagnostic assessment in the aged. There was evidence of the importance of evaluating the relationship of morale to the nature and effectiveness of adaptive techniques in the contemporary aging experience.

SOCIAL PSYCHOLOGY

Previous notions to the effect that arbitrary retirement per se results in unfortunate consequences require qualification, according to this study. It was found here that it was the man who arrived at retirement through conflicting internal and external pressures who seemed to suffer the most ill effects (Yarrow *et al.*, 1963).

The familiar sociological groupings of educational and occupational levels and ethnic classifications were not found to be related to highly differentiated patterns of function. In short, there appeared to be a "leveling" which may have resulted partly from the tendency for these men to drop their specializations, to find similar hobbies, to use common recreations afforded by the culture and to engage in many "maintenance" activities of the household. Inner resourcefulness in finding sustaining involvements was by no means the sole property of the more educated among these men.

Factors of the immediate environment were found to be very closely related to the aged person's behavior and attitudes. As the environment shows qualities of deprivation or displacement of the person (in loss of intimate persons, loss of income, in cultural displacement), the attitudes and behaviors of the aged show more deteriorative qualities and/or depressive manifestations. Losses of significant persons are especially associated with deteriorative functioning. In light of the findings on the effects of the immediate environment, the question of life setting influences might be refined. It seems probable that different life settings (group or family culture, education, *etc.*) build up, selectively and specifically, different strengths and vulnerabilities in the individual; also that different settings of earlier adult years make the occurrence of certain environmental circumstances in old age more or less likely.

INTERCORRELATIONS

Here we can only detail a few of the more provocative and significant findings, or lack of findings, of interrelationships between the various disciplines.

There was a general absence of correlations between physiological variables (*e.g.*, EEG measurements) and the general intellective factor. The interdisciplinary investigation failed to provide a neurophysiological basis for the apparent decline in speed of response in the healthy aged.

It was of considerable interest that psychiatrically evaluated depression was significantly associated with mean reaction time. This finding is consonant with most writings reporting relationships between depression and psychomotor and physiological retardation. There was not, however, any relationship between depression and cerebral circulatory, metabolic or electrical measurements.

Coupled with the findings that health status and increased arterial blood pressure also significantly correlated with mean reaction time, the question arose as to whether the hypothesized slowing of speed as a CNS process characteristic of aging required qualification. In any event, it is most important to consider this question since it is reasonable to suppose that effects intrinsic to aging are less likely to be subject to modification than are the causes and effects of morbid states.

Individuals evaluated as showing senile qualities were found to show statistically significant reductions in cognitive test scores compared to their non-senile peers but senile quality did not affect speed of response. There was some evidence to support the belief that cerebral arteriosclerosis with consequent reduction in cerebral blood flow and oxygen consumption was one pathway in production of manifestations of senility, perhaps prodromal to the development of an organic brain disorder. However, senile manifestations could not be totally explained in this way. There were individuals with early senile manifestations who did not have diagnosed arteriosclerosis or evidence of cerebral circulatory or metabolic changes. We are left with the realization that both senility and arteriosclerosis are fairly common occurrences in old age and that they may not, in fact, bear any essential pathogenic relationship to each other. It would seem reasonable to conclude, however, that when arteriosclerosis does occur with sufficient intensity cerebral circulation and metabolism are affected and senile manifestations may be produced (Butler et al., 1965). Other pathways to senility are possible. Either a non-vascular, neuronal degeneration, or a functional basis may be hypothesized.

Significant relationships which were found between measures of cerebral physiology and measures of social functioning were unexpected. Specific dimensions of organization of daily activity, maintenance of goals in living and maintenance of social contacts, as well as a summary score of social responsiveness, each significantly was associated with one or more of the physiological measures of cerebral blood flow, cerebral oxygen consumption and cerebral glucose consumption.

A significant association was found between contemporaneous environmental deficits as measured by the social psychologist and depressive trends as evaluated by the psychiatrist. A significant correlation was found between mean reaction time and severity of environmental deficits. It is suggested that the effects of losses may be mediated through the depressive state of the individual which in turn may be responsible for the slower reaction time.

SUMMARY

Old age is a period of rapid, profound and multiple changes of varying intensities, physiological and social, which influence subjective experience, behavior and adaptation. Characteristics possessed prior to

old age modify the extent and the nature of these influences but do not fully account for the changes themselves. Clarification of the nature of these changes and their age-specificity is exceedingly difficult since chronological aging is imbedded in a matrix of many other factors ranging from social to physiological.

In general this sample, as might have been expected from its selection for medical health and social competence, was quite different from other samples of aged reported previously. The belief, for example, that cerebral blood flow and oxygen consumption necessarily decrease as the consequence of chronological aging per se was not confirmed: rather it was found that when such changes did occur they were the probable result of arteriosclerosis. Although some EEG changes occurred, particularly a showing in peak frequency, they were minimal and again became marked largely in the presence of arteriosclerotic disease. Cognitive performance in this sample compared favorably with the young but the psychologists found evidence of some slowing in speed processes as a consequence of aging. Moreover, psychometric tests appeared unusually sensitive to the presence of minimal disease states including arteriosclerosis. Whether alteration in speed is an intrinsic process associated with aging and whether it is a centrally-occurring process may require further clarification. Environmental deficits, health status, arterial blood pressure, depression (and indirectly audition) were major factors that did influence both mean reaction time and a general speed factor which was extracted by means of a principal component analysis from the psychometric data.

Social, personality, and health variables would therefore appear to be of considerable importance towards explaining the manifestations of aging. Indeed, it was very striking to us that in a population purposely biased in its selection for medical health and community-residence the powerful influences of these factors would still be revealed.

It is a fundamental problem in geriatric medicine, including psychiatry, to determine how to extract aging from other factors producing overt manifestations of disturbance. It is of particular interest to the psychiatrist that disease, particularly arteriosclerosis, sensory deficits and social deprivation, has far-reaching effects; these findings are important both to evaluation and to the conduct of any treatment and care program (Butler, 1960). If arteriosclerosis should become preventable or reversible, for example, the entire façade of aging may change surprisingly.

Our broad conclusion may be stated as follows: As a consequence of a careful multidisciplinary pilot study, we have found evidence to suggest that many manifestations heretofore associated with aging per se reflect instead medical illness, personality variables, and social-cultural effects. It is hoped that future research may further disentangle the contributions of disease, social losses, pre-existent personality, so that we may know more clearly what changes should be regarded as age-specific. Indeed, various types of investigations, complementing one another, would be useful. Intensive studies, involving frequent contact over considerable periods of time, based upon the growing personal relationship between the investigator and the older person, would contribute to our understanding of the subjective experience of aging and approaching death (Butler, 1960, 1963). Longitudinal studies, of course, would enhance our opportunities of classifying changes as to whether they are age-specific, disease-linked, etc. If we can get behind the façade of chronological aging we open up the possibility of modification through both prevention and treatment. In our lifetime (if at all) it is not likely that the inexorable processes of aging will be amenable to human intervention but it cannot be too greatly emphasized that it is necessary to be able to recognize those factors which are open to change.

PART V

FAMILY RELATIONSHIPS

There is a growing literature now appearing in sociology dealing with family networks, the relations between parents and adult children, and the position of older people within the family. As a result, and unlike the situation that holds for other sections of this book, the group of papers to follow constitute a sampling from a very large number of possible inclusions.

The first paper by Sussman and Burchinal points up a major revision in sociological theories of family structure. Given the empirical evidence accumulated over the past two decades, the theory that the isolated nuclear family is the prevailing and functional form of the family in an industrialized society is shown to be in error; and the modified extended kin family is described as the most typical and the most functional, that is, a family system with complicated networks of aid and service activities in which nuclear units are linked together both vertically and horizontally.

The brief paper by Townsend extends the perspective of the family network by drawing attention to the high frequency of four-generation families now appearing in Western societies—a situation dramatized by the fact that 40 percent of persons aged 65 and over in the United States in 1962 had great-grandchildren—and discusses some of the implications for new patterns of family relationships as well as new experiences of aging.

The discussional papers by Sussman and Townsend are followed by six empirical studies, the first two focused on husband-wife relationships in middle age. Pineo's study is based on a second follow-up of 1,000 couples originally studied in engagement and again after a few years of marriage. The author reports a major loss of marital satisfaction at the time of sec-

ond follow-up, after 20 to 25 years of marriage, one he labels "disenchantment." In contrast, the brief paper by Deutscher paints a more positive picture and reports that the post-parental period of husband-wife relationships is not generally defined unfavorably by those involved in it.

Related to marital adjustment is, of course, sexual behavior. The selection that follows has been taken from the much-publicized work by Masters and Johnson on human sexuality. In the pages reproduced here the authors point to the relative paucity of data regarding the sexual behavior of older people; then describe some of the psychological and social factors, as well as health factors, involved in understanding the sexual behavior of the aging human female and the aging male.

In the paper by Neugarten and Weinstein, the focus is upon the role of grandparent. The data deal with the degree of comfort in the role expressed by grandmothers and grandfathers, the significance of the role in their lives, and differences in style in enacting the role. The "fun-seeker" emerged as a frequent style, one in which the grandparent-child relationship is characterized by "fun morality," a style which is more frequent in middle-aged than in older grandparents.

The selection by Reuben Hill is a partial report of a study of young married couples, parent families, and grandparent families. It represents one of the few investigations in which three generations of the same family line have been studied, and in which processes of decision-making differentiation of sex-roles, marital satisfaction, and other aspects of husband-wife relationships can therefore be viewed from a cross-generational point of view. One interesting finding is that the young married, and not the grandparent families are highest on vulnerability to problems requiring help; and it is the young married that receive most help from other family units.

The last paper in this section, by Shanas, is based on a survey of living arrangements and help patterns among older people and their adult children in three Western societies (United States, Britain, and Denmark) and shows how these patterns are related to social class. The empirical findings reinforce the theoretical position described in the Sussman paper: that the modified extended family is the basic social system in contemporary industrial societies; and that within this system, nuclear units are interlocked in a pattern of mutual aid which functions within all social classes.

(Other papers in this book also contain material regarding the family. In Part I "The Changing Age-Status System" includes a discussion of changes in timing of the family cycle and changing relationships between age groups within the family; and in the same Part, the paper by Neugarten and Gutmann on age-sex roles bears upon the marital roles of men and women in middle and old age.)

26

MARVIN B. SUSSMAN and LEE BURCHINAL

KIN FAMILY NETWORK: UNHERALDED STRUCTURE IN CURRENT CONCEPTUALIZATIONS OF FAMILY FUNCTIONING

Discrepancies between belief and practice of "ideal" and "real" behavior are common in our society. In family sociology the reason is "academic cultural lag"; the lag between apparently antiquated family theory and empirical reality. The theory stresses the social isolation and social mobility of the nuclear family while findings from empirical studies reveal an existing and functioning extended kin family system closely integrated within a network of relationships and mutual assistance along bilateral kinship lines and encompassing several generations. [1]

The major purpose of this paper is to reduce the lag between family theory and research in so far as it concerns the functioning of the American kin family network and its matrix of help and service among kin members. The procedure is to review relevant theory and conclusions derived from research on kin family networks completed by sociologists and an-

Abridged from *Marriage and Family Living*, 24, no. 3 (August, 1962), with the permission of the authors and the publisher. A longer article on the same subject by Dr. Sussman can be found in *Social Structure and the Family: Generational Relations*, Ethel Shanas and Gordon F. Streib, eds. (Englewood Cliffs, N.J.: Prentice-Hall, 1965).

[1] The authors adopt Eugene Litwak's interpretation of the modified extended family. It is one that "does not require geographical propinquity, occupational nepotism, or integration, and there are no strict authority relations, but equalitarian ones." (See Litwak, 1960 I, p. 385.) The components of the system are neolocal nuclear families in a bilateral or generational relationship. This system is referred to as the "kin family network."

thropologists. Appropriate modifications of existing theory which posits the notion of the isolated nuclear family are then suggested.

NUCLEAR FAMILY THEORY

Durkheim, Simmel, Toennies and Mannheim have stressed that the family in urban society is a relatively isolated unit. Social differentiation in complex societies requires of its members a readiness to move, to move to where there are needs for workers and where there are opportunities for better jobs.

American social theorists such as Linton (1959), Wirth (1938) and Parsons (1943, 1953, 1959; Parsons and Bales, 1955), support this position. Parsons suggests that the isolated nuclear family system consisting of husband and wife and offspring living independent from their families of orientation is ideally suited to the demands of occupational and geographical mobility which are inherent in modern industrial society. Major obligations, interactions and nurturance behavior occur within the nuclear family. While bonds exist between the nuclear family and other consanguineous relatives and affinals of the kin group, these lack significance for the maintenance of the individual conjugal family.

Family sociologists generally accept the isolated nuclear theory as promulgated above. They report the changes in the structure and functions of the American family system which have occurred as the system has adapted to the demands of a developing industrial society. There is general agreement that the basic functions reserved for the family are procreation, status placement, biological and emotional maintenance and socialization. However, these functions are generally analyzed in the context of the "isolated" nuclear family. The functions of intergenerational and bilateral kin family networks regarding the processes of biological and emotional maintenance or socialization are given little attention by theorists or analysts. The conclusion reached is that demands associated with occupational and geographical mobility have brought about a family pattern in urban areas consisting of relatively isolated nuclear family units which operate without much support from the kinship system.

DISCUSSION OF THE THEORETICAL ARGUMENT

A new empiricism emerging in the late 1940's questioned the persistence of the isolated nuclear family notion and presented evidence to support the viability of kin family network in industrial society.

The ideal description of the isolated nuclear character of the American family system cannot be applied equally to all segments of American society. Regional, racial, ethnic, and rural and urban, as well as socio-economic status differences in modified extended relations and family continuity patterns are known to exist. Family continuity and inheritance patterns of families in several social strata have been described (Warner and Lunt, 1941; Cavan, 1963, pp. 119–87). Among upper class families direct, substantial and continuous financial support flows from the parents, uncles, aunts, and grandparents to the children both before and after marriage. Only by receiving substantial kin support can the young high-status groom and his bride begin and sustain their family life at the financial and social level which is shared by their parents, other relatives and their friends. This support frequently includes obtaining a position for the husband in his or his in-law family's economic enterprise.

Members of lower class kin groups generally have few financial resources with which to assist married children. Among certain European ethnic groups some effort is made to assist the young couples at marriage; the notion of a dowry still persists. Generally, however, there is little knowledge, tradition or tangible forms of assistance transmitted to children which directly aids children in establishing or enhancing their socioeconomic status (Faris, 1947). Kin support in this class most frequently takes the form of providing services and sharing what financial resources are available at the time of crises or of exchanging nonmonetary forms of aid. Marginal financial resources and the impact of unemployment hits all kin members alike (Cavan, 1959).

The description of the isolated, nuclear American family system, if valid, is most suited to the white, urban, middle class segment of American society. Presumably, the leisure time of the members of these families is absorbed in the activities of secondary, special interest social groups. Since urban, lower-class family members participate less than middle class family members in voluntary organizations, it is believed that social activities of adult lower class family members are restricted to informal visiting patterns. Visiting with relatives would be a significant proportion of all of their social relations. However, prevailing sociological theory suggests that the disparities between an extended kin family system and the requirements of a mobile labor force and intergenerational family discontinuities generated by social mobility should be reflected in the lack of continuity among lower class families as well as among middle class families.

The degree to which urban lower or middle class families function as relatively isolated from their extended kin family systems is critical for all subsequent discussions of the question of kinship network and its matrix of help and service. Unless there is a reasonable frequent occurrence of primary group interaction among kin members, very likely there will be an insignificant help pattern.

The emphasis on the atomistic character of urban families has contributed to incorrect assumptions concerning interaction within the kinship matrix. It has led family sociologists to incorrectly assume that assistance among kin members was comparatively rarely sought or offered. A reconsideration of these assumptions is necessary. The bases of reconsideration are logical constructs and empirical realities set forth in the following data.

FAMILY NETWORK AND MUTUAL AID: CONCEPTUALIZATION AND RESEARCH

A theory is here considered to be composed of logically interrelated propositions which explain phenomena. Concepts are elements of a theory, defining what is to be observed. Concepts by themselves cannot be construed as a theory. They require integration into a logical scheme to become a theory.

The existence of a modified extended family with its intricate network of mutual aid in lieu of the isolated nuclear family notion is probably more of a conceptualization than a theory. However, it approaches the state of being a theory since it is not an isolated concept but is integrated with other propositions concerned with the maintenance over time of the family and other social systems of the society.

Family networks and their patterns of mutual aid are organized into a structure identified as a "modified extended family" adapted to contemporary urban and industrial society (Litwak, 1960 I; 1960 II). This structure is composed of nuclear families bound together by affectional ties and by choice. Geographical propinquity, involvement of the family in the occupational placement and advancement of its members, direct intervention into the process of achieving social status by members of nuclear family units, and a rigid hierarchical authority structure are unrequired and largely absent. The modified

extended family functions indirectly rather than directly to facilitate the achievement and mobility drives of component families and individual members. Its tasks complement those of other social systems. By achieving integration with other social systems, concerned with the general goals of maintenance and accomplishment of these systems, the extended family network cannot be considered as an isolated or idiosyncratic concept. Its elements require organization as logically interrelated propositions and whereupon it should emerge as a theory replacing the prevalent one of the isolated nuclear family.

Our concepts die hard and one way to speed their demise is to examine the evidence supporting the new ones. Evidence and measurement are difficult terms to define. When do you have evidence and when have you achieved a measurement? The reader will have to judge. The approach here is to examine the writings and research emerging from several disciplines. In some cases the work is focused on testing hypotheses or describing relationships relevant to the new conceptualization. In others, the discussions and findings emerge incidentally to the major purpose of the study. There are cases of serendipity. They occur more frequently than one would expect and add to the uncertainty of the notion of the isolated nuclear family.

One assumption of the isolated nuclear family conceptualization is that the small nuclear family came into existence in Western Europe and the United States as a consequence of the urban-industrial revolution. Furthermore its small size is ideally suited for meeting requirements of an industrial society for a mobile workforce. The effect of the urban-industrial revolution is to produce a small sized family unit to replace the large rural one. This assumption can be challenged. A study of different societies reveals that industrialization and urbanization can occur with or without the small nuclear family (Greenfield, 1961).

If household size reflects in any way the structure and characteristics of the joint extended family in India, then little changes have occurred in this system during the period of industrialization in India from 1911 to 1951 (Orenstein, 1961).

The uprooting of the rural family, the weakening of family ties, and the re-shaping of the rural family form into a nuclear type as a consequence of the industrial revolution are disclaimed for one Swiss town in a recent investigation. On the contrary many fringe rural families were stabilized and further strengthened in their kin ties from earning supplementary income in nearby factories. Able-bodied members obtained work nearby and no longer had to leave the family unit in search of work. Families which moved closer to their place of employment were accommodated in row houses; these units facilitated the living together of large family groups (Braun, 1960). These findings question the impact of industrialization upon the structure and functioning of the pre-industrial family.

It is difficult to determine if the conditions of living during the transition from a rural to an industrial society ended the dominance of the classical extended family and replaced it with a modified kin form, or if it was replaced by the nuclear one. The question is whether the modified extended family has existed since industrialization occurred; is it a recent phenomenon or an emergent urban familism, a departure from the traditional nuclear form; or is it non-existent? The evidence to support either of these positions is inconclusive. It remains however that the family network described variously as "an emergent urban familism" or "modified extended family" exists and functions in the modern community.

The family network and its functions of mutual aid has implications for the functioning of other social systems. With the growth of large metropolitan areas and concomitant occupational specialization, there is less need for the individual to leave the village, town, city or suburb of the urban complex in order to find work according to his training. Large urban areas supply all kinds of specialized educational and occupational training. The individual can remain in the midst of his kin group, work at his specialty and be the recipient of the advantages or disadvantages preferred by the kin family network. If individuals are intricately involved within a kin family network, will they be influenced by kin leaders and be less amenable to influence by outsiders; will they seek basic gratifications in kin relationships in lieu of the work place or the neighborhood; will they modify drastically current patterns of spending leisure time thus affecting current leisure forms and social systems (Haller, 1961)?

Empirical evidence from studies by investigations in a variety of disciplines substantiate the notion that the extended kin family carries on multitudinous activities that have implications for the functioning of other social systems of the society. The major activities linking the network are mutual aid and social activities among kin related families. Significant data have been accumulated on the mutual aid network between parents and their married child's family in a number of separate and independent investigations (Sussman, 1953 I, 1953 II, 1954, 1955, 1959, 1960, Sharp and Axelrod, 1956; Burchinal, 1959 I, 1959 II). The conclusions are:

1. Help patterns take many forms, including the exchange of services, gifts, advice and financial assistance. Financial aid patterns may be direct as in the case of the young married couples Burchinal interviewed; or indirect and subtle, such as the wide range of help patterns observed by Sussman, Sharp and Axelrod.

2. Such help patterns are probably more widespread in the middle and working class families and are more integral a feature of family relationships than has been appreciated by students of family behavior. Very few families included in

available studies reported neither giving nor receiving aid from relatives. However, these relationships until recently have not been the subject of extensive research.

3. The exchange of aid among families flows in several directions, from parents to children and vice versa, among siblings, and less frequently, from more distant relatives. However, financial assistance generally appears to flow from parents to children.

4. While there may be a difference in

High rates of parental support are probably associated with marriages of children while they are still in a dependency status; those among high school or college students are examples.

6. Research data are inadequate for assessing the effects of parental aid on family continuity and the marital relations of the couple receiving aid. Few studies report associations between the form and

TABLE 1

DIRECTION OF SERVICE NETWORK OF RESPONDENT'S FAMILY
AND RELATED KIN BY MAJOR FORMS OF HELP

MAJOR FORMS OF HELP AND SERVICE	DIRECTION OF SERVICE NETWORK				
	Between Respondent's Family and Related Kin Percent*	From Respondents to Parents Percent*	From Respondents to Siblings Percent*	From Parents to Respondents Percent*	From Siblings to Respondents Percent*
Any form of help.............	93.3	56.3	47.6	79.6	44.8
Help during illness.............	76.0	47.0	42.0	46.4	39.0
Financial aid..................	53.0	14.6	10.3	46.8	6.4
Care of children...............	46.8	4.0	29.5	20.5	10.8
Advice (personal and business)....	31.0	2.0	3.0	26.5	4.5
Valuable gifts.................	22.0	3.4	2.3	17.6	3.4

* Totals do not add up to 100 percent because many families received more than one form of help of service.
* Sussman, 1959, 338.

the absolute amount of financial aid received by families of middle and working class status, there are insignificant differences in the proportion of families in these two strata who report receiving, giving or exchanging economic assistance in some form.

5. Financial aid is received most commonly during the early years of married life. Parents are probably more likely to support financially "approved" than "disapproved" ones, such as elopements, interfaith and interracial marriages. Support can be disguised in the form of substantial sums of money or valuable gifts given at the time of marriage, at the time of the birth of children, and continuing gifts at Christmas, anniversaries or birthdays.

amount of aid given with the parents' motivations for providing aid. Additional studies on these points are necessary before the implications of aid to married children can be better known (Sussman, 1962).

Social activities are principal functions of the kin family network. The major forms are interfamily visitation, participation together in recreational activities, and ceremonial behavior significant to family unit. Major research findings are:

1. Disintegration of the extended family in urban areas because of lack of contact is unsupported and often the contrary situation is found. The difficulty in developing satisfactory primary relationships outside of the family in urban areas makes

the extended family *more important* to the individual (Key, 1961).

2. Extended family get-togethers and joint recreational activities with kin dominate the leisure time pursuits of urban working class members (Dotson, 1951).

3. Kinship visiting is a primary activity of urban dwelling and outranks visitation patterns found for friends, neighbors, or co-workers (Axelrod, 1956; Greer, 1956; Sussman and White, 1959; Bell and Boat, 1957; Reiss, 1959).

4. Among urban middle classes there is an almost universal desire to have interaction with extended kin, but distance among independent nuclear related units is a limiting factor (Frazier, 1957).

5. The family network extends between generational ties of conjugal units. Some structures are identified as sibling bonds, (Cumming and Schneider, 1961) "occasional kin groups"[2], family circles and cousin clubs (Mitchell I 1961, Mitchell II 1961; Mitchell and Leichter). These structures perform important recreational, ceremonial, mutual aid, and often economic functions.

Services performed regularly throughout the year or on occasions are additional functions of the family network. The findings from empirical studies are:

1. Shopping, escorting, care of children, advice giving and counselling, co-operating with social agencies on counselling and welfare problems of family members, are types of day-to-day activities performed by members of the kin network (Sussman I 1953; Leichter I and II, 1959, 1958).

2. Services to old persons such as physical care, providing shelter, escorting, shopping, performing household tasks, sharing of leisure time, etc. are expected

and practiced roles of children and other kin members. These acts of filial and kin responsibility are performed voluntarily without law or compulsion (Kosa *et al.*, 1960; Schorr, 1960; Townsend, 1957; Young and Willmott, 1957; Bott, 1957; Streib, 1958; Shanas, 1961; Kleemeier, 1961).

3. Families or individual members on the move are serviced by units of the family network. Services range from supplying motel-type accommodations for vacationing kin passing through town, to scouting for homes and jobs for kin, and in providing supportive functions during the period of in-migration and transition from rural to the urban pattern of living (Sussman and White, 1959; Mills *et al.*, 1950; Brown *et al.*, 1961; Rossi, 1955; Koos, 1946).

4. Services on occasions would include those performed at weddings or during periods of crisis, death, accident, disaster, and personal trouble of family members. A sense of moral obligation to give service or acknowledgement of one's kin appropriate to the occasion is found among kin members. The turning to kin when in trouble before using other agencies established for such purposes is the mode rather than the exception (Sussman, 1954; Bellin, 1960; Sharp and Axelrod, 1956; Wuarantelli, 1960).

5. General supportive behavior from members of the kin family network facilitate achievement and maintenance of family and community status.[3] Supportive behavior of kin appears to be instrumental

[2] Millicent Ayoub, "American Child and His Relatives: Kindred in Southwest Ohio," project supported by the Public Health Service, 1961. Dr. Ayoub is continuing her studies under the subtitle, "The Nature of Sibling Bond." She examines the solidarity or lack of it between siblings in four focal subsystems and at different stages of the life cycle.

[3] Barber, 1961. In this paper Barber challenges the current conceptualization of social class for designating an individual's position, and power within a community. He differentiates social class position, family status and local-community statuses into three types of social ranking. Each one has its own structure and functions; each allocates position, power and prestige; and each has its own range of variation. The family kin network and support received from it determines family status. President Kennedy's family and its extended family relations illustrates the point of this thesis.

252

in affecting fertility rates among component family members.[4]

A convergence of many of these findings occurs in the work of Eugene Litwak. In an extensive study of a middle class population Litwak tests several hypotheses on the functional properties of the isolated nuclear family for an industrial society: (a) occupational mobility is antithetical to extended family relations; (b) extended family relations are impossible because of geographical mobility. His findings summarized briefly are: 1) The extended kin family as a structure exists in modern urban society at least among middle class families; 2) Extended family relations are possible in urban industrial society; 3) Geographical propinquity is an unnecessary condition for these relationships; 4) Occupational mobility is unhindered by the activities of the extended family, such activities as advice, financial assistance, temporary housing, and the like provide aid during such movement; and 5) The classical extended family of rural society or its ethnic counterpart are unsuited for modern society, the isolated nuclear family is not the most functional type, the most functional being a modified extended kin family (Litwak, 1959–60; I 1960; II 1960).

CONCLUSIONS

There exists an American kin family system with complicated matrices of aid and service activities which link together the component units into a functioning

[4] Goldberg, 1960. Recent fertility research has focused upon the relationship of family organization to differential fertility since variations in family planning and family size cannot be explained by differences in socio-economic status. One variable of family organization is the family kin network. Goldberg observes, "—and incidentally one which may ultimately prove fruitful in cross-cultural studies, is a consideration of the relative benevolence of the environment in defraying the economic and social costs of having children. Here it is hypothesized that the greater the amount of help available from one's community or kinship system the weaker the desire to prevent or postpone pregnancy" (p. 9).

network. The network identified by Litwak as extended family relations is composed of nuclear units related by blood and affinal ties. Relations extend along generational lines and bilaterally where structures take the form of sibling bonds and ambilineages, i.e., the family circle or cousin club.

Major activities of this network are that members give to each other financial aid and goods of value, and a wide range of services at specific times and under certain conditions. The aid and service provided within the network supplement rather than displace the basic activities of nuclear family units. Kinship behavior assists more than negates the achievement of status and occupational advance of component families and their members.

The main flow of financial aid is along generational lines, from parents to young married children and from middle-aged parents to aged parents. Such aid is not restricted to emergencies, but may be given at various occasions such as support for education, to start a family, at time of marriage, to begin a career, and the like.

The network is used among middle class families as a principal source of aid and service when member families or individuals are in personal difficulty, in times of disaster and crisis, and on ceremonial occasions. There are some indications that established working class families are following the same pattern. Some situations cannot be handled by the nuclear unit alone, e.g., destruction of the family home by a tornado; while other situations involve more than one nuclear family or individual member, e.g., the death of an aging parent. In such situations these are mutual expectations of going to the aid of kin. Aid is sought from the most immediate kin chiefly along sibling or generational lines. Then it is followed by help from more distant kin.

In many instances everyday or weekly activities link together the members of the kin family network. Joint participation in leisure time activities are possible because of reduction of the work week. Visiting among kin is facilitated by high speed highways and other conveyances of a modern transportation system. Constant communication among kin members is possible by the widespread adoption on all class levels of the telephone as a household necessity.

The feasibility of the kin network in modern society is due to the existence of modern communication and transportation systems which facilitate interaction among members a bureaucratic industrial structure suited to modern society which removes the responsibility for job placement from the network will still permit the network to concentrate on activities intended to aid the social and economic achievement of network members,[5] and expansion of metropolitan areas in which individuals can obtain educational, occupational and status objectives without leaving their kin area. Kin members can live some distance from each other within the metropolitan area and still have relationships within the network. Nuclear units function autonomously. Decisions on what and when to act are responsibilities of the nuclear family. Influence may be exerted by the kin group upon the nuclear units so that the latter may make the "right" decision. However the kin group seldom directs the decision or action of the nuclear family in a given situation. Immunity from such control is guaranteed by legal and cultural norms which reaffirm the right and accountability of the nuclear family in such situations. The role of the family kin network is supportive rather than coercive in its relationship with the nuclear family.

[5] Mitchell (II, 1961), finds some integration of kinship and business activity. There is a tendency to "Throw business to kin members."

27

PETER TOWNSEND

THE EMERGENCE OF THE FOUR-GENERATION FAMILY IN INDUSTRIAL SOCIETY

The purpose of this paper is to call attention to a little-known fact about old people in industrial societies and to dwell upon its implications for our understanding of aging and the aged.

In 1962 a cross-national study of persons aged 65 and over was carried out in Denmark, Britain and the United States (Shanas *et al.*, 1968). Probability samples of around 2500 persons in each country were interviewed during the same period of the year. Questionnaires and methods of sampling, interviewing and analysis had been standardized.

One result surprised the investigators. A substantial proportion of the elderly populations were found to have great-grandchildren—as many as 40 percent in the United States, 23 percent in Denmark and 22 percent in Britain. What do these figures imply for our understanding of aging?

The existence on a substantial scale of families of four generations is a new phenomenon in the history of human societies. The emergence of a different structure brings new patterns of relationships but also different experiences of aging. How has it happened? This development is not attributable just to improvements in longevity. Average ages at first marriage have diminished and for women in the United States, for example, have been relatively low throughout this century. The age of parenthood has also been diminish-

ing. In the United States the median age of women at the birth of their first children was 23 for those born between 1880 and 1890 but is down to between 20 and 21 for the latest generations to marry. Because of the decreasing number of large families the median age at the birth of the last child has fallen more sharply. Earlier marriage, earlier childbirth and fewer large families inevitably contribute towards a narrowing of the average span in years between successive generations. The larger number of great-grandparents in the United States than in the European countries is attributable in the early decades of this century to the higher rates of marriage, the younger age at marriage and the birth to a larger proportion of women in the early years of marriage of several children.

It would of course be profitable to study the family life cycle in more detail. Among the British sample, for example, it seems that the women had become grandmothers on average at 54 years of age and great-grandmothers at about 72. The men had become grandfathers at 57 and great-grandfathers at 75. One immediate thought of relevance to our understanding of human personality is the scope that exists for structural variation in family building habits. Some women become grandmothers in their late thirties, others not until their seventies. These structural variations have been given little attention by sociologists and psychologists. If there are shifts of emphasis in family-building practices then there are likely to be big changes in the patterns of family relations

First published in the *Proceedings of the 7th International Congress of Gerontology, Vienna, 1966* (Vienna: Verlag der Wiener Medizinischen Akademie, 1966), pp. 555–58.

and in the types of relationship and of problems experienced by the elderly. With increasing age old people tend to find themselves nearer one of two extremes—experiencing the seclusion of the spinster or widow who lacks children and other near relatives, or pushed towards the pinnacle of pyramidal family structure of four generations which may include several children and their spouses and 20 or 30 grandchildren and great-grandchildren.

Previous theories about the changes that have taken place in family relations and in the care of the aged during the process of industrialization need to be qualified heavily. When we compare what the family does now with what it did a hundred or two hundred years ago we are not comparing like with like. Instead of 1 or 2 percent of the population being aged 65 and over there are 10 or 15 percent. In the former type of society old age may have a kind of pedestal prestige. Like the population age-pyramids that the demographers produce for us of pre-industrial societies the extended family may have only one surviving grandparent at the apex of a structure consisting of a large number of children and other relatives. Nowadays there may two, three or all four grandparents alive and often a great-grandparent too. The structure of the kinship network has changed and this has had important effects on the ways in which this network is broken into geographically proximate groupings and households.

The structure of the extended family—understood as a group drawn from the network of kin whose members meet every day or nearly every day and exchange a variety of services—has changed because of the pressures induced by changing mortality, birth and marriage rates. The relations between ascendant and descendant kin and affinal kin have been strengthened as compared with those with collateral kin. There is greater stability at the center. More people marry. More marry young. More survive as married couples until an advanced age. Consequently the number of middle-aged and elderly spinsters acting as universal aunts has diminished; there are fewer "denuded" immediate families (i.e. families of parents and unmarried sibling groups where at least one member is missing) and fewer extended families of certain types—such as widowed women linking with collateral married or unmarried kin for the purpose of rearing children and overcoming hardship. The broken marriage and the broken "home" are no longer dominant constituents of the extended family. A model type of extended family is beginning to replace a wide variety of families and households, ranging from lone individuals at one extreme to "kinship" tribes at the other. This family does not necessarily consist of *all* children and grandchildren of an old person, say, but only some of them.

What are the implications for old people in their relations with their families? They are dividing into two broad categories—those belonging to the third and those belonging to the fourth generation. Those belonging to the third generation more often have a surviving husband or wife than did persons of their age at the turn of the century. Fewer have single children remaining at home and grandchildren who are in their infancy. Since they represent the "younger" section of the elderly, fewer of their children have to look after them in infirmity, or illness, and they have more energy to spare for their grandchildren. In various ways it is likely that the rapid relative increase in importance of the third generation, with its younger age-span, will result in much greater emphasis being placed in the future than formerly on reciprocal relations between the third and fourth generations. This will alter, and complicate, the whole pattern of kinship activity. Moreover, a fourth generation of relatively frail people is also being established—for the first time on a fairly large scale.

The nature of the problems of old age is therefore changing. A common instance in the past has been the middle-aged woman faced with the problem of caring for an infirm mother as well as her young children. A common instance of the future will be the women of 60 faced with the problem of caring for an infirm mother in her eighties. Her children will be adult but it is her grandchildren who will compete with the mother for her attentions. The four generations of surviving relatives may tend to separate into two semi-independent groupings—each of two generations. Similarly, there may be a shift of emphasis from the problem of which of the children looks after a widowed parent to the problem of how a middle-aged man and wife can reconcile dependent relationships with *both* sets of parents.

Changes in population structure have far wider and deeper effects than I have been able to indicate here. Insufficient attention has been paid to them in discussing relationships between parents and their children, between husbands and

wives, between generations and generally among households and families. The data about the emergence of the four generation family suggest that the structure of the kinship network has been changing more rapidly than has been supposed. It is therefore likely that changes in family organization and relationships may have been affected less by changes in industrial and economic organization and more by changes in population structure. This may constitute an argument for reviewing and revising not only theories of change in the process of aging but also theories of urbanization and the social effects of industrialization. Individual aging is taking place in a situation of continuous sociostructural change rather than one of stability and we need to measure this change much more exactly if the question of process is to be properly explored.

28

PETER C. PINEO

DISENCHANTMENT IN THE LATER YEARS OF MARRIAGE

Since the time of Ernest W. Burgess' article "The Romantic Impulse and Family Disorganization" (Burgess, 1926) there has been an interest in family research in the process of disenchantment in marriage. Willard Waller, in *The Family, A Dynamic Interpretation* (1951), discusses the probable consequences of idealization in mate selection, emphasizing disillusionment and the growth of conflict. Recently Charles Hobart has presented empirical information showing disenchantment effects in the early years of marriage. In independent articles and with Clifford Kirkpatrick he has shown that an index of disagreement, which measures the accuracy of one spouse's estimate of the other's response to a series of questions, shows a phase movement during courtship (Hobart, 1958; Kirkpatrick and Hobart, 1954). The married phase typically shows more disagreement than the previous ones. For men, at least, there is a slight association between increases in such disagreement and the extent of premarital romanticizing.

E. E. LeMasters (1959), in another recent article in the *Midwest Sociologist*, discusses disenchantment as an aspect of divorce. Among his thirty divorced couples he reports a tendency to a non-specific disappointment in the spouse and in marriage as a cause of divorce.

LeMaster's work is concerned with disenchantment effects beyond the period of early marriage. That there is disenchant-

Abridged from *Marriage and Family Living*, 23 (1961): 3–11, with the permission of the author and the publisher.

ment after the marriage has endured for several years has not been shown in empirical work previously, to our knowledge. In part this is because for such a study longitudinal data are ideal and data of this kind are relatively scarce. But also the emphasis on romanticism in mate selection as the source of disenchantment may have dissuaded researchers from searching for effects well into the marriage.

In 1954, Burgess and his associates began a third wave of interviewing of the 1000 couples he and Paul Wallin had investigated for their verification study of the Burgess-Cottrell prediction instruments. The results of the initial interviewing and the first follow-up had previously been discussed in *Engagement and Marriage* by Burgess and Wallin (1953). The third interviewing, called the Middle Years of Marriage Study, was accomplished when the couples had been married up to 20 years. This paper is a report of some of the changes which occurred to the marriage between the early and middle years periods.

Four processes appear to dominate the data:

1. There is a general drop in marital satisfaction and adjustment, which we conceptualize as a process of disenchantment.

2. There is a loss of certain intimacy. Confiding, kissing, and reciprocal settlement of disagreements become less frequent; more individuals report loneliness. This loss of intimacy appears to be an aspect of disenchantment.

3. Personal adjustment and reports of personality characteristics are relatively unaffected by the process of disenchantment or loss of intimacy.

4. Certain forms of marital interaction are found to change as the frequency of sexual intercourse diminishes and the amount of sharing of activities drops, without any major link to disenchantment.

The evidence is presented in Table 1. As certain of the indices in the table are unfamiliar, a few comments on their performance are required. None of the new indices have been made with sufficient precision or have been tested enough to be considered more than short-term analytical devices, however.[1]

Peter C. Pineo
The Later Years of Marriage

CHARACTERISTICS OF THE INDICES INCLUDED IN TABLE 1

The scores classified as indices of marital satisfaction are highly intercorrelated and may all be said to measure a generalized

[1] The construction of the Marital Adjustment score is reviewed in Burgess and Wallin, 1953 as is that of Love, Permanence, Consensus, Own Happiness, and Sexual Adjustment indices. The Dominance score is discussed in Yi-Chuang Lu, 1952. The Index of Personal Growth is discussed in Dentler and Pineo, 1960. The Thurstone Neurotic Inventory is discussed in Burgess and Wallin, 1953 and elsewhere. Scoring instructions for the other nine indices may be obtained by writing to the author.

TABLE 1

STANDARDIZED MEAN GAIN FROM EARLY TO MIDDLE YEARS OF MARRIAGE FOR EIGHTEEN INDICES OF MARITAL SATISFACTION, MARITAL TYPE AND PERSONAL CHARACTERISTICS
(N = 400)

INDICES	GAIN FROM EARLY TO MIDDLE YEARS	
	Husbands	Wives
A. Marital satisfaction:		
Marital adjustment...............	−4.63*	−5.42*
Love............................	−2.01*	−2.87*
Permanence......................	−2.12*	−2.64*
Consensus.......................	−2.26*	−2.37*
Marriage complaints (absence of)....	−1.59	−2.09*
Own happiness...................	−1.13	−1.42
Sexual adjustment................	−1.14	− .93
B. Marital type:		
Sharing of interests and activities...	−3.84*	−4.56*
Frequency of sexual intercourse.....	−2.31*	−2.13*
Traditionalism...................	−1.86	−1.76
Attitudes to having children........	− .04	− .72
Dominance......................	.79	− .26
C. Personal characteristics:		
Idealization of mate's personality....	− .60	− .67
Personal growth gains due to marriage	− .16	− .36
Non-neuroticism or autonomy.......	− .24	− .12
Rating of own personality traits.....	−1.07	− .34
Rating of mate's personality traits...	.34	−1.31
Number of felt personality needs....	1.45	1.25

* Statistically significant changes at the .05 level of confidence or better; the standardized gains are numerically equivalent to z-scores between actual mean change and hypothesized no mean change.

$$\text{Gain} = \frac{\Sigma D}{\sqrt{\dfrac{\Sigma D^2 - (\Sigma D)^2}{N-1}}}$$

where D = (time period two score) − (time period one score).

marital adjustment or satisfaction. The marriage complaints score is based upon a long check list of possible complaints about the spouse on the marriage. Because the complaints cover many areas of marital life this index tends to be another, weaker measure of general adjustment.

Under the heading of "Indices of Marital Type" are listed five indices which measure something besides generalized adjustment, and for which no desirable and undesirable ends to the continuum each represents can immediately be named. Within any time period none is related to marital adjustment above the .40 level (Pearsonian correlation coefficient). While the median correlation of the satisfaction indices with marital adjustment is around .67, the median association with marital adjustment of the indices of marital type is around .22.

The index of Traditionalism consists of five, equally weighted questions concerning attitudes toward strong discipline of the child, independence for the wife, authority for the husband, sexual activity prior to marriage, and the sexual education of children. The total is felt to measure acceptance of "traditional" (i.e., patriarchal, restrictive) rules of marital behavior. The index has a positive association with marital adjustment, suggesting that within this cohort the traditional marriage was somewhat more satisfying for both husbands and wives than the nontraditional.

The scoring of "Sharing of Interests and Activities" comes from a long list of leisure activities which the respondents were asked to check as either engaged in alone, engaged in with the mate, or not engaged in. The score is the ratio of number of activities shared to the total number of activities undertaken. The lists were slightly revised in the middle years schedule and this may have contributed to the great drop shown in Table 1. Other information indicates that the drop must largely be real, however.

Three of the indices of personal characteristics derive from a single battery of questions. This is a list of ten personality traits, such as stubbornness or sense of humor. The respondent is asked to report, on a scale ranging from "very much so" to "not at all," how much both he and his mate, separately, possess each characteristic. The Rating of Own Personality is formed by equal weighting of the self-reports on all ten traits; the Rating of Mate's Personality is scored identically except that it is formed of the individual's rating of his mate rather than of himself.

For the Idealization of Mate index, which is perhaps misnamed, only five wholly negative traits are used. "Not at all" as a response is given the highest score and all items are weighted equally in the total. Only the rating of the mate is used.

The Personality Needs index comes from a check list of felt needs, such as needs for "someone who can give me self-confidence," "someone who makes me feel I count for something," "someone who sympathizes," etc. The respondents were asked to check any needs they felt they had, whether they were satisfied by the mate or not. The score is simply the number of such needs checked. It tends to be a measure of dependency, and in a cross-sectional analysis marital adjustment is found to be higher where the wife feels such needs and the husband does not.

The ratings of personality traits, the neurotic inventory, and the personal growth index are associated cross-sectionally from .30 to .55 with marital adjustment. On the whole the indices of personal characteristics associate more strongly than do the indices of marital satisfaction.

EVIDENCE OF DISENCHANTMENT

In Table 1 the standardized gains from the early to the middle years of marriage on these 18 indices of marital satisfaction, marital type, and personal adjustment are presented. Four hundred couples for whom schedules have been collected in both time periods are included. The standard error used in the standardization was calculated directly from the arithmetic differences between the middle years and the early years index scores.

Chance expectation would be that the "gains" would be found to fluctuate around zero.[2] In fact, however, virtually all are negative and 13 of the 36 show statistically significant drops. The drop in the marital adjustment score is roughly five standard deviations of the mean for both husbands and wives. On virtually all scores there was typically a move to the less desirable end of the continuum, as indicated by the negative signs.

The drops are particularly great and systematic within the category of indices of marital satisfaction. We conceptualize this process of dropping satisfaction as one of "disenchantment." The term "loss of satisfaction" is insufficient to express the fact that this is a process which appears to be generally an inescapable consequence of the passage of time in a marriage. In its recent usage the term "disenchantment" or its equivalent "disillusionment" has been used to refer to such a process without its origin necessarily having been in lack of realism or over-romanticizing in courtship. It must feel much like the classic disenchantment process to the individuals involved, even if its origin is different. Terms such as "disinvolvement," "individualization," "alienation," or "deterioration" have even stronger specific meanings than do "disenchantment" and so are less adequate to describe the general process.

There are two definite indications that

[2] In part, the 400 couples are not equivalent representatives of the two time periods. They are *all* who were contacted in the middle years, but only 400 of the 666 who were contacted in the early years. Put another way, all the 400 of the early years were to have at least 15 more years of married life; some of the 400 in the middle years may become divorced tomorrow. Investigation shows virtually no difference between, for example, the marital adjustment scores of the 400 used and the 266 unused from the early years. The differences cannot explain the observed losses between the time periods.

the loss in satisfaction is a general process, rather than several independent changes.

1. On the seven satisfaction indices, losses by husbands tend to associate with the losses by their wives. The median correlation between husbands' and wives' changes on these indices is approximately .30. This approaches the static husband-wife correlations for the same scores which range around a median of .42.

2. The change on any one score correlates with changes on the others. For example, just as the static scores on the indices tend to associate highly with the static marital adjustment score, so the changes on the indices associate with the changes on the marital adjustment score. The median correlation of change on the scores with change on the marital adjustment index is .41 for men. This approaches the median static correlation between the scores and marital adjustment of .68.

In an analysis in marital satisfaction, a general factor of reducing adjustment may be expected, just as an analysis by factor methods of cross-sectional data would tend to show a general factor of adjustment.[3]

THEORY OF DISENCHANTMENT

That there is a short-term disenchantment effect which derives from romanticism in mate selection seems likely. Essentially any misperception or misinformation in the selection process must bring about some reality shocks. But there are also aspects to the selection of a mate which cannot possibly be known to the individuals at the time of marriage. Insofar as personality changes and changes in environment must occur as time goes on, perfect mating could only occur with some element of luck. No couples during courtship could adequately forecast subsequent

[3] The assumption that marital adjustment is a "general factor" has not been proven at this time.

invalidism or chronic illness, for example.

We feel it is the unforeseen changes in the situation, personality, or behavior, which contribute most to the disenchantment occurring after five years of marriage. The effects of exaggerated idealization of the mate or of intense romanticizing probably are felt in the earlier years. Because the changes producing later disenchantment could not have been foretold, it is misleading to speak of "lack of realism" as the cause of later disenchantment.

Why is it that the unforeseen changes result in loss of marital satisfaction? Why do they not as frequently result in increases? The answer to these questions lies in the fact that mating occurs by personal choice. It is, moreover, a decision which may be deferred, even permanently. If mating were by random pairing, as many gains in the "fit" between husband and wife would occur as losses. But marriage by personal choice implies that a marrying group, at the time of marriage, has a self-contrived high degree of fit between the individuals involved. Individuals do not marry unless, to some extent, they feel they have more basis for union than would have occurred if their mating were determined by chance. The fit between the two is maximized before marriage will occur, as is the satisfaction such "fit" brings about. Subsequently a regression effect occurs. The deviant characteristics which provided the grounds upon which the marriage was contracted begin to be lost, as later changes tend toward the population mean and the couples become more and more like ones who married at random rather than by choice. Couples, for example, who might marry because of identical religious attitudes could only retain or lose this characteristic; they could not become more identical.

Similar disenchantment effects may be expected in other social situations. Friendships are formed by choice and on the basis of perceived valuable characteristics. Change will reduce the fit between friends, but friendships can be terminated so that the process probably does not frequently move to completion. Individuals also choose occupations somewhat on the perception of a degree of fit between their own personal characteristics and the role demands of the job. Here the commitment is often irreversible, as in marriage, so that the process of progressive loss of fit may move toward completion. Marriages are formed of individuals, while jobs involve an individual and an institution so that there is a lack of symmetry in the source of professional disenchantment which undoubtedly makes it differ from marital disenchantment.

Simply put, we argue that the grounds upon which one decides to marry deteriorate; the fit between two individuals which leads them to marry reduces with time. There is nothing in this argument which makes it necessary that satisfaction also reduce with time, however. The loss of fit could occur without reverberations in the amount of satisfaction, but our empirical finding is that satisfaction does progressively reduce as time passes. This suggests that the grounds upon which these couples married were sufficiently in phase with the actual experience of being married to maximize satisfaction at the beginning and to produce its gradual and progressive loss as the marriage wore on.

In any situation, such as marriage, in which individuals have made a major, irreversible decision to accept a long-term commitment and where the data upon which they decide are not or cannot be perfect, some process of disenchantment is to be expected. When fit and satisfaction are maximized at the point of accepting the commitment, they must, on the average, subsequently reduce.

29

IRWIN DEUTSCHER

THE QUALITY OF POSTPARENTAL LIFE

The life cycle of the family may be thought of as the sequence of realignments of family structure and relationships ranging from the time of marriage through the death of one or both partners. In a stable society, such a sequence remains relatively fixed. A body of cultural norms related to appropriate family organization and intra-family relationships develops. Obligations, responsibilities, and privileges appropriate to each phase of the family cycle become established, and anticipatory socialization for each phase takes place during the preceding period. When, however, the society itself is in a state of general transition rather than stability, the phasing of the family cycle may change, and discontinuities in socialization from phase to phase may occur.

This paper is concerned with an emergent phase of the family cycle referred to by Cavan as the postparental: "The postparental couple are the husband and wife, usually . . . in their forties and fifties. . . . The most obvious change is the withdrawal of . . . children from the family, leaving husband and wife as the family unit. . . ." (Cavan, 1963, p. 482) This new phase of the family cycle is, in large part, a consequence of the increasing longevity, coupled with a decline in the average number of children as compared with earlier generations.

In contrast to a dearth of research on the postparental period, clinical observations, speculations, and inferences from

Abridged from the *Journal of Marriage and the Family*, vol. 26, no. 1 (February, 1964), with the permission of the author and the publisher.

other kinds of situations are plentiful. Commentaries based on such sources tend to be polarized. On the one hand there are those who warn that this is a period which places a severe strain on both the individual adult and the husband-wife relationship; at the other extreme is the school of thought which suggests that this is the time when life reaches its fullest bloom and the husband-wife relationship is reinforced with renewed vigor.

There is, then, a substantial amount of disagreement regarding the quality of life during this newly evolving and yet largely unexplored phase of the family cycle. In addition, the opinions held by the experts are based to a considerable extent on experiences with clients or patients— a selectively disturbed segment of the population. The present paper reports the results of an attempt to locate and describe the quality of postparental life within one stratum of the urban population and among a more representative sample of that population.

Briefly, the investigator conducted a door-to-door survey in two socio-economic areas of Kansas City, Missouri. One of these areas can be described as upper-middle class and the other as lower-middle class. Approximately 540 households were contacted in these areas. A brief questioning at the door with anyone who answered was sufficient to determine whether or not the household met the operational criteria of postparental, i.e., husband and wife both alive and living together, both between the ages of 40 and 65, and having had from one to four children, all of whom had been launched.

The survey technique resulted in the identification of 33 postparental households. Efforts to obtain intensive interviews were successful in 31 of these households, with 49 of the spouses being interviewed. Most of these open-ended interviews, which lasted from one to three hours, were tape recorded. This paper examines the way in which these urban, middle-class couples orient themselves to a new phase in the family cycle: to what extent do they define the postparental situation favorably and unfavorably?

Evaluation	Total	Husbands	Wives
(+) Postparental is "better" than preceding phases....	22	8	14
Postparental is as "good" as preceding phases........	15	7	8
(0) Value orientation or changes not clear........	7	5	2
Postparental is as "bad" as preceding phases........	2	1	1
(−) Postparental is "worse" than preceding phases....	3	0	3
Total.................	49	21	28

DEFINITIONS OF THE SITUATION

The clearest clues to the manner in which postparental spouses evaluate their present situation lie in the place they reserve for it in their discussion of the total life line. This place was revealed by respondents in their discussion of such questions as, "If you could divide your life into parts, which part would you say was the best time?" and "which part was the worst time?" "How is your life different now from what it was when the children were at home?" "Now that the children have left, do you notice any difference in your husband (or wife)?" "How did you feel when the last of the children left home?"

"How is your life different now than it was ten years ago?"

As Table 1 indicates, clear evaluations of the postparental period as being "better" than life during earlier stages of the family cycle appear in 22 of the 49 interviews. Equally clear negative evaluations occur in only *three* instances. This sample provides little support for those observers who suggest that postparental life is a time of great difficulty. (It should be pointed out, however, that couples whose difficulties during this period were reflected in extreme husband-wife friction —so extreme that the couple no longer lived together—were selected out of this sample by definition.)

What kinds of comments provide the basis for the classification which appears in Table 1, and what lies behind the frequencies; i.e., what are the criteria by which people judge their lives as "better" or "worse"? Let us examine first the majority, for whom postparental life, far from being a time of crisis, is the "good" time—or, at least, better than the periods immediately preceding it.

For such people, it is a time of freedom —freedom from financial responsibilities, freedom to be mobile (geographically), freedom from housework and other chores, and finally, freedom to be one's self for the first time since the children came along; no longer do the parents need to lead the self-consciously restricted existence of models for their children. They can let their hair down: "We just take life easy now that the children are grown. We even serve dinner right from the stove when we're alone. It's hotter that way, but you just couldn't let down like that when your children are still at home."

These new-found "freedoms" are expressed in many ways by respondents. A newly postparental wife provides the following typical summary statement in response to the inquiry concerning how life is different now that the children are gone:

"There's not as much physical labor. There's not as much cooking and there's not as much mending and, well, I remarked not long ago that for the first time since I can remember my evenings are free. And we had to be very economical to get the three children through college. We're over the hurdle now; we've completed it. Last fall was the first time in 27 years that I haven't gotten a child ready to go to school. That was very relaxing."

In this group, typical male comments are "It took a load off me when the boys left. I didn't have to support 'em anymore. I wouldn't mind having a dozen if I could support 'em right." Or, as one businessman expresses it: "I think the happiest time was when our children came into the world, but I'm looking forward to our life together now; we're getting our dividends." In a manner of speaking, these become the years of the payoff.

The wives, on the other hand, respond typically in this manner:

"We're not tied down with children anymore, because they're all old enough to take care of themselves now."

"I don't have as many meals to prepare anymore, and my health is better now, and we have had more to live on in the past few years; our income is better now."

"We have given all for the children and that was the most important thing. We lived for the children, and after they were raised we looked for comfort for ourselves. Now when I make up my mind to get something important, I get it in time."

But even more important than these "freedoms" is the re-definition of self and the marital partnership which appears to result from them. It may be this new form of interpersonal relationship and self conception that is the real dividend for these particular families. They speak of "better" relationships with each other, of a sense of accomplishment—a job well done—and refer to postparental life as a time of "contentment" or "satisfaction."

As mentioned above, the "freedoms" culminate in the freedom to be oneself. Such a freedom could, of course, lead to either a strengthening or a weakening of the husband-wife relationship. For the moment only the former cases are considered:

"My husband was a very nervous, jumpy man when the children were younger. If he wanted to do something, he would do it. We would have an argument if I tried to stop him. Now he is altogether a different man. (Q.: What do you think brought about this change in him?) Well, I think that when the girls grew up and he saw how well I was trying to raise them that he was really proud of them. Of course, as a man grows older he doesn't want to go out so much. He gets to be more of a homebody."

Nor is this a one-way picture. This woman's husband also finds her more amiable now that the children are gone:

"We get along better—we always got along very well but we get along so much better since we're by ourselves. I know I appreciate and enjoyed her company more in the last year or two than I did before. The main change is like with myself; she's not as nervous since the children left home."

For some of the older postparental couples, retirement has accompanied the departure of the children, but the result is the same:

"The happiest time of my life? To tell you the truth, I believe it's right now. We're happier than we've ever been because we're together constantly, you know. He's home and I don't have to worry about him going out and going on the road, and I believe we're just the happiest now that we've ever been. Of course, we were happy when we had the children."

"Of course," they were happy; however, her husband, who commented that raising four children was a "hard row to hoe" agrees: "I think it's more like home since I retired. As I told you before, I'm really enjoying my life now." It is a long, hard row to hoe, not only economically, but emotionally as well. The prelaunching years are a time of uncertainty and of anticipation—will the children turn out all right? "You put part of the tension on the children in younger lives"—

"Just about now we have a comfortable home, two children, a grandchild, and I feel relaxed. That is a rather comfortable feeling—to be our age—to live for each other."

Things have not always been so good for this couple: "About ten years ago, my boy came home from the service, and I had a lot of worry and responsibility. Then, I had a teen-age daughter, and there was the uncertainty of their life." As one husband puts it, "Life didn't start settling down until the kids got grown up." He feels that now is the best time in life: "I'm more content, and there is more satisfaction."

Unfavorable evaluations made by postparents, although they rarely occur, bear examination in order to determine their quality. The difficulties appear to center around three areas: (1) the advent of menopause and other disabilities associated with the aging process; (2) the final recognition and definition in retrospect of oneself as a "failure," either in terms of the work career or the child-raising process; and (3) the inability to fill the gap—the empty place in the family which results from the departure of the children.

All of the respondents are familiar with the advent of menopause. To some it had no meaning or impact on their existence; to others it was a difficult time which had to be hurdled with a conscious effort; to a few it was a disrupting force which left a permanent impression on their lives and family relationships. Survival of the menopause is described by one respondent in terms of keeping "a healthy attitude:"

"I've had a little trouble with menopause. (Q.: Is menopause very bad?) Yes, it is sometimes. You just get so terribly depressed. You have all kinds of silly feelings. You hate your best friend, and you are irritable and critical and cross. You just feel crazy sometimes. But I make a joke out of it. You got to keep a healthy attitude."

Even more telling, however, is the final assessment—the summing up—which some respondents make of their own lives. Now, in late middle age, they gain some perspective on their own histories, and to a few, the story is a tragedy of unattained goals—of "failure." One kind of failure involves the shattering of hopes and ambitions for children:

"Things hurt you a little deeper when you get older. (Q.: What kinds of things?) Oh, if you have real trouble, it hurts you worse. If your children have traits— (Q.: What do you mean by traits?) Maybe you've been religious and gone to church and sent the kids to Sunday School regularly and, you know, put yourself out. Well, sometimes it ends up that the kids won't go near a church. They just say, 'I had all the church I need.' And education—well, you can't help but feel that they are foolish there. You have to know their personality. You can't make them over; you have to find out the hard way . . . (pause). . . . He had a voice like Nelson Eddy. Just beautiful. I tried to encourage him, but it didn't do any good. He would never do anything with it."

There are couples who have clung to marriage "for the sake of the children" or some other such rationale for as long as 25 years.

There is one respondent who illustrates in extreme form the kinds of limits which can be approached during this period; here is postparental life at its worst:

"(Q.: Both of your daughters are married?) Yes, both are married and have children. Yes, here I am fifty-five—fifty-five, but I don't feel old. I feel disgusted but not old. I would lay down and die if I wasn't a coward. I was kinda depressed when my first girl married. I thought that was the end. I just died. I don't even care very much how I look. Look, I'm thirty pounds overweight. My daughters were both nineteen when they married. I didn't want them not to marry, but I missed them so much. I felt alone. I couldn't play golf. I couldn't even play bridge. I don't have a profession, and I couldn't take just any job. . . . I wanted my girls to wait until they were 30 before they got married."

CONCLUSIONS

These, then, are the evaluative outlooks on postparental life, from its best face to its worst. If the sample employed for this analysis should prove to be typical of urban middle-class postparental couples, it can be concluded that the overwhelming majority of them define the situation favorably, although serious problems present themselves for a small minority. When this gross overview is examined for sex, age, and class differences, some variations appear. A larger percentage of wives evaluate the postparental period *both* more favorably and more unfavorably than do husbands. It would appear that this is a crucial time of life for the woman and that it is being clearly resolved one way or the other as far as she is concerned. It may be that the men have not yet been forced into self-evaluation or reconciliation to any major revisions in life. They are, for the most part, still employed in their occupations as they have been for many years, and the interviews reveal that in an overwhelming majority of cases, the children were closer to the mother and her primary responsibility. Her hand has been forced; her husband's showdown may lie in the near future when retirement comes.

Any explanation of the general bland-ness of the husband's interviews must be qualified in terms of some of the more universalistic sex-role characteristics in our society. Whereas a woman may be expected to be volatile, emotional, expressive, and sentimental, such qualities are hardly considered masculine. The interviews with husbands were characterized by a lack of emotional quality—of expressiveness. They were not nearly as communicative as their wives. This does not mean that their tendency toward neutral responses was an artifact of the methodology; the impression of the writer (and interviewer) is that it is more likely an artifact of the culture.

Insofar as the evidence obtained in this study is concerned, there seems to be no difference between older and younger postparental spouses regarding their evaluation of that time of life. In terms of class, however, a different picture presents itself. The upper-middle-class spouses have an appreciably more favorable outlook on postparental life than do their lower-middle counterparts.

Although the sample employed in the study is small, it does not suffer from representing only those people who seek help, and it does reveal some extreme differences. In addition, what little nonclinical research is available appears to agree with the present findings. Basing her conclusions on a study of 85 upper-middle-class women between the ages of 25 and 50, Gass found that they obtained little satisfaction from childrearing and that they were glad to be freed of the confining element of homemaking: "For these women, then, the fact that they were in their middle years increased, rather than decreased, their contentment" (Gass, 1959). Axelson studied postparental couples in two "medium sized communities" in Idaho and Washington at about the same time the field work for the present study was undertaken. His mailed questionnaire returns from over 800 parents of wedding-license applicants lead him to conclude that "this period of life seems as satisfying as earlier periods" (Axelson, 1960).

These data seem to indicate that the postparental phase of the family cycle is not generally defined unfavorably by those involved in it. This finding evidently holds true despite the relative newness of this phase of the family cycle and the assumption which might be made that little opportunity for role-taking or anticipatory socialization has existed (Deutscher, 1962).

30

WILLIAM H. MASTERS and VIRGINIA E. JOHNSON

HUMAN SEXUAL RESPONSE: THE AGING
FEMALE AND THE AGING MALE

THE AGING FEMALE

Theoretical knowledge and clinical experience related to sexual problems of the aging are totally inadequate to meet the requirements of men and women who currently are living within the framework of our newfound longevity. Any counselor facing problems created by the sexual tensions of menopausal or postmenopausal women finds himself seriously handicapped by the lack of a well-established body of literature on the subject.

Reports of the aging female's sexual activity have been limited largely to studies of the menopausal or immediate postmenopausal years. Possibly this investigative concentration on the climacteric age of 45 to 55 years has been stimulated by women's tendency to seek relief at this time from a variety of psychophysiologic problems. In order to establish the aging-female component of the study-subject population, 157 intake interviews were conducted with women beyond 51 years of age. One hundred fifty-two of these women contributed detailed sociosexual histories in response to team interrogation. From this material, together with that accumulated from seven years of clinical therapy of sexual inadequacy, the behavioral concepts expressed in this chapter have been drawn. The age distribution of the 152 women past 51 years of age and the level of their formal education are listed in Table 1. The subjects

Abridged from William H. Masters and Virginia E. Johnson, *Human Sexual Response* (Boston: Little, Brown and Co., 1966), chap. 15, pp. 238–47, chap. 16, pp. 260–70.

provided histories separately to both the male and female members of the interview team.

The degree of influence of sex-steroid withdrawal upon female sexual adjustment during the menopausal and postmenopausal years has not been established, although it is a popular practice to assign to the physiologic fact of steroid starvation most of the physical ills and psychosexual problems associated with these years. Many facets of the relationship between states of steroid starvation and female sexual response remain to be defined. Specific indications of postmenopausal physiologic involution of ovarian function may be corrected easily with adequate endocrine-replacement therapy. (Davis, 1965; Freeman and Pincus, 1963; Froimovich *et al.*, 1962; Masters, 1953, 1957) but even more necessary for maintained sexual capacity and effective sexual performance is the opportunity for regularity of sexual expression. For the aging woman, much more than for her younger counterpart, such opportunity has a significant influence upon her sexual performance.

As has been seen, endocrine starvation has an indirect influence upon, but certainly not absolute control over, female sexual capacity or performance. Steroid starvation also has an indirect influence upon female sexual drive. However, sex drive is but one in the total of physical and psychosocial factors influenced by the aging process.

It has become increasingly evident that the psyche plays a part at least equal to, if not greater than, that of an unbalanced endocrine system in determining the sex drive of women during the postmenopausal period of their lives. If endocrine factors alone were responsible for sexual behavior in postmenopausal women (whether menopause occurs by surgical or natural means), there should be a relatively uniform response to the physiologic diminution and ultimate withdrawal of the sex hormones. However, there is no established reaction pattern to sex-steroid withdrawal. For instance, clinical symptoms of menopausal distress vary tremendously between individuals, and, for that

TABLE 1

AGE AND EDUCATION OF 152 GERIATRIC FEMALE STUDY SUBJECTS

AGE BY DECADE	No. SUB- JECTS	EDUCATION			
		Grade School	High School	Col- lege	Gradu- ate School
51–60......	98	2	62	29	5
61–70......	37	1	28	6	2
71–80......	17	3	11	3	0
Totals....	152	6	101	38	7

matter, within the same individual as the demand arises for increased physical or mental activity (Masters and Ballew, 1965).

Elevation of sexual responsiveness rarely results directly from the administration of estrogen or estrogen-like products. Estrogenic compounds frequently do improve sex drive in an indirect contribution above and beyond the original intended purpose of insuring a positive protein balance in the aging female. A woman previously experiencing a healthy libido may become relatively asexual while contending with such menopausal discomforts as excessive fatigue, flushing, nervousness, emotional irritability, occipital headaches, or vague pelvic pain. This individual's personal eroticism may be restored to previously established response

levels following the administration of estrogenic preparations. The obviously increased sex drive well may have developed secondary to relief of the woman's multiple menopausal complaints, rather than as a primary or direct result of the actual adjustment of the individual's sex-steroid imbalance (Masters, 1957).

Personality studies of menopausal or postmenopausal women are more prevalent in the literature than are endocrine studies. In the opinion of Stern and Prados (1946) there is no correlation between the intensity of the type of physical symptoms usually related to hormonal withdrawal (hot flushes, for instance) and the severity of emotional disturbances occasioned by steroid starvation. They do feel, however, that among the many complaints presented by menopausal women the physical complaint of pelvic pain is the most intimately associated with the more severe forms of psychic maladjustment. Rosenzweig (1943) suggests that emotional disturbance during the menopause may represent a reaction of frustration to the representation of the menopause as the failure of the whole life cycle in respect to procreation. Shorr (1938) came to the conclusion that the emotional complications of the menopause are basically psychoneurotic in nature and are almost always exacerbations of similar disorder patterns developed earlier in the patient's life. Certainly, absence of a sense of well-being and general physical discomfort frequently present in the menopausal woman only would tend to heighten and reactivate established psychoneurotic behavior patterns of sexual origin. The average woman's psychosomatic symptoms fluctuate to the greatest extent in the menopausal years. It is to be expected that the sex drive, with its multiple related tensions, would reflect the instability of this age group.

During the climacteric either a return to or escape from the reproductive drive has been demonstrated by many women. Helene Deutsch (1945) has stated that during the preclimacterium many women develop an overwhelming desire to become pregnant once more, demonstrating in this manner an apprehensive feeling about the "closing of the gates." Other women welcome the advent of the climacteric with genuine pleasure but do not demonstrate an increased sex drive until menopause obviously is well established. These women usually have been burdened with either an excessive number of children or a financial situation too insecure to guarantee adequate family protection. They develop a resultant "freedom from fear of pregnancy" as the menses terminate.

Many a woman develops renewed interest in her husband and in the physical maintenance of her own person, and has described a "second honeymoon" during her early fifties. This expression of unleashed sexual drive occasioned by the alleviation of the "pregnancy phobia" is one of the most frequently occurring factors responsible for increased sexual tensions evident in the 50–60-year age group. Noteworthy is the obvious fact that the renewed husband-interest of the pregnancy-phobic individual reflects a baseline of pleasure and stability in the sexual relationship.

When the women who demonstrate the "freedom from fear" complex are added to those concerned with the "closing of the gates," the frequently increased levels of sexual activity during the late forties and early fifties noted by many observers is partially explained. It should be emphasized, however, that the woman who increases her sexual activity basically from a desire to conceive rarely has major interest in the sexual relationship per se. Thus, the marked increase in sexual activity of these two groups does not reflect parallel increase in sex drive.

Absolute contraceptive security has not been available in the past to women who are presently in the menopausal and postmenopausal age groups. Therefore, the pregnancy phobias, when they have developed, have been thoroughly understandable. When the 20–30-year-old women of today are in their late forties and early fifties, the expected increase in sex drive concomitant with release of pregnancy fears well may be a thing of the past. In today's society the young wife need have no fear of unwanted pregnancy, provided her religion tolerates the practice of contraception and she can afford to purchase the effective contraceptive materials presently available.

It also should be recalled that women beyond 50 years of age usually have resolved most of the problems associated with the raising of a family. Once the exhausting physical and extensive mental demands of brood protection have been obviated by the maturing of the family group, it is only natural that new directions are sought as outlets for unexpended physical energy and reawakened mental activity. Thus, a significant increase in sexual activity marks the revived sex drive of these middle-aged women. Frequently this is the time for casting about for new sexual partners or for the development of variations of or replacements for long-established unsatisfying sexual practices.

The Kinsey group has noted that a large part of the sex drive during the postmenopausal age is related directly to the sexual habits established during the procreative years (Kinsey *et al.*, 1953). The interview material suggests that a woman who has had a happy, well-adjusted, and stimulating marriage may progress through the menopausal and postmenopausal years with little or no interruption in the frequency of, or interest in, sexual activity. Additionally, social and economic security are major factors in many women's successful sexual adjustment to their declining years.

Needless to say, there is an increasingly large segment of the female population that is diametrically opposite to the reasonably adjusted individual described above. If a woman has been plagued by seeming frigidity, or by lack of regularly recurrent or psychosexually satisfactory coital activity during her active reproductive years, there is reason to believe that the advent of the postmenopausal years may serve to decrease sex drive and to make the idea of any form of sexual expression increasingly repugnant. This individual uses the excuse of her advancing years to avoid the personal embarrassment of inadequate sexual performance or the frustrations of unresolved sexual tensions.

There also remains the Victorian concept that older women should have no innate interest in any form of sexual activity. The idea that the postmenopausal woman normally should have little or no sex drive probably has arisen from the same source. Even dreams or fantasies with sexual content are rejected in the widespread popular belief that sexual intercourse is an unsuitable indulgence for any woman of or beyond middle age.

As emphasized by Newman and Nicols (1960), the sexual activity of the woman in the 70-plus age group unfortunately is influenced by the factor of male attrition. When available, the male marital partner is an average of four years older than the female partner. Many of the older husbands in this age group are suffering from the multiple physical disabilities of advancing senescence which make sexual activity for these men either unattractive or impossible. Thus, the wives who well might be interested in some regularity of heterosexual expression are denied this opportunity due to their partner's physical infirmities. It also is obvious that extramarital sexual partners essentially are unavailable to the women in this age group.

The trend of our population toward an aging society of women without men must be considered. Roughly 10 percent of women never marry. In addition, the gift of longevity has not been divided equally between the sexes. As a result, there is a steadily increasing legion of women who are spending their last years without marital partners (Mering and

Weniger, 1959). Many members of this group demonstrate their basic insecurity by casting themselves unreservedly into their religion, the business world, volunteer social work, or overzealous mothering of their maturing children or grandchildren. Deprived of normal sexual outlets, they exhaust themselves physically in conscious or unconscious effort to dissipate their accumulated and frequently unrecognized sexual tensions.

Masturbation presents no significant problem for the older-age-group women (Masters and Johnson, 1960, 1964). The unmarried female who has employed this method for relief of sexual tensions during her twenties and thirties usually continues the same behavioral pattern during her forties and through her sixties. When heterosexual contacts are limited or unavailable the widowed or divorced woman also may revert to the masturbatory practices of her teens and twenties when sexual tensions become intolerable. As might be expected, there is reduction in the frequency with which manipulative relief is deemed necessary beyond 60 years of age.

There seems to be no physiologic reason why the frequency of sexual expression found satisfactory for the younger woman should not be carried over into the postmenopausal years. The frequency of sexual intercourse or manipulative activity during the postmenopausal years is of little import, as long as the individuals concerned are healthy, active, well-adjusted members of society.

It would seem that the maladjustments and abnormalities of sex drive shown by states of hyper- or hyposexuality which develop during and after the menopause might best be treated by prophylaxis. If satisfactory counseling of sexual content were made more available to sexually insecure, uneducated, or inadequate women in the premenopausal years, there is reason to believe that the unresolved tensions of the later years might be reduced or, to a large extent, avoided. There is no reason why the milestone of the menopause should be expected to blunt the human female's sexual capacity, performance, or drive. The healthy aging woman normally has sex drives that demand resolution. The depths of her sexual capacity and the effectiveness of her sexual performance, as well as her personal eroticism, are influenced indirectly by all of the psycho- and sociophysiologic problems of her aging process. In short, there is no time limit drawn by the advancing years to female sexuality.

THE AGING MALE

Our aging population increasingly demands functional and functioning roles not only within community structure but in private life. Vocalization of these demands has stimulated renewed consideration of the inevitable adjustments of the aging process. Not the least of these adjustments are those related to physiologic and psychologic capacity for sexual performance.

Investigative scrutiny rarely has been directed toward the functional and functioning variations of the sexuality of the human male during and beyond his climacteric years. Much in the aging male's life is affected by psychosocial adjustments occasioned by sexual involution. Yet little scientific data has been established as a baseline from which his psychosexual needs may be interpreted and solutions to related problems suggested. Although the Kinsey group recorded data on over 5,000 white males, only 126 histories were obtained from men past 60 years of age (Kinsey *et al.*, 1948). Both Finkle *et al.* (1959) and Newman and Nicols (1960) in independent studies interviewed just over one hundred males beyond the age of 55 years. Although Stokes (1951) has assembled a massive amount of pertinent information, his statistics and conclusions have not been published to date (Stokes, 1963).

In short, clinical material gathered to evaluate sexuality of males in the geriatric population has been totally inadequate. This statement should not be construed as reflecting adversely upon prior investigations, but rather should serve to emphasize the difficulties inherent in any attempt to evaluate the aging male's sexuality. In order to understand the rigid social resistance expressed toward any investigation of the aging male's sexuality, it may be helpful to recall that Victorian influence upon our society has decreed for years that the aging male possesses little or no socially acceptable sexuality.

When this culturally resistant facet of human sexual experience was approached, the anticipated inadequacy of available clinical material was encountered; 245 men over the age of 50 years were interviewed. Of this total, 212 were sufficiently motivated to provide detailed sociosexual histories which dated from earliest recall to current state of sexual activity. Of the 212 aging men, 152 were members of marital units in which both partners were past 50 years of age and were willing to provide histories of sexual behavior. Full advantage was taken of the opportunity to crosscheck the sociosexual histories of the 152 men by comparing them insofar as possible with those obtained from their wives. There was marked correlation in material on sexual capacity and performance, including specifics of current frequency, techniques, mounting success, and patterns of satisfactory response. When an aging male or female cooperated to provide a history, the partner was interviewed immediately to avoid suggested or jointly prepared answers. It is from a review of this material, together with data acquired from seven years of clinical therapy of male sexual inadequacy that this chapter has been constituted.

The aging male's obvious reluctance to impart material with sexual orientation is evidenced by the fact that 245 men had to be interviewed in order to accumulate the 212 histories granted separately to both the male and female members of the interview team. The age distribution, by decades, of these 212 cooperative men and brief statistics relating to their formal education are presented in Table 2.

The bias toward higher levels of formal education than would be expected for the general population is obvious. Only 4 men failed to enter high school, and only a total of 39 (18 percent) failed to enroll in college. Despite the exceptionally higher levels of formal education apparent in the male study-subject population, only 39 men had sufficient incentive and security of sexual performance to cooperate actively with the study-subject group.

There is no question of the fact that

TABLE 2

AGE AND EDUCATION OF 212 GERIATRIC
MALE STUDY SUBJECTS

AGE BY DECADE	No. SUBJECTS	EDUCATION			
		Grade School	High School	College	Graduate School
51–60......	89	2	17	43	27
61–70......	71	0	8	51	12
71–80......	37	1	6	26	4
81–90......	15	1	4	9	1
Totals....	212	4	35	129	44

the human male's sexual responsiveness wanes as he ages. Particularly is this true if sexual responsiveness arbitrarily is defined in such general, clinical terms as (1) existing levels of sexual tension, (2) ability to establish coital connection, (3) ability to terminate coition with ejaculation, and (4) current history of masturbation and/or nocturnal emission. A major difference exists between the response patterns of the middle-aged male (41–60 years) and those of men past the 60-year landmark. This difference is reflected in the male over 60 years by loss of maintained levels of sexual tension and reduced reactive intensity during sexual expression. Not only does coital activity usually decrease but the incidence of masturbation and nocturnal emission also is slowed

with advancing years (Botwinick, 1959; Kinsey et al., 1948).

The aging male's sexual capacity and performance vary from individual to individual and from time to time in a particular individual. Obviously, capacity and performance are influenced directly by acute or chronic physical infirmity, or by the general physiologic involution of the total body. Possibly the greatest influence on geriatric sexual response may be inherent in the sociosexual environment within which a male lives during his sexually formative years. Kinsey et al. (1948) suggested this possibility and work with the present investigative population has tended to support their thesis.

The most important factor in the maintenance of effective sexuality for the aging male is consistency of active sexual expression. When the male is stimulated to high sexual output during his formative years and a similar tenor of activity is established for the 31–40-year age range, his middle-aged and involutional years usually are marked by constantly recurring physiologic evidence of maintained sexuality. Certainly it is true for the male geriatric sample that those men currently interested in relatively high levels of sexual expression report similar activity levels from their formative years. It does not appear to matter what manner of sexual expression has been employed, as long as high levels of activity were maintained.

The incidence of sexual inadequacy in the human male takes a sharp upturn after 50 years of age. As might be expected, secondary impotence increases markedly after this age and continues to increase with each additional decade. During the last seven years of experience in therapy for sexual inadequacy, 83 percent of impotent males have been past the age of 40 years at onset of treatment, and three of every four of these men were over 50 years of age. Of real interest is the fact that the male over 50 years old can be trained out of his secondarily acquired impotence in a high percentage of cases

(Carmichael and Noonan, 1941; Johnson and Masters, 1964, I and II; Masters and Johnson, 1961, 1965; Walker and Strauss, 1939).

Just as the secondarily impotent male over 50 years old can be reconstituted, so can the potent aging male's responsive ability, dormant for physical or social reasons, be restimulated, if the male wishes to return to active sexual practices and has a partner interested in sexual performance. If he is in adequate health, little is needed to support adequacy of sexual performance in a 70- or even 80-year-old male other than some physiologic outlet or psychologic reason for a reactivated sexual interest.

Briefly, if elevated levels of sexual activity are maintained from earlier years and neither acute nor chronic physical incapacity intervenes, aging males usually are able to continue some form of active sexual expression into the 70- and even 80-year age groups. Even if coital activity has been avoided for long periods of time, men in these age groups can be returned to effective sexual function if adequate stimulation is instituted and interested partners are available.

FACTORS IN MALE SEXUAL INVOLUTION

Under what physical conditions or psychic influences does the aging male progressively lose sexual responsiveness? Answers to these questions comprise information of extreme importance in both understanding and treating problems of geriatric sexuality. Although the sample is small and obviously is not representative, some suggestions worthy of consideration have emerged not only from intensive team interrogation of the aging male but in many instances from cross-interrogation of his spouse.

There are manifold physiologic and psychologic factors that contribute to involution of the aging male's sexual prowess. This becomes particularly apparent when interrogation is carried out in depth. Under detailed probing the individual basis for alteration in male re-

sponsive ability usually falls within one or more of six general categories: (1) monotony of a repetitious sexual relationship (usually translated into boredom with partner); (2) preoccupation with career or economic pursuits; (3) mental or physical fatigue; (4) overindulgence in food or drink; (5) physical and mental infirmities of either individual or his spouse; and (6) fear of performance associated with or resulting from any of the former categories. These six categories will be considered briefly but in specific terms.

Monotony in Sexual Relationship.— Loss of coital interest engendered by monotony in a sexual relationship is probably the most constant factor in the loss of an aging male's interest in sexual performance with his partner. This monotony may be the end-result of a sexual relationship which did not develop beyond the stage of dutiful indulgence and/or physical need for tension release. It also may develop from a relationship in which the sexual component did not mature or keep pace with other facets of marital progression.

Since the factor of overfamiliarity with the partner does influence sexual responsiveness, it should be considered in some detail. For generations, the mores of a patriarchal society have not confined the male to one sexual partner. When this attitude exists in the male partner, it may provide a built-in reaction of sexual restlessness after many years of partner restriction in a monogamous state. The female partner may lose her stimulative effect as her every wish, interest, and expression become too well known in advance of sexual activity, especially if the subconscious male focus has anticipated multiple-partner sexual variation. Although the younger woman to whom such an aging male turns may not in fact be as effective a sexual partner from a purely physical point of view, the mere lack of familiarity with the new personality creates an illusion of variation so attractive to the sexual demands of many males. For the aging male, the natural concomitant of this unconscious drive for variation is the possible development of a need for a change of outlet in order to create sexual tension or stimulate sexual capacity.

The complaint of sexual boredom frequently originates in the fact that the female partner has lost sight of the necessity for working at the marital relationship with the same interests in stimulating and satisfying her male partner that she originally may have demonstrated at the outset of marriage. The female partner who incites boredom may have lost herself in the demands of children, in social activities, in an individual career, or in any combination of interests extraneous to the marital focus. By their own admission many of the women interviewed no longer showed either sexual interest in or sexual concern for their husbands. It is the attitude of being taken for granted that the male apparently rejects, at least at a subconscious level. The ego of the aging male is especially vulnerable to rejection, either real or illusional.

Male Concern with Economic Pursuit. —Most men in the 40–60-year age group are reaching the competitive heights of their occupations and are contending with the greatest personal or family needs. They are engrossed with striving for the preeminence in their particular interest deemed necessary to provide that level of family financial security demanded by their socioeconomic structure. The competitive male world can be and frequently is allowed to become a demanding, all-consuming structure. This major diversion of male interest outside the home progressively reduces time available to the marriage. The male who is immersed in such an economic pursuit may make little or no effort to vocalize his occupational concerns to his female partner. Maintaining communication at any level permits sexual interchange to remain a natural occurrence rather than to become the result of a major effort of physical and mental reorientation.

There are additional factors in the vagaries of the competitive male world that should be considered. When the male has had a bad day, when things have not gone well, usually there is less interest in sexual activity than when he has experienced a most successful day. While a small percentage of the men interviewed reported finding comfort and reconstitution of ego within the realm of sexual release, it is certainly true that preoccupation remains a major deterrent to male as well as female sexuality.

Mental or Physical Fatigue.—Fatigue is an important element in the involution of male sexuality and exerts an ever-increasing influence during and beyond middle age. Mental rather than physical fatigue is the greater deterrent to male sexual responsiveness, although both are capable of major influence in lowering or aborting sexual tension.

If the middle-aged male has the type of employment that requires essentially a physical effort, he long since has conditioned his body to these physical demands and there usually is relatively little involution in sexual activity that results from such occupational efforts. The types of physical activity that have been reported directly to inhibit male sexual interest are those of unusual or excessive physical strain which are more often associated with recreation than with job demands. Rarely does the middle-aged male in our culture make any effort to maintain his physical being in good condition. Therefore, the type of activity associated with a weekend's recreation frequently is more exhausting than his routine job demands, particularly for the 50-plus age group. An aging male in poor physical condition, exposed to occasions of excessive physical activity, frequently complains of reduction in or complete loss of sexual responsiveness during the 24 to 48 hours immediately following such unaccustomed physical effort.

As stated, mental as opposed to physical

fatigue is the greater deterrent to sexual tension during the male's middle-aged years. Reflected from the competitive male world, the loss of sexual interest paralleling "the bad day at the office" initially results from mental exhaustion which only later may be translated into a physical counterpart. As the male ages, anything with which he habitually is preoccupied necessitates the expenditure of significant mental energy and subsequently reduces his sexual responsiveness. Occupational, financial, personal, and family emergencies universally are reported by the male geriatric research population to repress severely any existent sexual interest not only during the immediacy of the emergency but also usually for significant lengths of time thereafter. This sensitivity of male sexuality to mental fatigue is one of the greatest differences between the responsiveness of the middle-aged and the younger male.

Overindulgence in Food and Drink.—The aging male's excessive consumption of either food or drink has a tendency to repress his sexual tensions as it also lowers his capacity to feel or achieve in other areas. Many males have reported diminution of intensity in sensual focus, sometimes to a degree of anesthesia, as a result of overeating. However, the repression of sexuality is transient in nature unless the individual's eating patterns are grossly excessive and on a constant basis.

The syndrome of overindulgence has particular application to alcohol. While under its influence, many a male of any age has failed for the first time to achieve or maintain an erection of the penis. Secondary impotence developing in the male in the late forties or early fifties has a higher incidence of direct association with excessive alcohol consumption than with any other single factor. When a man is traumatized by the inability to achieve or to maintain an erection while under the influence of alcohol, he frequently develops major concerns for sexual performance and rarely associates his initial disability with its direct cause.

Not only does high alcohol ingestion directly reduce sexual tension in the aging male but also it often places upon him the additional indirect burden of concern for performance. He usually faces this secondary psychologic problem, if it persists, either by partial withdrawal from or by total avoidance of marital sexual exposure. His frequent solution to his erective concerns is to seek a sexual source unfamiliar with his personal concerns of sexual inadequacy. If, coincidentally, he refrains from adding excessive alcohol ingestion to the occasion of the first coital opportunity with the new partner, his solution probably will work. Thus a new problem within the marriage may arise. He is impotent with his wife but has confidence in his sexual performance elsewhere.

The alternative to the alcohol-dependent male with an impotence pattern is the picture of the true alcoholic. As this male progressively deteriorates physically and mentally, his sexual tensions simply disappear. Since the chronic or even acute alcoholic is in reality a mentally infirm individual, sexual involution under these circumstances will be discussed under the next heading of physical and mental infirmities.

Physical and Mental Infirmities.—Physical infirmities that can reduce or eliminate sexual capacity and performance obviously may develop at any age. However, onset incidence rises precipitously beyond the 40-year age mark and, of course, is particularly a factor after 60 years of age. Any physical disability, acute or chronic, may and usually does lower the sexual responsiveness of the involved male. If the physical distress is acute, pneumonia for example, lack of sexual tension usually is transient and is accepted without question by both husband and wife. If physical infirmity develops as a chronic or slowly progressive distress, emphysema for example, involution of sexual capacity is among the early debilitating effects of progressive reduction in physical efficiency. Longstanding chronic metabolic diseases such as diabetes are known for the high incidence of associated secondary impotence (Hastings, 1963; Rubin and Babbott, 1958).

Most forms of involutional psychopathology are associated with evidence of reduced sexual activity. There are, however, notable exceptions to the general rule of sexual regression for the male experiencing mental senility. The entire problem has had little definitive investigation.

In short, any acute or chronic distress, mental or physical in character, that reacts to impair the male's general physical condition or to reduce the efficiency of his body economy may be associated with lowered or absent sexual tensions.

Androgens and estrogen-androgen combinations are being used with increasing frequency in an effort to maintain the aging male in a positive protein balance, just as these steroids have been used in younger men with steroid imbalance (Heller and Maddock, 1947). There has been some evidence of reawakened sexual interest subsequent to effective steroid replacement in aging males. Clinical impression suggests that the obvious elevation of eroticism is not a direct effect of steroid replacement. Rather, it may be a secondary result of the obvious improvement in total body economy and of a renewed sense of well-being (Masters, 1957).

Beyond the 60-year age level, the physical infirmity of the female partner also is an ever-increasing factor. If the wife is physically infirm, the aging male is restricted in sexual opportunity. As previously mentioned, regularity of sexual expression is the key to sexual responsiveness for the aging male. With loss of sexual outlet, many aging males report rapid loss of sexual tension. It should be emphasized that this situation is not as acute for the aging husband with a physically infirm wife as it is for the aging wife with a physically infirm husband. In our culture, the aging man has much more opportunity for sexual outlet than does the aging woman.

Fear of Failure.—There is no way to overemphasize the importance that the factor "fear of failure" plays in the aging male's withdrawal from sexual performance. Obviously, any of the categories discussed briefly above would and do create in the aging male a fear of ineffective sexual performance. Once impotent under any circumstance, many males withdraw voluntarily from any coital activity rather than face the ego-shattering experience of repeated episodes of sexual inadequacy. Not infrequently they vocalize, and eventually come to believe, extraneous excuses for sexual withdrawal rather than accepting the clinical fact of a normal involutionary process.

Expressions of anger or personal antipathy toward a partner frequently are used as an escape from a feared loss of ability to perform adequately. Innumerable instances of the middle-aged male's turning to a younger female partner for sexual stimulation provide everyday cases in point. This clinical picture has been interpreted widely as the male's subconscious attempt to reestablish sexual potency in his own eyes, and to support his ego by proving repeatedly his sexual prowess. The fallible element in this solution is obvious when attempts to meet the increased demands of the younger partner often have changed the aging male's passing concern for performance into an established physiologic sexual inadequacy.

When aging males express a lack of interest in sexual performance or seek sexual stimulation extraneous to the marriage, their wives are left without true insight into their husband's fear of performance and may feel personally rejected by his withdrawal from marital sexual activity. If insight is present, the wives still fear to push the reluctant aging male into the possibility of recurrent episodes of erective failure. In any event, attempts at sexual performance usually are reduced in intensity and frequency, and the real factor of sexual stagnation takes over the marriage. When the aging male is not stimulated over long periods of time, his responsiveness may be lost.

There is every reason to believe that maintained regularity of sexual expression coupled with adequate physical well-being and healthy mental orientation to the aging process will combine to provide a sexually stimulative climate within a marriage (Johnson and Masters, unpublished). This climate will, in turn, improve sexual tension and provide a capacity for sexual performance that frequently may extend to and beyond the 80-year age level.

31

BERNICE L. NEUGARTEN and KAROL K. WEINSTEIN

THE CHANGING AMERICAN GRANDPARENT

Despite the proliferation of investigations regarding the relations between generations and the position of the aged within the family, surprisingly little attention has been paid directly to the role of grandparenthood. There are a few articles written by psychoanalysts and psychiatrists analyzing the symbolic meaning of the grandparent in the developing psyche of the child or, in a few cases, illustrating the role of a particular grandparent in the psychopathology of a particular child (Abraham, 1913; Ferenczi, 1913; Jones, 1913; LaBarre *et al.*, 1960; Rappaport, 1958; Thurston, 1941). Attention has not correspondingly been given, however, to the psyche of the grandparent, and references are made only obliquely, if at all, to the symbolic meaning of the grandchild to the grandparent.

There are a number of anthropologists' reports on grandparenthood in one or another simple society as well as studies involving crosscultural comparisons based on ethnographic materials. Notable among the latter is a study by Apple (1956; see also Nadel, 1953; and Radcliffe-Brown, 1950) which shows that, among the 51 societies for which data are available, those societies in which grandparents are removed from family authority are those in which grandparents have an equalitarian or an indulgent, warm relationship with the grandchildren. In those societies in which economic power and/or prestige rests with the old, relationships between grandparents and

Reprinted from the *Journal of Marriage and the Family*, vol. 26, no. 2 (May, 1964).

grandchildren are formal and authoritarian.

Sociologists, for the most part, have included only a few questions about grandparenthood when interviewing older persons about family life, or they have analyzed the grandparent role solely from indirect evidence, without empirical data gathered specifically for that purpose (Cavan, 1962; Von Hentig, 1946; Nimkoff, 1961; Smith and Britton, 1958; Streib, 1958). There are a few noteworthy exceptions: Albrecht (1954) studied the grandparental responsibilities of a representative sample of persons over 65 in a small midwestern community. She concluded that grandparents neither had nor coveted responsibility for grandchildren; that they took pleasure from the emotional response and occasionally took reflected glory from the accomplishments of their grandchildren.

An unpublished study by Apple (1954) of a group of urban middle-class grandparents indicated that, as they relinquish the parental role over the adult child, grandparents come to identify with grandchildren in a way that might be called "pleasure without responsibility."

In a study of older persons in a working-class area of London, Townsend (1957) found many grandmothers who maintained very large responsibility for the care of the grandchild, but he also found that for the total sample, the relationship of grandparents to grandchildren might be characterized as one of "privileged disrespect." Children were expected to be more respectful of parents than of grandparents.

The data reported in this paper were collected primarily for the purpose of generating rather than testing hypotheses regarding various psychological and social dimensions of the grandparent role. Three dimensions were investigated: first, the degree of comfort with the role as expressed by the grandparent; second, the significance of the role as seen by the actor; and last, the style with which the role is enacted.

The data came from interviews with both grandmother and grandfather in 70 middle-class families in which the interviewer located first a married couple with children and then one set of grandparents. Of the 70 sets of grandparents, 46 were maternal—that is, the wife's parents—and 24 were paternal. All pairs of grandparents lived in separated households from their children, although most lived within relatively short distances within the metropolitan area of Chicago.

As classified by indices of occupation, area of residence, level of income, and level of education, the grandparental couples were all middle class. The group was about evenly divided between upper-middle (professionals and business executives) and lower-middle (owners of small service businesses and white-collar occupations below the managerial level). As is true in other middle-class urban groups in the United States, the largest proportion of these families had been upwardly mobile, either from working class into lower-middle or from lower-middle into upper-middle. Of the 70 grandparental couples, 19 were foreign born (Polish, Lithuanian, Russian, and a few German and Italian). The sample was skewed with regard to religious affiliation, with 40 percent Jewish, 48 percent Protestant, and 12 percent Catholic. The age range of the grandfathers was, with a few exceptions, the mid-50's through the late 60's; for the grandmothers it was the early 50's to the mid-60's.

Each member of the couple was interviewed separately and, in most instances, in two sessions. Respondents were asked a variety of open-ended questions regarding their relations to their grandchildren: how often and on what occasions they saw their grandchildren; what the significance of grandparenthood was in their lives and how it had affected them. While grandparenthood has multiple values for each respondent and may influence his relations with various family members, the focus was upon the primary relationship—that between grandparent and grandchild.

FINDINGS AND DISCUSSION

Degree of comfort in the role.—As shown in Table 1, the majority of grandparents expressed only comfort, satisfaction, and pleasure. Among this group, a sizable number seemed to be idealizing the role of grandparenthood and to have high expectations of the grandchild in the future—that the child would either achieve some special goal or success or offer unique affection at some later date.

At the same time, approximately one-third of the sample (36 percent of the grandmothers and 29 percent of the grandfathers) were experiencing sufficient difficulty in the role that they made open reference to their discomfort, their disappointment, or their lack of positive reward. This discomfort indicated strain in thinking of oneself as a grandparent (the role is in some ways alien to the self-image), conflict with the parents with regard to the rearing of the grandchild, or indifference (and some self-chastisement for the indifference) to caretaking or responsibility in reference to the grandchild.

The significance and meaning of the role.—The investigators made judgments based upon the total interview data on each case with regard to the primary significance of grandparenthood for each respondent. Recognizing that the role has multiple meanings for each person and that the categories to be described may overlap to some degree, the investigators nevertheless classified each case as belonging to one of five categories:

1. For some, grandparenthood seemed to constitute primarily a source of *biological renewal* ("It's through my grand-

fathers perceive family continuity less frequently through their female than through their male offspring and that in a sample more evenly balanced with regard to maternal-paternal lines of ascent, this category would appear more frequently in the responses from grandfathers.

2. For some, grandparenthood affords

TABLE 1

EASE OF ROLE PERFORMANCE, SIGNIFICANCE OF ROLE, AND STYLE OF GRANDPARENTING IN 70 GRANDMOTHERS AND 70 GRANDFATHERS

	Grandmothers ($N=70$) N	Grandfathers ($N=70$) N
A. Ease of role performance:		
1) Comfortable–pleasant	41	43
2) Difficulty–discomfort	25	20
(Insufficient data)	4	7
Total	70	70
B. Significance of the grandparent role:		
1) Biological renewal and/or continuity	29*	16*
2) Emotional self-fulfillment	13	19
3) Resource person to child	3	8
4) Vicarious achievement through child	3	3
5) Remote; little effect on the self	19	20
(Insufficient data)	3	4
Total	70	70
C. Style of grandparenting:		
1) The Formal	22	23
2) The Fun-Seeking	20	17
3) The Parent Surrogate	10*	0*
4) The Reservoir of Family Wisdom	1	4
5) The Distant Figure	13	20
(Insufficient data)	4	6
Total	70	70

* The difference between grandmothers and grandfathers in this category is reliable at or beyond the .05 level (frequencies were tested for differences of proportions, using the Yates correction for continuity).

children that I feel young again") and/or *biological continuity* with the future ("It's through these children that I see my life going on into the future" or "It's carrying on the family line"). As shown in Table 1, this category occurred significantly less frequently for grandfathers than for grandmothers, perhaps because the majority of these respondents were parents, not of the young husband but of the young wife. It is likely that grand-

primarily an opportunity to succeed in a new emotional role, with the implication that the individual feels himself to be a better grandparent than he was a parent. Frequently, grandfatherhood offered a certain vindication of the life history by providing *emotional self-fulfillment* in a way that fatherhood had not done. As one man put it, "I can be, and I can do for my grandchildren things I could never do for my own kids. I was too busy with my business to enjoy my kids, but my grand-children are different. Now I have the time to be with them."

3. For a small proportion, the grand-parent role provides a new role of teacher or *resource person*. Here the emphasis is upon the satisfaction that accrues from contributing to the grandchild's welfare —either by financial aid, or by offering the benefit of the grandparent's unique life experience. For example, "I take my grandson down to the factory and show him how the business operates—and then, too, I set aside money especially for him. That's something his father can't do yet, although he'll do it for *his* grandchildren."

4. For a few, grandparenthood is seen as providing an extension of the self in that the grandchild is one who will *accomplish vicariously* for the grandparent that which neither he nor his first-genera-tion offspring could achieve. For these persons, the grandchild offers primarily an opportunity for aggrandizing the ego, as in the case of the grandmother who said, "She's a beautiful child, and she'll grow up to be a beautiful woman. Maybe I shouldn't, but I can't help feeling proud of that."

5. As shown in Table 1, 27 percent of the grandmothers and 29 percent of the grandfathers in this sample reported feel-ing relatively *remote* from their grand-children and acknowledged relatively *little effect* of grandparenthood in their own lives—this despite the fact that they lived geographically near at least one set of grandchildren and felt apologetic about expressing what they regarded as unusual sentiments. Some of the grandfathers mentioned the young age of their grand-children in connection with their current feelings of psychological distance. For ex-ample, one man remarked, "My grand-daughter is just a baby, and I don't even feel like a grandfather yet. Wait until she's older—maybe I'll feel different then."

Of the grandmothers who felt remote from their grandchildren, the rationaliza-tion was different. Most of the women in this group were working or were active

in community affairs and said essentially, "It's great to be a grandmother, of course —but I don't have much time. . . ." The other grandmothers in this group indi-cated strained relations with the adult child: either they felt that their daughters had married too young, or they disap-proved of their sons-in-law.

For both the men and the women who fell into this category of psychological distance, a certain lack of conviction ap-peared in their statements, as if the men did not really believe that, once the grand-children were older, they would indeed become closer to them, and as if the women did not really believe that their busy schedules accounted for their lack of emotional involvement with their grandchildren. Rather, these grandparents imply that the role itself is perceived as being empty of meaningful relationships.

Styles of grandparenting.—Somewhat independent of the significance of grand-parenthood is the question of style in en-acting the role of grandmother or grand-father. Treating the data inductively, five major styles were differentiated:

1. The *Formal* are those who follow what they regard as the proper and pre-scribed role for grandparents. Although they like to provide special treats and in-dulgences for the grandchild, and al-though they may occasionally take on a minor service such as baby-sitting, they maintain clearly demarcated lines between parenting and grandparenting, and they leave parenting strictly to the parent. They maintain a constant interest in the grandchild but are careful not to offer advice on childrearing.

2. The *Fun Seeker* is the grandparent whose relation to the grandchild is char-acterized by informality and playfulness. He joins the child in specific activities for the specific purpose of having fun, some-what as if he were the child's playmate. Grandchildren are viewed as a source of leisure activity, as an item of "consump-

tion" rather than "production," or as a source of self-indulgence. The relationship is one in which authority lines—either with the grandchild or with the parent—are irrelevant. The emphasis here is on mutuality of satisfaction rather than on providing treats for the grandchild. Mutuality imposes a latent demand that both parties derive fun from the relationship.[1]

3. The *Surrogate Parent* occurs only, as might have been anticipated, for grandmothers in this group. It comes about by initiation on the part of the younger generation, that is, when the young mother works and the grandmother assumes the actual caretaking responsibility for the child.

4. The *Reservoir of Family Wisdom* represents a distinctly authoritarian patri-centered relationship in which the grandparent—in the rare occasions on which it occurs in this sample, it is the grandfather—is the dispenser of special skills or resources. Lines of authority are distinct, and the young parents maintain and emphasize their subordinate positions, sometimes with and sometimes without resentment.

5. The *Distant Figure* is the grandparent who emerges from the shadows on holidays and on special ritual occasions such as Christmas and birthdays. Contact with the grandchild is fleeting and infrequent, a fact which distinguishes this style from *Formal*. This grandparent is benevolent in stance but essentially distant and remote from the child's life, a somewhat intermittent St. Nicholas.

Of major interest is the frequency with which grandparents of both sexes are either Fun Seekers or Distant Figures vis-à-vis their grandchildren. These two styles have been adopted by half of all the cases in this sample. Of interest, also, is the fact that in both styles the issue of

authority is peripheral. Although deference may be given to the grandparent in certain ways, authority relationships are not a central issue.

Both of these styles are, then, to be differentiated from what has been regarded as the traditional grandparent role—one in which patriarchal or matriarchal control is exercised over both younger generations and in which authority constitutes the major axis of the relationship.

These two styles of grandparenting differ not only from traditional concepts; they differ also in some respects from more recently described types. Cavan (1962), for example, has suggested that the modern grandparent role is essentially a maternal one for both men and women and that to succeed as a grandfather, the male must learn to be a slightly masculinized grandmother, a role that differs markedly from the instrumental and outer-world orientation that has presumably characterized most males during a great part of their adult lives. It is being suggested here, however, that the newly emerging types are neuter in gender. Neither the Fun Seeker nor the Distant Figure involves much nurturance, and neither "maternal" nor "paternal" seems an appropriate adjective.

Grandparent style in relation to age.— A final question is the extent to which these new styles of grandparenting reflect, directly or indirectly, the increasing youthfulness of grandparents as compared to a few decades ago. (This youthfulness is evidenced not only in terms of the actual chronological age at which grandparenthood occurs but also in terms of evaluations of self as youthful. A large majority of middle-aged and older persons describe themselves as "more youthful than my parents were at my age.")

To follow up this point, the sample was divided into two groups: those who were under and over 65. As shown in Table 2, the Formal style occurs significantly more frequently in the older group; the Fun Seeking and the Distant Figure styles occur significantly more frequently in the

[1] Wolfenstein (1955, pp. 168–78) has described fun morality in childrearing practices as it applies to parenthood. Perhaps a parallel development is occurring in connection with grandparenthood. As Wolfenstein has delineated it, fun has become not only permissible but almost required in the new morality.

younger group. (Examination of the table shows, furthermore, that the same age differences occur in both grandmothers and grandfathers.)

These age differences may reflect secular trends: this is, differences in values and expectations in persons who grow up and who grow old at different times in history. They may also reflect processes of aging and/or the effects of continuing socialization which produce differences in role behavior over time. It might be pointed out, however, that sociologists, when they have treated the topic of grandparenthood at all, have done so within the context of old age, not middle age. Grandparenthood might best be studied as a middle-age phenomenon if the investigator is interested in the assumption of new roles and the significance of new roles in adult socialization.

In this connection, certain lines of inquiry suggest themselves: as with other roles, a certain amount of anticipatory socialization takes place with regard to the grandparent role. Women in particular often describe a preparatory period in which they visualize themselves as grandmothers, often before their children are married. With the presently quickened pace of the family cycle, in which women experience the emptying of the nest, the marriages of their children, and the appearance of grandchildren at earlier points in their own lives, the expectation that grandmotherhood is a welcome and pleasurable event seems frequently to be accompanied also by doubts that one is "ready" to become a grandmother or by the feelings of being prematurely old. The anticipation and first adjustment to the role of grandmother has not been systematically studied, either by sociologists or psychologists, but there is anecdotal data to suggest that, at both conscious and unconscious levels, the middle-aged woman may relive her own first pregnancy and childbirth and that there are additional social and psychological factors that probably result in a certain transfor-

mation in ego-identity. The reactions of males to grandfatherhood has similarly gone uninvestigated although, as has been suggested earlier, the event may require a certain reversal of traditional sex role and a consequent change in self-concept.

Other questions that merit investigation relate to the variations in role expectations for grandparents in various ethnic and so-

TABLE 2

AGE DIFFERENCES IN STYLES
OF GRANDPARENTING*

	Under 65 (N=81)	Over 65 (N=34)
The Formal:		
Men	12	11
Women	13	9
Total	25(31%)	20(59%)
The Fun-seeking:		
Men	13	4
Women	17	3
Total	30(37%)	7(21%)
The Distant Figure:		
Men	15	5
Women	11	2
Total	26(32%)	7(21%)

* These age differences are statistically reliable as indicated by 2×3 chi-square test applied to the category totals (P = .02).

cioeconomic groups and the extent to which the grandparent role is comparable to other roles insofar as "reality shock" occurs for some individuals—that is, insofar as a period of disenchantment sets in, either early in the life of the grandchild or later as the grandchild approaches adolescence when the expected rewards to the grandparents may not be forthcoming.

When grandparenthood comes to be studied from such perspectives as these, it is likely to provide a significant area for research, not only with regard to changing family structure but also with regard to adult socialization.

32

REUBEN HILL

DECISION MAKING AND THE FAMILY LIFE CYCLE

THE FAMILY DEVELOP-
MENTAL APPROACH

The family development approach emphasizes the time dimension neglected by the other conceptual frameworks dealing with the family, but its focus is on the family as a small group, the nuclear family occupying a common household. The time units employed encompass the family life span expressed in stages of development but subdivided into years of marriage.

The approach is eclectic in its incorporation of the compatible sections of several other approaches to the study of the family. From rural sociology the family development theorists have borrowed the concept of stages of the family life cycle which they have greatly elaborated, giving the phasing of the life cycle a theoretical rationale. From child psychology and human development have come the concepts of developmental needs and tasks. From the sociologists engaged in work on the sociology of the professions we have borrowed the concepts of career, viewing the family as a convergence of intercontingent careers of the positions of husband and wife, later of parents and children. From the structure-function and interactional schools has been borrowed the trio of concepts, position, role, and norms, particularly as these involve age and sex roles and changing family size. The many concepts associated with the

Abridged from *Social Structure and the Family: Generational Relations*, ed. Ethel Shanas and Gordon F. Streib (Englewood Cliffs, N.J.: Prentice-Hall, 1965), chap. 6, pp. 114–26. Reprinted by permission of the publisher. © 1965.

family as a system of interacting personalities find their place in the modifications of the concept of role seen in role-playing, role-taking, reciprocity of roles, and role differentiation. These several concepts have been assembled together in a frame of reference that furnishes an opportunity for accretion of generalizations about the internal development of families from their formation in the engagement and wedding to their dissolution in divorce or death. The scope and organization of this framework may be described as follows:

"The family development approach views the family as a small group system, intricately organized internally into paired positions of husband-father, wife-mother, son-brother, and daughter-sister. Norms prescribing the appropriate role behavior for each of these positions specify how reciprocal relations are to be maintained, as well as how role behavior may change with changing ages of the occupants of these positions. This intimate small group has a predictable natural history, designated by stages beginning with the simple husband-wife pair and becoming more and more complex as members are added and new positions created, with the number in interpersonal relations reaching a peak with the birth of the last child, stabilizing for a brief period, to become less and less complex subsequently with the launching of adult children into jobs and marriage as the group contracts in size once again to the dyadic interactions of the husband-wife pair. As the age composition of the family changes, so do the age-role expectations for occupants of the positions in the family, and so does the quality of interaction among family members.

"Viewed social psychologically and developmentally, the family is an arena of interacting personalities, each striving to obtain the satisfaction of his desires. Parents often defer the satisfaction of their own immediate needs, however, in building complementary roles between themselves and their children. At some stages of development, parents and children are good company; at other stages, their diverse developmental strivings may be strikingly incompatible" (Hill, 1961, p. 63).

An immediate by-product of this conceptual framework has been its sensitizing effect upon researchers utilizing the family as the unit of study. Any research which seeks to generalize about families without taking into account the variation caused by the stages of family development represented in the sample will leave much variance unaccounted for, just as studies which ignore social class differences leave much unexplained. Buying patterns, saving patterns, and mobility patterns can be expected to vary greatly over the family life span, as will many other family behaviors as yet unassessed by family life-cycle categories.

Using the family developmental approach to behavior to analyze decision making in the family urges us to ask certain questions and to anticipate certain regularities. First of all, the approach divides the family cycle into stages of growth and development which have been demarcated by application of role theory to the changing positions in a family as it moves forward in time. The role content of the several positions in the family constitutes the *role complex* of the family at a given point in time. A stage of development would change, according to the framework, each time a fundamental change in the age role content in the positions making up the family

occurs, or in other words each time the family's role complex changes.

The theoretically most sophisticated schemes for differentiating stages of the family life span today utilize three sets of data as indicators of change in role complex:

A first criterion used for dividing up the life span is the observable "number of positions in the family," which permits inferring stages of "expansion," of "stability," and of "contraction" to be blocked off. Changes in stages of development (because fundamental changes in role complex occur) would be required by the birth of the first child, launching of first child into marriage, and launching of last child.

A second criterion involves the age composition of the family, which reflects indirectly the *family's complex of age role expectations in reciprocity* at any one time in the history of the family. This criterion requires that a stage be changed each time the role complex changes in any degree. If we were engaged in undertaking case studies of individual families, this procedure would be most interesting to follow, but in seeking to differentiate stages of development for large numbers of families it would be highly impractical to designate a new stage each time the complex of age role expectations changed, since there would be almost as many different combinations of stages (family careers) as there are families in the study. Duvall, reflecting the judgments of the various committees working on the problem since 1948, chose a simpler solution to the problem in her text (Duvall 1962). She suggests that it is sufficient to change stages of development each time the oldest child shifts from one significant age category to another. Of all the children, to be sure, the oldest child's development is the most significant for the shift in role content in the parents' positions, since his experiences present new and different problems which as yet the family has not encountered and bring about the most modification of role content in all other positions in the family. The significant age categories in which changes would be expected to occur in our society include: infant, preschool child, school child, adolescent, young adult, middle-aged adult, and aged adult.

A third criterion involves the change in the age role content in the husband-father position which occurs with his retirement from active employment. For the mother who has not been gainfully employed, her retirement from active mothering occurs with the launching of her last child into marriage and is captured in the shift in the family's role complex from the launching center to the post-parental stage.

Employing these three sets of readily available data of numbers of positions in the family, age composition of the family, and employment status of the father, several stages of the family life span can be differentiated, each representing a distinctive role complex, as follows: Stage I Establishment (newly married, childless); II New Parents (infant–3 years); III Preschool Family (child 3–6 years and possibly younger siblings); IV School-Age Family (oldest child 6–12 years, possibly younger siblings); V Family with Adolescent (oldest 13–19, possibly younger siblings); VI Family with Young Adult (oldest 20, until first child leaves home); VII Family as Launching Center (from departure of first to last child); VIII Post-parental Family, The Middle Years (after children have left home until father retires); IX Aging Family (after retirement of father).

SOME GENERALIZATIONS WHICH FLOW
FROM THE FRAMEWORK

The view of the stages of the family life cycle as distinctive role complexes opens up the way for anticipating the content of family interaction for each of these stages. If we begin by looking at the focus of this conference on the aging family, we can readily see that the aged generation will be disproportionately found in Stage IX, with some representatives still in Stage VIII. The numerical composition of the family for both of these stages, in contrast with those which preceded them, is simple and stable—two positions with only one interpersonal relationship to maintain, a companionate dyad. This can be quite a contraction for large families. For the family of ten persons in which the author grew up, for example, there was a contraction from forty-five interpersonal relationships, which constituted the number the author's parents coped with before launching their eight children into jobs and marriage, to one in the post-parental period. The parental role content of the two positions which are left in the family in the post-parental stage (Stage VIII), as opposed to the spousal role content, is in the process of continuous redefinition, and by the time the couple enters Stage IX, almost fourteen years later, the nurturant, guiding, and socializing content will have largely disappeared in favor of a more symmetrical set of norms of mutual aid and reciprocity in exchanges between the generations.

The stages of family development are suggestive also of contrasts in needs, in volume of plans, and in willingness to take risks in the form of purchases and other commitments which affect the direction of decisions in the family. At the beginning of the family's life span, in Stages I–IV, the family tends to be future oriented, living with rapidly expanding needs for shelter spaces, for facilities, durable goods, and means of transportation. Needs press heavily on resources as the ratio of dependents to earners mounts, and we would accordingly expect that the volume of plans and decisions to make residential moves, to remodel, to purchase goods, to change jobs, and to purchase protective insurances to be very high. We would also expect concomitantly that the willingness to accept help from kin and peers as well as the utilization of credit from commercial sources would also be greater than at any other period in the life span.

In Stages V–VI, the stages of rearing school-age and adolescent children, we would expect the family to be more oriented to the here and now, to have achieved some equilibrium of interaction, but to be still heavily pressed with high needs for housing and added facilities.

In Stage VII, the stage of launching children into jobs and marriage, the family undergoes maximum contraction in size and experiences an irregular but slow decline in pressure of needs on resources. In many families the wife-mother has returned to the labor force, providing a double income to equalize the costs of higher education and of marrying off the children. The uncertainties and ambiguities of in-law roles and of grandparental roles are introduced into the positions of the family heads during this period. There are also complications of establishing mutually agreeable helping patterns for the newly married children through gift giving, exchanges, and loans.

In Stage VIII the family enters a stage of recovery financially, often with two earners, with disposable income for the first time since Stage I. The disposable income may be invested for retirement, but may also be turned to upgrading the level of living of the post-parental couple and helping both married offspring and their own aged parents. For some mothers it is a period of retirement from the protective roles that have been central to the career of wife and mother, so that they experience many of the adjustments to loss of functions which the breadwinner experiences at retirement. Mothers who have entered the labor force, on the other hand, experience the adjustments of loss of functions when retiring from their jobs years later. We would expect for the family as a whole that this would be a period of continued high volume of economic activity and, therefore, of decision making.

In Stage IX, with both spouses retired,

we expect a net change in the direction of giving, restrictions on the helping of married offspring who are now economically established, and a reversal of roles with the aged receiving more help than they give. There will be sharply restricted economic activity over the years which remain. In this stage particularly we would expect the family to be more oriented to the past, making accordingly fewer attempts to structure the future.

From the standpoint of decision making, then, the framework has suggested a number of regularities which are relevant while leaving room for the discovery of many others. It has suggested that the sheer volume of economic activity will rise rapidly at the beginning of the life span of the family, level off, and then decline. Indeed, that is probably the excuse to call the family life span a life cycle, since so many behaviors are of this order: residential mobility, occupational mobility, complexities of family interaction owing to changing plurality patterns, and so on. Long-term as against short-run type planning will be expected to appear more in the early than in the middle and late stages of family development because of the different time orientations of the generations.

The framework does not tell us anything about the relative success the families will have in preplanning their economic activities at various points in the life span, nor whether families will be more or less rational in their decision making at the beginning, in the middle, or at the end of the life span. The framework tells us little indeed about expected changes in power allocation or the allocation of duties in the family over the life span, although some empirical studies using the framework have advanced some findings on these issues (Rollins, 1963, pp. 13, 20). These are among the discoveries we can anticipate in studying families empirically by stages of development.

EMPIRICAL FINDINGS

To answer the questions raised in this paper we should ideally have available longitudinal data on decision making over the entire life span of a cohort of couples who entered marriage in the same year. No such data have ever been collected in the history of family research, in part because of the cost and continuity of research organization required. The few data that we do have were collected in synthetic longitudinal studies of various types drawn from cross-sectional samples. A sample of couples of different durations of marriage is interviewed and the resulting responses aggregated as if they were drawn from a marital cohort moving over time. The study of decision making by Blood and Wolfe is of this type (1960, pp. 41–44). They demonstrate that the husband's power in the family structure increases from the honeymoon period, Stage I, where there are no children, to Stage II-III with young children, and declines slowly through the various subsequent stages of family development into the post-parental period, Stage VIII, after which it drops sharply as the husband retires in Stage IX. In recent years this same device of aggregating cross-sectional samples to construct the life cycle of families has been widely carried out in making generalizations about consumer behavior: the timing of home ownership, automobile ownership, the acquisition of television sets, automatic dryers, and so on (Clark, 1955, pp. 28–58, 61–66). The hazards of generalizing from such synthetic longitudinal studies have been covered in some detail elsewhere in which the author discusses the relative advantages and disadvantages of five methodological short cuts that have been devised to circumvent the costs and travail of longitudinal research with families (Hill, 1964).

In this paper we turn to the least unsatisfactory set of data available about decision making over the life cycle. We are drawing from data obtained from an intergenerational sample and are treating the data obtained from the youngest of three generations as representative of the early stages of the cycle, the data from the parent generation as representative of the middle stages, and the responses from the grandparent generation as depicting the last stages of development. By placing findings of the other two generations in juxtaposition with those from the grandparent generation, we can gain some idea of the distinguishing characteristics of decision making among older couples. The findings we cite are valuable in their own right but should be used cautiously when generalizing about changes in decision making over the life cycle. It would be more defensible to refer to our findings as changes in decision making over three generations.

The data which we shall use for an empirical description of decision making have been collected as part of the Minnesota Consumership Study. The areas of planning and decision making covered included eight recurring problems requiring long-range planning and fairly elaborate decision making: residential location, redecoration, remodeling, acquisition of durable goods and of automobiles, changes in the family's financial portfolio in savings, investments, insurance, provisions for retirement, and changes of occupation (change of job by husband, entering or leaving labor force by wife). Methods of data collection have included four semi-structured interviews with wives, one joint interview with both spouses, tests and questionnaires filled out by both spouses, and direct observation of stress situations by interviewers.

The choice of intact families drawn from three generations of the same family line assures us relative homogeneity of family culture. Moreover, it provides us with three contrast groups to highlight the differences in decision making over the life span. A description of the families selected will make this even clearer.

An intergenerational sample of intact families linked through three generations living within fifty miles of Minneapolis-St. Paul was obtained from area probability samples of the metropolitan area. Three hundred and twelve nuclear families, composed of 100 grandparent families, 105 parent families, and 107 young married families, survived four waves of interviews covering a year's observations. These families are ecologically dispersed within the metropolitan area and its hinterland; they are well distributed by social class and economic levels, but are somewhat more stable residentially than comparable families without three-generation linkages. The three generations have the following characteristics:

1. Age: Grandparents 60–80; parents 40–60; married children 20–30.

2. Ethnic make-up: Grandparents, ¼ Scandinavian, ½ other Northern European, balance Southern European; parents and children, similar.

3. Religious affiliation: ⅓ Catholic, ⅔ Protestant (Lutheran dominant), some Jewish. High continuity of religious affiliation from generation to generation.

4. Income: Grandparents, $1,000 to $6,000, ½ under $2,000; Parents, $1,000 to $20,000, ½ under $5,000; Married children, $2,000 to $10,000, ½ under $4,000.

5. Children in residence: Grandparents, no children at home; parents, ⅔ with children still at home; married children, 1/10 no children yet, ⅔ with children all below school age, ⅓ with children of school age under 12 years of age.

With this background let us turn to the performance of the three generations over a twelve-month period in 1958 to highlight the similarities and differences found among the three generations. We begin with a comparative picture of the financial and housing constraints operative on the three generations, as well as the types of problems perceived as requiring help over the twelve-month period. Second, we shall examine the location of power in decision making and degree of differentiation of sex roles by generation. Third, our research design permits us to examine within several areas of activity the volume of plans enunciated and actions taken, the planning horizons, the proportion of plans fulfilled, the degree of rationality in decision making, and the degree of satisfaction expressed with the actions taken. Our empirical overview will conclude with some of the correlates of planning, rationality, and satisfaction in the grandparent generation.

SITUATIONAL CONSTRAINTS AFFECTING DECISION MAKING

We must remember that each of the three generations has had a different history before entering the twelve-month period of observation. The grandparent generation is educationally, occupationally, and financially handicapped compared with the younger generations. Educationally grandfathers averaged 6 years of schooling, fathers 9 years, and grandsons 12.6 years. Occupationally the grandfathers began lowest on the scale and have made the slowest movement upward. There has been an acceleration of occupational upgrading generation by generation when each is compared year by year since marriage. In each successive generation, more of the wives have worked during the first several years of marriage and more have returned to work after their children grew up. In all economic matters we can say that the married child generation is destined to outstrip the previous generations based on the achievements of each generation during the first ten years of marriage. In home ownership the married child generation has already exceeded the grandparent generation (80 percent homeowners) and is where the parent generation was only after twenty years of marriage. In acquisition of durable goods the married child generation has overtaken the grandparent generation and is at a point in its inventory where the parent generation was after thirty-five years of marriage—the same can be said for bathroom and bedroom spaces in the home and other amenities. This has not been done at the expense of protective insurances or retirement provisions, for the married child generation is well along in the acquisition of a portfolio of insurances and investments. Over 50 percent have retirement provisions over and beyond Social Security and 95 percent have life insurance. This married child genera-

Class D areas compared with 50 percent among the parent generation.

We earlier indicated substantial differences in average income and in the range of income among the three generations, with grandparents averaging below-subsistence incomes (one-half under $2,000). We asked families for their subjective definition of the adequacy of their current income in terms of its sufficiency to buy necessities and luxuries. Table 1 tabulates the responses of the three generations in percentage form and suggests that the grandparent generation feels the financial squeeze more than the other two

TABLE 1

PERCENTAGE DISTRIBUTION OF RESPONSES ON ADEQUACY OF
FAMILY INCOME BY GENERATION

Responses	Grandparents Percent	Parents Percent	Married Children Percent
Total...	100.0	100.0	100.0
Do without many needed things..................	28.0	4.7	1.2
Have the things we need, but none of the extras....	23.5	5.9	4.8
Have the things we need, and a few of the extras...	30.5	61.0	76.0
Have the things we need, and any extras we want..	3.5	14.2	16.8
Have the things we need and any extras we want, and still have money left over to save or invest.......	14.5	14.2	1.2
Number of families.............................	85	85	83

tion starts its marriage with 82 percent covered, which is higher than their grandparents ever reached, and is as high as their parents achieved after thirty years of marriage.

The pressure of members on resources is greatest in the early stages of the life cycle. As the study began, the married children had the most children resident in the home (two) and had the fewest rooms per family (4.6). Grandparents had no children and had the next highest number of rooms (4.9). The parent generation had the most rooms (5.6) with two thirds of the families having a child still at home. In quality of housing, however, grandparents had the lowest rental values, and more of them lived in the lowest grade neighborhoods, two thirds in Class C and

generations. Half of them are barely meeting the necessities, but 14.5 percent are on easy street. Three-fourths of the married child group checked the median expression, "We have the things we need and a few of the extras." Only one couple in this generation, however, feels really "flush." The parents are not only factually beter off (in income, housing, and durable goods), but they feel more comfortable, distributing their answers towards the luxury end of the scale.

DEGREE OF INTERDEPENDENCE FOR MUTUAL AID

We have indicated earlier in this chapter that family development theory anticipates some reversals in dependency-interdependency relations among the generations by stage of development. In the last of the four interviews respondents in each generation were asked to give an accounting of help given and received during the year from all sources including immediate and extended kin, peers, church, social agencies, private specialists, and commercial sources in the problem areas of illness, child care, household man-

The three generations reported an involvement in a vast nexus of transfers of one sort or another during the year, over five thousand, of which 3,781 were quite clearly help exchanges. Table 2 has been

TABLE 2

COMPARISON OF HELP INSTANCES GIVEN TO HELP INSTANCES RECEIVED BY
GENERATION AND BY VARIOUS SOURCES OVER A YEAR'S PERIOD*

GENERATION	SOURCE OR RECIPIENT	PERCENT OF HELP INSTANCES:		TOTAL INSTANCES OF HELP
		Given	Received	
Grandparent	Total	100	100	....
	Other generations	47	65	521
	Peers	15	16	148
	Horizontal and vertical kin once removed	9	8	80
	All other agencies	29	10	206
	N =	574	381	955
Parent	Total	100	100	....
	Other generations	44	53	637
	Peers	17	21	246
	Horizontal and vertical kin once removed	14	20	212
	All other agencies	25	6	252
	N =	890	457	1347
Married children	Total	100	100	....
	Other generations	28	44	516
	Peers	22	20	316
	Horizontal and vertical kin once removed	25	27	380
	All other agencies	25	9	267
	N =	844	635	1479
	Total instances of help	2308	1473	3781

* Percents may not total 100 due to rounding.

agement, emotional gratification, and economic assistance.

When examined by vulnerability to problems requiring help, the parent generation was lowest in vulnerability (44.7 percent receiving no help of a stress or problem-area nature); the grandparent generation was next lowest (32.9 percent receiving no help due to crises). The married child generation with its infant-age dependents was most vulnerable (only 21 percent receiving no help of a crisis nature during the year).

prepared to demonstrate the social networks within which help is exchanged. First of all, we note that help exchanges within the vertical kin (giving and receiving help, other generations) exceeds all other categories in the social networks for each of the generations. This is especially true for the grandparents for whom 65 percent of the instances of help received was familial (from children, the parent generation, or grandchildren) compared with 53 percent for the parent generation and 44 percent for the married grandchildren. The child generation operates in a wider flung network of exchanges with a less concentrated pattern especially of giving within the vertical kin line (only 28 percent) and giving proportionately more than the other generations to horizontal and vertical kin once removed (siblings, cousins, aunts, uncles, nieces, and nephews), 25 percent compared to 14 percent for the parent generation and only 9 percent for the grandparents. To all other sources (religious organizations, health and welfare agencies, and other specialists), the grandparents

generations by type of help provided or received. The parent generation, within this narrower network, is again the most active in giving help and the married child generation the most frequent recipient of help. The grandparent generation both gave and received least of the three generations in help items of all kinds. The parent generation is the sociometric star of the interchanges, giving more to the married children and to the grandparents than either gives to the other. The parent generation also receives in exchange more from the grandparents and from the mar-

TABLE 3

COMPARISON OF HELP RECEIVED AND HELP GIVEN BY GENERATION FOR CHIEF PROBLEM AREAS*

	Type of Crisis									
	Economic		Emotional Gratification		Household Management		Child Care		Illness	
	Gave Percent	Received Percent	Gave Percent	Received Percent	Gave Percent	Received Percent	Gave Percent	Received Percent	Gave Percent	Received Percent
Total............	100	100	100	100	100	100	100	100	100	100
Grandparents......	26	34	23	42	21	52	16	0	32	61
Parents..........	41	17	47	37	47	23	50	23	21	21
Married children...	34	49	31	21	33	25	34	78	47	18

* Percents may not total 100 due to rounding.

give proportionately the most (29 percent) followed by the other two generations at 25 percent each. Age mates are least likely to be recipients of help for the parent and child generation, whereas for the aged generation the horizontal and vertical kin once removed are least seen as targets for help.

In general we note that help instances given exceed those received for all generations and for virtually all categories of the social network. The level of giving is highest for the parent generation and lowest for the grandparents. The child generation leads in volume of receiving as might be expected, given its heavy needs.

In Table 3 we have looked much more intensively at the 1,674 exchanges which occurred exclusively among the three

ried children than either grandparents or grandchildren receive in their interchanges. By area of need grandparents required more help in the problem of illness (61 percent), household management (52 percent), and emotional gratification (42 percent), whereas the married child generation received help especially in the problem areas of child care (78 percent) and of economic assistance (49 percent).

Perhaps the most interesting findings in Table 3 are those which compare percentages receiving and giving help in five categories by generation. The parent generation quite clearly gives more help than it receives in all five areas of exchange. The grandparents, in sharp contrast, receive substantially more help than they give in all areas except child care where they have, obviously, no need of help. The married child generation gives more than it receives in three areas—emotional gratification, household management, and illness. This generation, on the other hand, receives more than it gives in the economic-assistance and child-care areas. We get from this table a most interesting picture of changes in symbiosis over the generations. In the beginning of the life span the married child generation is apparently quite willing to receive various kinds of help and perceives itself more or less in equilibrium in its giving and receiving. It appears to benefit more from exchanges that are reciprocal than does the grandparent generation. The grandparents perceive themselves as both meager givers and high receivers, almost in a *dependency status*, whereas the parent generation, in contrast, is high in giving and modest in receiving, a *patron-type status*. Only the married child generation appears high both in giving and receiving, a *status* of *high reciprocity* and *interdependence* within its social network.

33

ETHEL SHANAS

FAMILY HELP PATTERNS AND SOCIAL CLASS IN THREE COUNTRIES

Sociological theory has long alleged that industrialization has had a disintegrating effect on the extended family. Just as the family unit in response to industrialization was said to have diminished in size, so also the functions of the family were alleged to have diminished in number and importance (See Parsons, 1943, 1959; Ogburn, 1934). Family sociologists followed the lead of the social theorists. Textbooks on the family have given wide currency to the belief that the conjugal nuclear family unit consisting of husband, wife and unmarried offspring is the ideal structure for meeting the demands of contemporary industrial society.

"The most important characteristic of the ideal-type conjugal family is that it excludes a wide range of affinal and blood relatives from its everyday affairs—there is no great *extension* of the kin network" (Goode, 1963, p. 240). In analyses of the family based upon these assumptions, old people and their place in the family are often ignored. If the old are mentioned at all, they are discussed as though they were outsiders to the total family con-

Adapted from the *Journal of Marriage and the Family*, vol. 29, no. 2 (May, 1967), with the permission of the author and the publisher.

The research for this study was supported first by the United States National Institute of Mental Health, Grant numbers M5509 (Denmark), M5511 (Great Britain), and M5630 (United States); then by the Community Health Services Division of the Bureau of State Services, United States Public Health Service, Grant numbers CH00052 (Denmark), CH00053 (Great Britain), and CH00053 (United States).

figuration who serve only to create problems for the middle generation and the young (see Schorr, 1960, pp. 12–13).

The traditional assumptions about the disintegration of relations between generations in modern society and the physical and social isolation of the old from the middle generation and the young are contradicted by empirical evidence. In an extended review paper Marvin Sussman has summarized numerous studies of the relationships of adult children and their parents in the United States. Sussman says:

"The extended kin network is the basic social system in American urban society within which parent-adult child relationships are identified, described, and analyzed. The network is a pervasive system and includes member nuclear units interlocked within a structure of social relationships and mutual aid.

"The empirical evidence is conclusive on the existence of an extended kin network in urban society. The evidence also refutes the notion that nuclear family units are isolated and dependent upon the activities of other institutions and social systems" (Sussman, 1965, p. 91).

The extended kin network as the term is used by Sussman and others describes a social system consisting of parents, adult children, grandchildren and other relatives. These persons do not necessarily live in the same household. In contemporary society the extended kin network is not dependent on a common roof. Nevertheless, the members of the network continue to see one another frequently and to assist one another in meeting the demands of everyday living. In the kin network old people, as parents and grandparents or as relatives by blood or marriage, interact with children, grandchildren and other kin. The role of the elderly within the network may be a positive rather than a negative one. The old are often the givers as well as the receivers of help. The elderly indeed may be accepted by their kin rather than avoided by them. Old people may be integrated into the contemporary extended family rather than segregated from it.

METHODS OF STUDY

The present paper is a report of the help patterns among older people and their adult children in three countries: Denmark, Britain, and the United States. The findings are from an extensive collaborative research program on the social and economic circumstances of old people.

The data come from interviews conducted in mid-1962 with nationwide probability samples of approximately 2500 persons aged 65 and over in each of the three countries. The questionnaire used in the study was developed jointly by the three research teams. All concepts and variables, both in the questionnaires and in the tabulations, were defined in the same way in each country. As far as possible, interviewers in each country received the same instructions and training.

The research was limited to old people in private households. In all three countries only small proportions of the elderly live in institutions, 5.3 percent in Denmark, 3.6 percent in Britain and 3.7 percent in the United States. In each of the three countries, similar kinds of old people are found in institutions—those who are infirm and who lack family members or family substitutes to help them. In each country, there were some persons in the samples who could not be reached by the interviewers or who refused to be interviewed. The overall completion rate,

allowing for losses in the screening and locating of the elderly, was 84 percent in Denmark and the United States, and 83 percent in Britain. Although some information was collected about non-respondents, it may be that these persons differ from country to country. The effect of such differences, if they exist, cannot be completely evaluated. Comparison of each of the samples interviewed with independent estimates of the older population in each country, however, show generally good agreement.

A DEFINITION OF SOCIAL CLASS

In order to facilitate comparisons between the three countries, we have used occupation as an index of social class. Occupation is necessarily a rough indicator of class position but it was the index most readily available to us for the three-country analysis. Men and single women are classified by their own jobs, married women and widows by the occupations of their husbands. We are aware that many women have been widowed for long periods and that there may have been changes in their style of living since widowhood. Nevertheless, it is doubtful that the family values associated with the class position of a couple would change radically in the woman's widowhood.

In the present analysis we have grouped old people into three broad class categories: white-collar, working-class and agricultural workers. Our white-collar workers are comparable to the usual "middle-class" category; our working class includes both blue-collar and service workers. The most ambiguous of our class divisions is that of agricultural worker. Because of the wide range of agricultural establishments in the three countries this category includes agricultural laborers, share croppers and farm owners who may range from small holders to large ranch owners. The chief value of the

297

category is that it allows us to separate those old people of primarily rural background from those of town or city background.[1]

THE PATTERN OF FAMILY HELP

Family help patterns in old age are influenced by many factors. Among the most important of these are family size and structure and family living arrangements. If an old person has no living kin there will be no one to help him should he need help. Further, it is certainly easier for the old person to either give or receive help if he lives with children or relatives or close to them.

Aging parents turn to their children for help in meeting many daily responsibilities. Where children are not available brothers and sisters are a source of social support to the elderly. Several studies of old people that have investigated the importance of adult children in the maintenance of family life in old age have concentrated on the key role of the daughter. The dependence of working class old people on a daughter is one of the major themes of several related studies of the elderly in East London (Townsend, 1957; see also Young and Wilmott, 1957). An American study of old people and their families suggests that irrespective of social class old people in the United States are more likely to ask their daughters rather

[1] The class categories are based on occupational groupings of the United States Bureau of the Census. In each country all persons were classified using the *Alphabetical Index of Occupations and Industries* of that Bureau. U.S. Bureau of the Census, 1960 Census of Population, *Alphabetical Index of Occupations and Industries* (Revised Edition) (Washington, D.C.: U.S. Government Printing Office, 1960). The occupations in each category are: white-collar: professional, technical workers, managers, officials and proprietors (except farm), clerical and sales workers; working class: craftsmen, foremen, operatives and laborers (except farm), private household workers and other service workers; agricultural workers: farm owners, managers, laborers and foremen.

than their sons to help them (Shanas, 1962, p. 113).

If children and relatives are so important in providing assistance to the elderly and if daughters may be more important than sons in giving help, then, in studying the effect of social class on help patterns our first general questions must be: Does the social class of an old person affect his chances of having living children, particularly a daughter, and does the social class of an old person affect his chances of having living siblings?

Help from children to parents in old age, and from parents to adult children, particularly economic help, is often given in the form of shared living arrangements. Very often neither adult children nor old parents consider this type of shared living "help." In addition, there are many services which parents and children perform for one another in a common household. Often having an old mother or an old father in the house to look after young children makes it possible for both parents to work. Similarly, living with adult children may make it possible for an old person to maintain himself without turning to sources outside the family for financial assistance or care in illness. Where an old person has no children, relatives may share housing and thus help one another. The second question to be considered therefore in the exploration of help patterns is: Does the social class of an old person affect his living arrangements?

Sussman and Burchinal have reported that family help patterns take many forms, including mutual aid both material and non-material (Sussman, 1965, pp. 68–69). Help not only goes from adult children to aged parents, it goes from parents to children. The third topic to be considered then is: Does the social class of an old person affect whether he is more likely to say he helps his children or that his children help him?

From the findings in these three areas, family size and structure, family living arrangements, and reported family help patterns, I shall make some summary statements about family help patterns in old age and social class.

THE FINDINGS

How does the social class of an old person affect the size of his immediate family, the chances of his having a surviving daughter, and the chances of his having living siblings? In each country, Denmark, Britain and the United States, old people background, fewer children than the average.

Between one-fifth and one-fourth of all old people have no surviving children. The absolute percentages of people 65 years and older without children are: Denmark, 18 percent; Britain, 24 percent;

TABLE 1

PROPORTION OF PERSONS AGED 65 AND OVER IN EACH TYPE OF
FAMILY STRUCTURE: BY SOCIAL CLASS

FAMILY STRUCTURE AND COUNTRY	WHITE COLLAR			WORKING CLASS			AGRICULTURAL WORKERS		
	Men	Women	All Persons	Men	Women	All Persons	Men	Women	All Persons
No children:									
Denmark..............	15	22	19	14	19	17	18	10	15
Britain................	23	35	30	18	19	19	21	a	18
United States..........	16	21	19	18	13	16	14	9	11
One son only:									
Denmark..............	13	11	12	10	9	9	7	10	9
Britain................	13	11	12	8	8	8	8	a	7
United States..........	12	8	10	5	7	6	7	5	6
One daughter only:									
Denmark..............	9	13	12	10	8	9	7	7	7
Britain................	14	9	11	11	11	11	6	a	8
United States..........	11	11	11	10	10	10	7	8	8
Several children, at least one daughter:									
Denmark..............	53	45	48	59	56	57	59	67	62
Britain................	45	39	41	55	54	54	59	a	65
United States..........	54	49	51	61	52	61	64	69	67
Two or more sons, no daughters:									
Denmark..............	9	9	9	7	8	7	9	6	7
Britain................	5	6	6	8	8	8	5	a	3
United States..........	7	11	9	6	8	7	8	9	8

a Percents not computed when base is less than 50.

with white-collar backgrounds have the smallest number of surviving children, those with working-class backgrounds a substantially larger number of children, and agricultural workers the largest families of all. The average number of children per old person in Denmark is 2.8; in Britain, 2.5; and in the United States, 3.1. In each country, however, old people of working-class and agricultural backgrounds have more children than the national average, old people of white-collar and the United States, 18 percent. Among older women in particular lack of children is related to social class position (see Table 1). In all three countries women of white-collar background are more likely than women of working-class or agricultural backgrounds never to have married and thus are more likely to be childless. Among older men childlessness and class position are less clearly related. In general, while family size among the aged seems to be related to their class position, no

299

straightforward case can be made from our findings that class position affects the probability of both older men and older women being childless.

Does the social class of the old person effect whether or not he has a surviving daughter? Both men and women of white-collar background are less likely than persons of either blue-collar or agricultural backgrounds to have surviving daughters. In each country, older persons of white-collar backgrounds are the most

brothers and sisters. In each country, irrespective of social class, roughly four of every five older men and women have living brothers or sisters. Birth control was not generally prevalent seventy-five years ago or more. Furthermore, mortality in this generation has undoubtedly obscured any class differences in family size.

To this stage, we have shown that the social class of an old person affects both the size of his immediate family and its

TABLE 2

PROPORTION OF MARRIED PERSONS AGED 65 AND OVER IN EACH TYPE OF
LIVING ARRANGEMENT BY SOCIAL CLASS

FAMILY STRUCTURE AND COUNTRY	WHITE COLLAR			WORKING CLASS			AGRICULTURAL WORKERS		
	Men	Women	All Persons	Men	Women	All Persons	Men	Women	All Persons
Living with spouse only:									
Denmark...............	82	87	84	83	85	84	72	81	75
Britain................	74	72	73	66	68	67	a	a	48
United States..........	82	85	83	78	82	79	68	77	72
Living with spouse and children:									
Denmark...............	14	7	11	14	11	13	25	16	21
Britain................	20	19	20	29	27	28	a	a	45
United States..........	11	9	10	18	13	16	22	14	18
Living with spouse, relatives and/or others:									
Denmark...............	4	5	5	3	3	3	3	3	3
Britain................	6	9	7	5	5	5	a	a	6
United States..........	7	6	7	5	5	5	11	9	10

a Percents are not computed when base is less than 50.

likely of all persons to have only a single surviving child, either a son or a daughter. Since it may be assumed that the children of middle-class people were less likely than the children of blue collar or agricultural workers to have died in infancy or in early childhood forty or fifty years ago, we can only conclude that, particularly if the first child in a middle-class family was a son, no further children were wanted.

While social class apparently effects the size of an old person's immediate family and his chances of having a surviving daughter, class position is not related to the old person's chances of having living

structure. Let us now consider a second topic: Does social class affect the living arrangements of old people?

In all three countries, Denmark, Britain, and the United States, most married old people live apart from their children and relatives. In western cultures, this is what old people want—to live independently in their own homes as long as possible. As the Austrian sociologists, Rosenmayr and Köckeis (1963), have put it, old people want "intimacy at a distance." In both Britain and the United States, however, social class affects the living arrangements of old couples (see Table 2). Elderly couples with a white-collar background are more likely than those with either working-class or agricultural backgrounds to live apart from children and relatives. In Denmark, in contrast to Britain and the United States, the difference in the proportion of older couples with white-collar and working-class backgrounds who live apart from children and relatives is negligible. Differences in living arrangements among old couples in Denmark are less between the middle-class and the working-class than between these two groups and agricultural workers. Old

sharing a home with adult children is a working-class phenomenon in both Britain and the United States. In Denmark, the differences in the proportion of older unmarried persons with white collar and working class backgrounds who live with their children is negligible. Unmarried persons of agricultural backgrounds, however, are again twice as likely as other older people to share a home with their

TABLE 3

PROPORTION OF UNMARRIED PERSONS AGED 65 AND OVER IN EACH TYPE
OF LIVING ARRANGEMENT BY SOCIAL CLASS

LIVING ARRANGEMENTS AND COUNTRY	WHITE COLLAR			WORKING CLASS			AGRICULTURAL WORKERS		
	Men	Women	All Persons	Men	Women	All Persons	Men	Women	All Persons
Living alone:									
Denmark...............	62	62	62	67	71	70	42	49	46
Britain.................	41	42	42	35	47	44	a	a	a
United States.........	54	51	52	47	36	39	64	55	57
Living with children:									
Denmark...............	15	18	17	18	15	16	29	41	35
Britain.................	30	33	32	46	41	42	a	a	a
United States..........	24	27	26	31	46	41	20	34	31
Living with relatives:									
Denmark...............	5	9	8	6	6	6	9	6	8
Britain.................	15	19	18	13	9	10	a	a	a
United States..........	18	15	15	13	11	12	11	9	10
Living with others:									
Denmark...............	18	11	13	9	8	8	20	4	11
Britain.................	14	6	7	6	3	4	a	a	a
United States..........	4	7	7	10	7	8	5	2	2

a Percents are not computed when base is less than 50.

couples with agricultural backgrounds are one and one-half times as likely as old couples of white-collar or working-class backgrounds to share a home with one of their children or their relatives.

The living arrangements of unmarried old people—the widowed and the single—are also effected by their social class but the pattern is not as clear-cut as that for married old people (see Table 3). A complicating factor is that many unmarried old people have no children and therefore cannot be expected to live with children. Nonetheless, it is obvious that

children. To some extent relatives tend to replace children for many childless persons. In both Britain and the United States, living with relatives is more common among unmarried persons of white-collar background than unmarried working-class persons (for American material see Cumming and Schneider, 1961). Once again, the differences between these two classes are negligible in Denmark.

The findings indicate that in Britain and the United States and to a lesser extent in Denmark the social class of an old person affects whether or not he lives with his children and relatives. In both Britain and the United States persons with white-collar backgrounds, whether married or unmarried, are the least likely of all persons to live with children. In Denmark, irrespective of whether old people are of white-collar or working-class background they live apart from their children and relatives in both the provincial towns and in the urbanized Copenhagen area.

an old person to have his nearest child one hour or more distant from him. There are some class differences, however, among those old people who live this far from their nearest child. In both Britain and the United States persons of white-collar backgrounds are the most likely of all old persons to report that they live an hour or more from their nearest child. In Denmark, persons of both white-collar and

TABLE 4

PERCENTAGE DISTRIBUTION: PROXIMITY OF NEAREST CHILD OF PERSONS
AGED 65 YEARS AND OVER BY SOCIAL CLASS

PROXIMITY OF NEAREST CHILD AND COUNTRY	WHITE COLLAR			WORKING CLASS			AGRICULTURAL WORKERS		
	Men	Women	All Persons	Men	Women	All Persons	Men	Women	All Persons
Same household:									
Denmark...............	16	17	17	17	16	16	31	31	31
Britain.................	27	43	36	42	45	44	a	a	49
United States..........	16	25	21	26	37	32	25	30	28
10 minutes or less distant:									
Denmark...............	30	30	30	32	36	34	34	29	31
Britain.................	22	20	21	23	25	24	a	a	21
United States..........	31	33	32	34	31	33	34	37	36
11–30 minutes distant:									
Denmark...............	22	23	23	26	26	26	18	21	19
Britain.................	18	14	16	16	15	16	a	a	14
United States..........	17	14	15	17	16	16	15	14	15
31–60 minutes distant:									
Denmark...............	16	15	16	11	11	11	8	11	10
Britain.................	13	9	10	8	7	7	a	a	5
United States..........	11	9	9	7	4	5	13	6	8
One hour or more distant:									
Denmark...............	16	14	15	14	11	13	9	8	8
Britain.................	20	14	17	11	8	9	a	a	11
United States..........	25	19	22	16	12	14	14	13	13

a Percents are not computed when base is less than 50.

Sharing a home with children and relatives is apparently a rural rather than a working-class phenomenon in that country (Stehouwer, 1963).

In each country, and for every social class, old people who live apart from children tend to have at least one child in the immediate vicinity. Between half and two-thirds of all old people with children, irrespective of class, either share a household with a child or live within ten minutes distance from a child (see Table 4). Further, in all three countries, despite their differences in size, it is unusual for

working-class backgrounds are equally likely to report that they live this far from their nearest child.

The living arrangements of old people are obviously affected by their social class. Let us now consider our final topic: Does the social class of an old person affect the help he gives to his adult children or receives from them?

When old people are asked about help from children it is likely to be formal help that they recall and report. "Living together" as a form of mutual aid tends to be ignored. We would therefore expect that working class persons in Britain and the United States, and persons of agricultural backgrounds in Denmark would be the most likely to underreport help which they receive from children. In both Britain and the United States old people of white-collar background, particularly men, are the most likely of all old people to report that they helped their adult children. Indeed, more of these persons say that they helped their children than report that their children helped them (see Table 5). Working-class men in the United States are also noticeably more likely to say that they gave help to their

in Britain and the United States white-collar parents are more likely to give help to children; working class parents, at least in Britain, are more likely to receive help. In each social class, and in every country, however, help flows in two directions: from parents to adult children, and from adult children to aged parents.

CONCLUSIONS

Family help patterns in old age in Denmark, Britain and the United States differ

TABLE 5

PROPORTION OF PERSONS AGED 65 AND OVER GIVING HELP TO CHILDREN OR
RECEIVING HELP FROM CHILDREN DURING PAST MONTH
BY SOCIAL CLASS*

HELP PATTERNS AND SOCIAL CLASS	DENMARK			BRITAIN			UNITED STATES		
	Men	Women	All Persons	Men	Women	All Persons	Men	Women	All Persons
Gave help to child:									
White Collar............	25	33	29	55	56	56	66	70	68
Working Class..........	17	28	23	42	47	45	57	58	57
Agricultural Workers.....	29	37	33	a	a	40	58	57	58
Received help from child:									
White Collar............	n.a.	n.a.	18	40	55	49	37	59	49
Working Class..........	n.a.	n.a.	17	45	55	51	45	59	52
Agricultural Workers.....	n.a.	n.a.	25	a	a	46	55	67	62

* Danish data are based on help given or received at any time, not only during the past month. Twenty percent in Britain and 28 percent in the United States who said they gave help to children, gave no help in the past month.
a Percents are not computed when base is less than 50.

children rather than received it. However, in Britain both working-class men and women were more likely to say that they received help from their children rather than that they gave help to children. What Danish data are available indicate that few Danish old people either give help to children or receive help from adult children. However, irrespective of class, elderly Danes are more likely to say that they help their children rather than that their children help them.

Despite our assumption that working-class old people in particular may underreport help from children, it appears that

by the social class position of the old person. The class position of old people affects primarily the size of their immediate families, their family structure and their living arrangements. While the social class of the old person affects the magnitude and direction of parent-child help in old age, old persons in every social class report that they help their children and that their children help them.

Old people of white-collar background were apparently limiting the size of their families forty or fifty years ago. As a result these persons are the most likely among the aged to have only one surviv-

303

ing child or no children at all. The dependence of older working-class parents on a daughter previously reported in the literature may simply mean that daughters are more likely to be available to working-class parents. Other evidence in this research program shows that where there are no daughters, help flows from sons to aged parents (see Shanas *et al.*, 1968, ch. 8). If there are no children, however, child-parent help must be non-existent. The mutual interdependence of the elderly middle-class husband and wife remarked upon by other investigators, then, may be simply a result of the family structure of the middle class (see Wilmott and Young, 1960; for an American study see Kerckhoff, 1965). Since these old people are likely to have only a single child or no children, circumstances may force them to depend upon one another far more than may be either usual or necessary among the elderly of other class backgrounds.

The living arrangements of old people differ by social class. Middle-class white-collar parents in both Britain and the United States are likely to live apart from their adult children. In Denmark, the differences in living arrangements are between persons of white-collar and working class background on the one hand and persons of agricultural background on the other. A possible explanation of these class differences in living arrangements, at least in Britain and the United States, is the difference in the size of the families of the white-collar and other classes. Old people with working-class or agricultural backgrounds have larger families than old people of white-collar background and thus even after 65 are more likely to have a young unmarried adult child still in the home. On the other hand, an economic explanation for the differences in the living arrangements of old people of various classes must not be ruled out. Living together in a joint household is often the way in which adult children and other relatives assist in the support of aged persons (Schorr, 1960, pp. 19–21). The fact

that more older couples and unmarried persons of white-collar backgrounds live alone, particularly in the United States, may simply reflect their more comfortable economic status.

While the social class of an old person affects the structure of his household in each of the three countries, the evidence is diametrically opposite to the common belief that aged parents within any social class are physically separated from their children. The immediate household of the old person differs by whether he is of white-collar or working-class background in Britain and the United States, and by whether he is of these or of agricultural background in Denmark. However, if an old person has children and there is no child in his household, one of his children is likely to live in the immediate vicinity. White-collar parents are the most likely of all parents to be at some distance from their nearest child, but even the great majority of these persons live close enough to an adult child to call on him for help if it is needed.

What then of social class and mutual aid between older parents and adult children?

The findings suggest a somewhat more complicated help pattern between the generations than is often assumed in the literature. The help which old people give their adult children varies from help with grandchildren, through gifts of cash, clothing, household objects and food, to assistance with home repairs, improvements, gardening and yard work, and help with housework, mending, sewing and cooking. The help which adult children give old people varies from economic support, to personal care, to help with transportation, outings, holidays, to gifts of cash, money and food and the same range of housekeeping and home chores listed above. Each generation turns to the other for assistance during illness and other emergencies.

Help goes from adult child to aged parent or from aged parent to adult child as needed. In both Britain and the United

States old people of white-collar backgrounds are the most likely of all people to be able to help their children. As a consequence more of them report giving help to children than report receiving help. Old people of working-class backgrounds need help from children. As a result, at least in Britain, more of them report that they receive help from children than that they give it. In contrast to Britain and the United States "Denmark seems to be a country in which the generations live in close contact with each other but with a relatively low degree of functional dependence" (Stehouwer, 1965, p. 159). In every social class, however, there is some

report of mutual help between parents and adult children.

The empirical findings on family help patterns by social class in old age reinforce the theoretical position advocated by Sussman, Litwak, and others (Litwak, 1965). The kin network and the modified extended family appears as the basic social system in contemporary industrial society. Within this system, nuclear units are interlocked in a pattern of mutual aid, which functions within every social class.

PART VI

WORK, LEISURE, AND RETIREMENT

The areas subsumed under this title are so broad and the literature so extensive that the papers included here can do no more than to alert the student to a few of the major issues. In sociology alone so much attention has been given to the work life and the place of work in the social structure that the study of occupations and professions has itself come to constitute a well-defined content area. At the same time there have been relatively few empirical studies in which the work career has been viewed as a whole, or in which the changing relations between the work role and other life roles have been seen from the perspective of the life cycle. Psychologists and educators have focused largely upon the early phase of the career and upon the problem of matching individuals to jobs, while social gerontologists have focused upon the retirement phase. Even in the mushrooming literature on leisure and on the effects of technological change and cybernation on work-leisure patterns, there are few empirical studies of the ways in which people of varying occupational levels and of varying ages actually spend their time and little recognition of time-use patterns as a significant dimension in the study of lives.

The paper by Becker and Strauss is based upon a model of the work organization as a complex network of interlocking career lines, with channels for upward, downward, and lateral movement, and with ever-changing configurations of institutional and personal needs in which socialization and the formation of adult identities take place. The paper sets forth some of the issues common to various occupational careers: recruitment, replacement, training, attachment and loyalties, timing in status passage, and severance, as these issues involve the individual

on the one hand and the work organization on the other. The paper focuses on the dynamics of flow and change, and in so doing conveys something of the complex social reality in which career lines should be viewed and in which the relationships between career movements, personality, and adult socialization might well be studied.

In the next paper Wilensky focuses attention upon the relations between the work life and other aspects of social participation. He differentiates *orderly* from *disorderly* work histories: the *orderly* is one in which a succession of jobs are functionally related and hierarchically ordered. He then presents data to show that in the middle mass of the population, the lower-middle and upper-working class levels, only 30 percent of men can be said to spend half or more of their work histories in an orderly career. The author then shows that men whose careers are orderly have stronger attachments to formal associations and to the community than men whose job histories are disorderly. When work ties are severed, whether at different periods in the life span or between different groups at one point in time, there is a decline in community participation. The data are presented for men aged 20 to 40 and for those aged 40 to 55. While the overall relationship holds for both age groups, certain differences are discussed by Wilensky in terms of historical and generational effects.

The paper by Belbin and Belbin is quite different in topic and in perspective. Its focus is upon a particular social problem related to the work career, namely that of retraining large numbers of middle-aged workers who are displaced as a result of rapidly-changing technology. In touching briefly upon a set of related psychological and sociological problems—the abilities of older workers to learn new skills, attitudes in the worker and employer that involve age-prejudice, special training methods, and government programs now appearing in various countries aimed at this problem— the authors point to a new set of research problems for persons they call industrial gerontologists.

The paper by Havighurst and Feigenbaum deals with leisure and life-styles in middle-aged men and women living in an urban midwestern community. Using a rating scale to evaluate the quality or level of performance in the use of leisure time, the authors relate this measure to performance levels in other social roles; show how leisure patterns vary in various social class groups and in community-centered and home-centered life-styles; and discuss the differences in utilization of leisure by well-adjusted and poorly-adjusted persons.

The two papers that follow deal with the problem of retirement. The brief excerpt by Epstein and Murray is taken from the report of a Social Security survey undertaken in 1963. It states succinctly some important findings regarding the changing nature of the work-retirement pattern, findings which have implications with regard to the changing value systems in America. For instance, men in more highly paid occupations have a lower retirement rate than other men; over all, the proportion retiring voluntarily doubled between the years 1951 and 1963; and

there are more and more older men who are well enough to work and who might find work if they wanted, but who prefer the leisure of retirement.

The longer paper by Maddox is an overview of the major social-psychological issues of retirement. It includes a discussion of changing values of work and the Protestant Ethic; the complex problems involved in substituting leisure for work as a major anchorage for men; the great differences in the meaning and significance of retirement for men whose career lines have been orderly or disorderly; and the problems of applying the disengagement theory of aging (a theory which is discussed at greater length in the papers of Part III) in understanding problems of morale in retirement.

The paper by Miller carries further the discussion of the relationship between work and leisure, and poses the problem involved for the older person in maintaining an acceptable self-concept after retirement. Miller conceptualizes the problem as one in which the retiree, in establishing a new social identity, must find an activity in which to participate and must create a rationale for the meaningfulness of that activity. This process involves experimentation with new roles and the accompanying threat that a social encounter may break down or that the older person may not be able to fulfill the new role expectations. Social embarrassment or anticipation of embarrassment then becomes a major issue not only for the older person but for the others with whom he interacts.

34

HOWARD S. BECKER and ANSELM L. STRAUSS

CAREERS, PERSONALITY, AND ADULT SOCIALIZATION

In contradistinction to other disciplines, the sociological approach to the study of personality and personality change views the person as a member of a social structure. Usually the emphasis is upon some cross-section in his life: on the way he fills his status, on the consequent conflicts in role and his dilemmas. When the focus is more developmental, then concepts like career carry the import of movement through structures. Much writing on career, of course, pertains more to patterned sequences of passage than to the persons. A fairly comprehensive statement about careers as related both to institutions and to persons would be useful in furthering research. We shall restrict our discussion to careers in work organizations and occupations, for purposes of economy.

CAREER FLOW

Organizations built around some particular kind of work or situation at work tend to be characterized by recurring patterns of tension and of problems. Thus in occupations whose central feature is performance of a service for outside clients, one chronic source of tension is the effort of members to control their work life themselves while in contact with outsiders. In production organizations somewhat similar tensions arise from the workers' efforts to maintain relative autonomy over job conditions.

Whatever the typical problems of an occupation, the pattern of associated problems will vary with one's position.

Reprinted from the *American Journal of Sociology*, vol. 62, no. 3 (November, 1956). © 1956 by The University of Chicago.

Some positions will be easier, some more difficult; some will afford more prestige, some less; some will pay better than others. In general, the personnel move from less to more desirable positions, and the flow is usually, but not necessarily, related to age. The pure case is the bureaucracy as described by Mannheim, in which seniority and an age-related increase in skill and responsibility automatically push men in the desired direction and within a single organization (Mannheim, 1953).

An ideally simple model of flow up through an organization is something like the following: recruits enter at the bottom in positions of least prestige and move up through the ranks as they gain in age, skill, and experience. Allowing for some attrition due to death, sickness, and dismissal or resignation, all remain in the organization until retirement. Most would advance to top ranks. A few reach the summit of administration. Yet even in bureaucracies, which perhaps come closest to this model, the very highest posts often go not to those who have come up through the ranks but to "irregulars"— people with certain kinds of experiences or qualifications not necessarily acquired by long years of official service. In other ways, too, the model is oversimple: posts at any rank may be filled from the outside; people get "frozen" at various levels and do not rise. Moreover, career movements may be not only up but down or sideways, as in moving from one department to another at approximately the same rank.

The flow of personnel through an organization should be seen, also, as a number of streams; that is, there may be several routes to the posts of high prestige and responsibility. These may be thought of as escalators. An institution invests time, money, and energy in the training of its recruits and members which it cannot afford to let go to waste. Hence just being on the spot often means that one is bound to advance. In some careers, even a small gain in experience gives one a great advantage over the beginner. The mere fact of advancing age or of having been through certain kinds of situations or training saves many an employee from languishing in lower positions. This is what the phrase "seasoning" refers to— the acquiring of requisite knowledge and skills, skills that cannot always be clearly specified even by those who have them. However, the escalator will carry one from opportunities as well as to them. After a certain amount of time and money have been spent upon one's education for the job, it is not always easy to get off one escalator and on another. Immediate superiors will block transfer. Sponsors will reproach one for disloyalty. Sometimes a man's special training and experience will be thought to have spoiled him for a particular post.

RECRUITMENT AND REPLACEMENT

Recruitment is typically regarded as occurring only at the beginning of a career, where the occupationally uncommitted are bid for, or as something which happens only when there is deliberate effort to get people to commit themselves. But establishments must recruit for all positions; whenever personnel are needed, they must be found and often trained. Many higher positions, as in bureaucracies, appear to recruit automatically from aspirants at next lower levels. This is only appearance: the recruitment mechanisms are standardized and work well. Professors, for example, are drawn regularly from lower ranks, and the system works passably in most academic fields. But in schools of engineering young instructors are likely to be drained off into industry and not be on hand for promotion. Recruitment is never really automatic but depends upon developing in the recruit certain occupational or organizational commitments which correspond to regularized career routes.

Positions in organizations are being vacated continually through death and retirement, promotion and demotion. Replacements may be drawn from the outside ("an outside man") or from within the organization. Most often positions are filled by someone promoted from below or shifted from another department without gaining in prestige. When career routes are well laid out, higher positions are routinely filled from aspirants at the next lower level. However, in most organizations many career routes are not so rigidly laid out: a man may jump from one career over to another to fill the organization's need. When this happens, the "insider-outsider" may be envied by those who have come up by the more orthodox routes; and his associates on his original route may regard him as a turncoat. This may be true even if he is not the first to have made the change, as in the jump from scholar to dean or doctor to hospital administrator. Even when replacement from outside the organization is routine for certain positions, friction may result if the newcomer has come up by an irregular route—as when a college president is chosen from outside the usual circle of feeding occupations. A candidate whose background is too irregular is likely to be eliminated unless just this irregularity makes him particularly valuable. The advantage of "new blood" versus "inbreeding" may be the justification. A good sponsor can widen the limits within which the new kind of candidate is judged, by asking that certain of his qualities be weighed against others; as Hall says, "the question is not whether the applicant possesses a specific trait . . . but whether these traits can be assimilated by the specific institutions" (Hall, 1948, p. 332).

Even when fairly regular routes are fol-

312

lowed, the speed of advancement may not be rigidly prescribed. Irregularity may be due in part to unexpected needs for replacement because a number of older men retire in quick succession or because an older man leaves and a younger one happens to be conveniently present. On the other hand, in some career lines there may be room for a certain amount of manipulation of "the system." One such method is to remain physically mobile, especially early in the career, thus taking advantage of several institutions' vacancies.

THE LIMITS OF
REPLACEMENT AND
RECRUITMENT

Not all positions within an organization recruit from an equally wide range. Aside from the fact that different occupations may be represented in one establishment, some positions require training so specific that recruits can be drawn only from particular schools or firms. Certain positions are merely way stations and recruit only from aspirants directly below. Some may draw only from the outside, and the orbit is always relevant to both careers and organization. One important question, then, about any organization is the limits within which positions recruit incumbents. Another is the limits of the recruitment in relation to certain variables—age of the organization, its relations with clients, type of generalized work functions, and the like.

One can also identify crucial contingencies for careers in preoccupational life by noting the general or probable limits within which recruiting is carried on and the forces by which they are maintained. For example, it is clear that a position can be filled, at least at first, only from among those who know of it. Thus physiologists cannot be recruited during high school, for scarcely any youngster then knows what a physiologist is or does. By the same token, however, there are at least generally formulated notions of the "artist," so that recruitment into the world of art often begins in high school (see Strauss's unpublished studies of careers in art and Becker and Carper, 1956). This is paradoxical, since the steps and paths later in the artist's career are less definite than in the physiologist's. The range and diffusion of a public stereotype are crucial in determining the number and variety of young people from whom a particular occupation can recruit, and the unequal distribution of information about careers limits occupations possibilities.

There are problems attending the systematic restriction of recruiting. Some kinds of persons, for occupationally irrelevant reasons (formally, anyway), may not be considered for positions at all. Medical schools restrict recruiting in this way: openly, on grounds of "personality assessments," and covertly on ethnicity. Italians, Jews, and Negroes who do become doctors face differential recruitment into the formal and informal hierarchies of influence, power, and prestige in the medical world. Similar mechanisms operate at the top and bottom of industrial organizations (Hall, 1948; Solomon, 1952; Hughes, 1943; Dalton, 1951; Collins, 1946).

Another problem is that of "waste." Some recruits in institutions which recruit pretty widely do not remain. Public caseworkers in cities are recruited from holders of Bachelor's degrees, but most do not remain caseworkers. From the welfare agency's point of view this is waste. From other perspectives this is not waste, for they may exploit the job and its opportunities for private ends. Many who attend school while supposedly visiting clients may be able to transfer to new escalators because of the acquisition, for instance, of a Master's degree. Others actually build up small businesses during this "free time." The only permanent recruits, those who do not constitute waste, are those who fail at such endeavors (Bogdanoff and Glass, 1954). Unless an organization actually finds useful a constant turnover of some

313

sector of its personnel, it is faced with the problem of creating organizational loyalties and—at higher levels anyhow—satisfactory careers or the illusion of them, within the organization.

TRAINING AND SCHOOLS

Schooling occurs most conspicuously during the early stages of a career and is an essential part of getting people committed to careers and prepared to fill positions. Both processes may, or may not, be going on simultaneously. However, movement from one kind of job or position or another virtually always necessitates some sort of learning—sometimes before and sometimes on the job, sometimes through informal channels and sometimes at school. This means that schools may exist within the framework of an organization. In-service training is not only for jobs on lower levels but also for higher positions. Universities and special schools are attended by students who are not merely preparing for careers but getting degrees or taking special courses in order to move faster and higher. In some routes there is virtual blockage of mobility because the top of the ladder is not very high; in order to rise higher, one must return to school to prepare for ascending by another route. Thus the registered nurse may have to return to school to become a nursing educator, administrator, or even supervisor. Sometimes the aspirant may study on his own, and this may be effective unless he must present a diploma to prove he deserves promotion.

The more subtle connections are between promotion and informal training. Certain positions preclude the acquiring of certain skills or information, but others foster it. It is possible to freeze a man at given levels or to move him faster, unbeknownst to him. Thus a sponsor, anticipating a need for certain requirements in his candidate, may arrange for critical experiences to come his way. Medical students are aware that if they obtain internships in certain kinds of hospitals they will be exposed to certain kinds of learning: the proper internship is crucial to many kinds of medical careers. But learning may depend upon circumstances which the candidate cannot control and of which he may not even be aware. Thus Goldstein has pointed out that nurses learn more from doctors at hospitals not attached to a medical school; elsewhere the medical students become the beneficiaries of the doctors' teaching (Goldstein, 1954). Quite often who teaches whom and what is connected with matters of convenience as well as with prestige. It is said, for instance, that registered nurses are jealous of their prerogatives and will not transmit certain skills to practical nurses. Nevertheless, the nurse is often happy to allow her aides to relieve her of certain other jobs and will pass along the necessary skills; and the doctor in his turn may do the same with his nurses.

The connection between informal learning and group allegiance should not be minimized. Until a newcomer has been accepted, he will not be taught crucial trade secrets. Conversely, such learning may block mobility, since to be mobile is to abandon standards, violate friendships, and even injure one's self-regard. Within some training institutions students are exposed to different and sometimes antithetical work ideologies—as with commercial and fine artists—which results in sharp and sometimes lasting internal conflicts of loyalty.

Roy's work on industrial organization furnishes a subtle instance of secrecy and loyalty in training (Roy, 1952). The workers in Roy's machine shop refused to enlighten him concerning ways of making money on difficult piecework jobs until given evidence that he could be trusted in undercover skirmishes with management. Such systematic withholding of training may mean that an individual can qualify for promotion by performance only by shifting group-loyalties, and that disqualifies him in some other sense. Training hinders as well as helps. It may incapacitate one for certain duties as well as train him for them. Roy's discussion of the managerial "logic of efficiency" makes this clear: workers, not trained in this logic, tend to see short cuts to higher production more quickly than managers, who think in terms of sentimental dogmas of efficiency (Roy, 1954).

Certain transmittable skills, information, and qualities facilitate movement, and it behooves the candidate to discover and distinguish what is genuinely relevant in his training. The student of careers must also be sensitized to discover what training is essential or highly important to the passage from one status to another.

RECRUITING FOR
UNDESIRABLE POSITIONS

A most difficult kind of recruiting is for positions which no one wants. Ordinary incentives do not work, for these are positions without prestige, without future, without financial reward. Yet they are filled. How, and by whom? Most obviously, they are filled by failures (the crews of gandy dancers who repair railroad tracks are made up of skid-row bums), to whom they are almost the only means of survival. Most positions filled by failures are not openly regarded as such; special rhetorics deal with misfortune and make their ignominious fate more palatable for the failures themselves and those around them (See Goffman, 1952).

Of course, failure is a matter of perspective. Many positions represent failure to some but not to others. For the middle-class white, becoming a caseworker in a public welfare agency may mean failure; but for the Negro from the lower-middle class the job may be a real prize. The permanent positions in such agencies tend to be occupied by whites who have failed to reach anything better and, in larger numbers, by Negroes who succeeded in arriving this far (Bogdanoff and Glass, 1954). Likewise, some recruitment into generally undesirable jobs is from the ranks of the disaffected who care little for generally accepted values. The jazz musicians who play in Chicago's Clark Street dives make little money, endure bad working conditions, but desire the freedom to play as they could not in better-paying places (Becker, 1951).

Recruits to undesirable positions also come from the ranks of the transients, who, because they feel that they are on their way to something different and better, can afford temporarily to do something *infra dig*. Many organizations rely primarily on transients—such are the taxi companies and some of the mail-order houses. Among the permanent incumbents of undesirable positions are those, also, who came in temporarily but whose brighter prospects did not materialize, they thus fall into the "failure" group.

Still another group is typified by the taxi dancer, whose career Cressey (1932) has described. The taxi dancer starts at the top, from which the only movement possible is down or out. She enters the profession young and goodlooking and draws the best customers in the house, but, as age and hard work take their toll, she ends with the worst clients or becomes a streetwalker. Here the worst positions are filled by individuals who start high and so are committed to a career that ends badly—a more common pattern of life, probably, than is generally recognized.

Within business and industrial organizations, not everyone who attempts to move upward succeeds. Men are assigned to positions prematurely, sponsors drop protégés, and miscalculations are made about the abilities of promising persons. Problems for the organization arise from those contingencies. Incompetent persons must be moved into positions where they cannot do serious damage, others of limited ability can still be useful if wisely placed. Aside from outright firing, various methods of "cooling out" the failures can be adopted, among them honorific promotion, banishment "to the sticks," shunting to other departments, frank demotion, bribing out of the organization, and down-grading through departmental mergers. The use of particular methods is related to the structure of the organization; and these, in turn, have consequences both for the failure and for the organization (Martin and Strauss, 1956).

ATTACHMENT AND SEVERANCE

Leaders of organizations sometimes complain that their personnel will not take responsibility or that some men (the wrong ones) are too ambitious. This complaint reflects a dual problem which confronts every organization. Since all positions must be filled, some men must be properly motivated to take certain positions and stay in them for a period, while others must be motivated to move onward and generally upward. The American emphasis on mobility should not lead us to assume that everyone wants to rise to the highest levels or to rise quickly. Aside from this, both formal mechanisms and informal influences bind incumbents, at least temporarily, to certain positions. Even the ambitious may be willing to remain in a given post, provided that it offers important contacts or the chance to learn certain skills and undergo certain experiences. Part of the bargain in staying in given positions is the promise that they lead somewhere. When career lines are fairly regularly laid out, positions lead definitely somewhere and at a regulated pace. One of the less obvious functions of the sponsor is to alert his favorites to the sequence and its timing, rendering them more ready to accept undesirable assignments and to refrain from champing at the bit when it might be awkward for the organization.

To certain jobs, in the course of time, come such honor and glory that the incumbents will be satisfied to remain there permanently, giving up aspirations to move upward. This is particularly true when allegiance to colleagues, built on informal relations and conflict with other ranks, is intense and runs counter to allegiance to the institution. But individuals are also attached to positions by virtue of having done particularly well at them; they often take great satisfaction in their competence at certain techniques and develop self-conceptions around them.

All this makes the world of organizations go around, but it also poses certain problems, both institutional and personal. The stability of institutions is predicated upon the proper preparation of aspirants for the next steps and upon institutional aid in transmuting motives and allegiances. While it is convenient to have some personnel relatively immobile, others must be induced to cut previous ties, to balance rewards in favor of moving, and even to take risks for long-run gains. If we do not treat mobility as normal, and thus regard attachment to a position as abnormal, we are then free to ask how individuals are induced to move along. It is done by devices such as sponsorship, by planned sequences of positions and skills, sometimes tied to age; by rewards, monetary and otherwise, and, negatively, by ridicule and the denial of responsibility to the lower ranks. There is, of course, many a slip in the inducing of mobility. Chicago public school teachers illustrate this point. They move from schools in the slums to middle-class neighborhoods. The few who prefer to remain in the tougher slum schools have settled in too snugly to feel capable of facing the risks of moving to "better" schools (Becker, 1952). Their deviant course illuminates the more usual patterns of the Chicago teacher's career.

TIMING IN STATUS PASSAGE

Even when paths in a career are regular and smooth, there always arise problems of pacing and timing. While, ideally, successors and predecessors should move in and out of offices at equal speeds, they do not and cannot. Those asked to move on or along or upward may be willing but must make actual and symbolic preparations; meanwhile, the successor waits impatiently. Transition periods are a necessity, for a man often invests heavily of himself in a position, comes to possess it as it possesses him, and suffers in leaving it. If the full ritual of leavetaking is not allowed, the man may not pass fully into his new status. On the other hand, the institution has devices to make him forget, to plunge him into the new office, to woo and win him with the new gratifications, and, at the same time, to force him to abandon the old. When each status is conceived as the logical and temporal extension of the one previous, then severance is not so disturbing. Nevertheless, if a man must face his old associates in unaccustomed roles, problems of loyalty arise. Hence a period of tolerance after formal admission to the new status is almost a necessity. It is rationalized in phrases like "it takes time" and "we all make mistakes when starting, until . . . ."

But, on the other hand, those new to office may be too zealous. They often commit the indelicate error of taking too literally their formal promotion or certification, when actually intervening steps must be traversed before the attainment of full prerogatives. The passage may involve trials and tests of loyalty, as well as the simple accumulation of information and skill. The overeager are kept in line by various controlling devices: a new assistant professor discovers that it will be "just a little while" before the curriculum can be rearranged so that he can teach his favorite courses. Even a new superior has to face the resentment or the cautiousness of established personnel and may, if sensitive, pace his "moving in on them" until he has passed unspoken tests.

When subordinates are raised to the ranks of their superiors, an especially delicate situation is created. Equality is neither created by that official act, nor, even if it were, can it come about without a certain awkwardness. Patterns of response must be rearranged by both parties, and strong self-control must be exerted so that acts are appropriate. Slips are inevitable, for, although the new status may be fully granted, the proper identities may at times be forgotten to everyone's

embarrassment. Eventually, the former subordinate may come to command or take precedence over someone to whom he once looked for advice and guidance. When colleagues who were formerly sponsors and sponsored disagree over some important issue, recrimination may become overt and betrayal explicit. It is understandable why those who have been promoted often prefer, or are advised, to take office in another organization, however much they may wish to remain at home.

MULTIPLE ROUTES AND SWITCHING

Theoretically, a man may leave one escalator and board another, instead of following the regular route. Such switching is most visible during the schooling, or preoccupational, phases of careers. Frequently students change their line of endeavor but remain roughly within the same field; this is one way for less desirable and less well-known specialties to obtain recruits. Certain kinds of training, such as the legal, provide bases for moving early and easily into a wide variety of careers. In all careers, there doubtless are some points at which switching to another career is relatively easy. In general, while commitment to a given career automatically closes paths, the skills and information thereby acquired open up other routes and new goals. One may not, of course, perceive the alternatives or may dismiss them as risky or otherwise undesirable.

When a number of persons have changed escalators at about the same stage in their careers, then there is the beginning of a new career. This is one way by which career lines become instituted. Sometimes the innovation occurs at the top ranks of older careers; when all honors are exhausted, the incumbent himself may look for new worlds to conquer. Or he may seem like a good risk to an organization looking for personnel with interestingly different qualifications. Such new phases of career are much more than honorific and may indeed be an essential inducement to what becomes pioneering.

Excitement and dangers are intimately tied up with switching careers. For example, some careers are fairly specific in goal but diffuse in operational means: the "fine artist" may be committed to artistic ideals but seize upon whatever jobs are at hand to help him toward creative goals. When he takes a job in order to live, he thereby risks committing himself to an alternative occupational career; and artists and writers do, indeed, get weaned away from the exercise of their art in just this way. Some people never set foot on a work escalator but move from low job to low job. Often they seek better conditions of work or a little more money rather than chances to climb institutional or occupational ladders. Many offers of opportunities to rise are spurned by part-time or slightly committed recruits, often because the latter are engaged in pursuing alternative routes while holding the job, perhaps a full-time one providing means of livelihood. This has important and, no doubt, subtle effects upon institutional functioning. When careers are in danger of being brought to an abrupt end—as with airplane pilots—then, before retirement, other kinds of careers may be prepared for or entered. This precaution is very necessary. When generalized mobility is an aim, specific routes may be chosen for convenience' sake. One is careful not to develop the usual motivation and allegiances. This enables one to get off an escalator and to move over to another with a minimum of psychological strain.

Considerable switching takes place within a single institution or a single occupational world and is rationalized in institutional and occupational terms, both by the candidates and by their colleagues. A significant consequence of this, undoubtedly, is subtle psychological strain, since the new positions and those preceding are both somewhat alike and different.

CLIMACTIC PERIODS

Even well-worn routes have stretches of maximum opportunity and danger. The critical passage in some careers lies near the beginning. This is especially so when the occupation or institution strongly controls recruitment; once chosen, prestige and deference automatically accrue. In another kind of career the critical time comes at the end and sometimes very abruptly. In occupations which depend upon great physical skill, the later phases of a career are especially hazardous. It is also requisite in some careers that one choose the proper successor to carry on, lest one's own work be partly in vain. The symbolic last step of moving out may be quite as important as any that preceded it.

Appropriate or strategic timing is called for, to meet opportunity and danger, but the timing becomes vital at different periods in different kinds of careers. A few, such as the careers of virtuoso musical performers, begin so early in life that the opportunity to engage in music may have passed long before they learn of it. Some of the more subtle judgments of timing are required when a person wishes to shift from one escalator to another. Richard Wohl, of the University of Chicago, in an unpublished paper has suggested that modeling is a step which women may take in preparation for upward mobility through marriage; but models may marry before they know the ropes, and so marry too low; or they may marry too long after their prime, and so marry less well than they might. Doubtless organizations and occupations profit from mistakes of strategic timing, both to recruit and then to retain their members.

During the most crucial periods of any career, a man suffers greater psychological stress than during other periods. This is perhaps less so if he is not aware of his opportunities and dangers—for then the contingencies are over before they can be grasped or coped with: but probably it is more usual to be aware, or to be made so by colleagues and seniors, of the nature of imminent or current crises. Fortunately, together with such definitions there exist rationales to guide action. The character of the critical junctures and the ways in which they are handled may irrevocably decide a man's fate.

INTERDEPENDENCE
OF CAREERS

Institutions, at any given moment, contain people at different stages in their careers. Some have already "arrived," others are still on their way up, still others just entering. Movements and changes at each level are in various ways dependent on those occurring at other levels.

Such interdependence is to be found in the phenomenon of sponsorship, where individuals move up in a work organization through the activities of older and more well-established men. Hall (1948) has given a classic description of sponsorship in medicine. The younger doctor of the proper class and acceptable ethnic origin is absorbed, on the recommendation of a member, into the informal "inner fraternity" which controls hospital appointments and which is influential in the formation and maintenance of a clientele. The perpetuation of this coterie depends on a steady flow of suitable recruits. As the members age, retire, or die off, those who remain face a problem of recruiting younger men to do the less honorific and remunerative work, such as clinical work, that their group performs. Otherwise they themselves must do work inappropriate to their position or give place to others who covet their power and influence.

To the individual in the inner fraternity, a protégé eases the transition into retirement. The younger man gradually assumes the load which the sponsor can no longer comfortably carry, allowing the older man to retire gracefully, without that sudden cutting-down of work which frightens away patients, who leap to the conclusion that he is too old to perform capably.

In general, this is the problem of retiring with honor, of leaving a life's work with a sense that one will be missed. The demand may arise that a great man's work be carried on, although it may no longer be considered important or desirable by his successors. If the old man's prestige is great enough, the men below may have to orient themselves and their work as he suggests, for fear of offending him or of profaning his heritage. The identities of the younger man are thus shaped by the older man's passage from the pinnacle to retirement.

This interdependence of career may cross occupational lines within organizations, as in the case of the young physician who receives a significant part of his training from the older and more experienced nurses in the hospital; and those at the same level in an institution are equally involved in one another's identities. Sometimes budding careers within work worlds are interdependent in quite unsuspected ways. Consider the young painter or craftsman who must make his initial successes in enterprises founded by equally young art dealers, who, because they run their galleries on a shoestring, can afford the frivolity of exhibiting the works of an unknown. The very ability to take such risk provides the dealer a possible opportunity to discover a genius.

One way of uncovering the interdependence of careers is to ask: Who are the important *others* at various stages of the career, the persons significantly involved in the formation of one's own identity? These will vary with stages; at one point one's agemates are crucial, perhaps as competitors, while at another the actions of superiors are the most important. The interlocking of careers results in influential images of similarity and contrariety. In so far as the significant others shift and vary by the phases of a career, identities change in patterned and not altogether unpredictable ways.

THE CHANGING WORK WORLD

The occupations and organizations within which careers are made change in structure and direction of activity, expand or contract, transform purposes. Old functions and positions disappear, and new ones arise. These constitute potential locations for a new and sometimes wide range of people, for they are not incrusted with traditions and customs concerning their incumbents. They open up new kinds of careers to persons making their work lives within the institution and thus the possibility of variaton in long-established types of career. An individual once clearly destined for a particular position suddenly finds himself confronted with an option; what was once a settled matter has split into a set of alternatives between which he must now choose. Different identities emerge as people in the organization take cognizance of this novel set of facts. The positions turn into recognized social entities, and some persons begin to reorient their ambitions. The gradual emergence of a new speciality typically creates this kind of situation within occupations.

Such occupational and institutional changes, of course, present opportunity for both success and failure. The enterprising grasp eagerly at new openings, making the most of them or attempting to; while others sit tight as long as they can. During such times the complexities of one's career are further compounded by what is happening to others with whom he is significantly involved. The ordinary lines of sponsorship in institutions are weakened or broken because those in positions to sponsor are occupied with matters more immediately germane to their own careers. Lower ranks feel the consequences of unusual pressures generated in the ranks above. People become peculiarly vulnerable to unaccustomed demands for loyalty and alliance which spring from the unforeseen changes in the organization. Paths to mobility become indistinct and less fixed, which has an effect on personal commitments and identities. Less able to tie themselves tightly to any one career, because such careers do not present themselves as clearly, men become more experimental and open-minded or more worried and apprehensive.

CAREERS AND PERSONAL IDENTITY

A frame of reference for studying careers is, at the same time, a frame for studying personal identities. Freudian and other psychiatric formulations of personality development probably overstress childhood experiences. Their systematic accounts end more or less with adolescence, later events being regarded as the elaboration of, or variations on, earlier occurences. Yet central to any account of adult identity is the relation of change in identity to change in social position; for it is characteristic of adult life to afford and force frequent and momentous passages from status to status. Hence members of structures that change, riders on escalators that carry them up, along, and down, to unexpected places and to novel experiences even when in some sense foreseen, must gain, maintain, and regain a sense of personal identity. Identity" is never gained nor maintained once and for all" (Erikson, 1950, p. 57). Stabilities in the organization of behavior and of self-regard are inextricably dependent upon stabilities of social structure. Likewise, change ("development") is shaped by those patterned transactions which accompany career movement. The crises and turning points of life are not entirely institutionalized, but their occurrence and the terms which define and help to solve them are illuminated when seen in the context of career lines. In so far as some populations do not have careers in the sense that professional and business people have them, then the focus of attention ought still to be positional passage, but with domestic, age, and other escalators to the forefront. This done, it may turn out that the model sketched here must undergo revision.

35

HAROLD L. WILENSKY

ORDERLY CAREERS AND SOCIAL PARTICIPATION: THE IMPACT
OF WORK HISTORY ON SOCIAL INTEGRATION
IN THE MIDDLE MASS

Durkheim's and Mannheim's ideas about careers as a source of social integration are put to the test among 678 urban white males of the upper-working and lower-middle classes, aged 21–55. Data suggest that chaotic experience in the economic order fosters a retreat from both work and the larger communal life. Even a taste of an orderly career enhances the vitality of participation: compared with men who have chaotic work histories, those who spend at least a fifth of their worklives in functionally-related, hierarchically-ordered jobs have stronger attachments to formal associations and the community. Their contacts with kin, friend, and neighbor are at once more integrated, wide-ranging, and stable. Their "occupational community" is stronger. These contrasts are especially marked among young, high-income college men—a vanguard population. Although men with work histories that fit the model of "career," comprise only a tiny slice of the labor force in modern societies, they may be strategic for social order.

It is clear that *class cultures* (sustained by similar levels of income and education and common absorption of the mass media) and *ethnic-religious cultures* (sustained by common descent and early socialization) significantly shape social rela-

Abridged from the *American Sociological Review*, vol. 26, no. 4 (August, 1961), with the permission of the author and the American Sociological Association.

This paper is part of a larger study of "Labor and Leisure in the Urban Community" made possible by grants from the National Institute of Mental Health (M-2209), 1958–60, and a fellowship at the Center for Advanced Study in the Behavioral Sciences, 1956–57. For description and theoretical background of the study, see Wilensky, 1960. I am indebted to Albert J. Reiss, Jr., and Morris Janowitz for critical readings of an early draft, and to John C. Scott, Michael T. Aiken, Paul R. Kimmel, Betty Burnside, and other members of our labor-leisure seminar for research assistance, especially in the difficult task of coding complete work histories.

tions. It is also clear that *occupational cultures* (rooted in common tasks, work schedules, job training, and career patterns) are sometimes better predictors of behavior than both social class and pre-job experience. The question of which is most important in determining specific types of social relations remains quite open. The evidence, while scanty, suggests that wherever work ties are severed, there is a decline in community participation—whether we consider variations over the life span of persons or variations among groups at one point in time. For instance, excluding churches, there appears to be a general curve of participation in formal associations which closely parallels a job satisfaction curve—a sharp drop in the early 20's, especially among hard-pressed married couples, a climb to a peak in the middle years, a slight drop-

321

off and then a final sag in the 60's—and these cycles seem to be interdependent, although good longitudinal data are as usual lacking (Wilensky, 1961). More important, those persons and groups with the most tenuous ties to the economic order—from men squeezed out of the labor market (older workers and retirees, the unemployed) to "unemployables" who seldom get in (skid row bums, adolescents of the slum)—are also those who are most isolated in community and society.[1]

Plainly, Durkheim's view that in modern society workplace and occupational group draw the person into the mainstream of social life deserves further elaboration and test. This is perhaps the central problem of the sociology of work—the effect of the division of labor on social integration, or more precisely the conditions under which work role, occupational association, and career are most and least effective as bonds of solidarity either within workplace or between workplace and larger units, or both (Cf. Durkheim, 1947).

The guiding hypothesis of the present study is this:

The vitality of social participation, primary and secondary, and the strength of attachment to community and to the major institutional spheres of society are in part a function of cumulative experience in the economic system. Participation in community life is a natural extension of participation in the labor market; orderly and pleasant experiences in the latter provide motive and opportunity for the former. Specifically, *where the technical and social organization of work* (1) *offers*

---

[1] On the effect of unemployment, see Bakke, 1934 and 1940; Zawadski and Lazarsfeld, 1935; Eisenberg and Lazarsfeld, 1938; Komarovsky, 1940. Cf. Kornhauser, 1959. On the position of youth, see Eisenstadt, 1956. On the decline of participation with aging, see citations in Wilensky, 1961. None of these studies, however, tells us whether re-employment brings a return to previous participation levels, none deals with the impact of other forms of economic deprivation or discontinuity (e.g., continuous employment, but chaotic "careers").

much freedom—e.g., discretion in methods, pace or schedule, and opportunity for frequent interaction with fellow workers who share common interests and values, (2) *necessitates sustained and wide-ranging contact* with customer or client, making the work role visible to the community and (3) *provides an orderly career* in which one job normally leads to another, related in function and higher in status, then work attachments will be strong, work integrated with the rest of life, and ties to community and society solid. Conversely, if the task offers little workplace freedom (assembly-line workers, dentists, accountants and many engineers), if the job demands no customer or client contact and yields no readily visible status claim ("burr knocker" in a job shop, "console operator" in an insurance office), if the work history is punctuated by unexpected periods of unemployment, disorderly shifts among jobs, occupations, and industries, then work attachments will be weak, work sharply split from leisure, and ties to community and society uncertain.

In short, to the extent that men are exposed to disciplined work routines yielding little gratification and have "careers" which are in no way predictable, their retreat from work will be accompanied by a withdrawal from the larger communal life—and this will apply to the middle class as well as the working class.

In order to tackle these and similar problems, we have in the past two years interviewed about 1500 men in various occupational groups, strata, and workplaces. This paper deals with 678 white males of the "middle mass" and the effect of their career patterns on the kinds and strength of their ties to community and society.

"CAREER" AS A SOCIOLOGICAL PROBLEM

There is uncommon agreement that the study of types and rates of mobility is crucial to an understanding of modern society. And there are hints that worklife mobility may be more fateful than inter-generational mobility (Wilensky and Edwards, 1959). It is therefore remarkable that detailed work histories which cover a decade or more have been reported in only about a dozen studies.[2] These studies have located types of job histories in various strata, and they leave no doubt that modern adult life imposes frequent shifts between jobs, occupations, employers, and workplaces; but they tell us little of the consequences for person and social structure.

Let us define career in structural terms. A career is a succession of related jobs, arranged in a hierarchy of prestige, through which persons move in an ordered (more-or-less predictable) sequence. Corollaries are that the job pattern is instituted (socially-recognized and sanctioned within some social unit) and persists (the system is maintained over more than one generation of recruits).

It has long been recognized that careers in this sense are a major source of stability. Every group must recruit and maintain its personnel and motivate role performance. Careers have served these functions for organizations, occupational groups, and societies, and in cultures as diverse as those of medieval Europe, Soviet Russia and the United States. Careers also give continuity to the personal experience of the most able and skilled seg-

[2] E.g., Davidson and Anderson, 1937; Form and Miller, 1949, pp. 317–329; Lipset and Bendix, 1952, pp. 336–374, 494–504; Warner and Abegglen, 1955; the U.S. Bureau of Labor Statistics series on work histories of skilled populations, and the earlier Works Progress Administration studies. For the complete list see Wilensky, 1960. The Six City Survey of Occupational Mobility, although based on only one decade, contains the most adequate data and most extensive and representative sample. From it we can say that in most cases changing jobs means changing *both* occupation and industry, and, projecting the data, the average worker will hold 12 jobs in a 46-year worklife and only one man in five will remain at the same occupational level throughout his worklife—*if* the decade 1940–50 is typical, *if* the Census categories are meaningful, etc. Palmer, 1954; Reiss, 1955, pp. 693–700; and Jaffe and Carleton, 1954.

ments of the population—men and groups who otherwise would produce a level of rebellion or withdrawal which would threaten the maintenance of the system. By holding out the prospect of continuous, predictable rewards, careers foster a willingness to train and achieve, to adopt a long time perspective and defer immediate gratifications for the later pay-off. In Mannheim's phrase, they lead to the gradual creation of a "life plan" (Mannheim, 1940, pp. 56, 104–6, 181).

Most men, however, never experience the joys of a life plan because most work situations do not afford the necessary stable progression over the worklife. There is a good deal of chaos in modern labor markets, chaos intrinsic to urban-industrial society. Rapid technological change dilutes old skills, makes others obsolete and creates demand for new ones; a related decentralization of industry displaces millions, creating the paradox of depressed areas in prosperous economies; metropolitan deconcentration shifts the clientele of service establishments, sometimes smashing or restructuring careers; recurrent crises such as wars, depressions, recessions, coupled with the acceleration of fad and fashion in consumption, add a note of unpredictability to the whole. There are many familiar variations on the main theme: in industries such as construction, entertainment, maritime, and agricultural harvesting, the employment relationship is typically casual. In food processing and the needle trades, drastic seasonal curtailments are common.

All this is easy to see among populations that are depressed, deprived, or marginal—non-white victims of racial discrimination, underdogs on relief rolls, miners stuck on a played-out coal patch, the chronically unemployed among the old, sick, or disabled.

But what about the vanguard population—the great middle mass around which *Fortune* magazine's portrait of the "soaring sixties" is drawn? What portion of the growing middle—the lower middle class and upper working class—can be said to have orderly careers? This paper will show that a majority of the middle mass experiences various degrees of disorder in the work history. At the same time it will test several hypotheses about the functions of predictability by comparing the behavior of men with disorderly work histories with that of the more fortunate, the men of orderly career. It will give special attention to those at higher education and income levels. Assuming that the middle mass will grow in size and influence, that education and income levels will continue to rise, and assuming (with less confidence) that job histories will become more like careers, we may thereby come to some hints of the direction of social change.

DIMENSIONS AND MEASURES OF CAREER

Although we have many sophisticated discussions in the sociological literature (Hughes, 1958; Becker and Strauss, 1956, pp. 253–63; Martin and Strauss, 1956, pp. 101–110, and Goffman, 1952. See also Dubin, 1958, ch. 15, and Gross, 1958), two difficulties have discouraged the full and systematic exploration of the problem of "career": (1) conceptualizing both career pattern and social participation; (2) gathering and processing data beyond crude levels. In handling careers as a source of social integration, I have given special attention to one dimension of job history beyond direction and amount of movement: the degree of orderliness—i.e., how well it fits the model of "career." Complete work histories and information on each job, employer, and job change were recorded in a detailed interview. In coding, we first aimed to rank all jobs in four classes according to society-wide judgments of occupational prestige: upper-middle (high non-manual), lower-middle (low non-manual), upper working (high manual), lower working (low manual). Detailed instructions covered

major classification problems: e.g., foremen were coded as high manual; all service occupations, farm employment, and highest military rank achieved were distributed among the four categories (e.g., farm owners or managers on farms of 100 acres or more were counted as low non-manual, on farms of 50–99 acres, high manual, all other farm employment, low manual). Where detailed instructions did not cover the case, the following additional information was used (in the priority listed) to fit jobs in: (1) the North-Hatt scale (e.g., service jobs like detective were counted low non-manual; playground director, policeman, Greyhound bus driver, railroad conductor, high manual; below, low manual); (2) data on education and training—e.g., all ambiguous jobs which might be skilled manual (requiring six months or more training on or off the job) were counted low manual if no special training was indicated in a separate battery on training; (3) job status or training inferred from the *Dictionary of Occupational Titles;* (4) data on changes in rates of pay and reasons for leaving (used as a last resort to indicate direction of movement).[8]

Combining direction with orderliness, the job histories were then coded as follows:

1. *Orderly horizontal progression. Orderly.*—The skills and experience gained

[8] We excluded low-status "clerical" jobs held for less than two years when respondent was under 21 (e.g., errand boy), as well as "moonlighting" (covered in a special battery, which showed that 36 percent of the middle mass have at some time held secondary jobs). A code for worklife mobility covered all cases: on *distance,* much (clerk to college-educated engineer, non-manual to manual), some (non-college accountant to sales clerk, semiskilled operative to foreman) or none (stable high non-manual, stable low manual, etc.); and on total *pattern,* four types of *up,* four *stable,* 11 *fluctuating,* six unstable or *highly fluctuating,* and four types of *down.* Based on a 15 percent check (102 cases), the code as a whole has 85 percent reliability; all but four of the disagreements, however, were choices between detailed codes within the major categories, "fluctuating" or "unstable," and could not affect this analysis.

324

on one job are directly functional to performance in subsequent jobs and jobs are arranged in a hierarchy of prestige. Indicators: (a) an expert on occupations could defend the sequence as an ordered, more-or-less predictable pattern *or,* as a last resort only, (b) R planned the sequence, sees one step leading to another (coder read seven questions that would indicate this). And *horizontal progression:* some evidence of increased job status within one occupational stratum. E.g., carpenter's apprentice, journeyman, foreman in construction firm. These are functionally related, hierarchically-ordered jobs that do not cross-cut occupational strata.

2. *Orderly vertical progression.*—At least half of the years covered in the work history are in jobs that are functionally related and arranged in hierarchy of prestige, and the mobility pattern cuts across occupational strata.

3. *Borderline orderly vertical progression.*—At least a fifth but less than half of the worklife is in jobs that are functionally related and arranged in a hierarchy of prestige. The mobility pattern cuts across occupational strata.

4. *Disorderly horizontal movement.*—Less than a fifth of the worklife is in functionally-related, hierarchially-ordered jobs —i.e., by no stretch of the imagination could the history be classified as a fifth or more orderly. Mobility pattern does not cut across occupational strata.

5. *Disorderly vertical movement.*—For at least four-fifths of the worklife, jobs are neither functionally related nor hierarchically ordered. Cuts across occupational strata.

6. *One job for entire worklife.*

In order to avoid exaggeration of labor-market chaos, coders were instructed to resolve doubts in favor of orderliness. Similarly, "some orderly" was combined with "orderly," on the assumption that a modest amount of job predictability can go a long way to integrate a man into the social system. From inspection of detailed tables it appears that these borderline cases do occupy a middle ground with respect to the dependent variables.[4]

This entire coding effort was guided by the assumption that what several students have viewed as "bureaucratic" vs. "entrepreneurial" or "old middle class" vs. "new" (Miller and Swanson, 1958; Mills, 1951; Corey, 1935), is better treated as types of careers that cross-cut organizations large and small, bureaucratic and not, as well as diverse age grades and economic strata. For instance: "bureaucracies" come and go. In many sectors of the economy mergers, relocations, and shutdowns (rooted in the population shifts and technological changes discussed above) reach big firms and high-seniority workers, and, sometimes, as the business press notes, they take their toll in executive careers, too. Even in the more stable bureaucracies, some layers of personnel (e.g., foremen) have quite chaotic job patterns. In the little leagues, too, there are great variations: a well-located, well-run service station may prosper for years, another may be the scene of recurrent bankruptcies.

The concept, "disorderly work history" (counterposed to "career"), takes account of these variations, permits determination of the incidence of real careers, and brings a broad range of cases into view. Table 1 shows that in the middle mass—a relatively secure population, well off by American standards—only 30 percent can by any stretch of the imagination

[4] A 15 percent check showed over 90 percent reliability—and much of the disagreement was between orderly vertical and borderline orderly. For various reasons the 21 men in the "one job only" category were eliminated. A separate analysis, comparing one-job men with the rest of the middle mass shows similar distributions on all participation measures but two: one-jobbers have a wider range of secondary contacts and a lower range of primary contacts. To include them as "orderly horizontal" would slightly strengthen the case.

be said to act out half or more of their work histories in an orderly career. If we count the lower class, excluded from this sample, it is apparent that a vast majority of the labor force is going nowhere in an unordered way or can expect a worklife of thoroughly unpredictable ups and downs.

Comparing men with orderly careers and those with disorderly work histories, the data show an almost even distribution among a variety of social characteristics (direction and distance of mobility, father's occupation, percent of worklife

contact and amount of *time* in each; (2) the *range* of participation; (3) *role integration*—the degree of *coherence* of the pattern; and (4) the *stability or duration* of relationships. Together these constitute an index of the vitality of objective participation, the dimensions and measures of which are discussed below. Unless otherwise specified, coding reliability on a 15 percent check was over 95 percent.

SECONDARY ATTACHMENTS

From detailed information on each organization to which the respondent be-

TABLE 1

DISTRIBUTION OF THE MIDDLE MASS BY TYPE OF WORK HISTORY

	Number	Percent
Orderly:		
Orderly horizontal progression...........	88	13
Orderly vertical progression..............	116	17
Borderline:		
Some orderly vertical progression........	223	33
Total orderly.......................	427	63
Disorderly:		
Disorderly horizontal..................	36	5
Disorderly vertical.....................	194	29
Total disorderly....................	230	34
One job only...........................	21	3
Grand total........................	678	100

self-employed, religion, age, occupational stratum, income, education)—although high-income college men do have a decided edge among the orderly. Thus, as an independent variable, orderliness crosscuts traditional categories of sociological analysis; if it has an impact on social life, that impact is distinctive.

DIMENSIONS AND MEASURES OF OBJECTIVE SOCIAL PARTICIPATION

The research aimed to analyze social relations with an eye to their capacity for linking the person and his immediate family to the larger communal life. Four dimensions were found useful in approaching this problem: (1) *the number of roles* played (groups participated in, primary, informal, or secondary), *the frequency of*

longs plus a battery on organizational and community activities, the following indexes were developed.

1. *Number of memberships.*—Each organization counts one point for a quartile ranking. Church counts one only if respondent reported a current religious preference and attended church services at least once a month. Men in the two highest quartiles (three organizations or more) were scored High.

2. *Frequency of contact and time spent.* For each organization other than church, we asked when it held regular meetings, how many of the last six the respondent attended, whether this was usual, etc. In the absence of precise information, we counted a meeting as worth two hours. We similarly elicited data on time spent on organizational activities other than

regular meetings—committee work, phone calls, money-raising, etc. We then estimated the usual hours per month for all organizational activity. This measure avoids the common tendency to overestimate levels of participation. Excepting regular church services, we found that almost 4 in 10 of the middle mass, a relatively active population, spend less than 30 minutes a month on all organizational activity; median time is about two hours. (Compare their median estimated time watching TV—about 48 hours per month.)

3. *Range of secondary participation.*— A man may play many roles in many groups, interact at a high rate, and devote much time to it—all with family and relatives living in a homogeneous neighborhood. If our interest is in the integrative potential of social ties, we must note, too, the participation pattern of miners, longshoremen, and others who are surrounded by men like themselves, and who, in lodge and union, at home and at the bar, reinforce their common alienation and isolation.

Accordingly, special attention has been given to the range of social relations, primary and secondary. "Range" is the variation in *interests* (concern for or stake in the course of events), *values* (affectively-toned, group-shared desires which serve as criteria for choice among ends) and *status* (prestige levels) represented by all the roles the person plays. This aims to permit classification of respondents from "community isolation" through ever-wider circles of involvement. Two operational criteria were used for secondary range: (a) heterogeneity of membership to which exposed; (b) number of major institutional spheres to which exposed.

a. *Heterogeneity:* the degree to which the respondent's organizations provide opportunity for interacting with people who differ from him in important social characteristics. All types of organizations were put in four categories according to heterogeneity of their members in occupation, income, education, ethnicity or religion or race, age or life cycle, and sex —in that order of importance. The categories are: *narrow range or least heterogeneity of membership* (e.g., exclusive craft unions, professional groups, property-owners associations, business pressure groups, etc.); *medium-restricted range* (e.g., minority defense organizations, like the NAACP or Polish National Alliance, ambiguous multicraft unions, church-connected organizations, workplace-based leisure associations); *medium range* (e.g., inclusive labor unions, service clubs and civic groups, PTA, church, youth-serving groups, non-neighborhood card and social clubs, fraternal organizations, etc.); *broad range* (tolerance organizations, charitable organizations, political parties, etc.). In the scale developed, minimum exposure was required; if respondent attends none of the last six meetings or answers "don't know," if he names church preference but never attends, he receives no points. Otherwise, the more range, the more points. Pre-coded lists were made up in difficult cases (e.g., unions). Coding reliability for a 15 percent check of the detailed code was 81 percent. The lowest two quartiles (0–11) were counted as low range, the highest two (12–42), high range.

b. *Number of institutional spheres covered* by respondent's membership— economic, political-military, educational, religious, public welfare, recreation-aesthetic. The major and peripheral functions and purposes of each type of organization were listed on a chart, with three points for a major function in a given sphere (e.g., labor unions are mainly economic), one point for peripheral functions (unions, one for political, and one for welfare). Maximum respondent score in any sphere is three. The detailed code has a reliability of 84 percent. The scoring system, with a minimum exposure criterion, yields a dichotomy of 0–7 vs. 8–18.

4. *Attachment to the community.* Except among officials and community elites there are few obvious and direct attachments to the communities constituting a metropolis. On the assumption that schools and churches are major transmitters of the most widely-shared community values, and the private welfare structure is another potential source of contact, we used voting in the most recent school election and size of contribution to church and charity as indicators of community attachment. A high score goes to men who remember the school election and say they voted to increase school taxes (40 percent of all). A charitable contribution of at least $100 was scored high. (The median amount is $100 to $199; the median slice of annual family income is 1.8 percent.)

PRIMARY AND INFORMAL RELATIONS

The study assumes that "primary" relations vary in their potential for expanding the person's horizons; some ties to kin and friend are more parochial than others. Accordingly, the interview included many questions on the number and group contexts of leisure-time activities, number of persons known well, the last time the respondent got together socially with neighbors, relatives not living with him, fellow-workers, people in the same line of work, and others, a complete battery on each of three best friends, and two questions on income and location of relatives.

The major dimensions and measures of objective primary relations used for this analysis follow:

1. *Range of primary relations* (see secondary range above).—The minimum exposure counted was "got together socially within the past two months." The range score begins with one point for living with wife and children, moves up to four points for recent contact with people in the same line of work who work elsewhere or "other" friends (cross-neighborhood, former workplace, etc.). Contact with often-seen relatives earns from one to four points. (If almost all or about half live in the neighborhood and most are in the same income bracket, it is worth only one point; if few or no relatives contacted are neighbors and some are financially much better or worse off, then the respondent gets three points.) Fellow workers in the same type of work get three points, those in a different line get four points.

The top two quartiles score 8–18, a high range; the rest, low.

2. *The coherence and integration of primary and secondary roles.*—A segregated role is one in which the behavior expected and preferred in one group has nothing to do with the behavior expected and preferred in any other group. For instance, when an occupational role (banker) becomes so elaborated that its rights and obligations come to embrace the behavior expected in other role systems (country club, family, Republican Party), we speak of "integrated roles." It is assumed that those roles that are most integrated are most effective in social control; from the viewpoint of the person such roles reduce conflict and choice and make for an easy falling in line. Here are the measures of role integration:

a. *Work associates and leisure-time friends.*—The degree to which social relations at work overlap those off work was used as the first index. We coded the number of three best friends in the same workplace or occupation or both, how often each is seen socially outside of work, and other leisure contacts with other work associates. A strong "occupational community" (at least one best friend from work or in the same line of work who is seen socially at least once a week) covers 199 cases—29 percent.

b. *Friendship circles.*—The attack on traditional theories of urbanism and the rediscovery of Cooley's primary group have diverted attention from several crucial contrasts between modern and premodern patterns of friendship—among them, the tendency for urban-industrial populations to be linked in open networks rather than circles. Almost one-fifth of the middle mass have two or three best friends, none of whom know one another well; another six percent have no friends or only one. The modal case names three best friends, two of whom know each other well; this or better was scored as high integration.

c. *Overlapping friendship and membership.*—Those who have at least one membership in common with one best friend are scored high on integration.

3. *Duration of friendships.*—A crude measure of stability of primary ties was the number of best friends who have been known for ten years or more. To score "high vitality" the respondent had to have either (1) one or two best friends, each known that long; or (2) three best friends, two of whom are of ten years' duration.

In sum: this study assumes that any social tie integrates. But those relationships that are wide-ranging, most coherent and stable are most effective in binding the person and his immediate family to community and society.

Specific hypotheses derived from these ideas about careers and participation are listed below with the findings.

THE MIDDLE MASS SAMPLE

The analysis is based on a multi-stage probability sample combining the use of city directories with block supplementation and segmentation procedures. The population sampled consisted of all private dwelling units within the tracted areas of the tri-county Detroit Standard Metropolitan Area and, within the selected dwelling units, those white, male members of the labor force who were 21 to 55 years old, ever married, who fell into the "middle mass."

The middle mass is a residual category. We eliminated the lower half of the working class by requiring a minimum family income of $5,000 in any one year of the past five; we cut out the upper-middle class by applying the usual criteria of authority and skill. Upper-middle class *authority* was indicated by size of firm of

owner (e.g., 25 or more employees), number of subordinates of manager or official (e.g., 100 or more) or control over client and monopoly of vital service among professionals. Upper-middle class *levels of skill* involve mastery of an abstract, codified body of knowledge (e.g., minister, architect or professor)—and imply a college education usually going beyond the bachelor's degree, or executive training after college. In order to eliminate upper middles, interviewers were given a list of specific occupation-education categories which were ineligible. Occupational categories which remained—clerks, salesmen, craftsmen, foremen, small proprietors, semimarginal- or would-be-professionals and technicians, managers and officials with high income—constitute the core of the middle mass.

In designing the sample we noted that in a 1958–59 Detroit area sample about 10–15 percent of the eligibles in such middling occupational categories reported family incomes of $10,000–15,000. Therefore, we settled for an arbitrary top income limit for "lower-middle class" of $13,000—representing two-thirds of those who fit the occupation-education criteria (one standard deviation from the mean).

Thus, by use of selector questions, we bracketed in white, male members of the labor force, 21 to 55 years old, ever married, whose family incomes in any one of the past five years reached $5,000 or more but never topped $13,000. I think that this procedure yields a reasonable cross-section of the upper-working and lower-middle class—men at the bottom of various ladders leading upward, and some on their way down, too.

Eligible men of the middle mass were found in 39 percent of the 2137 occupied dwelling units visited. Of a total of 678 respondents, 47 percent were coded as white collar and 53 percent as blue collar. Their median age, 39; median family income in 1959, $7,650. Nearly three in five live in the suburbs.

The interview period was late January through March, 1960. Most interviews were done by graduate students in the Detroit Area Study, the rest by professional interviewers. Median interview time: one hour and 48 minutes.

The analysis concentrates on one dimension of career, orderliness, as it affects the objective vitality of social participation. Critical ratios of the differences in proportions were computed and treated as one-tail tests; percentage differences serve as a measure of the strength of relationships. The case rests upon the size and consistency of predicted differences within a homogeneous sample in which broad controls for race, family income, occupational stratum, age, marital status, and location were built in by selection. In testing hypotheses, three social characteristics that other studies have shown to be related to participation—education, income, and age—will be used as analytical controls. Then the conditioning effect and the independent effect of each of these will be examined.

FINDINGS

I. *Men whose careers are orderly will have stronger attachments to formal associations and the community than men whose job histories are disorderly.* The data, summarized in the top half of Table 2, generally support the hypothesis. Of 72 possible comparisons of the orderly and disorderly (six dimensions of participation for 12 education-income-age categories), 24 comparisons show percentage differences in the unexpected direction. The overall net difference in the predicted direction is eight percent. The results for each dimension of secondary attachment follow:

A. *Men with orderly careers will have more memberships in formal associations and attend more meetings (including church services) than men with disorderly work histories.*—All but one of the 12 comparisons conform in direction to the

hypothesis—a net average difference of 13 percent. p < .01.

B. *Men with orderly careers will average more hours a month in all activities of formal associations (excluding church services) than men with disorderly work histories.*—Differences are in the predicted direction in 10 of the 12 comparisons; the net average in predicted direction is 12 percent. p < .03. Using a measure which sifts out the activists, 29 percent of the orderly appear in the highest quartile (10 or more hours per month) compared to 19 percent of the disorderly.

C. *Men with orderly careers will range widely in their secondary attachments more often than men with disorderly work histories: the participants among the former will be exposed to organizations representing a greater variety of values, interests, and status levels.*—Using the two indexes—heterogeneity of membership and number of institutional spheres covered by the respondent's memberships—the hypothesis is restated:

1. *The memberships of the orderly will offer greater opportunity for interacting with persons who differ from themselves in important social characteristics.*—Differences are in the predicted direction in seven of the 12 comparisons. p < .03. The net average in the right direction is 10 percent.

2. *The memberships of the orderly will expose them to more of the major institutional spheres of the society.*—Only five of the 12 comparisons conform in direction; the net average difference is +2 percent. The results do not even approach significance.

D. *Men with orderly careers will have stronger attachments to the community than men with disorderly work histories.* Two indicators:

1. *The orderly will more often support local schools; they will remember the last school election and report that they voted in favor of increased school taxes.*—Eight of the 12 comparisons conform in direction—a net average of 8 percent. p < .05.

2. *The orderly will more often report a*

TABLE 2

ORDERLY CAREERS ARE ASSOCIATED WITH STRONG ATTACHMENTS TO FORMAL ASSOCIATIONS AND THE COMMUNITY, AND HIGH VITALITY OF PRIMARY PARTICIPATION, CONTROLLING FOR EDUCATION, INCOME, AND AGE

	LESS THAN 12 GRADES				HIGH SCHOOL GRADUATE				SOME COLLEGE OR MORE				NET AVG. % IN PREDICTED DIRECTION	p<**
	Under $8000		$8000 and Over		Under $8000		$8000 and Over		Under $8000		$8000 and Over			
	Under 40	40 and Over	Under 40	40 and Over	Under 40	40 and Over	Under 40	40 and Over	Under 40	40 and Over	Under 40	40 and Over		
	1	2	3	4	5	6	7	8	9	10	11	12		
Formal associations and community														
IA No. of memberships	22%*	− 2%	2%	6%	3%	38%	9%	12%	6%	17%	31%	17%	13%	.01
IB Frequency, time—organizations	12	10	25	2	4	27	9	22	− 9	17	23	− 3	12	.03
IC₁ Secondary range—heterogeneity	− 4	− 1	18	35	− 7	27	27	8	4	27	− 4	− 9	10	.03
IC₂ Secondary range—institutional spheres	7	− 9	− 2	24	−18	30	−13	− 5	− 9	7	26	− 9	2	.30
ID₁ Community attachment—school tax	12	− 1	14	−16	21	− 5	4	39	3	−13	27	12	8	.05
ID₂ Community attachment—charity	10	12	4	3	− 3	−18	7	......	18	−11	38	− 2	5	.10
Net avg. percentage in predicted direction	10	2	10	9	......	16	7	13	2	7	24	1	8	......
Primary participation														
IIA Primary range	20	3	21	42	8	− 8	15	24	2	−47	22	19	10	.01
IIB Role integration—occupational community	23	11	35	3	1	......	14	25	− 4	20	8	15	13	.01
IIC Friendship circles	2	18	9	16	13	−17	1	35	− 2	11	17	− 5	8	.02
IID Stability of friendships	14	− 4	5	8	2	3	−11	− 9	−12	4	− 1	23	4	.40
IIE Overlapping friendships and memberships	3	− 9	13	−18	18	18	−12	4	− 7	17	5	......	3	.50
Net avg. percentage in predicted direction	12	4	17	10	8	− 1	1	16	2	1	10	10	8	......
N***	(69)	(86)	(31)	(46)	(83)	(51)	(66)	(47)	(61)	(13)	(53)	(37)	(643)	......

* Percent in predicted direction (proportion by which orderly exceed disorderly in high vitality or strong attachment). Each figure is based on a fourfold subtable.

** The method for computing this combined probability is described in R. A. Fisher, *Statistical Methods for Research Workers*, Edinburgh: Oliver and Boyd, Ltd., 1944, 9th edition, pp. 99–101.

*** N's on which percentages are computed vary slightly within columns due to different response rates for different measures.

contribution of $100 or more to churches and charity in the past year.—Seven of the comparisons are in the right direction. p < .10. The net average is +5 percent. Using more stringent measures of community attachment—$200 or more or more than 1.8 percent of family income—this small net average is wiped out and the pattern is insignificant. Orderliness predicts voluntary giving of modest amounts; it does not predict the donation of large sums or (taking account of ability-to-contribute) efforts going beyond the median.

II. *Men whose careers are orderly will evidence greater vitality of primary relations (a pattern of contact with kin, friend, and neighbor which ranges into the wider community) than men whose work histories are disorderly.*—(It is assumed that the latter often retreat to family-home localism, a leisure style which, is relatively isolated, although it may include many relationships and frequent interaction.) The data, presented in the lower half of Table 2, generally support the hypothesis. Of 60 possible comparisons of orderly and disorderly (five dimensions of primary relations for 12 education-income-age categories), only 13 show percentage differences in the unexpected direction. The net average difference in the predicted direction is eight percent. Below is an analysis of sub-tables for each hypothesis specifying each dimension of primary group vitality.

A. *Compared with men whose work histories are disorderly, men whose careers are orderly will have a wider range of primary contacts—a pattern generally going beyond family and relatives in the same neighborhood and income bracket, and beyond others in the same neighborhood or type of work.*—Ten of the 12 comparisons conform in direction to the hypothesis—a net average difference of 10 percent. p < .01.

B. *Men whose careers are orderly will integrate work and non-work roles to a greater extent than men whose work histories are disorderly; their best friends will more often be persons in the same*

workplace or same line of work and they will more often see work associates socially.—All but one of the 12 differences are in the right direction. p < .01. The net average difference is +13 percent. When a looser definition is applied (no best friends from work, but sees people from work at least once a week) the net difference goes down to 7 percent. The complementary hypothesis that *disorderliness leads to a sharp split between work and leisure (no fellow-worker friends, no contacts) is supported but not as strongly as the above.

C. *Men with orderly careers will have two or three best friends who know each other well more often than those with disorderly work histories.*—Nine of the 12 comparisons are in the right direction. p < .02. Net average difference: 8 percent.

D. *Men with orderly careers will have more long-lasting friendships than men with disorderly work histories.*—Differences are in the predicted direction in eight of the 12 comparisons. p < .40. Net average in the right direction: only 4 percent. A complete history of the picking up and dropping of friends would be better than number of years each best friend was known, which is too much a function of age.[5]

E. *Men whose careers are orderly will have best friends in clubs and organizations more often than those with disorderly work histories.*—Seven of the 12 comparisons conform in direction. p < .50. The net average difference is only 3 percent.

The conditioning effect of major social characteristics.—What about education, income, and age (variables known to be related to social participation)? How do they condition the impact of an orderly career on the vitality of participation?

[5] As in the case of the occupational community, however, college men with high incomes and orderly careers score strong; not one such person in 71 cases falls in the category "short-term friends or no best friends." Contrast low-income older men with less than high school, and disorderly work histories: 14 percent fit the category (five in 35 cases).

Table 3, controlling for these variables one at a time, shows that education, income, and age for the most part have weak and somewhat erratic conditioning effects. *Education* is most consistent: in five of six measures of secondary attachment a high school diploma or some college experience strengthens the tendency of the orderly to participate most; in three of five measures of primary participation (range, integration, circles), education weakens this tendency. *Income* has its strongest effect on the relationship between orderliness and range of social contacts—the more income, the sharper the contrasts. (E.g., controlling for age and

education among men with $8,000 or more, the net average difference between orderly and disorderly in percent whose primary contacts range widely is 24.) The only aspect of participation for which *age* has an appreciable effect on the hypothesized relationship is that for secondary range.

In general, these control variables boost the effect of an orderly career most among younger, high-income college men and with respect to support of schools, contributions to church and charity, and primary range—the measures most clearly

TABLE 3

PERCENT DIFFERENCE IN PREDICTED DIRECTION FOR EACH DIMENSION OF THE
VITALITY OF PARTICIPATION, CONTROLLING SINGLY FOR
EDUCATION, INCOME, AND AGE

			GRADES OF SCHOOL COMPLETED				TOTAL FAMILY INCOME		AGE	
		Without Controls	11 or Fewer	12 (HS Grad.)	More Than 12	Under $8,000	$8,000 and Over	Under 40	40 and Older
			Formal associations and community							
IA	No. of memberships	14%*	5%	14%	17%	13%	15%	14%	14%
IB	Frequency, time—organizations	13	10	13	3	11	14	12	14
IC₁	Secondary range—heterogeneity	6	6	11	....	1	14	2	12
IC₂	Secondary range—institutional spheres	....	2	− 5	4	− 4	4	− 4	6
ID₁	Community attachment —school tax	11	3	14	12	7	16	15	3
ID₂	Community attachment —charity	11	14	− 1	17	8	10	15	2
			Primary participation							
IIA	Primary range	13	15	9	5	4	25	14	12
IIB	Role integration—occupational community	7	9	7	4	4	10	9	4
IIC	Friendship circles	6	9	6	5	4	12	4	10
IID	Stability of friendships	6	12	− 2	12	6	3	5	4
IIE	Overlapping friendships and memberships	2	− 3	7	....	4	− 1	3	− 1
	N	(643)**	(232)	(247)	(164)	(363)	(280)	(363)	(280)

* All percentages refer to how much the men with orderly careers exceeded those with disorderly work histories in strong attachment or high score.
** N's on which percentages are computed vary slightly within columns due to different response rates.

TABLE 4

COLLEGE EDUCATION AND AN ORDERLY CAREER ARE BETTER PREDICTORS OF
STRONG ATTACHMENTS TO FORMAL ASSOCIATIONS AND THE
COMMUNITY THAN INCOME AND AGE

		WORK HISTORY		GRADES OF SCHOOL COMPLETED			FAMILY INCOME		AGE	
		Orderly	Dis- orderly	11 or Fewer	12 (HS Grad.)	More Than 12	Under $8,000	$8,000 and Over	Under 40	40 and Over
IA	No. of memberships...	55%	41%	37%	54%	60%	47%	54%	50%	50%
IB	Frequency, time—or- ganizations.......	54	41	38	54	60	47	52	53	46
IC₁	Secondary range—het- erogeneity.........	58	52	57	54	58	57	55	55	57
IC₂	Secondary range—in- stitutional spheres..	55	55	54	56	55	54	57	54	56
ID₁	Community attach- ment—school tax...	44	33	34	42	46	39	41	39	41
ID₂	Community attach- ment—charity.....	78	67	69	75	80	69	81	69	81
	N.............	(420)**	(223)	(232)	(247)	(164)	(363)	(280)	(363)	(280)

* All percentages refer to proportions scoring high vitality or strong attachment.
** N's on which percentages are computed vary slightly within columns due to different response rates.

TABLE 5

AN ORDERLY CAREER IS A BETTER PREDICTOR OF HIGH VITALITY OF
PRIMARY PARTICIPATION THAN EDUCATION, INCOME. OR AGE

		WORK HISTORY		GRADES OF SCHOOL COMPLETED			TOTAL FAMILY INCOME		AGE	
		Orderly	Dis- orderly	11 or Fewer	12 (HS Grad.)	More Than 12	Under $8,000	$8,000 and Over	Under 40	40 and Over
IIA	Primary range......	55%*	42%	45%	51%	57%	49%	52%	57%	42%
IIB	Role integration—oc- cupational commu- nity............	33	23	33	29	25	29	30	32	27
IIC	Friendship circles....	80	74	79	75	80	79	76	79	76
IID	Stability of friend- ships............	55	49	56	48	56	50	56	40	69
IIE	Overlapping friend- ships and member- ships............	49	47	48	45	52	50	46	46	51
	N.............	(420)**	(225)	(232)	(247)	(164)	(363)	(280)	(363)	(280)

* All percentages refer to proportions scoring high vitality or strong attachment.
** N's on which percentages are computed vary slightly due to different response rates for different measures.

reflecting community attachment. (For instance: on local charity, the young, high-income college men with orderly careers have a 38 percent edge over their disorderly counterparts—or, by the criterion of a $200 annual contribution, a 58 percent edge. There are similarly strong relationships between orderliness and a "yes" vote on school taxes.)

Perhaps this is a hint that the stratification system functions most clearly with respect to community-oriented behavior and among those who range informally across strata. In other contexts—with respect to the more private associations which lie between the nuclear family and community institutions—the stratification order and the criteria on which it is based are reinterpreted and their impact lessened.

The relative effect of social characteristics and work history.—Tables 4 and 5 compare, without controls, the effect of career, education, income, and age. Table 4 shows that orderliness comes close to education in importance as a predictor of secondary participation and is clearly more important than income or age. (Note that comparing the "some college" men with the "less than HS" brings a 24 percent difference on number of memberships. If career type were equally refined —e.g., by dropping the "borderline orderly" category—we might achieve more than 14 percent, but sample size does not permit it.) In its effect across all measures of primary participation, career type is more important than any of the other variables. (See Table 5. While the differences here between orderly and disorderly are small but consistent, the differences by education, income, and age are both small and erratic.)

Tables 6 and 7, which pile one variable on top of another and contrast the extremes, permit us to examine further the interplay of all four variables. We see that their cumulative impact on most dimensions of participation is quite strong.

SUMMARY AND INTERPRETATION OF FINDINGS

Orderly experience in the economic system is associated with many social ties which range broadly and at the same time overlap. Men who have predictable careers for at least a fifth of their worklives belong to more organizations, attend more meetings, and average more hours in organizational activity. Their attachments to the local community are also stronger— indicated by support of local schools and, to a lesser extent, by contributions to church and charity.

In both formal and informal contacts, the men of orderly career, more than their colleagues of chaos, are exposed to a great variety of people: the fellow-members they see in clubs and organizations represent many social and economic levels; frequently-seen relatives and close friends are more scattered in space both social and geographical, cutting across neighborhoods, workplaces, occupations, or income brackets. Finally, the total participation pattern of the orderly is more coherent: close friends tend to form a circle and they overlap work contacts. (The data do not support the view that best friends share voluntary association memberships.) There is some indication that these friendships, anchored in workplace, forming a leisure-time clique, may also be longer-lasting.[6]

The effect of work history, while reinforced by other social positions and biographical facts, seems to be distinct. Or-

[6] In Table 2, wherever any sizable differences appear, the young orderly more often have stable friendships than the older orderly—until we come to the college-educated, high-income group where the *older* orderly have a 24 percent edge. Perhaps the young in this category are Organization Men on the make, who have many lightly-held attachments, while their older colleagues are settled into comfortable high-seniority positions requiring little moving about among residences and workplaces.

TABLE 6

PERCENT OF MEN WITH STRONG ATTACHMENTS TO FORMAL ASSOCIATIONS AND COMMUNITY, AND PERCENT DIFFERENCE IN PREDICTED DIRECTION AS WE ADD EDUCATION, INCOME, AND AGE TO AN ORDERLY CAREER

	IA No. of Membs.	IB Freq., Time —Orgs.	IC₁ Sec. Range —Heterog.	IC₂ Sec. Range Inst. Spheres	ID₁ Com. Attachm. —School Tax	ID₂ Com. Attachm. —Charity	N*
Orderly..........	55%	54%	58%	55%	44%	78%	420
vs.	14%**	18%	6%	.....	11%	11%	
Disorderly........	41	41	52	55	33	67	223
	$p<.001$***	$p<.10$	$p<.20$	.....	$p<.02$	$p<.08$	
College or H.S. orderly.........	61	59	58	55	47	79	293
vs.	26	27	4	2	15	18	
Less than H.S. disorderly.........	35	32	54	53	32	61	105
College or H.S. high income orderly.........	65	61	57	57	52	84	153
vs.	30	28	—2	1	18	28	
Less than H.S. low income disorderly.........	35	33	59	56	34	56	79
College, high income young orderly.........	67	69	50	66	63	87	29
vs.	33	33	—14	9	35	37	
Less than H.S. young, low income disorderly	34	36	64	57	28	50	44

* N's may vary slightly from column to column due to cases not ascertained on dependent variables.

** Percent in predicted direction (proportion by which orderly exceed disorderly in high vitality or strong attachment).

*** Chi square test of significance.

TABLE 7

Percent of Men with High Vitality of Primary Participation, and Percent Difference in Predicted Direction as We Add Education, Income, and Age to an Orderly Career

	IIA Primary Range		IIB Role Integ. Occup. Com.		IIC Friendship Circles		IID Stability Friendships		IIE Overlapping Friendships and Memberships		N*
Orderly................	55%	18%**	33%	10%	80%	6%	55%	6%	49%	2%	420
vs.											
Disorderly............	42		23		74		49		47		223
	p<.01***		p<.02		p<.10		p<.20		p<.80		
College or H.S. orderly........	56		30		78		52		49		293
vs.											
Less than H.S. disorderly.........	37	19	25	5	74	4	49	3	50	— 1	105
College or H.S. high income orderly........	60		33		78		55		46		153
vs.											
Less than H.S. low income disorderly.........	41	19	25	8	76	2	49	6	52	— 6	79
College high income, young orderly.........	67		36		81		45		50		29
vs.											
Less than H.S., young low income disorderly....	47	20	25	11	86	— 5	34	11	49	1	44

* N's may vary slightly from column to column due to cases not ascertained on dependent variables.

** Percent in predicted direction (proportion by which orderly exceed disorderly in high vitality or strong attachment).

*** Chi square test of significance.

derliness is unrelated to three indicators of early socialization (religion, father's occupation, and intergenerational mobility). It is also unrelated to distance and direction of worklife mobility and portion of worklife self-employed. Finally, work history is clearly a better predictor of participation than income or age.

With respect to associational ties, educational background and work history seem to constitute a developmental sequence. The more education, the more motivation and opportunity for a career both at work and in voluntary organizations—and the higher educated men with orderly careers are apparently making a life plan of both. If we give a man some college, put him on a stable career ladder, and top it off with a nice family income, he will get into the community act. Give a man less than high school, a thoroughly unpredictable sequence of jobs, a family income of five to eight thousand and it is very likely that his ties to the community will be few and weak.

The sub-tables on which Table 2 is based permit some refinement of this rough sketch. Considering both primary and secondary participation, an orderly career shows its greatest and most consistent effect in columns 1, 3, 8, and 11, and little or no effect or one that is inconsistent in columns 2, 9, and 12. Six of these seven columns are at the extremes of education—"college" vs. "less than high school." But they come in pairs of best and worst at both levels. Orderly careers count among *young* high-income college men, but not among the *older* high-income college men.[7] Orderliness counts among the *young* low-income men who never completed high school but not among their *older* counterparts. Since "old" in this sample is 40–55, the explanation may be life-cycle differences in aspirations and generational differences in

experience. In stage of the life cycle, the older men are now in their peak earnings period (whatever the level); their youthful aspirations, if unfulfilled, are now being scaled down. Whether education and income are high or low, the balance between rewards and demands is tolerable.

In political and economic experience, the older group is a product of the Great Depression. These massive forces apparently overcome the effect of orderliness in the career: What's a little unpredictability in jobs, compared to the general chaos of the 1930's? What's a little job chaos compared to the days when they were hard-pressed family men just starting out? Contrast the young: in terms of stage in life cycle, whatever the income or education, their aspirations are likely to soar high in relation to rewards; in terms of generation, their demand for good jobs, stable careers, and general security is as urgent as it is plain. Disorderliness in the work history activates the already established predisposition to pull away from community life—a predisposition rooted in life cycle stage and political generation.

Generational differences may also explain why, among high school graduates, orderliness counts in columns 8 and 6 but not in columns 5 and 7. In relative educational opportunity and attainment, and for their generation, men 40 years and over who graduated from high school are like the young high-income men who have had "some college";[8] their behavior should be similar. Thus orderliness increases the vitality of both primary and secondary participation among the older high-income high school graduates and

[7] In column 12 there are five exceptions—positive results for two dimensions of secondary attachment and three dimensions of primary relations. Their import is diminished, however, by skewed distributions and a small N.

[8] It is important to remember that "college men" in the middle mass are typically professionals, technicians, or supervisors of the "semi-" variety—and their education is a neat fit. The modal case had one to three years of college; only 30 percent of the "some college" have a bachelor's degree. It is impressive that merely a taste of college—even among those who did not quite make it through—sorts out the college men from others. Both self-selection and training are doubtless among the causes.

does something for secondary participation among the older low-income high school graduates. Orderliness has little or no effect on anything among the younger counterparts.

SOME IMPLICATIONS

1. If work role, occupational association, and career are central variables in the sociology of work, we must develop typologies of each and put them to sociological use. The orderliness of the work history—i.e., the degree to which it fits the model of career—is one useful concept in that effort. When the idea of career is taken seriously and applied to large populations, we see that few men are gripped by careers for the entire worklife, only a minority for as much as half the worklife. We see, too, that in the perspective of decades, the pattern and sequence of jobs may have more impact on a man's social life than any one of the many positions he picks up and drops on the way.

2. With regard to participation, the types of social relations covered by "primary" and the types of formal organizations covered by "secondary" (we have tapped everything from a "Marital Therapy Club" to "Joe's Regulars," a semiformal, bar-connected drinking club)—these are the stuff of the discipline. The labor-leisure study suggests the theoretical relevance and operational feasibility of concepts such as range of participation and role integration. The results support two apparently contradictory assumptions that have been made: that role integration and a wide range of attachments are compatible and have similar effects. There may be an upper limit beyond which strong role integration blocks exposure to diverse values, interests, and strata, and a broad range of participation produces severe role conflict with a consequent withdrawal, but at the medium levels tapped by our measures, and in the middle mass, coherence and range go together.

3. The data are consistent with a major assumption of the study: with advancing

industrialism and urbanism, traditional indicators of social class—present income and occupational category of self or father—no longer discriminate among styles of leisure and degrees of social integration for a growing middle mass. As determinants of social relations, media exposure, and consumption, these "class" variables are becoming less important than career pattern, mobility orientation, and work milieu—and the associated educational experiences.

4. The data are consistent with the guiding hypothesis: chaotic experience in the economic order fosters a retreat from both work and the larger communal life. It may be that the economic and non-economic spheres are so interdependent that this causal formulation cannot be tested—that an orderly career facilitates participation, participation boosts chances for an orderly career, and both are affected by underlying processes of personal self-selection and organizational recruitment. Three considerations, however, suggest that the causal sequence is: education → orderly career → participation, whatever the interaction of these variables once the process is under way. First, preliminary analysis not here reported shows that "pre-occupational leisure training" in adolescence (e.g., parental participation when respondent was a teenager, respondent's own activities at that time) does not affect later participation. Second, several crude indicators of early socialization are unrelated to work history, so the argument that personality pre-dispositions cause both orderliness and participation seems weak. Although an intensive psychological analysis might explain part of the variance, these men are *not* merely recapitulating family history. Finally, the structural forces shaping adult life—economic crises in economy and firm, life cycle stage—seem to account for the reported variations by age, income, and education

339

in the relation of work history to participation.

In so far as job patterns in modern economies become more orderly and more of the population achieves the position of the young, high-income, "some college" men of the middle mass, participation in community life is likely to increase, whatever its quality. It is quite possible, however, that other structural changes—in the content of jobs, the schedule of work, hours of leisure and the agencies that serve it—will offset those labor force trends that make for more predictable careers. It is possible, too, that the generations will again be divided by different trauma: most of the men in our sample did not grow up in the Affluent Society; a little orderliness for them may go further in stimulating community participation than a lot of orderliness will do for a generation with its eyes glued to the television screen and its energies devoted to the ardent consumption of "goodies" pouring from automated industry.

36

EUNICE BELBIN and R. M. BELBIN

NEW CAREERS IN MIDDLE AGE

One question which must have been encountered by almost every gerontologist
is from what age does the study of aging
commence. This seemingly straightforward question is likely to elicit a devious
reply and one that will vary with the
specialty of the gerontologist. Aging begins from birth. But, as gerontologists,
our interests are likely to be confined
only to part of the aging process. Our
common interest would seem to lie in the
study of diminishing capacity. On this
criterion, the study of the problems of
age and adaptation to new work will
oblige us to consider age groups younger
than those which figure in most gerontological studies. The problems to which
we shall refer are likely to be evident not
only in the 50's and 60's age groups, but
also in the 30's and 40's and may, in certain classes of industrial work, manifest
themselves as early as the late 20's.

It may be diminishing capacity or it
may be prejudice which accounts for the
employment difficulties of middle-aged
workers. But whatever the interpretation,
it seems that these difficulties are being
magnified by rapid changes in the occupational structures of industrial societies.
There is growing recognition that redundant middle-aged workers face hardship and downgrading even in full employment economies. Our object in this
paper will be to consider the contribution
that can be made by training the middle-
aged for new work, to review the prog-

First published in the *Proceedings of the 7th
International Congress of Gerontology*, Vienna,
1966 (Vienna: Verlag der Wiener Medizinischen
Akademie, 1966), pp. 71–82. Abridged.

ress that has already been made and to
assess to what newer areas of study we
should devote our attention.

The job prospects of re-employment in
so far as age is a significant factor depend
on the extent to which the worker is considered sufficiently flexible and adaptable
to meet the demands of a new situation.
The greater the amount of skill involved,
the more important flexibility, adaptability and trainability become. And today
skill is at a premium; the completely unskilled jobs which for long have been
the traditional refuge of the older or incapacitated worker are being steadily
whittled away. The industrial gerontologist must therefore orientate his efforts
around problems of adjustment between
men and jobs. He will need to further his
interest in and support for programs
aimed at retraining redundant mature
adults for new and more highly skilled
work. Unless this need is generally appreciated we shall witness the emergence of
middle-aged workers as an under-privi-
leged group. Economically viable solutions must be found rather than charitable
ones. The first step in this direction is to
recognize that retraining is the means by
which adult workers can continue to adjust themselves to the exigencies of a rapidly changing society.

In a number of countries the challenge
to retrain the middle-aged has been accepted and this is now being followed by
the adoption of important policies and
programs: *In the U.S.A.* by the Manpower Development and Training Act; *in
Great Britain* by the Industrial Training
Act and by the expansion in the number

of Government Training Centers for Adults; *in France* by the program of the Federation of French Industries (C.N.-P.F.) and by the great work of the F.P.A. with now almost 100 centers throughout France for the vocational training of adults; *in Sweden* by an extensive public program whereby fully 1% of the adult population is being retrained for new industrial skills.

Efforts in these countries are relatively well publicized and documented. Other examples, less well-known, may be cited from countries widely separated both in their geography and in their culture patterns: *Norway* has successfully trained 400 adult workers for the merchant marine. Recruits for training up to the age of 59 years have been drawn from occupations as diverse from each other and from seafaring work as agriculture, forestry, building, and even office work. *Costa Rica* is establishing a National Institute of Apprenticeship with special programs of accelerated training for adults. *Poland* is building up teaching units in its Workers Technical Colleges specializing in the teaching of adults.

These programs seem to be developing on a wide front. In this way a contribution is being made not only to the personal well-being of the middle-aged but also to the economic growth of the countries concerned.

Nevertheless, the increased provision of retraining facilities does not remove the problems associated with aging and adaptation. Indeed it has served to highlight them. Where reliable figures have been collected on admission rates, performance during training, and success in subsequent placement, age has invariably stood out as a significant factor. It is here that we must ensure that there exists a strong body of facts. Those who are formulating new programs must have at hand the results of research if these programs are not to fall short of their objectives.

The first problem to consider is that of older worker pedagogy. Are programs for the middle-aged to be based on methods used for young recruits? If not, how should they differ and why?

In the United Kingdom, much of our knowledge of the way in which performance changes with age stems from the Nuffield Research Unit into Problems of Aging which operated in Cambridge during the 1950's under Dr. A. T. Welford. What we have learned during the last few years is how to put such knowledge to good effect. The results of applied studies have confirmed the value to be gained from studying intensively the nature of the difficulties in adult training. These difficulties include: (1) *among manual skills*, that of establishing a controlled performance where some form of speed stress is present; and the difficulty of discarding wrongly learned responses; (2) the difficulties in acquiring skills *where memorizing is entailed*. Here there are the problems of mental interference, characterized by the presence of irrelevant or distracting stimuli which cause forgetting; (older people are especially liable to disruption of short-term memory traces). (3) Further difficulties occur in skills which entail the *development of understanding*. These skills are likely to increase with automation as manipulative skills tend to diminish. There is here the problem of finding a suitable framework in which effective assimilation can take place. (The older learner is depressed by situations which he finds difficult to comprehend, yet unmotivated by those which he regards as child's play.)

These are but a few of the difficulties encountered in adult training. Research in Great Britain has concentrated on a practical means of overcoming such psychological difficulties by the redesign of training methods.

Work in this area has allowed us to reach two important generalizations about training methods:

1. Serious problems do exist which, if ignored, are liable to lead to failures in training and to discrimination against the middle-aged entrant. For example, the

difficulties of middle-aged trainee sewing machinists have resulted in a policy which is now prevalent throughout the clothing industry in many countries of excluding all entrants over the age of 25. The effect of this has been to unbalance the age structure of the industry and in some cases to cause acute labor shortage.

2. Where an appropriate method of training can be developed, older trainees often achieve results comparable with those of their younger colleagues. Training method appears to be far more crucial for the old than for the young.

From a practical point of view the specific requirements of the middle-aged learner include (1) first, and perhaps rather surprisingly, long and uninterrupted learning sessions; (2) greater consolidation of learning before attempting new aspects of the skill—accomplished best perhaps by what we have termed cumulative part learning; (3) the need for accurate responses and rapid feedback during learning in order to avoid the difficulties of unlearning; (4) self structuring of the learning program within his own time limits and avoidance of competition which is likely to produce "paced" conditions; and (5) above all—the need for active mental participation during learning. This is best achieved, perhaps, by deductive or inferential learning—learning by discovery rather than learning by imitation or by rote.

Our next and as yet unsolved problem takes us into the realms of social psychology. Evidence is now gathering that it is a formidable problem to steer older workers into training. This is evident from the sharp discrepancy which exists between the ages of entrants to training programs designed for adults and the ages of those who are available for training.

In the United States about 39 percent of the labor force is over 45 as compared with 11 percent of those receiving training under the Manpower Development and Training Act. In Great Britain the proportion is smaller; under 5 percent of those being retrained in Government Training Centers are aged 45 or over. In France the figure for the corresponding training body, F.P.A., is insignificant and even for those over 35 years of age the figure is less than 4 percent.

The shortage of older workers in these training programs can only partly be explained by age discrimination. A more liberal policy on recruitment now prevails but it has not resulted in any sharp increase in the number of older workers being trained. On the other hand there is a good deal of evidence from case studies of retraining to indicate that anxiety about "making the grade" exerts a major influence in discouraging adults from participating in such programs. The longer the gap between previous learning and the new training situation, the more serious this problem becomes. The very fact that a mature adult has been separated from learning for a long period may indicate an attitude of avoidance and disinclination towards learning. The adult who avoids training is likely to have been an early "casualty" or "drop-out" from the school educational system. The less skilled and less literate see no hope of learning new skills by the techniques of the once-rejected classroom or by methods of training which they associate with schoolroom tuition.

Hence, it is not surprising to find in some countries that downgrading is automatically accepted—or even sought—by the older workers themselves. Of 331 men rendered redundant by the closure of two British Railways Workshops, not one accepted opportunities for retraining. In Arizona, it was necessary to contact 900 migrant families in order to enroll 75 adult trainees. And when a group of older railway workers in Great Britain applied to an engineering firm, it was for *un*-skilled work. It was management in this case who eventually persuaded them to enter a training school, where, perhaps as a result of new and stimulating techniques of training they are once again doing semi-skilled work.

But reluctance to enter training is not confined to the unskilled and the poorly educated. There is a general reluctance on the part of the middle-aged industrial worker to present himself for retraining. Attention has been drawn to the fact that high seniority men are less likely to volunteer than low seniority men, believing that they may continue to enjoy the protective features of a seniority system. And we have observed in our recent studies that the man who has enjoyed the status which skill confers is loth to admit that his skill is really obsolete. He lacks confidence that he can acquire the same degrees of perfection in a new skill, especially if he is to be taught "by the youngster down the road." He prefers to stay in his old job until that job disappears.

Some unwillingness to enter training seems to be associated with fear of selection methods and aptitude testing. Traditional selection methods often prove a psychological as well as an attainment barrier to those whose acquaintance with paper and pencil techniques was never a close or affectionate one. It has recently been shown, however, that Mental and Aptitude Test scores can rise on average as much as 20 points for the 45 year-olds after 20 weeks of Vocational Training on activities quite unrelated to those measured. Thus the value of such tests may need reappraisal on technical grounds alone.

Although there are a number of factors in the training environment liable to discourage the mature worker, the core of the problem is likely to be one of emotional adjustment.

The most promising means of ensuring re-orientation towards training on an individual basis would seem to be through personal counseling. As yet we are on the threshold of our knowledge of how counseling work can be adapted to the special needs of the middle-aged worker. There is certainly a need for an integrated service which could take account of informa-tion on established skills, personality and physical fitness on the one hand and job opportunities, job demands and general employment trends on the other. Clearly this is a field in which a great deal of research and development will be demanded in future years.

A second possibility is to explore the cultivation of social norms in bringing about higher participation rates in training. The older worker is reluctant to enter as a lone individual into training situations which he considers more appropriate for younger men. But studies of retraining within an organization or of retraining programs that have been taken into isolated communities have shown remarkably high older person participation rates. The common feature seems to be that retraining has become socially acceptable; the older participant is conscious that he is not an isolated individual but has peers who are also receiving training. We may surmise from this that training is more effective where it can be taken to the group and less effective where older people are recruited individually to form a new group. Policies for area redevelopment are therefore likely to prove attractive for redundant older workers.

In cases where it is impracticable to get older workers to enter into group training situations, account might be taken of recent advances in Home Study methods whereby adults are allowed to combine systematic Home Study with periodic practical training and group tutorials. A study this year in Great Britain has shown that the results of such methods can be comparable with results gained from attendance at formal courses.

This particular study has also shown that by far the most successful Home Study students were those who had maintained some form of learning activity after leaving school, even though this learning consisted of subjects quite unrelated to their course in Boiler Fuel Efficiency, for example: first aid, music, languages, wireless telegraphy, and so on.

We must remember that in studies of adult retraining we have in many countries been dealing with the products of the depression years, those whose education was terminated prematurely, those who had less opportunities for equality of education, and those too, who for reasons stated earlier, had little inclination to pursue postschool education. Many of the future problems of adult reluctance or inability to learn might be solved if today's young worker could build continued learning so fully into his habit pattern that he took it for granted. This can only be done if training and retraining is organized on a periodic basis throughout working life. This is important if we are to prevent present generations of younger workers from having difficulties when they become older.

These matters relate to developments that have either emerged at the present time or which are likely to assume increasing industrial importance during the immediate future. But we must avoid becoming so preoccupied with them that we lose sight of other problems that belong to the less immediate future and yet which we begin to see in our midst. It seems opportune to turn to the occupational problems of the middle-aged in relatively high grade jobs.

The effect of more widespread higher education and of improved facilities for vocational training is creating a new set of problems due to increased competition arising for better jobs. Graduates are now being recruited into jobs for middle-management and even for supervisory level jobs.

To illustrate the problems among the higher echelons, the Institute of Directors in Great Britain has estimated that 2000 directors and managers are becoming redundant each year as a result of mergers and dismissals and are usually finding great difficulty in obtaining any form of comparable employment. Very few are graduates.

Older people who have held relatively high grade jobs, whether directors, managers, supervisors or even skilled workers appear to be difficult to place in new jobs when their technical qualifications are rather lower than would be normal in the jobs they have previously held. Their experience too may count for little where it has been gained in one firm. In fact, older worker experience is often something of a myth. One is reminded of the retort to the man who claimed 20 years' experience: "You mean one year's experience repeated 20 times." Those in higher occupational grades also appear then to have a need for retraining at various periods throughout their working life as a safeguard against the obsolescence of their skill or a loss in its market value.

But there is still a residue of age discrimination which is exercised in higher grade occupations against older people who cannot be faulted on any of the above points. The core of the problem seems to rest with the notion that however satisfactory an individual in, say, his 50's might be in his present job, he will not be able to extend his concepts, to adapt and modify behaviour developed in a previous situation to take account of the needs of the new situation.

How true is this generalization? A progressive inability with age to organize new data can certainly be indicated at the sensory level. For example, adults who have gained sight after being blind from birth have shown an impairment in adapting to the visual environment and in overcoming reliance on touch and, in fact, never attain normal visual ability. This lack of adjustment is evident from age 20, but much more marked in later decades.

Is it not likely that some similar impairment underlies a failure to organize new data at higher cognitive levels? Here the evidence is uncertain. At the higher cognitive levels the exceptions are more striking than at the sensory levels. While lack of adaptability is very evident in many from middle maturity, yet some older people show exceptional powers of adaptability.

It seems consistent with the evidence to argue that trainability, adaptability and flexibility of mind have a certain common physical basis which physical aging affects unfavourably, but that this can be compensated by practice in modifying and adapting behaviour. This practice in modifying and adapting behaviour tends to be lost with age as the environment of mature adults and the elderly becomes increasingly stable.

As yet we have virtually no knowledge of what would happen if these two trends could be counterposed. What would we expect to happen if the environment of adults became less stable with age and required an increasing measure of learning and adjustment? We can only guess at the answer.

In this notion of two forces counterposed, one of the forces, that of the environment, is subject to man's control. The possibilities that are developing of changing jobs in middle life and the facilities that are being developed for learning new skills (arising out of the needs of modern society) promise to modify one of these forces. Learning in middle age and even late maturity may no longer become an exceptional activity. It is our hypothesis that such activity will not only improve the vocational qualifications of adults but prolong that flexibility of mind which is rated so highly in the changing of jobs.

To sum up, we have seen from our excursions into the occupational problems of the middle-aged that, irrespective of the grade of skill or education, real security of employment must rest on the ability to move from one job to another, and here training of the middle-aged in new skills has a vital role to play. A new outlook should pervade education and training. We should get away from the ritual of the long learning period with formalized qualifications. Facts will soon become outdated. We must re-orientate our thinking towards acceptance of learning throughout life in a flexible pattern of work and study.

The industrial gerontologist will see the immensity of the challenge that presents itself. Our focus on the problem of being able to train a middle-aged worker for a specific job can be seen as only one fragment of a much larger picture. To develop a program that will be equal to the needs of the situation we shall need to build up an inter-disciplinary approach. We shall need to predict how far an individual can develop new skills and abilities having regard to his current abilities and job history. We shall need to identify job facilities that can use to maximum his previous experience while furthering his occupational prospects. We must learn to identify the emerging pattern of occupational change that can justify long-term programs of individual training and development. And we must be able to apply the most up-to-date knowledge of selection, training and placement techniques in equipping older workers for tomorrow's jobs.

These are some of the matters around which industrial gerontologists may feel motivated to conduct their research in the future.

37

ROBERT J. HAVIGHURST and KENNETH FEIGENBAUM

LEISURE AND LIFE-STYLE

Leisure has generally but vaguely been seen as a source of satisfaction and even of delight. In a society in which most people had to work, and to work hard and long, leisure was scarce and was regarded either as a reward to be earned by work and to be enjoyed because one had worked so hard for it or a good thing conferred by inherited wealth or by marriage to wealth.

With the coming of more leisure in the lives of the common people, not all the rosy promises have been realized. Some people have found themselves with more leisure than they really wanted. The values of increased leisure to welfare and the quality of living of society as a whole have been seriously questioned. It is clear that modern leisure is not an unmixed blessing. This suggests the desirability of studying the uses that people make of their leisure, what satisfactions they get out of it, and how it fits into the rest of their lives.

Using the concept of "life-style" to describe a person's characteristic way of filling and combining the various social roles he is called on to play, we may see how leisure fits into it. To do so, the Kansas City Study of Adult Life interviewed a sample of men and women aged from forty to seventy to get an account of the way the person spent his time and the significance to him of his major social roles—those of parent, spouse, homemaker, worker, citizen, friend, club or association member, and user of leisure time. About a quarter of the interview was devoted to leisure. The individual was asked about his favorite leisure activities, what they meant to him, why he liked them, whom he did them with, as well as a number of questions about vacations, reading, television, radio, and movies, and what he did around the house.

On the basis of this interview, ratings were made of the competence of the individual in his social roles. Rating scales were devised to represent the general American expectations or definitions of these roles.[1] The rating scale for user of leisure time follows:

a) *High (8–9).*—Spends enough time at some leisure activity to be rather well known among his associates in this respect. But it is not so much the amount of leisure activity as its quality which gives him a high rating. He has one or more pursuits for which he gets public recognition and appreciation and which give him a real sense of accomplishment.

Chooses his leisure activities autonomously, not merely to be in style. Gets from leisure the feeling of being creative, of novel and interesting experience, sheer pleasure, prestige, friendship, and of being of service.

b) *Above average (6–7).*—Has four to five leisure activities. Leisure time is somewhat patterned, indicating that he has planned his life to provide for the satisfaction of the needs met through these activities.

Leisure interests show some variety.

Abridged from the *American Journal of Sociology*, vol. 64, no. 4 (January 1959). Copyright 1959 by The University of Chicago.

[1] For the other role-performance scales and for the pattern analysis mentioned later see Havighurst, 1957.

Displays real enthusiasm for one or two—talks about them in such a way as to indicate that he has put considerable energy into acquiring proficiency or the requisite understanding and skills and prides himself on it.

c) *Medium (4–5).*—Has two or three leisure activities which he does habitually and enjoys mildly—reading, television, radio, watching sports, handwork, etc. May do one of these things well or quite enthusiastically, but not more than one. Gets definite sense of well-being and is seldom bored with leisure.

Leisure activities are somewhat stereotyped; they do not have a great deal of variety.

d) Below average *(2–3).*—

(1) Tends to take the line of least resistance in leisure time. Needs to be stimulated. Looks for time-fillers.

May have one fairly strong interest but is content with this one which brings him some sense of enjoyment. Leisure time is usually spent in passive spectatorship. *Or:*

(2) May have very little spare time. What time he has is taken up with activities related to his job or profession or with work around the house viewed as obligatory and not as a pastime.

e) *Low (0–1).*—

(1) Apathetic. Does nothing and makes no attempt to find outside interests. *Or:*

(2) Tries anxiously to find interesting things to do and fails to find them. Is bored by leisure and hurries back to work. Dislikes vacations and cannot relax.

The procedure in studying life-style was based upon the use of the scores for performance in the eight social roles. A life-style was defined as a pattern of role-performance scores shared by a group of people.

Among 234 persons in the Kansas City Study of Adult Life, there were twenty-seven specific patterns, or life-styles, each characterizing from 8 to 34 members. The specific patterns were grouped into four major groups, and these four groups may be regarded provisionally as life-style groups. Their characteristic role-performance scores are shown in Figure 1. The names given to the life-style groups, and a brief description of each, follow:

A. *Community-centered.*—This is a pattern of uniformly high performance scores in all eight social roles. It is called "community-centered" for the sake of contrast with the following group, though the performance scores in the community roles of citizen, club or association member, and friend are not higher than those in the family areas. The social class distribution of these people in the Kansas City Metropolitan Area is shown in Table 1.

B. *Home-centered high.*—These people have performance scores in the roles of parent, spouse, homemaker, worker, and user of leisure time which are about the same as those of the community-centered, but they fall far below in the roles of friend, citizen, and club or association member. These people and the community-centered group have the highest personal adjustment scores and the highest scores on a rating of manifest complexity of life-style.

C. *Home-centered medium.*—These people have a family-centered pattern, though below that of the home-centered high group in role-performance scores.

D. *Low level.*—This is a pattern of generally low role-performance scores, with the family and work roles somewhat above the other roles. This group has very low scores on personal adjustment and on complexity.

The community-centered style of leisure emphasizes activities engaged in away from home. The individual uses entertainment institutions, such as the theater or the concert or social institutions, such as the country club, Rotary, chamber of commerce, Red Cross, etc., as the context for a major part of it. People employing the community-centered style of leisure tend to be autonomous, that is, to "choose activity with purpose and regard for its function in one's personal life" and to engage in activities that have some element of novelty. They are more instrumental and more inclined to "play a game or participate in an activity for some goal beyond the game or activity (philanthropic activity, etc.)." "Benefit for society" was given quite often as the motive.

Community-centeredness is the favorite leisure style of upper-middle-class people.

ple whose leisure is spent mostly around the house. This style is strongest in lower-middle- and working-class individuals and falls off in the lower-class, where family values lose some importance and the few

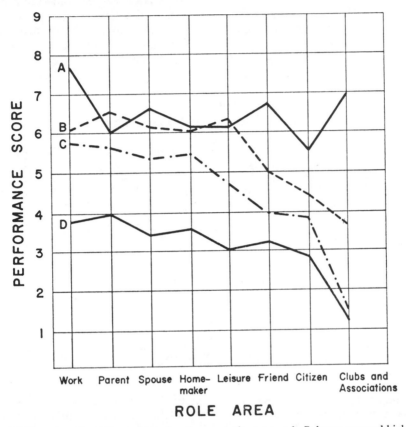

FIG. 1.—Life-styles of middle-aged people: *A*, community-centered; *B*, home-centered high; *C*, home-centered medium; *D*, low level.

Being successful in business or a profession induces them to join business and social organizations where they interact with each other to form wider circles of social and business contacts. Membership in the country club is part of their proper and accepted style of living. The community-centered individuals also tend not to have young children at home, which allows freedom for outside activity.

In contrast are the home-centered peo-

pastimes become sex-differentiated, the men going fishing alone or to the bar or poolroom with the "boys."

Leisure activities are engaged in jointly by the members of the family for the majority of the home-centered, whether it be a church outing, a fishing trip, or watching television. Sex-differentiated activities, such as sewing and embroidering for the women and carpentry and "fixing around the house" for the men, still allow for conversation and interaction between the spouses. Friendship and sociability are cultivated by visits from neighbors rather than through any membership other than church or perhaps a fraternal organization. For some people the family-centered style was not one of choice but of necessity, owing to the presence of young children.

A number of activities such as fishing and traveling during vacations were common to both leisure styles, with some differentiation as to the manner of them. In the community-centered style travel consists of going to resorts and sightseeing, while for the people engaged in home-centered leisure travel consists of a car trip to visit working-relatives in other cities. For the working-class members of the home-centered style travel may be quite circumscribed; one spoke of "taking a trolley trip to see the city."

In spite of the relationship between life-style and social class position, there were people whose life-styles did not correspond with their class positions, as would be expected in a society with a considerable degree of social mobility. From Table 1 it appears that some ten percent of the population may have patterns above their class level and five percent below it.

Two examples, one of a community-centered man with a high rating as a user of leisure and the other of a high leisure home-centered man, may further the reader's image of the difference between the two styles of leisure.

Mr. X is a fifty-year-old executive vice-president of a bank, with a pattern of leisure activities which is the prototype of the community-centered style of leisure. He is president of one country club, a member of another, a Shriner, and a member of the executive council of a national Boy's Club movement and of a number of charity organizations. Mr. X's favorite leisure activity is to go on trips during his vacation, to New York City to see the Broadway theater, and to see exhibitions of modern art. He is active in encouraging the local art museum to acquire examples of modern art. He enjoys playing golf once or twice a week at the country club, playing cards, painting his garage, and entertaining business people both at home and at the club. He does not own a television set, preferring the good music on the radio. He goes with his wife to the movies and to all the musical comedies

TABLE 1

SOCIAL CLASS DISTRIBUTION OF LIFE-STYLES

(Percent)

Social Class	Sex	Community-centered	Home-centered High	Home-centered Medium	Low Level	Un-grouped	Total Group
U & UM.....	M	7	3	1	0	2	13
	F	6	3	3	0	1	13
LM..........	M	8	11	10	3	1	33
	F	5	4	17	3	4	33
Working......	M	4	8	18	8	2	40
	F	2	5	23	7	3	40
Lower........	M	0	0	6	7	1	14
	F	1	0	5	7	1	14
Total group	M	19	22	35	18	6	100
	F	14	12	48	17	9	100

NOTE: The actual distribution of individuals in the Study Sample was the basis for this table, but the figures have been adjusted to fit the true social class distribution of adults in the Kansas City Metropolitan Area, as determined by Richard Coleman (unpublished working paper in the files of the Committee on Human Development, The University of Chicago).

that come to Kansas City. As for friends, Mr. X calls ten to twelve couples "close." He met them through various activities: "My business connections here at the bank, civic clubs, church, etc." With his wife he goes out to eat once a week and entertains other couples.

In contrast to Mr. X, Mr. Y, a fifty-eight-year-old social worker, is an example of an individual who employs the home-centered style of leisure. His favorite activity is gardening, in which he spends one-half hour to an hour a day during the growing season. Mr. Y's hobby is model railroading, which he engages in with his wife in the basement of his home. He also does some woodworking and woodcarving and manual work around the home. Once in a while he reads historical fiction. The television set plays for two hours an evening, showing sports events, quiz shows, and plays. With his wife he reads, plays cards, does model railroading, and takes walks. Living in a neighborhood of younger adults, he claims that he has few friends and that a large part of his time is spent taking care of the two children of his son. Mr. Y's "going out" consists only of movies (with wife) and American Legion meetings once a month.

The differences between the home-centered high, home-centered medium, and low-level life-styles as far as leisure is concerned are mainly those between high, medium, and low ratings on the scale of competence as a user of leisure. A higher role performance is associated with the following variables: autonomy, creativity, getting strong pleasure from the activity, instrumental, high energy input, ego integration, vitality, and expansion of interests and activities.

Have those whose leisure is home-centered different personalities from the community-centered? Or is the difference caused by some external factor, such as residence in a suburb versus residence in an apartment area in the center of the city, or having several young children versus having one or none? It has been

suggested by David Riesman (1957) and by Margaret Mead (1957), among others, that the trend toward suburban living and the trend toward larger numbers of children are making for values and leisure activities that are more home- and family-centered.

Riesman speaks of "suburban styles of life and thought" and stresses the suburban constriction of leisure to the family and the living-room–garden–television set, at the expense of theater, concert hall, downtown meetings, country clubs, and heterogeneous social groups. Margaret Mead says that the generation which has married since the war is much more concerned with home and family life than earlier generations and is busy trying to turn home life into "a self-rewarding delight."

To explore the differences between home-centered and community-centered people, we compared a community-centered group with a similar number of home-centered people, equating the groups for age and socioeconomic status. There was no difference between the two groups in the proportions of suburban dwellers and the proportions who lived in single-family houses with gardens and recreation rooms. However, the home-centered had more children living at home. This suggests that the presence of children in the home, together with the desire to have children and to have a home-centered life, are more influential than the actual physical location of one's house in determining leisure style. It should be borne in mind, however, that Kansas City does not have many apartment dwellings for upper-middle-class people near the city's center.

The foregoing facts point to the conclusion that the personality, more than the situation, determines the leisure style.

It has been assumed up to this point that there was a close correlation between personal adjustment and performance in the leisure role. The correlation coefficient is .32 for men and .33 for women, with socioeconomic status partialed out. Clearly, there are some exceptions to this rule. Study of these exceptions may teach us something more about the value of leisure.

Accordingly, we selected the cases which showed most markedly a high adjustment—low leisure performance combination and those who combined low adjustment with high leisure performance. There were nine of the former and twelve of the latter in the sample of 234 people. The criterion for the high adjustment—low leisure combination was an adjustment score of 6 or above on the ten-point adjustment scale and a score of 5 or below on the ten-point leisure performance scale. The criterion for the low adjustment—high leisure group was an adjustment score of 4.5 or below and a leisure score of 6 or above.

The content of the leisure and the significance ratings of the leisure activities of the low leisure—high adjustment people were similar to the general pattern of people with low leisure and low adjustment scores. There are low significance ratings as to the autonomy of the leisure activity, the creativity expressed in it, some apathy with respect to the activity, and either a decline in leisure interests or no expansion of interests.

These are people who get along very well with little or no leisure. They show a great deal of vitality in the instrumental activities of life. The men are busy with their jobs and the women with their children, allowing little time for leisure and restricting them to leisure activities near home. Six out of the nine in the group are females and follow this pattern. Their leisure activities are centered either at home, where they sew, watch television, and take care of the children, or in the church. The relationship between the spouses is good, and there is a general feeling of contentment and emotional security. It is this basically which accounts for the high adjustment scores of the group.

The group of individuals with high leisure scores and low adjustment tend as a whole to be maladjusted socially or occupationally and attempt to get through leisure what they cannot get in the other roles. They use their leisure as a compensation to make up for their deficiencies and to give their life some meaning.

The men in the group, often alienated from work, from spouse, or from the "community," attempt to adjust to this alienation by engaging in leisure activities where they invest a lot of energy and through which they can enjoy themselves and see themselves as socially acceptable. One is a factory manager. He finds no satisfaction in this position but rather pictures himself as an intellectual and therefore spends a great deal of time reading. A second, an amateur pilot, directs his leisure away from a home where some emotional difficulties exist. Another man was trained as an engineer and has shifted over the years from one job to another, finally going into a business with his wife, which he does not enjoy. Like the factory manager, he pictures himself as a scholar and spends his leisure time reading oriental history.

The women in the group have difficulty in relating to their husbands and are emotionally insecure; there are degrees of feelings of unwantedness and not being loved. They concentrate their energies into a single activity which they engage in alone and where they can achieve a great deal of proficiency, such as sewing, embroidery, or petitpoint, or in church activities where they can spend time with the "women" and achieve the feeling of "doing something worthwhile."

CONCLUSIONS

1. The most successful life-styles, as judged by the level of role-performance scores, have concomitant patterns of leisure activity. The community-centered life-style includes a leisure pattern which spreads from the home out through a variety of community circles. On the

other hand, a successful home-centered life-style contains a home-centered leisure pattern. These successful leisure patterns tend to be autonomous, creative, instrumental, vital, and ego integrative, whether they be community-centered or home-centered.

The lower-level life-styles are lower in performance in roles external to the home than in the home roles. They also have lower-level leisure styles, with lower scores on the values listed in the preceding paragraph.

2. The two major types of leisure style, the community-centered and the home-centered, appear to be equally accessible to middle-class people, but rarely are working-class people community-centered. An individual with a large family of children is more likely to be home-centered. However, his place of residence —whether in a suburb, single-family home, or city apartment—does not seem to affect his leisure style to any great degree. The personality of the individual appears to find its own leisure style.

3. There are a few exceptional cases where the life-style and the leisure style are not in close relation. One group of such cases consists of about five percent of adults. They are people with little or no leisure activity who have a successful life-style and good personal adjustment. These men and women generally invest most of their energy in work or in home and children, with little time and inclination for leisure.

Another group consists of about six percent of adults. They have a high level of leisure activity but are dissatisfied or inadequate workers or parents or spouses who attempt to compensate with a high leisure performance.

38

LENORE A. EPSTEIN and JANET H. MURRAY

EMPLOYMENT AND RETIREMENT

Retirement is an issue faced by most people some time in their sixties. It is a major step, which affects the individual and also the society of which he is a part. On the aggregate level, retirement decisions affect the labor force, the market, and the cost of public and private retirement insurance programs. The "decision" has not been a real one for many—those who could not get jobs if they wanted them either because of market conditions or because of their own poor health or disability. With the growth in public and private retirement benefits, however, more and more of the aged have a real choice: work or retirement.

Retirement can be defined in a number of ways. The most inclusive measure, for example, would include all those who did not work full time the year around—that is, 35 or more hours a week and 50 or more weeks in the year. According to this measure, almost 9 out of 10 men aged 65 and over in the survey were retired. A rather different measure counts all persons receiving some type of retirement benefit, even though they may still be working; it excludes persons who do not qualify for a retirement benefit, even though they may have stopped working. Eight out of 10 men aged 65 and over had retired according to this measure. An-

Adapted from *The Aged Population of the United States: The 1963 Social Security Survey of the Aged*, U.S. Department of Health, Education, and Welfare, Social Security Administration, Office of Research and Statistics, Research Report no. 19 (Washington, D.C.: U.S. Government Printing Office, 1967), pp. 4, 13, 102–5. The principal author of Part III of Report 19, from which much of this chapter was taken, was Dr. Erdman Palmore.

other measure includes only those who did not work at all in the preceding year—about two-thirds of all aged men in 1963. A measure important in the analysis, the proportion who did not work or worked less than 6 months at full-time jobs during 1962, counted as retired 83 percent of the men aged 65 or over and 95 percent of the women.

OCCUPATIONAL DIFFERENCES IN RETIREMENT RATES

Since men in the more highly paid occupations (professional and technical workers, managers, officials, and proprietors) generally have more savings and other resources for retirement income than do men in the jobs drawing lower pay, one might expect that they would be more likely to retire. The evidence from this, and from other surveys as well, indicates that the reverse is true: men in the better-paid occupations have a lower retirement rate than other men.[1]

[1] The survey collection on which these findings are based took place in early 1963, with most of the information relating to the year 1962. The Bureau of the Census was responsible for the sample design and the collection and tabulation of the data. The universe was composed of the civilian population aged 62 and over residing in the 50 states and the District of Columbia. Institutional residents were included. The basic interview unit for the survey was an "aged unit," defined as a married couple, either member of which was aged 62 or older, or a nonmarried person who was aged 62 or older. About 8,500 aged units consisting of about 11,000 aged persons was the expected sample size; altogether, useful questionnaires were completed for 7,515 aged units, a completion rate of about 88 percent.

Fewer than a third of the professional or technical workers, for example, who had worked at regular full-time jobs within the preceding five years had stopped working full time in 1962. In contrast, about two-thirds of the craftsmen and foremen had stopped working full time. Similar findings were made in a 1952 study of the aged (Steiner and Dorfman, 1957).

Within each occupational group, OASDHI beneficiaries[2] were more likely than nonbeneficiaries not to be working full time. But among beneficiaries and nonbeneficiaries, the better-paid occupational groups had the lowest retirement rates. The 1957 survey made by the Social Security Administration showed a similar pattern among beneficiaries. The pattern probably results from a combination of several factors. The higher paid men, in general, have less physically demanding work, their jobs are more interesting and more rewarding, and they have better health.

Among men aged 62 and over, a substantial majority of those who were partially retired (working less than 35 hours a week) continued in the same broad occupational group they were in when they worked at regular full-time jobs. However, the amount of shifting into new occupations after partial retirement was considerable. A fourth of the clerical and sales workers, for example, and about an eighth of the craftsmen and operatives said they had become professionals, managers, or proprietors after partial retirement. Since professional and managerial jobs generally require extensive training and experience, most of the reported shifts from the lower-paid occupational groups were probably into small-farm or small-business ownership. Altogether, more than a fourth of the part-time workers came from a different broad occupa-

[2] In this report the current terminology to cover Social Security benefits, OASDHI, has been adopted although the health insurance provisions were not enacted until 1965. The initials stand for "Old Age, Survivors, Disability, and Health Insurance." (Ed.)

tional group. The proportion would have been substantially greater if a finer occupational breakdown had been used.

REASONS FOR RETIREMENT

Men who had stopped working at a regular full-time job within the past five years were asked why they had stopped. Only 28 percent of the wage and salary workers aged 65 and over retired for such voluntary reasons as desire for leisure, being needed at home, or dissatisfaction with their job. The rest had retired for such compelling reasons as poor health, a compulsory retirement age, or being laid off.

Some might argue that the men who retired because of being laid off or reaching compulsory retirement age should be considered voluntary retirees on the assumption that they could get another job if they wanted, but the assumption is rather unrealistic for most of these men. Although there are no recent data, a 1952 study (Steiner and Dorfman, 1957, p. 49) found that only 12 percent of the men who had retired under compulsory retirement systems later returned to work. More than half the retirees were not well enough to get another job; 11 percent were well enough to work and interested in working but could not find suitable employment.

Also, some might maintain that those who retired because of poor health but on their own decision rather than their employer's should be classified as having retired voluntarily. Eighty-five percent of those who named poor health as the reason for retiring considered their retirement voluntary on this basis (Palmore, 1964, Table 4). Since more than half of these retirees, however, were not well enough to get another job, poor health was classified, for this analysis, as an involuntary reason for retirement.

When the reasons for retirement given the the 1963 survey are compared with those reported in earlier surveys, certain trends appear. In a comparison of the reasons for retirement given by full-year OASDHI beneficiaries in the 1951 survey made by the Social Security Administration and in the 1963 survey, it was found that the proportion retiring voluntarily had doubled between 1951 and 1963 If the reasons given in the 1963 survey by men who had retired within the past 5 years are compared with the reasons given by all retired men in the 1952 study referred to earlier (Steiner and Dorfman, 1957, p. 48), the same pattern results: increasing proportions retiring for voluntary reasons.

Further evidence that voluntary retirement is increasing is the marked growth since 1951 in the proportion of beneficiary men not employed but well enough to work who are not interested in going back to work. This proportion was less than a third in the 1951 survey, but it had increased to 52 percent in 1957 and to 54 percent in 1963.

The growth in voluntary retirements may partly explain the trend toward more retirement in general among men. There seem to be more and more aged men who are well enough to work and who might get some kind of job if they were interested, but who prefer the leisure of retirement.

39

GEORGE L. MADDOX

RETIREMENT AS A SOCIAL EVENT
IN THE UNITED STATES

I

Departure from the world of work, with the implication that the separation is intended to be permanent, is an event of considerable social and personal significance in our society. Historically, work has been a central life task and interest of American males as well as a source of income. Work outside the home has assumed importance as a source of personal and social identity for many American females in recent decades. However, the significance of retirement for the female, as compared with the male, has not been systematically explored and currently remains primarily a matter of conjecture. For this reason, in this brief discussion, attention will be directed to the retirement of males.

For better or worse, retirement is a rite of passage, usually an informal one, between productive maturity and nonproductive old age. For some employees, usually those with long years of service for a particular employer and typically (although not exclusively) those in the middle and upper ranges of status, the transition from the world of work to the world of nonwork is marked by a public ceremony and the presentation of a memento. For most employees, however, this significant transition appears to be unceremonious, perhaps almost intentionally so, as though retirement were an event

Abridged from *Aging and Social Policy*, ed. John C. McKinney and Frank T. de Vyver (New York: Appleton-Century-Crofts, 1966), chap. 4, pp. 119–35. Reprinted as abridged by permission of Appleton-Century-Crofts.

which one does not wish to mark especially. At any rate, retirement is not ordinarily an event which is noted in the daily newspapers as being of public interest. For some employees, retirement may be unintentional and unmarked, as in discovering that the loss of the last job and subsequent failure to be reeemployed constitute their retirement.

Predictably, an event of such personal and social significance might be expected to generate a substantial descriptive and interpretative literature (Donahue *et al.*, 1960). In fact, the primary task of this presentation will be the identification and assessment of the messages about retirement as a social event in the United States suggested by research. By way of previewing what is to follow, it will be argued that retirement lives up to its advance billing as a troublesome personal and social problem. But current interpretations of retirement are seriously marred by the inadequate attention to variations both in the social context within which retirement takes place and in the personal biographies of the elderly individuals. Too often retirement is treated implicitly as a fact with a given meaning, rather than as a sociological variable to be understood within the social life-space of an individual.

II

Although most retirees in our society depart from the world of work at about the same point in the life cycle, they do not leave for identical reasons. Many retirees, perhaps as many as one-half, leave the work force for reasons of poor health;[1] unless they have special scarce skills, most of the remainder are removed from the world of work more or less willingly, by the inexorable operation of established retirement procedures. One still encounters arguments about whether individuals whose health does not disqualify them from working can perform adequately in the modern industrial environment; the cumulative evidence indicates that the elderly worker's potential is, in fact, rather consistently underrated (Welford, 1963).

As it turns out, the argument is largely irrelevant because, given a labor market characterized by a sustained high level of unemployment and little immediate prospect that this situation will change, there is little bidding for the services of elderly workers.[2] The contemporary economic situation is one characterized by a surplus of manpower which reflects the combination of spectacular technological innovations in the work place and increasing life expectancy. Currently there is no certainty even that available manpower under sixty-five years of age can be utilized in conventional productive positions in the labor force. Consequently, arguments

that assume continuing full employment have a somewhat academic sound. Arguments about strategies for keeping the young off the labor market longer, for making early retirement less painful, or for spreading the work through shorter workweeks or more holidays seem more to the point, at least for the current generation of older workers. Although discussion of what constitutes an equitable distribution of work among persons of various ages continues, current strategies do not favor the older worker.

The most immediate consequence of retirement for the worker and his household is economic (Kreps, 1966).[3] For purposes of understanding the economic problems of retired individuals, it is important to distinguish between the permanent impoverishment of a substantial minority for whom retirement is just one more economic insult and the relative economic deprivation of a presumed majority of retirees. In the case of the former, satisfactory resolution of their economic situation is clearly not a matter of manipulation of the retirement age, of more permissive retirement policies, or of improved social security benefits. A frontal attack on the social factors associated with perpetuation of a cycle of poverty is called for in the long run. In the short run, the hard core of permanently impoverished elderly persons must be optimistically viewed as a temporary problem necessitating a humane program of economic relief as a matter of social justice.

In the long run, there are many indications that a social philosophy appropriate for an affluent society with a humane tradition will continue to develop. In all probability, appropriate mechanisms for guaranteeing minimum access to social facilities and resources will also continue to emerge. For the elderly these guarantees

[1] Data from systematic surveys which would permit firm conclusions about the relevance of poor health as a factor in retirement are limited. Slavick and Wolfbein, in Tibbitts, 1960, summarize research by P. O. Steiner and Ralph Dorfman indicating the % males not in the labor force had retired because of poor health, and by Margaret L. Stecker indicating that % of the male social security beneficiaries of this category were unable to work. Stecker's report, "Why Do Beneficiaries Retire?" May, 1955, indicates the experience of OASDI beneficiaries as of 1951 and may be compared with a more recent but similar report by Palmore, "Retirement Patterns Among Men: Findings of the 1963 Survey of the Aged" (August, 1964). In both instances about 40 percent of the male retirees indicated that poor health was the principal explanation of their retirement.

[2] Jaffe, "Population, Needs, Production, and Older Manpower Requirements," 1963, speaks for the apparent majority when he argues that all persons over sixty-five could be withdrawn without affecting per capita production of goods.

[3] See also C. A. Leninger, in Orbach and Tibbitts (1963), which reports aspects of the excellent work by James Morgan, Martin David, Wilbur Cohen, and Harvey Brazer, Income and Welfare in the United States (New York: McGraw-Hill, 1962).

will include improved social security benefits, greater and more widespread access to health and educational facilities, and, for a substantial percentage of aging workers, the prospect of a guaranteed annual wage.[4] Our economic resources are sufficiently great and the shared ethic which informs our public policy sufficiently humanitarian to provide a reasonable guarantee of continuing and increasing access of the retired individual to the fruits of our economic productivity. What proportion of our resources is to be committed to the achievement of minimum economic security for all elderly persons, and how and with what effect, will continue to be discussed, sometimes debated. Nevertheless, the prospect is encouraging that, in the future, retirement will not in itself mean severe economic deprivation for the elderly individuals in most households. This fact alone makes and will continue to make the idea of retirement less forbidding than it has been in the past.[5]

III

Retirement from the world of work is more than a matter of economics, important as economics may be in creating personal troubles for older males who are

[4] For a popular but concise summary of the evidence which suggests the probability of reducing the uncertainty that has plagued the working man, particularly the older worker, see A. H. Raskin, 1964.

[5] For example, Morgan *et al.*, (1962), p. 440, in their report of a survey of the general retirement outlook among heads of households thirty years of age and older, illustrate the positive relationship between economic resources and optimism about retirement. Among respondents, 22 percent of those with neither pensions nor social security expected that "things will be all right" in retirement; among those with social security only, 66 percent were optimistic; and among those with both social security and private pensions, 76 percent were optimistic. Moreover, in the comparison of reasons for retirement among male OASDI beneficiaries made possible by the reports of Stecker, 1955, and Palmore, 1964, the number of individuals in good health who reported retiring voluntarily increased from 3.8 percent in 1951 to 19 percent in 1963.

separated from the work force. Retirement is a social as well as an economic event. Consequently, improvement in economic security for retirees will tend to reduce the negative effect associated with departure from the work force, but by how much is not obvious. The contemporary American worker approaching retirement has been socialized in a milieu which has defined work as a central life task and interest for the male. In addition to his source of income, a man's job means a point of personal and social anchorage with considerable significance, both for the emergence and maintenance of a satisfactory self-identity and for the experience of adequate social intercourse with his family and peers.[6]

Thus the argument has followed—and with considerable justification—that any tampering with the work role, the great balancing factor of life, runs the risk of creating a profound alienation and disequilibrium among the affected individuals (see Friedmann, 1961). In an environment characterized by a religious devotion to work (see Tilgher, 1962) and peopled by individuals dedicated to conspicuous production as an important means of self-identification and self-justification, retirement would be expected to have social as well as economic significance. There are continuing expressions of concern with ways to keep elderly males in the work force in spite of the fact that their productive capacity is not bid for and with multiplying activities for the elderly which have the form and appearance of productive work (Donahue, 1955). This concern not only motivates attempts to increase income among retirees but also illustrates residues of a cultural heritage in which work is a central life task and interest.

[6] The centrality of the work role for males in our society is an assumption well grounded theoretically and empirically. See, for example, Nosow and Form, 1962, Chapters I and II.

This characterization of the contemporary social milieu would lead one to expect retirement to be a troublesome challenge to the retired individual's conception of himself as an adequate, worthwhile individual, even if his income were reasonably adequate. Whereas the characterization is correct historically and in its general emphasis, especially when applied to the contemporary generation of workers in or approaching retirement, it is deficient in specific detail. Job-related work as a central life task and interest to be valued per se is, after all, a culture-specific phenomenon whose historical emergence can be traced to Protestant theology in the Reformation period in general and to Calvinism in particular (Tilgher, 1962). If the phenomenon is culture-specific rather than a culture-universal reflecting some sort of instinct for workmanship, then one may entertain the possibility that, since the conditions which brought the notion into existence no longer pertain, emphasis on work as the primary source of meaning and satisfaction may no longer have its original significance. Evidence is accumulating that just such a reappraisal may have been taking place in recent decades.

Robert Dubin presents evidence indicating that among selected industrial workers work is not the central life interest and the work place is not the locus of the most rewarding social experiences for the worker (Dubin, 1956; Riesman and Bloomberg, 1962; Friedmann and Havighurst, 1954). Remunerative work may be required by society, he contends, but this no longer guarantees that it will be viewed as valuable by workers. Specifically, Dubin found that only one in ten industrial workers in his survey sample perceived their important primary social relationship to be located in the work place; instead, the job was endured as a necessary condition to secure satisfaction elsewhere. It is important to note that Dubin was describing not the elderly worker but the industrial worker without

regard to age. A generalization of this suggests the possibility that increasingly the greatest sense of loss associated with retirement will be economic, as subsequent generations of workers, exposed to a cultural tradition in which work as the central life interest has weakened, approach a permanent separation from the world of work.[7] Mounting evidence suggests that already to some extent, and probably to a greater extent in the future, the economic aspects of retirement among blue-collar workers may overshadow the negative social reactions to retirement. At the present time such a conclusion does not, however, seem warranted with regard to the minority middle and upper status white-collar workers in the labor force. Although the relevant evidence is sketchy, the very individuals who, half a century ago, were considered to be candidates for a leisure class characterized by conspicuous leisure may now be the unexpected candidates for a "working" class characterized by conspicuous occupational involvement.

Contemporary discussions of the changing meaning of work emphasize that the emerging crisis about work as a life task and interest has ceased to be peculiarly a problem of the old in the modern industrial era. Technology has served man notice that he must find a home, a new anchorage point for himself, outside the world of work, certainly by the time of retirement if not before then. But what that home will be remains to be seen. Georges Friedmann (Tibbitts, 1960,

[7] For example, Friedmann and Havighurst, 1954, and Riesman and Bloomberg, 1962. Margaret Gordon, "Work and Patterns of Retirement," 1961, describes a firm with a flexible retirement policy and a generous private pension plan in which only a third of the employees who reached the age of sixty-five elected to continue working. Moreover, Donahue, Orbach, and Pollak, in Tibbitts, 1960, p. 368, report studies in which from one-fourth to one-third of selected groups of older employees elected early retirement; in the case of certain governmental civil service employees as many as 59 percent elected early retirement.

Ch. 8) toys with the notion that increasing free time makes possible self-expression through political action, a possibility which has concerned some who observe the elderly as frustrated and alienated participants in political activity in the United States. To date, however, these observers do not feel that an effective political bloc of elderly persons is likely to appear or could be sustained even if such appeared (Pinner *et al.*, 1959; Campbell, 1962). Others have expressed some hope that the free time increasingly at the disposal of all adults in our society might be something more than free-from-work or recreation time against the prospect of returning to work. As a case in point, Sebastian de Grazia is quite pessimistic about the possibility of free time's becoming discretionary time, the use of which would result in substantial self-fulfillment and, hence, satisfaction for the contemporary individual who has much free time to spend and the prospect of even more. The reasons for this pessimism are three: (1) the absence of a strong cultural tradition of leisure; (2) a preoccupation with the accumulation of "things," and with wanting "things" which cost money, work, and time and hence lead to moonlighting, overtime, and a working wife rather than to the development of a tradition of leisure and (3) the suspicion that leisure, that is, discretionary time utilized for self-fulfillment as distinct from off-work time, may be beyond the capacity of most people (de Grazia, 1962, pp. 300 f., 369 f.).

A key point in the pessimistic argument of de Grazia, Riesman, G. Friedmann, and other observers of work and leisure in the United States is that a great fracture has appeared in the ethos which historically made work a major anchorage for the male. Off-work time, condemned in the nineteenth century as idleness, has achieved an increasingly respectable status. And work, which is still an important stabilizing force in contemporary

life, has an uncertain future. The situation is further complicated by an unequal distribution of work and leisure, and hence income, over the work life of an individual, and by an inverse relationship between income and the amount of leisure preferred. Leisure per se is not perceived in the typical instance as an attractive form of income, although various mechanisms, such as the guaranteed annual wage, contribute to a change in this direction, at least among blue-collar workers. It is important here to note again that the issue of how to make life socially and economically bearable, if not interesting, when one is not working is visibly a current problem of the elderly. But it is not their problem alone, and this fact will become more evident as off-work time increasingly accumulates for individuals at every age level.

IV

The apparent failure of many industrial workers to find their work a stable and satisfying anchorage point has understandably led to discussions about constructive uses of free (or discretionary) time that might supply the meaning in life which work does not. The prospect that a satisfactory separation is possible, at least in the short run, is not very bright. Wilbert E. Moore (1963, pp. 37 ff.) has succinctly suggested why this is so. His argument focuses attention on the difficulty, if not the impossibility, of arbitrarily separating a social role from the social life-space available to an individual.

Moore argues that the use of discretionary time is a problem when work is a problem. An individual's interests are most likely to be sustained and his aspirations realized when his important social roles have been extensively meshed in a network of satisfying social relationships. In fact, he continues, one index of social participation and integration of an individual might be a "perceived scarcity of time scale," with perception of scarcity positively associated with both social participation and integration. In his discussion of "the orderly career," Wilensky (1961) provides additional insight into the importance of focusing on the work role within, not apart from, its total social context—that is, work experience in which some meaningful positioning of self in relation to others and reasonable advancement are both probable and predictable.

An orderly career is experienced by approximately half the individuals currently in the labor force. Predictably, the individuals most likely to experience an orderly career hold prestigious and economically rewarding positions, whether white-collar or blue-collar. Predictably also, one of the characteristics of such individuals is an above-average exposure to education. Prestige, money, and education are, in turn, important social resources known to be positively correlated with participation in voluntary organizations, general involvement in community activity, and access to power structures.[8] For some men, work becomes the opportunity for participation in a network of social relationships which extend beyond the work place but which are not initially independent of it. Moreover, prestige, money, and education are personal as well as social resources in that they enhance the probability of ego gratification, of a sense of control over the environment, and of a variety of satisfying skills that do not necessarily require interaction with other individuals (e.g., reading and hobbies). In sum, these resources maximize the probability that an individual will develop a satisfying self-image and that he will be able to maintain a satisfying conception of himself even in the event of change.

In a society in which the work role is increasingly irrelevant as a source of satisfaction for many workers and in which the prospect of a disorderly career remains a common fate, a pessimistic forecast about the personal and social consequences of retirement seems quite realistic. Such pessimism would seem warranted even if adequate provision were made for retirement income by one or another mechanism. But it is equally important to note that this forecast applies not to workers in general but to specific workers, particularly those whose work experiences have not served to integrate them in a network of satisfying social relationships in the preretirement years. It is necessary, therefore, to discuss not only the differential meaning of work with occupation controlled but also the differential social participation and integration likely to be correlated with this placement. The need of this kind of specification and differentiation in discussions of retirement as a social event may seem painfully obvious. Yet it is equally obvious that discussions of the social aspects of retirement typically treat this social event as though it had the same, or at least a similar meaning for all workers.[9]

Neither Moore nor Wilensky extrapolates his argument to include the elderly person. If this were done, one would expect that an individual's being elderly, or retired, or both, would not in itself be a sufficient determinant of the probable degree of social participation and integration or of a positive self-concept. Rather, one would expect that the presence or absence of an orderly career in the life experience, together with its implied correlates, would constitute a crucial antecedent variable.[10]

[8] Prestige, money, and power are essential ingredients in the determination of the shorthand designations used to position individuals in a stratification system by social class. While both Wilensky and Moore correctly resist the simple equation of orderly career and a superordinate social class position, the probability of their positive correlation is high.

[9] A notable exception is, of course, the work of Friedmann and Havighurst, 1954.

[10] This is in fact essentially the argument developed in the work of John McKinney, Ida Harper Simpson, and Kurt Back, 1966.

Failure to conceptualize reaction to retirement as a variable (rather than as a social event with a single meaning) related to the particular configuration of experiences which constitute an individual's biography has been a crucial flaw in many studies of retirement. Another flaw of equal importance has been the frequent failure to introduce as an intervening variable the opportunities and constraints in the specific social milieu into which an individual retires. Current critical discussions generated by the proposal to interpret growing old as a process of disengagement have highlighted the unfortunate consequences for adequate understanding of the aging process which follow from these flaws in interpretation.

V

The concept of disengagement has been introduced to identify the model process of mutual withdrawal of aging individuals and society and to describe the state of affairs most likely to produce mutual satisfaction. Retirement is one of the components of the disengaged process and state as initially described by Cumming and Henry (1961), the original proponents of the concept; the positive contribution to the maintenance of morale among elderly males which they implicitly attribute to retirement is of special interest here.

Cumming and Henry have noted "the common reduction in life activities and in ego energy found in most but not all older persons." Moreover, they have proposed that this process of social and psychic withdrawal is to be explained as much, if not more, by psychological events indigenous to the individual as by societal reactions involving the exclusion of the older person from social interaction within the society. Disengagement is intrinsic, hence inevitable. Consequently this process, of which retirement is an integral part, is not only said to be a correlate of successful aging; it is also purportedly a condition of successful aging.

While retirement may lower morale temporarily, they argue, this event is not a problem for most men in the long run *if* health care and economic independence are guaranteed and *if* there is satisfactory integration into an appropriate network of social relationships.

The adequacy of the disengagement interpretation of the aging process as initially described by Cumming and Henry is currently under critical review by them (both of them have had further thoughts)[11] and their colleagues (Havighurst *et al.*, 1963), as well as others (Rose, 1964, Maddox, 1964, II). A quite basic objection to the disengagement formulation is its tendency to treat as relatively insignificant those variations in the constraints of social environment and in the cumulative patterns of experiences which constitute the biographies of individuals.

The possibility has not yet been adequately explored that an individual's life style—reflecting, for example, an orderly career and its correlates—developed during his mature years might be an important variable intervening between his response to retirement and the hypothesized intrapsychic processes of withdrawal. Evidence suggests that retirement of an orderly, career is not likely to have the same meaning as it does for a lower-class male with minimum education and the experience of a disorderly career.[12] Where-

[11] See, for example, Henry, 1963, and Cumming, 1963, 377–393. In fairness to these authors, it should be pointed out that one chapter (XII) in their monograph suggests some conditions under which the course of disengagement would be modified. The main thrust of their original argument, however, is essentially reductionistic; disengagement is said to be inevitable because it is intrinsic.

[12] The Duke University Work and Retirement Study, McKinney *et al.*, 1966, and research reported by Kerckhoff, 1964, lend empirical support to this expectation. See also Friedmann and Havighurst, 1954.

363

as the individual who has experienced a disorderly career may indicate a more favorable preretirement attitude toward his departure from the work force, especially if there is a reasonable prospect for economic security, the individual who has experienced an orderly career brings to this change of status substantially superior personal and social resources, and hence a substantially superior capacity to explore alternatives and, if appropriate, to make compensatory adjustments. With advancing age, which implies a relative decrease in physical resources, the capacity for changing one's "main bets" and for rearranging the "side bets" diminishes in the typical case.[13] However, neither theory nor such evidence as is available encourages one to treat the experience of retirement either as though it had a common, nonsocial explanation or as though it had common meaning and import for individuals with substantially different personal and social resources.

A second objection to the interpretation of the aging process suggested by disengagement theory is the inadequate attention given to variations in situational constraints. Developmental theorists of various persuasions are far too prone to equate observed situational adjustments of individuals with the behavior which would be observed even if the constraints were different. For example Rose believes that "it is a matter mainly of social fact, not so much of natural inevitability, that the American reaching the age of 65 shifts into a social role of disengagements" (Rose, 1964; Blau, 1961).

In sum, despite an extensive literature on retirement which provides many impressions, explanation of the observed variations in the social consequences of retirement in our society remains to be explored systematically. The available re-search has been hampered by substantial methodological problems and, too often, by a simplistic perspective which has not given adequate attention to variations either in personal biography or in situational constraints. One conclusion seems clear, however: to continue to speak of retirement as though it were a single experience with a predictable consequence serves no useful purpose.

VI

Increased economic security is a reasonable prospect for the majority of the elderly approaching retirement. With increased economic security, the negative effect commonly associated with permanent departure from the world of work may be reduced, although probably not eliminated. For many elderly workers, retirement clearly marks their increasing obsolescence and is not a welcome rite of passage. Whatever the origin and justification of concern about the social status of the elderly, consequential efforts at improvement lie not so much with what is done with the current generation of retirees as with what is planned for those who constitute future generations. The matter of education is a case in point.

In discussions of the relevance of education for the problems associated with retirement, manipulation of exposure to formal instruction is commonly mentioned as one strategy for delaying the entrance of the young into the labor force and, hence, for reducing the pressure for removal of the elderly. Such a strategy might be dismissed both as being unlikely to produce the desired effect on the availability of jobs in a shrinking job market and as being very likely to produce equally undesirable effects among the young who wish, for whatever reason, to begin working. There are two, more adequate reasons for focusing our attention on education in terms of increasing the average years of school completed and of improving its quality—specifically, the improvement and increased flexibility of work-

[13] See Becker, 1964. Becker conceptualizes the differential capacities for change in terms of the existing commitments and resources of individuals which make the "side bets" more or less possible and probable.

related skills which will maximize the opportunity for employment, and the development of personal resources which enhance the capacity for satisfying discretionary-time activities.

Our educational problems are complex. Focusing attention on education as one mechanism for dealing with some problems associated with retirement is intended to emphasize the developmental nature of behavior, not the simplicity of educational problems as compared with those of retirement. A new and independent status for the retired elderly will simply be more likely if the personal and social resources appropriate to this status are developed in the younger years.

Reduction of the number of individuals with grossly inadequate exposure to the

educational system may be expected to increase the number of those with the knowledge, skills, and attitudes which either make them fit the needs of the current labor market or, more important, provide them with the resources to adapt with minimum effort to the changing needs of that market. Moreover, in a world in which the ratio of hours spent in the nonwork and work roles is changing dramatically in the direction of nonwork, the necessity of having the educational system address itself to the development of personal and social skills which are relevant for living as well as for making a living is increasingly clear.

40

STEPHEN J. MILLER

THE SOCIAL DILEMMA OF THE AGING LEISURE PARTICIPANT

In anticipation of the day when the worker retires, the day he will lose his occupational identity and functional role, he is encouraged by his family, friends, and even employer, to adjust by spending his leisure time in some activity which holds meaning for him. It is assumed that the problem of retirement adjustment will be solved if the individual will engage in some sort of activity which will fill his leisure time. Such an attitude to the value of leisure for adjustment during old age takes little note of the associational aspects and social needs of life. For example, solitary leisure will not provide a person with the opportunity for interpersonal contacts and might well only increase withdrawal from social participation. Even those activities which provide interpersonal contacts may not provide a social group which will replace former co-workers. A recreational group may facilitate the development of an identity, but, as Cavan notes, the identity may well be limited and may not be expressible in any group except the recreational group itself (Cavan, 1962, pp. 529–30).

If leisure activities are to provide a new role, the retired person must engage in some meaningful activity, appropriate in terms of cultural values, which will afford him a rationale for a social identity and a concept of self. In the case of the retired person participating in leisure activity, this poses a dilemma—that is, he must jus-

Abridged from *Older People and Their Social World: The Subculture of the Aging,* ed. Arnold M. Rose and Warren A. Peterson (Philadelphia: F. A. Davis Co., 1965), chap. 5, pp. 79–92.

tify an identity in terms of his leisure activity which is by definition "superfluous in character, extraordinary . . . and stands apart from work." "While [leisure] has a definite value," writes Cavan, "to make a career of recreation, hobbies, and the like, goes against deeply instilled values."

THE TRADITION OF LEISURE AND THE AGING

Work and leisure are complementary components of human activity. The style and pattern of both are reflections of the culture of the time and subject to the societal ideology, development, and organization which are characteristic of that culture. "The problems faced in studying leisure," writes Gross, "are both consequence and cause of the problems faced in studying work, for one is usually defined as the absence of or preparation for the other" (Gross, 1961, p. 2). In the light of the complementary nature of work and leisure, a consideration of the leisure activity of the aging must also be concerned with the social developments which affect work and the cultural values which dominate the social circumstances. Historically, three work-leisure traditions are discernible: (1) pre-industrial: traditional work alleviated by related customs, practices, and rites; (2) industrial: the polar opposition of work and leisure, and (3) post-industrial, or contemporary: the integration of work and leisure (Larrabee and Meyersohn, 1960; Riesman, 1950).

The pre-industrial culture, based on an agricultural economy and rural in character, lacked (with few exceptions) any commercial recreation or organized leisure which would draw the person away from his work and family. Clement Greenberg notes that most work during this period was "work on the land . . . adulterated more or less by irrational practices—customs, rites, observances— that, conceived of originally as means of helping work . . . actually furnished occasions *inside* work for relief from the strain of its purposefulness" (Greenberg, 1953, p. 58). The cultural tradition did not separate work and leisure, nor did the demands of labor segment the life of the person into a world of work and another of the family (Dulles, 1950). The place of finding some activity which would amuse or occupy the old was non-existent, for the old remained functional until failing health forced withdrawal from most, if not all, activity.

The rise of industrialization and the accompanying urbanization not only affected the economy of Western culture but had a decided impact, one still felt on the social life of the person. Work, which required organization and structure to assure efficiency and production, became the central life interest, regulating economic, social, and family life. Unlike the pre-industrial period, the place of work was no longer the home but a place removed from home and family. The extended family was becoming a thing of the past and its social life, which the aged had previously enjoyed, was rapidly curtailed. "To the exact end of greater productivity," writes Greenberg, "capitalism, Protestantism, and industrialism have brought about a separation of work from all that is not work which is infinitely sharper and more exclusive than ever in the past" (1953). The time not occupied by work, that is, leisure, became diametrically opposed to productive labor, and the Puritanical tradition emphasizing work as the major cultural value was established. In this period, a man's work as the basis of his social identity has its roots,

and his functional role, in terms of cultural values, emerges. In accordance with the structured nature of work, labels were attached to various types of work placing men in categories and locating them in the patterned activities of society. The functional role and occupational identity of the person were readily available for evaluation by his social audience. A man's conception of himself, developed and reinforced by his recurrent social relationships, was directly influenced by his work (cf. Hughes, 1951, pp. 313–23).

A society which emphasizes efficiency and production will define the value of the person in terms of his ability to play a functional role in the industrial system. When, as in the case of growing old, an individual is subject to limitations which presumably reduce his ability to play such a role, he must be removed and replaced —hence, the development of an industrial policy toward old age requiring occupational retirement at some point in the life cycle. The industrial changes not only established the occupational role as the basis for social identity but also developed the manner in which that identity could be subverted. The constituent elements of work—a work group and a work situation —are the basis of a culturally approved and personally acceptable self-concept. These are lost to the older person when he is retired from the vocational world to which he has belonged. In place of work, the retired worker is offered leisure which is the opposite of work and of doubtful, if not negative, cultural value. In such cultural circumstances, leisure participation cannot reduce the problem of finding a new identity and role. The lack of an occupational identity is culturally characteristic of the old, and leisure activity only supports the position of the old as non-meaningful, non-functional or, at best, superannuated.

In post-industrial society, or, for the

purposes of this study, in the "American" pattern of work and leisure, work remains as the basis of social identity. However, the nature of work has changed. The boredom of routine and the performance of repetitive tasks has been noted and acknowledged—in fact, work no longer requires the degree of routine and structuralization that was necessary during the early phases of industrialization. The nature of contemporary work has led to attempts to make work meaningful and reduce fatigue and boredom, though, as Riesman notes, "by and large [they] succeeded only in making it more time-consuming and gregarious but not more challenging" (1960, p. 367). Whatever the reasons, though apparently they are functional, a characteristic of the twentieth century is the re-introduction of leisure into work. Gross explains the situation in terms of the concept of adaptation as follows: "Work results, inevitably, in fatigue and often in boredom, and one of the forms of leisure—recreation—is essential here insofar as it restores, though, it is recognized, it may not always do so" (1961, p. 5). The nature of work has come a full cycle and is marked by related customs, practices, and rites, furnishing occasions of leisure inside work to alleviate fatigue and boredom.[1] Outside work, Rose indicates that "the opportunity to engage in something creative, even if only in a hobby association, provides a compensation for the deadening effect of working on a simple repetitive task . . ." (1956, p. 330).

In addition to the reduction of opposition between work and leisure, a cultural value which affects the American pattern of life is the contemporary emphasis on action. In much the same manner as work and leisure were earlier opposed, activity of any sort is valued over non-activity. "People who are not active," writes Buhler, "are made to feel useless, indeed, even worthless" (Buhler, 1961 I, p. 35). Hence, in terms of the contemporary scheme of work and leisure, in which leisure has become a value, the older person showing an interest in some activity, no matter what, is less subject to social labeling as "non-functional," "ineffectual," and so on, than one who disengages himself from activity. It would appear, therefore, that leisure has the potentiality to reduce the social loss to which the aged are subject and facilitate adjustment. This new social situation of the aging is a way open to those of the aging who wish to remain socially active but resist the cultural trends which are making the elderly more segregated from other age categories. They may employ their leisure as an opportunity to establish an identification with other groups in society. That is, they may reduce their social loss by participating in activities which are respected in general by others as well as by those of their own social category or group.

THE RATIONALE FOR LEISURE

The problem of social adjustment faced by the leisure participant is apparently rooted in the lack of social substance (meaning) or cultural value of the majority of ways in which he might occupy his leisure time. In the light of the values which are characteristic of the American pattern of life, the person who is now free of work should be socially able to overcome the problem by spending his leisure in some activity which holds meaning for him and is generally respected by others. If this were the sole dimension of the problem, then participation in systematized leisure groups would not only fulfill the social needs of the older person, but facilitate the development of a new social identity as well. However, the work which the person is ultimately free of is

[1] The image of the congenial group at the office water-cooler, the coffee break, and even the office Christmas party, which is fast disappearing, are examples. Of course all such customs and practices are not occasions of leisure but may as well be worker rebellion, "goofing off," etc. Cf. Riesman, 1960, p. 372.

exactly that which has allowed him to justify leisure or, as Mead has put it, work is not only necessary to obtain the means but the right to leisure (1957).

An employed person, prior to his retirement with its loss of occupational identity, is free to use his leisure time any way he chooses. No matter how far removed from work, so long as the leisure activity is not otherwise culturally defined as deviant, a rationale is readily available to justify its legitimacy. The interrelationship of work and leisure as a necessary condition for adjustment to and performance of work plus the value placed on activity are the constituent elements of that rationale. Those who are engaged in work are not required to justify their leisure since socially supportive factors, occupational identity, and the halo effects of labor operate on the social circumstances to do just that. On the other hand, the older person operates without such support. For example, the employed person occupied in leisure activity of some sort will, more often than not, be perceived by others as engaged in "recreation" whereas the retired person engaged in the same activity will be perceived as occupying his "free" time. In other words, the numerous activities in which the older person may participate, thereby reducing the degree of his social loss, may have no further cultural value than that they are "activity."

A career of leisure (play) is characteristic of the socially immature (children) or the socially superannuated. For the aging individual, it can only serve to add to his social loss, negating any social benefits that might be derived from remaining active by serving to reinforce a definition of him as superannuated. There are other leisure interests—for example, genealogy, the writing of an ethnic cook book, family history or autobiography, to mention a few encountered by the writer—which are often considered to be interests peculiar to people nearing the end of life, the assumption being that such interests

are reflections of a concern with perpetuating life in some manner or with death itself. It is also likely that participation in groups created for, and composed of, older people only which offer an old age identity—for example, the Golden Age Club or Senior Citizens—only aggravate the social situation of the aged by reinforcing the stereotype of the older person as one set apart from those who are not old. This is one of the factors in the development of an aging subculture. The older person, in order to establish a new identity and acceptable self-concept on the basis of leisure must first establish a rationale for the activity on which he bases that new or altered identity. He must legitimatize it in some manner other than in those terms which sanction leisure for the very young and old. The leisure activity of the retired and elderly must, therefore, be in some way appropriate in terms of traditional and contemporary values which do not apply specifically to the aging but to the population in general.

The retired leisure participant is in the unique position not only of having to find an activity in which to participate but, once having found such an activity, if he wishes to reduce his social loss, also of establishing a meaningful rationale for participating in that activity at all. The current compatibility of work and leisure offers the older person an opportunity to change his social situation—that is, to establish the cultural value of his leisure which will act as the basis for a social identity. He may do so by introducing, in much the same fashion as leisure has been introduced into work, aspects of work into his leisure. The person may choose among the alternative avocations available to him those which offer the possibility of establishing a rationale, in keeping with the cultural and social circumstances, which will serve to legitimize a social future. The problems posed by aging and retirement have been well documented, but the manner in which the aging introduce aspects of work into leisure and establish an appropriate rationale for this has, to the writer's knowledge, been explored only incidentally.

The attitude regarding meaningful leisure participation and the elements of a rationale are expressed in the following comments of the wife of an aging leisure participant: "Hobbies are eccentric when you never make anything [useful] out of them or get anything [monetary] out of them." It is not simply participation in *some activity* which is desirable but participation in activity with culturally acceptable manifest goals, or at least with latent implications of being useful and/or gainful in some way.

A notable example of the way in which such a rationale for useful and gainful activity may be established is the case of the aging American collector of coins, stamps, books, antiques, and what have you. The gainful rationale for a leisure activity is similar to the major perspective to these modern collectors which parallels and reflects the current and growing interest of the general population in the stock market, investment programs, etc., and is focused on the monetary and investment aspects of collecting. The following comments by a collector with some thirty years' experience bring this out:

"It [leisure] can be commercial. When I started [collecting] people took the time and trouble of assembling a collection. The real interest was research and the arrangement of your collection . . . the originality of showing, too. Only a little attention, if any, was paid the expense of collecting. Now, thousands and thousands of people, because of the publicity that has been given to the value of coins and stamps, have gone into collecting. They [collectors] go to banks and to the mints and buy coins and put them away for the future or sell them. In other words, they are *investors* and *speculators.*"

In addition to the collector who may also be an investor and speculator, there are, for example: (1) persons who buy, restore or otherwise improve, and sell antiques, household goods, appliances, etc.; (2) the handicraftsman, who may find a market, or at least a demand, for what he makes; and (3) the do-it-yourself person who manages to supplement the neighborhood or community demand for the skilled labor which is becoming increasingly expensive and difficult to find. These examples certainly do not exhaust the variety of activities which lend themselves to a gainful rationale; they are illustrative of the way in which personally meaningful activity can be infused with the aspects of work which are culturally understood and accepted. It is interesting that many of the retired individuals who are so engaged deny that their activity is work in the traditional sense. The activity is enjoyable, interesting, or challenging, only incidentally profitable, and rarely, if ever, demanding. If what is labeled leisure were to be defined as work, the person would be expending himself entirely in work without leisure and operating in a manner contrary to the American pattern of work and leisure.

Other types of activity, though in no way economically productive, are contributory to the general good and may be exploited by the person as a basis for a new social identity. Those who offer their leisure service to others—the retired cabinet-maker who supplements the efforts of the high school manual arts teacher, or the older woman who becomes an integral part of the community hospital as a volunteer—enjoy high public esteem by acting in a subordinate auxiliary role to more essential work roles. These activities and the roles which the aged may assume in them are part of larger work systems which lend them vicarious status, authority, and other meaningful satisfactions which operate to the social advantage of the participants, allowing them to establish a useful rationale for their leisure.

Though slightly more difficult for the participant to legitimize, activity which is educational or develops a skill or talent also provides a social future since there exists the potentiality for its future productive application.

The economic perspective on leisure reflects a contemporary cultural value, an economic ethic, so to speak, while the supplemental nature of other useful activities meets certain societal needs. Activity in these spheres will be defined as acceptable if presented in the appropriate terms. It will not be perceived as far removed from work since, like work, it offers a reward for labor or is contributory to work in some way, factors which can be employed in evaluating the worth of the individual. Any activity presented in these terms has recognizable goals which lend it meaning and, therefore, is considered as an understandable activity in which to engage. In much the same manner as the person preparing for an occupation attempts to determine the worth of the activity on which his identity will be based, the aging retired person establishes the worth of his avocational activity to legitimize a base for a new social identity—that is, to justify a career of leisure.

THE PORTENT OF EMBARRASSMENT

The rationale for leisure, once established, provides a background for the social participation of the involuntarily retired person which allows the projection of a meaningful and acceptable social future on which may be based a new identity. However, the person is not entirely free of the social implications of his retirement and advanced age. He has not left his occupational role in a way which reflects favorably upon his ability to perform a work role, in particular, and other social roles, in general—that is, he is still, though somewhat less, vulnerable to the stigma attached to retirement (cf. Goffman, 1952, 1955). In addition, he must continue to operate in an age-graded so-

cial system which defines the aging as people who are most likely to fail. Once the person has selected a leisure activity which offers him a social future and identity, that social future remains subject, within the leisure group, to the implications of retirement and aging.

If a rationale is to be maintained and an identity developed, the person, once he participates in some activity, must be capable of supporting a role in the group throughout the social interactions and performances required of a participant. Identity, writes Gross and Stone, "must be continually reaffirmed, must be maintained, and provision made for repair in case of breakdown" (Gross and Stone, unpub.). The result of identity breakdown—a social occurrence which belies what the person has announced he is, and what he is capable of, by assuming the role of participant—is embarrassment. In turn, embarrassment makes continued role performance difficult and undermines the foundation of the new identity.

The results of embarrassment are most often treated in terms of their implications for the continued social participation of the person. That is, once an embarrassing encounter or performance has taken place the question is, what are the social implications for the person (cf. Gross and Stone, unpub.; Goffman, 1952, 1955, 1956). The implications of embarrassment may also be considered in a related though somewhat extended manner: A person who is aware of some socially restrictive factors to which he is subject may anticipate the embarrassing encounter and subsequent identity breakdown, and choose either to curtail or end participation entirely. That is to say, embarrassment not only has implications for continued but also for initial social participation as well. In any analysis of the leisure careers of the aging the factor of social embarrassment, including both actual and anticipated embarrassing encounters, is particularly important. The implications of actual embarrassment for social performance have been treated elsewhere by others and apply equally to the situation of the aging leisure participant; the writer will concern himself with anticipatory embarrassment, that is, the portent of embarrassment, as a correlate of social participation and its implications for social performance.

The obvious implication of the portent of embarrassment is that it may result in the aging person excluding himself from social interaction with others not of his social category. The frequency of possibly embarrassing encounters would be higher for the person participating in the social system at large than for the person limiting his participation to groups which are composed of members who share his circumstances, problems, and concerns—that is, a group of older people. The portent of embarrassment operates, in addition to the circumstances noted by Rose (1965), to facilitate the development of a subculture of the aging. It is sufficient for the purposes of this essay, since Rose discusses the subculture of the aging at length, to note that the positive affinity many other people have for each other may well be the result of negative expectations of social participation with persons not of their social category or group. A similar argument may be offered in explanation of the apparent decline in social participation of people as they grow older —that is, they become increasingly aware of the possibility of social embarrassment and make preparations accordingly.

In the work conducted by the writer, those of the aged who were only somewhat active offered the obvious reasons, such as, health, expense, transportation, as explanations of their limited participation. These recurrent themes, however, seemed to be but reflections of a more socially based reason for non-participation. In general, non-participation or limited participation was a matter of choice resulting from a feeling of inability to meet the demands of participating. The person who embarks on a leisure career is announcing who he is and what he is capable of; he is committing himself to a role which requires he meet the expectations of others. If he feels or finds that he is unable to meet these expectations, or expects to encounter difficulty which would subvert his identity, role, and self-concept, he is likely to choose not to make such a commitment or limit his participation of those aspects of an activity which reduce the possibility of identity subversion and embarrassment.

As observed by, or told to, the writer, the instances of embarrassment which caused the aging leisure participant particular concern, and were usually accompanied by decreased commitment or participation, were one or more of the following types: (1) an inability to reciprocate due to family, economic, or health circumstances which could be attributed to aging; (2) requests for the performance of a task which the person was assumed prepared for, or capable of, because of his age and experience but for which he was not—that is, the peculiar position of the older person as a novice and subordinate to the younger participants; and (3) faux pas which announced to other participants that the person and his knowledge were superannuated ("How would you like some young wiseguy to tell you things aren't done that way anymore?") The portent of embarrassment, anticipation of the occurrence of such social incidents, has, for at least a minority of the aging, a decided effect on the pattern of their participation. It influences a number of variables usually employed to measure social participation —for example, number and type of voluntary associations, frequency of attendance at meetings, number of contacts with others engaged in the activity, and the social category of those who are contacted.

It is possible that the portent of embarrassment may assume such proportions that it inhibits entirely participation in any specific activity. If a person, under these circumstances, withdraws from the activity but replaces it with another which reduces the portent of embarrassment (assuming a rationale to which he may subscribe is available), he continues to minimize his social loss and retains a base for an identity.[2] On the other hand, the person who withdraws and has no suitable replacement places himself in a situation in which he is subject to the additional stigma of non-activity. The attempt to erase the stigma of non-participation usually results in solitary activity of some sort, for example, reading. A number of aging leisure participants who were interviewed had done this and employed health, expense, and transportation, as an understandable rationale for non-participation in systematized or group leisure.

The aging are not operating alone to avoid embarrassing encounters and reduce the portent of embarrassment. The aging participant is perceived as the person most likely to fail and "becomes defined as someone who must not fail, while at the same time arrangements are made to decrease the chances of his failing" (Goffman, 1952, p. 499). The arrangements made by other participants to assure that embarrassment will not occur is not the result of an altruistic or patronizing concern with the problems faced by the aging. Embarrassment not only incapacitates the embarrassed person but others with whom he is interacting as well. When the identity of the aged participant is subverted, it is difficult for others to continue interacting and inhibits the social performances of all participants. "Embarrassment," writes Gross and Stone, "exaggerates the core dimensions of social transactions, bringing them to the eye of the observer in an almost naked state, for

[2] The portent of embarrassment offers an interesting scheme for the analysis of the acceptance of some and the rejection of other activities by the aging.

embarrassment occurs whenever some central prop in the transaction has unexpectedly given way so that the whole encounter collapses" (Gross and Stone, unpub. p. 2). The occurrance of embarrassment incapacitates all the performers for the continued and possibly future performances of their roles by disrupting identity and destroying the assumptions the performers have made about each other—assumptions on which they operate socially.

In the specific social system in which the older person is active, the portent of embarrassment may, and often does, result in his being excluded from interaction with other participants not of his social category. The result is increased interaction between the aging who share a common situation and the development of a group identification of the aging within the system. However, in systems which are not specifically for one social category, it is necessary for purposes of structure and cohesion that the roles played by the various participants be integrated into the role-scheme of the system.

The anticipation of social difficulty for and with the aging by other participants encourages them to make available to the older person a role which he is capable of assuming, or at least less likely to fail at playing. The problem of embarrassment and its ramifications are avoided by providing the aging participant with a social role within the system which he can maintain—that is, an identity system of interactions and performances of which he is capable. The older person is induced to assume this role identity by others who ascribe the necessary attributes to him and interact with him as if he did possess these attributes.

There are numerous cases which illustrate the action taken to avoid embarrassment for and with the aging. The family in need of home improvements, which the aging handy-man who services the neighborhood is not capable of carrying out, may call him in for consultation before hiring an outside firm or tradesman to do the work. If the handy-man had not been involved in some manner, by implication his identity would have been subverted and future interaction with him impossible. On the other hand, if he had been expected or allowed to do the work, the anticipated unfavorable outcome would have been equally embarrassing and ended the relationship. The solution was the ascription of certain qualifications as an expert to the handy-man, attributes inducing him to assume a role which he was capable of performing and allowing him to maintain his identity.

To be a member of a subordinate auxiliary group is also defined in a way which allows for a supportable identity for the older person. The main organization which the auxiliary group serves has a staff with occupational and professional roles which operate to delimit the activity of the older person. For example, the hospital volunteer is prohibited by their operational codes to assume the role of doctor, nurse, or of any other ancillary hospital personnel—only those activities which may be and are delegated to the volunteer are undertaken. The tasks delegated—for example, personal contact with the patient or with the family of the patient—comprise a role, status, or relationship, and are never such as to make great demands on the person. In more formal recreation, i.e., systematized leisure, possibly the most important roles the older person may play are that of "recruiter" and "socializer." By recruiting and socializing new members the aging participant not only facilitates the entrance of the novice into the activity group, but also contributes to group structure and the efforts of the group to perpetuate itself. Other roles for which the aging are considered suited and likely not to fail at are "learned elder," "keeper of the tradition," and, for those who have specialized and are recognized as proficient, "expert" or "resource person."

Though participants in social and leisure groups attempt to induce the aging participant to assume roles which lessen the portent of embarrassment, as noted earlier, the reasons are not patronizing. In addition to the services mentioned, such roles for the aging act to reduce the demands made on the time and energy of other participants. The roles have intrinsic value and are not artificially created to meet the needs of the aging. In these terms, the "most challenging problem of solving the present roleless role of the aging" is not so much *inventing* new leisure patterns and functional roles for the aging—which will only become culturally defined as "for the old"—as determining what roles presently exist in the social system, related to a specific sub-system and offering vicarious satisfactions, that can reduce the socially debilitating loss accompanying occupational retirement.

PART VII

THE IMMEDIATE SOCIAL ENVIRONMENT

A large number of empirical studies of aging are now appearing which demonstrate a point that any social scientist regards as a truism: namely, that the individual's behavior varies directly with the characteristics of his immediate social environment. In making selections for this section, the problem has not been to provide evidence of this fact, but only to illustrate some of the parameters of the social environment that have thus far been investigated.

The first brief paper by Williams and Loeb sets forth the concept of social life space as it may be useful in organizing various items of information about an individual's social behavior and in pointing to a method of studying consistency and change in the social aspects of the life-cycle. (The concept has been elaborated, for example, in studying the social systems or social networks of older people, reported in the book by Williams and Wirth, *Lives through the Years*, 1965.)

Rosow's paper deals with the dimension of residential density or concentration: that is, the proportion of old people residing in the immediate housing area, as this dimension relates to patterns of informal associations. Based on a study of 1200 older people, middle class and working class residents of several hundred apartment buildings in Cleveland, the paper presents a number of interesting findings regarding friendship and neighboring patterns in different social classes, in men compared to women, in persons who vary in health, in work status, and in marital status, all in relation to degree of density. Of particular relevance here are two of Rosow's major findings: first, that the number of old people's friends varies directly with the proportion of older neighbors available; second, regardless of the number, friends consist disproportionately of older rather than younger neighbors. (The last finding is of interest also because of its implications regarding age-grading. Old persons are shown to choose their associates primarily from among other old people; and the assumption that residential proximity results in friendships between younger and older people is not borne out.)

The paper by Lowenthal and Haven is a tightly-woven summary of findings from an extensive study of 280 healthy and mentally impaired elderly persons in San Francisco regarding the social factors related to adjustment. The distinction is drawn between three definitions of adjustment: subjective (defined in terms of morale or self-esteem); professional (defined by psychiatrists); and social (defined by the ability to maintain oneself in the community versus being confined in a mental hospital); and the factors associated with adjustment are shown to be different in each instance. (One important implication is that mental illness differs in kind, not merely in degree, from demoralization.) The paper highlights the importance of intimate social relationships by showing that the presence of a confidante is of crucial significance in assisting the older person to adjust to the social stresses of aging. In other words, presence or absence of a confidante emerges as a critical element of the social environment.

The next two papers illustrate how behavioral changes occur in older people when their living arrangements are altered. The paper by Aldrich and Mendkoff is based on a study of relocation in which a group of disabled persons were moved from an institution in which they had lived for varying lengths of time, and shows that for patients over 70 the death rate within the first three months after relocation was $3\frac{1}{2}$ times the expected rate. The author points to the role of emotional stress in precipitating death and gives a number of case reports as examples of various emotional reactions. The findings from this study, while striking, are in general agreement with other studies which show high death rates following certain types of relocation, as when persons enter mental hospitals, nursing homes, or homes for the aged. (The present study has the advantage that data were available for calculating expected death rates as well as actual death rates, thus providing a certain baseline for helping to answer the question, Are such high death rates related in truth to the change in social environment, or is it that the people who find their ways into institutions are closer to death than other people? In this study, change seems to be the relevant factor.)

The paper by Carp is another assessment of the impact of changed housing; but in this instance, the changes are in the opposite direction. Several hundred older people were studied when they applied for apartments in a new high-rise residence being completed by a city housing authority. After a period of 12 to 15 months, a followup was made both on the group who now lived in the new facility and on a similar group whose applications had been unsuccessful. (This study, like Aldrich's, has the advantage of base-line data by which to assess change.) Assessments of change were made in terms of directly expressed satisfaction with the new housing, changes in life style (number of services people felt they needed; budgeting arrangements; patterns of so-

cial interaction; views of themselves; feelings about health). Changes were consistently in the direction of good adjustment for the group who had moved.

Perhaps in these and other such studies the important variable is whether the move is involuntary, as in the Aldrich study, or voluntary, as in the Carp study. Despite the contrasting effects, both studies illustrate the importance of living arrangements as a significant dimension of the social environment and show that the behavior of older people changes in direct response to change in their social situations.

The last two readings in this section are of a somewhat different character. In the examples of diaries taken from Peter Townsend's *The Family Life of Old People* can be caught something of the flavor of the daily life of one man and one woman who live in Bethnal Green, a working-class area of London. Indirectly, the diaries refer to the concept of the social life space as described in the Williams and Loeb paper, first paper in this section, for they show that social life space can be understood from accounts of the daily round of activities.

The final selection is a short story, this time of an aged woman who is persuaded to move from her own home into the home of her daughter. Written in the first person singular, the story conveys something of the complex reactions of a sensitive old woman who feels caught in a well-intended but uncomfortable situation in which she feels she is playing a "game." The story illustrates how fragile the social world of an older person may be and how a small event can alter the balance toward distress or comfort.

41

RICHARD H. WILLIAMS and MARTIN B. LOEB

THE ADULT'S SOCIAL LIFE SPACE AND SUCCESSFUL AGING: SOME SUGGESTIONS FOR A CONCEPTUAL FRAMEWORK

Studies of the psychological and social aspects of aging have been concerned with three general problems: (1) how to define and analyze the major variables in adult personality as they change with age in the later years; (2) how to define and analyze variables in the social situations of persons in these years; and (3) how to establish normative concepts and normative data concerning degrees of "adaptation," "adjustment" or "success" in the process of aging. Each problem presents numerous difficulties in conceptualization and in methods of gathering and processing appropriate data. The relation between the three problems presents special difficulties of its own. The present discussion proposes some concepts which, it is felt, might be useful in clarifying this relation.

The social sciences have done relatively little research and have evolved relatively little by way of a systematic conceptual scheme for describing and evaluating the social life of a particular person. Sociologists have tended to do research either on large-scale societal and institutional patterns, or on small group processes, usually under rather artificial conditions. They have tended to neglect the analysis of immediate social systems as they surround and influence given subjects on a day by day basis. It does seem possible and desirable to develop a conceptual framework which will allow for generalizations comparing individual patterns of social relations. In order to de-

Paper presented at the Annual Meeting of the American Gerontology Society, Chicago, 1956.

velop such a framework one starts with the individual and works out to his broader social relations rather than starting with society and working toward the individual.

We may begin by asking such questions as: With whom does a given person interact and with how many people does he interact? How often and how long? How intimate is he with whom in his social world? Are the people active in his social environment similar to himself or is there a range or variety of such persons? Is he sometimes subordinate, sometimes peer, and sometimes superordinate, or is one position dominant in his social activities?

From answers to questions such as these a social map may be projected. It is this map which we think of as an individual's "social life space." From a study of these maps we can explore systematically the social reality within which an individual lives, the bases of his interaction with other individuals, and the degree of congruence between images he has of himself and the images others have of him.

We can assume that there is a pattern or order in these interactions. An individual has few or many individuals with whom he interacts; he may interact with greater or lesser intensity; his interactions may be simple or varied, that is, the people he interacts with may be similar or of a great variety. Number, intensity, and complexity may then be thought of as three major dimensions which make up an individual's social life space. Furthermore, this space may well vary in relation to age, sex, social class, and personality structure.

For the dimension of *number* we can find out how many contacts he has with how many other individuals. He may interact with a few people often, many people rarely, or some people sometimes. Concerning the dimension of *intensity* one can set up measures for the degree of intimacy he has with the people with whom he interacts. By intimacy one might use the notion of empathy, or the degree to which projection of self onto the other is accurate. One could also inject the notion of the sharing of emotional life. Or one might adopt the approach of Erving Goffman and look at the amount of "back stage" interaction as opposed to "on stage" or "face saving" behavior. The dimension of *complexity* refers specifically to the degree of variety of social relationships a person experiences. Are his contacts with people of the same or both sexes? Do they include people of the same age, older and younger? Are there in this spectrum people whose roles are primarily grandparent, parent, child, single, married, etc., Are there people who differ from the subject under study by occupation? Do they live in the same or different neighborhoods? Are all his contacts in the same social class or does he maintain relationships to those of higher and lower social status? These and similar categories make up the possible variety in modern life. To what extent does he use these available resources? What kind of a pattern of social life is characteristic of a given individual?

We can go a step further and ask: what is an appropriate or healthy pattern of social life for an individual of given age, sex, social class, and physical health status. In relating the life space to age, sex, social class, and personality, we might expect to establish some norms for healthy, or at least appropriate social life spaces. In assessing an individual's social life space we shall have to pay attention not only to those interactions which are found, but also to those which for him are humanly and socially possible. This is especially true in the study of aging. It is suspected that there is a tendency toward constriction of the social life space in the aging process, but we do not know its extent, nor when it is pathological. One might test the hypothesis that is widely held, at least on an implicit basis, that continuous stimulation and social interaction may be necessary to continued vitality. At the descriptive level one can delineate the structure and functions of an individual's present social life space and at the evaluative level one can develop norms to assess the adequacy of social behavior and the use made of potential social resources. Furthermore, one can perhaps isolate the pathogenic social life spaces, some of which might be universal and some of which might be pathogenic only for a given age, sex, social class, and personality constellation. For example, one can isolate such a pattern as that of a few relationships, high intimacy, low variety as seen in the aged man whose only contacts are with his wife and brother. Then there is the man with many contacts but none he can count on, even though they are of both sexes, many ages, and different occupations. How bleak it is to describe the lonely person with a few casual friends of the same age and sex, but with whom no intimacy or interdependence can be found; and how full is the life of the man who has many friends of many varieties with some of whom he is on fairly intimate terms. One can, however, also test the notion that each of these patterns may be healthy or appropriate in certain circumstances.

The concept of "successful" aging, and related concepts of health or pathogenic factors, may be approached both analytically and empirically. Analytically, successful aging would mean that a person is able to maintain an optimal position within his social life space in relation to his psychological and biological capacities. Some balance is maintained between inner resources and the immediate social systems surrounding the person. Shifts in

380

either aspect of this balance can produce stress. There is a continuum from "success" to "failure" in the way such stresses are met.

We can presume from our general knowledge of social and cultural systems that successful aging, as abstractly defined, can have a variety of contents. There will probably be significant variations in this respect by sub-groups, perhaps particularly by social classes and by careers and career clusters. We can also expect some margin of idiosyncratic variation. Hence, we should not establish specific criteria of success in terms of its content, a priori.

For operating within this conceptual framework some methodological items must be spelled out in greater detail. From the Study of Adult Life in Kansas City we have taken from Dr. Robert J. Havighurst's research the notion of social roles as a way of categorizing the organized segments of social behavior of the individual. These social roles may also provide the bases of the organization of data from which to study social life space. We may, for example, look at a person's activities in terms of the following social roles: (1) family of procreation roles, such as parent, grandparent, aunt and uncle, etc.; (2) family of orientation roles —adult child of aging parents, sibling, etc.; (3) societal roles, such as worker, citizen, friend, group, association or church member. Each of these roles involves relations with others on a mutual basis. For each role one can, as Dr. Havighurst has done, measure the adequacy of performance. In addition, one can draw the outline of social life space and relate the adequacy of role performance to the shape of the map.

In assessing the adequacy of role performance we look for the amount of participation in each role, the richness or the creative aspect of participation, and the complexity of participation patterns. To do this adequately, we not only want to get the description and evaluation of role activities by self-report, we also want to obtain from significant others in the person's social life space a description and evaluation of the subject's activities. These descriptions and evaluations may be made more meaningful when the individual studied is also asked to discuss the significant others who are evaluating and describing him. This provides us with self-other images and the expectations involved in them.

A person's social life space is related not only to present but to past experiences. The career of an individual may be thought of as a series of life spaces. Although one must always doubt the accuracy of a report on past experiences, it is possible that if we describe life career in terms of social roles and significant changes in roles or role activity and relate them by date or age, we might be able to draw outlines of past social life spaces and extract developmental stages. By doing cross-sectional and longitudinal studies as in the Kansas City study we can describe the various social life spaces of different types and individuals. From this kind of study it is hoped to derive standards so that we can begin to set up norms for different types of people at different ages. We can, in effect, postulate that for certain types at a given age, a certain life space is appropriate and should be achieved. In essence to achieve an appropriate social life space becomes an important developmental task.

This analysis of social life space complements the analysis of adult personality patterns and gives us usable sociological conceptualizations adequate to encompass the psychosocial complexities of individual adaptation. This conceptual framework then not only provides a way of organizing personal social data but to the extent that it does so successfully it may be a basic contribution to sociological theory and to conceptualization concerning the relationships of the individual to the total society.

42

IRVING ROSOW

HOUSING AND LOCAL TIES OF THE AGED

Professional people (medical practitioners, gerontologists, social workers, etc.) who work directly with the elderly are convinced that neighbors of different ages develop viable social relationships and mutual support. Such friendships, they believe, sustain the morale of older people as well as contribute to their youthfulness and independence. They therefore conclude that residential proximity of the generations should maximize the social integration of the aged.

Social theorists take the opposite view. They feel that informal association develops around similar statuses, of which age is one extremely powerful factor. Consequently, social structure reinforces age-grading, erects barriers to intergenerational relations, and focuses friendship within age groups. Accordingly, residential proximity should not integrate the old and the young. Local friendships should develop more *within* than *between* generations, and old people are more likely to have friends of their own age than they are to have younger ones.

This analysis results in two hypotheses. First, the number of old people's friends will vary with the proportion of older neighbors. Second, regardless of the number, these friends will consist disproportionately of older rather than younger neighbors.

Reprinted from *Patterns of Living and Housing of Middle-aged and Older People: Proceedings of Research Conference, 1965* (Washington, D.C.: United States Department of Health, Education, and Welfare, 1965), chap. 5, pp. 47–57.
This subject is explored more fully in the author's *The Social Integration of the Aged* (New York: The Free Press of Glencoe, 1967).

These were the basic hypotheses in a study of 1,200 older people—middle-class and working-class residents of several hundred Cleveland apartment buildings. The apartments varied in the proportion of older tenants—literally, the percentage of households with an aged member (a man 65 or older, a woman 62 or older).

Normal . . . . 1 to 15 percent of households having an aged member

Concentrated . . . . 33 to 49 percent of households having an aged member

Dense . . . . 50+ percent of households having an aged member

In the working class, public housing projects were used, and only *Normal* (1% to 15%) and *Dense* (50+%) buildings were available. In the middle class, all types of apartments were used, but a special middle-class group of residents of four retirement *Hotels* (75+%) was added. Because these categories differ in residential density (or concentration) of the aged, we refer to them as "density" areas or groups. Thus, to test our hypotheses, our independent variable is the residential density of old people (of two social classes), and our dependent variables are the number and age of their neighbor-friends.

In our sample, preliminary analysis has verified two basic propositions about friendship and social class. First, the middle-class person is significantly more likely to have more than one friend than is the person in the working class. Second, in the working class there is greater local dependency for friendships than in the middle class. The specific evidence shows that the middle-class member enjoys a larger number of good friends than does his working-class counterpart. As a func-

TABLE 1

DENSITY GROUPS' AVERAGE NUMBER
OF NEIGHBOR-FRIENDS

Class	Normal	Concentrated	Dense
* Working..........	1.52	....	2.12
** Middle...........	1.33	1.46	1.64

* On original distributions, linear regression X^2, 1 d.f. = 24.5 p < .001.
** On original distributions, linear regression X^2, 1 d.f. = 110.2 p < .001.

tion of this greater circle of friends, he also has more friends in his neighborhood or section of town than does the working-class individual.

Although in our sample the working class made more friends in the preceding year than the middle-class group, this seems largely artifactual, resulting from the special conditions created by retirement public housing. When the effect of

this factor is removed to approximate more typical residential conditions, then middle-class people apparently form slightly more new friendships in any given period of time than those in the working class. The working-class person, however, is far more dependent than the middle-class on neighbors as a source of friendships and social life. Consequently, in making new friends, those in the working class are also far more sensitive to variations in the age composition of local residents. Further, friendship and socializing with neighbors, especially among the most socially dependent older people, were clearly consequential for morale. If social policy about the age composition of residential settings affects their integration into local friendship groups, then factors governing their morale are amenable to planned intervention.

Our central hypotheses were definitively confirmed. The number of old people's local friends does vary with the proportion of old neighbors, and these friends are basically drawn from older neighbors. The common assumption that residential proximity readily stimulates friendships between the generations is not borne out by the facts. The contrary premise is essentially sound and correctly predicts the observed pattern. The number of old people's local friends varies directly with

TABLE 2

AGE OF NEIGHBOR-FRIENDS BY SOCIAL CLASS AND DENSITY

NEIGHBOR'S AGE	WORKING CLASS*		MIDDLE CLASS**		
	Normal Percent	Dense Percent	Normal Percent	Concentrated Percent	Dense Percent
Young..........	19	4	49	24	16
Old.............	81	96	51	76	84
Total friends.	(258)	(328)	(343)	(454)	(499)

* In the base data, X^2, 1 d.f. = 31.0 p < .001.
** In the base data, X^2, 2 d.f. = 122.4, p < .001.

the proportion of age peers. Regardless of the number of friends, the aged select their friends overwhelmingly from older rather than younger neighbors, and this tendency increases with the residential density of old people. The proportion of people named as neighbor-friends who are old increases with residential density from 81 percent to 96 percent in our two working-class areas and from 51 percent to 84 percent in the middle-class areas. Therefore, the proportion of aged in the immediate environment governs the relative size of the potential friendship field, and actual friendships are concentrated among age peers disproportionately more

come. (For purposes of this study, persons with loss in three or four of these areas were considered to have "high role loss.") People with high local contact (visiting or associating with neighbors at least four times a week) were compared with those having less frequent local contact.

The results show that the working class is not only more dependent on neighbors for friendship formation, but its entire social life is more residentially centered than that of the middle class. Consequently, the neighborly activity of manual workers is more responsive to density increases than that of nonmanual groups. In areas

TABLE 3

OBSERVED (O) AND EXPECTED (E) PROPORTION OF OLDER FRIENDS

	WORKING CLASS		MIDDLE CLASS		
	Normal Percent	Dense Percent	Normal Percent	Concentrated Percent	Dense Percent
Old neighbor-friends (O).	81	96	51	76	84
Aged households (E)....	14	67	12	40	60
Difference...........	67	29	39	36	24
z Value*.............	33.5	11.6	23.0	16.3	10.9

* All z values are significant beyond the .0001 level.

than the opportunity for such friendships increases.

This expresses the basic general principle that friendships are formed between persons of similar status, notably of age, but also of sex, marital status, social class, beliefs, and life style. Our data confirmed this directly for sex, marital status, and social class.

RESIDENTIAL DENSITY AND ROLE LOSS

The analysis turned to an intensive study of the subgroups whose interaction with neighbors was most affected by differences in residential density. This focused on those factors related to frequency of interaction, particularly the loss of various social roles through illness, widowhood, retirement, and extreme reduction in in-

of high density of old people, the overall proportion of workers with high local contact (4+ per week) is 30 percent higher than in low-density areas, while the corresponding gains in the middle class run only about 10 percent.

This general picture is modified when we consider the interaction between density and role loss. We assume that, regardless of other factors, high role loss generally confines the social arena of old people and makes them increasingly dependent on the immediate environment for their social activity. Because of the basic class differences in local dependency, loss of roles should have a greater impact on the local interaction of the middle class than on that of the working class. Thus, high role loss should increase the effects of high density more in the middle class than in the working class, and this is essentially what happens.

In the working class, high role loss adds very little to the incidence of high local contact (4+ per week) related to greater density alone. In the middle class, increased density has no effect on frequent interaction of people with low role loss, but those with high role loss double their high local contact as density rises. It increases from 21 percent of those in *Normal* areas to 44 percent of the *Hotel* residents. Thus, in the middle class, those who become more locally dependent use the greater social opportunities afforded by rising density in the manner, but not the degree, of working-class persons, rather than in that of other middle-class people who have lost few roles. This indicates that, even in the middle class, social integration through local friendships is possible for the most problematic alienated groups.

Various demographic factors and specific role losses have unequal importance in people's response to growing social opportunities represented by greater density. Certain characteristics stimulate disproportionate social activity as density rises, so that they predispose people to more intensive neighboring as the proportion of aged increases. In both classes, the most sensitizing variable is age itself. It increases the local contacts of those over 75 significantly more than those under 75.

Similarly, with greater density, women's social activity increases more than men's. This reflects the persistence of earlier sex role differences in which women are more locally oriented than men, and the self-selection of older apartment residents in which women systematically outnumber men. Hence, the increasing preponderance of neighbors of the same age and sex, as density rises, reinforces the basic sex role distinction. With greater density, men increasingly *deviate* and women *conform* to the social composition of their neighbors. Women respond more than men to the growing social oppor-

tunities in denser areas. Of course, when age and sex are considered together, this reinforces their separate effects.

Marital status is also related to rate of local contact, especially in the middle class. Generally, married people are significantly less dependent on local associations than are the maritally unattached. The single and widowed are, with one exception, extremely sensitive to density differences. The sole discrepancy appears among working-class women. Their basic local orientation is so strong that density alone accounts for differences in their neighboring—married and unmarried women respond to density differences in identical fashion. Marital differences generally add little to the sex factor but do amplify differences due to age.

Health presents an anomalous picture. We expected poor health to increase people's local dependence and their response to density, but this was not the case. For working-class individuals, density effects were similar for those in good and in poor health. In the middle class, those in good health were insensitive to density variations, although of those in poor health, the proportion with high local interaction increased from 22 percent in the *Normal* to 41 percent in the *Hotels*. The overall pattern, however, was most equivocal and the unhealthy showed no systematically greater local contact than the healthy. Poor health might restrict outside social life, but it had limited local effect, making itself felt only in conjunction with other disadvantages of age, sex, or lack of marital attachment. It had significantly less independent force than any of these factors.

Whether breadwinners worked or were retired had varying significance for the neighboring activity of the sexes. Our data were too sparse for analysis of the working class, virtually all of whose members were retired. In the middle class, however, there was no relationship between density and local social contacts of men, regardless of their employment status. Whether or not they worked, however, did have significance for self-supporting women. While they were still working, their neighboring was not affected by density, but after they retired, the proportion with high local contact increased progressively with density from 21 percent of those in *Normal* areas to 58 percent of those in the *Dense*. Hence, while women breadwinners worked, their local associations resembled those of men, but when they retired, their social activity shifted to the basic pattern of other women.

Thus, these discrete factors differentially predispose people to respond favorably to density opportunities. Age (76+), sex (women), and marital status (maritally unattached) are strong sensitizing variables, especially when they occur in combination. Retirement is highly selective in its effects, integrating previously self-supporting middle-class women into local social life. Health is surprisingly weak, except, possibly, for middle-class women. These sensitizing factors tend to have greater consequences for the working class than the middle class as density rises. They account for gains in incidence of high local contact of up to one-half in the working class, in comparison with gains in the +20 to 30 percent range for the middle class.

In general, the data confirm our basic analysis. The active local social life of the working class centers on the place of residence, while that of the middle class covers a larger sphere with less focus on the immediate environment. Consequently, greater residential density of older people increases the local integration of workers more than middle-class persons. Because the local orientation of working-class persons is so pervasive, role losses do not shrink their social world as much as that of middle-class members. Thus, even though middle-class people who lose roles

do respond to growing density opportunities, seldom does even a bare majority of them develop the high contact levels that typify the working class in *Dense* areas.

Within these social class differences, however, role loss and lower status do intensify the sensitivity to residential density. Those whose lives are the least disrupted and who retain their earlier roles and affiliations show the least local dependency, but those with the greatest disruption and the lower status positions respond most strongly to the greater social opportunities in denser areas.

The most problematic groups in both social classes are the most disadvantaged, those whose lives have been most disrupted and who have been most alienated from previous group supports. Under favorable conditions, these people can be reintegrated into local friendship groups, but the relative increase in their local ties is generally correlated with rising density. While this may not affect all the alienated equally, significant inroads on their social isolation can be made through local friendships. However, our data show that half measures are relatively ineffective, and strong concentrations of old people are a necessary condition. Very high residential densities of the aged, encompassing at least half the households in an apartment building, are necessary to produce significant gains in local social ties. Weaker concentrations have negligible effects and are inadequate to generate and sustain pervasive gains for the most problematic groups.

Integration into local friendship groups is clearly a function of density and social class, as well as of those factors which intensify the effects of density. But what is the response of people to their local social life? Are they satisfied or dissatisfied with their activity?

FUNCTIONS OF FRIENDSHIP

As a general proposition, the desire for more contact with intimates is inversely related to the actual frequency of seeing them. For example, the wish to see children more often is strictly a function of frequent contact, increasing from 30 percent of those who see them weekly to 82 percent of those who see them less than once a month.

This attitude toward children, however, clearly does not apply to friends. There is absolutely no correlation, for example, between amount of social activity with neighbors and desire for more friends. One-third of the respondents want more friends regardless of amount of contact with neighbors. Obviously, relations with children and with friends or neighbors are qualitatively quite different and are not to be casually equated. The sheer meaning of friendship and its function in people's lives varies considerably. People have decidedly different preferences about friends and the arena of social intercourse, whether this be in the immediate neighborhood or further afield.

Practitioners tend toward extreme views about friendships. Some regard them as a *sine qua non* of "adjustment" while others feel that disengagement and withdrawal are the normal, healthy developments in old age. These are overgeneralized views which fail to discriminate sufficiently between the various functions that friendship may serve for different people. The premises of the present study are not so arbitrary. We know that role loss can be severely demoralizing and that these losses can be partially compensated by local friendships. The basic problem, however, is whether everyone is interested in such compensation and desires friends, including local ones. Certainly, on our data, this is no universal imperative, for not everyone wants close contact with neighbors.

It is possible to assess people's social activity in terms of the functions of friendship in their lives. We abstracted five groups in our sample that encompass 88 percent of our respondents. This grouping was based on the amount of contact people had with neighbors and their desire for more friends.

The largest group (32% of the sample) was the *Cosmopolitan*. This group, largely middle class, had the least contact with neighbors and no desire for more friends. They led an active, diversified social life outside the neighborhood and were strictly oriented to these external interests and associations. Insofar as they avoided local involvements, they were completely indifferent to the suitability of their residential area. If there is any prospect of failing health which might restrict mobility, a residence close to an outside reference group, either children or friends, might be more appropriate for this group's needs.

The second group (only 4%), strongly working class, was the *Phlegmatic*. This group had low contact with neighbors, no good friends, and wanted no friends. Beyond routine visits with children, they were socially inactive. They were passive, apathetic, and wanted no social intercourse, but they were not demoralized and they had little need for social support in the immediate environment. Because they were not interested in friendships, almost anywhere they lived would be acceptable, although they seemed eminently suited to *Normal* areas.

The third group (19%) was the *Isolated*. This group had low contact with neighbors and strongly wanted more friends. They were average in almost all respects, except that they were frustrated because of their social isolation. This frustration was intensified by the limited social opportunities where they lived. They wanted more friends and missed social contacts. This group, more than any other, stood to gain more from the potential friendships in *Dense* areas.

The fourth group (23%) was the *Sociable*. These people had high contact with neighbors and wanted no more friends. They were disproportionately working class and mainly women (87%). They led a very active social life, which included organizational activity, as well as contact with their children, friends, and neighbors. They were satisfied with their social activity and had no desire for more friends. Their social proclivities, skills, and energy assured their full exploitation of social opportunities in *Dense* areas. They were, however, less dependent on optimal friendship conditions than any other group and even with fewer friends, could probably contrive some satisfying social life in less favorable settings.

The fifth group (10%) was the *Insatiable*. They had high contact with neighbors but wanted still more friends. Their social activity and interaction were extremely high and fully as great as the *Sociable* group. Even this did not satisfy them, because high role loss left them extremely threatened and demoralized. They used friendships and activity to cope with their anxiety and alienation, and the pursuit of these distractions had a frenetic quality. They exemplified the general relationship between demoralization and desire for more friends. Friendships were not so much an intrinsic pleasure as a form of defense against anxiety. Though serving this secondary, nonsocial purpose, their social contacts gave them important support. Consequently, their need for reassurance from highly intensive social activity also made the *Insatiables* prime candidates for *Dense* residential settings.

These five groups show that friendships serve a range of functions which have different implications for possible integration into local groups. The *Cosmopolitan* and *Phlegmatic* want no more friends, local or otherwise, and they avoid involvement with neighbors. They are satisfied with their social life as it is and are not problematic for social integration. The other three groups, however, are problematic. The *Isolated*, the *Sociable*, and the *Insatiable* all want an active social life

which includes contact with neighbors. The capacity of their local environment to provide social opportunities and to absorb them may be a significant factor in their fate, as illustrated by the *Isolated*.

*RELATION TO DENSITY
  AREAS*

The significant problem is to determine where these three problematic groups are found. In what density areas are they living? Of all those who are interested in local friendships, what proportion in each area is *Isolated*?

Our data show that in both social classes *Dense* areas produce *Isolated* residents only half as frequently as less concentrated apartments. In the working class, 29 percent of the subjects living in *Normal* density areas and 13 percent of those living in *Dense* concentrations of old people are *Isolated*. In the middle class, over 50 percent of those in the *Normal* and *Concentrated* areas, but only about 25 percent in the *Dense* and *Hotels* are *Isolated*. Thus, as density declines, the proportion of *Isolated* doubles in both classes.

To pursue this implication further, we eliminated those who purposely avoid local involvements—the *Cosmopolitan* and *Phlegmatic*—and recomputed our original sociometric data on the number of neighbor-friends. For those interested in neighboring—the *Isolated*, the *Sociable*, and the *Insatiable*—the average number of neighbor-friends was significantly larger. This was true for all density areas. The effect of high density on friendships remained strong and became even stronger in the middle class. Thus, the elimination of those who avoid neighboring strengthened the effect of density among those in the middle class who are interested in socializing, even though the class pattern does not encourage neighboring.

*EFFECT OF DENSITY
  ON MORALE*

A further problem is the effect on morale when the socially predisposed—the *Iso-*

lated, the *Sociable*, and the *Insatiable*—live in areas where their desires conform with or deviate from local social opportunities and existing interaction patterns. Do the prevailing social norms have the same consequences for them under all conditions? Do the *Isolated*, for example, feel better or worse in *Dense* rather than in *Normal* areas? Similarly, do the *Insatiable* have similar morale in *Normal* and *Dense* settings? Implicitly, is morale affected simply by the correspondence between desires and behavior, or is the relation between activity and the social norm a significant element of the problem?

We suggested three hypotheses: (1) *For the Isolated, morale will decline as density rises.* They desire interaction, but their own activity remains low. As density increases, the social life around them increases, but because they do not share in this, their sense of deprivation should rise in accordance with density. Consequently, this should depress their morale. (2) *For the Sociable, morale will remain constant with rising density.* Norms of low association are not particularly stringent, and high interaction should seldom invoke strong counter pressures. By associating mainly with others who are equally willing to interact, the *Sociable* are insulated from low-activity standards. Their deviation is rewarded rather than punished by the contacts and may be reinforced by the support of a subgroup of social activ-

ists. Consequently, interaction tends to insulate them and make them independent of low-activity norms. Their morale, therefore, should not vary with rising density. (3) *For the Insatiable, morale will rise with increasing density.* They want more and more friends. Hence, as the potential friendship field and social opportunities become larger, their morale should improve with rising density.

Our data confirmed all three hypotheses, although the results were weaker for the third than for the others. As density increased, the morale of the *isolated* declined. That of the *Sociable* did not vary, while—with one anomaly—the morale of the *Insatiable* rose. In eight out of nine comparisons the trends were in the predicted directions.

One definite implication about the *Isolated* group is that half do have the capacity to be socially integrated under favorable conditions, i.e., in *Dense* areas. When social opportunities exist, they can take advantage of them. The other half cannot exploit these without assistance. They need some kind of help in obtaining friends and becoming integrated into groups. If such assistance is not available, these people would be less demoralized if they were to live in less concentrated areas.

43

MARJORIE FISKE LOWENTHAL and CLAYTON HAVEN

INTERACTION AND ADAPTATION: INTIMACY
AS A CRITICAL VARIABLE

INTRODUCTION

This paper is a sequel to previous studies in which we noted certain anomalies in the relation between traditional measures of social deprivation, on the one hand, and indicators of morale and psychiatric condition, on the other, in studies of older populations. For example, lifelong isolates tend to have average or better morale and to be no more prone to hospitalization for mental illness in old age than anyone else, but those who have tried and failed to establish social relationships appear particularly vulnerable (Lowenthal, 1964 II). Nor, with certain exceptions, do age-linked trauma involving social deprivation, such as widowhood and retirement, precipitate mental illness (Lowenthal, 1965). While these events do tend to be associated with low morale, they are by no means universally so. Furthermore, a voluntary reduction in social activity, that is, one which is not accounted for by widowhood, retirement or physical impairment, does not necessarily have a deleterious effect on either morale or on professionally appraised mental health status (Lowenthal and Boler, 1965).

In analyzing detailed life histories of a small group of the subjects making up the samples for these studies, we were struck by the fact that the happiest and healthiest among them often seemed to be people who were, or had been, involved in one or

Reprinted from the *American Sociological Review*, vol. 33, no. 1 (February, 1968).

This research program has been supported by National Institute of Mental Health Grant MH-09145.

more close personal relationships. It therefore appeared that the existence of such a relationship might serve as a buffer against age-linked social losses and thus explain some of these seeming anomalies. The purpose of the present study is to explore this possibility. In doing so, we shall first illustrate how two rather conventional measures of interaction and role status are related to three measures of adaptation which represent different frames of reference. Taking advantage of the panel nature of the data, we shall further document these relationships by analyzing the effect of social gains and losses on adaptation. We shall then show how the presence or absence of a confidant serves as an explanatory variable in the overall trends and deviations noted in the relationships between the more conventional social measures and adaptation. Finally, we shall describe briefly the characteristics of those who do and do not have a confidant, and discuss the implications of these findings for adult socialization and adaptation.

THE CONCEPT OF INTIMACY

As we explored the literature prior to analyzing our own material on intimacy, we were struck by the paucity of references to the quality, depth or reciprocity of personal relationships in social science materials. In their studies of the relationship between social interaction and adjustment, sociologists traditionally have been concerned with the concepts of isolation and anomie, often gauged or inferred from low rankings on quantitative indicators of social roles and contacts; that is, with questions such as how many roles a person fills, how much of his time is spent in interaction with others, and the relationship to the subject of persons with whom this interaction takes place. Several of these studies have established a modest relationship between social isolation and maladjustment (see Lowenthal, 1964, II). With a few exceptions noted below, they have not taken into account the quality or intensity of the individual's relationships with others.

Psychologists have been concerned with dyadic relationships, including the parental and the marital, but although there are references in the literature to Freud's possibly apocryphal mention of the capacity for love as a criterion of mental health, one finds little research directly related to qualities or behavior reflecting the capacity for intimacy or reciprocity. Nor do the traditional personality tests often tap characteristics relevant to such concepts. Some research on animal and human infants, however, has explored this dimension. Harlow and Zimmermann (1959) have shown that infant monkeys spend a great deal more time with a cloth mother surrogate than with a wire surrogate, regardless of which mother provides the milk. They conclude, as have Spitz and Wolf in their studies of human infants (Spitz and Wolf, 1946), that the need for love is instinctual. Ferreira (1964) drawing on his own research and that of Bowlby (1958), concludes that the need for intimacy is "primary and of an instinctual nature . . . the intimacy need may represent a more basic instinctual force than oral or even nursing needs."

It is primarily the psychoanalysts and the analytically-oriented psychologists who, largely on the basis of clinical insights, have stressed this capacity or need, often implying that from its development and fulfillment grow all other forms of social growth and constructive social action. One of the fundamental precepts of

Angyal's theory is that "existing in the thought and affection of another really is a very concrete level of existence. . . ." He goes on to say that the establishment and maintenance of such a close relationship is "the crux of our existence from the cradle to the grave" (Angyal, 1965, p. 19). Erikson postulates the capacity for intimacy as one of the major developmental tasks of life, ideally to be achieved in the establishment of a close relationship with a person of the opposite sex in late adolescence and early adulthood (Erikson, 1959). While our data support this view, it seems clear that there are other viable forms of intimacy which are not necessarily experienced as substitutes for, or supplements to, a stable heterosexual relationship.

In the light of the general paucity of research on the problem of intimacy, it is not surprising that it has not been systematically explored in relation to older populations. Rosow's important study of friendship patterns under varying age-density conditions (1967) does not take the depth of these relationships into account. Arth (1962), in his study of friendships in an aging population, is concerned with "close" friendships, but he does not define closeness. Blau's pioneering study of structural constraints on friendships of the aged (1961) documents the importance of prevailing age-sex-marital status patterns in the establishment of friendships, but it does not discuss the quality or intensity of these relationships.

Obviously, this is a delicate area to explore with field research methods, and our own approach was a simple—if not crude—one. The analysis rests largely on responses to the question: "Is there anyone in particular you confide in or talk to about yourself or your problems?" followed by a description of the identity of the confidant. Still, the findings tend not only to confirm the insights of clinicians and the rather sparse observations of other researchers, but also to clarify some of the puzzling deviations we have noted in our own work in regard to the relationships between social measures, on the one hand, and adaptation, on the other.

THE SAMPLE

The sample on which this report is based consists of 280 sample-survivors in a panel study of community-resident aged, interviewed three times at approximately annual intervals. The parent sample included 600 persons aged sixty and older, drawn on a stratified-random basis from 18 census tracts in San Francisco. The sample of 280 remaining at the third round of interviewing is about equally divided in terms of the original stratifying variables of sex, three age levels, and social living arrangements (alone or with others). As might be expected, the panel differs from elderly San Franciscans (and elderly Americans), as a whole, by including proportionally more of the very elderly, more males, and more persons living alone. Largely because of the oversampling of persons living alone, the proportion of single, widowed, and divorced persons, and of working women, is higher than among elderly Americans in general. Partly because of the higher proportion of working women, their income level was higher than average (44 percent having an income of over $2,000 per year, compared with 25 percent among all older Americans). The proportion of foreign born (34 percent) resembles that for older San Franciscans in general (36 percent), which is considerably more than for all older Americans (18 percent). While some of these sample biases may tend to underplay the frequency of the presence of a confidant, we have no reason to believe that they would influence findings from our major research question, namely the role of the confidant as an intervening variable between social resources and deprivation and adaptation.

MEASURES OF ROLE, INTERACTION AND ADAPTATION

The two conventional social measures to be reported here are number of social roles[1] and level of social interaction.[2] Men tend to rank somewhat lower than women in social interaction in the younger groups, but up through age 74, fewer than 17 percent of either sex rank "low" on this measure (defined as being visited [only] by relatives, contacts only with persons in dwelling, or contacts for essentials only). Isolation increases sharply beginning with age 75, however, and in that phase women are slightly more isolated than men (32 percent compared with 28 percent), possibly because of the higher proportion of widows than of widowers. In general, because they are less likely to be widowed and more likely to be working, men have more roles than women at all age levels, and this discrepancy becomes particularly wide at 75 or older, when 40 percent of the men, compared with only 15 percent of the women, have three or more roles. Among men, a low level of social interaction and a paucity of social roles tend to be related to low socioeconomic status, but this does not hold true for women.

The principal measure of adaptation in this analysis is a satisfaction-depression (or morale) score based on a cluster analysis of answers to 8 questions. For a subsample of 112, we shall also report ratings of psychiatric impairment by three psychiatrists, who, working independently, reviewed the protocols in detail but did not see the subjects. We thus have a subjective indicator of the sense of well-being, and a professional appraisal of mental health status. A third measure, opinion as to whether one is young or old for one's age, is included to round out the adaptation di-

[1] Roles include parent, spouse, worker, churchgoer and organization member.

[2] Ranging from "contributes to goals of organizations" to "contacts for the material essentials of life only." All measures of interaction and adaptation reported here pertain to the second round of follow-up.

mension with an indication of what might be called the respondent's opinion as to his relative deprivation—that is, whether he thinks he is better or worse off than his age peers.

As is true for the social indicators, there are age, sex, and class differences in regard to these adaptation measures which we shall have to bear in mind in analyzing the relationship between these two dimensions. Among men, morale deteriorates evenly with advancing age, from somewhat over one-third "depressed" among those under 65 to about three-fifths among those 75 or older. The youngest women are more depressed than the youngest men (47 percent depressed), but there is no increase—in fact there is a slight decrease—in depression among the 65-74 year old women. The oldest women, however, are nearly as depressed as the oldest men. There are no consistent age or sex trends in regard to whether the subject thinks he is young or old for his age—a slight majority of both sexes at all age levels consider themselves young.

Mental health status, as judged by psychiatrists, indicates that if all age groups are combined, men are psychiatrically more robust than women. This is especially true for the oldest group (75 or older), where four-fifths of the men, compared with only two-fifths of the women, are considered unimpaired. The sex difference is reversed, however, in the middle age-range (65-74), where men are judged to be more impaired than women (44 percent, compared with 29 percent rated impaired). While at first glance this discrepancy might be interpreted as a consequence of psychic crises relating to retirement, detailed analysis of a large psychiatrically hospitalized older sample (Lowenthal and Berkman, 1967; Simon, et al., pub. pending) indicates that retirement rarely precipitates psychiatric disorder. But this same analysis does demonstrate clearly that physical deterioration in the elderly is frequently accompanied by psychiatric impairment. The sharp reversal of sex differences in mental

health status in the middle age group may, therefore, be associated with the earlier onset of physical impairment among men. The fact that the death rate for men between 65 and 74 is considerably greater than for women may, in turn, on the principle of survival of the fittest, account for the oldest men's (75 or more) again being judged of more robust health than women.

In view of the association between physical and mental health in the elderly, and of the association between poor health and low socioeconomic status, it is not surprising that there is also some relationship between low socioeconomic status and psychiatric impairment, though this association is more marked for men than for women. Low morale, on the other hand, is related to low socioeconomic status among both men and women.

RELATIONSHIP BETWEEN SOCIAL
MEASURES AND ADAPTATION

As Table 1 indicates, there is a clear and consistent relationship between social resources and good morale, and between social deprivation and low morale. Low social interaction, in particular, is strongly related to depression. While high ranks on both social measures' contribute to the sense of relative privilege (feel young for age), a low rank is not related as consistently to a sense of relative deprivation as it is to poor morale. A high rank on the two social measures is more closely associated with professional ratings of good mental health than with the respondents' own reports on mood and a sense of relative advantage or deprivation. A low rank on social measures, however, is not consistently or markedly related to a rating of impairment. In other words, social resources and social deficits appear to influence self-appraisals of mood, comparison of self with others, and professional appraisals of adaptation in different ways. Social roles and high interaction are apparently considered to be indicators of, or associated with, mental health—but their absence is not necessarily construed as indicative of impairment. The pattern of association between the social indicators and morale is just the reverse. Social deficits—at least as indicated by the social interaction measure—are more highly correlated with a depressed state than are social resources correlated with a satisfied state. The sense of relative privilege is enhanced by social advantage, but social disadvantage does not necessarily evoke a

TABLE 1

SOCIAL INDICATORS AND ADAPTATION

	SOCIAL INTERACTION		ROLE STATUS	
	High	Low	High	Low
	%	%	%	%
Psychiatric status:				
Unimpaired.......	73	42	90	61
Impaired.........	27	58	10	39
Opinion of own age:				
Young...........	65	39	67	57
Not young........	35	61	33	43
Morale:				
Satisfied.........	58	15	60	46
Depressed........	42	85	40	54

sense of relative deprivation, at least insofar as this sense is reflected by feeling average or old for one's age.

If we compare these social indicators, as reported at the second follow-up, with those reported at the first follow-up approximately one year earlier, we find that several changes took place. These trends were on the order of those noted for other variables used in the panel questionnaire (Lowenthal and Berkman, 1967). Social interaction and role status closely resemble each other with respect to change, with 14 and 15 percent, respectively, "improving," and 20 and 21 percent, respectively, "deteriorating." The broad patterns of relationship between change in social resources and the three indicators of adaptation resemble those

which emerged in the more static picture shown in Table 1. Social losses are related to poor morale, but gains are not related to high morale. Gains are, however, highly correlated with good psychiatric status, though again decrements are not so strongly associated with poor status. Improvements in role and social interaction are related to a sense of relative advantage, as indicated by feeling young for one's age, but losses do not markedly contribute to a sense of relative deprivation (feeling old). This again suggests that a professional's judgment of mental impairment rests on factors other than the absence of indicators of health; an individual's subjective sense of well-being does not automatically result from supplying the role and interaction deficits that often are associated with low morale.

On the other hand, maintaining the status quo in social interaction and role is related to good adaptation, regardless of which indicator of adjustment is used. In fact, on four of the six correlations, stability proves to be more highly associated with good adaptation than does "improvement." At the same time, we note that sizeable proportions of those who suffered social decrements are well-adapted, ranging from one-third to over half, depending on the adaptation measure used. Clearly, our conventional measures alone do not fully explain the relation between the individual's position and behavior in his social milieu, on the one hand, and his adjustment, on the other.

Pursuing our hypothesis with regard to the potential importance of a confidant as a buffer against social losses, we turn to Table 3, which shows the current presence or absence of a confidant, and recent losses, gains, or stability in intimate relationships, in conjunction with the three adaptation measures. As the first column shows, the presence of a confidant is positively associated with all three indicators of adjustment. The absence of a confidant is related to low morale. Lack of a present confidant does not, however, have much bearing on the individual's sense of relative deprivation, or on the psychiatric judgments of mental impairment. We suggest, though with the present data we cannot fully document, two possible explanations for these findings. First, as we have previously noted (Lowenthal, 1964), there are some lifelong isolates and near-isolates whose late-life adaptation apparently is not related to social resources. The sense of relative deprivation, at least for older persons, no doubt applies not only to current comparisons with one's peers, but also to comparisons

with one's own earlier self. This would contribute to an explanation of the fact that some older people without a confidant are satisfied. They do not miss what they never have had. Our second explanation echoes the old adage that it is better to have loved and lost than never to have loved at all. The psychiatrists, in rating mental health status, may take *capacity* for intimacy into account, as indicated by

TABLE 2

THE RELATION BETWEEN CHANGE IN SOCIAL MEASURES AND ADAPTATION

	SOCIAL INTERACTION			ROLE STATUS		
	Increased	Decreased	Unchanged	Increased	Decreased	Unchanged
	%	%	%	%	%	%
Psychiatric status:						
Unimpaired.....	(32)	42	30	(11)	(45)	35
Impaired........	(68)*	58	70	(89)	(55)	65
Opinion of own age:						
Young..........	70	49	63	53	55	63
Not Young......	30	51	37	47	45	37
Morale:						
Satisfied........	47	35	58	50	47	53
Depressed.......	53	65	42	50	53	47

* Percentages are placed in parentheses when the numbers on which they are based are less than 20; the N's for the percentages in parentheses range from 14–19.

TABLE 3

THE EFFECT OF A CONFIDANT ON ADAPTATION

	CURRENT PRESENCE OF CONFIDANT		CHANGE IN CONFIDANT PAST YEAR		
	Yes	No	Gained	Lost	Maintained Same Confidant
	%	%	%	%	%
Psychiatric status:					
Unimpaired.........	69	60	(60)	(56)	80
Impaired...........	31	40	(40)	(44)	20
Opinion of own age:					
Young..............	60	62	42	49	61
Not young..........	40	38	58	51	39
Morale:					
Satisfied............	59	41	44	30	68
Depressed...........	41	59	56	70	32

past relationships such as marriage or parenthood. The respondent, in a more or less "objective" comparison of himself with his peers, may also take these past gratifications into account. However, such recollections may well be less serviceable on the more subjective level of morale and mood.

The right side of the table, showing

TABLE 4

EFFECT ON MORALE OF CHANGES IN SOCIAL INTERACTION AND ROLE STATUS, IN THE PRESENCE AND ABSENCE OF A CONFIDANT

	SOCIAL INTERACTION			
	Increased		Decreased	
	Has Confidant	No Confidant	Has Confidant	No Confidant
	%	%	%	%
Morale:				
Satisfied......	55	(30)	56	13
Depressed....	45	(70)	44	87
	ROLE STATUS			
	Increased		Decreased	
	Has Confidant	No Confidant	Has Confidant	No Confidant
	%	%	%	%
Morale:				
Satisfied	55	(42)	56	(38)
Depressed	45	(58)	44	(62)

change and stability in the confidant relationship, dramatically exemplifies the significance of intimacy for the subjective sense of well being: the great majority of those who lost a confidant are depressed, and the great majority of those who maintained one are satisfied. Gaining one helps, but not much, suggesting again the importance of stability, which we have noted in relation to other social measures. Maintenance of an intimate relationship

also is strongly correlated with self-other comparisons and with psychiatrists' judgments, though losses do not show the obverse. This supports our suggestion that evidence of the *capacity* for intimacy may be relevant to these two more objective indicators of adaptation.

The great significance of the confidant from a subjective viewpoint, combined with the fact that sizeable proportions of people who showed decrements in social interaction or social role nevertheless were satisfied, raised the possibility that the maintenance of an intimate relationship may serve as a buffer against the depression that might otherwise result from decrements in social role or interaction, or from the more drastic social losses frequently suffered by older persons, namely widowhood and retirement. To test this hypothesis, we examined the morale of changers on the interaction and role measures in the light of whether they did or did not have a confidant.

THE INTIMATE RELATIONSHIP AS
A BUFFER AGAINST SOCIAL
LOSSES

As Table 4 shows, it is clear that if you have a confidant, you can decrease your social interaction and run no greater risk of becoming depressed than if you had increased it. Further, if you have no confidant, you may increase your social activities and yet be far more likely to be depressed than the individual who has a confidant but has lowered his interaction level. Finally, if you have no confidant and retrench in your social life, the odds for depression become overwhelming. The findings are similar, though not so dramatic, in regard to change in social role: if you have a confidant, roles can be decreased with no effect on morale; if you do not have a confidant, you are likely to be depressed whether your roles are increased or decreased (though slightly more so if they are decreased). In other words, the presence of an intimate relationship apparently does serve as a buffer against such decrements as loss of role or reduction of social interaction.

What about the more dramatic "insults" of aging, such as widowhood or retirement? While a few people became widowed or retired during our second follow-up year (and are therefore included among the "decreasers" in social role), there were not enough of them to explore fully the impact of these age-linked stresses. We therefore have checked back in the life histories of our subjects and located persons who retired within a seven-year period prior to the second follow-up interview or who became widowed within this period. Though our concern is primarily with social deficits, we added persons who had suffered serious physical illness within two years before the second follow-up contact, since we know that such stresses also influence adaptation.

Table 5 indicates that the hypothesis is confirmed in regard to the more traumatic social deprivations. An individual who has been widowed within seven years, and who has a confidant, has even higher morale than a person who remains married but lacks a confidant. In fact, given a confidant, widowhood within such a comparatively long period makes a rather undramatic impact on morale. Among those having confidants, only 10 percent more of the widowed than of the married are depressed, but nearly three-fourths of the widowed who have no confidant are depressed, compared with only about half, among the married, who have no confidant. The story is similar with respect to retirement. The retired with a confidant rank the same in regard to morale as those still working who have no confidant; those both retired and having no confidant are almost twice as likely to be depressed as to be satisfied, whereas among those both working and having a confidant, the ratio is more than reversed.

Although relatively few people (35) developed serious physical illness in the two-year period prior to the second follow-up interview, it is nevertheless amply

clear that a confidant does not play a mediating role between this "insult" of aging and adjustment as measured by the depression-satisfaction score. The aged person who is (or has recently been) seriously ill is overwhelmingly depressed,

TABLE 5

EFFECT OF CONFIDANT ON MORALE IN THE CONTEXTS OF WIDOWHOOD, RETIREMENT AND PHYSICAL ILLNESS

	Satisfied	Depressed
	%	%
Widowed within 7 Years:		
Has confidant..........	55	45
No confidant..........	(27)	(73)
Married:		
Has confidant..........	65	35
No confidant..........	(47)	(53)
Retired within 7 Years:		
Has confidant..........	50	50
No confidant..........	(36)	(64)
Not retired:		
Has confidant..........	70	30
No confidant..........	50	50
Serious physical illness within 2 Years:		
Has confidant..........	(16)	(84)
No confidant..........	(13)	(87)
No serious illness:		
Has confidant..........	64	36
No confidant..........	42	58

regardless of whether or not he has an intimate relationship. Superficially, one might conclude that this is a logical state of affairs. A social support—such as an intimate relationship—may serve as a mediating, palliative or alleviating factor in the face of social losses, but one should not expect it to cross system boundaries and serve a similar role in the face of physical losses. On the other hand, why doesn't one feel more cheerful, though ill, if one has an intimate on whom to rely for support, or to whom one can pour out complaints? At this point we can only conjecture, but one possible explanation is that serious physical illness is usually accompanied by an increase in dependence on others, which in turn may set off a conflict in the ill person more disruptive to his intimate relationships than to more casual ones. This may be especially true of dependent persons whose dependency is masked (Goldfarb, 1965). A second possibility is that the assumption of the sick role may be a response to the failure to fulfill certain developmental tasks. In this event, illness would be vitally neces-

TABLE 6

CHARACTERISTICS OF PERSONS
HAVING A CONFIDANT

	PERCENT WITH CONFIDANT		
	Men	Women	Total
Sex:			
Men.............			57
Women...........			69
Age:			
60–64...........	50	72	62
65–74...........	68	75	72
75+.............	55	59	57
Marital status:			
Single..........	36	67	46
Married.........	74	81	77
Separated–Divorced....	50	57	54
Widowed........	50	65	62
Socioeconomic status:			
High...........	69	77	73
Low............	38	56	47
Educational level:			
Less than 8 years..	51	67	56
8 years.........	58	62	60
More than 8 years.	61	70	67
Occupational level:			
Blue collar.......	48	67	55
White collar......	65	69	67
Social interaction:			
High...........	62	72	68
Low............	39	50	44
Role status index:			
3–5 roles........	71	84	76
0–2 roles........	45	62	55

sary as an ego defense, and efforts of intimates directed toward recovery would be resisted (Lowenthal and Berkman, 1967). A third possibility is that illness is accompanied by increased apprehension of death. Even in an intimate relationship, it may be easier (and more acceptable) to talk about the grief associated with widowhood or the anxieties or losses associated with retirement than to confess one's fears about the increasing imminence of death.

CHARACTERISTICS OF PERSONS
HAVING A CONFIDANT;
CONFIDANT IDENTITY

In turning to the question of who does, and who does not, maintain an intimate relationship, we found sex and marital status differences that were not unexpected, and some discrepancies with respect to age and socioeconomic status that seemed, at first glance, puzzling. Despite the fact that there were about twice as many widows as widowers in this sample, women were more likely to have a confidant than were men (69 percent, compared with 57 percent). Age trends are irregular. Both persons under 65 and those 75 and older were less likely to have a confidant than the 65 to 74 year olds. Women are more likely than men to have an intimate relationship at all age levels, and the differences between the sexes are especially pronounced in those under 65, where nearly three-fourths of the women and only half the men reported that they have a confidant. These findings tend to support those of Arth (1962) and Blau (1961) in regard to the social capacities and advantages of women. The married are notably more likely to have a confidant than those who are not; single persons are most deprived on this score, and the widowed fall between. Persons above the median on our socioeconomic measure are considerably more likely to have a confidant than those below it, and the differences are more marked for men than women. Education makes surprisingly little difference for either sex, but occupational differences are marked for men.

As to the identity of the confidant, among the nearly two-thirds of the sample who do have a confidant, the identity of this person is fairly evenly distributed among spouse, child and friend. Siblings or other relatives as confidants are comparatively rare. Among women in general, husbands are least frequently mentioned, while wives are the most important for men. This is not only because women are more likely to be widowed, for if we look only at those who are married, or still married, men at all age levels are more likely to report a spouse than are women. Women are about twice as likely as men to mention a child or another relative, and more likely to name friends.

In view of the frequently noted class differences in social interaction (Blau, 1961; Rosow, 1967), it does not surprise us that more than half again as many of those above the median on our socioeconomic measure have a confidant than do those below the median. The generally reported wider range of friendship patterns among the higher socioeconomic groups does not prepare us for the class differences in the identity of confidants reported by this older sample, however. More than three times as many of the higher class report a spouse than do those of lower socioeconomic status (28 percent compared with 8 percent). While this tendency holds among both sexes, the discrepancies are most dramatic among men (36 compared with 2 percent). Conversely, more than twice as many of the low socioeconomic group report a friend, and again it is men who account entirely for the discrepancy. Women of higher status are slightly more likely to have a friend as confidant than are women of lower status. Analysis of detailed life history interviews available for a subsample provide some evidence that the lesser importance of the spouse as confidant among the men of the lower socioeconomic group is connected with problems of masculine role and identity, low-status males considering close association with women a sign of male weakness. This he-man theory gains some support in the fact that among men, not having a confidant is more related to blue collar occupational status than it is to little schooling. Men in the blue collar occupations, whether skilled or unskilled, would obviously—at least in the United States—have less opportunity to associate with women than would white collar males.

In these same life history studies, we have noted some examples of "a regression or escape into intimacy" with advancing age. That is, people who have maintained both intimate and other types of social relationships may, on retirement, for example, or after the departure of children from the home, withdraw to a situation where a close relationship with the spouse is, in effect, the only social contact. But this is by no means the rule. In general, the more complex the social life, the more likely is there to be an intimate relationship, no doubt, in part, because of the larger pool of social resources from which a confidant may be drawn. Among persons having three or more social roles, for example, three-fourths have a confidant, whereas among those having two or fewer social roles, only slightly more than half have a confidant. Similarly, two-thirds of those on the highest level of social interaction have an intimate relationship, while the majority of those whose interaction is limited to being visited by relatives do not. Such resources, however, are more important for men than for women.

IMPLICATIONS

This study indicates that when two conventional indicators of social role and interaction are used, the significance for adaptation of being socially deprived or advantaged varies in accordance with the degree of subjectivity of the adjustment measure used. Social resources are more related to professional appraisals of good health than to subjective appraisals of high morale; social deprivation, on the other hand, is associated with subjective reports of poor morale, but not with professional assessments of poor mental health. A more objective self-report involving comparisons with others resembles the psychiatrists' judgments; that is, being socially privileged enhances one's evaluation but being socially underprivileged

399

does not deflate it. Regardless of the indicator of adaptation which is examined, however, the deviant cells are sizeable.

To help explain these variations, we went on to show that the maintenance of a stable intimate relationship is more closely associated with good mental health and high morale than is high social interaction or role status, or stability in interaction and role. Similarly, the loss of a confidant has a more deleterious effect on morale, though not on mental health status, than does a reduction in either of the other two social measures. We suggested that while psychiatrists may take the capacity for an intimate relationship into account in their professional judgments, awareness that he has such a potential does not elevate an individual's mood if he has recently lost a confidant. Finally, we have noted that the impact on adjustment of a decrease in social interaction, or a loss of social roles, is considerably softened if the individual has a close personal relationship. In addition, the age-linked losses of widowhood and retirement are also ameliorated by the presence of a confidant, though the assault of physical illness clearly is not.

In view of the apparently critical importance of an intimate relationship, the sex and class differences we have noted in the reporting of the presence or absence of a confidant provoke speculation. In the youngest age group (those between 60 and 64, presumably a period where the pool of potential confidants is greatest), nearly half again as many women as men reported an intimate companion. We are reminded, in this connection, of the observations of psychoanalyst Prescott Thompson in regard to age trends in the significance of interpersonal communication among spouses. In early periods of the adult life span, he suggests, communication problems may well have been obscured by the pressures and distractions of job and children; as the empty nest and retirement phases approach, awareness of deficiencies in this respect may become acute (Thompson and Chen, 1966). Significantly, it is the wives who are most likely first to become conscious of the problem, and to be able to talk about it (Thompson, 1966).

There seems little doubt that, to some extent, marital status is an indication of the capacity for intimacy. We have seen that the married are most likely to have a confidant, whether spouse or some other. Among those not married and living with spouse when we interviewed them, widows and widowers were most likely to have a confidant, single persons least, and the divorced and separated fell between. Finally, the class and sex differences we have noted suggest that the lower class men may harbor a concept of virility which discourages the development of types of intimacy other than the purely sexual. Thus, with the waning of sexual potency or the loss of a partner with advanced age, they are left with fewer alternatives for an intimate relationship than are women.

At this stage of our knowledge, we can only wonder whether women's greater sensitivity to close relationships, and, as we have seen, their greater versatility in the choice of objects for such relationships, has any causal connection with their greater adaptability for survival. Not only is the overall death rate higher among men, but among them, and not among women, the suicide rate increases rapidly with age. And despite their greater potentiality for remarriage, it is among men, not women, that widowhood is more likely to trigger mental illness. Conversely, the few instances where retirement precipitates mental disturbance tend to be found among working women rather than men, suggesting that an important source of frustration and conflict may lie precisely in the incapacity, or lack of opportunity, to carry out the special feminine task of developing and sustaining intimate relationships (Lowenthal and Berkman, 1967). We are reminded once more of Angyal's guiding thesis that the maintenance of closeness with another is the center of existence up to the very end of life (Angyal, 1965).

44

C. KNIGHT ALDRICH and ETHEL MENDKOFF

RELOCATION OF THE AGED AND DISABLED:
A MORTALITY STUDY

The findings of several studies have suggested that relocation is not without risk to the aged. Lieberman (1961) observed that the death rate for elderly people shortly after admission to homes for the aged is high. Whittier and Williams (1956), Kay, Norris and Post (1956), and Camargo and Preston (1945) reported an even higher early mortality among elderly patients confined to hospitals for the mentally ill. According to medical folklore, the stress of retirement from an active life may precipitate death. However, the studies of McMahan and Ford (1955) and Thompson and Streib (1958) do not substantiate this position.

The view that emotional stress can precipitate death has been supported by observations in concentration camps and prisoner-of-war camps. Nardini (1952) noted that despair, depression and apathy, with their associated lack of an outlet for hostility, appeared to precipitate death in prison camps. Schmale (1958) and others have reported on the relationship of separation and depression—of feelings of helplessness and hopelessness—to the onset of disease.

Since declining health in an elderly person often brings about the decision to place him in an institution, it is usually difficult to determine to what extent the high initial death rate in institutions is related to physical factors or to the psychologic effect of change. When a patient moves from a family setting to an institution, it is also difficult to determine whether any associated psychologic stress

Reprinted from the *Journal of the American Geriatrics Society,* vol. 11, no. 3 (March, 1963).

is primarily related to separation from the family or whether it is crucially related to relocation in a new environment and away from familiar surroundings, including friends.

The closing of the Chicago Home for Incurables provided us with an opportunity to study aged in-patients who were relocated from one institution to another without regard to their state of health or family relationships but solely as a result of administrative necessity. Admissions to the Home for Incurables were stopped in 1958. The relocation process began in 1959 and lasted approximately two years. At the beginning of the project, 233 disabled persons, of whom 162 were aged 70 or older, had lived in the Home from one to forty-five years. Transfer was made primarily to other nursing homes of substantially the same or better quality in the same community.

In this study we attempted to find answers to the following questions:

1. Does relocation affect the death rate of elderly and disabled persons?

2. Does the anticipation of relocation affect the death rate?

3. Does the patient's psychologic adjustment affect his chances of survival?

SETTING AND PATIENTS

Although modern rehabilitation techniques were virtually absent in the Home, the patients were generally satisfied with the care and services available to them. Since many patients suffered from several types of disability and the primary diagnosis in others was obscured by secondary problems, detailed classification by diagnosis was not undertaken. An estimated 40 percent primarily suffered from neurologic conditions, including cerebrovascular accidents; about 25 percent were principally handicapped by bone and joint disease; about 12 percent had cardiac disease; another 12 percent had disorders classed as senility or generalized arteriosclerosis; and the remaining 10 percent had miscellaneous illnesses. The patients required varying degrees of nursing care, and by the time this study began they had become accustomed to their routine schedules. Prior to the closing of the Home they had assumed that they would

TABLE 1

DEATHS DURING FIRST YEAR FOLLOWING RELOCATION, DISTRIBUTED ACCORDING TO AGE GROUPS

Age of Patients	No. of Patients	Survived	Died	Mortality
35–49......	17	15	2	12%
50–59......	20	16	4	20%
60–69......	22	16	6	27%
70–79......	45	30	15	33%
80–89......	56	31	25	45%
90+.......	20	14	6	30%
Total....	180	122	58	32%

receive care in the same institution for the remainder of their lives.

Although there was no formal announcement of the closing, the rumor soon spread to the patients. When admissions were discontinued and a new social worker began to arrange plans for relocation, an atmosphere of apprehension developed. As a result of a strike of nonprofessional employees at the Home soon after the news of the merger, 57 patients were placed elsewhere without time for a thorough investigation of their needs or the relationship of their needs to the relocation plan. However, after the strike was over, planning could be carried out more effectively and casework was apparently helpful in reducing anxiety and apprehension regarding the transfers. A home recently opened in the neighborhood accepted 28 patients from the Home for Incurables as well as many employees and some of the activities various religious groups had sponsored. Thus in many ways the stress of relocation was reduced.

Meanwhile the social worker recorded her observations concerning each patient's adjustment to the institution prior to the news of its closing, and his or her adaptation during the period in which relocation was being considered.

FINDINGS

On May 1, 1959, there were 233 patients in the Home, but 51 died there before relocation could be carried out. Of the remaining 182 patients, 163 were transferred to 56 nursing homes or homes for the aged in the Chicago area; 4 were placed in hospitals; 6 were accepted by relatives and friends; and 9 (all under 70 years of age) were removed to independent living in the community. Follow-up reports on 180 of the 182 one year after relocation, revealed an over all death rate of 32 percent. The death rates for men and women were 34 percent and 31 percent respectively. Table 1 shows the distribution according to age at date of discharge. Except for patients past the age of 90 years,[1] the death rate was progressively higher in each age group.

In order to estimate the death rates that could have been anticipated had the Home not closed, the records of the Home were examined for ten years prior to the closing of intake (1949–1958) and calculations of the annual survival rate for patients in each age decade were made for each year of residence in the Home.[2]

Examination of these data indicated that

[1] Four of the group more than 90 years old died in the first three months of the second year.

[2] Inasmuch as follow-up data were not available for the 1949–58 group, patients who left the Home alive were included as deaths. Since a fraction of those who left alive did not leave because of serious illness and may have survived past the year in which they left, the expected death rate developed from these figures may be slightly higher than it would have been if the dates of all deaths had been available.

after the first year of residence, in which the death rate was higher than in subsequent years, the year of residence was not a significant factor in the survival rate. For example, a patient in the eighth decade of life had virtually the same chance for survival whether he had been in the Home two, three, four, five or any subsequent number of years. By summation of the data for the period 1949 to 1958 (in which there was no appreciable change in the over-all death rate) it was possible to calculate the expectation of death for any individual in any age group who had been in the Home more than one year. None of the patients in the study group had been in the Home less

The actual and expected death rates in the last nine months of the year were approximately the same; in the first three months of the year the actual death rate for patients over 70 was about three and a half times as high as the expected death rate, and for all patients it was more than three times as high as the expected death rate.

TABLE 2

COMPARISON OF CALCULATED ANTICIPATED DEATH RATES AND ACTUAL DEATH RATES DURING FIRST YEAR FOLLOWING RELOCATION, DISTRIBUTED ACCORDING TO AGE GROUPS

Age of Patients	Anticipated Mortality (%)	Actual Mortality (%)
Under 70........	13	20
70–79..........	19	33
80–89..........	28	45
90+...........	28	30
All 70 and older..	23	38
All ages........	19	32

TABLE 3

DISTRIBUTION OF DEATHS DURING FIRST YEAR, ACCORDING TO TIME ELAPSED AFTER RELOCATION

Months after Relocation	Deaths of Patients Less than 70 Yrs. Old	Deaths of Patients 70 Yrs. and Older	Total Deaths
1	2	6	8
2	1	10	11
3	1	10	11
4	2	2	4
5	2	2	4
6	0	4	4
7	2	5	7
8	0	3	3
9	0	0	0
10	0	2	2
11	1	1	2
12	1	1	2

than one year, so our computations did not include those who were in the first year in residence.

A comparison of anticipated and actual death rates (Table 2) indicated that, except for patients in the tenth age decade, the actual rate was substantially and significantly higher than the anticipated rate $[x^2 = 11.06$ (df = 3) p < .02].

Analysis of the deaths according to the months elapsed since relocation (Table 3) showed that the number of deaths in the first three months was substantially higher than during the remainder of the year.[3]

The significant increase in the death rate, therefore, occurred primarily in the first three months following relocation.

Determination of the possible effects on the patients of the news that relocation was anticipated, was more difficult. Since more than half of the patients left within a year after they knew of the relocation plans, we could not obtain complete and comparable figures on the death rate following the news and before relocation. We obtained an approximate assessment, however, by comparing the number of persons who died in the Home during the year May 1, 1959–April 30, 1960 with the number remaining in the Home on April 30, 1960. The results of this comparison are listed in Table 4. Although the actual

[3] Seasonal factors did not appear to be an influence in determining the distribution of deaths.

death rate was somewhat higher than the expected death rate for each age group, the differences were not statistically significant [$\chi^2 = 5.74$ (df $= 3$) p $=$ N.S.].

Two determinations (A and B) were made in an effort to assess the effects of personality adjustment on mortality.

A. For the first determination, we obtained descriptions of each patient's adjustment to the Home prior to the news of its closing. Thirty-eight patients showed reactions that were psychotic or prepsychotic; 52 showed clearcut evidence of depression or neurotic reactions; 30 were consistently angry and demanding; and 49 displayed relative equanimity. Table 5 lists the mortality rates in the first

and overtly depressed patients was three times as high as that for patients who had made a satisfactory adjustment to their disabilities and to institutional life, and more than twice as high as that for patients who had made an overtly angry or demanding adjustment. After correction for age, these differences were found to be statistically significant [$\chi^2 = 12.65$ (df $= 4$) p $< .02$].[4] Unfortunately, we were not able to obtain accurate information about the causes of death, and so did not attempt to correlate death rates with organic disease entities.

B. For the second determination, we evaluated the response pattern of each patient who was sufficiently aware of the

TABLE 4

DEATHS WITHIN THE HOME DURING PERIOD OF ANTICIPATION OF RELOCATION. MAY 1, 1959–APRIL 30, 1960

Age of Patients	No. of Patients	Survived	Died	Actual Mortality	Anticipated Mortality
Under 70.............	32	24	8	25%	13%
70–79................	32	21	11	34%	19%
80–89................	43	29	14	33%	28%
90+................	12	7	5	42%	28%
All 70 and older........	87	57	30	34%	23%
All ages..............	125	87	38	30%	19%

TABLE 5

DEATHS DURING FIRST YEAR FOLLOWING RELOCATION, DISTRIBUTED ACCORDING TO PATTERN OF ADJUSTMENT TO THE HOME BEFORE THE NEWS OF ITS CLOSING

Type of Adjustment	No. of Patients	No. of Deaths	Mortality
Satisfactory.........	49	6	12%
Angry and demanding	30	5	17%
Neurotic or depressed	52	19	37%
Psychotic or near psychotic............	38	24	63%

year following relocation for each of these groups.

The death rate for the psychotic or near-psychotic elderly patients was the highest for any group. Of the remaining patients, the death rate for the neurotic

news of relocation to respond in a discernible manner. Although many persons showed evidence of multiple patterns of response, we arbitrarily classified each patient according to his more characteristic pattern. The results, summarized in Table 6, indicate that the survival rate was highest for patients who took the change in their stride or were overtly angry; patients who became anxious but did not withdraw, survived reasonably well; and patients who regressed, became depressed or denied that the Home was closing, survived less well. After correction for age, these differences were found to be statistically significant [$\chi^2 = 11.43$

[4] Fifteen patients were not included, either because of mental retardation or because their physical condition made it difficult to assess adjustment patterns adequately.

404

(df $= 4$) p $< .05$]. The psychotic, helpless and mentally retarded groups were
not included in this assessment, and data
were not obtained on 13 patients who
were relocated shortly after they learned
that the Home was closing.

CASE REPORTS

Case I illustrates a reaction of depression
to the news of relocation in a woman
whose prior adjustment had been satisfactory. (Since she died before relocation,
her data are not included in Tables 5 and
6.):

Miss E. W., aged 85, had been in the
Home for twenty-four years following a
back injury. She walked with a cane and
had been an active and alert participant,
requiring no nursing supervision. She was
anxious about the Home's closing, expressed fear of any change in her situation, and became depressed and withdrawn. After arranging her belongings
and taking care of her personal affairs, she
withdrew further and lost all interest in
the daily activities of the Home. She frequently spoke of death and stated that she
had no reason to live. While efforts were
being made for transfer, she died, apparently of arteriosclerosis.

Case II pertains to the relocation of a
woman with a compulsive adjustment before the news, and regression afterwards:

Miss M. K., aged 67, had been in the
Home for twenty-three years following
a fractured hip. She cared for herself according to a rigid routine, and disliked
deviating from it in any way. She was
careful not to reveal her feelings and was
guarded in her relationship with others.
She was a religious woman, and often said,
"God gives the heaviest cross to the
people he likes best." She responded to
news of the relocation with anxiety, tears,
and some denial of the need to plan. Her
most evident reaction was regression.
Whereas she had regularly been in a
wheelchair and had walked somewhat
with crutches, she now remained in bed,
demanding more care. With the assistance

of relatives, a nursing home was selected,
but the day after she was transferred she
died.

Case III represents a satisfactory adjustment before the news of relocation,
and depression afterwards:

J. H., a 73-year-old man with left hemi-
plegia, required nursing care, but was able
to sit up in a wheelchair. He read a great
deal, and was mentally alert and active.
He responded to the news of the Home's

TABLE 6

DEATHS DURING FIRST YEAR FOLLOWING RE-
LOCATION, DISTRIBUTED ACCORDING TO
PATTERN OF ADJUSTMENT TO THE NEWS OF
THE HOME'S CLOSING

Type of Adjustment	No. of Patients	No. of Deaths	Mortality
Philosophical........	17	0	0%
Angry..............	17	1	6%
Anxious............	40	6	15%
Regression..........	11	3	27%
Depression..........	27	11	41%
Denial..............	7	5	71%

closing by crying, depression and loss of
interest in his everyday activities. He
stated the staff would never be able to
find another place for him like the Home
for Incurables. He was placed in a nursing
home, where he died two months later.

Case IV illustrates an adjustment that
was angry and demanding before the
news of relocation, with depression afterwards:

Miss N. S., aged 81, had been in the
Home for twenty-seven years with a
spinal deformity. She was a controlling
person who required little nursing care in
spite of rather serious disability. She was
alert, sewed her own clothes and read and
wrote a great deal. She was not easy to
get along with and would frequently
argue with her roommates. On hearing of
the Home's closing, she became more in-

secure and depressed. Her physical complaints increased, and she repeatedly said, "I have lived too long." She was apprehensive lest she make the wrong decision for relocation. Although transferred to an excellent home where the personnel attempted to help her overcome her apprehension about the transition, she complained about the food, the facilities and the other patients. She died following an upper respiratory tract infection, twenty-six days after transfer.

Case V is an example of a patient who appeared gradually to displace her anger regarding several relocations in new facilities. (Several persons of this type required multiple transitional placements before a satisfactory adjustment could be made.):

Mrs. J. L., aged 89, had been in the Home six years. She was ambulatory, cared for herself and made daily trips in the neighborhood. Her primary reaction to the move was regression, and she took to her bed with many physical complaints. After transfer to a nursing home, she complained so bitterly about the new home that she was again transferred. She again objected strongly, and her helplessness continued until a third placement was made. Although essentially similar in physical features and facilities to all three previous homes, the new placement was much more to her liking. Twenty-eight months after the original placement she was reported to be active and in good health.

Case VI. For this elderly patient, relocation paradoxically seemed to stimulate eventual improvement in spite of an initial depression:

Mrs. M. D., aged 83, had been in the Home for three years with arthritis. She was customarily a controlling and manipulating personality, but occasionally was withdrawn and depressed. She refused to remain out of bed except for brief periods, demanded care and attention from the nursing staff and, although she

could walk to the bathroom, frequently asked for a bedpan in her room. She became depressed when relocation was imminent, complaining that "No one understands me or is interested in me," and indicated her wish to die. She remained unhappy and in bed during her first placement, and was soon transferred to another home. She was more satisfied with this home, and twenty-seven months after the original placement was reported to be regularly up in her wheelchair, taking better care of herself than before, and in general showing improvement.

Case VII. Most of the patients who improved, however, were in the younger age group:

Miss D. S., aged 60, had been in the Home for fourteen years with a diagnosis of multiple sclerosis. She was withdrawn, never left her room, and for the most part stayed in bed, reading and smoking constantly. Her primary response to the news of the relocation was anxiety. She was interested in the details of the new placement, however, and purchased an adjustable wheelchair. She now shares a room with another patient, shows more interest in others, walks to the bathroom and takes a daily bath, and is happier and more relaxed.

For one couple and two other patients, the closing of the Home led to marriage and independent living. The couple were aged 50 and 51 respectively; one suffered from rheumatoid arthritis and one from muscular dystrophy. A 39-year-old man with cerebral palsy married a woman with the same disease, who lived elsewhere. A 38-year-old woman with Friedreich's ataxia married an orderly at the Home. After a year, all three marriages appeared to be successful and all three families were living independently.

DISCUSSION

In contrast to the reasons for the initial admission of an old person to a nursing or old people's home, the reasons for relocation in our study bore no relation to the physical health of the patient or the situation within the family. In all cases the homes to which patients were transferred provided medical, nutritional and nursing care that was equal to or better than the care available at the Home. Therefore, we believe that the increase in the number of deaths in the year following relocation is attributable to the social and psychologic effects of the change. Our findings indicate that these effects can be lethal.

The effects of relocation on the mortality rate were concentrated in the first three months following departure from the Home. After that, the rate returned to the figure that past experience would lead us to expect. Since patients either die or become adapted within three months, efforts to assist adaptation to relocation should be concentrated within this period.

Our statistics did not permit us to draw definite conclusions about the effects of anticipation of relocation on mortality. The approximation shown in Table 4 suggests a possible relationship, but any difference in values was not statistically significant. The somewhat arbitrary time-period chosen as the basis for the comparative statistics in Table 4 may be misleading, since there had been no definite announcement of the Home's closing, and since the time provided for preparation for relocation varied widely among the patients.

Furthermore, we could not measure the effect of preparatory casework help. Subjectively, casework was apparently helpful in the patient's preparation for relocation and probably was helpful in reducing mortality. Our observations lead us to believe that relocation should be carried out expeditiously, as soon after announcement to the patient as compatible with proper planning and preparation.

The patient's psychologic adjustment, both before and after the news of relocation, is a significant factor in predictions regarding survival. Our finding that over half of the psychotic or near-psychotic patients died in the first year after reloca-

tion is consistent with the findings of Camargo and Preston (1945) and Whittier and Williams (1956). The psychotic patients were older than the non-psychotic ones on the average, and were unaware or less aware than the others of the impending relocation. We do not have specific figures for comparison, but it was the opinion of the Home's staff that the rate of psychosis had been reasonably steady throughout the years. However, since the deaths among psychotic patients were not as frequent in the period preceding relocation, we believe that the change of surroundings was a definite factor in increasing the mortality.

Nonpsychotic patients who expressed anger and those who avoided conflict by accepting their disabilities and the relocation philosophically, were more likely to survive than patients who retreated from the conflict situation by regression or denial and those who directed their anger against themselves and became depressed. However, respiratory, nutritional and autonomic factors secondary to or associated with depression will have to be investigated carefully before we can conclude that hostility turned inwards or the loss of the will to live are in themselves lethal.

Case work or psychiatric help in preparing elderly and disabled patients for relocation, therefore, should be primarily directed towards helping them recognize and accept, rather than conceal, their anger at the prospect. Our findings suggest that in these circumstances, preparatory psychologic help can be life-saving. Ideally, for control purposes, we should have limited the casework help to alternate residents of the Home; practical and humane considerations, however, did not permit casework to be withheld from any group of patients. Therefore, it was not possible to determine whether the death rate for any subgroup would have been materially higher without such preparation.

Despite conscientious efforts, the dangerous effects of relocation cannot be completely eliminated. The best prevention is not to relocate elderly and disabled people. This type of prevention is not always possible, however. The danger remains greatest among helpless and psychotic elderly people who, on the basis of practical considerations, are most likely to require relocation in other institutions.

45

FRANCES M. CARP

EFFECTS OF IMPROVED HOUSING ON THE LIVES OF OLDER PEOPLE

THE PROBLEM

Many people over 60 express dissatisfaction with the situations in which they live. They feel that their lives, generally, would be much better if only their housing were improved. Often the possibilities are limited by finances. The depression hit members of this generation at a critical point in their earning years, and inflation diminished whatever they were able to save.

For some individuals the primary difficulty is physically substandard or inconvenient housing. For others the frustration is primarily social, involving isolation from old friends and contemporaries, or intergeneration conflict and the feeling of imposing or being imposed upon.

The critical question is: *If pleasant living quarters are made available, in proximity to other people in the same age range, will the later years of these people be better?* While most studies have shown positive associations between housing and health or adjustment, a few have reported negative findings and others ambiguous ones.

Given the aim of reducing major frustrations of these later years, and recognizing that many people in this age span perceive either the physical or social situations in which they live as being especially thwarting, it does not necessarily follow that moving to a different environment will achieve the goal. Increase in satisfaction cannot be assumed, even if the new surroundings are designed according to the special needs and desires of the group.

First of all, are people of this age group able to make the change to modern equipment and to a new social situation? Operating pushbutton stoves may prove too much of a challenge. Living up to a fine modern apartment may become taxing. Neighbors may prove to be as incompatible as relatives. Availability of other people may be overwhelming. Once in the tailormade setting, a person advanced in years may look back regretfully at what he left. In an alien land of technical modernity with its constant demands of cleanliness and beauty, in an area densely populated by strangers, he may view his former residence nostalgically as being less demanding and far more comfortable.

Relative fixity of the older personality and life pattern is commonly assumed, though evidence seems inadequate to attribute this to chronological age as such. If older people are able to make the adjustment to a new environment, will their enjoyment of life increase, or will more basic dissatisfactions simply take new surface forms? Displeasure with housing may be an expression of a more general frustration at growing old and one which can-

Reprinted from *Patterns of Living and Housing of Middle-aged and Older People: Proceedings of Research Conference, 1965* (Washington, D.C.: United States Department of Health, Education, and Welfare), pp. 147–59.

The research reported here was supported by the Hogg Foundation for Mental Health and by the U.S. Department of Health, Education, and Welfare, and is reported more fully in *A Future for the Aged: The Residents of Victoria Plaza* (Austin: University of Texas Press, 1966).

not be alleviated by changed living quarters. The effort and expense involved in relocating older people may not be justified, if reduction in complaints about residence is matched by increased discontent in other areas.

In addition to expressed pleasure or displeasure with the housing itself, will there be other changes? Does improving the living situation have a consistent impact on physical and mental health, on attitudes toward others, on self-concept, on patterns of day-to-day living? Both for those who must make plans for aged people and for those interested in more theoretical aspects of aging, it is important to determine which behavioral characteristics are intrinsic to aging and which are relatively dependent on environmental circumstances.

The difficulty of isolating the effects of housing *per se* is obvious. Many variables related to housing—such as age, socioeconomic status, and health—also affect satisfaction and well-being. Public housing tenants have been recommended as subjects for studies of environmental impact, because the range of difference in such characteristics is usually smaller, which tends to minimize their effect on measures of morale or adjustment.

It was possible for this study to extend itself a little further in controlling the effects of extraneous variables. In 1960, the San Antonio Housing Authority completed a high-rise residence designed for, and limited to, older applicants for public housing. Apartments had special design features as well as a community center. To provide a base from which to measure change resulting from living in the new environment, 352 (nearly all) qualified applicants were interviewed. As many as possible were tested before the building was completed and before they were advised regarding their acceptance as tenants.

A common weakness in studies appraising programs of housing (and of recreation, occupation, and nutrition) has been the unavailability of preliminary data

from which to assess the direction, extent, and quality of change in people resulting from altered circumstances. Usually, it has not been possible to obtain comprehensive descriptions of subjects prior to the environmental changes under evaluation, which obscures the validity of conclusions regarding cause. Some programs for the aged may be judged to have improved happiness or competence, whereas, in reality, a process of selectivity rather than of change was operating. Others may have been discounted and discarded for the same reason. Here, "baseline" data were collected on qualified applicants, and changes from that baseline were measured for those who obtained improved housing and for those who did not. Selection of tenants was made by Housing Authority personnel according to Housing Authority standards and was completely separate from this study (Netter, 1962; San Antonio Housing Authority, 1959, I and II).

After the period of 1 year to 15 months, followup data were collected on people who had lived in the new facility and on a similar group of people who had applied unsuccessfully for apartments there. Comparison of changes in these groups minimized mistaking initial differences for results of improved living and recreation condition. The analysis of covariance model used for data processing took into account initial differences between the subgroups. These, incidentally, proved be be few in number and small in size. Even on the characteristics included in the legal requirements of the Housing Authority, selectees did not differ significantly from nonselectees (Carp, 1966). This probably reflects the efficiency of the initial Housing Authority screening of applicants for eligibility for public housing and the inutility of the eligibility standards for the further discrimination among the qualified.

This, then, was an assessment of the impact of changed housing on older people. Physically and socially, the new housing was planned to meet the expressed needs

410

of people who were to live in *Victoria Plaza*, a high-rise public housing apartment building for the aged. The study attempted to ascertain whether the plan was successful in providing a more satisfying living situation. It also evaluated more general changes in attitudes, life style, and mental health.

SUBJECTS

Not only were the "ins" and "outs" quite similar, but in general background and current demographic characteristics they were very much like the majority of people in their age range (Carp, 1961). Therefore, careful generalization seems justified, not only to elder applicants for public housing but to other groups as well.

These people were old by the calendar (average age 72+ when first contacted), but most were "middle-aged" in their own eyes. They were poor (all applicants for public housing) but, surprisingly, they were probably no more so than many people in their age group (their median income of $94.40 per month was similar to that of the United States census for people of their age who were on Social Security). No one was affluent—nor was anyone extremely poor. The range of income was restricted by Housing Authority requirements: an income "ceiling" in the legal requirements for eligibility; a "floor" in the necessity to pay at least minimum rent—which was higher for *Victoria Plaza* than for other public housing in the area.

Though probably above average in intelligence, as measured by standardized tests (verbal I.Q. 112 for a sample of 104), they were no better educated than was typical for their generation (8th grade). Forced into dependency, they were reluctant to be social burdens and had strong needs to stand on their own. They accepted inevitable physical and sensory losses and complained little of ailments, although they resented the inaccessibility of the little medical attention they needed and the lack of such things as new eye-

glasses and dentures which could make life more comfortable and enjoyable. Though neurotic-type complaints "bothered" them somewhat more than physical ailments, all indexes showed them to be in unexpectedly sound mental health.

Overwhelmingly interested in religion, they tended to participate in religious activities to the limit of their resources of transportation, money, and pride. They regretted and resented the meagerness of attention received from religious institutions and people. Common to everyone in the group was the desire to find a better place to live, one which could be paid for personally, and one which could be lived in as the individual wished and without imposing on other people.

Their need for more adequate housing was unquestionable. The typical applicant lived in an "apartment," usually one small room partitioned out of a larger one on the second or third floor of an old house. Often, antiquated wallpaper hung from two walls and the others were of unpainted fiberboard. Cooking arrangements might consist of a two-burner stove in one corner of the room, refrigerator space in the downstairs kitchen, and garbage cans in the alley. Bathrooms usually were shared by all the occupants of a floor.

Social contact was limited for most applicants. One woman had spoken to no one, except the boy who delivered her groceries, for the three months previous to her first research interview. This isolation was not of her own choosing but because her "apartment" was up three rickety, poorly lit flights of stairs. She had broken her hip several years earlier and feared another fall, particularly since her medical insurance was inadequate and she had no family to help her in case of emergency.

The need to move was often as compelling for applicants with adequate physical housing, because of crushing loneliness or wounding interpersonal relationships. Some applicants felt that their presence imposed a burden upon younger households; some knew that other people took advantage of them. A 75-year-old woman who had given her home to her daughter and son-in-law lived in the maid's room in the garage—and did a maid's work. She was so afraid her son-in-law would find out about her application for public housing and somehow foil her efforts to get away from him that she would not allow the interviewer near her home. She made elaborate excuses to her daughter in order to go out to meet the interviewer. She lived in dread lest a phone call from the Housing Authority be intercepted. The research staff suspected her of being paranoid, but the son-in-law's reaction at the time of her move into the *Plaza* fully justified the woman's concern.

Some applicants feared the loss of the shelter they had, because old buildings were being razed to make way for new ones or for parking lots or expressways. Other old persons anticipated eviction or higher rent if the landlord learned of the application for public housing. The interviewer was sure one applicant was paranoid in his desire to hide his public housing application, until she caught the landlady reading the residents' mail.

RESEARCH DESIGN

Comprehensive descriptive material—background and current—was obtained from qualified applicants for housing in *Victoria Plaza* before it was known which ones would be assigned apartments. A year after the first occupants moved into *Victoria Plaza*, followup interviewing and testing was begun to determine not only how residents liked the *Plaza* after having lived in it, but also to find what impact it might have had on their way of life, general adjustment, and attitudes toward themselves and others.

In light of their similarities and differences as applicants, comparison of changes over this period of time for those who had lived in *Victoria Plaza* and those who had not seemed the safest way to assess the impact of residence. Of the original group of 352 applicants, 295 were restudied; 190 had lived in *Victoria Plaza* for 1 year to 15 months; 105 had remained in substandard and/or socially impoverished situations.

The design followed an analysis of covariance model. In data treatment, a multiple-regression approach (Bottenberg and Ward, 1963) was used with continuous and ordered variables, the McNemar Test of Change (McNemar, 1962) with dichotomous variables. These tests minimize the assumptions which must be made about the nature of the variables and permit testing of sex as well as housing effects. All changes and differences in change for the residents and the nonresidents are statistically significant at the 5 percent level—most of them at or beyond the 1 percent level. All are attributable to housing, not sex, difference.

DIRECTLY EXPRESSED SATISFACTION WITH HOUSING

About nine months after they moved in, apartment occupants had been asked to rate, on a 5-point scale, their satisfaction with *Victoria Plaza* as a place to live. Only three women were not "satisfied" or "very well satisfied." One person moved out in the period between interviews, while about one in every three of the unsuccessful applicants moved one or more times during that period.

This might have sampled a "honeymoon" phase. However, when a similar question was put to them about 3 months later in the regular followup interview, only one woman reacted negatively. These favorable ratings seemed reasonably honest reflections of feelings. Residents' occupancy of living space in the *Plaza* was secure. There was no longer pressure—as there may have been while they were applicants—to give responses which might improve their chances of obtaining apartments. From the beginning it was obvious that they were delighted with their good luck and appreciative of the many changes brought about in their lives. This first flush of enthusiasm, far from dying down or swinging back toward disillusionment, seemed only to deepen with continuing experience.

Residents did not feel that the building, their own apartments, the Senior Community Center in the same building, or the other people living in it, were perfect. They did not expect Utopia, however, and most were wryly aware that they were not without fault themselves. Even more important in determining the unanimity of their satisfaction with *Victoria Plaza* was the dramatic improvement it represented over what they had had immediately before. They had moved from substandard housing to a freshly completed, totally modern apartment building, and they appreciated and enjoyed the convenience, cleanliness, and beauty. From social isolation or resentment-producing interpersonal situations, they had been transported into the midst of a bountiful supply of people, yet they had considerable control over their own privacy and choice of associates. They were genuinely pleased and grateful for these marked improvements in determining realities of their day-to-day living.

Some of the "special design" features of the building evoked negative comments. Low clothes rods (to reduce stretching) drooped clothes on the floor. High refrigerators (to eliminate stooping) were difficult to see into and messy to defrost. Back-control panel stoves seemed less safe for older people because of their poor vision and unsteadiness.

The most pervasive dissatisfaction was over lack of privacy. This related to characteristics of the building itself, particularly the location and draping of windows. It was expressed in complaints about tours through the new facility and about nonresident elder citizens who made use of the Senior Center. Also, it tied in with the fact that gossip was most frequently mentioned when residents were asked to name the "worst thing" about the *Plaza*. These criticisms were given in an effort to improve future facilities and were not indicative of a desire to leave. During the first 18 months only one person moved out voluntarily, for reasons other than ill health or physical incapacity.

Housing had practically disappeared as a "major problem" among residents, while

TABLE 1

SATISFACTION WITH HOUSING AND
LIVING ARRANGEMENTS

Variables	F	Chi-Square
↓ Major problem: housing.		79.23**
↑ Satisfaction with living arrangements........	19.76**	
↑ Evaluation of housing...	31.28**	
↑ Housing value for cost..	15.26**	
↑ Evaluation of neighborhood...............	12.78**	

** Significance at or beyond the .01 level.
↑ Increased for residents relative to nonresidents.
↓ Decreased for residents relative to nonresidents.

NOTE. All tabular material in this paper is reported more fully in *A Future for the Aged; The Residents of Victoria Plaza.* Austin, University of Texas Press, 1961.

it continued to plague those who continued to live elsewhere (table 1). Direct evaluations of their housing by residents were drastically different from those they had made a year earlier, though evaluations of nonresidents were not appreciably altered. Residence in *Victoria Plaza* had a tremendous impact on satisfaction with arrangements for eating, sleeping, garbage disposal, and maintenance. *Plaza* dwellers were unanimously delighted with these conveniences, regardless of their evaluations earlier. No matter how an individual described his living conditions at the time of the initial interview, and given only the fact that he was to move into the Plaza, one could predict his followup evaluation perfectly. Nonresidents' views of their housing and living conditions were also predictable but in a different way—they did not change. These results suggest that the earlier judgments by applicants were realistic and that, rather than expressing generalized dissatisfaction, they related to the specifics of the environment.

CHANGES IN LIFE STYLE

Services wanted.—Residents showed a dramatic decrease in the number of services they felt they needed (table 2). In the final interview, fewer than 20 percent

TABLE 2

SERVICES WANTED

Services	Chi-Square	Residence by Sex
↓ Number wanted........	123.12**	
↓ Recreational...........	114.45**	
↓ Instructional..........	31.17**	
↓ Housekeeping.........	94.31**	
↓ Transportation........	13.46**	
↓ Medical..............	10.80**	
↑ Cafeteria..............	51.62**	
↑ Beauty shop..........		64.15**

** Significance at or beyond the .01 level.
↑ Increased for residents relative to nonresidents.
↓ Decreased for residents relative to nonresidents.

of the people in *Victoria Plaza* expressed the need for one or more services, though over three-fourths of the same people, as applicants, had named some. The pattern of change is interesting. In the second interview, fewer residents mentioned recreational, instructional, housekeeping, transportation, and medical services. On the other hand, an increased number of residents wanted a cafeteria or other food service, and more women residents expressed the desire for a beauty shop.

Budget.—The period between interviews was one of a slightly rising cost of living. This was reflected in the tendency for nonresidents to increase their food budgets by about 50 cents a month (table 3), while residents, on the average, spent $3.65 less per month for food. (As applicants, both groups had averaged about $24.50 per month for food.) This greater

resistance by *Plaza* dwellers to rising costs was probably related to the pressure of other demands on fixed incomes. Food budgets were surely more limited for the 50 percent who had to pay more rent to live in *Victoria Plaza.*

The new contagion to "keep up with the neighbors" was also probably related. Previously, hand-me-down clothing and old furniture had been suitable, but these were no longer acceptable. Housing Authority personnel had been concerned over the possibility that old people would not want to give up belongings too cumbersome or too dirty for the new building, but their tendency to buy new ones "on time" was perhaps a greater hazard.

Though residents expressed increased satisfaction with their income, they were

TABLE 3

LIVING COSTS

Items	F	Chi-Square
↑ Food costs............	6.62**	
↓↑ Cost of housing.......	91.11**	
↑ Satisfaction from money	35.28**	
↑ Financial security.....		91.00**
↑ Major problem: money.		31.29**

** Significance at or beyond the .01 level.
↑ Increased for residents relative to nonresidents.
↑↓ Relative increase or decrease differed according to amount of rent paid by applicant.

also more likely to consider it as a "major problem" than they had previously or than the nonresidents did. Apparently, they enjoyed what their money bought for them, but the new style of life tempted them with new ways to spend, and in some instances "rainy day" sums or "burial money" was depleted.

Activities and relationships with others. —Residents showed many changes in the pattern of their lives, generally toward increased activity and social interaction (table 4). Memberships in clubs and participation in less formal group activities multiplied. Furthermore, the residents were not surfeited—the number of groups they wanted to join also increased. The number of leisure activities, and the proportion of social and active pastimes to solitary and inactive ones, increased. The amount of time spent sleeping and resting, or time "doing nothing" or simply not accounted for, decreased.

While there was a tendency for nonresidents to have fewer friends at followup than at baseline data collection time, residents had more friends and more contact with friends. Family contacts of residents decreased relatively but not absolutely. Satisfaction with family, as well as

clined in importance with nonresidents, although church attendance remained as it had been. Residents reported more "calls" from clergy and laymen, probably because of their increased visibility and accessibility.

TABLE 4

ACTIVITIES AND RELATIONSHIPS WITH OTHERS

Variables	F	Chi-Square
↑ Memberships		11.05**
↑ Time at meetings	5.93**	
↑ Leadership roles in organizations		11.98**
↑ Memberships wanted		81.19**
↑ Activities compared to 55	30.67**	
↑ Number of leisure activities	9.41**	
↑ Percent active activities	6.01**	
↑ Percent social activities	12.83**	
↑ Time at hobbies	8.31**	
↓ Time sleeping	7.86**	
↓ "Lost" time	23.02**	
↑ Number of close friends	13.88**	
↑ How often visit friends	24.33**	
↑ How often friends visit	11.42**	
↑ Visitors: neighbors vs. family		47.55**
↑ Phone relatives	11.81**	
↑ Attitude: family	10.37**	
↑ Attitude: friends	42.76**	
↓ Major problem: companionship		10.42**
↑ Attitude: religion	7.36**	
↑ Calls from church people		31.71**
↓ Disengagement score	6.74**	

** Significance at or beyond the .01 level.
↑ Increased for residents relative to nonresidents.
↓ Decreased for residents relative to nonresidents.

TABLE 5

MORALE

Indexes	F	Chi-Square
↑ Age identification (middle-aged)		6.50*
↑ Feel about accomplishments in life	5.79*	
↑ Attitude: work	13.87**	
↑ Attitude: usefulness	8.06**	
↑ Attitude: happiness	24.79**	
↑ Attitude: total	45.78**	
↓ Major problem: personal adjustment		5.18*
↑ Happiest period (present)	15.51**	
↑ Percent of favorable adjectives	8.68**	
↓ Number of major problems	5.52*	

* Significance at the .05 level.
** Significance at or beyond the .01 level.
↑ Increased for residents relative to nonresidents.
↓ Decreased for residents relative to nonresidents.

On a Disengagement Index, residents had lower scores, nonresidents slightly higher scores, at followup than at baseline. These scores reflect the interviewers' judgments of the nonresidents as people who showed diminished involvement over the intervening period with people, material possessions, and activities—and of the residents as people who were maintaining and even increasing involvement.

Views of themselves.—Though they were a year or more older, an increased number of residents still thought of themselves as "middle-aged" (table 5). Their evaluations of their accomplishment in life were higher than they had been a year earlier. Residents had more optimistic opinions of their ability to work and of their general usefulness, while those of nonresidents had declined.

with friends, improved for residents. Nonresidents showed no change in contacts with kin or in attitudes toward family or friends.

Patterns of church attendance did not change for either group. Religion, however, became even more important to residents. For a number of them, *Victoria Plaza* literally seemed the answer to prayer. During the same period, religion de-

Residents considered themselves happier than they had earlier—nonresidents, less happy. Compared to a year earlier, less than half as many residents, but twice as many nonresidents, worried about their personal adjustment. In describing themselves, residents chose a larger percentage of adjectives with positive connotations. Fewer residents could name any problem

TABLE 6

HEALTH

Indexes	F	Chi-Square
↑ Rating of health.......	6.41*	
↑ Attitude: health........	5.93*	
↓ Major problem: health..		5.90*
↓ Neurotic problems......	5.98*	
↓ Time on health care....	5.53*	

* Significance at the .05 level.
↑ Increased for residents relative to nonresidents.
↓ Decreased for residents relative to nonresidents.

of major proportions. Fewer said the present was the unhappiest time of life; more, that it was the happiest. All of these trends were reversed for nonresidents.

Health.—Living in *Victoria Plaza* affected health, or at least most people's feelings about their health (table 6). Nonresidents consistently showed a tendency to change for the worse on items related to physical and mental well-being. Residents improved. These tendencies were observed also on the more objective items. Residents, for example, decreased time spent in health care and reduced their requests for medical services. Requests for medical care increased among nonresidents.

SUMMARY

Changes consequent upon moving to *Victoria Plaza* were obvious in all measures of satisfaction, attitude, life style, and adjustment. They were consistently in the direction of "good adjustment" insofar as this is defined for adults in general—away from passivity, seclusiveness, or disengagement. These changes, together with the continuing enthusiasm of residents, strongly suggest that *Victoria Plaza* was a success in meeting the needs of this group of "middle-aged" people, and that the impact of environment should not be underestimated, even with people in the later years of life. Only a second followup of these people, over a longer period of time, can determine the extent of a Hawthorne Effect (Roethlisberger and Dickson, 1939). Only a new study of different old people in another setting can test the generality of these findings.

46

PETER TOWNSEND

EXAMPLES OF DIARIES KEPT BY OLDER PEOPLE

The following diaries were selected from twelve that give some illustration of the patterns of daily life of old people in Bethnal Green. With a few minor alterations to conceal identity and correct spelling and punctuation they are printed as written. Among a few simple instructions people were asked to note the time of day when getting up, having breakfast, calling on relatives and friends, etc., and to note in particular whom they met and what they did together. Altogether 20 people, selected to represent as fair a cross-section as possible of those interviewed, were approached. A few refused because they were unable to write and a few because they did not want to do it. Twelve kept a diary for a whole week.

WEEK'S DIARY NO. 1
MARCH 21–27, 1955

Mrs. Tucker, 16 Bantam Street, aged 60, living with infirm husband in terraced cottage

MONDAY

7:45 a.m.—I got up, went down and put my kettle on the gas—halfway—then I raked my fire out and laid it, swept my ashes up and then cleaned my hearth. Then I set light to my fire, then sat down for a while, then I made tea and me and Dad had a cup.

9:20 a.m.—I went out for the *Daily Mirror* and fags for Dad. About eight people said "Good morning" with a nice smile, then I replied back. Then I went

Reprinted from Peter Townsend, *The Family Life of Old People* (London: Routledge and Kegan Paul, 1957), app. 3, pp. 249–55.

home and prepared oats and bread, butter and tea and me and Dad sat for breakfast. When we finished I cleared away and swept and mopped my kitchen out.

11:15 a.m.—I started to get dinner on, then Mrs. Rice, a neighbour, asked me to get her coals in, and she will take my bagwash, also get my dog's meat. We had a nice chat about Mother's Day. I showed her my flowers and card which Alice sent. It was very touching, a box of chocs from John, stockings and card from Rose, card and 5s. from Bill, as I know they all think dearly of me.

1:00 p.m.—My daughter Alice came with baby. We had dinner together.

2:00 p.m.—My daughter Rose and husband came. I made them a cup of tea and cake.

3:15 p.m.—Dad and I sat to listen to radio.

5:00 p.m.—We both had tea, bread and cheese Dad, bread and jam myself. When finished I cleared away again.

7:00 p.m.—My son John and his wife called to see if we were all right before they went home from work.

8:00 p.m.—I did a little mending.

10 p.m.—We went to bed.

TUESDAY

8:00 a.m.—I put kettle on. While waiting for it to boil I lit my fire, swept up, cleaned my hearth, then made my tea and sat for a while.

9:00 a.m.—I went for the *Mirror*. I had a chat with Mrs. Hoover. She told me about her husband being queer, I felt very sorry for her, although I have my own bad. Then I got my potatoes and went home, had breakfast, plate of oats for Dad and me.

10:10 a.m.—I cleared my kitchen up and went out for stewing meat around the corner at Stans, only 1*s.* 6*d.* Came back and put it on.

11:30 a.m.—I went around to see my little granddaughter Carol in Tudworth St. A lady asked me how I was. She told me when her boy was three she used to miss the food off the table such as spam or pies, she spoke to him about it, he was feeding his pussy, he said. She gave him a bit to *give* his pussy and, as he called it, a rat came out of a hole and we had a good laugh. Then I came home with my granddaughter. I am happy when she is here and so is Dad.

1:00 p.m.—We had dinner, then I read the paper.

4:30 p.m.—My daughter came. We had tea together, then she took baby home.

5:30 p.m.—Listened to wireless.

7:00 p.m.—My son and wife called in. Stayed till 8, then went home.

9:00 p.m.—We went to bed.

WEDNESDAY

7:45 a.m.—We were up as I had to go to Doctor's with Dad. We just had a cup of tea and off we went at 9. Then we came home to Quaker Oats and bread and butter—that was 10 o'clock. I lit my fire, then cleared my kitchen up.

11:00 a.m.—I went to the chemist first, then got my potatoes and a little piece of meat. I made a lot of it, I put it through the mincer with other little things and made a nice pie.

1:00 p.m.—We had dinner and a cup of tea and my daughter stayed with baby Carol. Nobody came after 6 o'clock, except my son John came with his wife to say good night before they went home from work.

9:00 p.m.—We went to bed: I didn't feel so well with my back.

THURSDAY

7:00 a.m.—I got up a bit early as it was early closing and I can't rush about and I can't always expect the children to be right on spot every time, so while God above gives me a little health and strength I must use it.

10:00 a.m.—I went for my shopping which didn't last long as I don't get my money till Friday and Saturday, so we make the best of it.

12:30 p.m.—We had dinner, then had a rest. My daughter came with baby then.

2:30 p.m.—I fed my dog and cats, then a neighbour asked me to have her key and see her coals in, as she was visiting a sick friend.

5:00 p.m.—My grandson came to see me. He loves to have tea with me. He went home at 8 o'clock.

9:30 p.m.—We went to bed.

FRIDAY

7:30 a.m.—I got up, lit my fire, had a cup of tea and then washed my woollens out, and then I started to do my bedroom, that lasted up till 11:15, then I got ready and went to the post office with Dad. I got a few errands on the way and some fish and chips for dinner, then I fed my birds, cat, dog, had a rest, then went out. (Two married daughters and three grandchildren came and had a midday meal.)

3:30 p.m.—We went and sat in the park, had a little stroll, then home to tea.

5:00 p.m.—We had egg, bread and butter for tea.

6:30 p.m.—John and wife came as they always do, then I washed up and cleared up my kitchen. Listened to wireless all night, in between I did a bit of ironing.

10:30 p.m.—We went to bed.

SATURDAY

7:00 a.m.—I got up, fed my birds, gave the dog a cup of tea, then had a cup myself, I then got water for cleaning. My back and legs don't keep good, so I have to mop out with Dettol.

9:30 a.m.—I went with Dad to the post office and got a few things on the way.

11:30 a.m.—I went out to get meat for Sunday and potatoes. On my way back I met my brother, I hadn't seen him for two years. I went and had a drink with him, he was ever so pleased to see me. I hurried back because I left my three grandchildren indoors. I have them on Saturday while my daughter Rose is on the stall with her husband in Bethnal Green Road, but I am pleased to have them. I sent them to the pie shop. I made them hot cups of tea when they came back.

4:30 p.m.—We all went for a stroll to Woolworths (in Hackney) and looked at stalls and shops.

6:30 p.m.—Their mother took them home.

9:30 p.m.—Dad and I had a walk. Had one drink, then home for the wireless, then to bed.

SUNDAY

9:00 a.m.—Up and had breakfast, egg, bread and butter, fed my birds, dog, cats, then I ground all the hard bread I collected from my daughters through the mincer for the little birds outside. I bagged it up and that lasted all the week putting a bit out every morning.

10:30 a.m.—I got my dinner all on, then cleared up.

1:30 p.m.—Dinner and then a rest.

6:00 p.m.—Tea. My son (George—eldest) came with his wife and baby. Brought a box of chocolates. They stayed till 10 o'clock. (Also Alice, Rose and John.)

10:30 p.m.—Went to bed, as we missed the papers very much.

WEEK'S DIARY NO. 2
MARCH 21–27, 1955

Mr. William James, aged 73, widower, lives alone in two-room flat on first floor in Gretland Street. Formerly a market porter.

MONDAY

7:45 a.m.—Got up, made a cup of tea.
8:00 a.m.—Started to clear the place up. Cleared the fireplace out. I had the sweep

coming between 9:30 and 10 and they are very strict on time. And at 9 had some bread and marmalade for quickness and he came at 9:45. He stayed about 20 minutes—another 5s. gone. Well, I had to sweep up and clear the place up and got out at 11:15.

11:15 a.m.—Went to the paper shop, got my *News Chronicle* and my rations of 20 Woodbines and went to my daughter's place in Thirsk Street at 11:45. Sat down for a while and had a smoke.

12:15 p.m.—Washed her breakfast things up, swept the kitchen up and then had another sit down talking to Mr. Bird (budgie). Then found some cold meat, so I boiled some potatoes and had some dinner with a nice cup of tea.

1:30 p.m.—Sat down and read the paper and listened to the wireless and of course dozed off till 3:00 p.m. Got up, washed up and got ready for the girl to come home at 4:20, made a cup of tea, then the grandchildren came home at 4:40 and you know what they are for talking and at 5:30 I went home, buying the paper as I go along. Got home 5:50.

5:50 p.m.—First thing light the fire, then lay the table, make the tea, boil an egg and finish up with marmalade. Then sat down and read the paper. Then got up, washed up, had a wash, sat down till 9. Then went to the club and had a chat and a game of cards till 11, then home and so to bed 11:30.

TUESDAY

8:00 a.m.—Got up, made a cup of tea. After that cleared the stove out, chopped some wood and laid the fire for tonight, swept the room and dusted the place up and also did my bedroom. Made the bed and finished that job.

9:30 a.m.—Had some breakfast. I boiled an egg and some toast, also a slice of marmalade, and ate a lot of marmalade because I think it is good for the bowels. After breakfast had a smoke for a while, then washed up and put the things away, then went out.

11:00 a.m.—Got my paper, went to the baker's and got one small loaf. Met a couple of my friends and had a chin-wag and got round to the girl's place at 11:45. Had a look to see if there were any potatoes—none, so I went to the butcher on the corner, bought one small lamb chop and 4 lbs. of potatoes and went home loaded. Cooked my dinner and sat down and had a smoke and read the paper till 2. Then washed up and went to my daughter-in-law in Flower Street. My eldest grandchild was there, he is a lovely boy, he likes to hear me sing, he keeps on saying 'more'. Well, I got a nice cup of tea, then went home at 4:00, put the things on the table ready for the girl and her two nippers for their tea, for I tell you they come home hungry, they are good eaters. And after their tea a lot of talking and larking about. I went home at 5:30, buying my paper as I go home. Lit the fire, turned on the wireless, had my tea of bread and jam, sat down and read the paper till my son Arthur came. He comes every Tuesday. We talked till 8:00, then washed up and had a wash and went to the club at 9:00. Met my old chinas, and a game of cards with a couple of glasses of beer and home at 11:00. A couple of biscuits and into bed at 11:40.

FRIDAY

8:00 a.m.—Got up as usual. Put the kettle on for a cup of tea, after that cleared the grate out, chopped the wood and laid the fire ready for the evening. Swept the kitchen and my bedroom, then put the duster all round. Then got my breakfast.

9:50 a.m.—For breakfast I had a fried egg and one tomato. I am not a great lover of tomatoes but still they go down all right. After that washed up, had a wash myself and out we go. Went to the paper shop, got my cigs and paper, went over to the fish shop, bought a plaice for 1/6 and also a bloater for my tea. Crossing over the road saw one of my friends.

Had a chat for a while and then round to Thirsk St. and I bought a small loaf as I came along, the time nearly 12:00. Then washed her things up, made the fire, put some potatoes on, washed my fish, put it in the oven, mashed my potatoes and you have a nice dinner. That over sat down, and read and a smoke at 2:00, got up at 3:00 and had a clean up, then went to the door for a while waiting for the girl to come along and when I saw her coming along get inside and put the tools on the table for a cup of tea, that is near enough 4:30. 10 minutes later in come the two hungry merchants and then we got more school for tea and 5:30 I went home. No papers—oh dear! That's done it. Well, go indoors, light the fire, lay the table and have my tea which was a bloater and very nice too! Put the wireless on for the news, and you don't get much out of that. Then sat down till 8:00 with a nice Woodbine. Then washed up and cleared the deck. Had a wash and shave and at 9:00 round to the club. Then we had a good chat—what cards! Oh yes, a nice game of cribbage, and our usual couple of drinks and when the bell rings that's your lot. Homeward bound and had a couple of biscuits and so to bed 11:40.

SATURDAY

8:00 a.m.—Got up, made a cup of tea, put a kettle of water on and scrubbed the stairs down at 9:00. Went out and did some shopping. I bought one long cut loaf 8*d.*, bacon ⅛, 4 eggs, ½—3/6 the lot, and ¼ marge 9*d.* Went home and had a rasher and one egg for breakfast. After that washed up, swept the place out, then I went to the paper shop and got Woodbines but no papers. Well, my friend comes every Saturday morning at about 11:30 and we sat down and had a chat about anything, you might say the weather and the strike,[1] which I think was very unjust as there was such a lot of sport. At 12:30 we went out to the P.H. and had a couple of drinks. I left him at 2:00.

[1] A printing strike, when no newspapers were published.

On the way home I bought one small chop and one kidney for dinner which was O.K. Put the wireless on and heard the boat race—some race! Well, sat down for a while and a smoke, then boiled a kettle of water, washed up everything, made my bed, then waited for football, that lasted till 4:45. Then went and paid Oxford House loan club which is a Xmas club for my son and daughter. Went to the paper shop and had a talk with the gov'nor. Got back in time for the football results and at 6:00 had some tea. I don't go to the daughter's house on Saturday or Sunday but will tell you tomorrow where we go. That will be Sunday. Well, after tea put the wireless on to the Home Service, washed up, put the things away and listened to the wireless till 9:00. Then went to the club. No cards Saturday and Sunday. Piano playing and anybody who can sing a song, but it makes a nice evening till 11:00 and then home and finished with the wireless at 12:00, then bed.

SUNDAY

8:30 a.m.—Got up, made a cup of tea, sat down for a few minutes, then started to work on the grate. Cleaned it out, chopped the wood and made the fire. Went out and bought one small bottle of O.K. sauce, 1/–. Spoke to Mr. Gold for a while, then went home and started on the breakfast. I cooked egg and bacon and I think it makes a nice Sunday morning's meal. Well, after filling my tummy I went to work, washed up and swept up and cleared the place in general. All that done have a wash and change and get round to my eldest boy, Flower St. I go there to dinner every Sunday 1:30. I stopped there talking and chinwagging, then the woman next door came in: she and her husband had been down the Row and Petticoat Lane, and showed us what they bought, ash trays and small things like that and my word she can't half jaw. Then Betty the grandchild made a cup of tea, had that with a jam tart. Well, at 4:30 I said, 'Annie, I'm going to slip off the side', and when I was going she gave me two bananas and two long rolls for my tea, very nice too. I just had a slow walk home, got home at 10 past 5. On goes the wireless and tea at 6.00. Finished tea, sit down till 7:30, then washed up, cleared the deck and out at 8:30 to the club, because being Sunday they close earlier. I get home about 10:30, turned on the wireless with a few biscuits till about 11:45, then to bed.

421

47

HOWARD WEBBER

GAMES

My name is Eleanor Vernor, and I am an old woman. I live now with my daughter and her husband. Until my daughter came to get me, I was alone in the house where I had passed nearly my entire adult lifetime. In the last of those years, the house had fallen into some disrepair. Paint was needed on all the wood, the windowpanes were loose in their frames because the putty had become brittle and had fallen away, some of the screens had holes in them, and the corner of one of the porches was sinking. But it was not a disreputable house, though it was too big for me, having held at one time, besides me and my daughter, my husband and an aunt of mine whom we had brought to live with us much as my daughter has brought me to live with her. We had altered the house, worn it down and built it up in a thousand ways, and it was a monument to all of us. I had always assumed I would die in it.

I do not remember having lived in any other house. I remember other rooms, particularly from my childhood, but I can only conceive of them as being arranged in the pattern of that house, so that it is as if the furniture, the decoration, and even the placement of the windows and doors had varied but the essential house had always been with me. I believe that if I had ever become blind, my memory would have served for sight, and as I grew older that thought comforted me. And as long as I was able to

see, the appearance of the house would have comforted me also, for it suited the way in which I have come to look at the world. One sloughs off many customs and impostures, and the house as well no longer felt it must hide its naturalness or correct every lapse of posture. It was a good house, full of time.

Then Laura decided I was no longer able to live alone, and I have now a single bedroom to myself in her new house that smells of paint and impermanence. I have wondered who it was who told her—the neighbors, perhaps: Mr. and Wrs. Wrigley, whose Saint Bernard yearned to sleep on my porch swing; the Esmonds, whose voices were so loud; Mrs. Britten, whose yardman was always running her mower into the flower bed that edged my property on her side—and I have wondered which one of the embarrassing little incidents it was she learned of. They were all squabbles of one kind or another. The milkman had begun counting out the wrong change for me. The postman had held back my mail. The paper boy had delivered my newspaper or not, as the inclination struck him. And the clerks at the grocery store had amused themselves by playing petty tricks on me, breaking a few of my eggs as they packed the carton in a bag, or speaking so softly I could not hear them. The milkman wanted money, the postman and the newspaper boy convenience, the clerks amusement. To keep me from insisting on justice and courtesy, they relied on the precariousness of an old person's reputation, on the skepticism with which the word of the old is regarded, on my fear and feebleness. But I caught each of them up, and I did insist.

When I was young, I used to discount what the old ladies I knew said. I heard their tales of injustice with a smile working at the corners of my mouth. Outrage screwed their faces up even more than age had already, and, breathless and palsied, they showed in their passion a presumption that amused me. But now I was discovering that the old ladies were right, having become one myself; there is no end to the advantage people will take of you if they can. I could not let that advantage be taken. So much seemed to depend on standing firm—my self-respect, the possibility for a reasonable life in the years ahead, even the balance of my mind. Yet I recalled my own smiles of years ago, and I was not surprised when Laura came to my door one afternoon.

I was in one way pleased to see her. I had known that the aspect of things changes from year to year, that it is like the examples of optical illusions one used to see in books or magazines—the clever patterns that shifted inward or outward according as one happened to look at them. I could not submit to the milkman's cheating, but I could tell what he was thinking of me. As I ran out and called back the postman, I had the dreadful feeling that when I spoke my words to him they might emerge as noise or light or delicate puffs of smoke. I could picture the wide-mouthed, close-eyed face of the paper boy exploding into a joke-store bouquet of plastic pansies. The clerks I could imagine slowly rising on their billowing aprons into the sky, like Baptist angels. I do not mean that I had lost hold. I do not think one ever loses one's intelligence, and visions play in the attics of everyone's mind. What I mean is that my visions, so far as I could tell, were different now, that maybe I had my own code of justice now, which was unlike Laura's, or my own twenty years ago, or sixty years ago. When she came, I thought, Now I don't have to worry about the meaning of these new illusions. Now

Laura will take care of the world outside.

As soon as I opened the door, Laura said she had been struck with a sense of missing me and had decided on impulse to ride up and see me. She talked about the time when she was a little girl, and recalled how she had depended on me. She mentioned the complexity of her present life and the pace of the world. She spoke of doing things for others, and the importance of family. In time, Peter, my son-in-law, came in. "Laura needs you," Peter said. "She won't admit it, but it's really true."

It was clear that Peter and Laura had considered in advance what to do and say —I saw that without difficulty. So that I could think, I went off and made tea for the three of us. By the time I returned, I had understood they were trying to deceive me. Not that the evidence was in any way obscure; I simply couldn't, at first, bring myself to accept their astonishing conviction that I was susceptible to that kind of deceit. They took their tea and began talking again, but I wouldn't allow it. I broke in and made the suggestion myself that I go back with them. It was the only way I saw to cut off the pretense. I did return with Laura and Peter, but the pretense was merely beginning.

It is games, really, that we have played —games about who I am. The aim of them all was that I am as young as Laura and Peter, as free, as carefree, as strong, as recollected. They must soon have known that I knew they were trying to deceive me, and their encouragements and deferences and accommodations became an elegant play among us. I was never tired because I am old but because I had walked too much or there had been a draft upon my legs, and my turn came when I said, "Yes, yes, that is exactly what it is." If I couldn't open the olive jar, the packers of olives were taken to task for affixing the covers too tightly. If I lay awake at night, it was the unseasonable weather that was blamed. Every one of my acquiescences in these pretenses brought me sadness.

The evening I got here—I remember I was wearing a gray suit that I had decided to give to the Salvation Army but that Laura had laid out for me to wear on our trip—I was ill at ease. I stood in their strange kitchen and wondered whether I should sit or offer to make dinner or go to my room. There had been a haste about our departure, and now there was shame in the air. Laura and Peter put on their serious expressions and began again telling me how fond they were of me. I remember wishing they had told me instead that they could imagine how it is to have to give up dreaming and the possibility of justification that the future allows, to have to tolerate a mind that on occasion cannot follow the slight movements of the present moment, and, finally, to have to give up authority and independence. But I said nothing. Later on, we talked again. "Do whatever you like, as you like it," they told me. "Keep your own hours. Go shopping, have friends in." Then they sent me to bed. And I said a pleasant "good night" as I went. I was caught in the trap of the games already.

I stayed in it, even though some of them were quite cruel. I used to paint—water colors—years ago, and they brought down some of my best work, which had been hanging on the walls of my home, and hung these pictures in my bedroom here. Then they bought me brushes and colors and paper, and I, who had vowed that when my hand wavered I would cheerfully give up painting and content myself with admiring what I had done at my best, had no choice but to take it up again, having not painted a stroke for ten or more years. I puttered with the paints, but that was not enough. They made me go on. They went so far as to frame one of my wretched efforts and put it on the wall with the others. They admired it ex-

travagantly, but if I had dared, I would have burned it, and the good ones with it. As it was, I became a little surly, but even that satisfaction was removed, for they ascribed my humor to a new variety of medicine I was taking.

I like my daughter and my son-in-law. There is a lot of my husband in Laura. He has been dead for many years, but I have not forgotten him. To others, I suppose he must have seemed ineffectual. He dressed carelessly, and, whatever he was doing, moved by indirection. He was a master of the precisely inappropriate word, forgot people's names, occasionally fell asleep at parties, and lost his wallet or his car keys time after time. But when he finally blundered into the clear truth about any human situation, he did, during all the years I lived with him, what was kind and right, unfailingly. And Laura's aim is often wide of the mark, but her mark is the same as his was.

As for my son-in-law, the only thing I really know about him is that my daughter loves him. He is very youthful and energetic. He speaks respectfully to me, awkwardly, and frequently. I have the feeling that if I knew him better I would have many more grounds for liking him.

Laura and Peter do not disappoint me. What has disappointed me is the way things are—the subtle conspiracy of my weakening nerves and tendons and of the alteration in my outward flesh and of my changing disposition that has cut me off from the continent of the young and put me on the ancient island where I am. And yet, island and continent are both part of the world of the living. The changeless old are not changeless at all. They live, they are real, authentic, and the same combinations of circumstance form on one side as on the other.

As my months with Laura and Peter passed, and the games thronged our days until it was wearisome to be in one another's presence, I almost began to look upon myself as they did—changeless, timeless, exiled on my island. But happenings go on, even for the old, and the happening that brought me back to myself began with Mrs. Hartwell, who is even older than I.

Mrs. Hartwell—her first name is Eva, but I never call her that—lives four blocks away. She is with her son and his wife and has in their house a room quite like my own. It was Laura who learned about Mrs. Hartwell and from time to time took me to sit in her son's garden with her. She herself is not able to move about much any more. It is a pleasant garden, and when Laura and Mrs. Hartwell's daughter-in-law settled us there and left, we were perfectly alone, not being able to see more than the tops of the surrounding houses above all the trees. In an hour, the young people returned, and Laura and I went home.

"Dear Mrs. Vernor," Mrs. Hartwell always began when we were by ourselves, "how are things with you these days?"

And then we talked about our situations. There are two children in Mrs. Hartwell's house, and that is her advantage in many ways. Her son and his wife do not have as much time to contrive as Laura and Peter do. There is not as much routine. Best of all, the children do not know enough to engage in duplicities, and she and they are friends. On the other hand, she has been quite ill and dreads the time when she may have to go to a hospital. Also, her daughter-in-law somehow has the idea that Mrs. Hartwell's poor health jeopardizes the children, and all the dishes are sterilized whenever she is unwell. She is always trying to seem better than she really feels.

When I first began to visit Mrs. Hartwell, our conversations were limited to those matters one can discuss with an intelligent person about whom one knows almost nothing. They would have sufficed. Mrs. Hartwell was not in my debt, nor was I in hers; we had common problems; and, altogether, we were able to speak freely and enjoyably. Later, though, as we began to learn more about each other, we confided more and ranged

further. We talked a great deal about our childhoods. She remembered a school much like the one I went to. She could still call up her teachers' names, the procedures of the classroom, what the children wore and did, what games they played.

"Did you by any chance ever play marbles, Mrs. Vernor?" she said to me one day.

"Why, yes," I said. "I was a champion player."

"What a coincidence," she said.

And for the next few minutes we compared our merits as marbles players. We both, it seemed, had been little girls gifted at the game. I had prided myself on never having to buy any new marbles. I had had a reserve of marbles that I kept in three cloth bags, I remembered. I never used these in play and, in fact, never touched them except occasionally to turn them over in my fingers and admire them. She recalled that the time had come when it was difficult to find any boy who would risk his marbles against her, she won so consistently. She had begun to have to play with a handicap, such as her boulders against someone else's agates.

Our talk moved to other matters, and I thought no more about marbles until I next came to see her. She was waiting for me in the garden, and she had an embroidered purse in her lap. I did not notice it in the beginning, and our conversation at first was quite usual. It lagged after a while, though, and we sat for a time in silence. Mrs. Hartwell broke the pause by holding up her purse and shaking it. I thought she wanted me to admire it, and I passed some compliment, but I saw then that was not what she had in mind.

"What do you suppose is inside?" she asked me.

I had no idea, of course, and said so, but instead of telling me, she put the purse

425

down and started philosophizing in some way about friends and friendship.

"What's wrong?" I said.

"Nothing's wrong," she said. "I'm trying to tell you that this purse is full of marbles."

"Marbles?" I said.

"I got them from the children," she said. "They lent them to me so we could play. I told them you wanted to."

For a minute, I thought I was witnessing some kind of disintegration in Mrs. Hartwell. I was shocked and saddened. But then, seeing her sitting there looking like herself, her hands folded around the purse, her face composed and earnest, I knew that could not be so. "If you want to play, let's play," I said.

"Don't do it unless you really do want to," she said.

"I do," I said, and by that time I did indeed, though it surprised me to discover it.

Our chairs were always set upon a sandy oval where a folding table was sometimes put for outdoor entertainments, and this surface, with a little digging, made an entirely adequate ring. I moved my chair across from Mrs. Hartwell's and scooped out the sand with my hand. We divided the marbles, and hesitantly, as when one takes up a song that others are singing, began a game. We had to crouch in our chairs in order to reach the ring, but we played leisurely, breaking off now and then to rest. Before long, I was enjoying myself, and I believe Mrs. Hartwell was, too. I could not help feeling that what we were doing was a justification of ourselves as reasonable human beings, entitled to our wishes.

Each of us won about as often as the other that day. Allowing for age and lack of practice, Mrs. Hartwell had not exaggerated her prowess, but then, neither had I my own. We were careful to finish playing long before we began to expect the two young people. The marbles were returned to Mrs. Hartwell's purse, I filled in the ring, and when Laura and Mrs. Hartwell's daughter-in-law came, we were exactly as they had found us every other time.

When I visited Mrs. Hartwell again, I felt uneasy about our little indulgence. I looked immediately to see whether the purse was again in her lap, and it was. She, however, behaved so naturally—when we were alone, opening it in the middle of a story she was telling, and counting the marbles into two piles with perfect self-possession—that I could not remain disquieted. Once more we moved our chairs, and once more I prepared the ring.

This day, I won the first few games, but then Mrs. Hartwell, saying "Knuckles down," set out to recoup her losses. She recovered her eye and, when her turn came, fired off a peerless shot. Then she fainted. It was only vertigo, I believe, for she was quite all right in a few minutes, but at the time I could not know she would be, and I had to call for help. At first, though I suppose her daughter-in-law and Laura saw what we had been doing, they were occupied in reviving Mrs. Hartwell. It was after she was herself again that the awkwardness came.

"Mother," Laura said, looking at me. It was an entirely equivocal word in that circumstance, but my conscience led me to take it badly, and I was ashamed.

Laura and I made a hasty departure. My embarrassment did not abate when we were back at her house. Laura and Peter were very kind to me through the evening, but that only made me feel worse. A day passed, and I hardly went out of my room. Another day came, and in the morning Laura told me she would be taking me to see Mrs. Hartwell at three.

I pretended I did not feel well and told her I wouldn't be able to go. She cocked her head at me, the way her father used to, conjuring him into my mind with that small gesture. I gave in.

When I actually got in the car and then got out at Mrs. Hartwell's, when I passed through the house, when I came out on the lawn and saw Mrs. Hartwell sitting in her chair, I was in anguish. The young people left quickly, but at the last moment Laura pressed my hand. I went forward, though I did not look at Mrs. Hartwell.

"Mrs. Vernor," she said to me.

So I looked at her. The purse was in her lap.

"How are things these days?" she said, motioning me to my chair.

On the seat of it was an old evening bag of mine that Laura had stuffed into one of my suitcases when I moved to her house. I opened it, and, of course, it was filled with marbles.

Since then, the pretenses that had con-fined my life have been receding. My essential situation is the same. I am not free or carefree or strong or recollected. But something has happened at the core of things. I feel better. Mrs. Hartwell and I do not play marbles any more, for that was a silly business. It is not at all silly to feel better, though, and when I am alone I think often how some slight event can shift a whole structure of circumstance so that the balance is somewhat away from distress.

PART VIII

AGING IN OTHER SOCIETIES

Studies of human behavior in different societies have helped the social scientist understand the relations between culture and personality and have helped him shake free his hypotheses about human behavior from particular sets of cultural biases. These points are as important in studying middle age and aging as in studying child development. The five papers in this section illustrate some of the insights that are emerging, as a small but growing number of investigators are turning attention to the crosscultural method in studying patterns of aging.

In the first paper Clark raises the question: why is it that anthropologists in the past have focused attention upon the early part of the life-cycle, to the neglect of the latter part? The author argues that persons in any given society must learn the "proper" manner of growing old; movement from middle age to old age in modern American society represents a dramatic cultural discontinuity for most persons. Individuals who fail to reorder their values and their behavior in prescribed ways, and who cling to values more characteristic of American culture 25 years ago than of today, turn out to be today's best prospects for geriatric psychiatry according to the author. While this paper contrasts two time periods in America rather than two different societies, it points up the close relationships between culture, personality, and mental health.

The paper by Gutmann illustrates the use of projective techniques in a crosscultural psychological study of aging. In an earlier study based on a sample of middle-aged and older urban American men, the author reported age differences which indicated a developmental progression toward greater passivity and ego-regression in old age. Here, again using the Thematic Apperception Test along with an extensive interview, he collected comparable data on a group of Mayan Indian men and reports age differences in ego style remarkably similar to those found in the American sample. This study supports the hypothesis of developmental influences in personality throughout the life cycle.

The paper by Barker and Barker shows the differences in patterns of social participation in older people who live in a small Midwest town in United States and those in a small English town. It demonstrates that differences occur between groups of people who share the same general value patterns but who are responding to different social forces; and it shows that the immediate social structure of the community produces quite different behavior in otherwise similar groups. The paper is included also because of the unique research method involved in the approach of psychological ecology. While the method is laborious, it is unusually promising because it offers a way of comparing social-cultural settings in terms of actual opportunities and expectations for social interaction. In operationalizing their concepts and in developing new methods of quantification, the Barkers have built an empirical as well as a conceptual bridge between the behavior of individuals and measurable aspects of the social setting in which the behavior occurs.

The paper by Talmon analyzes the influence of ideological and social-structural factors on aging in collective settlements in Israel. While older people in the Kibbutz generally maintain productive roles in the economy as long as possible and retire gradually and while they remain full members of a cohesive community, nevertheless many older persons experience aging as a difficult and painful process of reorientation marked by severe intergenerational tensions. The author points out that the Kibbutz is a future-oriented, youth-centered society in which the major rewards are given for hard physical work and productivity; these values make it difficult for older persons to maintain feelings of worth.

The last paper in this group is addressed to the commonly-held thesis that the status of the aged was or is higher in pre-industrial societies than in contemporary urban societies and that current problems of the aged are consequences of urbanization and industrialization. Harlan finds that the social status of the aged in three traditional villages in India is actually quite low and not in keeping with the prevailing hyothetical norms which prescribe high status for the aged. In studying the power, prestige, authority, and security of older persons in the villages, he concludes that aging in pre-industrialized societies is fraught with as many problems as aging in our own culture.

Cross-cultural studies in themselves do not, of course, overcome the problem of distinguishing the effects of historical and cultural change from "inherent" or developmental processes of aging. Even when similar age differences are found in various societies, as in Gutmann's study of Kansas City and Mayan men, it would be premature to attribute the similarity to universality of aging processes. Given the rapid social change going on in all parts of the world, it is likely that even in the "simple" societies now available for study by anthropologists, young adults hold values and attitudes that may distinguish them from older adults. As a consequence age differences discovered in such societies may reflect cultural change just as is true in industrialized societies. Comparative studies based on cross-sectional samples, while they may be the best available and while they go far toward broadening the perspective of the student of aging, are thus far only partially helpful in elucidating the interplay between cultural and biological factors. The problem of isolating "inherent" age changes must depend, in the last analysis, upon crosscultural and comparative studies which are longitudinal rather than cross-sectional. Meanwhile, comparative cross-sectional studies such as these reported in the following group of papers provide our best clues to the problem.

48

MARGARET CLARK

THE ANTHROPOLOGY OF AGING: A NEW AREA FOR
STUDIES OF CULTURE AND PERSONALITY

Anthropologists are relative newcomers to the field of aging studies and this is somewhat odd for two reasons. First of all, the aged are no strangers to us; ethnographers have traditionally relied heavily on the memories, knowledge, and insights of old informants for a good deal of their cultural data. Much of what we have learned in preliterate societies about the ways of man and the varieties of his culture we owe to the accumulated experiences and recollections of the elderly.

In the second place, anthropologists have long claimed the study of cultural patterning of the human life cycle, with its various phases, transitions, and rites of passage, as one of their special concerns. To be sure, early life has been given careful scrutiny: infancy, childhood, adolescence, the early adult years—all these have received meticulous ethnographic attention. However, if one is to judge from typical anthropological accounts, the span of years between the achievement of adult status and one's funerary rites is either an ethnographic vacuum or a vast monotonous plateau of invariable behavior. Occasional exceptions to this tendency in ethnography are found in reports on societies where age-grading is an inescapable feature of the culture, and where the elderly as a formal group play

Abridged from *The Gerontologist*, vol. 7, no. 1 (March, 1967).

This study is part of a larger interdisciplinary research program conducted at the Langley Porter Neuropsychiatric Institute under Public Health Grant No. MH-09145, with supplementary support from the California Department of Mental Hygiene.

critical roles in political or economic organization. Perhaps the most classical of such accounts is Warner's ethnography of the Murngin of Australia (Warner, 1958). A recent example of such work is Spencer's (1965) study of gerontocracy among the Samburu. LeVine (1965) has summarized some of these studies of age-graded societies in Africa, pointing particularly to the fact that, within many extended family units in such cultures, obligations between young and old

". . . beyond the nuclear family engender antagonisms which may ultimately be registered in homicide, suicide, litigation, and other forms of interpersonal conflict" (LeVine, 1965).

Leo Simmons (1945) was the first to introduce a cross-cultural perspective to gerontological studies. In his major work, he posed the following question:

"What in old age are the possible adjustments to different environments, both physical and social, and what uniformities or general trends may be observed in . . . cross-cultural analysis? More specifically, what securities for long life may be provided by the various social milieus and what may the aged do as individuals to safeguard their interests?"

Simmons' work was an analysis of the impact of 109 specific cultural traits (such as principal food source, matrilocal versus patrilocal residence, forms of marriage, inheritance and succession, and specific religious beliefs and practices) on the status of the aged. Correlations between these traits and the status and condition of elders were studied among 71 separate primitive people; the material was abstracted from the Yale Human Relations Area Files.

The focus of Simmons' work was on social status of the aged and its relationship to material culture and formal social structure. Thus, he was able to show, for example, that aged women tend to retain property rights more readily than men in simple hunting, fishing, and gathering societies, while it is aged men who preserve the greatest advantage in the control of property in farming and herding societies.

With the growth and development of the field of social gerontology, there is today a revived interest in the relationship between cultures and patterns of individual aging. There are two groups of behavioral scientists—none of them anthropologists, however, who are now engaged in crosscultural studies. But, curiously, research by anthropologists in the field of aging has been very sparse, although several exceptions may be noted. Norbeck (1953) has written on age-grading in Japan, including some data on old age. Henry (1963) has devoted a chapter in a recent book to a commentary on what he calls "human obsolescence" in American society. Arth (1965) has recently completed a year's study of intergenerational relations in an Ibo village in eastern Nigeria; his report is now in preparation. Current work on the anthropological aspects of geriatric psychiatry is being conducted by von Mering (1966) at the University of Pittsburgh.

Other writings by anthropologists in the field of aging have been in the nature of reports of observations incidental to research focused on some other central problem. (Simmons' data, in fact, were almost entirely of this kind.) Examples in recent publications are by Cowgill (1965) from his work in Thailand, and Shelton (1965) from his Ibo field notes. A group of such serendipitous papers were collected by Kleemeier (1961); these include brief essays or miscellany on cultural aspects of aging by Holmberg (Peru), Hughes (St. Lawrence Island Eskimos), Smith (Japan), Rustom (Burma), and Rowe (India).

The research reported in this paper adds to the accumulating evidence that the transition from adult to elderly status is a critical period of socialization whose norms and goals are rigorously structured by culture, just as is the transition from childhood to adulthood. This social metamorphosis of later life may be equally as crucial for the individual's subsequent emotional stability and equally as demanding in terms of reorganization of goals, values, and sanctioned social behavior. Yet, anthropologists have rarely discussed it.

There seem to be two reasons why this is so. First of all, within the discipline of anthropology, it is the student of culture and personality who would be most likely to observe and record information on the cultural patterning of aging and its impact on the individual. The field of culture and personality is largely an American product, however, and aging is not a popular topic in American thought. To contemplate later life is often seen as a morbid preoccupation—an unhealthy concern, somewhat akin to necrophilia. Since anthropologists are indeed creatures of their own culture, it may be that prevailing American attitudes toward aging are manifesting themselves in unconscious decisions by ethnographers to ignore this aspect of the life cycle.

A second factor seemingly related to the dearth of culture and personality studies of later life has a more rational basis. Early students in the field long tended to accept a view of personality as a system which is open during infancy and childhood, but closed and fixed fairly early in life, thenceforth becoming relatively impervious to the ordinary experiences of adult life. This idea was a direct borrowing from psychoanalytic theory, as described by Fromm-Reichmann (1950):

". . . Freud taught that all our relationships with other people, including the relationship of the mental patient with his doctor, are patterned by our early relationships with the significant people of our environment in infancy and childhood."

In this tradition, Honigmann (1954) listed the following among what he called "some basic postulates" in culture and personality research:

"Many patterns are learned early in life and remain to influence all further learning. From this postulate derives the importance attached to early experiences for an understanding of human behavior."

More recent advances in personality psychology seem to have made less impression on anthropologists than did the earlier psychoanalytic formulations. Work in the field of ego psychology, for instance, has led its adherents to a more flexible conception of personality. As early as twenty years ago, Allport wrote on the "functional autonomy" of adult personality:

"The dynamic psychology proposed here regards adult motives as infinitely varied, and as self-sustaining, contemporary systems, growing out of antecedent systems, but functionally independent of them" (1937).

More recently, Neugarten has observed that

"changes in personality occur with the passage of time—not only as the child becomes the adolescent, and the adolescent, the adult, but also as the adult moves from youth to middle age to old age. . . . We do ourselves a disservice to assume that relationships found to hold between various classes of phenomena in the child or in the adolescent hold, also, for the adult" (1966).

Within recent years this more current view of personality has been recognized by anthropologists; for example, Hsu (1961) has said:

". . . the term 'personality' possesses connotations that often lead the student to regard it as a complete entity in itself. Instead of seeing personality as a *lifelong process of interaction* [emphasis mine] between the individual and his society and culture, he thinks of it as being some sort of reified end-product (of very early experiences according to orthodox Freudians, of somewhat later sociocultural forces according to many Neo-Freudians and social scientists), which is ready to act in this or that direction regardless of the sociocultural fields in which it has to operate continuously. . . . The one-sided finished-product view of personality . . . must be resisted."

There is good evidence, as Barnouw (1963) claims, that students of culture and personality may fall prey to

"the fallacy of misplaced concreteness. . . We must grant that personality may change over time. Despite much carryover, the adult is a different person from the child. . . . Thus, there are both consistency and change in personality, just as there are both consistency and change in culture."

In spite of these disclaimers, there has still been no significant expansion in the culture and personality field to include studies of the last half of life. Still under the major influence of the Freudian view of human behavior as rooted in personality components formed and fixed in early childhood, personal change in adult life is seen as essentially superficial. The assumption persists that human beings are basically unchanging, at least in their deeper and "more important" aspects. This orientation has led students of culture and personality to confine their work to four major areas: (1) the enculturation of children and adolescents, and the role of child-rearing practices in the determination of adult personality, (2) status personality characteristics, as influenced by sex roles and class or caste differences —these, too, thought to be group differences for which the individual is shaped quite early in life; (3) modal personality or national character, usually derived from studies of young or middle-aged adults (those whose personalities are now assumed by the observer to be "fixed" or "set" into a particular shared pattern through common early life experiences); and (4) individual deviance (mental illness, criminality, sexual inversion, and the like) and its cultural interpretation. Nowhere in this conception of the field is there a place for studies of later life and the ways in which culture continues to pattern normative behavior, even to the moment of death.

This particular orientation in personality and culture studies seems to me to have imposed serious limitations on work in the field, in that it has tended to blur our understanding of cultural forces impinging upon adult individuals during the course of the life-span and to force us to think of changes in character structure during those years as "anomalies that need to be explained away," as Becker (1964) has said.

I have no wish to minimize the patent significance of early life experiences as patterned by culture in the development of the individual. But I do want to emphasize the fact that this development does not stop at any particular point in the life cycle. As this report will show, culture continues to prescribe certain changes in individual behavior and experience throughout the life-span.

The program of Studies in Aging of the Langley Porter Neuropsychiatric Institute is not primarily an anthropological investigation, but its two large cohort samples of community and mentally hospitalized aged have provided a wealth of information on the shaping power of culture upon individual patterns of adaptation to old age. These nearly 1200 Ss have been drawn from the population of San Francisco, a city with an enormous variety of subcultural and ethnic communities. In addition to this, since these two samples were selected to represent a range from mental health to illness, they offer an excellent opportunity for the study of adaptive and maladaptive modes of aging and the cultural factors influencing those modes. The following two case histories will illustrate this.

Mr. Spenser was born and reared in a rural village in Sussex, England. His father was a prototype of the English eccentric —self-styled inventor, tinkerer, mastermind of numerous projects which would "benefit all mankind" and recluse from an indifferent, unappreciative humanity. In this rural English setting, Mr. Spenser's father was patiently tolerated—and even prized as something of a village institution. But when Mr. Spenser himself grew into much the same kind of older man as his father had been—with the single difference that Mr. Spenser had early immigrated to the United States and was now growing old in a populous American city —all of this madcap wizardry and ceaseless puttering brought him into trouble with his American-born wife and the City Health Department.

Mr. Spenser had crammed into a three-storied house scores of pets—birds, rats, cats (whom he was training to live peaceably together as his contribution to world peace)—junk of all varieties, over a thousand cactus plants, his paintings, his sculpture, and buckets of his formula for "plastic stone," which Mr. Spenser was sure would revolutionize the building industry. The squalor was so outlandish that Mrs. Spenser refused to stay in the house any longer and moved into the building next door where she lived separate from her husband. In an attempt to force Mr. Spenser to conform a bit more to minimum standards of sanitation, his wife finally had him hospitalized for psychiatric observation.

After six months in a state mental hospital, Mr. Spenser was discharged. Since his release, he has tried to comply somewhat with the demands made upon him by his wife and the Health Department. But he still trains kittens to walk a tight-rope and, of course, he is still working on his many inventions. He is very proud of his release from the hospital, interpreting it as his personal victory over foolish psychiatrists and a vindictive wife.

An interesting parallel to this case is that of Mrs. Rena Trocopian:

Mrs. Trocopian was born and reared in Armenia and brought to the United States as a young bride for the young Mr. Trocopian who had preceded her and had made arrangements to wed her through a native marriage broker. As a small child, Mrs. Trocopian had witnessed the slaughter of her parents in the religious wars that raged in Armenia at that time. In consequence, Mrs. Trocopian was reared by her grandmother, an elderly woman of strong character, who was respected in the peasant village of the homeland as a folk-curer of considerable gift and esoteric knowledge. This old woman was the repository for all the traditional herbal remedies and was held in an awe bordering on fear by the ordinary villagers, who attributed such medical skills less to intellect and learning than to a possible indulgence in the black arts. As Mr. Spenser modeled his old age upon his father's, so Mrs. Trocopian, after a lifetime of service to a demanding, vituperative husband, struggled to attain the privileged and respected status of a great sorceress. "I am very talented," she said, "creative; I have a strong mind to overcome the weak. I could have been a physician. I am strong in my mind, both a scientist and a poet. I can create energy. I have the power to heal." But, unfortunately for Mrs. Trocopian, there was no place in her new world for her to reincarnate her old grandmother. Her strange ideas and her insistence upon them led her into conflict with her relatives and neighbors. Finally, her feelings of resentment against her Anglo-Saxon neighbors and her unappreciative family burst into open suspicion and hos-tility, resulting in her admission to a psychiatric hospital. She was released a year later, but has ever since been morose and preoccupied with aging and death.

Both of these cases provide interesting examples of the difficulties that arise from acculturation, when one tries to import models of adaptation to aging which are in conflict with prevailing norms. It should be noted that, in later life, both Mr. Spenser and Mrs. Trocopian showed personal characteristics deemed appropriate to the role of the aged person within their parent cultures. They were both unable, however, to emulate the aged role as defined and prescribed by American culture; the resulting conflicts with society led them into psychiatric institutions.

A comparative study of mentally-healthy and mentally-ill samples also affords evidence of how very similar conflicts are created *within* American culture simply by virtue of the fact that our culture demands major reorientations in values as people grow old. Perhaps a brief digression at this point can clarify a bit better how the dominant values of American culture work against the aged.

Most of us are sharply aware of how rapid advances in technology and medicine have opened up possibilities for the fullest realization of our potential longevity. The old are everywhere, and more and more so. The old have never been the problem they are today because, quite simply, they were never around in such numbers as they abound today. But the problem is far more than an arresting biological statistic. These numerous old people would be *no* problem were it not for the definition of old age—the expectations, requirements, and limitations—that American culture has imposed upon this period of life.

I have already mentioned how Simmons has examined the bewildering variety of definitions of aging in many cultures and how these definitions can be reasonably understood in the light of the social group's economy, history, religion, and the like. For most of these societies, "old age" is defined in functional terms—this is to say, when biological deterioration sets in, as this affects productivity, mobility, strength—in short, when the individual's capacity to contribute to the work and protection of the group to which he belongs is substantially changed. Beyond this, the culture will also prescribe what is to be done with such an individual: exposure, increased protection, contempt, or high honor. But in our own culture—one that has raised the awareness and measurement of time to a high art—old age has come to be increasingly defined in *formal* terms, according to a birthdate on a calendar. Ours is more a social definition of old age, based on chronology, more and more removed from the realities of physical debility. Moreover, with the intensification of social and economic problems, such as automation, unemployment, and increasing competition for the remaining jobs, there are current signs of setting this "retirement age" at an even earlier stage in the life-span—at 60 or even 55.

There are profound implications to these simple, hard facts. In essence, our culture is presently creating a new life-era—a new phase of considerable duration in the life cycle—but, as yet, has not developed any major institutions that can give purpose and meaning to life in these extended 20 or 30 years. In many simpler cultures, the old are the about-to-die. It seems that something of this code still lingers, atavistically, with us, despite the fact that our so-called "dying" people may go on living far beyond the formally defined onset of such a status.

Within any culture, certain social roles —age, sex, familial, or occupational—may be the locus of especially acute stresses. The stress in point in this discussion is the contradiction between a particular set of dominant cultural values in the United States and the physical and social restraints of old age.

As a part of the Geriatrics Research Program of the Langley Porter Neuropsychiatric Institute, we conducted in 1963–64 a set of intensive attitudinal interviews with 80 persons over the age 60. Half of these were community Ss, whose later lives had been free of any medical treatment for mental or emotional problems; the other 40 were hospitalized Ss, who had been institutionalized for psychiatric disorder for the first time after the age of 60. Most of these patients were given a psychogenic diagnosis. At the time of interview, two-thirds of the hospitalized Ss had been released from the hospital and one-third were still institutionalized.

The interview schedule contained a set of questions dealing with self-image and the criteria used by the S in making a self-judgment. All available data on self-perception for the members of the sample were subjected to qualitative content analysis. This analysis yielded six general criteria used by members of the sample as bases for self-esteem. These, in order of their frequency of mention, were as follows: (1) independence, (2) social acceptability, (3) adequacy of personal resources, (4) ability to cope with external threats or losses, (5) having significant goals or meaning in later life, and (6) ability to cope with changes in the self.

Responses falling within each of these areas were then examined for underlying value-orientations. (Note that the term *value-orientation* is defined here as a perception of reality, including notions of cause and effect, that influences the selection from available modes, means, and ends of action.) For each of the six areas, the orientations characteristic of the community sample on the one hand and the hospital sample on the other were defined. This procedure consisted of determination of central tendencies or characteristic configurations of value-orientation within the community and hospitalized subsamples. I found that, while there was overlap

438

between the two groups, approximately three-fourths of the community sample was oriented in ways that I have called "adaptive," while more than three-fifths of the hospitalized Ss subscribed to those orientations labeled "maladaptive."

The results of this comparative procedure were as shown in Table 1.

The ability to be independent, to provide for one's own needs, is an important value to the majority of all the elderly people in our sample, regardless of their state of mental health. This theme is recited over and over again in the inter-

community Ss are more likely to esteem themselves for being congenial, as attractive as possible, pleasant, easy to get along with, and supportive of others. The mentally ill characteristically perceive social approval as deriving from entirely different sources. They are skeptical of the idea that others will accept them simply for being pleasant or agreeable—in fact, they often mention this as a sign of weakness. Self-esteem of hospitalized Ss is

TABLE 1

DIFFERENCES BETWEEN ADAPTIVE AND MALADAPTIVE PERSONAL
VALUE-ORIENTATIONS IN AN AGED AMERICAN SAMPLE

Principal Areas of Concern To Both Groups	Adaptive Value-Orientations (Mentally-Well Group)	Maladaptive Value-Orientations (Mentally-Ill Group)
Independence	Pride in autonomy and concern for freedom of others	Avoidance of dependency out of fear and mistrust of others
Social acceptability	Congeniality	Status and achievement
Adequacy of personal resources	Conservation	Acquisition
Ability to cope with external threats or losses	Action if appropriate; resilience if loss is inevitable	Aggressiveness, regardless of the situation
	Harmoniousness	Control
	Emphasis on the existential	Emphasis on the instrumental
Having significant goals or meaning in later life	Relaxation and cooperation	Ambition and competitiveness
Ability to cope with changes in the self	Emphasis on continuity	Emphasis on progress
	Skill in substitution	Continued pursuit of earlier goals
	Reasonable level of aspiration	High level of aspiration

views, but if we look at the underlying value-orientations, the *reasons* for wishing to be independent, an important difference between the mentally-well and -ill Ss becomes apparent. The community aged want to be independent to avoid inconveniencing others. Among the mentally ill, a fear and mistrust of others makes the goal of independence a defense against malevolence or neglect. They strive not so much for the positive value of autonomy as against the dangers of dependency.

Social acceptability is a second source of self-esteem in the sample, but the two groups differ in their conceptions of the appropriate means for achieving it. The

rather contingent upon the belief that an individual must be superior to others in some way in order to gain or preserve social acceptance. They must have status, wealth, power, or recognition for some talent, special ability, or other outstanding trait; they must command respect from a position of strength.

Adequacy of physical and financial resources is a common goal for the aged. Beliefs regarding the proper means to this end, however, differ with mental health. Community subjects perceive as one of the tasks of old age the conservation of self and resources. They deem it unlikely that their store of health or wealth will be replenished, and therefore, emphasize an economy of the resources that remain. By contrast, the mentally-ill members of the sample more frequently reflect a view of life as a state of unlimited resources and new opportunities. They are oriented toward acquisition; a failure to muster new resources is often perceived by them as a character defect.

In coping with changes in the external world, we see another major difference in value-orientation between the community and hospitalized *Ss:* the healthy "don't fight City Hall" and the disturbed do. There seems to be a difficulty among the mentally ill in distinguishing between circumstances that can be changed and those that cannot. The mentally-healthy aged seem able to meet unpleasant but alterable circumstances with action, and inalterable ones with flexibility and forbearance. The mentally ill, by contrast, value aggressiveness as such; they are instrumentally-oriented. They must *do* something, and they are less likely to admit that there are circumstances beyond their control. Harmonious co-existence with the inevitable is the goal of the mentally healthy.

Self-esteem among this group of older Americans is also influenced by the fruitfulness of a search for meaning in one's life in the later years. But community and hospitalized *Ss* have quite distinct characteristic orientations in this sphere. The mentally well are oriented toward relaxation, which includes such traits as release from compulsion, lower level of excitability, and a broader perspective which they call by different names: wisdom, maturity, peacefulness, or mellowing. They feel released and freed in some basic sense from earlier social imperatives. The mentally-ill group are still driven to compete; ambition is a central value, and failure to achieve leads to self-recrimination.

The final goal of this aged sample is ability to cope with changes in the self, whether physical, cognitive, or social. Again, I found differences between community and hospitalized *Ss* in the value-orientations brought to bear on this task.

The community *Ss* are more likely to emphasize those characteristics of themselves that are continuous or evolving. They conceive of life as a "holding action." They emphasize what they still have, rather than what they have lost. And, perhaps more important, they are able to substitute a new set of achievable gratifications and sources of pride to replace old ones which are no longer available to them. Failure to perceive alternatives, however, characterizes the hospital sample and may lead to a retrospective or deteriorative view of the self.

There are also differences in levels of aspiration: the mentally healthy have more modest expectations of life and themselves than do the mentally ill, who seem to feel that they must ever strive for perfection. They seem to believe seriously in the Cinderella legend—for them, the life story should have a happy ending, ambition should triumph, and all their dreams come true. This expectation keeps them oriented toward a diminishing future, and time becomes an enemy. For the more present-oriented community *Ss*, time is an old friend—what remains of it is to be cherished and enjoyed.

In looking at these contrasting orientations, I was struck by the fact that the value-orientations which are associated with the maladapted aged in this sample are strikingly similar to values found by a number of observers to be characteristic of American culture generally. Although some writers, such as Riesman (1954) and Whyte (1956), have seen a somewhat different set of goals emerging in our contemporary society, dominant American values have been described by Kluckhohn and Kluckhohn (1947), Mead (1943), Gorer (1948), Hsu (1961), and others as including achievement and success, movement, aggressiveness, acquisition (rather than possession) of money, activity and work, individualism, competence and control, progress, and orientation toward the future. These values were reported to be dominant in American society during the period just prior to

World War II—that is, at least until about 25 years ago. That was the era during which the members of this now elderly sample were at the prime of life. At that time the present values of the mentally-ill Ss in this sample were modal. Yet, now we find that the individualistic, competitive, aggressive, future-oriented and acquisitive American of 25 years ago—that person who rigidly clings to those values in his old age—is today's best prospect for geriatic psychiatry.

It seems to me that these findings can be interpreted in either of two ways: First, it may be, as Riesman and Whyte have suggested, that American society is undergoing a rapid shift in dominant value-orientations, leaving the Protestant Ethic behind, replacing the individualism with affiliation, and substituting a consumer morality for a production morality. If this is so, then it may be that the mentally-healthy Ss in my sample are merely those who have followed the trend of the times, while those who become mentally ill in late life are anachronistically fixated on a now-obsolete set of values.

One the other hand, it may be that American society even today has different norms for the aged from those prevailing for young or middle-aged people. If this is the case, then we can think of aging in our society as representing a culturally prescribed value-shift imposed upon those entering old age status. There is some independent evidence that the latter is, in fact, a true explanation. David Gutmann recently conducted an analysis of TAT data from middle-aged and aging white males aged 40 through 70 of middle class status, and resident in Kansas City, Missouri. All his Ss were rated as being free from diagnosable psychiatric illness. His analysis of projective materials indicated the following differences between younger and older Ss:

". . . where younger men tended (as estimated from their TAT results) to be freely assertive, older men tended to be passive and accommodating; where young-

er men seemed to be concerned with gaining respect from others, older men projected a concern with being loved by others; where younger men sought to change the environment, older men projected a need to change themselves to conform to what they saw as external mandates and external necessities; where younger men seem to look for external challenge and opposition . . . , older men projected a wish for tranquility . . . ; where younger men generally sought to extend their sphere of mastery, older men seemed more concerned with retrenchment . . . ; where the ego defenses of younger men [featured] intellectualization, rationalization, and compulsivity, . . . the defenses of older men tended to substitute for action—faced with troubling events older men might rely on 'internal alteration' of the environment." (Gutmann, 1967).

In sum, both Gutmann's analysis and mine agree on the pattern of orientations which are characteristic of mentally-healthy older Americans in this decade. However, the orientations that he found modal for younger mentally-healthy Ss (those 40 to 50) are nearly identical to the configuration I found associated with mental illness among the aged. To go a step further in generalization, it seems likely that patterns of value appropriate to the middle-aged in our society are deemed inappropriate (or prove dysfunctional) for the elderly.

One may reasonably conclude that the accession to the status of old age in American society represents a dramatic cultural discontinuity, in that some of the most basic orientations—those relating to time perspective, competitiveness and cooperation, aggression and passivity, doing and being—must be changed at that stage of the life cycle if adaptation is to occur. Abrupt changes in the demands made on the aging individual require marked shifts in value-orientations. Yet, as we know, values are among the most tenacious of human sentiments. They are the building blocks, not only of self-esteem, but also of the very definition of reality. Any individual at any age finds it difficult to withstand such a massive reordering of his behavioral world. The old people in our hospitalized sample were unable to make such shifts, and aging adaptation with them failed. On the other hand, those who either had a broader and more flexible spectrum of value-orientations in *middle* life, or who have been able to effect a shift of values in *later* life seem to be meeting the problems of aging today with less danger of psychiatric hospitalization.

But the stress induced in American society by hard cultural imperatives to develop new orientations in later life impinges upon community as well as upon hospitalized Ss. How is it, then, that some older people withstand it so well? A partial answer was once suggested by Benedict, who remarked that cultural discontinuities—such as those accompanying adolescence in our society—always involve strain for the individual; however, when persons confronted with such discontinuities are fortified by "a solid phalanx" of social grouping, "they can often swing between remarkable extremes of opposite behavior without apparent psychic threat" (Benedict, 1938). In an analysis reported elsewhere (Clark & Anderson, 1967), I found that community Ss in this sample have more social relationships and are more active in those relationships than the hospitalized Ss now discharged and having similar opportunities for interaction. A significant reference group, then, may protect the aging individual against the stresses of cultural discontinuity.[1] But where the aging individual is released from earlier adult roles without either real or symbolic interrelationships upon which to build self-esteem, he often suffers a serious, stress-ridden discontinuity.

In order to learn if this kind of trau-matic aging is specific to our culture, it would be to our advantage, as anthropologists, to examine aging in societies where the values our aged are pressed to adopt in later life are already the *core* values of the culture. Would we find comparable discontinuities where continuity and conservation are modal values for even the young and middle-aged?

Let us examine just two of the contrasting pairs of value-orientations discussed above: first, acquisition versus conservation. Foster has observed what has great relevance to the point here. According to him, the culture of some peasant societies (his study communities are Mexican and Egyptian) is pivoted on an "Image of Limited Good."

"By 'Image of Limited Good' I mean that broad areas of peasant behavior are patterned in such fashion as to suggest that peasants view their social, economic, and natural universes—their total environment —as one in which all of the desired things in life such as land, wealth, health, friendship and love, manliness and honor, respect and status, power and influence, security and safety, *exist in finite quantity* and *are always in short supply*, as far as the peasant is concerned. Not only do these and all other 'good things' exist in finite and limited quantities, but in addition *there is no way directly within peasant power to increase the available quantities*" [emphasis his] (Foster, 1965).

[1] Nadel, in a classic paper on witchcraft in Africa, was able to demonstrate that there is less "hostility of the old toward the young" and fewer "frustrations springing from such envy of youth" in societies where the elders form a clearly defined age-grade: "The Korongo [a group with little intergenerational conflict] have six age classes, as against three among the Mesakin [with high conflict], so that in the former tribe the various phases of individual life are much more faithfully represented; also, the rights and responsibilities changing with age are more evenly spaced. . . . The Korongo also specifically name their sixth and last grade the age class of 'old men,' the criterion now being the visible physical decline of the really old" (Nadel, 1952).

442

Foster goes on to observe that because of the static nature of the economic system in these peasant societies, such American virtues as competition, acquisition, exploitation of the environment, and socioeconomic mobility are held by everyone to be social evils because such things are gained only at the expense of others. If however, we were to substitute the words "American aged" for "peasants" in the quoted passage, it would still be quite true, although peasant peoples, according to Foster, hold the "image of limited good" all their lives, while Americans must learn it as a new and alien concept as they enter late life.

To turn to another value-dimension, a comparative study of societies marked by an acceptance of the inevitable and the patterns of aging found in them would be enlightening. Saunders, studying the Spanish-speaking people of the Southwest, notes the fatalism of these people as:

". . . their somewhat greater readiness toward acceptance and resignation than is characteristic of the Anglo. Whereas it is the belief of the latter that man has an obligation to struggle against and if possible to master the problems and difficulties that beset him, the Spanish-speaking person is more likely to accept and resign himself to whatever destiny brings him. With his eyes on the future, the Anglo tells himself and his friends that 'while there's life there's hope.' . . . The Spanish-speaking person, by contrast, is likely to meet difficulties by adjusting to them rather than by attempting to overcome them. Fate is somewhat inexorable, and there is nothing much to be gained by struggling against it" (Saunders, 1954).

Once again, we can see that what American aged must so painfully *learn* in their later years the elderly of certain other cultures have known as "reality" from their earliest days.

CONCLUSION

Personality is rather an on-going process of interaction between the sociocultural world and the internal life of the individual—a process that continues *throughout the life cycle*. As anthropologists, we have learned little about the last half of that process and the diverse ways in which different cultures may pattern it.

The research reported here suggests that a person not only must learn how his culture defines the "proper" manner of growing up; he must learn the "proper" manner of growing old—and failures to perceive or conform to these cultural dicta may bring him into serious conflict with society.

49

DAVID L. GUTMANN

AGING AMONG THE HIGHLAND MAYA:
A COMPARATIVE STUDY

The study of TAT responses and other psychological data from middle-aged and aging men resident in the urban United States has led to developmental hypotheses concerning the ego psychology of the aging process (Gutmann, 1964; Neugarten & Gutmann, 1958). Briefly, mature and aging American men seem to move through three major ego states, each representing a distinctive integration of drives, defenses, and self-other definitions. In the first stage, termed alloplastic mastery, the emphasis is on control of outerworld affairs, in pursuit of achievement and independence. In the second stage, termed autoplastic mastery (or passive mastery), the emphasis is on accommodation to the outerworld and on changing the self, rather than the external domain. Thought substitutes for action, and philosophic resignation begins to substitute for achievement and autonomy drives. In the last stage, termed omniplastic mastery (or magical mastery), security and self-esteem are maintained by the regressive defensive strategies of denial and projection, rather than through instrumental action against either the outer world or the self. To a statistically significant degree,

Adapted from the *Journal of Personality and Social Psychology*, vol. 7 (1967), no. 1. Copyright 1967 by the American Psychological Association and reproduced by permission.

This research was supported by a Career Development Award from the National Institute of Child Health and Human Development (National Institutes of Health) and by a faculty research grant from the Horace H. Rackham School of Graduate Studies, University of Michigan.

younger American men (aged 40–54) are characterized by alloplastic mastery, while older men (55–70) are characterized by autoplastic and omniplastic mastery.

The age differences—from greater to lesser autonomy, from greater to lesser objectivity, etc.—suggested a replication, though in reverse chronological order, of the maturational stages of early life and thereby pointed to possible developmental explanations of the observed age differences. If intrinsic, developmental factors do exercise some influence over the direction of psychological change in later life, their presence could best be demonstrated through data gathered over a variety of cultures, different from the urban United States and from each other in terms of value systems, socioeconomic organization, and especially the social supports provided older men. Should equivalent psychological states be found in age peers across such diverse cultures, the developmental hypothesis would receive strong support.

METHOD

This paper reports results from one such study, a series of intensive interviews carried out with 40 men of the Highland Maya group, preliterate, subsistence-level corn farmers resident in the remote Mexican province of Chiapas. Interviewing was carried out in the Tzeltal-speaking village of Aguacatanango (32 interviews) and in the Tzotzil-speaking town of Zinacantan (8 interviews). Subjects were typical villagers, ranging in age from 30 to 90 (though only 2 men were younger than 35 and only 3 men were over 75). Some subjects spoke the contact language, Spanish, but interviewing generally required the aid of local interpreters, who also recruited subjects. The interviews were given prior to the administration of projective tests, and various approaches were used to insure reliable personality data; for example, no rigid schedule was followed, and the investigator tried to remain sensitive to personal and implicit drifts in the subject's conventional responses—as much as possible he picked up on and tried to amplify the respondent's personal feelings about the facts that he was reporting. Also, in order to clear the air, the investigator invited respondents to interview him, telling them that he would give them the kinds of frank answers that he hoped to get. Areas covered with most subjects included personal history, with special emphasis on important figures and important deaths; views of the future; views of old men's roles; the way in which contentment was gained, lost, and restored; dreams; and the loss and conservation of vitality in later life.

In general, the hypothesis was that dimensions suggested by the mastery typology would accommodate the interview data, and that these dimensions would discriminate age groups in predictable ways. For example, younger men (aged 30 through 49) should be concerned with their productive and competitive relationship to the outerworld, whereas older men (in their 50s and early 60s) should be less involved with production, competition, and future opportunity. It was predicted that these older men, like their American age peers, would handle their concerns in more autoplastic ways, that is, through comparative retrenchment accommodation, and self-restriction. Finally, the prediction was that the oldest men (in their late 60s and 70s) would define both pleasure and pain in immediate, body-centered, and oral terms; and that they would defend and comfort themselves in irrational ways, through denials and distortions of troubling reality.

In order to avoid halo effects, each question and the data that it elicited was dealt with individually, across interviews. The mastery typology suggested categories for ordering the data, and each response was assigned to that category best representative of the dominant theme that it expressed. The data generated by those questions which discriminated age groups will be reported. Given the open, unstructured nature of the interviewing, each question was not routinely put to each respondent. Accordingly, the respondent N varies for each question, and in no case equals the sample N of 40.

RESULTS

PSYCHOSEXUAL REGRESSION

The most striking age trend found in these data is towards a passive-dependent and explicitly oral stance among older Highland Maya men. This movement, toward passive-incorporative and away from instrumental orientations, comes out most clearly in replies to questions dealing with pleasure, displeasure, and vitality.

Responses to the question, "What are the things in your life that give you pleasure?," were grouped by three major categories: pleasure in productive work, pleasure in maintaining the status quo ("I am happy when I and my family are healthy."), and pleasure in passive receptivity. Sixty percent of the younger men (aged 30–49) are found in the production-centered category: they are happy tilling their corn fields, selling their goods in the market, fattening animals, and so forth. A few declare themselves dissatisfied with their present work, but with work per se; they still hope to find employment more productive and less gruelling than their present tillage. By contrast, older men (aged 50 through 90) visualize contentment in other than achievement and production terms: only 29% of them cite productive work as a source of contentment. For some of the older men

TABLE 1

AGE AND THEMATIC DISTRIBUTIONS*

	Age 30-49	Age 50-90
1. Responses to question, "What makes you happy?" [N=34]		
a. Productive work	9	6
b. Maintaining status quo	0	6
c. Passive receptivity	4	9
2. Responses to question, "What makes you unhappy?" [N=28]		
a. Interruptions and risks of production	10	2
b. Illness	1	7
c. Anaclitic losses	0	8
3. Responses to question, "How do you restore contentment?" [N=28]		
a. Reliance on instrumental action	8	5
b. Reliance on omnipotent figures	2	5
c. Reliance on oral supplies	1	7
4. Subject's views concerning the loss, conservation, and restoration of vital forces: [N=28]		
a. Denial of loss and/or externalization of cause (e.g. illness)	9	3
b. Irreversible attrition	3	4
c. Oral equivalent (forces maintained or restored by food)	2	7
5. Dreams: [N=15]		
a. "Mastery" dreams: work, acceptance of loss	5	2
b. Passivity: before death or external attack	1	7
6. Questions asked of interviewer: [N=27]		
a. Objective questions	6	5
b. Both objective curiosity and self-referent questions	2	3
c. Concrete, self-referent questions	3	8
7. Explanations of significant deaths (Age and cause distribution): [N=29]		
a. "Prosaic" and/or impersonal causes (illness, murderous assault)	11	11
b. Supernatural, personally referent causes (envy, witchcraft, retribution for sins, etc.)	0	7

* The distributions of responses shown in this table were tested for statistical significance, as reported in the original version of this paper.

(grouped in the status quo category) contentment involves staving off physical threats of one sort or another; they are happy if they are not ill or if they stay out of trouble. But the largest block of oldest men—41%—define contentment in oral, sensual terms and are therefore grouped in the passive-receptive category. For this group happiness comes from something beautiful or when one is visited by friends or relatives, drinks with friends, listens to the music of marimba, or has sufficient food.

Thus, as summarized in Part 1 of the table, the age shift in terms of contentment, though not statistically significant, is from achievement, from the rewards of productive work (herds of animals, tiled roofs), to a more custodial "getting by" orientation, and finally to a receptive, oral posture where the next meal or the next bit of affection is the focus of interest.[1]

Responses to the question, "What makes you unhappy?," were accommodated by these categories: interruptions and risks of production, illness, and anaclitic losses. Seventy-nine percent of the younger men are found in the interrup-

[1] Simmons (1945) cites data from a wide range of preliterate cultures in support of the contention, also stated here, that food becomes increasingly important to older people. He proposes that orality among the aged has a completely rational basis, as a strategy for prolonging life: "A dominant interest in old age is to live long, perhaps as long as possible. Therefore, food becomes a matter of increasing concern [p. 12]." However, as suggested here, the increased interest in food is linked to a general passive-receptive posture, which informs many interests and activities of later life besides the preparation and ingestion of food. If this is so, then the transcultural interest in food among the aged has less circumscribed, more irrational roots.

tions of production category, and this group clearly visualizes frustration and pain in terms of what might be called a production-competition syndrome: they are bothered if their work does not produce capital or if they lack investment capital (to buy animals and new land), but they also tend to be frightened of the murderous envy generated by the competitive struggle in their society. (Like many preliterate people, the Highland Maya fear ambush and witchcraft from neighbors and relatives envious of their accumulated wealth.)

By contrast, only 12% of the older men are found in the production-competition category; their complaints refer instead to the anaclitic losses category, and 47% of them are found there. Thus, the older men are made unhappy by fairly immediate physical and emotional deprivations: the loss of physical comfort (as in illness), the loss of loved and/or nurturant figures, and the loss of oral supplies ("I am unhappy when there is not enough corn and beans.").

In sum, younger men's discontents refer to a relatively wide sphere of economic and interpersonal activities. They worry about markets and about the competition, envy, and retaliation that result from the striving orientation. For older men, the relevant world seems to have shrunk down to the narrower precincts of the family, the circle of friends, necessary supplies, and their own bodies.[2] It is in these more restricted terms that they define discomfort (see Part 2 of the table).

Responses to the question, "When you are unhappy, how do you make yourself happy again?" are more clearly diagnostic of the age shift from productive to passive-receptive interests. In all three major ways of restoring lost contentment are found: reliance on instrumental action, reliance on omnipotent figures, and reliance on oral supplies. A plurality of the sample, who claimed that they rely on their own actions and resources to restore contentment, fall in the first category:

"When I am discontented, I go back to work"; "I take a trip, I look for work"; "I cure myself and so am happy again"; etc. The next largest group of subjects, in the second category, claim to restore contentment through reliance on some powerful external figures: "I burn my candle to the Virgin, so the envy that is around us is pushed away"; "The doctors give me a medicine for it and tell me that I will live for a long time"; "If there were armed soldiers in the village, there would be peace here and so I would be content again"; etc. Finally, many respondents mention food, drink, and medicine as means of restoring contentment and so are found in the third category: "When I have my corn and beans, and my tortilla, I grow happy again"; "Well, a little drink will warm the body and drive away the sadness. One drinks with friends and calls for marimba music"; "The doctor gives me a tonic to make me feel better"; etc.

Seventy three percent of the younger men and only 29% of the older men are found in the first category, involving instrumental action against the causes of

[2] It can be argued that the grievances of older men refer to realistic problems—the losses of health, vitality, and intimates necessarily attendant on aging—and not to more intrinsic shifts at the irrational levels of personality. It does not say much about the psychology of older men that they get sick more often than younger men, and that they complain about their ills. However, if all references to illness are left out of the statistical comparison (see Part 2 of the table), the remaining grievances cited by older men—object loss (death) and oral insupply—reflect the already noted passive-receptive concerns.

Also, the experience of death is not age graded for the Highland Maya: the infant mortality rate is very high, and young men experience death as frequently or more frequently than do older men. Accordingly, older men's emphasis on object loss as a cause of discontent suggests the greater sharpness rather than the greater frequency of this experience for them. In sum, irrational or psychological vulnerability may account for much of the generational difference in the causes of discontent.

discomfort. Eighteen percent of younger men and 29% of older men are found in the second category, involving reliance on powerful external figures. Nine percent of younger men and 41% of older men are found in the third category, involving restoration of contentment through oral intake. The significant age shift, then, is from reliance on internal or "self" resources to dependence on external sources, in the form of powerful persons or strength-giving foods and tonics (see Part 3 of the table).

The age shift to an explicitly oral orientation also comes out in older men's responses to the linked questions, "Are your forces declining?"; and "Can the forces be restored?" Respondents' beliefs concerning the loss, conservation, and restoration of vitality are grouped under three categories: denial and externalization, irreversible attrition, and oral equivalent. Denial and externalization groups those respondents who either deny that their forces are diminishing or who impute responsibility for such loss to accidental, possibly reversible, processes, such as illness. These men seem to suggest that the loss of forces is not an intrinsic process, with its own scheduling, but is the product of fortuitous events. Sixty four percent of the younger men and only 21% of the older men are found in this category. The men grouped in the irreversible-process category refer to a natural event, an inevitable concomitant of aging: "The blood gets tired"; "Your strength goes out with your sweat"; etc. These men do not seem to believe that the forces can be restored or the process reversed. Twenty one percent of the younger men are found here, as against 29% of the older men.

The third group see physical strength and energy as an oral equivalent and imply that the correct foods and medicines will conserve or partly restore the forces that are lost: "We start losing our forces after 40. Only rich men who eat greens and vitamins continue to grow strong and fat after 40." Only 14% of the younger men are found in this group, as opposed to 50% of the older men. Thus, to a statistically significant degree (see Part 4 of the table), older men see physical energy and well-being as a concrete quality that resides in food or in medicinal tonics. Younger men reluctantly note their declining vigor, but do not concretize vital force into an entity existing apart from the body processes that produce it—an entity that can be put back into the body through the mouth.

The older men's preference for passive-receptive modalities is reflected in their dreams. In all, 15 men reported dreams. Seventy one percent of the dreams reported by older men involved helplessness before external or internal attack; they were dying, etc.: "Sometimes in my dreams they throw me into a canyon or into the water"; "I dream that I will die and that I am sad. I ask, 'Who will support my daughters?' "[3] By contrast, younger men's dreams are generally more benign and suggest that the ego is on top of potentially troublesome issues: in one case a man dreams that he is working; in four cases the dreamer meets a deceased kinsman, recognized in the dream as dead. Such dreams may represent attempts to come to terms with loss: "My mother comes to me and only looks at me without saying anything"; "I dream that my father visits my house, and I tell him that I am content with my family and my work."

Thus, to a significant degree, young men tend to have mastery dreams, while older men tend to have dreams in which they are passive and overwhelmed. The dream, like other forms of fantasy, is the portrait of a wish, and these dreams may convey the older men's unconscious wish to be dominated, much like a child, by powerful external forces.

[3] Robert Butler, a psychoanalyst, has done extensive studies of aging in this country. He reports that the assassin dream is very common among his older American subjects.

448

Psychosexual regression towards oral-aggressive and oral-incorporative positions may have consequences for ego process, as well as ego interests. Older men's responses to at least two questions suggest regressive thought and defensive processes, involving the erosion of ego boundaries and heightened cognitive subjectivity.

The subjects' questions reflect their concerns and the terms in which they comprehend the world. Thus, the age-graded trends in thinking are first illustrated by the questions asked by those subjects who interviewed the investigator. These questions could be grouped into two major classes: "objective" or "self-referent." The objective questioners recognized that he came from a different society, and they took him as an informant on work and living conditions in that society. The more subjective, self-referent questioners tried to understand him in terms of their own fears and suspicions: they saw him as someone who might either help or harm them.

To a significant degree, younger men are found in the objective category: they wanted to know about the investigator's work, pay, and training. These younger men were intrigued rather than put off by the fact that he was a foreigner: for them it implied new work styles and new opportunities. By contrast, 50% of the older men (and only 20% of the younger men) group in the more subjective category, in that they tended to ask situation-bound, self-referent questions. They wanted to know why he asked questions, and who would hear his tapes. As a foreigner, he was something of a threat; being different, he was also morally deviant. Thus, some elders stated that he was a loafer because he did not work hard to grow corn. Accordingly, while the younger men tried to understand him in his own terms, the older men to a significant degree saw him as someone to be judged against the values and moral standards by which they judged themselves (see Part 6 of the table).

The shift in later life towards more referential thinking may influence older men's conceptions of death. Most subjects reported the deaths of friends and family members, and most subjects attributed the death to some cause: illness, physical assault, witchcraft, or other supernatural agency ("Perhaps it is a punishment for my sins."). Explanations concerning supernatural agency, and especially witchcraft, are especially meaningful to 44% of the older respondents: one reports, "My brother was fooling around with a married woman, and her husband put a stick in the road, and he tripped on it and that caused my brother to die." By contrast, even where the deceased had been murdered, *no* younger man claims that witchcraft was involved. Three younger men cite murder as the cause of a death, but in these cases the murder was carried out in a prosaic way, as with a shotgun or machete. In one case, a younger man denies that witchcraft killed his step-father, even though other people suspected it: "I got home and my stepfather was already dead. Many people were crying, and some were talking about witches, but I knew that the old man drank too much."

The heightened belief in witchcraft suggests a more primitive phrasing of the acquisitive motivations among older men: the younger man's decorous pursuit of land, animals, and tiled roofs *via* productive labor may become the older man's more directly oral-sadistic readiness to appropriate angrily, to swallow up all good things, and to envy those who possess what he lacks.

There is some Rorschach evidence for this speculation: older men tend to see biting, contending animals and demons in the cards. But the Rorschach taps unconscious processes; these primitive wishes are experienced projectively, as an external threat, a property of the witch who murders out of envy.[4] Possibly, there is a return in later life to more archaic ego states, where the "good" is perceived as "inside," and the "bad" is experienced as alien and "outside."

In any event, the older man's sensitivity to witchcraft points to some primitivization of ego functions: in later life the boundary between self and other, between emotion and the object of emotion, may begin to break down. Phenomena are understood in terms of their relevance for the older observer, and death is the signature of personal malice, envious thoughts, rather than natural, impersonal process.

THREE CASE STUDIES

Three protocols, one from each major age period, are presented to illustrate the ways in which the age-discriminant responses fit together in the individual interview.

Don Hermelindo Aguilar is 46 years old and a life-long resident of Aguacatanango. His opening question concerns the investigator's work: "What is your work —your project? What do you learn from it?" Reviewing family history, he gives a younger man's "objective" explanation of his father's death: his father was killed by a son-in-law in a dispute over some lime trees. The subject misses his father deeply because he now serves in the village government, and, were he alive, his father would advise him about his duties. However, the subject's dreams suggest that he

can get along, as a man in his own right, without his father's help: "I dream that my father visits my house. 'How are you?' he says. 'Very well,' I answer. My father says, 'I see that you have work and what to eat. Now I am going to another place for I am already far away from here.'"

Regarding contentment, the subject says, "We always think of our work, where we make our money. We think, 'Is there enough to eat?' We think every day of work, of getting corn and beans."

The subject's problems are met by direct action: "If there's not enough to eat, then we go out and work some more." As for the decline of his "forces," the subject mentions only that he sometimes feels cold and that he has trouble getting out of bed and getting to work in the early morning.

Don Alcadio Gomez is 55 years old. His questions are fairly direct and personal, indicate some suspicion, and do not go much beyond our immediate contact: "Am I 55?" He asks, "Why do you need these talks? What do you need from me? It's easier to talk about one's life if there's a drink to start with." Reviewing his life and the significant deaths in it, the subject says that his parents died of fever, but that his three children were killed by witchcraft of envious people. He seems to be trying to fend off any blame for these deaths: "*We* don't know how it happens, *we* just do our work and try to get something for our families and then somebody might die." Discussing the important people in his life, the subject refers mainly to his mother: he had been working in the coffee plantations far from the village but, "My mother was always crying, so I returned from the *finca* to help her."

Orally receptive themes pervade his version of contentment: "I am happy eating, not being sick, and working happily." He also mentions the pleasure he gets from drinking and listening to the marimba in the company of his friends. He is made unhappy "by the death of loved ones," and by the threat from unknown

---

[4] There are, of course, other possible explanations of this age-graded tendency toward witchcraft explanations: while all villagers believe in witchcraft (and younger men do the dirty work of killing known witches), younger men might be more knowledgeable about the gringo view of death and so feed it back to the investigator. By the same token, the older men may feel freer to speak of these "secret" things, as they no longer compete with the investigator as a peer; for them, confession is not equated with shameful submission. However, younger men mention ordinary murder with about the same frequency that older men mention witchcraft murder. It is not the readiness to discuss murder, but to blame the witch, that distinguishes older men.

enemies: he fears being shot from ambush and is reluctant for this reason to travel on the road. Contentment is restored by work, liquor, and God: "I put my faith in God's hands. I beg God for relief; what if they kill me, what if I die? It is all in God's hands, and so I feel better, happy with God." Predictably, Don Alcadio dreams that a man has come to kill him.

Don Cyrilo Aguilar, aged 66, is a sad and dignified man who asks if there are aged men like himself in the United States and if the investigator plans to help them. He then makes his self-concern more explicit by asking for medicine, for his own pain.

Reporting the death of his children and grandchildren, Don Cyrilo cites witchcraft, explaining that he once led a religious faction that was opposed to other village factions and thus made enemies. He fears imminent death, probably from the same agents, and advises his sons not to fight when he is gone. His gloomy prediction may be based on his father's fate: unlike the younger Don Hermelindo, who recalls the competent role-model parent, Don Cyrilo remembers his father as a victim, thrown into a pot of boiling cane juice by envious co-workers in the sugar plantations.

The subject has a custodial view of contentment: he is happy being without sickness or pain. He is unhappy when he remembers his dead grandchildren, whom he once embraced. Contentment is restored only by passive and incorporative means: "I stay quiet," meaning that he does nothing provocative, and he prays to his favorite saint. When too much troubled by grief, Don Cyrilo drinks for 2 days, "until there is no more pain," and then returns to work. His dreams alternate between images of death, magical escape, and oral comfort:

"I dream that they are cutting meat and that they gave me the meat as a gift. . . . I dream that I run from something. I escape through a crack in the wall. A man tries to catch me, and I can't run. Then, sud-

denly I fly away. A woman calls me, but I don't want to go to her. . . . I am offered food. They offer me grains of corn. I put it in a pocket and eat it."

Clearly, oral intake is recruited to the service of defensive denial, for Don Cyrilo uses the imagery of his dream to describe the comfort that comes from liquor: "After two days of drinking, I don't feel alive. *It's just like flying.*" Along the same lines he asks, "Are there any medicines to restore the forces?"

In these three representative men we see the benchmarks of allo-, auto-, and omniplastic mastery. Don Hermelindo, the youngest, is involved in production and in his prestigeful role in the village government; difficulties are handled through work and through emulation of successful men. Don Alcadio, 9 years older, is still involved in competitive, productive striving, but he is also terrified of the more primitive implications of that striving. The oral calculus—"If I have something good, it was taken from him and he will envy me"—begins to order his understanding of events. His world is personalized, full of "envious ones." His solution is to passively put his fate in the hands of the omnipotent *Tata Dios* (Father-God) and to abide by his larger will. Finally, the eldest, Don Cyrilo, fears death on both realistic and superstitious grounds. He falls back on various autoplastic and omniplastic tactics to deny fear and to frustrate the assassin. He avoids provocation ("I stay quiet."). He enlists the help of powerful *Santos,* and he bolsters himself with potent oral allies: liquor gives him wings to fly from death; good food gives temporary pleasure; medicines restore lost forces.

This is an admittedly small sample on which to base generalizations, but there are, overall, some provocative similarities between the United States and Mexican data. The age differences found in the interview data from middle-aged and older Highland Maya men replicate, in a broad thematic sense, age differences found in projective data from a sample of urban American men of similar age composition. Men of both societies seem to move at a similar pace through successive alloplastic, autoplastic, and omniplastic ego stages such that equivalent libidinal, defense, and cognitive shifts are found in both sets of data. These shifts are towards explicitly oral definitions of pleasure and pain, simplistic defensive tactics of denial and projection, and subjectivity of thinking.

Similar shifts have been found in projective materials from the Lowland Maya of the Yucatan, a group distantly related to and geographically separate from the Highland Maya (Gutmann, 1966).

The sociocultural factors common to these three diverse societies are negligible. Accordingly, the cross-cultural similarities begin to suggest intrinsic developmental influences on the psychology of men in middle and later life.

50

ROGER G. BARKER and LOUISE SHEDD BARKER

THE PSYCHOLOGICAL ECOLOGY OF OLD PEOPLE IN MIDWEST, KANSAS, AND YOREDALE, YORKSHIRE

This paper reports an ecological study of the old people of a Kansas and of a Yorkshire town. It deals, in particular, with the place of old people in the two community systems. The study is a part of a more comprehensive, comparative investigation of psychological ecology in America and England (Barker, 1960; Barker & Barker, 1961 II).

The town of Midwest is a county seat in eastern Kansas: Yoredale is a market town of North Yorkshire and the location of a Rural District Council. Both towns are rural distribution centers, comparable in industry, governmental institutions, and in nearness to cities. Midwest has a population of 715; Yoredale, a population of 1300. By careful selection the investigators aimed to eliminate community differences with which the study was not concerned.

The data to be reported were gathered from September, 1954 through August, 1955. The methods and concepts used will be briefly described, since they are in some ways unique.

Reprinted from the *Journal of Gerontology*, vol. 16, no. 2 (April, 1961).

The collection and analysis of the data reported here was aided by grants from the Carnegie Corporation of New York, the Ford Foundation, and the National Institutes of Health (M1513). A more detailed presentation of the concepts used in this research, and further developments of the methods, are presented in Roger M. Barker, *Ecological Psychology: Concepts and Methods for Studying the Environment of Human Behavior* (Stanford: Stanford University Press, 1968).

METHOD

BEHAVIOR SETTINGS

The community behavior systems of Midwest and Yoredale have been described in terms of the *behavior setting*. The following description of this unit has been adapted from a previous study (Barker & Wright, 1955).

When a mother writes, "There is a baseball game in progress on the playground across the street," she does not refer to any individual's behavior, but to the behavior of the children en masse. The same is true of a newspaper item which reports, "The annual fete held in the St. Ambrose Church garden was a great success." These are behavior settings.

Behavior settings are highly visible behavior phenomena; laymen mention them in conversation and in writing as frequently as they do individual persons. The ten behavior settings of Midwest in which the old people of the town spend the greatest amount of time are: Streets and Sidewalks; Poole's Grocery; Kane's Grocery & Feed Store; The Midwest Weekly Newspaper Office; Murray's Grocery Store; Cabell Department Store; Mack's Shoe Repair Shop; Graham's Lumber Yard; French & French, Attorneys & Abstract Co.; and Pearson's Dairy Farm. The ten behavioral settings most extensively inhabited by Yoredale's old people are: Streets and Sidewalks; Market Day; Webber Bakery; Maynard, Milk Retailer & Dairy; Dale's Cafe; Harbor & Lawson, General Draper; Red Lion Pub

& Dining Room; Kings Arms Pub & Dining Room; Three Tuns Pub & Dining Room; and Pied Bull Pub.

Behavior settings such as these are entities with features which can be identified as precisely as those of organisms, mountain ranges, or gas jets.

Behavior settings are behavior entities, but their laws of operation are not the laws of individual psychology. In the functioning of the Pearl Cafe in Midwest, for example, the availability and the price of food, the season of the year, the prevailing temperature, the size, lighting and ventilation of the building, the state laws concerning hygienic practices, the customers, and the employees are all involved. We have only the beginning of an understanding of how these incommensurate phenomena are combined into the reliable, nonerratic entity known so well to Midwest residents. None the less, behavior settings are, even now, useful units for the ecological study of behavior.

The research reported here deals only with public, non-family behavior settings, i.e., with settings outside the homes of Midwest and Yoredale.

MEASURES OF INVOLVEMENT IN BEHAVIOR SETTINGS

The basic data used to measure the impact of the behavior settings of the towns upon their aged residents were:

1. Territorial range. Territorial range refers to the number of behavior settings a person or a group of persons inhabits in any capacity during a year. Data to be presented will show that the 162 old people of Midwest had a territorial range of 462. This means that some Midwest residents 65 years of age or older were observed to be present in 462 of the behavior settings of Midwest during the year of the study. It is sometimes convenient to express the territorial range as a per cent of the total number of settings in the town. This per cent is called the *territorial index*.

2. Occupancy time. Occupancy time refers to the number of hours a person (or the members of an identified class of persons) spends in a behavior setting, or a territorial range of settings, during a year. During the year of study, Midwest old people spent 89,050 hours in the 462 behavior settings of their territorial range. The occupancy time of Midwest by its aged was, therefore, 89,050 hours, or 9.5 per cent of the total occupancy time of all Midwest behavior settings by all the town's residents.

3. Exposure time. The occupancy time divided by the number of persons in the class under consideration provides a measure of the average amount of time each person is exposed to the influence of settings within the territorial range in question. For the old people of Midwest, the exposure time was 550 hours per year. This is the mean amount of time the old people of Midwest spent in the town's behavior settings.

4. Zones of Penetration. The residents of Midwest and of Yoredale not only inhabit settings for different amounts of time, but also participate in them in different capacities and with different degrees of involvement and responsibility. Six degrees of the latter have been defined, and are represented as zones of increasing centrality. The more central the zone, the deeper the penetration and the greater the involvement and responsibility of its occupants in the functioning of the setting. These zones are as follows (adapted from Barker & Wright, 1955):

Zone 0. Stranger. Settings which the person, or class of persons, does not inhabit.

Zone 1. Onlooker. This is the most peripheral behavior setting zone; persons within it are inhabitants of the behavior setting, but they take no active part in the standing pattern of behavior.

Zone 2. Audience or Invited Guest. The inhabitants of this zone have a definite place; they are welcome, but they have little power in the setting. At most they can applaud or express disapproval.

Zone 3. Member or Customer. Occupants of Zone 3 have great potential power, but usually little immediate power. They are the voting members, or the paying customers who ultimately make or break the setting.

Zone 4. Active Functionary. The inhabitants of this zone have an active part in the operation of the setting, but they do not lead it. Included here, for example, are store clerk, church deacon, organization secretary. Active functionaries have direct power over a limited part of the setting.

Zone 5. Joint Leaders. Persons who enter Zone 5 lead the setting jointly with others; they have immediate authority over the whole setting, but their power is shared with others. Examples: Mr. and Mrs. Cabell who jointly own and operate the Cabell Department Store; the president of the high school drama club and the sponsoring teacher.

Zone 6. Single Leader. Zone 6 is the most central zone. Here are the positions of all persons who serve as single leaders of behavior settings. These single leaders may have helpers or subordinate leaders in Zone 4. Persons in Zone 6 have immediate authority over the whole setting.

In the data to be presented, we have for certain purposes combined penetration zones 1 and 2, which incorporate the more passive positions within settings, into a single *onlooker-guest* zone; and we have combined zones 4 to 6, which include the more active, responsible positions, into a single *performance* zone. Persons who penetrate a setting to zones 4, 5, or 6 are termed *performers*. These are the people who carry the responsibility of seeing that the setting functions.

5. Action Pattern Characteristics. The standing behavior patterns of behavior settings have many discriminable features. We have rated them on 13 variables called action patterns. The action patterns are as follows (the abbreviations used in the figures are given in parentheses): Art (Art), Business (Busi), Education (Educ), Government (Gov't), Nutrition (Nutr), Orientation (O), Personal Appearance (Pers App), Philanthropy (Phil), Professional Leadership (Prof Lead), Physical Health (Phys Heal), Recreation (Recr), Religion (Relig), Social Interaction (Soc). The ratings, ranging from 0 to 14, indicate the degree to which the behavior described by a variable occurs within a setting. The ratings of the behavior setting Presbyterian Worship Service, for example, are: Art, 6; Business, 0; Education, 3; Government, 1; Nutrition, 0; Orientation, 1; Personal Appearance, 2; Philanthropy, 3; Professional Leadership, 1; Physical Health, 0; Recreation, 1; Religion, 8; Social Interaction, 6.

Action pattern ratings of 6 and above have special significance, for within this range an action pattern is so prominent a feature of the total behavior pattern of a setting that it is commonly seen as one of the major "purposes" of the setting. We have called these ratings *prominent action patterns*. Examples of behavior settings receiving ratings of 6 or greater on the action pattern Recreation are: High School Boys Basketball Game; Circus; Town Band Concert.

The degree to which an action pattern occurs within a single setting is indicated by the rating just described. When all the behavior settings of a town, or of a particular territorial range, are considered, one of the following measures is used: 1) The *territorial range* (or index) of an action pattern refers to the number (or per cent) of settings within which the action pattern occurs. The territorial index of the action pattern Recreation in Midwest was 81, meaning that 81 per cent of Midwest's 579 settings received some rating for Recreation. 2) The *occupancy time* of an action pattern is the sum of the occupancy times of the settings within which the action pattern occurs. Occupancy time can be expressed, too, as a per cent of total occupancy time of *all* settings in the town or territorial range. The occupancy time of Recreation in

Midwest was 84, meaning that 84 per cent of the occupancy time of all of Midwest settings, namely, 938,636 hours, occurred in settings that received some rating for Recreation. 3) The *exposure time* of an action pattern is obtained by dividing its occupancy time by the total number of persons who inhabit the territorial range involved. The occupancy time of Recreation in Midwest was 135,138 hours. Midwest's 715 inhabitants, therefore, experienced an average exposure to this action pattern of 189 hours per year. The ex-

TABLE 1

POPULATION (P), TERRITORIAL RANGE (TR), AND TERRITORIAL INDEX (TI) OF AGE GROUPS IN MIDWEST AND YOREDALE

AGE GROUP	MIDWEST			YOREDALE		
	P	TR	TI	P	TR	TI
Aged (65 years and over)............	162	462	80	178	332	67
Adult (18–64 years)	375	578	99	770	491	99
Adolescent (12–17 years)............	50	464	80	107	329	
Older School (9–11 years)............	26	389	67	51	274	67 55
Younger School (6–8 years)............	28	359	62	72	251	51
Preschool (2–5 years)	50	363	63	81	214	43
Infant (under 2 years)............	24	329	57	41	125	25
All ages............	715	579	100	1300	494	100

posure time tells us nothing about the distribution of exposure times among Midwest inhabitants.

RESULTS

TERRITORIAL RANGE

The territorial ranges of the old people, and of all other age groups in Midwest and Yoredale, are given in Table 1. According to these data: 1) the old people of Midwest have a larger territorial range, and index, than those of Yoredale; 2) this relationshop holds true, too, for other age groups; 3) the relative deficit in the territorial range, and index, of Yoredale age groups decreases from infancy to adulthood, and increases again in old age to al-

most exactly that occurring in adolescence; and 4) the old people of Midwest and Yoredale stand in almost identical relationships to the other age groups of their towns with respect to the extent to which they range over the behavior areas of the towns.

In interpreting these data, it is essential to bear in mind that the smaller territorial ranges of Yoredale age groups occur in spite of greater populations at each age. The question arises why Midwest's 162 old people inhabit a greater number (and greater per cent) of Midwest's 579 settings than Yoredale's 178 old citizens inhabit of Yoredale's 494 settings. On the basis of population pressure one might expect the contrary to occur, for there are 3.6 behavior settings for each Midwest old person to inhabit, on the average, and 2.8 for each Yoredale old person. In spite of this, Yoredale old people live within 67 per cent (332) of the settings of their town, while Midwest old people inhabit 80 per cent (462) of the settings of theirs. Thus, the range of behavior settings is more restricted both absolutely and relatively for the aged of Yoredale than for the aged of Midwest.

DEPTH OF PENETRATION

Data regarding depth of penetration by aged citizens into the behavior settings of Midwest and Yoredale are shown in Table 2.

These data refer to maximal penetration, and tell nothing about the frequency with which old people enter zones peripheral to the zone of maximal penetration. Old people may or may not inhabit the more peripheral zones. Table 2 is not, therefore, a frequency distribution of zone occupancy; it refers only to maximal penetration depth.

These data tell us that the old people of Midwest penetrate their town's behavior settings to peripheral levels (zones 1 and 2), and to performance levels (zones 4, 5 and 6) more frequently than do the old people of Yoredale. This is true in terms of both absolute numbers of settings and per cent of settings. Yoredale old people, on the other hand, are more frequently noninhabitants of the town's behavior settings (zone 0), and more frequently penetrate to Zone 3, the level of members. In other words, Yoredale old people are more often than Midwest old people either solidly within behavior settings as members, or completely outside of settings. Midwest old people, on the other hand, are more often either on the fringes of behavior settings (as onlookers and guests) or active, responsible functionaries within the settings.

BEHAVIOR SETTING EXPOSURE TIME IN OLD AGE

Behavior setting exposure time, it will be recalled, is the number of hours per year a person, or the average number of hours the members of a class of persons, is exposed to whatever occurs within the be-

TABLE 2

PENETRATION OF BEHAVIOR SETTINGS BY THE AGED CITIZENS OF MIDWEST AND YOREDALE

MAXIMAL PENETRATION ZONE	MIDWEST		YOREDALE	
	Number of Settings	Percent of Settings	Number of Settings	Percent of Settings
0 (Stranger).........	117	20	162	33
1 (Onlooker)........	65	11	1	0+
2 (Guest)...........	80	14	41	8
3 (Member).........	176	30	212	43
4 (Functionary).....	64	11	44	9
5 (Joint Leaders)....	49	8	27	5
6 (Single Leader)....	28	5	7	1

NOTE.—The table is to be read as follows: Old people do not enter 117 (20 per cent) of Midwest's behavior settings and do not enter 162 (33 per cent) of Yoredale's settings; they are onlookers only in 65 (11 per cent) of Midwest's settings and in 1 (0 per cent) of Yoredale's settings; and so on.

These differences between towns are not peculiar to the old inhabitants. Data that are too extensive to be presented here show that at every age (except adulthood) Midwest citizens are more frequently performers, and more frequently onlookers and guests than Yoredale citizens; and that they are less frequently members (except in infancy) and strangers. The unreported data show, too, that in all of these respects the old people of both towns closely approximate adolescents in behavior setting penetration.

TABLE 3

BEHAVIOR SETTING EXPOSURE TIME BY AGE GROUP, AND FOR ALL AGES, IN MIDWEST AND YOREDALE

AGE GROUP	EXPOSURE TIME	
	Midwest	Yoredale
Aged..............	550	415
Adult.............	1526	1322
Adolescent.........	2808	1978
Older School........	2190	1577
Younger School.....	1900	1558
Preschool...........	413	547
Infant.............	211	359
All ages...........	1313	1195

havior settings of a town, or territorial range within a town. The exposure times of the old people of the towns, of other age groups, and of the total populations are given in Table 3.

These data show that the aged citizens of Midwest are exposed to the behavior settings within their territorial range for an average of 550 hours per year, and that the exposure time for the old people of Yoredale is 415 hours. The lower exposure time of Yoredale old people is in accord with that of the other age groups and of the whole population, but the degree of the deficit is greater. The exposure time of Yoredale old people is 75 per cent as great as that of Midwest old people, instead of 91 per cent when all citizens are included. In other words, insofar as behavior setting exposure time is concerned, Yoredale old people differ

457

from Midwest old people relatively more than Yoredale differs from Midwest.

The deficit of Yoredale old people is greater relative to the level of exposure for all ages, also. In Yoredale the exposure time of old people is 35 per cent as great as that of the community as a whole, while in Midwest it is 42 per cent as great. Yoredale old people differ from the town as a whole relatively more than Midwest old people differ from Midwest as a whole.

In both towns the regression in behav-

for ratings of 6 and greater. There is clearly great similarity between the old people of Midwest and Yoredale in the *relative* degree of their exposure to different action patterns.

The data of Figure 1 show, too, that the old people of Midwest are exposed to most action patterns for a greater length of time than are the old people of Yoredale. On only one action pattern, Nutrition, is the Yoredale exposure time greater than the Midwest at both rating levels. In the case of Art, the Yoredale aged have

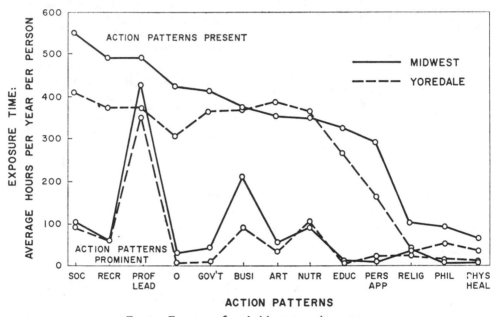

FIG. 1.—Exposure of aged citizens to action patterns

ior setting exposure time is approximately to the level of preschool children.

ACTION PATTERN EXPOSURE TIME
IN OLD AGE

The exposure times of the aged of Midwest and of Yoredale to the 13 different action patterns studied are shown in Figure 1 for ratings of 1 and greater (i.e., action pattern present) and for ratings of 6 and greater (i.e., action pattern prominent). The correlations between action pattern exposure times in the two towns is .96 for ratings of 1 and greater, and .93

greater exposure at the lower rating level and less exposure at the higher rating level than the aged of Midwest.

Exposure of the aged and of the total populations to action patterns rated 1 and greater are presented in Figure 2. The correlations between the exposure times of the aged and of the total populations on action pattern ratings of 1 and greater are .96 and .99 for Midwest and Yoredale respectively; they are .98 for both towns on action pattern ratings of 6 and greater. It is evident that the old people of Midwest and Yoredale mirror the total population of the towns so far as exposure to action patterns is concerned. Data which are too extensive to be presented here indicate that this is also true, in general, for other age groups.

It was pointed out earlier that regression in old age occurs to the level of adolescents in the case of territorial range and behavior setting penetration, while in the case of behavior setting exposure time regression occurs to the preschool level. Other data not presented here show that exposure to most action patterns regresses in old age to the level of preschool children. It appears that the old people of both Midwest and Yoredale maintain their contacts and positions within behavior settings on a higher level than they maintain the duration of their contacts. Our field observations lead us to believe that the lower exposure times in old age occur because a smaller proportion of aged than of adults inhabit settings, and those aged who do inhabit settings stay a shorter length of time.

SUMMARY OF RESULTS

The aged citizens of Midwest and Yoredale live in environments that are much alike in the *relative* magnitudes of their behavior setting measurements (territorial range, penetration, and action patterns). This means that, despite differences in ab-

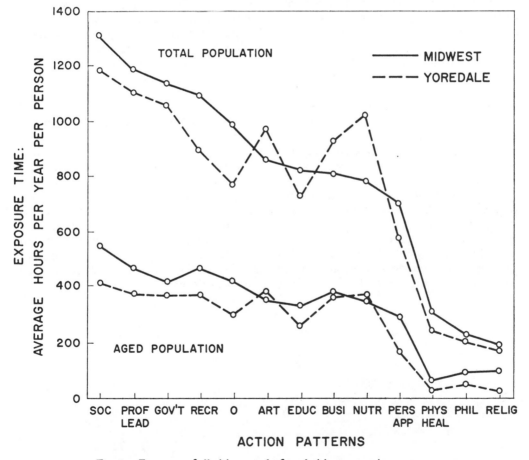

Fig. 2.—Exposure of all citizens and of aged citizens to action patterns

solute magnitudes (i.e, despite differences in the size of environments) the measurements show that the environments of the old people of Midwest and Yoredale are quite similar.

The environments of the old people of both communities differ from their respective communities in the same direction. The measures are all smaller than either the corresponding total community measures or the measures for the adult citizens. In this respect, the environments of the old people of both towns "regress," i.e., differ from the community at large and from adults in the same way that the environments of children differ. Such regression in old age is indicated in both Midwest and Yoredale by all of the measures used. The regression occurs in both towns to the preschool levels in the case of behavior setting exposure times, and to adolescent levels in the case of territorial range and penetration variables.

The environment of the old people of Midwest is greater in territorial range (extent), in penetration (depth), and in exposure to behavior settings and action patterns (duration) than the environment of Yoredale old people. The absolute amount of regression in all environmental measures is greater in Yoredale than in Midwest.

These differences in the environments of the aged inhabitants of the towns are not peculiar to this age group. The same sorts of differences occur at almost all ages, but the degree of the difference is greater at the youngest ages and in old age. It appears, therefore, that most of the differences in the environments of the old people of Midwest and Yoredale are due to conditions common to all ages, conditions which operate in proportion to the extent to which persons deviate in age from adulthood.

DISCUSSION

The data assembled on the psychological ecology of the citizens of an American and an English town reveal systematic differences that invite theoretical explanation. According to a theory of behavior-setting dynamics outlined elsewhere which appears to be promising (Barker, 1960, Barker & Barker, 1961 II), Midwest citizens are under greater pressure than Yoredale citizens to participate widely and deeply in the behavior settings of the town. This difference in pressure is exhibited with special clarity in deviant groups, such as old people and children, which are in varying degrees unsuited to the demands of the behavior settings. This may be the source of the wider, deeper, and temporally longer environment of Midwest old people, and of the lesser regression of Midwest old people from the community norms, as compared to Yoredale aged. According to this theory, Midwest old people are not different from Yoredale old people in their motives, abilities, and basic ideologies, and they would behave as Yoredale old people behave under the lesser pressures of Yoredale.

The data make it clear, however, that in the environments actually prevailing, life is different for the aged citizens of Midwest and Yoredale.

51

YONINA TALMON

AGING IN ISRAEL, A PLANNED SOCIETY

This paper analyzes the influence of ideological and structural factors on the process of aging in collective settlements in Israel.[1] The collectives have solved many of the basic and most persistent problems of aging. Aging members enjoy full economic security. Communal services take care of them in case of ill health or infirmity. Retirement from work is gradual and does not entail an abrupt and complete break from work routines. Aging members are not cut off from community life. Social participation serves as an alternative avenue of activity and provides respected substitute functions. In many cases it compensates the aging member for his gradual loss of competence and status in the occupational sphere. What is most important, grown-up children are expected to live in the community founded by their parents. Parents are able to maintain close and constant relations with their children without losing their independence. Elderly and old people are thus spared much of the insecurity and isolation, the futile inactivity and dependence entailed in aging.

Analysis in this paper is based on a research project conducted in one of the four federations of collectives. The number of collectives in our sample is twelve, or one in six of all the collectives affiliated with the federation. The project has combined sociological and anthropological field methods. The data obtained from

Abridged from the *American Journal of Sociology*, vol. 67, no. 3 (November, 1961). Copyright 1961 by The University of Chicago.

This research was partly supported by a grant from the Research Council of the Federation of Labor.

the questionnaires, from various types of interviews, and from the analysis of written materials were examined and carefully interpreted by direct observation. We did intensive and systematic field work in the collectives in the sample.

Our initial project dealt with aging primarily within the framework of the developmental cycle of the family and its effects on intergenerational continuity. We were able to deal with other aspects of aging by doing additional research. Documentary material of various sorts, concerned with aging, which appeared in the last five years, was subjected to systematic content analysis. Some of the hypotheses derived from the initial project and from the additional analysis of publications were put to further test in a subsample of two collectives (see Talmon-Garber, 1957, 1958).

SOURCES OF STRAIN

The ambivalent position of old age in a future-oriented and youth-centered society (Kluckhorn, 1954) is one of the main sources of strain of aging in the collectives. The founders had dissociated themselves from Jewish traditional life and had rebelled against the authority of their elders, most members having been trained in radical non-conformist youth move-

[1] The main features of collective settlements (*Kvutzot* or *Kibbutzim*) are: common ownership of property except for a few personal belongings and communal organization of production and consumption on an equalitarian basis. All income goes into the common treasury, each member getting a very small annual allowance for personal expenses. The community is run as a single economic unit and as a single household.

ments whose values and patterns of behavior have had a decisive and indelible influence on communal life. The original revolutionary ideology was reinforced by the personal experience of rebellion. All this glorified youth as full of potentialities, free, and creative, and emphasized discontinuity.

The appearance of the second generation in time naturally brought to an end the disrupting of intergenerational ties. Children are expected now to settle in the collective founded by their parents and to continue their life work there; the family of orientation is no longer considered an external and alien influence. The continuity of the collective depends on intergenerational continuity, and the second generation is called upon to be responsible for maintaining and developing the heritage of the first (Talmon-Garber, 1958; Sarell, 1961).

This new ideology of continuity is just beginning to take root. It is, as yet, of only secondary importance because the collective movement, constantly seeking reinforcement from the youth movements, relies on youth-centered appeal and continues to preach rebellion and discontinuity. Since this spirit predominates, aging is looked on as a process of steady decline, a gradual fall from grace.

The central position accorded to work and the exceptionally high evaluation of productivity lead to the same effect. The founders of the collectives have undergone a process of voluntary de-urbanization and proletarization which reversed the traditional Jewish hierarchy of occupational prestige. Retraining for hard physical labor and settlement on the land were imperative for survival in the difficult conditions of settlement. Strenuous work, a dire economic necessity, has become much more than that: it has been endowed with deep meaning and dignity and invested with a quasireligious seriousness, as an important instrument for the realization of social and national ideals as well as an ultimate value in itself. The idealized figure of a farmer-pioneer tiller of the soil has become one of the main symbols of personal redemption and of national revival.

Work and productivity, in all collectives, has become a compelling drive (Spiro, 1956, p. 17). Absence from work even for a legitimate reason engenders a feeling of discomfort and a sense of guilt; an individual who shirks his work responsibilities is severely criticized. The position of a lazy or incompetent worker is precarious, regardless of his other accomplishments and achievements. The position of any member in the collective is determined primarily by his devotion to his work and the excellence of his performance, and those engaged in physical labor in agriculture enjoy highest prestige.

Retirement from work is gradual. Aging members are not suddenly relieved of their major social function but undergo a steady and cumulative decline in occupational status. Inevitably, as they lose their capacity for hard work and find it increasingly difficult to excel in their tasks, they gradually become part-time workers and are eventually transferred to lighter tasks, sometimes in a less arduous non-agricultural occupation. If an aging member happens to hold a managerial position he relinquishes it in due time, for most work branches require a full-time manager. Old people often wander from one work assignment to another, doing odd jobs here and there.

Aging members thus gradually cease to be self-supporting, and grow more dependent on communal institutions and require more services. Even though most have earned their keep in many years of hard and devoted work, they cannot face declining productivity without misgivings; the constant emphasis on productivity and self-maintenance discourages any too easy adjustment to growing dependence. Moreover, unlike dependence on a state pension or on an old-age insurance scheme, dependence on the collective is not neutral and anonymous. The aging member sometimes experiences it as a direct personal dependence on his fellow members. No wonder, then, that many of the elderly refuse to make use of their right to part-time work and continue to work full time as long as they possibly can.

The objective need for hard productive labor and the ideological emphasis on it in agriculture put elderly members at a considerable disadvantage. Moreover, the constantly changing rationalized and mechanized economy of the collectives puts a premium on up-to-date specialized training, with which long experience gained during many years of practical work often cannot compete. Inasmuch as long experience engenders rigid adherence to routine and hampers adjustment to new techniques, it is a liability. Elderly people are thus severely handicapped. Younger people, stronger and more flexible, are often better trained and more up to date.

Paradoxically, the emphasis on equality, another important value, further harasses elderly members. Social status in the collective is a function of ability, not of age; young people enjoy social equality with their elders, and there are few symbols of deference. Aging members have no claim to vested positions; their contributions in the past do not entitle them to special consideration, and they are judged on their merits.

The fear of losing one's position in the occupational sphere is a major source of insecurity of the aged and a cause of much anxiety and discontent. Analysis of self-images of aging members and of the stereotypes employed to describe old age indicates clearly that retirement is crucial in heightening the awareness of the onset of old age. Many members defined the reduction of their hours of work as the beginning of the end (Blau, 1956; Philips, 1957).

Gradual retirement spares the workers the shock of an abrupt and total loss of their major social function and enables them to adjust to retirement stage by stage. Moreover it enables the community

to utilize the productive capacities of all members fully and spares aging members the long period of involuntary idleness. It should be stressed, however, that full retirement at a fixed age has one important advantage over gradual retirement.[2] Complete retirement constitutes a clear-cut break; gradual retirement spares the worker a major crisis, but at the same time subjects him to difficult and recurrent changes, a long process of continuous reorientation and readjustment.

The rivalry between old and young can be fully analyzed only when viewed against the wider ramifications of the relationship between successive generations. The second generation is expected to stay in the collective founded by their parents. This pattern of familial continuity enables the parents to maintain close contacts with their children, but it engenders considerable strain in the occupational sphere. Occupational opportunities are rather limited in the collective. Members of the second generation have to compete directly with the first generation for the available jobs (see Gluckman, 1955, pp. 56–57). As members of the collective they are in free competition with the older generation, a competition in which the most suitable candidate usually wins— and the better worker is more often than not the younger.

The fear of blocking the channels of advancement often leads to a policy of early replacement of older members by younger, even if the aging workers are more suitable and more qualified for the job. The anomalous age distribution and incomplete generational structure of the collectives are of utmost importance in

[2] On the influence of full retirement at a fixed age on morale see Friedman and Havighurst, 1954; see also Tibbitts, 1953. Most researches emphasize the grave difficulties entailed in adjustment to total retirement. There is, however, some evidence that these difficulties are overstressed. See Streib, 1955–56.

this matter. The founders of a collective are usually young people, of the same or similar age and unattached. At this initial stage there are no aging parents and no young children in the collective. When additional groups and individuals join the founders at different stages of community development the age distribution becomes more varied. When the one-generation structure becomes two-generational, a number of old parents will be found in most established collectives. These parents live in the collective and enjoy the status of "member's parent" but do not as a rule become full members: they are marginal, and the generation structure remains for a considerable time truncated and incomplete. It is only when the original founders become grandfathers and grow old that the collective develops into a full-scale three-generational structure.

The uneven and discontinuous age distribution and the incomplete generational structure have many repercussions on the process of occupational allocation. Adolescents born in the collective begin to come of age when all members of the first generation are still in possession of their full working capacities and hold most jobs which require specialized skill and experience. The process of taking over is a prolonged one; in collectives which have ceased to expand and have not evolved special mechanisms to speed up the taking-over process, the restriction of occupational opportunities is felt very keenly. Any attempt of the aged to hold on to their positions limits the occupational choices open to the second generation. The young people resent being hemmed in and being unduly restricted. They become restless and in some cases leave their parents' collective in search of better openings. Thus severe and protracted blocking of avenues of occupational mobility endangers intergenerational family continuity.

Our material indicates the growing importance of parent-children relationship in the process of aging. The center of gravity often shifts to the familial role: in many cases it is more important than the substitute functions provided by participation in public affairs. At first this seemed surprising. The family in the collectives has delegated most of its functions to the community (Talmon-Garber, 1956), and members' needs are provided by communal institutions. The main socializing agencies are the peer age-group and the specialized nurses, instructors, and teachers. Children are partly segregated from their families, mutual and direct dependence between parents and children being restricted. Since only very few primary familial roles have been left to the family, it seemed reasonable to expect the family to be of only secondary importance. Paradoxically, this limitation of functions seems to have a beneficial effect on family relations: insofar as the family has ceased to be the prime socializing agency it escapes, to some extent, the inevitable ambivalence felt toward agents of socializations, for parents do not have to perform the two-sided role of ministering to their children's needs, on the one hand, and thwarting their wishes, on the other. Parents do not carry the main responsibility for disciplining their children and can afford to be permissive, all of which limits the areas of potential conflict. Since occupational allocation is not familial, it does not affect the relationship between parents and children, and occupational rivalry between generations does not penetrate the family nor disrupt its unity. Moreover, it is mainly within the family that both parents and children have intimate relations, unpatterned by their position in the community and are free from routine duties; only in the family do they get love and care which they do not have to share with many others.

To the elderly, the gradual withdrawal from the occupational sphere enhances the importance of the family. Curtailment of outside activities brings about a concomitant decline in the number and intensity of outside contacts, but they may seek solace and emotional security in their relationship with their children. Grandchildren thus become a major preoccupation, especially with aging women.

Elderly people render their children many small but important services. Although children are looked after mainly by communal institutions the need for aid is not completely satisfied. Children come to their parents' flat after work hours, and the parents look after them during the afternoon and take them to the children houses at night and put them to bed. But if they are very tired after a day's work, the parents may find it difficult to cope with their children without some rest. Parents who have a number of young children will find the afternoon noisy and hectic, and now grandparents may be a great help. They take their grandchildren for walks. They help with older children after the birth of a new baby. They take over the care of children when their parents go on vacation. Whenever either parent is absent from the collective attending refresher courses for specialized training or seminars of advanced studies, the grandparents replace the parent and compensate the children for the temporary separation. They help regularly, but do so especially during emergencies.

Grandparents' needs are provided for by communal institutions. But they, too, often need help, especially when they are incapacitated or very old. Children visit their parents regularly and help with the nursing during illness. They bring in food from the communal kitchen to their parents' flat whenever the parents are unable or disinclined to eat in the communal dining hall, and they carry the parents' clothes to and from the communal laundry. These small domestic and personal services grow very important when the parents are old or infirm; they are indispensable when there is only one widowed and very old parent left.

It should be stressed that the services that children render to their parents are on the whole not very irksome or time-consuming, being auxiliary functions. The old parents' primary needs are provided for by the collective so that they retain to the very last a semi-independence. In the support and care of aged relatives the children only supplement collective institutions. Their limited liabilities and duties do not, in most cases, interfere with their normal life routines. The curtailment and limitation of obligations seem to reinforce rather than weaken family relationships. As a rule, it does not undermine the sense of responsibility toward old parents; quite the contrary; the children are able to help spontaneously and generously. The relationship is free of the feeling of resentment and of the sense of guilt engendered by too heavy responsibilities (Townsend, 1957, pp. 164–65; Rosenmayer, 1958).

The ties between aging parents and children are, thus, firmly based on reciprocal services, on a constant give-and-take of small but significant and continuous services. During the first and middle stages of aging services flow mainly from parents to children, who receive more help than they give. It is only during the last stages of aging that the asymmetrical exchange is reversed in favor of the parents, but it seldom becomes completely one-sided. Only in cases of long-term infirmity do aged parents impose severe strain on their families.

The importance of the interrelation between parents and children can be clearly demonstrated by examining the problems of aging of unmarried and childless members, on the one hand, and of parents whose children have left the collective on the other hand. Needless to say, we do not find here the extreme isolation and bitter loneliness found elsewhere (Townsend, 1957, pp. 166–82). Old people remain full members of a cohesive community and continue to participate in its life. Their diminishing participation in the occupational sphere may be partly counterbalanced by enhanced participation in communal affairs. They are surrounded by friends and neighbors. Yet in spite of all these benefits and substitute functions, most of those who have no children living nearby in the same collective feel very lonely and discouraged, especially so if they have no other relatives in the collective.

Increasing age enhances the importance of geographical proximity and daily face-to-face contact.[3] The aged find it increasingly difficult to get about and visit their relatives who live elsewhere; they need daily care and company. The social and health services and their friends and their neighbors take on some of the functions of children, but this substitute aid can not completely fill the gap. Old parents have no qualms about accepting personal services from their children since the relationship is based on reciprocity and deep affection, but they feel unhappy if they have to trouble a nurse more often than do other old people. Accepting aid from neighbors occasionally, they regard it as not quite right to depend on them for regular services, and they are not completely at ease even with very close and old friends.

Some of the childless old members attach themselves to the family of a friend or a neighbor, as additional or substitute grandparents. This creates a basis of common interest and co-operation and enables them to accept the help offered not as a favor but as part of a mutually satisfactory relationship. In some cases the problems are solved by bonds of enduring friendship and mutual aid between two old and childless people. These alternatives offset certain of the difficulties but they do not entirely replace the family.

Relations with children who live in the same collective are essential to the well-being and happiness of the aged. The services that they render to their children give them a hold on life, and the help extended to them by their children is not just a fulfilment of professional duty or a personal favor but a reciprocation of past services and a reaffirmation of a diffuse and comprehensive lifelong loyalty, a recurring symbolic expression of attachment and affection.

There is thus a marked contrast between the interests of old members in the occupational sphere and their interests as members of families. As workers they would like to slow up replacement of old workers by younger ones. But as parents they want their children to achieve their occupational aspirations without delay and press for their assignment to desirable and important jobs as soon as possible. Thus parents pay the price for family continuity by undergoing difficulties in the occupational sphere, for family continuity can be maintained only at the cost of early replacement.

A smooth process of aging entails both disengagement and re-engagement. It depends primarily on a smooth retirement from work, a successful reorientation to civic and domestic relationship, and, in addition, to leisure activities (Michel, 1954; Havighurst, 1957, II). The elderly, having more free time, are often at loss how to use it and need advice. Life in the collectives is work-centered: work for many was an all-absorbing and often deeply satisfying activity. They had little time and perhaps no great need to develop hobbies. Retirement creates a void not easily filled, and their main problem is to find a new balance between work and social participation on the one hand, and study and recreation, on the other.

We must take into consideration the overemphasis on planning which is typical of recently founded revolutionary societies. Consciously or unconsciously, the members assume that all human problems can be solved by comprehensive social reorganization. Sooner or later they learn that social planning cannot cure all ills.

---

[3] See Litwak, 1960, I. Litwak advances the hypothesis that close relations with kin can be maintained in spite of distance or of breaks in face-to-face contact. However, his sample did not include people over forty-five years of age, and he himself noted that older people might vary significantly in this respect. His analysis of patterns of geographical mobility of extended families indicates a tendency to move closer together in the later stages.

It very often involves the sacrifice of certain ends in the interest of others, and in the course of solving a problem, new ones often are engendered. Members of the collectives are surprised and deeply disappointed when it becomes obvious that total social planning leaves many problems unsolved and even causes new and unforeseen strains; they are easily discouraged and prone to be impatient. Even those who in the process of aging seem well ordered and well balanced very often feel defeated. In many cases we found a considerable discrepancy between our evaluation of the degree of adjustment achieved by an elderly member, on the one hand, and his own self-evaluation, on the other.[4] We found that many of the aged tended to underrate advantages and overrate disadvantages: many took the amenities provided by the community for granted and magnified their difficulties.

The overemphasis on planning has yet another important consequence: the aged tend to rely on organizational changes rather than on ideological reorientation and personal resocialization. They do not fully realize the need for a deliberate cultivation of flexibility in role (Havighurst, 1954), hence a certain rigidity and failure to undertake long-range preparation for the inevitable change.

The importance of structural position is clearly expressed in the differences between aging men and aging women in the collectives (see Talmon-Garber, 1959). We were led by our data to expect that women find it more difficult to adjust to aging than men. Climatic conditions, hard labor, and the negative attitude toward beauty care contribute to a comparatively early onset of aging. Most elderly women drift away from agriculture and child care to service institutions, such as the communal kitchen and laundry, where work is often hectic and full of tension or monotonous and boring and of low prestige. Women, we find, are less inclined than men to participate in communal affairs, and few manage to find a suitable substitute role in this sphere. Most seek comfort in their relationship with their kin and usually cling to the familial roles more than do the men. However, since activities in the family are limited they cannot in most cases fully compensate the women for withdrawal in other spheres. Women tend to engage in leisure pursuits more than men, but there is as yet little systematic cultivation of them in the collectives. Thus women in the collectives apparently have less chance to achieve a balanced and well-ordered old age than men,[5] and we therefore expected them to be more critical of the collective than were aging men.

This hypothesis was examined in our inquiry in the subsample of two long-established collectives. The sample included half of all the members above fifty years of age: the average age of the women was fifty-seven, while that of the men was fifty-eight. The respondents were asked to evaluate the position of aging members in the collective. Table 1 indicates the difference between the statements of men and women.

As shown here, fewer women than men have an unqualified favorable evaluation of the position of aging people in the collective and more women are very critical of the collective. When asked to compare the position of aging men and aging women about 70 percent of the women and 62 percent of the men felt that women have a more difficult time than men: only 6 percent of the women

[4] The investigator assessed the degree of adjustment by extent of participation in the main institutional spheres, basing his examination on a set of fixed indicators. His judgment in each case was compared with the self-assessment by the elderly person.

[5] Men have a more difficult adjustment to aging than women in working-class families (see P. Townsend, 1957, chap. vi). There is little comparative material on retirement of women and its effect on their adjustment to aging.

and 10 percent of the men stated the reverse.

The connection between the system of values and the strains entailed in aging is conclusively demonstrated by comparing members' parents who are only quasi-members with elderly people who are founders of the collective and full members in it. Members' parents do not serve on committees; they are partly isolated and do not participate as much as full members in the collective's social life.

ferences. Members' parents in the sample are older than aging members: their average age is about sixty-four. They numbered fourteen men and nineteen women.

Members' parents, it is seen, who are in a less advantageous position in the collective, express a markedly more favorable evaluation of the position of aging people in the collective than the better situated and more privileged aging members. This seemingly paradoxical finding can be accounted for only if we take into consider-

TABLE 1

ATTITUDES OF AGING MEMBERS AND AGING PARENTS OF MEMBERS
TOWARD THEIR POSITIONS IN COLLECTIVE

Group	No.	Appreciative of Collective (Percent)	Critical of Collective (Percent)	Very Critical of Collective (Percent)
Aging members:				
Men	42	31	45	24
Women	39	18	44	38
Total	81	25	44	31
Parents of members	33	67	24	9

Moreover, many do not fully identify themselves with the collective and find it difficult to get used to its way of life. On the face of it, one would expect quasi-members to be less adjusted than full members who have more substitute functions and are better integrated in the collective. Analysis soon revealed, however, that members' parents are on the whole, much happier and more contented than the others. Many, indeed, describe their life in the collective in glowing terms.

By contrast, aging members are much more aware of the disadvantages. Their praise of the collective is guarded and qualified and they will always point out the need for further planning and reorganization. Table 1 also shows these dif-

ation the ideological and structural position of the two groups. Members' parents are not imbued with the prevalent faith in youth, work, and productivity, and being marginal they are less susceptible to the pressure of public opinion. Having come to the collective after, or near, retirement they are grateful for the possibility to work part time and do not regard this as a comedown. As they do not set their hopes high, they are easily satisfied and enjoy many of the amenities of aging in the collective without suffering from the concomitant strains. But the aging members, who are an integral part of the system and adhere to the dominant values, find it much more difficult to avoid the inherent pressures and strains.

52

WILLIAM H. HARLAN

SOCIAL STATUS OF THE AGED IN THREE INDIAN VILLAGES

The problematic status of the aged in contemporary urban-industrial societies frequently is contrasted with the high prestige, power, authority, and security which the aged are presumed to hold in pre-industrial village societies, such as those of China and India, or of Europe before 1750. It is stated that the once-high position of the aged was undermined by changes in the family and community resulting from urbanization and industrialization; current problems of the aged are explained in terms of these changes. Statements by Davis and Coombs (1950) exemplify this view:

"In general the respect and power commanded by the aged is greatest in static agricultural and familistic societies. . . . The head of the family has authority; he is the head not merely of an immediate family but of a larger joint family; his authority is buttressed by his close and long association with other members of the family . . . which creates in them ingrained habits of respect and subordination. . . . In our own case: the old are a problem partly because . . . this type of society alters the status of the aged. . . . It tends to make them more useless and insecure. . . ."

Williams (1951) emphasizes similar conceptions:

"In comparison with past periods of our own society and with traditionalized rural societies of present times . . . the elders in America have little functional

Abridged from *Vita Humana*, 7 (1964): 239–52, with the permission of the publisher, S. Karger, Basel/New York.

place in the kinship system and occupy a position of relatively low prestige or esteem. . . . The modern urban family is incompatible with the traditional roles. . . . The elderly person is . . . bereft of social function and life rationale. . . ."

Comparable views have been stated by Epstein (1931), Frank (1943), Dunham (1945), Moore (1950), Smith (1950), Simmons (1952, 1960), the *White House Conference* (1961), and by numerous others, and have become firmly rooted in current gerontological thought. They are reiterated frequently, but rarely questioned.

Changes in kinship and family organization do occur in conjunction with urbanization and industrialization, and the extended family system tends to be modified toward the nuclear or conjugal family form (Burgess, 1960, 1963). However, these statements do not compel agreement with the proposition that the status of the aged was or is higher in pre-industrial societies, nor with the contention that current problems of the aged are consequences of urban-industrialism.

This paper undertakes to examine these latter propositions in the light of two previously-unreported studies of the aged in North Indian villages, supplemented by pertinent data from a well-known monograph concerning a South Indian village.

THE OLD MEN OF THE VILLAGE BURAIL

DESCRIPTION OF VILLAGE

Burail stands on the plains of the Punjab, 160 miles northwest of New Delhi, near the provincial capital city of Chandigarh (Singh, 1962). At the Census of 1961 its population was 3,081 persons, living in 566 households. Four-fifths (760) of the men were engaged solely in agriculture, and one-fifth (198) were occupied in village crafts such as carpentry, weaving, and pottery-making, or in shop-keeping. Most of the houses are of simple adobe construction, with a few of brick, all tightly grouped along narrow, winding streets.

The village is on a low hill near the center of its partially-irrigated fields. It has no electrical, telephone, or sanitary system; water for household use is obtained by rope and bucket from deep wells. A rough dirt path leads out to an asphalt road one-half mile away, and thence to the fringes of the city at a distance of two miles more.

The chief features of village social structure are twelve castes typical of this region of India; these are divisible into three dominant land-owning castes, and nine smaller landless castes of laborers and craftsmen. Caste status is the major index of occupation and economic condition and of social relationships within the community (cf. Lewis, 1958). Despite proximity to a city, Burail remains essentially an agricultural, peasant village; the evidences of urban influence are surprisingly few.[1]

In 1961, the lists of the village patwari (accounts-keeper) showed 152 men of 60 years of age and over. For study, a sample of 50 men was selected to represent various castes and age groups over 60. All were members of households, usually of three generations. One-half were married and living with spouse; 22 were widowers,

[1] A few men have bicycles, and the village council head operates a small gasoline-powered grinding mill; there are a few manually-operated ropemaking and cane-pressing machines, but no others. Cows and water buffalo are kept in household compounds, and occasionally within the house. Some young men wear Western-style clothing, but the older men and all women wear traditional garments. See Dube (1955), Marriott (1955), Srinivas (1960), Lewis (1958), Beals (1963).

and three had never married. Forty men continued to work more or less regularly at their customary occupations, while 10 could perform only light or occasional duties because of illness. Interviews were conducted in the local dialect, at the subjects' houses, using a standard schedule of 62 items.

FAMILY STATUS AND RELATIONSHIPS

Traditions of great antiquity, sanctioned in contemporary law, define the model or normative form of the joint family in India (Mandelbaum, 1949). The family is considered to consist of a number of nuclear units living as a single

TABLE 1

STATUS AS HEAD OF FAMILY IN RELATION TO AGE

AGE GROUP	NUMBER		PERCENT	
	Head of Family	Not Head of Family	Head of Family	Not Head of Family
60–65......	13	11	54.1	45.9
66–70......	5	8	38.4	61.6
71–75......	2	5	28.6	71.4
76–80......	1	3	25.0	75.0
81–over....	0	2	0.0	100.0

household, holding all property in common; the men are related as fathers and sons, or as brothers; the women are their wives or unmarried daughters. Authority in matters of property, marriages, work, and discipline resides with the eldest male, who is entitled to respect and obedience. These are norms of the orthodox Hindu family, widely held to be the ideal toward which all should strive.

By these standards, all or nearly all of the old men of Burail should have occupied positions as heads of joint families, with corresponding authority, prestige, power, and security. This expectation was not supported by the data of the study, as indicated in Table 1. When asked, "Who is the head of your family?", only 21 men so identified themselves; 29 named an-

470

other person, usually a married son. Thus, a majority were in fact subordinated to the control of another person within the household. It appears that the shift from dominant to subordinate status had occurred before age 65 in most instances: only eight of the 26 men over age 66 continued to be heads of families. The traditional family norms were not observed in practice. The common view of gerontologists and others as to the high status of the aged within the family of pre-industrial society is not valid with reference to a majority of these men.

Some understanding of these facts is gained by considering the relation between marital status and headship of the joint family. Of the 21 men who were heads-of-family, 14 were married and living with spouse; but of the 25 widowed and single men, only three were heads-of-family. Approximately twice as many men whose wives were living had retained the position of family head as had widowers or single men. From other sources (Indra, 1963; Mandelbaum, 1949) we learn that the wife of the eldest male acts, during her lifetime, as intermediary between her husband and other members of the household, especially daughters-in-law and grandchildren, communicating their requests to him and informing him of complaints or irregularities of behavior. When she dies, however, the wife of the eldest son begins to demand recognition as the new intermediary; but because she traditionally has little or no direct communication with her father-in-law, this new role evolves through her relationship with her husband, who gradually assumes the authority and prestige of his widowed father. As a consequence, the family patriarch is reduced in status and becomes a dependent in the household of his eldest son. In Burail his decline is symbolized by his relegation to such peripheral tasks as taking cattle to pasture, gathering firewood, and tending small children.

Status as head of the joint family, with its associated authority and prestige, is not automatically retained by old men in

Burail by reason of age alone; it appears to be determined by several factors, including marital status and the pattern of intergenerational and interpersonal relationships.

PHYSICAL CARE AND FEELINGS OF SECURITY

The assumption that physical and mental security in old age are inherent in the traditional family system was referred to previously. In Burail, 22 of the 50 old men stated that they were "often" or "always" ill, and of these, 15 complained that they were not properly cared for by their families. They said that when other members of the household were busy in the fields, they were left alone and without food during the day, sometimes on cots in the cattle sheds, and were neglected in other ways. Their complaints were unlikely to arise from circumstances in which family concern was centered upon a member with high prestige and authority who derived therefrom a feeling of security. Similarly, statements by 40 of the men that they worried about family problems and often were unable to sleep for this reason reflect anxieties of a type and degree not to be expected among secure old people.

The study leads to two conclusions regarding the status of the old men of Burail within their families: first, their status was not uniformly high, but varied with age, physical health, material condition, and interpersonal relationships; and second, only a minority of the men had continued to enjoy prestige, authority and security beyond the age of 60.

FORMAL VILLAGE LEADERSHIP

Traditional village panchayats (councils) in India were substantially modified under British rule and have been partially supplanted since 1947 by the institution of elected councils and other local representative groups. Older men would be expected to be prominent in these bodies if they in fact had prestige and the respect of the community. In Burail this expectation was not borne out: only 17 of the 50 men were members of all-village groups, fewer than the number of family heads. The village council was led by a man of less than 50 years of age. Table 2 shows that organization membership was inversely related to chronological age: only eight men over age 66 were organization

TABLE 2

ORGANIZATION MEMBERSHIP IN
RELATION TO AGE

Age Group	Number of Men	Number of Organization Members	Percent Organization Members
60–65........	24	9	37.5
66–70........	13	6	46.1
71–75........	7	2	28.6
76–80........	4	0	0.0
81–over.......	2	0	0.0

TABLE 3

ORGANIZATION MEMBERSHIP IN
RELATION TO INCOME*

Annual Income (in Rupees)	Number of Men	Number of Organization Members	Percent Organization Members
Less than 500..	4	0	0.0
501–1,000...	15	3	20.0
1,001–1,500...	11	4	36.3
1,501–2,000...	6	3	50.0
2,001–over....	14	7	50.0

* Total family income for the year, including cash equivalents of commodities exchanged by barter. The mean income was approximately Rupees 1300, or $260, averaging $43 per person per year.

members, and none in the two oldest age categories.

Two other types of factors appeared to be more closely associated with village leadership than age: socioeconomic status and education. Table 3 indicates that the proportion of organization members among the old men varied directly with family income: no man of the lowest income category held such membership,

whereas 50% of the two highest income groups were members. Income depends mainly upon land ownership, which is closely related to caste status. These interrelated factors were of greater importance than age in determining village leadership.[2]

A second factor, education, had a similar bearing upon formal leadership roles. The 15 men who had ever attended school were classified as educated. Of these, 13 were organization members; but of the 35 men who had no education, only four were members. Education formerly was a prerogative of the upper castes, and its importance cannot be separated from that of socioeconomic status, but it is

TABLE 4

CONSULTATION ON VILLAGE PROBLEMS
ACCORDING TO INCOME*

Annual Income (in Rupees)	Number of Men	"Never" Consulted	"Often" Consulted	"Always" Consulted
Less than 500...	4	4	0	0
501–1,000....	15	10	3	2
1,001–1,500....	11	3	6	2
1,501–2,000....	6	0	3	3
2,001–over.....	14	0	3	11

* Total family income for the year; see table 3.

clear that the two factors jointly were more influential in relation to choice of leaders than the factor of age.

INFORMAL LEADERSHIP FUNCTIONS

Older men might be expected to exercise an indirect voice in village affairs through advice given in informal consultation. An index of the extent to which they functioned in this capacity was provided by responses to the question, "Are you consulted regarding village prob-

[2] Lewis (1958, pp. 26–31, 125–30) states that older men in the village of Rampur retain ceremonial leadership, while middle-aged men dominate secular affairs. He includes age among the criteria of leadership, but his classification of village leaders by age does not include any over age 65.

472

lems?" As shown in Table 4, 17 men said they "never" were consulted, and 18 that they "always" were consulted; the close connection of this role with socioeconomic status is evident. The data do not indicate the types of problems concerning which consultation occurs, nor whether the advice given is followed. But men of upper-caste, land-holding families are taken into account primarily because of these attributes and not because of their age.

Neither formal nor informal village leadership is vested in the old men of Burail. Prestige, power, and authority derive from ascribed status in the hierarchical structure of the village. Insofar as older men occupy positions of leadership

same, and Rattan Garh is also a traditional agricultural community. There were 66 women in the village over age 50, of whom 60 were interviewed, using a schedule similar to that used in Burail. The age, marital status, and family income classifications of the women are given in Table 5. There are differences in these characteristics from the corresponding data from Burail, but they are not crucial for the present purpose.

TABLE 6

HEAD OF FAMILY IN RELATION TO MARITAL STATUS OF THE WOMEN

Head of Family	Woman Married or Remarried	Woman Widowed or Divorced	Total
Husband........	29	0	29
Son............	9	12	21
Woman herself...	3	4	7
Daughter-in-law..	1	1	2
Daughter........	0	1	1

TABLE 5

AGE, MARITAL STATUS, AND FAMILY INCOME OF THE WOMEN*

Age	Number	Marital Status		Family Income (in Rupees)	
50–60...	23	Married	40	0– 500	17
61–70...	16	Widowed	17	501–1,000	14
71–80...	15	Remarried	2	1,001–1,500	10
81–90...	3	Deserted	1	1,501–2,000	10
91–over..	3	Unmarried	0	2,001–over	9

* Total family income for the year; see table 3.

in affairs beyond those of the family, they do so in consequence of attributes other than chronological age. There is little reason to think that the situation is much different today from that which has existed in the village for many generations.

THE OLD WOMEN OF RATTAN GARH[3]

Description of village. Rattan Garh is 18 miles southwest of Burail, in a similar geographic setting, although more remote from an urban center. Its population of 820 is about one-fourth that of Burail. The dominant land-owning caste is the

[3] All numerical data and quotations in this section are from Indra (1963). Her study also was directed by Dr. M. L. Sharma of the Punjab University.

FAMILY STRUCTURE

The patterns of family organization in Rattan Garh are quite at variance with the ideal norms. As shown in Table 6, in 13 instances in which the husband was present, he was not the head-of-family; this was one-third of the cases in which both husband and wife were living. Most often, this role had been assumed by a son in lieu of the father, but three married women and four widows had become family heads; the latter cases probably were due to illness of the old man or to absence of a son. In 19, or nearly one-third of these village families, authority did not reside with the eldest male; as in Burail, the deviation from the hypothetical joint family pattern is quite clear.

The effect of death of spouse upon the elderly woman in Rattan Garh is described as follows: ". . . the old woman whose husband is alive and head-of-family is very well adjusted . . . the old woman and man are considered the two wheels of the family tumbril—if one is broken, the other finds it extremely difficult to pull on . . . So long as he lives, no one dares neglect her; but as soon as the husband dies, the old woman is left alone to suffer the pangs and agonies of widowhood."

INTRAFAMILIAL RELATIONSHIPS

As in Burail, the loss of status by old women did not begin with the death of the husband, but often with the coming of a daughter-in-law into the household. In Rattan Garh, it was said that the daughter-in-law "usurps the position" of the old woman; she "poisons the ears of her husband (i.e., the eldest son) against the old woman." Such was the "clash of personalities in most families" that the son and daughter-in-law "always want to get rid of aged persons." Widows were humiliated to be told by their sons that if they wished to remain in the household "you will have to live particularly and quietly . . . Otherwise, take your clothes and go wherever you like." The bitterness of some old women concerning their status was vividly stated, including clearly paranoid types of reactions. Among women who had daughters-in-law, 13 said they were "good," while 29 considered them "bad."

PHYSICAL CARE AND SECURITY

Old women in Rattan Garh often sought to insure physical care and attention by somewhat coercive techniques of control over the household. These included the keeping of property under lock and key, burying family jewelry and gold in secret places, and letting it be known that the family member who was most attentive to her needs would receive these possessions at her death. The assumption implicit in these measures seemed to be that they were necessary to avoid neglect in times of illness or with advancing years.

Upper caste women did not work outside the household in Rattan Garh, but lower caste women continued at their traditional and often menial occupations about the village until they were no longer able to work. Their tasks included work in the fields, cutting fodder for cattle, and collecting wood and dung for fuel, in addition to care of the household.

Twenty-nine of the women, or nearly half, stated that they could not sleep well because of worry and the "unsympathetic attitude" of the family toward them.

The old woman in Rattan Garh maintains her status "if her spouse is alive, if she is physically able to perform some beneficial function for the family, if she behaves well toward other members of the family, and if she has valuable material in her possession." These are critical qualifications of the conception that authority, prestige, and security automatically accrue to the aged in village society. It would be more correct to say that in Rattan Garh the old women, particularly those of low socioeconomic position, occupy a very tenuous status in old age, and that their difficulties are not instigated by outside forces—nor are they new in the long history of the Indian family.

COMPARISONS WITH A SOUTH INDIAN VILLAGE

Few of the published studies of Indian villages give specific attention to the older segments of the population. The most extensive discussion is that of Dube (1955) concerning Shamirpet in South Central India, which he speaks of as representative of the villages of that area. In population, physical plan, and geographic setting it has sufficient resemblance to Burail to make comparisons meaningful.

Dube forcefully describes the discrepancies between the ideal norms of family life in Shamirpet and the actual practices. He speaks of "four basic principles" which are subscribed to by the entire community: respect for age, respect for kinship position, superiority of males, and restriction of certain information to the family group. He says that "in their idealizations, the different sections of the population show striking similarities; but in their attitudes and reactions to specific social situations the different levels present remarkable contrasts." The ideals are "considerably diluted" at intermediate social levels, and at lower levels are "diluted so much that it is difficult to find any traces of them in actual practice." The conception of family solidarity is reduced, in the latter instance, to "a meaningless ideal." Respect is shown to older people on ritual occasions, "but in everyday life one can ignore these considerations." Abuse may be showered upon parents: "one may spit at them, or throw dust at them, or strike them"; the offender may apologize, but "can repeat it when he is provoked again" without reaction from the community.

The eldest male is the nominal head of the family in Shamirpet, but "in many cases the *de facto* head of the family may be a son." Disruptions of the joint family are common: more than 75% of the men had established separate households within five years after marriage. The author attributes this largely to conflicts between mother-in-law and daughter-in-law of the types which were observed in Burail and Rattan Garh.

Two further comments by Dube are instructive. He states that parents dominate the family until middle age, but "with approaching old age they gradually recede to the background. Nominally they remain the heads of the family, but their sons are left more or less free to conduct the management of the family property and profession as they like." With regard to participation in community interests, it is stated that the older people "generally stay at home. The middle-aged people have in effect the controlling hand in village affairs; the truly aged retire into insignificance and fade away."

CONCLUSION

We return to the questions posed at the outset: whether the status of the aged was or is higher in pre-industrial than in urban-industrial societies, and whether contemporary problems of the aged are consequences of urban-industrialism.

There are close parallels in the status of the aged in Burail, Rattan Gahr, and Shamirpet, and in none of them is that status high. Each village is a pre-industrial agricultural community, little affected by urbanization; yet in each the aged occupy a precarious position. Status difficulties arise from various circumstances, among them personal illness, death of spouse, intra-family conflicts, the demands of younger persons, and economic adversity. All of these are understandable apart from consideration of remote processes of urbanization and industrialization; they may be characterized as inherent in traditional family and village life, and have precedents running deep into the history of Indian society.

The studies described here pertain to only three villages within a single society, but they indicate a need to re-examine current assumptions as to the origins of the problematic status of the aged, keeping in mind three heuristic principles. *First*, generalizations concerning the status of the aged should be based upon representative sampling of all socioeconomic levels, in both traditional and contemporary societies. *Second*, a clear distinction must be maintained between hypothetical norms of family life with regard to the authority and prestige of the aged, and the actual relationships and behavior within a given society. *Third*, caution must be exercised in attributing to the economic and social changes accompanying urbanization and industrialization the whole responsibility for problems of role and status which confront the aged in contemporary urban society.

Programs intended to alleviate the problems of older people might proceed along somewhat different lines if additional inquiry produces further evidence of the need to qualify the frequently-asserted propositions with which this discussion has been concerned.

PART IX

TIME, DYING, AND DEATH

The terminal phase of the life cycle is receiving increased attention from social scientists. While this may be caused by the student interested in the sociology of knowledge, it is nevertheless striking that in the past few years there has been a sudden multiplication of studies of perceptions of time, finitude, attitudes toward death, and other psychological and sociological aspects of death and dying (an interest which is reflected also in the professional literature of physicians, psychiatrists, nurses, and clinical psychologists). The six papers that follow illustrate some of the diverse approaches that are now being pursued.

The paper by Wallach and Green reports an empirical study of differences between the young and the old in the way they perceive the passage of time. The study indicates that time moves more quickly for the old, presumably because they have little time left to live and therefore attach greater value and significance to the passage of time than do young people.

In the next paper Butler postulates a universal occurrence in older people of the life review, an inner experience of reviewing one's life preparatory to death; he describes some of the constructive and destructive effects upon personality that may occur. The paper points to the functional qualities of reminiscence in the aged and to the need for studying the psychology of the aged in understanding the life cycle. In contrast to the quantitative method used by Wallach and Green, this paper is based upon clinical evidence gathered by the psychoanalyst as he treats aged patients.

Issues relating to religious beliefs and religiosity are closely associated with issues relating to perceptions of time and preparation for death. The next paper in this section deals, therefore, with religiosity in older people. Moberg, in reviewing the empirical studies that have thus far appeared, draws attention to various dimensions of religiosity and indicates that some of the discrepant research findings regarding the role of religion among elderly people are due to the fact that various investigators have focused upon different dimensions: religious feelings, religious beliefs, religious practices, religious knowledge, and the effects of religion upon adjustment. The paper indicates some of the complexity of the issues that face the researcher in this field with regard to conceptual frameworks as well as methods of measurement.

In the paper that follows Lieberman reports a set of data which indicates that systematic psychological changes are measurable in aged persons many months prior to death, changes which are not simply the result of physical illness. (Persons who became seriously ill and recovered did not exhibit psychological changes similar to those in persons whose death was imminent, even when they were the same age.) The findings lead him to suggest that in the age range over 70, distance from death may be a more crucial dimension of time than chronological age, a suggestion that has important implications for a possible reconceptualization of time, aging, and life cycle.

In the reading by Glaser and Strauss the perspective is more sociological. Dying is perceived as a status passage, with the dying person moving from one status to another in socially regulated ways. The paper illustrates the research method of participant observation in studying sequential events in natural situations. In this instance, death is perceived as a social event and is analyzed as it occurs in one of its common social settings, the hospital.

Blauner's paper moves further into the sociologist's realm and focuses upon the ways in which the wider society deals with death and on the impact of death upon the social structure. It includes a discussion of the funeral as a social ritual, generational continuities, and the status of the aged as the latter relates to the society's views of death; and it provides a discussion of the interplay between social-structural and psychological factors.

(The paper by Aldrich and Mendkoff in Part VII is also relevant to this section in relating increased death rates to residential relocation of aged persons.)

53

MICHAEL A. WALLACH and LEONARD R. GREEN

ON AGE AND THE SUBJECTIVE SPEED OF TIME

Although the hands of a clock circle the face at the same rate for all observers, time will seem to move more quickly to one person than to another. It is a cultural adage that time seems to go faster if we are busy; slower, if we are idle. But is it being busy, itself, that is the important factor; or is it that being busy may make time more valuable? It is the purpose of this report to question the cultural adage by considering persons whose level of activity has dropped, but for whom the value of time nevertheless has increased. If activity level is the more important factor, then for such persons time should seem more static and slow than before. If the value of time as such is the more important factor, then for such persons time should seem more swift and hasty than before.

In some cases activity and the value of time seem closely related. Kluckhohn (1954) contrasts the dynamic, hasty conception of time found in the urban middle-class American adult with the static, slow conception of time found among the Spanish-Americans in our Southwest. The former individuals are much busier than the latter, much more concerned with getting things done. The need to fill time with various hectic activities makes time more precious and the passage of time more significant for the urban middle-class American than for the Span-

Reprinted from the *Journal of Gerontology*, vol. 16, no. 1 (January, 1961).

This investigation was supported by Research Grant M-2269 from the National Institute of Mental Health, Public Health Service, conducted under the auspices of The Age Center of New England, Inc.

ish-American. A similar point is made by Hall (1959).

At another level of personality, Knapp and Garbutt (1958) have found that persons high in need for achievement tend to think of time in more swift, hasty terms than do those low in need for achievement. As these investigators point out, the high need achiever's aim is to fill time with as many personal accomplishments as possible, with the result that time has a high value for him. We might well expect such a person to perceive time as more swift and dynamic than does the person lower in achievement need.

Turning to a different case, when a person reaches old age, he tends to become much less active than he was in his prime; he finds himself idle; and even is said to "have time on his hands." The cultural adage of time going more quickly if one is busy would, therefore, lead to the prediction that time should seem more static and slow to an old than to a young person. This prediction, however, is based upon the assumption that a person's activity level, rather than the value of time, is the more important determinant of the subjective speed of time. Yet old age presents a situation where the value of time seems to be greater, even though the aged individual is less busy and active than before. Time is running out for the older person as death approaches. While a minority of old people may be impatiently waiting for death and feel time to be long, the majority probably cleave to life and regret the shortness of the time that remains. For the older individual, then, much time has been used up and little remains. For the younger adult, on the other hand, time is a matter of less concern. He still presumes himself to have a great deal of it, so that as a commodity time is relatively cheap.

If the degree of value of time, rather than a person's level of activity, is the more important determinant of the subjective speed of time, then the prediction would be that time should seem more swift and hasty in old age than in young adulthood. The present experiment evaluates this prediction by determining the extent to which time seems swift or static to older and to younger persons who have been matched as well as possible for education and intelligence.

METHOD

SUBJECTS

A total of 278 persons served as Ss in the present research: 118 young adults in their freshman or sophomore year of college at the University of Connecticut, and 160 older persons available through The Age Center of New England, Inc., a non-profit gerontological research organization in Boston. The young adults consisted of 48 men and 70 women, while the older persons included 65 men and 95 women. The median age of both the older men and older women was 71 years (interquartile range 66 to 74.5 years for the males; 65.5 to 74.5 years for the females). The age range for the young adults, in turn, was approximately 18 to 20.

The median level of education for the older men was 14 years of schooling or the sophomore year of college (interquartile range, 12 to 16 years of schooling); while for older women, the median was 12 years of schooling or the senior year of high school (interquartile range, 12 to 16 years of schooling). The older samples thus were well above the average for their age group in educational level.

The intelligence level of the older samples can be evaluated from their scores on the vocabulary subtest of Wechsler's intelligence test for adults (Wechsler, 1944); a subtest which is highly corre-lated with the overall score on the Wechsler. While vocabulary scores were not available for all older Ss, for 64 of the 65 older men the median vocabulary score was 36 (interquartile range 32 to 39); for 79 of the 95 older women, the median was 35 (interquartile range 30 to 38). Reports by Dana (1957) and others indicate that these vocabulary scores of our older Ss exceed, if anything, those of college students.

The older Ss, finally, were non-institutionalized, in apparently good physical health, and quite capable of handling the experimental tasks given them. Most of the older males (over 75%) were retired, and very few older persons of either sex had any present family responsibilities.

In sum, the younger and older adult samples used in this study probably constitute groups which are quite similar in educational and intellectual status. Both the college students and the older adults were above the population average of their respective age groups regarding education and intelligence.

PROCEDURE

The instrument used was Knapp's time metaphor test (Knapp & Garbutt, 1958), administered individually to older Ss and to small groups of the young Ss. The instructions, printed at the top of the response sheet, were as follows:

"Time is an aspect of our experience of which we are all in some degree and in different ways aware. Below are listed 25 phrases which might be employed by a poet or a writer to symbolize his sense of time. I should like you to read through this list of phrases and then indicate before each how appropriate you think this phrase is in evoking for you a satisfying image of time. First select the five phrases that seem to you most appropriate and before each place the number "1." Then pick out the next five most appropriate phrases and before them place the number "2." Continue this process until you have placed the number "5" before the five least appropriate phrases in your opinion. Please be sure to evaluate these phrases on the basis of how well they express *time* to you rather than on the basis of how pleasing you find them as literary images."

The list of 25 metaphors appeared below these instructions on a single sheet. They were arranged in a random order with regard to meaning. This order, the same as that used by Knapp and Garbutt, is shown by the list numbers in Table 1. Knapp and Garbutt, in their factor analysis of ratings of these metaphors by male college students, obtained one major factor which concerned swift vs. static meanings of time, and no other equally large factor. The first aim in the present study was to replicate Knapp and Garbutt's results concerning this factor with separate factor analyses for young men, for young women, for older men, and for older women. If the factor structure for

these four groups proved to be the same and similar to Knapp and Garbutt's, we wished to combine the groups and perform a new factor analysis on all Ss as one group. We then planned to construct individual factor scores for all Ss on the swift-static factor emerging from this combined factor analysis, and to compare young adults and older persons on this dimension.

RESULTS

FACTOR ANALYSES AND FACTOR CONSTRUCTION

The metaphor ratings were intercorrelated separately for each of the four groups of Ss—young adult males, young adult females, older males, and older females. Each of the four correlation ma-

TABLE 1

UNROTATED FACTOR LOADINGS OF THE 25 METAPHORS ON THE FIRST FACTOR

NUMBER ON LIST	METAPHOR	LOADINGS			
		For Young Males	For Young Females	For Older Males	For Older Females
25	a galloping horseman.........	+83	+56	+71	+68
21	a fleeing thief................	+77	+58	+68	+66
7	a fast-moving shuttle.........	+76	+67	+67	+82
9	a speeding train..............	+74	+71	+75	+70
2	a whirligig...................	+66	+47	+51	+71
22	a devouring monster..........	+49	+17	+33	+46
6	a bird in flight..............	+35	+25	+51	+44
14	a space ship in flight..........	+35	+32	+65	+69
13	a dashing waterfall...........	+32	+55	+33	+52
8	a winding spool..............	+22	+26	+17	+07
18	marching feet................	+22	+37	+11	+19
1	a large revolving wheel........	+05	+37	+50	+35
23	a tedious song...............	−11	−25	−23	−22
15	wind-driven sand.............	−21	+06	−13	−04
16	an old woman spinning........	−24	−27	−14	−20
11	a burning candle.............	−28	−42	−24	−41
24	a string of beads.............	−34	−38	−43	−44
4	budding leaves...............	−36	−29	−35	−53
5	an old man with a staff.......	−44	−53	−37	−38
17	drifting clouds...............	−46	−31	−33	−55
12	a stairway leading upward......	−52	−48	−34	−50
19	a vast expanse of sky.........	−54	−61	−70	−76
3	a road leading over a hill......	−55	−49	−42	−61
10	a quiet, motionless ocean......	−65	−46	−58	−70
20	the Rock of Gibraltar.........	−72	−41	−51	−43

trices was then factor analyzed by Thurstone's (1947) complete centroid method. The unrotated loadings of the 25 metaphors on the first factor extracted are presented in Table 1.

For the sample of young adult males, the first factor accounts for 25% of the total variance (the next strongest factor accounting for 7%); for young adult fe-

TABLE 2

Unrotated Factor Loadings of the 25 Metaphors on the First Factor, Arranged in Order of Magnitude of Loading, for All Subjects Combined (N = 278).

Number on List	Metaphor	Loading
7	a fast-moving shuttle..........	+76
9	a speeding train...............	+74
25	a galloping horseman..........	+69
21	a fleeing thief.................	+65
2	a whirligig....................	+61
14	a space ship in flight..........	+57
13	a dashing waterfall............	+44
6	a bird in flight................	+43
22	a devouring monster..........	+38
1	a large revolving wheel........	+31
18	marching feet.................	+23
8	a winding spool...............	+16
15	wind-driven sand..............	−06
23	a tedious song.................	−18
16	an old woman spinning........	−23
11	a burning candle..............	−36
24	a string of beads..............	−38
4	budding leaves................	−42
5	an old man with a staff........	−44
12	a stairway leading upward......	−44
17	drifting clouds................	−46
20	the Rock of Gibralter..........	−50
3	a road leading over a hill.......	−54
10	a quiet, motionless ocean.......	−63
19	a vast expanse of sky..........	−68

males, the first factor accounts for 19% of the variance (the next strongest factor, for 7%); for older males, the first factor accounts for 22% of the variance (the next factor, for 9%); and for older females, the first factor accounts for 28% of the variance (the next factor, for 8%).

Inspection of the loadings of the various metaphors on this first factor for each of the four groups indicates that the structure of this factor is highly similar for all groups. It is also similar to the first factor reported by Knapp and Garbutt.

Its positive end tends to be defined by such metaphors as "a fast-moving shuttle," "a fleeing thief," "a galloping horseman," and "a speeding train." Its negative end tends to be defined by such metaphors as "a quiet, motionless ocean," "a road leading over a hill," "the Rock of Gibraltar," and "a vast expanse of sky." This factor might perhaps best be characterized as "swift vs. static," and is indeed the factor we had hoped would emerge from each of the four analyses. The second factors emerging from each of the four factor analyses were different in structure from group to group, and hence could not provide a basis for group comparisons.

The high degree of similarity of structure of the first factor for all four groups not only is evident from inspection, but is also indicated by the degree of agreement among these four groups in rankings of the metaphors according to their order of magnitude of loading on this first factor. Kendall's coefficient of concordance is .95, indicating high agreement (Walker & Lev, 1953).

We then proceeded with the next step: namely, the combining of all 278 Ss in a new factor analysis. The metaphor ratings for all Ss were now intercorrelated and factor analyzed by Thurstone's complete centroid method, with results for the first factor as shown in Table 2. This first factor extracted accounts for 24% of the total variance, the next strongest factor accounting for 6%. As would necessarily be the case, the unrotated loadings in Table 2 for this first factor are highly similar to the analogous loadings in Table 1.

Individual factor scores were constructed for all 278 Ss on this first factor by weighting an S's rating of 1 through 5 for each metaphor by the size of that metaphor's positive or negative loading on the factor. After an S's rating for each metaphor was multiplied by that metaphor's loading on the factor, the 25 products were algebraically summed to yield that S's factor score. (It should be noted that standard deviations of ratings for the various metaphors were highly similar.)

With positive loadings at the swift end of the factor, and with ratings of 1 given to those metaphors S considered most appropriate as descriptions of time, a positive factor score means that S tended to consider static metaphors more appropriate than swift ones.

GROUP COMPARISONS

Table 3 presents median factor scores on this dimension of the swift vs. static meaning of time for male and female younger and older Ss. It is apparent that young adults of each sex tend to consider static metaphors more appropriate than swift ones for describing time, while older persons of each sex tend to consider swift time metaphors more appropriate than static ones.

DISCUSSION

For older individuals, in comparison with younger, level of activity is much reduced but the general value of time is probably higher. The findings hence indicate that the subjective speed of time is more directly influenced by the degree of value of time than by a person's level of activity as such. A first reading of Knapp and Garbutt's findings with respect to need achievement (time seems more swift to high need achievers), as well as the cultural adage (time seems more swift if one is busy), might have led us to expect younger rather than older persons to consider time more swift. If need achievement directly determined the subjective speed of time, this speed should decrease when, as the individual enters old age, former achievement pressures are relaxed. As Knapp and Garbutt themselves point out, however, need achievement's influence on the subjective speed of time is mediated by another factor: the value and significance of time for the individual. The value of time, in turn, may be affected by determinants other than one's need for achievement and how busy or active one is. The present study has pointed to one such additional determinant: the time that has already been used up

and the scarcity of time that remains when a human being becomes old.

It also has been noted by Hoagland (personal communication) that the present findings are consistent with what would be expected from the fact that metabolic activity slows down with increasing age (see, e.g., Hoagland, 1943). A slower metabolic rate means that less subjective time will pass per unit of clock

TABLE 3

SWIFT VS. STATIC MEANING OF TIME, BY AGE AND SEX

	Young Adults	Older Persons
Median factor scores[a]:		
Males	+ 3.47	− 2.95
Females	+ 3.05	− 1.79
Combined sexes	+ 3.31	− 1.85
Sample Ns:		
Males	48	65
Females	70	95
Total	118	160
Mann-Whitney tests of sex differences:		
z	0.69	0.17
p	n.s.	n.s.

Mann-Whitney test of age difference, combined sexes............ $z = 4.03$, $p < .0001$

[a] Negative factor scores indicate preference for swift metaphors.

time, thus making clock time appear to be "a fleeing thief."

SUMMARY

In an experiment using 278 older and younger adults of both sexes, it was demonstrated with Knapp's time metaphor test that older persons consider swift metaphors more appropriate for describing time, while young adults consider static metaphors more appropriate. This finding suggests that the subjective speed of time is more directly influenced by the value of time than by a person's level of activity as such, for while activity level decreases in old age, the value of time seems to increase.

54

ROBERT N. BUTLER

THE LIFE REVIEW: AN INTERPRETATION OF REMINISCENCE
IN THE AGED

This paper postulates the universal occurrence in older people of an inner experience or mental process of reviewing one's life. I propose that this process helps account for the increased reminiscence in the aged, that it contributes to the occurrence of certain late-life disorders, particularly depression, and that it participates in the evolution of such characteristics as candor, serenity, and wisdom among certain of the aged.

Allusions to a life-reviewing process are common in the literature of various historical periods:

"They live by memory rather than by hope, for what is left to them of life is but little compared to the long past. This, again, is the cause of their loquacity. They are continually talking of the past, because they enjoy remembering."—ARISTOTLE, *Rhetoric* [367–347 B.C.].

"Mem'ry's pointing wand, that calls the past to our exact review."—COWPER, *Task* [1784].

"What makes old age hard to bear is not a failing of one's faculties, mental and physical, but the burden of one's memories."—MAUGHAM, *Points of View* [1959].

Intimations of the existence of a life review in the aged are also found in psychiatric writings—notably in the emphasis upon reminiscence—and the nature, sources, and manifestations of the life review have been studied in the course of intensive psychotherapeutic relationships (Butler, 1960). But often the older person is experienced as garrulous and "living in the past," and the content and significance of his reminiscence are lost or devalued. Younger therapists especially, working with the elderly, find great difficulties in listening (Butler, 1961).

The prevailing tendency is to identify reminiscence in the aged with psychological dysfunction and thus to regard it essentially as a symptom. One source of this distorted view is the emphasis in available literature on the occurrence of reminiscence in the mentally disordered and institutionalized aged. Of course, many of the prevailing ideas and "findings" concerning the aged and aging primarily stem from the study of such samples of elderly people. Since the adequately functioning community-resident aged have only recently been systematically studied (Rechtschaffen, 1959) and intensive study of the mentally disturbed aged through psychotherapy has been comparatively rare, these important sources for data and theory have not yet contributed much to an understanding of the amount, prevalence, content, function, and significance of reminiscence in the aged.

Furthermore, definitions and descriptions of reminiscence—the act or process of recalling the past—indicate discrepant interpretations of its nature and function. Reminiscence is seen by some investigators as occurring beyond the older person's control: It happens to him; it is

Abridged from *Psychiatry, Journal for the Study of Interpersonal Processes*, vol. 26, no. 1 (February, 1963). Copyright 1963 by The William Alanson White Psychiatric Foundation, Inc.

spontaneous, nonpurposive, unselective, and unbidden. Others view reminiscence as volitional and pleasurable, but hint that it provides escapism. Thus purposive reminiscence is interpreted only as helping the person to fill the void of his later life. Reminiscence is also considered to obscure the older person's awareness of the realities of the present. It is considered of dubious reliability, although, curiously, "remote memory" is held to be "preserved" longer than "recent memory." In consequence, reminiscence becomes a pejorative, suggesting preoccupation, musing, aimless wandering of the mind. In a word, reminiscence is fatuous. Occasionally, the constructive and creative aspects of reminiscence are valued and affirmed in the autobiographical accounts of famous men, but it must be concluded that the more usual view of reminiscence is a negative one.

In contrast, I conceive of the life review as a naturally occurring, universal mental process characterized by the progressive return to consciousness of past experiences, and, particularly, the resurgence of unresolved conflicts; simultaneously, and normally, these revived experiences and conflicts can be surveyed and reintegrated. Presumably this process is prompted by the realization of approaching dissolution and death, and the inability to maintain one's sense of personal invulnerability. It is further shaped by contemporaneous experiences and its nature and outcome are affected by the lifelong unfolding of character.

THE SIGNIFICANCE OF DEATH

The life review mechanism, as a possible response to the biological and psychological fact of death, may play a significant role in the psychology and psychopathology of the aged.

The following dream, related by a 70-year-old-man, illustrates the awareness of approaching death:

"I dreamt that I had died and my soul was going up and when I did reach the top I saw a great, huge statue—or living man—sitting there, and then a second man came over to me and asked 'What do you want?' I answered, 'I want to get in here.' So the big man said, 'Let him in.' But then the second man asked, 'What did you do in the other world?' I told him a great deal about myself and was asked, 'What else?' I told of an occasion in which I helped an old lady. 'That's not enough. Take him away.' It was God judging me. I was very afraid and woke up."

The interrelationship of awareness of impending death and recall of past inadequacies is shown in the following case history.

"A 70-year-old retired and widowed mother came from another city to visit her son and showed no inclination to return home. Six months later, the son, anxious about his depressed, irritable mother, brought her to me. She reluctantly accepted a psychotherapeutic relationship: Frightened and guarded, overly suspicious, she continually described her worthlessness; she considered herself so unworthy that she was not able to attend church. I had two impressions—that she was wrestling with guilt concerning past wrongs, acts both committed and avoided, and that she was afraid of death and judgment.

"In one interview, she suddenly appeared to confirm these impressions, which up to then had not been presented to her. She asked about privileged communication—that is, whether I would testify in a court of law against her if she were indicted for her past misdeeds, an unlikely event. Later in the hour she said, 'I am worried about my granddaughter—that something does not happen to her.' She did not explain but added, 'I wonder if she will be able to face her final examinations and graduation day.' [Since her granddaughter is an excellent student, she had little reason to worry.] Still later in the hour she said, 'My doctor referred to these black spots on my head as God's subpoenas.' [She was referring to brown, not black, senile freckles on her scalp.] She went on to explain that she had been having difficulties getting her hair done properly and perhaps this was because she was contagious."

The significance of death is often inappropriately minimized by psychiatric writers, reflecting the universal tendency to deny its reality; it is also sidestepped by some writers through the use of such psychoanalytic constructs as castration anxiety, which has been held to be the basic fear. Fear of death is often conceptualized as merely manifest and not authentic (Grotjahn, 1940).

The relation of the life-review process to thoughts of death is reflected in the fact that it occurs not only in the elderly but also in younger persons who expect death—for example, the fatally ill or the condemned. It may also be seen in the introspection of those preoccupied by death, and it is commonly held that one's life passes in review in the process of dying. One thinks of the matador's "moment of truth" during the *faena*. The life review, Janus-like, involves facing death as well as looking back. Lot's wife, in the Bible, and Orpheus, in Greek mythology, embodied an association of the ideas of looking death in the face and looking back.

But the life review is more commonly observed in the aged because of the actual nearness of life's termination—and perhaps also because during retirement not only is time available for self-reflection, but also the customary defensive operation provided by work has been removed.

In extreme cases, severe consequences of the life review seem to be quantitatively related to the extent of actual or psychological isolation. The writings of Cannon (1942), Richter (1957), Adland (1947), Will (1959), and Fromm-Reichmann (1959) suggest a relationship between isolation, or loneliness, and death.

"The feeling of unrelatedness is incompatible with life in the human being," writes Will (1959, p. 218).

Reviewing one's life, then, may be a general response to crises of various types, of which imminent death seems to be one instance. It is also likely that the degree to which approaching death is seen as a crisis varies as a function of individual personality. The explicit hypothesis intended here, however, is that the biological fact of approaching death, independent of—although possibly reinforced by—personal and environmental circumstances, prompts the life review.

MANIFESTATIONS OF THE LIFE REVIEW

The life review, as a looking-back process that has been set in motion by looking forward to death, potentially proceeds toward personality reorganization. Thus, the life review is not synonymous with, but includes reminiscence; it is not alone either the unbidden return of memories, or the purposive seeking of them, although both may occur.

The life review sometimes proceeds silently, without obvious manifestations. Many elderly persons, before inquiry, may be only vaguely aware of the experience as a function of their defensive structure. But alterations in defensive operations do occur. Speaking broadly, the more intense the unresolved life conflicts, the more work remains to be accomplished toward reintegration. Although the process is active, not static, the content of one's life usually unfolds slowly;[1] the process may not be completed prior to death. In its mild form, the life review is reflected in increased reminiscence, mild nostalgia, mild regret; in severe form, in anxiety, guilt, despair, and de-

[1] The term "life review" has the disadvantage of suggesting that orderliness is characteristic. The reminiscences of an older person are not necessarily more orderly than any other aspects of his life, and he may be preoccupied at various times by particular periods of his life and not the whole of it.

pression. In the extreme, it may involve the obsessive preoccupation of the older person with his past, and may proceed to a state approximating terror and result in suicide. Thus, although I consider it to be a universal and normative process, its varied manifestations and outcomes may include psychopathological ones.

The life review may be first observed in stray and seemingly insignificant thoughts about oneself and one's life history. These thoughts may continue to emerge in brief intermittent spurts or become essentially continuous, and they may undergo constant reintegration and reorganization at various levels of awareness. A 76-year-old man said:

"My life is in the background of my mind much of the time; it cannot be any other way. Thoughts of the past play upon me; sometimes I play with them, encourage and savor them; at other times I dismiss them."

Other clues to its existence include dreams and thoughts. The dreams and nightmares of the aged, which are frequently reported (Perlin and Butler, 1963), appear to principally concern the past and death. Imagery of past events and symbols of death seem frequent in waking life as well as dreams, suggesting that the life review is a highly visual process.[2]

Another manifestation of the life review seems to be the curious but apparently common phenomenon of mirror-gazing, illustrated by the following:

"I was passing by my mirror. I noticed how old I was. My appearance, well, it prompted me to think of death—and of my past—what I hadn't done, what I had done wrong."

One hospitalized 80-year-old woman, whose husband had died five years before her admission, had been discovered by

[2] Various sensory processes are involved. Older people report the revival of the sounds, tastes, smells of early life, as: "I can hear the rain against the window of my boyhood room."

her family berating her mirror image for her past deeds and shaking her fist at herself. She was preoccupied by past deeds and omissions in her personal relationships, as evidenced by this excerpt from nursing notes:

"Patient in depths of gloom this morning—looking too unhappy for anything. Patient looked angry. I asked her with whom. She replied, 'Myself.' I asked, 'What have you done that merits so much self-anger so much of the time?' She replied, 'Haven't you ever looked yourself over?' In the course of conversation I suggested she might be too harsh with herself. At this she gave a bitter laugh and stuck out her chin again."

Later in her hospitalization she purposely avoided mirrors.

Another patient, 86 years old and periodically confused, often stood before the mirror in his hospital room and rhythmically chanted either happily or angrily. He was especially given to angry flare-ups and crying spells over food, money, and clothes. When angry he would screech obscenities at his mirror image, so savagely beating his fist upon a nearby table that the staff tried to protect him by covering the mirror. But in contrast to the first patient he denied that the image was himself, and when an observer came up beside him and said, "See, this is me in the mirror and there you are in the mirror," he smiled and said, "That's you in the mirror all right, but that's not me."

ADAPTIVE AND CONSTRUCTIVE
MANIFESTATIONS

As the past marches in review, it is surveyed, observed, and reflected upon by the ego. Reconsideration of previous experiences and their meanings occurs, often with concomitant revised or expanded understanding. Such reorganization of past experience may provide a more valid picture, giving new and significant meanings to one's life; it may also prepare one for death, mitigating one's fears.[3]

The occasions on which the life review has obviously been creative, having positive, constructive effects, are most impressive. For example:

A 78-year-old man, optimistic, reflective, and resourceful, who had had significantly impairing egocentric tendencies, became increasingly responsive in his relationships to his wife, children, and grandchildren. These changes corresponded with his purchase of a tape recorder. Upon my request he sent me the tapes he had made, and wrote: "There is the first reel of tape on which I recorded my memory of my life story. To give this some additional interest I am expecting that my children and grandchildren and great-grandchildren will listen to it after I am gone. I pretended that I was telling the story directly to them."

Ingmar Bergman's very fine, remarkable Swedish motion picture, *Wild Strawberries*, provides a beautiful example of the constructive aspects of the life review. Envisioning and dreaming of his past and his death, the protagonist-physician realizes the nonaffectionate and withholding qualities of his life; as the feeling of love reenters his life, the doctor changes even as death hovers upon him.

Although it is not possible at present to describe in detail either the life review or the possibilities for reintegration which are suggested, it seems likely that in the majority of the elderly a substantial reorganization of the personality does occur. This may help to account for the evolution of such qualities as wisdom and serenity, long noted in some of the aged. Although a favorable, constructive, and positive end result may be enhanced by favorable environmental circumstances,

[3] For example, Joyce Cary's *To Be a Pilgrim* (London, Michael Joseph, 1942) concerns an insightful old man "deep in his own dream, which is chiefly of the past" (p. 7) and describes the review of his life, augmented by the memories stimulated by his return to his boyhood home.

such as comparative freedom from crises and losses, it is more likely that successful reorganization is largely a function of the personality—in particular, such vaguely defined features of the personality as flexibility, resilience, and self-awareness.

In addition to the more impressive constructure aspects of the life review, certain adaptive and defensive aspects may be noted. Some of the aged have illusions of the "good past"; some fantasy the past rather than the future in the service of avoiding the realities of the present; some maintain a characteristic detachment from others and themselves. Although these mechanisms are not constructive, they do assist in maintaining a status quo of psychological functioning.

PSYCHOPATHOLOGICAL MANIFESTATIONS

As indicated earlier, the many and varied behavioral and affective states resulting from the life review can include severe depressions, states of panic, intense guilt, and constant obsessional rumination; instead of increasing self-awareness and flexibility, one may find increasing rigidity. The more severe affective and behavioral consequences apparently tend to occur when the process proceeds in isolation in those who have been deeply affected by increasing contraction of life attachments and notable psychosocial discontinuities, such as forced retirement and the death of the spouse. But, again, while environmental circumstances are important, it is in character and its life-long unfolding that the unfortunate manifestations of the life review mainly originate.

In a recent series of articles on the aged appearing in a national magazine, a 70-year-old woman in a mental hospital is quoted, "Some nights when I can't sleep, I think of the difference between what I'd hoped for when I was young and what I have now and what I am" (*Life*, 1959, p. 67). The most tragic situation is that of the person whose increasing—but only partial—insight leads to a sense of total waste: the horrible insight just as one is about to die of feeling that one has never lived, or of seeing oneself realistically as in some sense inadequate.[4]

Because the affective consequences are not all readily attributable to definitive losses, the painful accompaniments of the life review are often hard for the observer to understand. It is often extremely difficult for the reviewer to communicate his insights because of the unacceptability to him. When he can communicate them, it is also extremely difficult for the observer to comprehend and face them. The more tragic manifestations are the most difficult—at times impossible—to treat. I believe that this situation is one contribution to increased suicide rate found in old age.[5]

One group of persons who seem to be especially prone to anxiety, despair, depression, or the extreme kind of total catastrophe outlined above, consists of those who always tended to avoid the present and to put great emphasis on the future. These people made heavy investments in and commitments to the future: The future would bring what they struggled to achieve, and it would be free of that which they dislike but have tolerated in the present. This places a considerable strain upon old age, which cannot often deliver; the wishes cannot be met. The poet Adah I. Menken clearly stated this idea in the line, "Where is the promise of my years, once written on my brow?" (Menken, 1888, p. 37).

Another group that appears to be especially prone to some of the more severe manifestations and outcomes of the life review consists of those who have consciously exercised the human capacity to injure others. These people, in whom guilt is real, can see no way of reversing the process; they do not imagine forgiveness and redemption. Still another group

[4] Samuel Beckett's one-act play *Krapp's Last Tape* dramatically illustrates the life review (*Krapp's Last Tape and Other Dramatic Pieces*; New York, Grove Press, 1960).

[5] One may compare this with Durkheim's concept of anomie (Émile Durkheim, 1960).

that appears especially vulnerable to the consequences of the life review may be best described as characterologically arrogant and prideful. This group may overlap with the previous group, but not all its members necessarily have undertaken directly hurtful actions. Their narcissism is probably particularly disturbed by the realization of death.

The following case illustration concerns a person whose life and personality probably involve a merger of all of the factors predisposing one toward psychopathological complications resulting from the life review.

Mrs. G, a 69-year-old married woman, developed a depression six months prior to hospitalization; her depression had been unsuccessfully treated by electroshock, tranquilizers, and heeded recommendations that she take vacations and move to a new environment. She was agitated, suspicious, delusional, nihilistic ("This is the end of the world"), self-derogatory, and self-accusatory, and revealed suicidal ideas. She was embittered and hostile, particularly toward her husband, with whom she was often combative. She was preoccupied with thoughts of death. She had lived for nearly 20 years across the street from a hospital morgue; her physician had sensed this to be disturbing to her and had therefore recommended moving, which she did. She refused psychological testing, explaining, "Why should I be uncomfortable during the little time remaining?" She had a fear of cancer, and once stated, "You can see your funeral go by but still not believe it." She viewed her situation as futile and increasingly refused to talk in any detail about herself to others, including members of her family.

She was in good physical health although she showed increasing preoccupation with her gastrointestinal tract. Upon admission, symptoms suggesting the possibility of a malignancy required investigation. The examinations were all negative, but the patient became increasingly "fixated" upon her lower bowel.

There was no evidence of organic mental changes, including confusion. She became essentially mute several weeks after her admission; she refused to recognize her psychotherapist as a therapist and refused to cooperate with nursing personnel or the ward administrator. She felt no one "could understand." She assaulted others and herself; she would smash her fist at her head and body until she was a frightful sight to behold, with extensive ecchymoses and hematomas all over her body. She refused to eat or drink and continued to lose weight; she rarely slept, day or night. Upon the firm insistence of the administrator that she would be sedated and fed intravenously or by tube, she responded by maintaining a minimum intake of food and fluid. Occasional sedation interrupted her sleeplessness. Otherwise, she did not materially change at that time, and continued to be assaultive toward family members and staff, and to be self-abusive. Because of her years and the remarkable amount of self-destructiveness, she created considerable anxiety and despair in the staff, which eventually was reflected in terms of considerable anger and rage at her. It was exceedingly difficult to break through this kind of bind. Her threat of suicide made the situation for the professional staff even more difficult. However, during the course of a year she improved to the extent that she was no longer as self-punitive or assaultive.

On one occasion she communicated to the Director of Psychotherapy her concern with "God's wrath" and at various times gave intimations of her severe and intense sense of guilt about both past actions and past omissions. Her wish to kill herself seemed quite clear in both direct and indirect statements.

Her past history strongly suggested that she had never realized her potentialities as a person and had never achieved an individual sense of identity. Her premorbid personality was characterized by dependency, indecisiveness, self-centeredness, stubbornness, and a lack of generosity, despite the fact that she had stayed home to care for her mother and father after the other siblings had married. An attractive woman, she did not marry until a year and a half after her mother's death, when she was 47; her husband was then 60. Behind a dignified and passive façade lay a formidable character. She was the quiet but potent center of opposing family forces; her gift was the masterly regulation of these forces. Moreover, she had become increasingly isolated in the three years prior to admission.

In addition to whatever irrational and unconscious feelings of guilt the patient may have experienced, it appeared quite clear that she had in fact done or omitted to do things that justified her sense of guilt. From indirect intimations and direct communications, it became apparent that she was engaged in a process of reviewing her past life but that despite the presence of professional people she was unwilling to review her life with them.

Her therapist concluded that "all of these changes, especially the more restricted life, might have brought on an opportunity for the patient to inquire about herself; that is, to do some introspective thinking. Such introspection might have led to some thoughts about the uncertainty of her future, as well as some unpleasant traits of her personality, and it is this kind of inquiry that might have led to her depression."

The terrifying nature of some of the insights accompanying aging can also be seen in the following illustration from James's *The Beast in the Jungle*. In it James delineated the nature of the "beast" of insight, and of detached, egotistic, intellectualizing John Marcher, upon whom the beast descended. In this profoundly disturbing creation, Marcher's illumination grows to the point of "gazing at [what] was the sounded void of his life," and "leaving him stupefied at the blindness he had cherished."

It is evident that there is a considerable need for the intensive detailed study of aged persons in order to obtain information concerning their mental functioning, the experience of aging, approaching death, and dying. Behavior during aging may be clarified by the revelations of subjective experience. Because of the garrulity, repetitiveness, and reminiscence of the aged, it is not always easy for investigators or therapists to listen; but for those who will listen there are rewards. The personal sense and meaning of the life cycle are more clearly unfolded by those who have nearly completed it. The nature of the forces shaping life, the effects of life events, the fate of neuroses and character disorders, the denouement of character itself may be studied in the older person. Recognition of the occurrence of such a vital process as the life review may help one to listen, to tolerate and understand the aged, and not to treat reminiscence as devitalized and insignificant.

Of course, people of all ages review their past at various times; they look back to comprehend the forces and experiences that have shaped their lives. However, the principal concern of most people is the present, and the proportion of time younger persons spend dwelling on the past is probably a fair, although by no means definite, measure of mental health. One tends to consider the past most when prompted by current problems and crises. The past also absorbs one in attempts to avoid the realities of the present. A very similar point has been made by others in connection with the sense of identity: One is apt to consider one's identity in the face of life crisis; at other times the question of "Who and what am I?" does not arise.

At present, not enough is known about the mental disorders of the aged and how they differ from the manifestly similar disorders of younger age groups. It is known, however, that late life is the period when people are most likely to develop mental disorders—specifically, organic disorders and depressions. The question arises as to whether the life review is related to the increased occurrence as well as the character and course of these disorders.

The current nosology distinguishing the so-called exogenous or reactive depressions from the endogenous depressions may be clarified and explained in part by the concept of the life review. Endogenous depressions, which operationally are those which are least easily comprehensible in terms of environmental variables, may owe their existence to the inner process of life review. The relationships of and distinctions between depression and despair need study. The role of guilt especially requires investigation. Recently, Busse suggested, in connection with "so-called normal elderly persons," that "guilt as a psychodynamic force of importance is infrequently seen in our subjects of elderly persons living in the community. It appears that old people become involved in very little guilt-producing behavior" (Busse, 1959, p. 390). This sanguine idea seems questionable. Not only do older people appear to maintain the capacities to undertake hurtful actions and to feel guilt but also they have not lost the past, which, indeed, comes back forcibly. It is essential to accept the occurrence of reality-based as well as imagined guilt (Buber, 1957).

The oft-stated impression that the aged have relatively greater impairments of recent than remote memory—an impression not substantiated by any experimental data since "remote memory" is difficult to test—may reflect the older person's avoidance of the present as a consequence of the life review.

Other writers have offered constructs pertinent to the aged which probably relate to the life review process. The atrophy of the capacity to project oneself into the future, described by Krapf

(1953), may be another way of discussing the life review; here stress is upon the absence of a process rather than upon the presence of another, active, substitutive process. Balint has written of the *Torschlusspanik* (literally, the panic at the closing of the gate) (1951), which may be related to the state of terror already described in the extreme unfolding of the life review and may also be germane to the "time panic" which has been described by Krapf.

Intimations of the life review are also found in the literature of psychotherapy; indeed, the dangers involved when an older person reviews his life have been cited as either a contraindication to, or a basis for modification of technique for, psychotherapy in this age group. Rechtschaffen wrote, "also to be seriously considered in this regard is the emotional price paid when a patient reviews the failures of his past. It must be exceedingly difficult for a person nearing death to look back upon the bulk of his life as having been neurotic or maladjusted." It is this consideration that led Grotjahn to suggest that it was important for the aged person to integrate his past life experiences as they have been lived, not as they might have been lived (Grotjahn, 1951). It is curious, and probably reflective of psychiatrists' own countertransference concerns, that the dangers of reviewing one's life in psychotherapy should be emphasized; underlying is the implication that truth is dangerous.[6] The existence of a life review occurring irrespective of the psychotherapeutic situation suggests that the aged particularly need a participant observer, professional or otherwise, and that the alleged danger of psychotherapy should be reevaluated.

Past and current forms of, or views about, the psychotherapy of the aged might well be evaluated in terms of their relation to the life review. The "Martin Method," for example, may have been successful because of the enthusiasm, interest, and support provided in this inspirational catechismic form of therapy, but perhaps also because the client was asked to relate his life history in detail, including the seemingly irrelevant side thoughts or images, which might help in understanding "subconscious complexes."

Goldfarb and his associates, on the other hand, propose a technique based upon illusion—namely, creating the illusion of mastery in the patient. Goldfarb's brief therapy is oriented neither toward insight nor toward discharge, but rather toward amelioration of disturbed behavior (Goldfarb, 1956).

One might also speculate as to whether there is any relationship between the onset of the life review and the self-prediction and occurrence of death. Another question that arises is whether the intensity of a person's preoccupation with the past might express the wish to distance himself from death by restoring the past in inner experience and fantasy. This may be related to human narcissism or sense of omnipotence, for persons and events can in this way be recreated and brought back. At the same time a constructive reevaluation of the past may facilitate a serene and dignified acceptance of death.[7]

The phenomenon of mirror-image gazing is of both practical and theoretical interest. In addition to affording one a diagnostic clue to the existence of the life-review, it may provide an unusually excellent experimental basis for the study and further elucidation of the changing concepts of self- and body-image, and the phenomenon of depersonalization, that accompany the rapid, profound, and mul-

---

[6] In the atmosphere of hospital units for the mentally disturbed aged are to be found the notions that the aged "can't stand the truth," must be protected from "bad news," and need to be reassured about their "conditions," and, curiously, that therapy may prove too "disturbing." I submit that the hospitalized aged, already disturbed, need honesty.

[7] However, I do not intend to imply that a "serene and dignified acceptance of death" is necessarily appropriate, noble, or to be valued. Those who die screaming may be expressing a rage that is as fitting as dignity.

tiple bodily and mental changes in the aged (Werner *et al.*, 1961).

Certain schizophrenic and neurotic patients are also known to seek out and gaze at their images in the mirror, talk to their images, and reveal many similar behavioral manifestations. The French psychiatrist Perrier has stated flatly that the schizophrenic does not recognize himself in the mirror; he considers that this symptom shows that the patient has neglected and lost his ego (Perrier, 1955). Schulz has described a 25-year-old female patient whose depersonalization—she felt her right arm was not connected to her body—ceased when she was reassured about her body integrity by looking in the mirror (Personal Communication). The experience of a probably paranoid schizophrenic observing himself in mirrors is also excellently described in a novel by Simenon (1958).

Schulz also reported a neurotic patient who would examine himself in the mirror while shaving and experience the recurring inner questions, "Is that me?" and "Who am I?," probably illustrating his concern about his identity. In this connection, one observes that adolescents frequently spend time examining themselves in mirrors; and analysands, especially female, often report mirror-gazing in their childhood, especially during pubescence. Persons of certain narcissistic character-types describe disrobing before a mirror and deriving great pleasure in self-observation; occasionally there are reports of actual or wished-for orgastic experiences. The theme of the mirror as revealing character is ancient, ranging from the stories of Narcissus and Snow White to the use of the mirror as a chastity test in the *Arabian Nights* tales.

Memory is an ego function whose neurophysiological mechanisms remain hypothetical and inconclusively demonstrated. It serves the sense of self and its continuity; it entertains us; it shames us; it pains us. Memory can tell us our origins; it can be explanatory and it can deceive. Presumably it can lend itself toward cure. The recovery of memories, the making the unconscious conscious, is generally regarded as one of the basic ingredients of the curative process. It is a step in the occurrence of change. Psychotherapists tend to associate self-awareness with health, and lack of awareness with morbidity.

Probably at no other time in life is there as potent a force toward self-awareness operating as in old age. Yet, the capacity to change, according to prevailing stereotype, decreases with age. "Learning capacity" falters with time, and it is fair to say that the major portion of gerontological research throughout the country is concerned almost enthusiastically with measuring decline in various cognitive, perceptual, and psychomotor functions. Comparable attention toward studies of the individual, of growing wisdom, of the meaning of experience, is not ordinary. It is therefore of interest to notice the positive, affirmative changes reported by the aged themselves as part of their life experience, and to find constructive alterations in character, possibly as a consequence of the life review. The relationships of changed functions to aging per se and to diseases, psychosocial crises, and personality remain obscure. There is at least reason to observe that personality change can occur all along the life span, and that old age is no exception. Change obviously cannot be attributed only to professional effort, and changes in behavior outside of professional effort and beyond professional understanding should not be casually categorized as either unreal or "spontaneous." It is necessary to study the changes wrought in life by experience, eventful or uneventful, by brief or enduring relationships with other human beings, or even through images evoked by hearing or reading of the experiences or efforts of others.

In the course of the life review the older person may reveal to his wife, children, and other intimates, unknown qualities of his character and unstated actions of his past; in return, they may reveal heretofore undisclosed or unknown truths. Hidden themes of great vintage may emerge, changing the quality of a lifelong relationship. Revelations of the past may forge a new intimacy, render a deceit honest; they may sever peculiar bonds and free tongues; or they may sculpture terrifying hatreds out of fluid, fitful antagonisms.

Sameness and change may both be manifestations of the active process of ego identity. Erikson writes, ". . . identity formation neither begins nor ends with adolescence: it is a lifelong development largely unconscious to the individual and to his society" (Erikson, 1959, p. 113). He also writes that "early development cannot be understood on its own terms alone, and that the earliest stages of childhood cannot be accounted for without a unified theory of the whole span of pre-adulthood" (Erikson, 1959, p. 121). Similarly, it may be argued that the entire life cycle cannot be comprehended without inclusion of the psychology of the aged.

55

DAVID. O. MOBERG

RELIGIOSITY IN OLD AGE

Geriatricians and gerontologists hold divergent opinions about the importance of religion in the later years of life. The differences reflect a combination of facts and personal biases. Religious persons tend to praise the influence of religious faith and practice and to believe that people become more religious as they approach death, while secularists are prone to believe religiosity declines and to condemn the "ill effects" of both personal and organized religion.

There is no question about the relative importance of the church among voluntary association memberships of the aged. Study after study in various parts of the nation and in different types of communities have found that the aged (like most younger people) are more apt to be church members than members of any other one type of voluntary organization and, indeed, than of all other associations together. Disagreements arise, however, on several topics: What are the trends of personal religion over the life cycle? (Are the aged more likely to be church members than middle-aged and young adults? What is their comparative rate of participation in the church?) What are the effects of church participation? (Does it promote personal adjustment or does it reflect a search for security by maladjusted persons?) What are the characteristics of religious faith among the elderly? (Do they revert to the religion of their childhood? Are they progressively emancipated from traditional religion?)

Reprinted from *The Gerontologist*, vol. 5, no. 2 (June, 1965).

Contradictory answers to questions of these kinds are based not only upon the personal opinions of experts but also upon empirical data from research surveys of behavioral scientists. The confusion that results leads to both traditionalistic attempts to perpetuate past practices and radical proposals that religion be drastically changed or else ignored entirely in geriatric programs.

The confusion of gerontologists about the role of religion is readily transferred to geriatricians, for scientific generalizations eventually influence practical action.

After considerable study and research, I have concluded that the confusion and contradictions about religion in old age are a product of more than a simple lack of research on the subject. The concept of "religion" is very broad, and it is defined in the research operations of social scientists in a variety of ways. The "religiosity" of scientist A is so greatly different from the "religiosity" studied by scientist B that they are not dealing with the same subject even though the same words may be used in their reports. Examination of the "operational definitions" (questions asked and other techniques used to describe and classify people's religious behavior) of relevant research projects reveals several types of "religiosity."

The best analysis of this conceptual problem is the five-fold classification of "dimensions of religiosity" developed by Professor Glock of the Survey Research Center at the University of California (Berkeley). I shall briefly describe each of his five modes or types of religious expression and then summarize some findings on each dimension from studies about religion in old age.

DIMENSIONS OF RELIGIOSITY

Glock's (1962) analysis of the "core dimensions of religiosity" within which "all of the many and diverse manifestations of religiosity prescribed by the different religions of the world can be ordered" provides the most satisfactory extant frame of reference for studying and assessing religion scientifically.

1. The *experiential* dimension reflects the expectation that religious persons "will achieve direct knowledge of ultimate reality or will experience religious emotion," although the emotions deemed proper or experienced may vary widely from one religion or one person to another. Subjective religious experience or feeling is difficult to study but may be expressed chiefly in terms of "concern or need to have a transcendentally based ideology," cognition or awareness of the divine, trust or faith, and fear.

2. The *ideological* dimension concerns beliefs that the followers of a religion are expected to hold (official doctrine), the beliefs they actually hold, the importance or saliency of beliefs, and their functions for individuals.

3. The *ritualistic* dimension has to do with the religious practices of adherents to a religion. It includes public and private worship, prayer, fasting, feasting, tithing, participation in sacraments, and the like.

4. The *intellectual* dimension deals with personal information and knowledge about the basic tenets and sacred writings of one's faith. Again official expectations and the actual achievements of constituents tend to diverge considerably and need to be clearly distinguished from each other. Misconceptions, intellectual sophistication, and attitudes toward both secular and religious knowledge are important aspects.

5. The *consequential* dimension "includes all of the secular effects of religious belief, practice, experience, and knowledge on the individual." It includes all specifications of what people ought to do and to believe as a result of their religion. In Christianity it emphasizes the theological concept of "works" and especially Christian perspectives on man's relationships to other men, in contrast to his relationships to God. Rewards and punishments, expectations and obligations, commandments and promises are all aspects of this measure of religiosity.

Obviously, there are distinctions both in kind and in degree within each of the five dimensions. Just as religiosity itself is not a unilateral concept, each of its major dimensions may also be complex and multidimensional. The areas of religious commitment are all inextricably bound up with each other in real life; none can be studied effectively without recognition of and consideration for the others.

The attempt to clarify the present status of knowledge about religion in old age through use of Glock's dimensions is not simple, as we shall see in the following summary. A wide variety of techniques has been used. Measuring instruments and operational definitions of concepts have not been the same; therefore the actual phenomena studied are not identical even when presented under the same terms. The studies have had divergent objectives and in many additional ways have not been directly comparable. Can order be introduced into such a conglomeration of findings and interpretations?

RELIGIOUS FEELINGS

On the basis of her 25 years of medical practice, Dr. Nila Kirkpatrick Covalt (1960), Director of the Kirkpatrick Memorial Institute of Physical Medicine and Rehabilitation in Winter Park, Florida, stated that she found no evidence to support the common assumption that people turn to religion as they grow older. Patients do not talk with their physicians about religion. The religious attitudes of most old people are those they grew up with. Patients' thoughts, visions, and dreams when regaining consciousness are often given a spiritual significance, Dr. Covalt stated, but

"I recall no person who called out to God or audibly prayed when he knew he was dying. Usually these persons are exerting every bit of energy in a struggle to keep alive."

At least the overt manifestations of their feelings do not indicate a high degree of experiential religiosity.

Contrary evidence is also available, however. The panel of persons in the Terman Gifted Group apparently had greater interest in religion in 1960 (at their median age of 56) than they had in 1940 and 1950 (Marshall & Oden, 1962). Over half (54.1%) of 210 people past age 65 in a Chicago working-class area said religion had become more helpful over the preceding decade; 30.1% said that it had not become more helpful, and 6.2% said that there had been no change (9.6% gave no answer) (O'Reilly & Pembroke, n.d.).

Jeffers and Nichols (1961) found in their study of 251 persons in North Carolina past age 60 that religion means more to most Ss as the years go by and the end of life approaches and that this is especially true of disabled persons for whom the end is more imminent. Similarly, 57% of 140 retired Negroes in South Carolina reported that religion and the church held more meaning since retirement than they did before; 42% reported that they held the same meaning, and only two persons said they held less meaning (Lloyd, 1955).

A large study of 1700 elderly Minnesotans found that only from 7 to 19% of the subcategories of men and from 2 to 5% of the women reported that religion does not mean much to them. In contrast, 52 to 55% of the men and 66 to 71% of the women reported religion was the most important thing in their lives (Taves & Hansen, 1963). Among the 143 older people in a rural New York community, the church and clergy were much more important than formerly to 34 persons,

somewhat more important to 28, about the same to 56, somewhat less important to 10, and much less important to only 7. Corresponding answers about the meaning of God and religion ranged from 46 who said they held much more meaning than formerly, through 25, 59, and 3 in the respective intermediate categories, to only 1 who said they held much less meaning (9 gave no response). Yet only 13 mentioned religion as one of the things that provided them the greatest satisfaction (Warren, 1952).

Wolff's (1961) summary of psychological aspects of aging includes the statement that geriatric patients have ambivalent feelings toward life and death and may turn toward religion, which "gives them emotional support and tends to relieve them from the fear that everything soon will come to an end."

The contrasting results of studies which refer to religious feelings of the aged may result from a basic difficulty in scientific research on religious feelings. American societal expectations hold that religion is helpful in any time of trouble. Anyone who expresses a perspective contrary to the position that religion helps the aged may feel that he is in danger of being socially rejected for his seemingly heretical views. With the fear of such reprisals, biased responses to questions about religious feelings may distort the results of questionnaire as well as interview studies. A type of self-fulfilling prophecy mechanism also may be at work: the expectation that religion will help may lead the person to receive genuine help through religious channels or at least to feel as if he had.

While the bulk of the evidence available to date indicates that religious feelings increase for more people than those for whom they decrease, we must retain an open mind on this subject while awaiting additional research.

RELIGIOUS BELIEFS

There is some evidence from public opinion survey data that belief in life after death may increase with age; at least a higher proportion of old people than of younger generations believe that there is a life after death. Older people also are more certain that there is a God and apparently are more inclined to hold to traditional and conservative beliefs of their religion (Gray & Moberg, 1962).

A study of 496 persons in New York City, 325 of whom were Jewish, found that the proportion who believed in a life after death (heaven) increased from 30.1 to 40.5% from ages 30–35 to aged 60–65. Non-belief for the same age categories diminished from 36.1 to 25.1, with the remainder uncertain (Barron, 1961, pp. 164–183). The nationwide *Catholic Digest* (Anon., 1952) survey revealed that 81% of the respondents aged 65 and over compared to 79% of all and 76% of those aged 45–54 thought of God as a loving Father. Belief in God was held the most certainly by persons aged 65 and over, and a somewhat higher proportion of the aged (56%) than of the total sample (51%) believed one should prepare for life after death rather than be concerned with living comfortably. This lends some support to the opinion of Starbuck (1911), the pioneer in the psychology of religion, that religious faith and belief in God grow in importance as the years advance. His research data were skimpy and his highest age category was "40 or over," but his conclusion has been adopted so widely that Maves (1960) has called it a "part of the folklore of the psychology of religion."

Surveys have revealed that older people as a whole tend to have more conservative religious perspectives than younger adults. Indirect evidence of this also comes from St. Cloud, Florida, where more than half the population in the mid-1950's was aged 60 and over. Its churches were generally more fundamentalistic than was usual in peninsular Florida, and over one-third were evangelical and sectarian (Aldridge, 1956).

Whether the differences in religious beliefs between the generations are a result of the aging process or of divergent experiences during the formative years of childhood and youth, which are linked with different social and historical circumstances, is unknown. Longitudinal research might reveal considerably different conclusions from the cross-sectional studies which provide the foundation for current generalizations about age variations in the ideological dimension of religion.

RELIGIOUS PRACTICES

The ritualistic dimension has received considerable attention from social scientists, perhaps because the observation of most religious practices is relatively simple. The findings are not wholly consistent, however.

All American studies which have come to my attention indicate that more of the formal social participation of the elderly, as well as of other age groups, is in the church than in all other voluntary community organizations together. This holds true whether measured by membership, attendance, or other indicators. For example, 87% of 1,236 persons aged 60 and older in two Kentucky communities participated in the church, 35% in Sunday school, and 8% in other church activities. The next highest participation was 6% in "service and welfare organizations." As also is consistently true, women participated in the church to a somewhat greater extent than men, 94% compared with 85% of the men in a Lexington sample and 93 and 73%, respectively, in a Casey County sample (Youmans, 1963).

The highest Chapin social participation scores for religious participation among the heads of households in four rural New York communities studied in 1947–1948 were found among men aged 75–79, followed closely by those aged 45–54. Among homemakers in the same study, the highest scores were found among those aged 70–74 and 75–79, with women aged 60–64 in third place and 45–54 fourth. Female participation in religious organizations exceeded that of males at every age, but male participation exceeded that of the females in nonreligious organizations (Taietz & Larson, 1956). (Chapin scores are based upon a combination of membership, attendance, financial contributions, committee positions, and offices held.)

The peak of intensity of social participation, based on Chapin's scale among 1,397 persons aged 10 and over in two North Carolina localities, came at ages 55 to 59 with a sharp drop thereafter. Four-fifths of this participation was in religious activities, and six-tenths of the persons participated only in churches and their auxiliary organizations (Mayo, 1951).

Some studies have revealed increases in religious practices in old age. Public opinion poll data indicate consistently higher figures for church attendance, Bible reading, and prayer among persons aged 50 and over than among younger groups (Toch, 1953). Age among 597 institutionalized women aged 65 or older living in Protestant homes for the aged was positively correlated with increased religious activities as well as with increased dependence upon religion (Pan, 1954). Contrasting evidence from other samples of older people suggests that the relative youthfulness of the "over 50" group compared to samples with a higher minimum age and the unusual environmental circumstance of residents in Protestant church homes, which facilitate participation in organized religious activities, may account for the variation between these two studies and others reported below.

A survey of 100 first admisions of persons aged 60 and over to a county hospital found evidence which was interpreted tentatively as contrary to the common assumption that people become more interested in religion as they grow older. Several were found to attend church less frequently than at age 50, and few attended more often than before

(Fiske, 1961). (The report sensibly qualifies the finding by suggesting that a change in behavior does not necessarily imply, less concern with spiritual matters. It refers to a University of Chicago study which found that the decrease in church attendance among aging persons is accompanied by increased listening to religious programs on radio and television.)

In the "Back of the Yards" Chicago study (O'Reilly & Pembroke, n.d.) approximately equal proportions of men attended church more (34%) and less (32%) than they did before the age of 65, but among women the respective figures of 27 and 46% indicate a decrease in attendance. Increasing age among Catholics in Fort Wayne, Indiana, was associated with decreasing church attendance, chiefly because of poor health (Theisen, 1962). Fichter's (1954) study of 8,363 active white Catholic parishioners found that the percentage who received monthly Communion diminished fairly consistently in each 10-year category from age 10 to 60-and-over. However, a higher percentage of the eldest category (86.6) made their Easter duties (confession and Holy Communion) than any other age except the youngest (ages 10–19, 92.1%), and only the youngest exceeded the elderly in the percentage attending Mass every Sunday (92.8 versus 90.9%). Physical disabilities may account for differences. Although variations over the total life span cannot be accounted for solely on the basis of age, both the young and the old were significantly more religious as measured by these practices than persons aged 30–39, who had the lowest record for both sexes (63.4% made their Easter duties, 69.3% attended Mass every Sunday, and 31.6% received monthly Communion).

Only 4% of a representative stratified sample of people aged 65 and over studied in 1948–1949 in a small midwestern city rejected religion and the church, but an additional 18% had no church affiliation and no attendance, and 15% had only a passive interest. The other 63% participated in religious activities frequently and actively. Most people evidently continued to carry on the religious habits of their middle years, but they also customarily dropped gradually out of church leadership positions after the age of 60 (Havighurst & Albrecht, 1953). In a metropolitan Kansas City study (Cumming & Henry, 1961) the proportions of persons aged 50 and over who seldom attended church was lowest at age 60–64 in both sexes and reached its highest figure among those aged 75 and over (64.3% of the men and 75.0% of the women).

Senior citizens surveys of a cross-section of the population aged 65 and over in Long Beach, California (McCann, 1955), and Grand Rapids, Michigan (Hunter & Maurice, 1953) indicated a definite tendency of the aged to attend church less often than they did ten years earlier, and increasing non-attendance accompanied increasing age. Problems of physical mobility and finances were among the most significant factors related to declining attendance. Listening to religious services on radio or television and "lost interest" followed health or physical condition in importance among the reasons respondents gave for attending church less often than they had a decade earlier; where the former is a major reason for decreased attendance (17.1% of the Long Beach and 33.9% of the Grand Rapids sample), non-attendance can hardly be accepted as an indicator of a loss of religiosity.

Fifty-five per cent of 131 aged members of two urban Baptist churches in Minnesota attended church every Sunday. The percentages ranged from 71.4 among the 14 persons aged 80–84 to 20 among the 5 aged 85–89. Nearly half (45.6%) of the persons aged 75 and over attended church every Sunday, compared with 64.5% of those aged 65–69 and 60.5% of those aged 70–74. The evidence pertinent to attendance at other church activities clearly supported the hypothesis that participation declines in old age. This decline was even more pronounced in regard to holding lay leadership positions, which reached its peak in both churches at the age of 25–44. Only 4.6% said that they were more active in the church now than they were in their fifties, but 72.5% said that they were less active than in their fifties (Moberg, 1965).

The survey (Barron, 1961) of 496 residents of New York City (325 of whom were Jewish, 98 Roman Catholic, 65 Protestant, and 8 of other or no faiths) found only insignificant differences between the age categories 30–35, 40–45, 50–55, and 60–65 in the proportion that attended church or synagogue "often" in contrast to "sometimes" and "hardly ever" or "never."

The strongest criticism of the "contemporary folklore that 'older' people are more religious than others . . . , and that there is a turning to religion in old age" comes from Orbach's (1961) interpretations and research. In support of his position, Orbach appealed to sociological interpretations of the functions of religion in our "youth-centered society," evidence of the significance of religious beliefs, feelings, and conversion among the young rather than the aged, and empirical findings from studies like those mentioned above which indicate that participation in religious activities decreases in old age.

Since other studies are weak on the levels of both sampling and the analysis of relevant sociological variables other than sex, Orbach made a careful analysis of five probability samples of 6,911 adults aged 21 and over who resided in the mid-1950's in the Detroit Metropolitan Area. Church attendance on a five-point scale from once a week to never was related to age in five-year intervals with sex controlled. Age *per se* was found to be unrelated to changes in church attendance; there was no indication of an increase in attendance in the later years, although the data suggest that there is a polarizing effect in which intermediary categories of "casual" and "cursory" churchgoers tend to shift into a dichotomous distribution of regular church attenders and non-attenders.

When the data were grouped into four age categories (21–39, 40–59, 60–74, 75 and over), the most striking finding was the constancy of attendance in all age groupings, with the one exception of significantly increased non-attendance among the oldest group, which can be attributed at least partly to the effect of age on physical health. Multivariate analysis of church attendance in relationship to age with religious preference, sex, and race as control variables found only Protestant Negro males and Jewish males and females to show increased attendance with age. The small number of cases of Negro males in the oldest age category and the historical decline of Jewish orthodoxy, which is directly reflected in the age groupings, may account for these exceptions to the general pattern of declining attendance as age increases. When other sociological variables were controlled, the relationships between age and attendance were mixed and inconsistent and lent no support to the hypothesis that religiosity increases with age.

The bulk of reliable evidence thus indicates that church attendance of people generally remains fairly constant but tends to decline in the later years compared with younger ages. It is hazardous, however, to assume that church attendance is anything more than a crude indicator of religiosity; it is only one subdimension of religious practices, which themselves comprise but one of Glock's five major dimensions of religious commitment.

Orbach (1961) states that "participation in religious bodies through attendance and involvement in ceremonial worship is perhaps the most crucial and sensitive indicator of overt religiosity." This may apply satisfactorily to the most sacramentally oriented religions—those which believe that the religious institution is the channel of God's grace and that salvation is bestowed upon the individual only through institutionalized participa-

tion in church rituals. It probably does not apply to non-sacramental Protestants and to Jews. Orbach (1961) also wisely reminds us that "objective criteria such as attendance cannot replace study of the area of religious beliefs and attitudinal changes or approximate the subjective aspect of inner religious feelings." Attendance is easier to study, but it should be used as a measure of religiosity only provisionally and with a clear recognition of attendant dangers.

Although church attendance tends at most to remain constant with increasing age in cross-sectional studies of the population and more often to decline, regular listening to church services and other religious broadcasts on the radio and reading from the Bible at least weekly have been found to increase among the elderly with advancing age (Cavan, Burgess, Havighurst, & Goldhamer, 1949). Evidently religious practices outside the home diminish while those within the home increase. Physical condition may be the chief intervening variable responsible for such trends. Comparative studies reveal that participation in other social organizations declines at a much more rapid rate than participation in the church.

RELIGIOUS KNOWLEDGE

Relatively little research has been done on age differences in the intellectual dimension of religiosity among older adults. I have been unable to locate any published research which bears directly upon this topic.

EFFECTS OF RELIGION

Although many of the other dimensions of religiosity have been only crudely defined, they have been used as independent variables in research designed to discover the effects of religion upon other aspects of personal and social life. Examples of some of these explorations of the consequential dimension of religion will be presented here.

A number of studies have demonstrated that church members hold a larger number of memberships in voluntary community associations and other organizations than those who are not members and that lay leaders in the church are more active in non-church organizations than are other church members (Moberg, 1962), but relatively little attention has been given to age variations in this pattern.

A national survey of adults (Lazerwitz, 1962) in the spring of 1957 related the age of persons with Protestant and Catholic religious preference to the number of voluntary association memberships they held. It was found that the lowest membership levels prevailed among Protestants in the youngest (21–24) and oldest (60–64 and 65 and over) categories and the highest membership rates at ages 30–59. Among Catholics the highest percentage of persons with no organizational memberships was at ages 65 and over and 45–49, with the greatest number of memberships at ages 35–44. Most of the Protestants and Catholics who seldom or never attended church also lacked membership in voluntary associations, while most of those who attended faithfully had one or more such memberships.

Other studies support the conclusion that there is a positive correlation between church participation and other formal social participation at all ages. It is not unreasonable to think that associating with people in church-related activities and organizations contributes to knowledge of other voluntary organizations; friendships in the church with persons who are members of other groups may lead to social participation in them. The lower organizational membership levels of Catholics hence could result from their lesser stress upon "fellowship" in the church as compared to Protestants, as well as from their somewhat lower position in the social class structure of American society.

Barron's (1961) New York City study included a question about the respondent's self-image, "Would you say you are a religious person, or doesn't religion mean very much to you?" Of all the respondents, 44.7% responded affirmatively and 25.2% expressed an irreligious self-image. Among the 116 persons aged 60–65, however, the respective percentages were 55.1 and 19.9 (25.0% were undecided compared with 30.1% in the total sample).

The most significant aspect of the chronological age distribution in answer to this question was the steadily increasing proportions of the religious self-image and the steadily declining proportions of indecision regarding the self-image in the ascension of chronological age.

The relationship of religion to personality problems has been observed and commented upon by a number of behavioral scientists. Religion was the preferred topic of discussion in group therapy sessions with geriatric patients at a state hospital. Religious beliefs and faith in God helped disorganized members to overcome their grief when unhappy, lonesome, and despondent. They were eager to discuss a better life after death; other members sensed the support religion gave them because they themselves also received greater "Ego strength" from religion. Delusions and hallucinations involving religious symptoms were, however, not accepted by other members of the group as true and correct; when they occurred the possibility of a mistake or incorrect interpretation was discussed (Wolff, 1959).

Elderly patients who have ambivalent feelings toward life and death often want to die, since they believe they have nothing for which to live. Yet as they sense death is approaching, they may become disturbed and insecure, want others near at all times, and fear the dark. They may attend church more often than previously, confess, and ask that their sins be forgiven. They thus turn toward religion, which gives them emotional support and relief from the fear that everything soon will end (Wolff, 1959 II).

Fear of death was one topic probed in a study of 260 community volunteers aged 60 and over in North Carolina. Such fear was found to be significantly related (at the 1% level of confidence) to less belief in life after death and less frequent Bible reading (Jeffers, Nichols, & Eisdorfer, 1961). Swenson's (1961) psychological study of 210 Minnesota residents aged 60 and over similarly found a significant relationship between death attitudes and religiosity as measured by both religious activity and the MMPI religiosity scale, a measure of devotion to religion. "Persons with more fundamental religious convictions and habits look forward to death more than do those with less fundamental convictions and less activity. Fearful attitudes toward death tend to be found in those persons with little religious activity. . . . It seems logical to infer that the eschatologically oriented person contemplates death in a positive manner."

These findings support the conclusion that a sense of serenity and decreased fear of death tend to accompany conservative religious beliefs. This does not necessarily prove, however, that religious faith removes the fear of death. It is conceivable that attitudes toward death of the religiously faithful differ from those of nonreligious people because of differences in their social integration (Treanton, 1961); the religious have a reference group that gives them support and security and the nonreligious are more likely to lack such social support. Swenson's finding that fear of death is related to solitude supports this hypothesis; social isolation may be an intervening variable explaining the observed relationships.

The traditional cultural definition of death complicates research on this subject among people of Christian convictions. The faithful believer is expected so to rest upon the promise of his salvation that he has no fear of death; he is expected to see death as a portal to immortality. His affirmation that he does not fear the advent of death could be an expression of a neurotic personality which disguises death and pretends that it is not a basic condition of all life (Fulton, 1961). Feifel (1956) has hypothesized that "certain older persons perceive death as the beginning of a new existence for the purpose of controlling strong anxieties concerning death." While this hypothesis may be perceived by some religious people as an impudent attack upon the genuineness of religious faith, it may also be viewed as a compliment to it. If the hypothesis is verified, one of the social-psychological functions commonly attributed to religion by even the most faithful when they seek comfort in biblical teachings about the resurrection will have received scientific support.

Happiness was significantly related to frequency of church attendance among both Catholics and non-Catholics in the Chicago "Back of the Yards" study. The "very happy" attended church the most frequently, the "moderately happy" the next most frequently, and the "less happy" persons attended the least of all. Lonely Catholics tended to be less active in the practice of their religion, but the relationship was not statistically significant (O'Reilly & Pembroke, n.d.).

Feelings of satisfaction and security were provided older persons by religion and church participation in a small midwestern community studied by McCrary (1956). Yet in her general medical practice in Muncie, Indiana, Dr. Covalt (1958) observed little or no relationship between religion and good adjustment to illness. The patient who brought a Bible to the hospital with him thereby gave the physicians a sign of anticipated trouble for the stable, secure person did not bring a Bible. These insecure individuals often were members of fringe-type religious sects. They were uncooperative, did not carry out instructions, fought the nurses, complained about even the most minor matters, and unpleasantly hindered their own recovery.

Contradictory evidence thus emerges on the matter of whether religion performs such functions as promoting happiness, increasing personal security, combatting loneliness, and removing the fear of death. Several of these concepts are reflected in studies of personal adjustment or morale in old age. To discuss the techniques and findings of these in any detail is impossible in the short space available here, but a brief summary of some of the major studies will help to illuminate this aspect of the consequential dimension of religion. More thorough surveys are found in Gray and Moberg (1962) and Maves (1960).

These studies generally have found that there is a direct relationship between good personal adjustment and such indicators of religiosity as church membership, church attendance, Bible reading, regular listening to radio church services, belief in an after life, and religious faith. Yet a carefully planned experimental design to explore this relationship further, with the use of the Burgess-Cavan-Havighurst Attitudes Inventory as the measure of personal adjustment, revealed that controlling other factors which also are linked with good adjustment removed the correlation between adjustment and church membership (Moberg, 1953). The relationship observed in cruder studies must be a result of linking with church membership certain other factors which contribute to adjustment rather than a result of church membership in and of itself.

Further analysis (Moberg, 1956) through additional experimental designs demonstrated that religious activities (church attendance in the past and present, lay leadership in the church, grace at meals, reading from the Bible and other religious books, family prayers, etc.) were significantly correlated with high adjustment scores. It was concluded that either those who are well-adjusted engage in many religious activities or else engaging in many religious activities contributes to good adjustment in old age.

Similarly, an experimental design (Moberg, 1953 II) to analyze the relationships between adjustment and leadership in the church, as indicated by office-holding and committee work in the past and present, revealed that personal adjustment was positively related to lay leadership. An investigation (Moberg, 1958) of Christian beliefs about sin, prayer, the future, the Bible, and Jesus in relationship to personal adjustment also revealed a positive relationship between holding conventional Christian beliefs and good adjustment in old age when other factors were controlled. The evidence from these experimental designs, based upon institutionalized persons in homes for the aged, a county home, and a soldiers' home, supports the conclusion that religious beliefs and activities, in contrast to church affiliation *per se*, contribute to good personal adjustment in old age.

This conclusion is supported by additional studies of elderly people. The most significant of these (Moberg & Taves, 1965) involves over 5,000 persons aged 60 years and over interviewed in five surveys in four midwestern states. It was found that the adjustment scores of church "leaders" (church officers and committeemen), other church members, and non-church members were significantly different, with the leaders consistently highest and non-members lowest. Cross-tabulations of the data for 1,340 urban respondents in one of the states demonstrated that these differences remained statistically significant at the .001 level when analyzed within categories of sex, age, education, marital status, home ownership and type of residence, participation in civic, social, and professional organizations, organizational activity levels compared to those during the respondents' fifties, self-rating of health, and self-identification of age. Only in the area of employment were the variations non-significant, but even these were in the anticipated direction, so the hypothesis that

506

church participation is related to good personal adjustment in old age was overwhelmingly supported by the evidence.

A study (Oles, 1949) of Orthodox Jews aged 65 and over also found that adjustment was related to religious adherence. No non-religious persons were in the well-adjusted category; all were intensely or fairly religious. Three-fourths of the fairly adjusted group were intensely or fairly religious, but only 35% of the poorly and very poorly adjusted group were.

Religious beliefs and activities seem, on the basis of these and other studies, to be positively related to good personal-social adjustment in old age. Contrary evidence, but on a somewhat different basis, comes from Barron's (1961) New York City study. Only 39% mentioned that religion and the church gave them the most satisfaction and comfort in their lives today. This was exceeded by being home with the family, keeping house, "doing things I like to do by myself at home," having relatives visit, and spending time with close friends. Worry about getting older was significantly less among these who found religion comforting only for the age group 40–45; the comparative figures for all ages indicate that 37% of those who derive comfort from religion worry about aging compared with 40.6% of those who do not find religion comforting. Both of these measures of religiosity are very limited, but this finding suggests the need for further research before making sweeping generalizations about the impact of religion upon personal adjustment.

Another consequential aspect of religion is the large number of retirement homes and communities, nursing care facilities, social clubs, literary projects, counseling centers, volunteer services programs, educational activities, and other programs by and for the aged which are under church sponsorship (Culver, 1961). While these, like all human behavior, are based upon a wide range of economic, social, political, psychological, and humanitarian interests, the very fact that religiously based institutions are their sponsors demonstrates this to be a consequence of organized religion. Religious beliefs, feelings, knowledge, and practices undoubtedly are an underlying factor in much of the humanitarian work that is done through other institutional structures as well. The educational and inspirational work of the church often is directly oriented toward such goals; to whatever extent it is effective, it serves as an enlightening and motivating influence in society, and more often produces change through its constituents than through formal institutional action. This aspect of the consequential dimension of religious commitment is obviously very difficult to study empirically because it is so intricately woven into the total fabric of society.

INTERRELATIONS OF THE DIMENSIONS

Some studies have shown both the interconnectedness and the relative independence of various dimensions of religious commitment. The biserial correlation coefficient between the religious activity and religious attitude scores in the Chicago Activities and Attitudes Inventories by Burgess, Cavan, and Havighurst, for example, was significant at the .001 level of confidence in a North Carolina study (Jeffers & Nichols). The correlation coefficient between attitudes toward religion and frequency of attendance at religious services in the original Chicago study was .55 among 1,024 males and .37 among 1,894 females (Cavan et al., 1949). In a study (Moberg, 1951) of 219 institutionalized aged persons, the product-moment correlation of a religious activities score and a religious belief score was .660 with a standard error of .038.

Such relationships are the kind one would expect; if a person has religious faith, he is more apt to participate in the personal and social activities which simultaneously nourish that faith and are consequences of it. Belief in life after death thus is significantly associated with more frequent church attendance, more frequent Bible reading, a greater number of other religious activities, a feeling that religion is the most important thing in life, less fear of death, and stronger religious attitudes than are found among those who lack such a belief (Jeffers *et al.*, 1961).

Nevertheless, it is a fallacy to assume that *all* dimensions of religiosity are highly intercorrelated. Hospitalized old people, we know, are somewhat more likely than the elderly in the community to identify with a religious group, but they also are considerably less likely to attend religious services than nonhospitalized old people (Fiske, 1960). To judge the totality of the religiosity of a person on the basis of one of the five major dimensions of religious commitment or, as is a common practice, of but one subdimension thereof, can lead to serious errors. Religious preference, church attendance, religious self-identification, and other simple indicators of religiosity must be used with great caution of interpretation. Religious commitment is a complex phenomenon with many ramifications. Until research has demonstrated the ways in which and the extent to which the experiential, ideological, ritualistic, intellectual, and consequential dimensions of religious commitment are inter-correlated, it is wise to refrain from jumping to conclusions about any of them on the basis of evidence only from another.

SUMMARY AND CONCLUSIONS

Research to date seems to indicate fairly conclusively that ritualistic behavior outside the home tends to diminish with increasing age, while religious attitudes and feelings apparently increase among people who have an acknowledged religion. To use Kuhlen's (1962) words in his summary of research findings on adult religion,

". . . in all studies examined, with the exception of those relating to church attendance, trends indicate an increased interest in and concern about religion as age increases, even into extreme old age" (p. 23).

In other words, religion as a set of external extradomiciliary rituals apparently decreases in old age, while the internal personal responses linked with man's relationships to God apparently increase among religious people. Thus both disengagement from and re-engagement with religion are typical in old age!

We have seen that some religious practices decline in the later years, but religious feelings and beliefs apparently increase. These contrasting tendencies account for most of the apparently contradictory statements about the place of religion in old age. The use of non-comparable "indicators" or "measures" of religiosity has led to confusion. More research is needed on the major dimensions of religiosity; it will have implications for the specialist in geriatrics as well as for churchmen and gerontologists.

This distinction is related to the age-old contrast between faith and works. Most of the objective practices ("works") of religion become increasingly difficult to perform in old age as the body and mind gradually show the effects of the aging process. Yet in his "spirit" the religious person may remain devout; his religious beliefs and feelings can become more intense even though his institutionally-oriented religious practices diminish.

Recognition of these distinct dimensions of religiosity thus helps to resolve differences of opinion about the role of religion among the elderly. Research can clarify the subject further; it also can lead to more realistic and wholesome relationships between clergymen and psychologists, social workers, and medical personnel and to keener awareness of the religious implications of geriatric practice.

508

56

MORTON A. LIEBERMAN

PSYCHOLOGICAL CORRELATES OF IMPENDING DEATH:
SOME PRELIMINARY OBSERVATIONS

The purpose of this study was to determine whether systematic psychological changes occur in older people prior to death and to distinguish such changes from those occurring in illnesses which are not terminal. Underlying this investigation is the question of whether the deteriorative psychological changes usually associated with longevity may be better understood in a framework where time is measured in terms of distance from death.

The author's interest in examining psychological changes preceding death was stimulated by the observation that the chief nurse in a home for the aged could predict the death of residents with remarkable accuracy several months prior to any marked physical changes. Nevertheless, she could identify no regularities in the pattern of change nor any cues other than that a person nearing death "just seemed to act differently."

Systematic observations of an individual's psychological state before death have rarely been reported in the literature. Beigler (1957), who used data collected in clinical interviews with physically ill Ss, noted a marked increase in anxiety several months prior to death. Kleemeier (1961 II) reported observations on intellectual changes in an aged population approximately two years prior to death. Obrist, Henry, & Justiss (1961), who reported on the same population, found characteristic EEG changes preceding death. In a recent study Jarvik and Falek

Adapted from the *Journal of Gerontology*, vol. 20, no. 2 (April, 1965).

(1963) observed intellectual changes similar to those reported by Kleemeier. These studies suggest two alternative approaches to the study of psychological changes which occur prior to death. The first study suggests a phenomenological investigation in which a process involving an individual's sensing and reacting to a biological change is an issue. The latter three studies suggest that psychological changes which occur prior to death be viewed as a general system decline which may be measured either psychologically or physiologically. Awareness was not a crucial factor in the design of these studies.

The present study employed psychological measures which primarily reflected the second of these approaches. Four tasks were used to assess several aspects of the individual's adequacy of ego functioning and affective states.

MATERIALS AND METHODS

TESTS

Brief performance tasks were administered every three to four weeks to a group of elderly Ss over a two and a half year period. The tasks were ones that were not radically affected by repeated administration and were not known to show significant improvement with practice. They were the Bender-Gestalt test, the Draw-A-Person test, a time reproduction task, and a simple projective test in which the individual was asked to respond to 12 line drawings. Six scores were derived from these four tasks (intercorrelations between the six scores were low and ranged from a -0.01 to $+0.56$ [average, 0.19], with only one statistically significant). The tests are described below:

1. Bender-Gestalt figures were used as a copying task with no time limit. The adequacy of the reproduction was interpreted as a measure of organization-disorganization. Poor scores on this test have been associated with psychiatric disability, organic brain damage, less adequate reactions to physical stress, and inability to cope with cognitive complexities of the physical environment. The test was scored for the number of errors according to the system suggested by Pascal & Suttell (1951). Scores obtained from the present population ranged from 3 (an almost perfect reproduction, reflecting high organization) to 200 (a grossly unrecognizable reproduction of the test figures, indicating considerable disorganization).

2. The size of the Bender-Gestalt reproduction was used as an indicator of ego energy (Bender, 1938), that is, available energy that is free for dealing with stimuli from the outer world (Hartman, 1951). Evidence that the size of Bender-Gestalt drawing reflects this concept is based on comparisons of different psychopathological groups. A score for each performance was derived by measuring the area enclosed by each of the nine figures, and summing the nine into a total score. Scores ranged from 9 square in. to 64 square in. (The actual area of the nine figures in the standard designs is 29.3 square in.) All area scores were converted by means of the square-root transformation prior to statistical analysis.

3. The free drawing of a human figure (DAP) was used as a means of assessing capacity to integrate stimuli in the sense of reflecting a measure of ego sufficiency-insufficiency (Modell, 1951; Swenson, 1957). Although the figure drawings are open to a wide range of interpretations, Swenson's review of the current literature on the use of this test suggests that such an interpretation as the one made here best fits the current empirical evidence. Scores were based on a frequency count of body parts shown and on the size rela-

tionships of body parts. One point was given for each body part and one point for each correct size relationship. The scores obtained from the present population ranged from 1 (a simple oval with no differentiated body parts) to 22 (a well-articulated drawing of the human figure). High scores indicate complex figures and were interpreted to reflect ego sufficiency.

4. The Ss were asked to estimate the passage of a 60-sec. interval. The time interval was signaled by a red light which the Ss were instructed to turn off at the end of 60 sec. Two contiguous trials were used. The task was suggested by the work of Feifel (1957), who found that, for a similar population of institutionalized aged Ss, the length of the estimated passage of time correlated with measures of optimism and pessimism. The longer the time estimate, the more optimistic was the person's mood. Estimates for our population ranged from 2 sec. to 87 sec.

5 and 6. Twelve simple line drawings of the human figure (portraying a range of postures) were shown to the Ss one at a time. They were asked to tell what they saw and to describe the feeling and action states represented in the drawings. Two measures were derived from this test, the degree of affectivity and the intensity of activity. Activity ascribed to the stick figures was measured on a five-point scale from 0 to 4 (zero indicated a lack of attributed activity, 1–4 indicated the intensity of activity involved, e.g., a score of 1, given to a figure standing, to 4, for a figure running and jumping). Affect scores were based on the number of affective responses attributed to the 12 stick figures. Scores ranged from 0 to 30 for activity and from 0 to 12 on affect.

TESTING PROCEDURE

The tests were administered in the same order for all Ss over all trials. During the two and a half years of data-gathering, two examiners were used. One served about a year and the other a year and a half.

The degree of judgment involved in scoring these tasks is relatively minimal. Interscorer reliability was computed for all tasks in which there was some aspect of judgment (the Bender-Gestalt performance, DAP complexity score, and the activity and affect ratings), and correlations ranged from a low of 0.84 for the judgment of activity level from responses to the stick figures to 0.96 for adequacy of reproduction of the Bender-Gestalt.

SUBJECTS

The sample consisted of volunteers who had been residents in the same home for the aged for at least one year but less than three years. The residents were told that the investigator was interested in developing psychological tests specific to an aged population. Fifty persons volunteered, from whom 30 (17 women and 13 men) were selected. Those who had any incapacitating physical illness or gross neurological or psychiatric disorders were eliminated. Ss were tested every three to four weeks and were paid a small amount of money after each trial.

The results reported as based on 25 Ss—four dropped out or died before a sufficient number of trials could be gathered, and 1 S died five months after the end of the two and a half year study period.

All 25 Ss were born in Eastern Europe. All but one migrated to the United States prior to World War I; five before 1900, 19 prior to 1914, and one in the middle 1920's. Most had been (or were married to) small storekeepers or craftsmen. Educational level was difficult to determine with any precision, but generally seemed equivalent to an 8th grade education.

RESULTS

Results are reported in terms of comparison between two groups of Ss—a Death-Imminent group and a Death-Delayed group. The Death Imminent (DI) group consisted of 8 Ss who died less than three months after completing at least five trials on the measures used in this study.

The Death-Delayed (DD) group was composed of 17 Ss who were still living a year after they had completed at least ten trials. For the Death-Imminent group (DI), the time from last trial to death ranged from 2 to 11 weeks, with a mean of 5.4 weeks. All Ss in the Death-Delayed group (DD) lived at least 52 weeks after completing the last trial.

Table 1 shows the age and sex distribution of Ss for both groups.

TABLE 1

AGE AND SEX DISTRIBUTION OF THE DEATH IMMINENT (DI) AND DEATH DELAYED (DD) GROUPS

	AGE (YRS.)			
	70–74	75–79	80–84	85–89
DI:				
Males........	....	2	....	1
Females......	1	2	1	1
DD:				
Males........	....	2	3	2
Females......	2	4	3	1

INITIAL DIFFERENCES BETWEEN THE DEATH-IMMINENT AND THE DEATH-DELAYED GROUP

To determine whether the DI and DD groups differed at the onset of the experimental period, a series of t-tests on the scores of the first trial were computed. Only one significant difference was found at a 5% level between the DI and DD groups. The Death-Imminent group had an initially smaller Bender-Gestalt area score than did the Death-Delayed group.

RELATIONSHIP BETWEEN CHANGES IN PERFORMANCE LEVELS AND IMMINENT DEATH

The major hypothesis of the study—that systematic psychological changes occur prior to death—required a method for comparing the direction of changes in test scores between the DD and DI groups.

In order to make such a comparison, the following transformations of the test scores were carried out:

a) Ss' baseline performances varied considerably on all six measures. Rank order of scores rather than raw scores were used to analyze change over time. The raw scores were ranked with a rank of 1 given to the poorest performance. Thus, scores for each S were represented by six sets of ranks, one for each variable.

used because the smallest number of trials for any S was 5), and an average rank score computed for each fifth. To illustrate, S # 6M of the DD group had the following set of scores on the Bender-Gestalt performance:

Date	4/61	6/61	7/61	10/61	11/61	1/62
Score	180	125	188	137	82	163
Rank	2	6	1	5	10.5	3

Date	2/62	7/62	8/62	10/62	1/63	3/63
Score	140	123	91	82	97	65
Rank	4	7	9	10.5	8	12

Thus, each fifth of S # 6M consists of two or three trials (unequal number of trials were grouped randomly) as follows:

Time	I	II	III	IV	V
Average rank	3	7.8	4.7	9.8	10

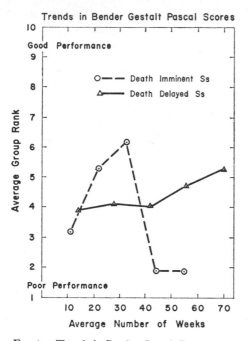

Fig. 1.—Trends in Bender-Gestalt Pascal scores over time for the DI and DD groups. Each point ⊙ for the 8 DI Ss is an average group rank representing one-fifth of all trials for each DI S; each point △ for the 17 DD Ss is an average group rank representing one-fifth of all trials for each DD S. High ranks indicate good performance, low ranks, poor performance.

b) Number of completed trials also varied considerably because of illness, vacations, and occasional refusals, as well as death. For the DI group, the number of completed trials ranged from 5 to 18; for the DD group, from 9 to 21. In order to compare the direction of change between the DI and DD groups, each S's set of ranks was divided into fifths (fifths were

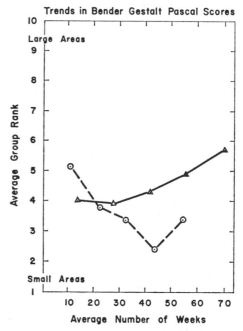

Fig. 2.—Trends in Bender-Gestalt area scores over time for the DI and DD groups. Each point ⊙ for the 8 DI Ss is an average group rank representing one-fifth of all trials for each DI S; each point △ for the 17 DD Ss is an average group rank representing one-fifth of all trials for each DD S. High ranks indicate large drawings, low ranks, small drawings.

512

The averaging also served to minimize the effects of the high intra-individual response variations observed in most *Ss* over all six measures.

A more detailed statement on intra-individual variability and age can be found in an earlier paper (Lieberman, 1962). In that study it was suggested that response fluctuation of an aged population is not influenced by the time interval between test sessions or by motivation. It was also determined that variability cannot be considered a trait of individuals but rather that degrees of variability (in relationship to the other *Ss*) vary from person to person on specific tasks. It was

c) To obtain group scores, the average ranks of each *S*'s fifths were summed for the DI and DD groups.

Figures 1–6 summarize the results of these data manipulations. They indicate the direction of performance changes over time.

These data suggest that on the Bender-Gestalt Pascal scores (Fig. 1), in the size

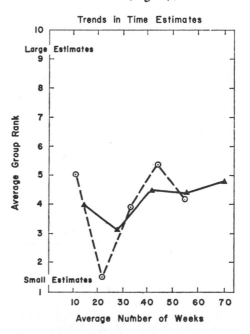

Fig. 4.—Trends in Time estimates of a 60-sec. interval over time for the DI and DD groups. Each point ⊙ for the 8 DI *Ss* is an average group rank representing one-fifth of all trials for each DI *S*; each point △ for the 17 DD *Ss* is an average group rank representing one-fifth of all trials for each DD *S*. High ranks indicate large estimates of the standard time interval, low ranks, small estimates.

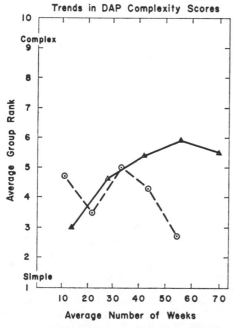

Fig. 3.—Trends in Draw-A-Person complexity scores over time for the DI and DD groups. Each point ⊙ for the 8 DI *Ss* is an average group rank representing one-fifth of all trials for each DI *S*; each point △ for the 17 DD *Ss* is an average group rank representing one-fifth of all trials for each DD *S*. High ranks indicate complex drawings, low ranks, simple drawings.

found that the degrees of intra-individual variability were roughly similar from task to task for the total population, when the fluctuations were measured relative to total possible scores on each test.

of the Bender-Gestalt reproductions (Fig. 2), and in the complexity of the DAP drawings (Fig. 3), the Death-Imminent group showed a pattern of declining (poorer) performance over time. In contrast the Death-Delayed group indicated a pattern of improving performance over time. Both groups generally showed similar curves on the Time Estimation Task

(Fig. 4), and number of affect responses to the Stick Figure Test (Fig. 5), while on the intensity of activity score (Fig. 6), in which both groups generally showed an increase, the Death-Imminent group reversed the direction after the 40th week.

(Although the three measures differentiating the DI from the DD group were

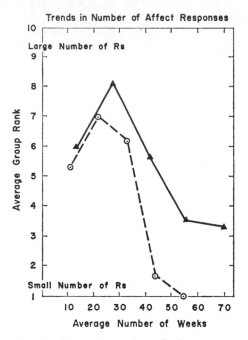

FIG. 5.—Trends in number of affect responses over time for the DI and DD groups. Each point ⊙ for the 8 DI Ss is an average group rank representing one-fifth of all trials for each DI S; each point △ for the 17 DD Ss is an average group rank representing one-fifth of all trials for each DD S. High ranks indicate a high frequency of affect responses to the Stick Figure test, low ranks, small number of such responses.

all based on drawings by the S, these tests have been shown by several investigators not to be significantly affected by differences in motor abilities. These measures were also not significantly intercorrelated [Bender-Gestalt Pascal scores with Bender-Gestalt size (0.22), Bender-Gestalt Pascal scores with DAP (0.33), and Bender-Gestalt size with DAP (0.28)].)

The graphs are based on average ranks; thus they cannot be used to compare dif-

ferences between the two groups at any one point in time. Differences between the groups, however, are represented by the direction of the lines. In interpreting the graphs, it should be noted also that the DD and the DI groups were not equivalent in length of time intervals. For the DI group each time point represents a range of 5 to 15 weeks with a mean of 11; for the DD group, a range of 10 to 20 weeks with a mean of 14. Thus, despite

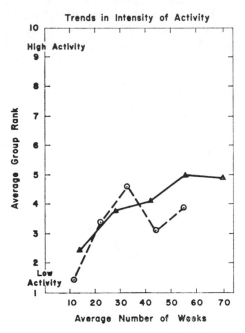

FIG. 6.—Trends in intensity of activity over time for the DI and DD groups. Each point ⊙ for the 8 DI Ss is an average group rank representing one-fifth of all trials for each DI S; each point △ for the 17 DD Ss is an average group rank representing one-fifth of all trials for each DD S. High ranks indicate high intensity of activity attributed to the stick figures, low ranks, low intensity.

the longer period of observation for the DD group and the increased age of the Ss, Figures 1, 2, and 3 suggest that the effects of practice were greater than the effects of aging measured over a two and a half year span. Decline in scores was associated with imminency of death and not with increase in age.

Another method used to compare the

two groups' change over time was to ask how many Ss in each group showed improved or declining performance. Comparisons of change over time were made by comparing the first half of each S's trials with his last half. Six 2 × 2 tables were set up. In each table the number of Ss in each group who showed declining scores was compared with the number who showed improving or stable scores. [Declining scores are defined as a mean

Over time, more Ss in the DI group showed a pattern of declining scores while more Ss in the DD group showed improved or stable scores.

The changes are illustrated by Figure 7, which shows a DI S's decline in DAP complexity score; in Figure 8 by a DI S's increasingly poorer performance on the

TABLE 2

NUMBER OF Ss SHOWING PERFORMANCE CHANGES

Test		Death-Delayed Group	Death-Imminent Group	Probabilities
Bender-Gestalt performance	Number declining	3	6	0.01
	Number not declining	14	2	
Bender-Gestalt area	Number declining	3	5	0.04
	Number not declining	14	3	
DAP complexity	Number declining	2	5	0.02
	Number not declining	15	3	
Amount of activity	Number declining	2	3	0.17
	Number not declining	15	5	
Number of affects	Number declining	12	5	0.78
	Number not declining	5	3	
Time estimation	Number declining	6	2	0.31
	Number not declining	11	6	

* Fisher exact probability test.

rank for the first half of trials larger by at least one than for the second half of trials. Improving scores are defined as a mean rank larger by at least one for the second half of trials. Stable scores indicate that the mean rank between the first and second half of trials did not differ by more than one.] The six 2 × 2 tables were evaluated by means of the Fisher exact probability test (Fisher, 1950). Three of the six measures significantly distinguished the DI from DD group (Table 2). These differences were all in the same direction:

Bender-Gestalt; and by Figure 9 which illustrates a DI S's decrease in the size of the Bender-Gestalt reproduction over time.

Results indicate that DD and DI groups could be distinguished by changes in the tasks reflecting the adequacy of ego functioning—Bender-Gestalt performance (organization-disorganization), DAP complexity (integrative capacity), and Bender-Gestalt size (ego energy), but were similar on measures of affect—time estimation (optimism-pessimism), and the activity and affect scores derived from the stick figure test. In addition to these analyses, the examiner's notes (observations on S's test behavior, mood, and "critical events" since the last testing session) and a content analysis of responses to the stick figure test were examined in an attempt to further differentiate the DD from the DI group. Over-all, few consistent differences could be found between the two

COMPLEXITY SCORE - FIGURES
SUBJECT #17 M

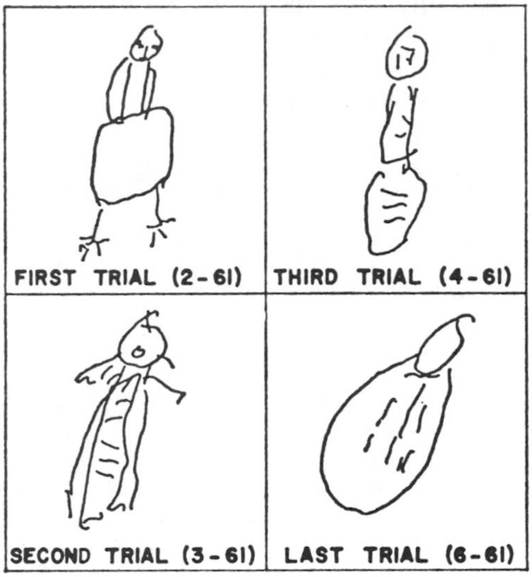

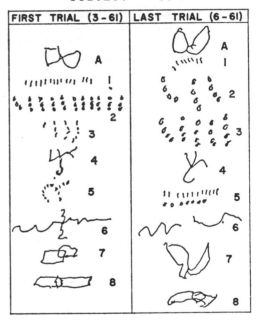

FIG. 7.—Illustration of a decline in complexity in DAP for a DI S. The four trials shown for S 17M indicate less complex drawings as S approaches death.

groups from this qualitative analysis. However, the data did indicate that: 1) Ss in the DI group frequently made more spontaneous comments which indicated that something was wrong, that something was "going on" and, at times, that they were going to die; 2) four out of the 8 Ss in the DI group gave responses to the stick figure test, on the trial preceding death, which indicated an increased frequency of depressive content when compared to the early trials. Depressive content, however, was no more characteristic of DI Ss than DD Ss. Further content analysis of the stick figure test did not

reflect responses which indicated increased anxiety or fear.

TIME OF DECLINING
PERFORMANCE

The scores of each S in the DI group were examined to determine if changes in performance level occurred at particular points in time. The small N and the degree of response fluctuation from trial to trial prevented a meaningful quantitative analysis. However, inspection of the sets of scores for each S suggested that major shifts of performance on the tests could

FIG. 8.—Illustration of a decline in Bender-Gestalt Pascal scores for a DI S. The first and last trial of S 15F indicate less adequate performance as the S approaches death.

be found as early as six to nine months preceding death. The earliest identifiable changes occurred in the Bender-Gestalt performance scores, followed by changes in the complexity of the drawn human figure, and, finally, by decreases in the size of the Bender-Gestalt figures.

516

The results already presented suggest that the DI and DD groups could be distinguished by the direction of performance changes over time, even though they were similar at the onset of the study in all but one of the variables. The next question is whether the Ss in the Death-Imminent group declined to a point prior to death where their performance on the tests was characteristically different from that of the Ss of the Death-Delayed group. The DD and DI groups were compared by choosing the last trial of each Death-Imminent S and matching the Death-Delayed Ss for number of trials (to control for effects of practice), that is, the tenth trial for all DD Ss was chosen for comparison with the last trial of the DI Ss. t-Tests were used but no significant differences were found in the comparison of absolute levels of performance on the six variables. The data suggest that what distinguished the two groups was the changing level of performance over time and not some absolute level of test performance at any single point in time. Thus, without sequential observation of Ss, it would be impossible (with the variables used here) to distinguish Ss whose death was imminent from Ss whose death lay in the distant future.

Changes in the test variables have been presented in relationship to time of death. Could such changes have occurred simply in relationship to illness states of the Ss? A partial answer can be suggested because 12 Ss of the Death-Delayed group suffered major illnesses and required hospitalization during the course of the study. It was reasoned that if declines in test performance reflected only states of illness rather than imminency of death the trial(s) preceding hospitalization would show a lower level of performance than other trials for the same S. Each S's mean score for all trials was used to divide, on each of the six measures, good and poor performances. With the use of this criterion, it was found that the trial preceding illness was as likely to be above the S's mean as below it. A second method of

analysis utilized the total set of trials in evaluating the effects of illness on performance. The sum of scores of all the trials prior to illness was compared with an equal number of trials after the acute phase of the illness had subsided. Only 7 of the 12 ill Ss could be used for this

SIZE CHANGE - BENDER GESTALT
SUBJECT #17M

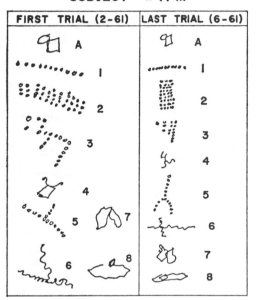

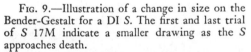

FIG. 9.—Illustration of a change in size on the Bender-Gestalt for a DI S. The first and last trial of S 17M indicate a smaller drawing as the S approaches death.

analysis. The other 5 had episodes of illness too early or too late in the series of trials for a pre-post comparison. Performance level was similar pre- and post-illness. These two analyses of the performance of Death-Delayed Ss who became ill and recovered suggest that illness *per se* was not the sole factor which affected the decline of performance found in the Death-Imminent group.

DISCUSSION

The findings of this study suggest that the terminal phase of life is characterized by specific psychological changes which may have broader implications for the study of aging.

In spite of the small N and the magnitude of the intra-individual variability, the results indicate that systematic psychological changes which occur many months prior to death are measurable. The observed psychological changes are not the simple result of physical illness. Ss who became seriously ill and recovered did not exhibit psychological changes similar to Ss whose death was imminent. The absolute level of ego functioning was also unrelated to impending death, which suggests that the absolute level at which aged Ss are able to cope with their environment is not associated with the distance from death, but instead it is the *change* of individual's level relative to his own initial performance which is related to death.

Prior to death, Ss showed changes (relative to their initial levels) toward a decreased level of organization as measured by the adequacy of the Bender-Gestalt reproductions, a decreased energy as indicated by measurement of the size of the Bender-Gestalt figures, and a lessened ability to integrate stimuli as shown by a decrease in the complexity of the figure drawings. Affective states or changes in affect were not found to be systematically related to approaching death.

This suggests that the psychological changes preceding death are best viewed in terms of the individual's lessened ability to cope adequately with environmental demands, particularly because of a lowered ability to organize and to integrate stimuli in his environment. Perhaps the aged individual, approaching his own death, experiences upheaval because of currently active disorganizing mental processes, rather than because he fears his approaching death. Thus, the disintegration is seen, here, not as a reaction to an unknowable, to-be-encountered event, but as a current experience of disruption in the individual's precarious equilibrium. The changes preceding death may repre-

sent a general system decline which might be reflected in a variety of physiological and psychological measures.

In this context of a current psychological experience of disintegration, some of the phenomena frequently observed and reported in the literature on the terminal phase of life become more understandable. Many observers have commented on the psychological withdrawal of the dying patient and have suggested that the withdrawal is functional in that it protects the individual from intense separation anxiety. The concept of disruption identified here suggests that such a withdrawal represents, rather, an attempt to cope with the experience of inner disintegration. The disintegration probably precedes the reduced emotional investment in others. Individuals approaching death pull away from those around them, not because of a narcissistic preoccupation with themselves, but because they are preoccupied with an attempt to hold themselves together—to reduce the experience of chaos. Some of the Ss were clearly aware of such a process. A number of them sensed some type of change and subjectively felt it to be different from that of illness. The labeling of this subjective experience, however, varied from one S to another; some could report only a vague sense of feeling "different"; others labeled it by saying that they were going to die. The evidence suggests that more thorough and sensitive phenomenological reports would be useful avenues of research in the terminal phase of life.

Investigators of psychological functioning in the very old have been impressed by the increased inter-individual differences over a wide range of psychological abilities. Explanations of these individual differences have run the gamut from the genetic-biological to personality. The present study may point to another area of explanation worthy of investigation. Variations in psychological abilities among a given age group may be explained, in part, as an effect of distance from death. A group of 70-year-old men, for example, may represent variations in distance from death of 1 to 15 years. If, as suggested above, imminent death implies an experience of psychological chaos and lessened psychological effectiveness, the man of 70 closest to death could be expected to perform differently from his age mate who will survive him by an appreciable length of time.

Chronological age (in itself a complex variable) has been shown repeatedly to correlate with many psychological functions. It is not unusual in samples of individuals 70 and above, however, to find the absence of any appreciable correlations between age and psychological functioning. This lack of relationship may in part be accounted for by the phenomenon suggested, namely, differences in distance from death. We are suggesting that in the age range over 70, distance from death may be a more crucial dimension of time than chronological age.

57

BARNEY G. GLASER and ANSELM L. STRAUSS

TEMPORAL ASPECTS OF DYING AS A NON-SCHEDULED STATUS PASSAGE

Our purpose in this paper is to conceptualize dying as a non-scheduled status passage. That is, we see a dying person as passing between the statuses of living and dead according to no man-made or imposed schedule. When study turns to the non-scheduled status passage, timing becomes a crucial problem and raises problems not considered in studies of scheduled passage, which tend to focus on how an occupant gets through the passage and what benefits and deficits he gets out of it. For the non-scheduled status passage, the important questions are how the occupant in passage, as well as those people around him, even know in the first place *when* he will be, and is, in movement between statuses. Further, how do these people define the succession of transitional statuses (which occur between the two principal statuses of living and dead) so as to establish where the person is when in passage, when the next transition might occur, where the next transition will take him, and how the occupant is to act and be treated by others at various points in the passage? Also, what happens when the occupant in passage and those around him have *different perceptions* pertaining to when the passage started and where he is going—and what kinds of interaction are consequent upon these differential perceptions? When differential percep-

tions of timing exist, then legitimation, announcement, and co-ordination of the passage become problematic, and interaction strategies to handle these issues become crucial (see Strauss, 1959, pp. 121–31). In contrast, how the person in a scheduled status should act and be treated, hence how his passage is legitimated, announced, and co-ordinated, is usually a matter of routine, even ceremonial, consensus.

METHOD

The material for this paper is drawn from a study of how hospital personnel handle terminal patients. The data were collected over a two-year period through field observations and interviews at a teaching hospital of a medical center, a veteran's hospital, a state hospital, a county hospital, a denominational hospital and a private hospital, all in the San Francisco Bay area. Co-operation was excellent, so that the field-workers were unimpeded and able to range widely. Participant observation is an especially reliable method of data collection when one is interested in sequential interactions within natural situations (Becker and Geer, 1957). It is also the most "adequate" and "efficient" method of obtaining information on many "properties of the same object" (Zelditch, 1962). In this paper we utilize our data to illustrate theoretical points.

LEGITIMATING THE PASSAGE

A central problem in viewing dying as a non-scheduled status passage is that of who can legitimately determine *when* the

Abridged from the *American Journal of Sociology*, vol. 71, no. 1 (July, 1965). Copyright 1965 by The University of Chicago.

This paper derives from an investigation of terminal care in hospitals supported by National Institutes of Health Grant NU 00047.

passage occurs. This determination typically cannot be left to just any relevant party, but is *the obligation* and *responsibility* of an institutionally designated legitimator: the doctor. He is someone with sufficient expertise, knowledge, and experience to be most able to judge accurately when the patient (the status occupant) is in passage, through what transitional statuses he is passing and will pass, how long a period he will be in each transitional status, and what his rate of movement will be between transitional statuses. Three interrelated problems of importance for which the doctor is held responsible are (1) defining temporal dimensions of the status passage, (2) timing announcements about the status passage to the patient and to other involved parties, and (3) co-ordinating the passage itself. In this first section we shall discuss the defining of the status passage; in the next the timing of announcements on the passage; and in the following section co-ordinating the passage.

Dying is divided by medical personnel into four death expectations, which we conceive of as the transitional statuses of dying that define the patient's status passage from living to dead: (1) uncertain about death and unknown time when the question will be resolved, (2) uncertain about death and known time when the question will be resolved, (3) certain about death and unknown time when it will occur, and (4) certain about death and known time when it will occur. In defining which dying or transitional status the patient is in and which he is passing to, it is often far easier for the doctor to say whether or not death is *certain* than at what *time* either uncertainty will be resolved or death will occur.

It is easier to establish certainty than time because of the two principal kinds of cues upon which the doctor bases his judgment: physical attributes of the patient and time references made about him. Physical cues, which vary in their severity from those that spell hope to those that indicate immediate death, for the

most part establish the certainty aspect of death expectations. As for temporal cues, they have many reference points. A major one is the typical progression of the disease against which the patient's actual movement is measured (he is "going fast" or is "lingering"). Another temporal reference is the doctor's expectation about how long the patient will remain in the hospital compared to how long he does remain. For instance, one patient's hospitalization was "lasting longer than the short while" that had been anticipated by the physician. Work schedules also provide a temporal reference: doctors adjust their judgment on whether or not the patient can continue being bathed, turned, fed, and given sedation regularly.

In combination, physical and temporal cues have interesting consequences. Since physical cues are easier to read, without their presence—which helps establish some degree of certainty about death—temporal cues remain rather indeterminate. That indeterminacy is reflected in such phrases as that the patient may die "some time" or "any time." As both types of cues accumulate, they can support each other: for example, a patient's condition becomes more grave as his hospitalization becomes longer. But physical and temporal cues can also cancel each other: thus undue hospitalization can be balanced and even negated by increasingly hopeful physical cues. When cues cancel each other, the more hopeful cue (he is going home sooner than expected) can be used to deny the less hopeful (he looks bad). As physical and temporal cues accumulate in severity and speed, respectively, deniability decreases, while a correspondingly determinate death expectation is gradually established. Then, doctor and staff are less likely to be surprised because of an inaccurate expectation.

While other parties to the status passage (including the patient) are not institutionally designated to define either the patient as dying or his current transitional status, they privately engage in trying to ascertain whether he is in passage and where he is, in order to guide their own behavior. For instance, nurses who have not received information from the doctor will try to read the same cues as he does, but their definitions will usually be imbued with *doubt,* especially when they try to ascertain the temporal dimension of the transitional status that the occupant is in or passing to and the period of time he will be in each status. If the doctor does tell them the patient is in passage and his definition of transitional status disagrees with their own, then they will usually accept his, since he is the responsible expert. However, in some cases of disagreement, experienced nurses will not change their view, since they feel familiar with the timing of this passage. While family and patient may never really believe that the latter is dying unless the doctor discloses the news, after a while they can hardly avoid the temporal cues—such as undue hospitalization—even though they are not expert at recognizing physical cues. Thus they may start suspecting the occurrence of dying however undefined such a status passage may be to them.

When establishing the various temporal aspects of the dying status passage, the doctor, as legitimator, may also set forth the probable sequence of transitional statuses that the patient is expected to follow. While the transitional status-sequence in dying is not institutionally prescribed, many typical ones are known that help the doctor to anticipate a schedule of periods in transitional statuses and rates of movement between them. For instance, there is the "lingering" pattern in which the patient stays in "certain to die but unknown when" status. Even in this case there are temporal limits to holding on to that status: though the patient is expected to remain for some time, after a while the nurses, doctors, and family may feel that he is taking more time than is proper in dying. Other sequences are the "short-term reprieve," in which the patient seems

"certain to die at a known time" but suddenly begins to linger for a while and then dies; the "vacillating" sequence, in which the patient alternates over and over from "certain to die on time" to lingering; and the "heroic" sequence, in which a patient in the "uncertain, unknown time of resolution" status passes to the "certain, known time of resolution" status, while the medical staff heroically tries to save him. This patient may then pass either directly to death or through both certainty statuses first.

ANNOUNCING THE PASSAGE

Since the behavior of others toward a status occupant is temporally oriented (Strauss, 1959)—that is, how long he has been in the status, when he will move on to another, what his rate and period of transition will be, and what his next status will be—it is crucially significant that announcement of dying, since it is an unscheduled status passage, be the obligation of the doctor. Only he is institutionally designated both to legitimate and to announce that the patient is dying. For in the end the doctor is the person held socially and perhaps legally responsible for the diverse outcomes resulting from changes in the behavior of the patient, of other parties to the patient's passage, and of the hospital organization occasioned by his legitimating and announcing temporal aspects of the dying. These outcomes can range from being most *beneficial,* as when the doctor announces to the staff that a patient is about to die in order quickly to co-ordinate heroic measures to save him, to being most *adverse,* as when a family, unaware that their relative is dying, is thereby given no time to prepare for his death and may be deeply shocked by the surprise of it, which, in some cases, can cause a family member to have a heart attack. The proper timing of announcements can forestall such surprises.

In view of his responsibility for the effects on all parties of changes in behavior of all parties, the doctor has many decisions to make about to whom, how much and when to announce. In some cases, he is guided, or forced, by hospital rules to make various kinds of announcements (principally to the family who "must be told something") at certain points in the status passage. In some hospitals, the doctor is required at least to legitimate for the medical staff a degree of the certainty dimension of the dying or transitional status by putting the patient on a critically, dangerously, or seriously ill list or by including the information on an admitting card. He will often be reminded of this rule "before it is too late." The patient's being posted on such a critical list usually requires an announcement of dying by the doctor to the family. If they are not on hand, a family member is sent a wire stating that "Your (kin) has been put on the critically ill list, please come at once." The doctor then has a talk with the family. After this announcement, the family is allowed to visit around the clock with the patient. Thus the family's awareness of dying changes its temporal approach to contact with the patient, because the hospital allows relaxation of the temporal aspect of visiting rules. This announcement also allows the family time to prepare for the demise of its relative and time to get estates and wills and other social and personal responsibilities properly in order.

When the patient passes from a dying status to death, only the doctor can pronounce death (a professional as well as hospital rule), and only he is supposed to announce death to the family. These two announcements must be made as soon as possible after death, both to forestall other parties from leaking the news, possibly irresponsibly, and to keep nurses and families fully abreast of developments as they happen so these people can adjust their behavior accordingly.

Since the doctor's responsibility is very great, he is allowed much discretion—unguided by formal rules—on when, what, and how to announce dying to others. Short of the critically ill list, which doc-

tors may try to avoid, doctors vary considerably as to whether or not they give nurses information; however, these variations are patterned under certain temporal conditions of the status passage. The temporal and physical cues on the patient's condition may be so obvious that the doctors feel that there is no necessity for informing the nurses about the patient's current and expected status. For instance, the patient is obviously near death, or obviously nothing more can be done for the patient, and now it is just a matter of waiting. Also, the doctor may be quite oblique in telling nurses about dying in the initial uncertainty statuses; but as the patient passes through the certainty statuses, the doctor becomes more direct and explicit about certainty as well as expected time of death. Thus he varies the clarity of his announcements in line with the patient's passage from one transition status to another.

Some doctors may try to avoid announcing to others altogether; but this is difficult, as we have seen, because these others are defining the dying on their own and basing their behavior on their own definitions. Thus the doctor is forced at points to make sure that the others' definitions are correct, so that their behavior will not result in adverse outcomes for the patient, themselves, or other parties. For example, a strategic passage in dying is from the transitional status of "uncertainty and time of its resolution known" to either of the two certainty statuses. Accompanying this passage is an important change in the goals of nursing care: that from working hard to recover the patient to routinely providing him comfort until death. If nurses perceive the passage inaccurately they can cease trying to save a patient, although he still may have a chance to survive. Therefore, the doctor will make sure the nurses realize that the patient is still in the uncertainty status until he himself is sure all hope is lost. He will often give them a time limit on when they may expect the outcome. If the doctor sees a nurse not wishing to accept the passage from uncertainty to certainty, he may delay telling her it is occurring or has occurred in order to keep her alert to possible reversals. However, if this delay interferes with her providing adequate comfort to the patient, say giving enough pain killers, he will have to tell her that the passage has occurred. Sometimes when a doctor will not stop his attempts to save a patient who is obviously lost, a nurse will have to tell him that the passage has actually occurred. She will tell him that more blood will do no good or that continuing the heart massage is useless. Conversely, often the doctor's actions are enough to announce this crucial passage to nurses: for example, he stops using equipment or giving blood transfusions. If a nurse does not understand and blurts out, "Do something, doctor," she will have to be told, "It's all over" or "There is nothing more to do."

Various temporal organizational conditions can literally wipe out a doctor's announcements if the hospital has no formal provisions for diffusion of information on dying. Thus doctors' announcements often are informal and directed at a few nurses in attendance. If these nurses do not informally pass on the information among themselves, it can be lost in the change of work shift or in the rotation of nurses between wings, wards, or patient assignments; and relevant parties will not be aware that the patient is dying. Dying is not the easiest news to pass on, especially if the doctor is vague or unsure in announcing it. Another organizational condition that may preclude a nurse from being "in" on the informal distribution of information about dying is the temporary assignment of students to a patient. Thus a student may have no idea her patient is dying and may be quite shaken to hear afterward that the patient has died.

Whether or not to announce dying to the patient can be quite problematic since the status passage may be inevitable as well as undesirable. While supposedly the doctor is allowed the maximum of discretion for each patient, it would appear that the professional rule is not to disclose dying to the patient, since surveys show that few American doctors do. Thus the dying patient typically knows neither his true transitional or dying status nor his rate of movement between statuses, and is thereby denied the time necessary to prepare himself for death and to settle his financial and social affairs. He therefore may either complete his status passage unaware that he ever was in passage between life and death or be very shocked almost at the end to discover he is and has been in passage for some time.

The doctor may have several temporal problems in deciding whether or not to disclose a patient's dying to him. Three problems are (1) spending enough time with the patient to judge how he will take the news; (2) timing a disclosure in order not to risk losing the patient's trust in his expertise and responsibility; and (3) deciding how much to tell the patient about the direction, periods of transition, and rates of movement of his passage.

Doctors often do not have enough time to spend with dying patients to make an adequate judgment as to whether or not, say, the patient will become despondent, commit suicide, or actively prepare for death. Under this condition, they prefer not to tell the patient. However, if the doctor realizes the patient is becoming aware that he is dying, the doctor may feel forced to disclose to the patient, and he must time the disclosure just right in order not to risk losing the patient's trust in his care. In disclosing, the doctor will typically leave out the temporal dimension of the dying status, as a way of softening the blow for the patient and perhaps giving him interim hope. The doctor will also avoid details of the illness that may give the patient temporal knowledge about his dying. He also may follow his disclosure with a temporal rationale, such as "You've had a full life," or "Who knows, maybe next week, next month, or next year there will be a drug that can save you." Leaving out the temporal dimension of the dying status also reduces chances of error, since, as we have seen, it is easier to judge certainty than time.

When the doctor decides not to inform the patient that he is dying, several temporal problems of announcement are created for other parties who must deal with the patient. One problem is how to ascertain whether or not the patient actually needs to be told, since he might really have discovered his passage on his own. If the doctor has decided the patient should not be informed, the nurses are not allowed to ask the patient if he is aware he is dying. Therefore, they may engage in endless debates, stimulated by changes in the patient's behavior, as to whether or not he "really knows." These debates may never be resolved and can even last long after the patient has died.

Two other temporal problems created for parties to the dying passage are those of handling unwitting and witting announcements to the patient. They must avoid providing temporal cues to the unaware patient that will clearly indicate he is dying. Because of the nature of his dying, this may be impossible. For instance, when the patient passes from "certain to die—time unknown" to "certain to die—time known," it may be important to move him to a dying room or to an intensive care unit. Implicit in these moves is a timing that indicates quite clearly to the patient that he soon will die. To counteract this realization, some nurses will mention that these spatial moves are done to provide the patient better care, as a way of trying to deny their temporal meaning to him. Another clear temporal cue to the patient is the appearance on the scene of a chaplain or priest, whom the nurses are supposed to call when the patient is still sentient and on the verge of death. It is difficult to forestall the patient's reading of this cue.

One way nurses avoid unwitting disclosures to a patient is to take a temporally neutral stand in the face of his questions about his condition: they say things like "We all die sometime," or "I could leave here and be killed walking across the street." Another strategy is to maintain, in all talk and work with the patient, a constant time orientation that is linked with his certain recovery. Thus he sees himself being constantly placed in the recovery status.

Sometimes nurses will wittingly break the institutional rule that only the doctor may disclose dying to the patient. In some hospitals, enforcement of this rule is based on legal action as well as less formal sanctions against the person who would disclose against the wishes of the doctor. A navy corpsman told us that disclosure would be grounds for a court-martial, and a nurse who discloses can lose her job in a hospital or her place in a referral system.

Several temporal conditions, however, may stimulate disclosure by nurses to unaware patients against the doctor's orders. One condition is that the family is with the patient while he is dying, and it is clear to the nurse that if the patient knew what was happening he could then take adequate farewell of his wife and children in such a manner as to benefit all—such as awarding social responsibilities to a son for care of the mother. It is also clear to the nurse that there is no time to convince a doctor of this pressing need for action, and that she must disclose either now or never. An inaccessible doctor may also force the nurse to disclose in order to accomplish an immediate medical treatment. She, like the doctor, may also be forced to tell a patient in order not to lose his trust if he is starting to realize his condition; otherwise, after he is certain enough of dying, not to have acknowledged it to him (or to disclose later) makes the nurse sound "phony." The patient will feel he is being "strung along" and "getting the run-around."

In spite of the doctor's announcement of dying to relevant parties, he cannot actually guarantee the occurrence of a transitional status or death since it is unscheduled. If the passage does not go through as announced, difficulties can be caused between the doctor and family and hospital personnel who might have a stake in the passage being finished and who are making plans accordingly. These parties may not trust the doctor's expertise in future cases. For instance, in an unexpected short-term reprieve sequence, a doctor announced that a patient would die within four days. This patient had no money but needed a special machine during his last days. A hospital at which he had been a frequent paying patient for thirty years agreed to receive him as a charity patient. He did not die immediately but started to linger indefinitely, even to the point where there was some hope that he might live! His lingering created a money problem that caused much concern among both his family and the hospital administration. Paradoxically, the doctor had continually to reassure both parties that this patient—who lasted one and one-half months—would soon die.

CO-ORDINATING THE PASSAGE

Our discussion has indicated that the essential element in shepherding the patient through the dying status passage is co-ordination of the definitions of the passage held by those parties involved, since these parties adjust their behavior according to their definitions. In order to work sufficiently well together, each relevant party must know how the others are defining the passage. It is the doctor's responsibility to make sure that everyone knows what they need to know at certain points during the status passage so that difficulties do not develop.

Since many people can be involved, diverse sets of patterned differential definitions can be the basis of co-ordination, each with its own mechanisms for shepherding the occupant from one transition-

al status to another. In this last section we have space to consider only a few temporal aspects of the co-ordination of passage under two patterned conditions: (1) only the doctor and his staff know of the passage; and (2) all parties, including the patient, are fully aware of the passage (see Glaser and Strauss, 1964). These two sets of differential definitions include the two basic alternatives considered by the doctor who is co-ordinating the passage: to tell or not to tell the patient.

OCCUPANT IS UNAWARE

When the patient is unaware that he is dying, the doctor and his staff have considerable control over the passage. However, since the patient cannot purposively help his own passage, his unawareness can present temporal problems to those in control—such as unduly slowing down or speeding up the passage. Some treatments to sustain life do not make sense to a patient who does not know he is dying.[1] He may refuse a medicine, a machine, an awkward position or a diet, thus shortening his life. A temporally oriented tactic to cope with the problem is proffering a momentary transitional status. The patient is delicately rendered a few cues that indicate he might die if he does not agree to the treatment. As soon as he takes the treatment, the proffered dying status is immediately withdrawn, say, by laughing it off. The reverse of this example is also true: an unaware patient may ask for treatment that would needlessly prolong his life into a period of uncontrollable pain or deterioration. Thus he may be denied treatment of this sort. These illustrations show that the patient will be managed by doctor and staff in ways enabling work to go on for the passage, while the patient's awareness remains unchanged despite changes in his transitional status.

Part of working with the unaware pa-

[1] Similarly it is difficult for polio patients who anticipate being cured to take full advantage of rehabilitation programs for the handicapped. Davis, 1960, p. 45.

526

tient while shepherding him through his passage consists of talking with him. Therefore, if he is to be kept unaware he is dying, the temporal dimension of this talk must be managed to prevent giving cues. The doctor and his staff will tend to manage their talk with the patient according to the transitional status they define him in and expect him to pass into. One strategy noted above is to use a constant time orientation that refers to one status only. Coexistent with this strategy may be another in which talk is managed on a present-future oriented continuum, so as not to raise a temporal reference for discussion that would lead the patient to suspect and schedule his dying. For example, when a patient is defined as certain to die in a few days, nurses will tend to focus their talk upon the immediate present. They discuss with him current doses of medication for pain relief, ask to fix his pillow, or focus upon matters relevant to his comfort. However, if they do not know when he is going to die, they will extend the temporal range implied in their talk. One nurse thus said, before leaving for a weekend, "See you next week." Another told her patient about his needing another x-ray in two weeks. Similarly, blood tests that will be done next week or the family's visit of next weekend will be discussed. Frequently the nurses cautiously manage such temporal references without clear intent. One young nurse told us how she used to chat with a young patient about his future dates and parties. After discovering his certain and near death, she unwittingly cut out all references to the distant future, because this kind of talk was "inappropriate" for a patient who is to die in a matter of hours or days.

When it is uncertain whether the patient will die but nurses know that a definite answer is soon coming, some will engage in faith-oriented talk about the near future. An example is, "You'll probably be going home soon after your operation." Such statements support the patient's hope about the near future—al-

though they do not actually detail exactly how he is going to live out his life. However, if the nurses are uncertain both about his death and about when the issue will be resolved, then their talk becomes less guarded. They tend to talk of the patient's return to home and work.

OCCUPANT IS AWARE

Once the patient is told by the doctor that he is dying—and recovers from the shock if the passage is both inevitable and undesirable—he must make the decision either to accept or deny dying. With this disclosure and acceptance or denial, the balance of control over the status passage can shift from the doctor and his staff to the patient.

If the patient *accepts* that he is dying, the doctor and his staff can help to prepare him for the passage on many levels—medical, psychological, social, and financial. And the more active the patient is in his preparation, the more others can help during the remaining time. In this way, the doctor and staff can regain a measure of control potentially lost at the initial disclosure, since they have had experience in helping other patients prepare—some are professional preparers, for example, chaplains and social workers—and the patients accept their aid.

Since the doctor has allowed everyone to know the patient is dying, there may be as much free discussion as people can reasonably take in helping prepare the patient. Family and patient can obtain fairly uncensored information on the latter's condition. The patient can focus his remaining energy on settling his affairs properly before death, instead of trying vainly to get well. One cancer patient whom we observed held off on sedation as much as possible so as to put his financial and social affairs in order with the aid of a social worker. Another told his son about various duties that would befall him as man of the house. One young man

527

tried to get his wife potentially married off to another man who worked in the hospital. Nurses and chaplains do not have to walk on "conversational eggs," but can devote themselves—if they can manage their own feelings—to helping the patient settle his affairs, discuss his past life and coming death, and make a graceful exit from life.

There is a temporal pitfall in this active preparation allowed by the fact that all people are aware. Typically the doctor will give both certainty and time dimensions of the patient's status passage to nurses, chaplains, and social workers, but not to family and patient. Thus patient and his helpers can talk politely past each other temporally; yet problems of preparation may arise. The social worker or chaplain who expects the patient to die in a month might wish to hurry up certain preparations in co-ordination with reviewing the patient's past life, such as, respectively, his making a will or taking up religion. But the patient, left to his own time orientation, may give himself a year or two and be in no rush for either his will or religion.

Acceptance of the passage does not always mean active preparation. The patient can fight dying, no matter how inevitable, and often with the help of others. In this situation, the doctor and his staff lose much control over the passage. For example, the dying patient may reject his doctor and with the support of family go to a quack or marginal doctor who will help him "beat this thing." One way a doctor can maintain and then regain much temporal control is to permit the patient to go for the "cure" with the idea of keeping a general watch over his physical condition and of preventing premature death. Thus it will only be a matter of time before the "cure" fails and the patient returns to his doctor. If the doctor does not give permission, the patient may be too embarrassed to return after the failure. Indeed, he might take complete temporal control over his passage by scheduling and committing autoeuthanasia

(suicide). Other patients will proceed directly to autoeuthanasia as a way of putting temporal order into an interminably unschedulable dying.

If the patient *denies* he is in passage, he sees himself in a living status—recoverable —although the surrounding people see him in a transitional status of dying. Then it is hard, if not impossible, to help the patient in his passage, and much control is lost. The doctor and staff must develop ways to do it unbeknownst to the patient. At the same time, the patient is trying to get the people around him to join in the definition that he will never have to leave his living status. Thus both the patient and the others are trying to obtain shared definitions: the patient to get everyone to deny his passage, the others to get him to accept it.

The dying patient may use several temporal strategies to get others to help deny his impending passage. One we have seen is that the patient thinks up his own time schedule, which can amount to living several years, and then gets nurses and family to engage in this time orientation which becomes, then, circumstantial proof to him that he is really not dying. The patient will also ask the doctor or nurses for explanations of extended hospitalization or slow recuperation in a way that begs for denial that he is dying. Another strategy is a game of temporal polarity—asking an extreme question that may force the doctor or nurse into a denying response. To the question, "Am I getting worse, the medicine is not working?" the staff may have to answer, "Give yourself a chance—medicines take a long time." So, the patient ends up with the idea that he has a long time.

It is also likely that the denying patient's passage will be lonely. Since he has been told he is dying, the staff will expect him to act according to the requirements of this status passage, in contrast to the unaware patient who is expected to go on as before. When he does not, because of his denial, he will frustrate their efforts to relate to him according to how he is

528

supposed to act (he will not let the pre-parers prepare him). They may give up, leave him alone, and turn to patients they can help. The source of their frustration is the differential defining by the patient, who sees himself as staying in his present recoverable status, and by the staff, who see him in passage toward death. Need-less to say, the denying patient is liable to complete his passage with neither prepa-ration for the change in status or under-standing of the effect of his dying on others.

CONCLUDING REMARKS

Other dimensions of status passage bring our own study into more precise focus. We have been writing about *unscheduled* passage. Another dimension is whether or not a status passage follows an institution-ally *prescribed transitional status-se-quence*. For instance, many of the ethno-graphic descriptions of growing up and aging and many descriptions of organiza-tional careers delineate prescribed pas-sages. (Such passages may or may not be precisely scheduled.) Transitional status is a concept denoting *social structural time*.[2] If we ask how a social system keeps a person in passage between two statuses for a period of time, the answer is: He is put in a transitional status or sequence of them which denotes a period of time that he will be in a status passage. Thus the transitional status of "initiate" will, in a particular case, carry with it the amount of time it will take to make a non-member a member—a civilian is made a soldier by spending eight weeks as a basic trainee.

[2] Transitional status, as a concept for handling social structural time, may be contrasted with the concepts suggested by Moore of synchroni-zation, sequence, rate, rhythm, routine, and re-currence. All help us talk of the social ordering of man's behavior, but the Moore concepts lack the requirement of linking a discussion to social structure. They must be applied to it, whereas transitional status requires that the analyst locate his discussion within social structure. We need many such concepts for handling time from a distinctly social structural view. See Moore, 1963, chap. i.

Another dimension of status passage is to what degree it is *regulated;* that is, to what degree there are institutionalized operations for getting an occupant in and out of beginning, transitional, and end statuses and keeping others informed of the passage. Rites of passage are instances of such regulated operations. It is notable in the case of dying that the non-sched-uled status passage involves both fairly regulated and fairly unregulated tem-poral elements. An example of the former is that at certain points in the passage the doctor must announce dying to a family member. An example of the latter is the typical problem: When (if ever) does the physician announce to a patient? To-gether the regulated and unregulated ele-ments of the non-scheduled status passage generate one structural source of differen-tial definitions among parties to the pas-sage. Further dimensions of status passage are to what degree the passage is con-sidered *undesirable*, whether or not it is *inevitable*, and the degree of *clarity* both of the relevant transitional statuses and of the beginning and end statuses of the pas-sage itself.

We believe that it is important to dis-tinguish clearly among such structural dimensions of passage, and among the various possible permutations. Thus dying in hospitals can be located in the follow-ing way: the status passage is non-sched-uled, non-prescribed, undesirable, and after a point, inevitable. The passage is sometimes regulated but sometimes not, and sometimes relatively unambiguous—except for its end status—and sometimes not.

A crucial step in the study of status passage is to compare different types in order to begin generating a general theory of status passage. Various combinations of the above dimensions provide both ways of tying different status passages and some of the conditions under which the pas-sage is managed. Differences between two sets of these conditions will, therefore, tend to explain why two types of status passages are managed differently.

For example, the *engagement* status passage between the statuses of single and married in America is usually institutionally non-scheduled like dying; but, unlike dying, it is desirable to the parties in passage. Therefore, because of its desirability, the status occupants are their own legitimators of when they are in passage, what the transitional statuses will be, and for how long a period they will be in each one. In contrast, in cases of undesirable or forced engagements, such as found in Europe and Japan among the upper class, the occupants are not their own legitimators.

The *defendant* status passage linking the statuses of citizen to prisoner is an undesirable, scheduled passage. Here we find that the definition of the transitional statuses of sane or insane usually lacks clarity. In contrast to dying, the institutional legitimator of these statuses is often not a clearly designated person. Should he be a lawyer, a general practitioner, or a psychiatrist, and if the latter, of what persuasion? Thus the person who would be a legitimator must develop tactics both to make his claim as such "stick" and to have his definition of the defendant's sanity status be accepted by the court. What are the characteristic tactics he uses?

Last, our study of a non-scheduled status passage highlights the usefulness of taking explicit account of the participants' differential concepts of transitional statuses and their timing in the study of *all* types of status passage and consequent behavior.

58

ROBERT BLAUNER

DEATH AND SOCIAL STRUCTURE

Death disrupts the dynamic equilibrium of social life because a number of its actual or potential consequences create problems for a society. One of these potential consequences is a social vacuum. A member of society and its constituent groups and relationships is lost, and some kind of gap in institutional functioning results. The extent of this vacuum depends upon how deeply engaged the deceased has been in the life of the society and its groups. The system is more disrupted by the death of a leader than by that of a common man; families and work groups are typically more affected by the loss of those in middle years than by the death of children or old people. Thus a key determinant of the impact of mortality is the age and social situation of those who die, since death will be more disruptive when it frequently strikes those who are most relevant for the functional activities and the moral outlook of the social order.

In modern Western societies, mortality statistics are more and more made up of the very old. The causes are obvious: The virtual elimination of infant and child mortality and the increasing control over the diseases of youth and middle life. Almost one million American males died in 1960. Eight percent were younger than 15 years. Fifty-five percent were 65 or

Excerpted from *Psychiatry, Journal for the Study of Interpersonal Processes,* 29 (November, 1966): 378–94. Copyright 1966 by The William Alanson White Psychiatric Foundations, Inc.

The reader is referred to the original paper, not only for more elaboration of the topic but also for a valuable bibliography of anthropological and sociological references.

older (29 percent were past 75), and another 18 percent were between 55 and 64. The middle years, between 15 and 54, claimed the remaining 19 percent of the deaths (United Nations, 1961, Table 15). As death in modern society becomes increasingly a phenomenon of the old, who are usually retired from work and finished with their parental responsibilities, mortality in modern society rarely interrupts the business of life. Death is uncommon during the highly engaged middle years, and the elderly are more and more segregated into communities and institutions for their age group.

Although accurate vital statistics for contemporary preindustrial societies are rare, the available data indicate that the primary concentration of death is at the opposite end of the life-span, in the years of infancy and childhood. For example, among the Sakai of the Malay Peninsula, approximately 50 percent of the babies born die before the age of three; among the Kurnai tribe of Australia 40 to 50 percent die before the age of 10 (Krzywicki, 1934, pp. 148, 271). Fifty-nine percent of the 1956 male deaths in Nigeria among the "indigenous" blacks were children who had not reached their fifth birthday. Thirty-five percent of an Indian male cohort born in the 1940's died before the age of 10 (United Nations, 1961, pp. 622–676). The same concentration of mortality in the early years was apparently also true of historical preindustrial societies.

Aside from this high infant and child mortality, there is no common pattern in the age composition of death in preindustrial societies. In some, there appears to be a secondary concentration in old age, suggesting that when mortality in the early years is very high, the majority of those who survive may be hardy enough to withstand the perils of middle life and reach old age.

In other societies and historical periods, conditions are such that mortality remains heavy in the middle years, and few people reach the end of a normal lifespan. Thus calculations of age at death taken from gravestones erected during the early Roman empire (this method is notoriously unreliable, but the figures are suggestive) typically find that 30 to 40 percent of the deceased were in their twenties and thirties; the proportion who died past the age of 50 was only about 20 percent (Russell, 1958).

The demographic pattern where mortality is high in the middle years probably results in the most disruption of ongoing life. Procedures for the reallocation of the socially necessary roles, rights, and responsibilities of the deceased must be institutionalized. This is most essential when the roles and responsibilities are deemed important and when there is a tight integration of the society's groups and institutions. Such is the situation among the LoDagaa of West Africa, where many men die who are young and middle-aged. Since the kinship structure is highly elaborated, these deaths implicate the whole community, particularly the kinship group of the bereaved spouses. The future rights to these now unattached women, still sexually active and capable of child-bearing, emerge as an issue which must be worked out in the funeral ceremonies through a transfer to new husbands (Goody, 1962, pp. 30, 73 ff.). In contrast, in modern Western societies, the death of a husband typically involves only the fragmented conjugal family; from the point of view of the social order as a whole, it makes little difference whether a widow replaces her deceased husband, because of the loose integration of the

nuclear family into wider kinship, economic, and political spheres.

Another way of containing the impact of mortality is to reduce the real or ideal importance of those who die. Primitive societies, hard hit by infant and child mortality, characteristically do not recognize infants and children as people; until a certain age they are considered as still belonging to the spirit world from which they came, and therefore their death is often not accorded ritual recognition— no funeral is held (Hertz, 1960, pp. 84– 85; Goody, 1962, pp. 208 ff.). Arles has noted that French children were neither valued nor recognized in terms of their individuality during the long period of high infant mortality:

"No one thought of keeping a picture of a child if that child had . . . died in infancy . . . it was thought that the little thing which had disappeared so soon in life was not worthy of remembrance. . . . Nobody thought, as we ordinarily think today, that every child already contained a man's personality. Too many of them died" (Arles, 1962, pp. 38 ff.).

One of the consequences of the devaluation of the old in modern society is the minimization of the disruption and moral shock death ordinarily brings about.

But when people die who are engaged in the vital functions of society—socializing the young, producing sustenance, and maintaining ceremonies and rituals—their importance cannot be easily reduced. Dying before they have done their full complement of work and before they have seen their children off toward adulthood and their own parenthood, they die with *unfinished business*. I suggest that the almost universal belief in ghosts in preindustrial societies[1] can be understood as an effect of this demographic pattern on systems of interpersonal interaction,

[1] After studying 71 tribes from the human area files, Leo Simmons generalizes that the belief in ghosts is "about as universal in primitive societies as any trait could be." See Simmons, 1945, pp. 223 ff.

and not simply as a function of naive, magical, and other "unsophisticated" world views. Ghosts are reifications of this unfinished business, and belief in their existence may permit some continuation of relationships broken off before their natural terminus.

More common in primitive societies is an ambivalent attitude toward the ghost. Fear exists because of the belief that the dead man, frustrated in his exclusion from a life in which he was recently involved, wants back in, and, failing this, may attempt to restore his former personal ties by taking others along with him on his journey to the spirit world. The elaborate, ritually appropriate funeral is believed to keep the spirit of the dead away from the haunts of the living,[2] and the feasts and gifts given for the dead are attempts to appease them through partial inclusion in their life. It would appear that the dead who were most engaged in the life of society have the strongest motives for restoring their ties, and the most feared ghosts tend to be those whose business has been the least completed. Ghosts of the murdered, the suicide, and others who have met a violent end are especially feared because they have generally died young, with considerable strength and energy remaining. Ghosts of women dying in childbirth and of the unmarried and childless are considered particularly malignant because these souls have been robbed of life's major purpose; at the funeral the unmarried are often given mock marriages to other dead souls. Ghosts of dead husbands or wives are dangerous to their spouses, especially when the latter have remarried (Frazer, 1936, pp. 103–260). The spirit of the grandparent who has seen his children grow up and procreate is, on the other hand, the least feared; among the LoDagaa only the grandparent's death is conceded to be a natural rather than a magical or malignant event, and in many societies there is only a perfunctory funeral for grandparents, since their spirits are not considered to be in conflict with the living (Goody, 1962; Levy-Bruhl, 1928, p. 219; Hertz, 1960, p. 84).

The relative absence of ghosts in modern society is not simply a result of the routing of superstition by science and rational thought, but also reflects the disengaged social situation of the majority of the deceased. In a society where the young and middle-aged have largely liberated themselves from the authority of and emotional dependence upon old people by the time of the latters' death, there is little social-psychological need for a vivid community of the dead. Whereas in high-mortality societies, the person who dies often literally abandons children, spouses, and other relatives to whom he is owing affection and care, the deceased in advanced societies has typically completed his obligations to the living; he does not owe anything. Rather, the death is more likely to remind survivors of the social and psychological debts they have incurred toward him—debts that they may have been intending to pay in the coins of attention, affection, care, appreciation, or achievement. In modern societies the living use the funeral and sometimes a memorial to attempt to "make up for" some of these debts that can no longer be paid in terms of the ordinary give and take of social life.

The disengagement of the aged in modern societies enhances the continuous functioning of social institutions and is a corollary of social structure and mortality patterns. Disengagement, the transition period between the end of institutional functioning and death, permits the changeover of personnel in a planned and careful manner, without the inevitably disruptive crises of disorganization and succession that would occur if people worked to the end and died on the job. The unsettling character of the Kennedy

---

[2] The most complete materials on ambivalence toward ghosts are found in Frazer, 1933, 1934, and 1936.

assassination for our nation suggests the chaos that would exist if a bureaucratic social structure were combined with high mortality in the middle years.[3]

For the older person, disengagement may bring on great psychological stress if his ties to work and family are severed more abruptly and completely than he desires. Yet it may also have positive consequences. As Robert Butler has described, isolation and unoccupied time during the later years permit reviewing one's past life (Butler, 1963). There is at least the potential (not always realized) to better integrate the manifold achievements and disappointments of a lifetime and, doing so, to die better. Under favorable circumstances, disengagement can permit a person to complete his unfinished business before death: To right old wrongs, to reconcile longstanding hostile relations with relatives or former friends; to take the trip, write the play, or paint the picture that he was always planning. Of course, often the finances and health of the aged do not permit such a course, and it is also possible that the general status of the aged in a secular, youth-and-life oriented society is a basic obstacle to a firm sense of identity and self-worth during the terminal years.

BUREAUCRATIZATION OF MODERN DEATH CONTROL

Since there is no death without a body—except in mystery thrillers—the corpse is another consequence of mortality that contributes to its disruptiveness, tending to produce fear, generalized anxiety, and disgust. Since families and work groups must eventually return to some kind of normal life, the time they are exposed to corpses must be limited. Some form of

[3] See Cumming and Henry (1961) for a theoretical discussion and empirical data on the disengagement of the old in American society. In a more recent statement, Cumming, 1963, notes that disengagement "frees the old to die without disrupting vital affairs," and that "the depth and breadth of a man's engagement can be measured by the degree of potential disruption that would follow his sudden death."

disposal (earth or sea burial, cremation, exposure to the elements) is the core of mortuary institutions everywhere. A disaster that brings about massive and unregulated exposure to the dead, such as that experienced by the survivors of Hiroshima and also at various times by survivors of great plagues, famines, and death-camps, appears to produce a profound identification with the dead and a consequent depressive state (Lifton, 1963).

The disruptive impact of a death is greater to the extent that its consequences spill over onto the larger social territory and affect large numbers of people. This depends not only on the frequency and massiveness of mortality, but also on the physical and social settings of death. These vary in different societies, as does also the specialization of responsibility for the care of the dying and the preparation of the body for disposal. In premodern societies, many deaths take place amid the hubbub of life, in the central social territory of the tribe, clan, or other familial group. In modern societies, where the majority of deaths are now predictably in the older age brackets, disengagement from family and economic function has permitted the segregation of death settings from the more workaday social territory. Probably in small towns and rural communities, more people die at home than do so in urban areas. But the proportion of people who die at home, on the job, and in public places must have declined consistently over the past generations with the growing importance of specialized dying institutions—hospitals, old people's homes, and nursing homes.[4]

Modern societies control death through bureaucratization, our characteristic form of social structure. Only a few generations ago most people in the United States

[4] Statistics on the settings of death are not readily available. Robert Fulton reports that 53 percent of all deaths in the United States take place in hospitals, but he does not give any source for this figure. See Fulton, 1965, pp. 81–82.

534

either died at home, or were brought into the home if they had died elsewhere. It was the responsibility of the family to lay out the corpse—that is, to prepare the body for the funeral. Today, of course, the hospital cares for the terminally ill and manages the crisis of dying; the mortuary industry (whose establishments are usually called "homes" in deference to past tradition) prepares the body for burial and makes many of the funeral arrangements. A study in Philadelphia found that about ninety percent of funerals started out from the funeral parlor, rather than from the home, as was customary in the past (Kephart, 1950). This separation of the handling of illness and death from the family minimizes the average person's exposure to death and its disruption of the social process. When the dying are segregated among specialists for whom contact with death has become routine and even somewhat impersonal, neither their presence while alive nor as corpses interferes greatly with the mainstream of life.

Another principle of bureaucracy is the ordering of regularly occurring as well as extraordinary events into predictable and routinized procedures. In addition to treating the ill and isolating them from the rest of society, the modern hospital as an organization is committed to the routinization of the handling of death. Its distinctive competence is to contain through isolation, and reduce through orderly procedures, the disturbance and disruption that are associated with the death crisis. The decline in the authority of religion as well as shifts in the functions of the family underlies this fact. With the growth of the secular and rational outlook, hegemony in the affairs of death has been transferred from the church to science and its representatives, the medical profession and the rationally organized hospital.

Death in the modern hospital has been the subject of two recent sociological studies: Sudnow (1965) has focused on the handling of death and the dead in a county hospital catering to charity patients; and Glaser and Strauss (1965) have concentrated on the dying situation in a number of hospitals of varying status. The county hospital well illustrates various trends in modern death. Three-quarters of its patients are over 60 years old. Of the 250 deaths Sudnow observed, only a handful involved people younger than 40. This hospital is a setting for the concentration of death. There are 1,000 deaths a year; thus approximately three die daily, of the 330 patients typically in residence. But death is even more concentrated in the four wards of the critically ill; here roughly 75 percent of all mortality occurs, and one in 25 persons will die each day.

Hospitals are organized to hide the facts of dying and death from patients as well as visitors. Personnel in the high-mortality wards use a number of techniques to render death invisible. To protect relatives, bodies are not to be removed during visiting hours. To protect other inmates, the patient is moved to a private room when the end is foreseen. But some deaths are unexpected and may be noticed by roommates before the hospital staff is aware of them. These are considered troublesome because elaborate procedures are required to remove the corpse without offending the living.

The rationalization of death in the hospital takes place through standard procedures of covering the corpse, removing the body, identifying the deceased, informing relatives, and completing the death certificate and autopsy permit. Within the value hierarchy of the hospital, handling the corpse is "dirty work," and when possible attendants will leave a body to be processed by the next work shift. As with so many of the unpleasant jobs in our society, hospital morgue attendants and orderlies are often Negroes. Personnel become routinized to death and are easily able to pass from mention of the daily toll to other topics; new staff members stop counting after the first half-dozen deaths witnessed (Sudnow, 1965, pp. 20–40, 49–50).

Standard operating procedures have even routinized the most charismatic and personal of relations, that between the priest and the dying patient. It is not that the church neglects charity patients. The chaplain at the county hospital daily goes through a file of the critically ill for the names of all known Catholic patients, then enters their rooms and administers extreme unction. After completing his round on each ward, he stamps the index card of the patient with a rubber stamp which reads: "Last Rites Administered. Date _____ Clergyman _____." Each day he consults the files to see if new patients have been admitted or put on the critical list. As Sudnow notes, this rubber stamp prevents him from performing the rites twice on the same patient. This example highlights the trend toward the depersonalization of modern death, and is certainly the antithesis of the historic Catholic notion of "the good death."[5]

The rationalization of modern death control cannot be fully achieved, however, because of an inevitable tension between death—as an event, a crisis, an experience laden with great emotionality—and bureaucracy, which must deal with routines rather than events and is committed to the smoothing out of affect and emotion. Although there was almost no interaction between dying patients and the staff in the county hospital studied by Sudnow, many nurses in the other hospitals became personally involved with their patients and experienced grief when they died. Despite these limits to the general trend, our society has gone far in containing the disruptive possibilities of mortality through its bureaucratized death control.

[5] Ed. note: See Glaser and Strauss, pp. 520–30, in this reader for another discussion of death in the hospital setting and its implications *re* rationalization of death control.

THE DECLINE OF THE FUNERAL IN MODERN SOCIETY

Death creates a further problem because of the contradiction between society's need to push the dead away, and its need "to keep the dead alive" (Borkenau, 1955). The social distance between the living and the dead must be increased after death, so that the group first, and the most affected grievers later, can reestablish their normal activity without a paralyzing attachment to the corpse. Yet the deceased cannot simply be buried as a dead body: The prospect of total exclusion from the social world would be too anxiety-laden for the living, aware of their own eventual fate. The need to keep the dead alive directs societies to construct rituals that celebrate and insure a transition to a new social status, that of spirit, a being now believed to participate in a different realm. Thus, a funeral that combines this status transformation with the act of physical disposal is universal to all societies, and has justly been considered one of the crucial *rites de passage* (Van Gennep, 1908; Warner, 1959; Habenstein, 1968).

Because the funeral has been typically employed to handle death's manifold disruptions, its character, importance, and frequency may be viewed as indicators of the place of mortality in society. The contrasting impact of death in primitive and modern societies, and the diversity in their modes of control, is suggested by the striking difference in the centrality of mortuary ceremonies in the collective life. Because death is so disruptive in simple societies, much "work" must be done to restore the social system's functioning. Funerals are not "mere rituals," but significant adaptive structures, as can be seen by considering the tasks that make up the funeral work among the LoDagaa of West Africa. The dead body must be buried with the appropriate ritual so as to give the dead man a new status that separates him from the living; he must be given the material goods and symbolic invocations that will help guarantee his safe journey to the final destination and at the same time protect the survivors against his potentially dangerous intervention in their affairs (such as appearing in dreams, "walking," or attempting to drag others with him); his qualities, lifework, and accomplishments must be summed up and given appropriate recognition; his property, roles, rights, and privileges must be distributed so that social and economic life can continue; and, finally, the social units—family, clan, and community as a whole—whose very existence and functioning his death has threatened, must have a chance to vigorously reaffirm their identity and solidarity through participation in ritual ceremony.

Such complicated readjustments take time, and therefore the death of a mature person in many primitive societies is followed by not one, but a series of funerals (usually two or three) that may take place over a period ranging from a few months to two years, and in which the entire society, rather than just relatives and friends, participates. The duration of the funeral and the fine elaboration of its ceremonies suggest the great destructive possibilities of death in these societies. Mortuary institutions loom large in the daily life of the community, and the frequent occurrence of funerals may be no small element in maintaining society continuity under the precarious conditions of high mortality.[6]

In Western antiquity and the middle ages, funerals were important events in the life of city-states and rural communities. Though not so central as in high-mortality and sacred primitive cultures (reductions in mortality rates and secularism both antedate the industrial revolution in the West), they were still frequent and meaningful ceremonies in the life of small-town, agrarian America several generations ago. But in the modern context they have become relatively unimportant events for the life of the larger society. Formal mortuary observances are completed in a short time. Because of the

segregation and disengagement of the aged and the gap between generations, much of the social distance to which funerals generally contribute has already been created before death. The deceased rarely have important roles or rights that the society must be concerned about allocating, and the transfer of property has become the responsibility of individuals in cooperation with legal functionaries. With the weakening of beliefs in the existence and malignancy of ghosts, the absence of "realistic" concern about the dead man's trials in his initiation to spirithood, and the lowered intensity of conventional beliefs in an afterlife, there is less demand for both magical precautions and religious ritual. In a society where disbelief or doubt is more common than a firm acceptance of the reality of a life after death, the funeral's classic function of status transformation becomes attenuated.

The recent attacks on modern funeral practices by social critics focus on alleged commercial exploitation by the mortuary industry and the vulgar ostentatiousness of its service. But at bottom this criticism reflects this crisis in the function of the

[6] I have been unable to locate precise statistics on the comparative frequency of funerals. The following data are suggestive. In a year and a half, Goody attended 30 among the LoDagaa, a people numbering some 4,000 (1962). Of the Barra people, a Roman Catholic peasant folk culture in the Scottish Outer Hebrides, it is reported that "most men and women participate in some ten to fifteen funerals in their neighborhood every year." See Mandelbaum (1959), p. 206.

Considering the life-expectancy in our society today, it is probable that only a minority of people would attend one funeral or more per year. Probably most people during the first 40 (or even 50) years of life attend only one or two funerals a decade. In old age, the deaths of the spouse, collateral relations, and friends become more common; thus funeral attendance in modern societies tends to become more age-specific. For a discussion of the loss of intimates in later years, see Moreno, 1960.

funeral as a social institution. On the one hand, the religious and ritual meanings of the ceremony have lost significance for many people. But the crisis is not only due to the erosion of the sacred spirit by rational, scientific world views. The social substructure of the funeral is weakened when those who die tend to be irrelevant for the ongoing social life of the community and when the disruptive potentials of death are already controlled by compartmentalization into isolated spheres where bureaucratic routinization is the rule. Thus participation and interest in funerals are restricted to family members and friends rather than involving the larger community, unless an important leader has died. Since only individuals and families are affected, adaptation and bereavement have become their private responsibility, and there is little need for a transition period to permit society as a whole to adjust to the fact of a single death.

In modern societies, the bereaved person suffers from a paucity of ritualistic conventions in the mourning period. He experiences grief less frequently, but more intensely, since his emotional involvements are not diffused over an entire community, but are usually concentrated on one or a few people (Volkart, 1957). Since mourning and a sense of loss are not widely shared, as in premodern communities, the individualization and deritualization of bereavement make for serious problems in adjustment. There are many who never fully recover and "get back to normal," in contrast to the frequently observed capacity of the bereaved in primitive societies to smile, laugh, and go about their ordinary pursuits the moment the official mourning period is ended. The lack of conventionalized stages in the mourning process results in an ambiguity as to when the bereaved person has grieved enough and thus can legitimately and guiltlessly feel free for new attachments and interests (Marris, 1958, pp. 39–40). Thus at the same time that death becomes less disruptive to the society, its

prospects and consequences become more serious for the bereaved individual.

SOME CONSEQUENCES OF MODERN DEATH CONTROL

I shall now consider some larger consequences that appear to follow from the demographic, organizational, and cultural trends in modern society that have diminished the presence of death in public life and have reduced most persons' experience of mortality to a minimum through the middle years.

THE PLACE OF THE DEAD IN MODERN SOCIETY

With the diminished visibility of death, the perceived reality and the effective status and power of the dead have also declined in modern societies. A central factor here is the rise of science: Eissler suggests that "the intensity of service to the dead and the proneness for scientific discovery are in reverse proportion" (1955, p. 44). But the weakening of religious imagery is not the sole cause; there is again a functional sociological basis. When those who die are not important to the life of society, the dead as a collective category will not be of major significance in the concerns of the living.

In modern societies the influence of the dead is indirect and is rarely experienced in personified form. Every cultural heritage is in the main the contribution of dead generations to the present society and the living are confronted with problems that come from the sins of the past (for example, our heritage of Negro slavery). There are people who extend their control over others after death through wills, trust funds, and other arrangements. Certain exceptional figures such as John Kennedy and Malcolm X become legendary as national symbols or role models. But, for the most part, the dead have little status or power in modern society, and the living tend to be liberated from their direct, personified influence. We do not attribute to the dead the range of material and ideal interests that

538

adheres to their symbolic existence in other societies, such as property and possessions, the desire to recreate the networks of close personal relationships, the concern for tradition and the morality of the society. Our concept of the inner life of spirits is most shadowy. In primitive societies a full range of attitudes and feelings is imputed to them, whereas a scientific culture has emptied out specific mental and emotional contents from its vague image of spirit life.

GENERATIONAL CONTINUITY AND THE STATUS OF THE AGED

The decline in the authority of the dead, and the widening social distance between them and the living, are both conditions and consequences of the youthful orientation, receptivity to innovation, and dynamic social change that characterize modern society. In most preindustrial societies, symbolic contacts with the spirits and ghosts of the dead were frequent, intimate, and often long-lasting. Such communion in modern society is associated with spiritualism and other deviant belief-systems; "normal" relations with the dead seem to have come under increasing discipline and control. Except for observing Catholics perhaps, contact is limited to very specific spatial boundaries, primary cemeteries, and is restricted to a brief time period following a death and possibly a periodic memorial. Otherwise the dead and their concerns are simply not relevant to the living in a society that feels liberated from the authority of the past and orients its energies toward immediate preoccupations and future possibilities.

Perhaps it is the irrelevance of the dead that is the clue to the status of old people in modern industrial societies. In a low-mortality society, most deaths occur in old age, and since the aged predominate among those who died, the association between old age and death is intensified. Industrial societies value people in terms of their present functions and their future prospects; the aged have not only become

disengaged from significant family, economic, and community responsibilities in the present, but their future status (politely never referred to in our humane culture) is among the company of the powerless, anonymous, and virtually ignored dead. In societies where the dead continue to play an influential role in the community of the living, there is no period of the lifespan that marks the end of a person's connection to society, and the aged before death begin to receive some of the awe and authority that is conferred on the spirit world.

The social costs of these developments fall most heavily on our old people, but they also affect the integrity of the larger culture and the interests of the young and middle-aged. The traditional values that the dead and older generations represent lose significance, and the result is a fragmentation of each generation from a sense of belonging to and identity with a lineal stream of kinship and community. In modern societies where mobility and social change have eliminated the age-old sense of closeness to "roots," this alienation from the past—expressed in the distance between living and dead generations —may be an important source of tenuous personal identities.

These tendencies help to produce another contradiction. The very society that has so greatly controlled death has made it more difficult to die with dignity. The irrelevance of the dead, as well as other social and cultural trends, brings about a crisis in our sense of what is an appropriate death. Most societies, including our own past, have a notion of the ideal conditions under which the good man leaves the life of this world: For some primitives it is the influential grandfather; for classical antiquity, the hero's death in battle; in the middle ages, the Catholic idea of "holy dying." There is a clear relationship between the notion of appropriate death and the basic value emphases of the society, whether familial, warlike, or religious. I suggest that American culture is faced with a crisis of death because the changed demographic and structural conditions do not fit the traditional concepts of appropriate death, and no new ideal has arisen to take their place. Our nineteenth-century ideal was that of the patriarch, dying in his own home in ripe old age but in the full possession of his faculties, surrounded by family, heirs, and material symbols of a life of hard work and acquisition. Death was additionally appropriate because of the power of religious belief, which did not regard the event as a final ending. Today people characteristically die at an age when their physical, social, and mental powers are at an ebb, or even absent, typically in the hospital, and often separated from family and other meaningful surroundings. Thus "dying alone" is not only a symbolic theme of existential philosophers; it more and more epitomizes the inappropriateness of how people die under modern conditions.

APPENDIXES

RESEARCH STRATEGIES

The following four selections deal with some of the major problems in research strategy that face the investigator interested in studying change over time and in drawing generalizations from given samples of middle-aged and older subjects.

The first is by Birren and has been taken from his longer chapter that constitutes the introduction to the *Handbook on Aging and the Individual* (ed. Birren, 1959). That *Handbook* and a companion volume, *Handbook of Social Gerontology* (ed. Tibbitts, 1960), went far in delineating the area of gerontology in the psychological and social sciences and are still standard references in the field. The pages excerpted here provide a conceptual context for the study of aging in distinguishing different kinds of aging, in the development of age scales, and in the general issues of research design.

The second, by Kuhlen, deals with the contradictory trends found in cross-sectional and longitudinal studies of aging, and with the effects of cultural (historical) change in contaminating both types of investigations. While the discussion is focused upon studies of intelligence, the points are equally cogent for studies of other psychological abilities and for studies of life-tasks and adaptational patterns.

Schaie's paper carries further one of the points made by Birren and elaborated by Kuhlen, namely the distinction between age *differences* and age *changes*. It introduces a model of developmental change that involves three dimensions: differences in maturational level (age), differences among generations (cohorts), and differential environmental impact (historical time of measurement). In so doing, the author sets forth a conceptual clarification that would lead to resolution of the discrepant findings that emerge from cross-sectional and longitudinal studies.

Riegel, Riegel and Meyer's paper is addressed to one of the most difficult problems in the field, the problem of attrition in any sample followed over time and the subsequent difficulties in drawing generalizations from those who survive (or those who continue to cooperate as subjects). The suspicion that survivors are different from non-survivors on many social and psychological as well as biological traits is here demonstrated to be true on the basis of empirical data. To the reader who is unsophisticated in statistics and who may be unable to follow the section on treatment of data, the first and last sections of the paper will nevertheless be of value.

NATURE OF RESEARCH ON AGING

The contribution of an investigator of aging in part depends upon his ability to subdivide the total field into units amenable to research with current methods and on his ability continually to link his results to a larger context. Broadly speaking, the purpose of research on aging is to be able to characterize the nature of the older organism and to explain how the organism changes over time, that is, to be able to make succinct statements explaining increasingly large numbers of facts about aging individuals. The role of the scientist studying aging appears to be no different from that in other fields of investigation. In the process of integrating disparate facts into verifiable generalizations there are alternating phases of conceptualization, fragmentation of problems, and experimentation.

THREE WAYS OF STUDYING AGING

The study of aging may be approached in three ways: (1) as a basic field of inquiry in its own right; (2) as a source of experiments for hypothesis testing within the conceptual framework of established disciplines; and (3) as an applied field in which to develop and evaluate methods of meeting the needs of older persons. As a basic field of inquiry the subject matter has a relatively primitive conceptual framework compared with established fields of inquiry like biochemistry, physi-

Abridged from *Handbook of Aging and the Individual,* ed. James E. Birren (Chicago: University of Chicago Press, 1959), chap. 1, pts. 3 and 4, with the permission of James E. Birren and the publisher. Copyright 1959 by The University of Chicago.

ology, psychology, and sociology. Since one must always have some prior knowledge in designing experiments, recourse is made either to descriptive studies or to experiments conceptualized within an established science. The study of aging tends, however, to emphasize the unity of science rather than the compartmentalization of knowledge.

TYPES OF STUDY

1. Research on aging falls into four general types. Studies of longevity constitute one of the more clearly recognized types in which length of life is regarded as dependent on a variety of independent variables such as genetic background, parental age, nutrition, and cultural differences. In human longevity, inferences about the influences of the independent variables are almost exclusively limited to those derived from statistical analyses, where animal studies allow for direct manipulation of selected variables.

2. Another type of study is concerned with differences with age in a broad range of biological, psychological, and social characteristics. Interest lies not only in how long individuals live but also in age differences in particular characteristics. Chronological age is used initially as the independent variable, but, as this type of investigation progresses, the resulting explanations do not usually include age or time. Differences associated with chronological age tend to be looked upon as unexplained differences, and age-related phenomena are considered only as sources of new information for other ways of systematizing knowledge.

3. A third general type of study is con-

cerned with problems of how a complex living organism moves forward with time. Interest lies in what might be called the properties of "chronicity" of the organism. The biological and behavioral chronology of the individual involves phases or stages of development and aging, such as pubescence and menopause, which have a distinct constellation of characteristics. The research task is to discern, within the range of individual difference in time of appearance, characteristic events or sequences. Time or age appears in explanations resulting from such studies, and the general implication of the approach is that any statement about living organisms has to be qualified in terms of the age of the organisms in mind.

4. A fourth type of study is concerned with the historical aspects of the experience of an individual or group. Thus human biography attempts to reconstruct the experience and trends of individual lives and is much concerned with what is unique in experience in the path through time. Hypotheses derived from biographical-historical studies can be tested in predictive longitudinal studies: the purported consequences of selected types of experience can be predicted and individuals followed. This type of study includes an identification of those aspects of the individual's biology and psychology which remain stable or characteristic of him in comparison with the group. Interest lies in identifying those aspects or patterns of the individual which will remain distinctive of him over the life-span.

These emphases on length of life, chronology of events, or age-associated changes have an effect upon research design and methods. For example, if we adopt the view that any age difference is an unexplained difference, we might say that we cannot study the adult organism without ruling out the effects of disease, since it may be influencing an observed difference. We are involved here in a circularity, although a diminishing one, since almost all diseases of the adult organism themselves show an interaction with age.

Thus disease may not be studied without respect to the age of the host. It is possible that we might choose to regard age in this context as standing for everything else we ought to know about the organism that is related to the disease.

It is not unreasonable to expect that some classes of function may show evolution or increased differentiation at a time when other processes show involution. Although both gains and losses in function may occur with advancing age, most published literature about postmaturational changes is concerned with analysis of decrements. Value judgments may enter into a different emphasis placed upon studies of increments or decrements in function, particularly in the psychological area, where an "emphasis on the positive" may appear to be more supportive to the aging individual; but studies of decremental changes need not imply inevitability. Our strategy in picking and designing a research project on aging should be less influenced by what is currently a positive or negative approach than by longer-ranged values, including unforeseen benefits from the likelihood of gaining systematic information.

THREE KINDS OF AGING

Closely related to studies of longevity is the problem of developing an index of physiological or biological age. By means of measurements of the individual at one point in time, or several in a longitudinal study, the problem is to assign him an index number which would reflect his position on a continuum between birth and death better than would chronological age alone. The kinds of measurements which would enter such an index would be most interesting. It is not likely that all changes in the aging adult are related to how long the individual will live. Thus some investigators may reasonably question to what extent selected psychological changes associated with age may be independent of biological factors known to be more closely related to length of life. Man is a talking, thinking, social person, but he is also a biological system with a species-specific life-span.

There is the general query of whether there are sequences of state or orderly patterns of change in the many biological, psychological, and social aspects of man which are so closely associated with his chronological age that they can be called "aging." A related question is whether, if such orderly patterns exist, they are at all related to one another. Man as a highly developed organism may be differently described from different scientific viewpoints, and we might speak of the *biological, psychological,* and *social ages* of an individual. The implications of each of these ages are somewhat different. In the first case, *biological age,* one of the intents might be to designate the position of the individual along his life-span—to designate his capacity for survival. Thus viewed, biological age would be correlated with chronological age, but also to some extent it would be independent of it, since it must also correlate with the life-span of the individual. Such a measure of biological age must be able to predict with a smaller error the residual life-span of the individual than prediction based upon chronological age alone. Tamplin (1959) described a method for evaluating physiological age in relation to mortality rates. Longevity is only one aspect of biological age, but it is perhaps the most reliable one.

Psychological age can be used to refer to the age-related adaptive capacities of the individual. A measure or index of psychological age would be based upon both the achievements and the potentials of the individual. Like biological age, psychological age can be thought of in terms of a number or index which summarizes the position of the individual in a multidimensional space. Presumably, a measure of psychological age would correlate highly with chronological age and also, but to a lesser extent, with residual life-span or biological age. From a measure of psychological age it should be possible to predict, within some error, the capacity of the

individual to adapt to familiar as well as unfamiliar environments. Psychological age may also be regarded as a measure of the capacity to modify the environment.

A measure of *social age* presumably would also be related to chronological age, somewhat to psychological age, and to a lesser degree to biological age. Social age would refer to acquired social habits and status—to the individual's filling the many social roles or expectancies of a person of his age in his culture and social group. A social age measure would be a composite index to the individual's performance of social roles. It is obvious that these concepts or ages overlap somewhat; thus the capacity to lead alternative social roles is jointly a psychological and a social aspect of aging. It is a matter of considerable importance how much the biological, psychological, and social aspects of aging are interacting.

DEVELOPMENT OF AGE SCALES

Admittedly, the concepts of *biological, psychological,* and *social age* are abstract, but they are not necessarily more abstract or less amenable to measurement than other concepts related to the circumstances of man's life-span. Since our statistical methods are sufficiently well developed, we could, if we chose, select that combination of measurements which yields the highest correlation with specified criteria in the three areas of biological, psychological, and social age. In the case of the narrow index of *biological age* described, the criterion is simple—length of life. Interest is concentrated on which measurements have highest predictive value of residual life-span. If, for example, there are a great many predictable but independent factors any one of which can terminate the life, then a mean value would be of little use. That is, a mean value describing the individual's position in a many-dimensional space would have less predictive value for length of life

547

than would the occurrence of a single extreme value in any one of the many dimensions. If this were found to be so, it would imply the unlikely fact that there were no contingencies in the probabilities of dying from various causes. The questions here are rather straightforward conceptually, although available data may not be in usable form. Diseases leading to death are evident states which reasonably might be predictable from measurements of precursor physiological states. Thus the research question is pushed one stage earlier in time: What are the contingencies among physiological measurements of aging persons prior to demonstrable disease? It is a matter for research to demonstrate whether or not there are general contingencies among diseases with age and in precursor physiological states in relatively healthy persons of different ages. At present, chronological age is our best general index to the residual life-span of apparently healthy individuals. If some combination of physiological measurements will predict residual life-span better than chronological age, presumably from the nature of the composite measurements, we could infer something about the mechanisms involved, and a further line of research could be developed which would attempt to alter the time course of these mechanisms.

Psychological age and *social age* tend to be more abstract than *biological age*, since the rather specific criterion measure, length of life, is less pertinent. Thus psychological age should be expected to be closely related to measures of adaptive capacity, and the task consists of identifying and measuring those aspects of adaptive capacity which show a change with chronological age. In comparison with psychological age, social age has the additional criterion of the extent to which the individual has acquired or performs the various social roles which his society and his immediate social group expect of a person of his age. The emphasis in psychological age is on the *capacity* to adapt, whereas in social age the emphasis is on

the *social output* or *performance* of the individual in relation to others. Since interpersonal relations are largely mediated through the use of language, we would expect that social-role performance may also improve with age, whereas the adaptive capacity of the individual, as in the rapid recognition of danger and the mobilization of effective responses, may decline. Viewing the individual in terms of his social age, we are faced with an organization of habit patterns which may be judged according to their appropriateness in some group. The individual may be simultaneously viewed in terms of psychological age or the processes by which he acquires, maintains, and modifies the habit patterns.

HIERARCHY OF "AGES"

In an expanding inclusiveness each index of aging described embraces the previous one but adds new aspects as well, chronological age being relevant to them all. Beginning with longevity and chronological age, we first subsume them under the concept "biological age," which may be empirically related to a cluster of measurements yielding a better prediction of residual life-span than chronological age alone. Biological age is in turn partly subsumed under the concept "psychological age," which is concerned with the capacity of the organism to adapt. At this level survival is no longer the sole important element; how well the individual adjusts to changing environmental conditions also demands attention. At the next level, *social age,* not only elements of survival and adaptive capacity but also the new aspect of the social roles of the individual are included. If we were to pursue an exhaustive series of investigations implied by the derivation of age scales or indexes of aging, it might be found that social age would be related to chronological age to only a small degree. This is to say that survival and some minimum level of health and capacity are necessary to subserve behavior but are not usually the limiting or sufficient conditions determining the social-role performance of people. Although the concept of "psychological maturity" is supposed to refer to a general characteristic of individuals, there may not be a general trait, and "maturity" may be specific to situations. We would not be privileged to speak of a general trait of "maturity" if evidence indicated that adequacy of behavior is situation specific. Similarly, if the adequacy of performance of one social role is unrelated to the performance of another, the concept of *social age* does not have much predictive and heuristic value: it would merely express a summation or mean adequacy in unrelated behaviors or social roles. These are matters for research and evidence; attempts to derive indexes of biological, psychological, and social age do not, however, bias against the finding that aging might be marked by specificity of changes rather than by changes in general properties of individuals. If research would show that the various biological, psychological, and social changes of age are relatively autonomous, we should drop the linking word "age" and resort to narrower non-overlapping terms to designate the various aspects of individuals which change with age. Furthermore, it would imply that effective research on aging could be more narrowly conceived.

RESEARCH DESIGN

The evolution of an investigator's research on aging often moves from the finding of a trait or characteristic which changes with age through a second stage of finding out what factors covary with it and, finally, to a stage of manipulating the isolated dominant factors. A study in which the investigator attempts to modify a relationship by perturbation or manipulation is more efficient than the study limited to a "natural experiment" or passive observation of the relationship as is often necessary in man. Although nonintrusive observation is not the most efficient method of research, there are many kinds of relationships which we could not

for ethical reasons perturb in man and yet are also not amenable to research in animals. However, there are usually more ways of studying an aspect of aging than an investigator can avail himself of because of his particular scientific lineage. He necessarily approaches a topic with selectivity in his prior factual knowledge, experience with particular methods of gathering data, more or less familiarity with statistical techniques, and also biases in what constitutes "important" and "good" research. Even if one is confidently, and perhaps justifiably, addicted to a line of research, it is helpful to know what the "line of research" consists of in contrast to other ways of studying the same topic.

CROSS-SECTIONAL AND LONGITUDINAL STUDIES

The basic method of the study of aging is the longitudinal method; if we wish to study age changes in individuals, we should follow individuals in time. Cross-sectional research on aging is a compromise or substitute for the ideal longitudinal study. Since longitudinal studies have practical disadvantages, investigators often use cross-sectional studies if the increase in error can be tolerated. The practical disadvantages of longitudinal research have been described by Jones (1958) and are of several types involving the (*a*) investigator, (*b*) subjects, and (*c*) support.

From a research point of view a 10-year period would seem to be a reasonable length of time to study aging in individuals. Yet this can be a long time in terms of the time perspective of the scientist, and to wait 5 or 10 years for results is a greater procrastination than many investigators can tolerate. Longitudinal research has administrative problems of keeping a professional staff together for long periods despite loss due to illness, change of position, and slackening of interest. In the case of the young investigator, his career advancement may require earlier tangible evidence of achievement. There is thus a professional risk involved for the research worker in addition to maintaining enthusiasm while deferring results for long periods. One method of meeting some of the problems is to intercalate cross-sectional studies on alternate years. In the "off-year," issues growing out of the longitudinal study can be investigated rather quickly as well as meeting some of the motivational problems of the staff.

Not only must the staff be kept intact; the population of subjects must be maintained. Subjects move, get sick, die, lose interest, or become unsuitable for study for unpredictable reasons. If the subjects are volunteers, there is a question whether their initial "altruism" will grow or diminish over a decade. It is likely that more effort has to be expended in longitudinal studies to cultivate and maintain subject interest and participation. Subject attrition must be anticipated, and a loss factor must be added to the size of the initial population.

Antiquation of methods in longitudinal research can prove a hardship to the investigator. The types of problems and methods selected in one decade may be obviated or dismissed in another. In some instances "satellite" cross-sectional studies may be carried out to determine the relation of the older to more contemporary measurements. Other than to be aware that it might happen, this is a problem which cannot be specifically anticipated. Institutional support may change over a decade, and the investigator contemplating longitudinal research may want to determine if the same facilities would be continuously available over a decade. Even 10 years is a long commitment for many institutions for budgets, space, and interest. Merely the space for record storage and maintenance can become a difficult issue. The above problems should not detract from the fact that the longitudinal method is the ideal method of studying human development and aging. A cross-sectional study may be accepted insofar as it may yield comparable results within some tolerable limits of error.

DIFFERENCES BETWEEN GENERATIONS

Both cross-sectional and longitudinal studies may be confronted with questions about differences in populations of the same age in different "generations." Successive generations have grown taller and heavier, and it is reasonable to suspect that many differences between young and elderly persons are not due to aging but to differences arising from shifts in nutrition, nature of the physical environment, education, public health, and attitudes. Adolescents today are not in all respects like adolescents three or four decades ago. Nor are these teenagers, 50 years from now, likely to resemble in all ways the current population now over 65. Generational differences are not entirely obviated by longitudinal study per se. It is conceivable that the rate of aging for many characteristics will be influenced by shifts in the age of onset of puberty, rate of growth, and nature of the environment.

In the last 100 years man's muscle power has tremendously decreased in importance. He now controls his environment largely by use of other energy sources than his own "horsepower." The consequence of this low-energy output for well-being is not clear, but it is suspected that this and other marked changes in activities must have an influence on our physical and mental well-being and the ways in which we age.

Most studies will contain mixtures of age trends and generational trends. It is possible that generational differences will maximize some and minimize other age differences. Perhaps more research will be done reporting age-specific data by cohort groups so that the two trends can be separated. The efficiency of longitudinal design may be increased by comparing present-generation young persons on the same measurements as the previous generations being followed longitudinally. An ideal solution would be continuous longitudinal studies in which new young subjects were being added continually. Put in terms of the above issues, the question may be asked whether individuals followed over their life-span today will show the same manifestations of aging as did previous generations.

COMPARATIVE STUDIES OF AGING

One of the most useful ways of finding out whether a relationship is an invariant one is to study it in different cultures or in different species. A comparative approach is beginning to be recognized in both biological and psychological studies of aging. Comfort (1956) has reviewed the attempts to relate length of life to attributes of different species of animals. One of the few cross-cultural analyses

of the psychological aspects of aging is seen in Figure 1, which presents the results of a test of adult intelligence given to the United States population and the German population. The test, the Wechsler Adult Intelligence Scale, was translated into German, and the scores were adjusted to give a maximum score of 100 between the ages of 20 and 34 years. Thus the same maximum level (i.e., 100) in the curves is without significance. The change from this level is not so restricted and is remarkably similar for the two populations. While longitudinal studies may require qualifications of the comparison and the inferences which may be drawn, the curves are an interesting example of a cross-cultural analysis of aging.

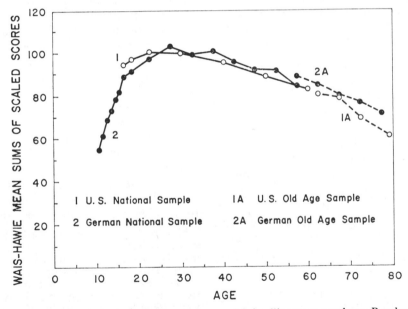

FIG. 1.—A cross-national comparison of scores on an adult intelligence test and age. Results are taken from the United States samples with the Wechsler Adult Intelligence Scale (WAIS) (Wechsler, 1955) and from the German samples with the translated test (HAWIE) (Wechsler, 1956). The German old age sample is from Riegel (1959). Both versions of the tests are adjusted to give a maximum score of 100 between the ages of 20–34 years.

RAYMOND G. KUHLEN

AGE AND INTELLIGENCE: THE SIGNIFICANCE OF CULTURAL CHANGE IN LONGITUDINAL VS. CROSS-SECTIONAL FINDINGS

A number of hypotheses may account for observed adult age trends in various psychological traits, and may serve to explain or reconcile the contrasting trends in mental abilities revealed by cross-sectional and longitudinal studies of aging. In a paper published some twenty years ago the writer (Kuhlen, 1940) emphasized the role of cultural change in *cross-sectional* studies, and concluded by stressing the merit of the longitudinal study as a means of minimizing the impact of that variable. In contrast, the present paper argues that cultural change contaminates *both* types of studies, but with opposing effects, such as to promote exactly the contradictions that have been found.[1]

In the comments to follow, this argument is pursued, first, by examining the nature of the data to be "reconciled"; second, by noting the character of some of the cultural changes that have been evident during the last 40 or 50 years; third, by suggesting ways in which such changes may have differential impact upon different age groups as they are studied in cross-sectional and longitudinal procedures; and, finally, by suggesting ways in which research designs and procedures of data analysis might provide a better perspective in this matter.

THE NATURE OF DATA ON "INTELLIGENCE"

Putting aside for present purpose any detailed consideration of what is meant by "intelligence," the term may be defined in

its barest operational sense: intelligence is what intelligence tests measure. Granting that this definition is a crude one, it is important to recognize that the basic data to be "reconciled" come from culturally based tests. It is well known that performance on such tests is influenced by cultural variables, by experience variables, and by personality and motivational variables; and that to a considerable degree such tests are broadly based *achievement* tests. This consideration is of first importance in evaluating longitudinal and cross-sectional data.

A second major consideration is that the trends suggested by current longitudinal studies are not yet determined with precision. We cannot be sure what it is we are contrasting when we compare the findings from longitudinal to the findings from cross-sectional data. Existing longitudinal studies of mental abilities suffer from one or more of the following deficiencies:

1. Abilities have usually been measured at only two, often widely-separated ages. In view of the fact that most functions

Reprinted from *Vita Humana*, vol. 6 (1963), no. 3, with the permission of the publisher, S. Karger, Basel/New York.

[1] The problem is, of course, intrinsic to aging studies generally, and in no sense peculiar to investigations of mental abilities. For example, *Kelly* (1955) noted in his presidential address to the APA some years ago that he found a trend toward increasing masculinity among women in a longitudinal study covering the age range from the 20's to the 40's, whereas *Terman and Miles* (1936) had found a trend toward increased femininity in a cross-sectional study. Similarly, young adults were found in a longitudinal study to become more liberal (*Nelson*, 1954; *Bender*, 1958) over a 14- or 15-year period whereas cross-sectional studies show trends toward conservatism.

studied are curvilinearly related to adult age, it is apparent that two points, which can establish only a straight line, are insufficient. Thus, Owens (1953) demonstrated that 50-year-olds did better than they themselves did at age 19; but previous studies indicate that performance on the *Army Alpha* test does not reach a peak until age 20.[2]

2. The tests employed in some studies are relatively homogeneous, and instead of yielding measures of "general" ability, may provide trends for some single function similar to vocabulary ability. This criticism may be made of the Bayley and Oden (1955) follow-up of Terman's gifted group, though it is to the credit of this study that the data were obtained at a number of age-points in the adult life span.

3. A third criticism applicable to certain longitudinal studies is that they are, in a sense, make-shift studies, capitalizing on existing initial data. Useful as such analyses may be for exploratory purposes, it is extremely likely that influences which operate at one age and not at the other may result in differences which are mistakenly attributed to age. Tests administered to *groups* during freshman week in college, for example, are seldom administered under conditions of high motivation. When these same subjects are retested individually and under vastly different conditions of motivation at a later time, important questions can be raised as to the meaning of the obtained differences.

4. The carefully designed longitudinal studies now in progress have not been pursued long enough to yield definitive data. Probably the most important studies are those underway at the University of California (Berkeley), which have revealed continued gains in intellectual ability up to around 30 years of age, as thus far reported. It is not yet known whether performance begins to decline as these groups move beyond age 30.

In evaluating the findings from current "two-point" longitudinal studies, it may be worth recalling an earlier semi-longitudinal investigation which is rarely referred to in current papers, but which provided longitudinal data at *several pairs of points* during the adult years. In 1934 Catharine Cox Miles published a brief paper reporting data from the Stanford Later Maturity Studies. She had retested, after two years, different age samples of the basic study group. Scores did not continue to rise, but paralleled rather closely the decrements apparent in the cross-sectional data. McCulloch (1957) used a very similar semi-longitudinal procedure in the study of age trends in 937 retarded adults. His summary curve, covering the age range of 16 to 60, showed a high point at 30, with decline thereafter. These studies suggest that longitudinal data may also reveal a downward turn after a peak in relatively young adulthood, just as do the cross-sectional studies.

It is noteworthy that the trend apparent in the Miles study, although true for the total sample of 190 Ss, was not evident in a subgroup of 135 Ss who had voluntarily returned to be retested because of their interest in the study. In fact gains, instead of losses, were evident for this group, except for the oldest members. Mean losses throughout the age range resulted for the total sample when those additional 55 subjects were included who agreed to be retested only after vigorous recruiting efforts. This is a rather important point since it suggests that those volunteering for longitudinal studies may be different Ss over time from those not volunteering.[3]

In contrast to the relatively tenuous longitudinal data now available, the cross-sectional data inspire more confidence in the curves they demarcate. The four prin-

[2] [Editor's Note: Owens did a second follow-up as reported in his paper, "Age and Mental Abilities" (Owens, 1966).]

[3] [Editor's Note: For more discussion on this point see the paper by Riegel, Riegel and Meyer, pages 563–70 of this book.]

cipal cross-sectional studies are the 1933 Jones and Conrad investigation of a rural Vermont population with the *Army Alpha* test; the Stanford Later Maturity Studies (Miles and Miles, 1932) involving a sample in California tested with a brief form of the *Otis;* the standardization data of the *Wechsler Bellevue Scale* (Wechsler, 1939); and the recent data of the *Revised Wechsler Adult Intelligence Scale* (Wechsler, 1958). In three of these studies performance reached a peak at age 20 and declined shortly thereafter. The 1955 *Wechsler* data, based on a stratified sample of the population, identified peak performance at around age 25, with linear decline evident shortly thereafter. Although there is a possible effect of cultural change in comparisons of the Wechsler data of the mid–1930's and the mid–1950's all four cross-sectional studies are consistent in showing an early adult peak performance, followed by regular decline.

Thus it may be argued that at the present time fairly adequate cross-sectional data are being compared with extremely tenuous longitudinal data; and the attempts to "reconcile" the findings or to draw firm conclusions may be somewhat premature.

CULTURAL CHANGE AND ITS IMPACT

There is now more "cognitive stimulation" in our culture than was true in earlier times. Older people when they were young not only received less stimulation through formal societal efforts (public schooling), but they were exposed to less informal stimulation through the media of mass communication. As is well known, length of schooling is highly correlated with measured intelligence; thus, "decline" in test performance evidenced in cross-sectional studies may be partially explained by the lower educational level of older individuals. It would seem clear that if intellectual stimulation is most important in younger years, older individuals, those who grew up at a time when verbal stimulation was relatively meager, would be handicapped.

If we consider the broad problem of cultural change as related to studies of aging, rather than considering only studies of intelligence,[4] further complications are encountered. Different aspects of the culture do not change to the same degree or in the same direction over the same period of time. An interesting illustration comes from a study published recently (de Charms and Moeller, 1962). As revealed in an analysis of children's readers, there is a marked curvilinear relationship over time in the pressure put upon children for achievement. The evidence suggests an increase in achievement pressure from 1800 to 1890, a steady decrease thereafter through the 1940's, and other evidence indicates a recent increase again in the last few years.

If such a curvilinear relationship between cultural trends and time characterizes the life spans of adults now living (instead of encompassing a century and a half, as in the foregoing illustration), then cultural change will have a differential impact upon different age groups in cross-sectional studies. However, cultural change will also produce age "gains" or "losses" throughout the age span studied in the longitudinal studies, depending upon the historical time setting in which the longitudinal measures are taken.

To take another example, some data suggest a turn away from religion during the first three decades of the twentieth century and a shift in the opposite direction during the last two decades. Thus if studies of age changes in religion had been conducted in 1930, one might well have expected, in a cross-sectional study, that older people would be *more* "religious" than those younger. At the same time, 1930, a longitudinal study might well have

[4] *Toch* (1953) has argued that cultural change is not a factor in certain types of psychological age data. Though he presents evidence from public opinion polls supporting his position, the evidence relates to a short span of years.

554

shown that, with age, people became *less* religious. The reverse might be expected in studies carried out in 1960—in which during the first half of the adult life span, a cross-sectional study might well show younger people more religious than middle-aged, whereas a longitudinal study might show that, as persons moved from early to middle adulthood, they became more religious.

It becomes evident from the foregoing that a longitudinal study will, under the cultural circumstances of the last several decades, result generally in data showing that older individuals are "better" in the respect being measured than they were when first tested at a younger age; whereas a cross-sectional study will put the older individual at a disadvantage compared to the younger person when they are both being tested at the same time.

That cross-sectional studies are influenced by cultural change has, of course, long been recognized. It is not so widely recognized that the longitudinal study may yield data spuriously favorable to the older individual when marked cultural change is occurring in a positive direction. Indeed, developmental psychologists appear to have become so enamoured of the longitudinal study that many view it as the design of choice for almost any problem. Yet a careful comparison of the advantages and disadvantages of the cross-sectional and longitudinal methods for research on aging will show the two methods to be fairly well balanced. For some purposes the longitudinal study is the only method of obtaining the desired data; for other purposes the cross-sectional study is the method of choice.

Two studies demonstrate the point that what appeared to be age trends in longitudinal data were instead artifacts of cultural change: Nelson (1954) tested college students with an array of attitude scales and retested them fourteen years later. Marked trends in the direction of increased liberalism were noted. However, at the second testing a new sample

of college students was obtained. The scores of this new group were about the same as those of the *re*test scores of the first sample. In another study by Bender (1958), Dartmouth College students were retested after a fifteen-year period with the *Allport-Vernon Scale of Values*. A marked trend in the direction of greater religious interest was noted. But again, test results from a new group of Dartmouth students tested at the time the first group was *re*tested suggested that the change in the first group was likely due to cultural change, not to age *per se*.

There seems little question that the tremendous changes in cognitive stimulation over recent decades can affect performance on intelligence tests just as dramatically as indicated in these attitude studies. Indeed, Tilton (1949) showed substantial gains in intellectual performance of World War II soldiers over World War I soldiers.

It might might well be asked why cultural changes should affect different age groups differently. Why are not people of all ages influenced to the same extent by the changing world in which they live? Several reasons suggest themselves. First, at least in the American culture, there are massive efforts to transmit the culture to the young through formal education. Thus the young get the quick advantage of new advances in knowledge. (A dramatic illustration is the fact that engineers can become rapidly outdated because of the rapid cultural change designated as "technical advance.") In addition to a very probable decline in learning ability with age, with handicaps especially evident when faced with new and different learning tasks, older people, as compared with younger, tend not to experience so directly the impact of cultural change. This is true, a) because of reduced need or motivation to learn (reflecting the decreased demand of the culture that they learn),[5] b) because of pressure of the work-a-day world, which denies the adult opportunities to interact with his broader environment, and c) because of the tendency of older persons to insulate themselves psychologically from new features of their environment. One notes, in this last connection, that as people become older they tend to live in an increasingly restricted social matrix. This circumstance probably results partly from losses in energy, and possibly from psychological trends such as increasing habits of conservatism, caution, and avoidance-tendencies—habits or practices which serve to reduce the anxiety generated by age-related losses. Despite these reasons, however, some of the cultural change reaches the older individual, with the result that compared to himself when younger, he is at a "higher" level.

DESIRABLE CORRECTIVES

While the arguments advanced above may explain why cross-sectional data may yield one type of age trend whereas longitudinal data may yield another, the basic question remains: What is the pattern of intellectual development and decline during the adult life span? As pointed out earlier, an answer to this question must necessarily await better data. If it should turn out that longitudinal data tend to show a peak at about age 30, the findings will be reasonably consistent with the cross-sectional data now available, and no reconciliation between the two types of studies will be necessary. If, however, longitudinal data should show that the peak is not reached until age 40, will this finding be due to practice effect, or to cultural change? Or do people actually continue to mature in the abilities measured by the tests? These questions cannot be answered in the absence of the data; yet when the data are in, they are likely to be subject to varied interpretations. Accordingly various procedures should be explored for checking on the effect of cultural change and other influences.

One approach is the systematic replication of studies across time and across cultures. Data presently available from both types of "replication," though admittedly sparse, tend to emphasize the influence of culture. Probably the major replication study across time is to be found in the Wechsler data of the 1930's and the 1950's, both sets of data based on substantial samples. In one case the peak of intellectual ability is shown at age 20; in the other, at age 25. Has the peak of the growth curve of intelligence shifted in approximately one generation? Or is there reflected here the greater verbal character of the culture, the increased levels of education (the larger proportions of the population in high school; the widespread training programs available to young people in industry, in adult education programs, as well as in college)? Perhaps in the United States the important changes in cognitive stimulation have occurred in the last two or three decades, with the onset of commercial radio in the early 1920's to the saturation of the American public with television in the 1960's. Hereafter such cultural changes may be less dramatic. Replication studies across time may thus provide intelligence test data of considerable relevance.

A second approach to the problem is to examine trends on individual test items, items which are judged to be especially reflective of cultural change. While there are important advantages in generalizing across groups of items, as sub-tests conventionally do, a detailed inspection of single *item* trends would yield useful insights.

Third, an analysis of the cultural, dietary, "life style," and other characteristics of subgroups of subjects showing differential age trends might prove to be instructive. Although test-retest correlations are high, even over thirty-year intervals, they are not so high as to preclude quite different trends for different individuals, especially when longitudinal studies suggest larger variance in distribution of scores at older ages. There may be some

[5] In the instance of "intelligence" tests, what is learned and practiced in adult years is often *not* the type of learning tested.

advantage at this stage of our research in relatively exploratory types of studies, in this respect. It is becoming increasingly evident that we need a better conceptualization of the aging process than is presently available. Age itself is not a significant theoretical variable, but is mainly an index of time—time in which other things of psychological importance happen. An empirical approach to the identification of age-related variables which may prove to be the important independent variables should not be neglected.

A fourth suggestion concerns the general design of studies. Cross-sectional and longitudinal studies are generally considered to represent different basic designs. The importance of cultural change in the outcomes of both types of studies, however, makes obvious the necessity of combining the two approaches. Given the substantial amount of time and money required for a longitudinal study, it would be wise if the investigators added the small amounts necessary to obtain cross-sectional data at the same time, as a check on the influence of cultural change. In this connection, it may also be noted that the design of many current studies does not provide for control over practice effects. The recent study by Jarvik, Kallmann, and Falek (1962) and some observations of William A. Owens (1962), as yet unpublished, suggest that practice effect on test-retest may be an exceedingly important influence even over ten-year intervals.

Finally, it may be that we need some new conception and definition of intelligence. Many psychologists still take a somewhat biological view of intelligence, and interpret cultural influences upon test performance primarily as a source of error. Perhaps studies of the central nervous system will eventually provide "answers" regarding the nature of intelligence. Be that as it may, current intelligence tests are fundamentally based in the culture; and the growth curves of intelligence obtained by means of the tests are to a considerable degree a function of the particular measuring instruments used. For

these reasons we shall probably never know the inherent nature of the intellectual growth curve through the use of such tests. Catharine Miles (1934) and Demming and Pressey (1957), among others, have pointed out that tests standardized on middle-aged adults rather than on children and adolescents would yield quite different "growth" curves.

New conceptions of intelligence may be emerging which place greater emphasis upon perception, thought processes, and reasoning; and which accord a greater role to experience and thus to cultural influences. For example, the distinction between "fluid" and "crystallized" intelligence, recently given elaboration by R. B. Cattell (1963), leads to specific predictions regarding the adult age trends. Cultural and personality variables are assigned an important role in the determination of crystallized ability.

To take another example, Piaget's work has received much attention in recent years. That American psychologists may be ready for a new look at the nature of intelligence is suggested not only by Cattell's research, but also by J. McV. Hunt's recent volume (1961) on intelligence and experience, and by the recent monograph (Kesson and Kuhlman, 1962) reporting a conference which focused on Piaget's views of cognitive development. Commenting briefly upon deficit, Hunt (1961, p. 297) notes that one of the contributions of Piaget's procedure "may be to help to clarify the nature of various kinds of psychological deficit. . . . The fact that logical operations clarify the variations in thought that occur with the development of thought suggests that they might help clarify the variations that occur with the dissolution of thought." New approaches to the definition of intelligence and to the study of cognitive functioning during the life span may serve to reconcile the findings of longitudinal and cross-sectional studies and thus to advance our understandings.

Almost as soon as objective measures were defined which could be used to index intellectual abilities and other cognitive functions, researchers began to express interest in individual differences on such measures. One of the most persistent of such interests has been the investigation of developmental changes in cognitive behavior. Most treatments covering age changes in cognitive behavior have closely followed the prevalent approaches in the description of developmental theories. Although great attention has always been paid to early development, and maturation during childhood and adolescence is fully described, very little is said about the further development of intelligence and other cognitive variables during adulthood or senescence. In fact, the concern with age changes in cognitive behavior during adulthood did not come to be of serious interest to psychologists until it became clear that the I.Q. concept used in age scales was inapplicable for the measurement of intelligence in adults. As a consequence of the work of Wechsler (1944) in developing special measures for the description of the intelligence of adults but also due to the earlier descriptive works of Jones and Conrad (1933) with the Army Alpha and that of the Stanford group working with Miles (1933), it soon became clear that somewhat different conceptual models would be required for the proper understanding of adult cognitive development.

Reprinted from *The Gerontologist*, vol. 7, no. 2, pt. 1 (June, 1967).

Preparation of this paper was supported in part by Public Health Services Research Grant HD-00367-02 from the National Institute of Child Health and Human Development.

It will be noted that emphasis has been placed upon the term "age changes." The literature on the psychological studies of aging has long been haunted by a grand confusion between the terms "age change" and "age difference." This confusion has beclouded the results of studies involving age as a principal variable and has loaded the textbook literature with contradictory findings and what will be shown to be spurious age gradients. This presentation intends to clarify in detail the relationship between age changes and age differences and to show why past methodologies for the study of age-related changes have been inadequate.

Much of the literature on aging and cognitive behavior has been concerned with describing how older individuals differ from their younger peers at a given point in time. Such a descriptive attempt is quite worth while and is necessary in the standardization of measurements. This approach, however, is restricted to a description of the very real differences between organisms of various lengths of life experience at a given point in time. Unless some very strong assumptions are made, these attempts beg the issue and fail to produce relevant experiments on the question of how the behavior of the organism changes over age. This is a strong statement, and it is not made rashly since it clearly questions much of the work in the current literature. But it is required since we find ourselves increasingly puzzled about the results of our own and others' studies of age differences. Let us be explicit in clarifying the basis of our concerns and in tracing the resulting implications for the interpretation of much of the data in the developmental literature.

A general model has been developed which shows how the previously used methods of developmental analysis are simply special cases which require frequently untenable assumptions. This model has been described elsewhere in more detail (Schaie, 1965). At this time, however, it would be useful to state the most important characteristics of a general model required for the explanation of aging phenomena as they pertain to the relationship between age changes and age differences.

Let us begin then by clearly distinguishing between the concepts of age change and age difference. Before we can do so effectively, we must also introduce some new concepts and redefine various familiar concepts. The concept of *age* is, of course, central to our discussion. It needs to be carefully delineated, however, and whenever used will be taken to denote the age of the organism at the time of occurrence of whatever response is to be measured. Even more precisely, age will refer to the number of time-units elapsed between the entrance into the environment (birth) of the organism and the point in time at which the response is recorded.

In addition, it is necessary to introduce two concepts which are relatively unfamiliar in their relevance to developmental study. The first of these concepts is the term *cohort*. This term has frequently been used in population and genetic researches and is useful for our purpose. The term implies the total population of organisms born at the same point or interval in time. Restrictions as to the nature of the population and the latitude in defining the interval in time designated as being common to a given cohort or generation must be determined by the special assumptions appropriate to any given investigation.

The second concept to be introduced is that of *time of measurement*. It will take on special significance for us as it denotes that state of the environment within which a given set of data were

obtained. In any study of aging it is incumbent upon the investigator to take pains to index precisely the temporal point at which his measurements occur. Such concern is most pertinent since changes in the state of the environment may contribute to the effects noted in an aging study.

With these definitions in mind let us now examine Figure 1 which will help us in understanding the distinction between age changes and age differences. Figure 1

Time of Testing		1955	1960	1965
	1910	Sample 3 Age 45 $A_1C_3T_1$	Sample 5 Age 50 $A_2C_3T_2$	Sample 6 Age 55 $A_3C_3T_3$
Time of Birth (Cohort)	1905	Sample 2 Age. 50 $A_2C_2T_1$	Sample 4 Age 55 $A_3C_2T_2$	
	1900	Sample 1 Age 55 $A_3C_1T_1$		

A - Age level at time of testing.
C - Cohort level being examined.
T - Number of test in series.

Fig. 1.—Example of a Set of Samples Permitting All Comparisons Deducible from the General Developmental Model.

contains a set of six independent random samples, three of which have a common age, three of which have been given some measure of cognitive behavior at the same point in time, and three of which have been drawn from the same cohort; i.e., whose date of birth is identical. If we compare the performance of samples 1, 2, and 3 we are concerned with *age differences*. Discrepancies in the mean scores obtained by the samples may be due to the difference in age for samples measured at the same point in time. But note that an equally parsimonious interpretation would attribute such discrepancies to the differences in previous life experiences of the three different cohorts (generations) represented by these samples.

If, on the other hand, comparisons were made between scores for samples 3, 5, and 6, we are concerned with *age changes*. Here the performance of the same cohort or generation is measured at three different points in time. Discrepancies between the mean scores for the three samples may represent age changes, or they may represent environmental treatment effects which are quite independent of the age of the organism under investigation. The two comparisons made represent, of course, examples of the traditional cross-sectional and longitudinal methods and illustrate the confounds resulting therefrom.

Lest it be thought that there is no way to separate the effects of cohort and time differences from that of aging, we shall now consider a further set of differences which may be called *time lag*. If we compare samples 1, 4, and 6, it may be noted that the resulting differences will be independent of the organism's age, but can be attributed either to differences among generations or to differences in environmental treatment effects or both.

Any definitive study of age changes or age differences must recognize the three components of maturational change, cohort differences, and environmental effects as components of developmental change; otherwise, as in the past, we shall continue to confuse age changes with age differences and both with time lag. Hence, it may be argued that studies of age differences can bear upon the topic of age changes only in the special case where there are no differences in genetically or environmentally determined ability levels among generations and where there are no effects due to differential environmental impact. It follows, therefore, that findings of significant age differences will bear no necessary relationship to maturational deficit, nor does the absence of age differences guarantee that no maturational changes have indeed occurred.

As a further complication, it is now necessary to add the notion that differences in the direction of change for the confounded developmental components may lead to a suppression or an exaggeration of actual age differences or changes. As an example, let us suppose that perceptual speed declines at the rate of one half sigma over a five-year interval. Let us suppose further that the average level of perceptual speed for successive five-year cohorts declines by one-half sigma also. Such decrement may be due to systematic changes in experience or to some unexplained genetic drift. Whatever their cause, if these suppositions were true, then a cross-sectional study would find no age differences whatsoever because the maturational decrement would be completely concealed by the loss of ability due to some unfavorable changes in successive generations.

As another example, let us suppose that there is no maturational age decrement but that there is systematic improvement in the species. In such a case successive cohorts would do better than earlier ones, and cross-sectional studies would show spurious decrement curves, very much like those reported in the literature for many intelligence tests.

One of the most confusing facets of aging studies therefore is the fact that experimental data may reveal or fail to reveal a number of different combinations of underlying phenomena. Yet the understanding of the proper conceptual model which applies to a given set of data is essential before generalizations can be drawn. Let us illustrate the problem by considering some of the alternative models that might explain the behavior most typically represented in the literature on developmental change. Reference here is made to cross-sectional gradients such as those reported by Wechsler (1944) or by Jones and Conrad (1933). These gradients typically record a steep increment in childhood with an adult plateau and steep decrement thereafter.

When we address ourselves to the question of what developmental changes are represented by such data, we face relatively little difficulty in determining whether maturational changes are contained in the age differences noted during childhood and adolescence. Our own children provide us with at least anecdotal evidence of the longitudinal nature of such change. Whether this portion of the developmental curve, however, is a straight line or a positive asymptotic curve is still in doubt. Also, it should be remembered that even if we agree upon the validity of evidence for maturational changes, we must still consider that such changes will be overestimated by cross-sectional data if there are positive cohort differences and/or negative environmental experience effects. Similarly, maturational growth will be underestimated in the event of cohort decrement or the effect of positive environmental influences.

For the adult and old-age portions of the developmental span, matters are much more complicated. While we can readily accept the fact of psychological maturational growth during childhood, similar evidence of maturational decline on psychological variables by means of longitudinal study remains to be demonstrated. As a consequence, we also must at least entertain models which would account for age differences in the absence of maturational age changes.

The detailed analysis of the general developmental model (Schaie & Strother, 1964) shows that it is possible to differentiate as many as 729 models to account for developmental change if one considers the direction and slope as well as the three components involved in developmental change gradients. Of the many possible models, three will be considered now which seem to be high probability alternatives for the classical textbook age-gradients. Our three examples are models which not only would fit these textbook gradients but would furthermore predict that the cross-sectional data depicted by the gradients could not possibly be replicated by longitudinal studies.

The first of these models might be called an "improvement of the species" model. It holds that the form of the maturational gradient underlying the typical representatives of the textbook gradients is positive asymptotic; i.e., that there is systematic increment in performance during childhood, slowing down during early adulthood, and that there is no further maturational change after maturity. The model further holds that the cohort gradient, or the differences between generations, should also be positive asymptotic.

Successive generations are deemed to show improved performance for some unspecified genetic or prior experience reason, but it is also assumed that improvement has reached a plateau for recent generations. The effect of the environment is furthermore assumed to be constant or positive asymptotic also. When these components are combined they are seen to provide a cross-sectional age gradient which shows steady increment during childhood, a plateau in midlife, and accelerating decrement in old age.

The same model, however, when applied to longitudinal data will predict steady increment during childhood, but slight improvement in midlife, and no decrement thereafter. The only reason the cross-sectional gradient will show decrement is that the younger generations start out at a higher level of ability and thus in the cross-sectional study the older samples will show lower performance. Of course, this means no more than that the older samples started out at a lower level of ability even though they showed no decrement over their life-span.

A second no less plausible alternative to account for the textbook age gradients might be called the "environmental compensation" model. This model also specifies a concave maturational gradient with increment in youth and decrement in old age, much as the cross-sectional gradient. In addition, however, this alternative calls for a positive environmental experience gradient. Here the effect of an environmental experience increases systematically due to a progressively more favorable environment. The effects of cohort differences in this model are assumed to be neutral or positive asymptotic.

If the second model were correct, then our prediction of longitudinal age changes would result in a gradient with steep increment in childhood but no decrement thereafter, since maturational changes would be systematically compensated for by a favorable environment. Since the environmental component of change over time is not measured in the cross-sectional study, assessment would be made only of the maturational decrement yielding information on the state of a population sample of different ages at a given point of time. But it would provide misleading information as to what is going to happen to the behavior of this population sample as time passes.

Third, let us propose a more extreme alternative which we might label the "great society" model. This model specifies a positive asymptotic maturational gradient; i.e., increment during childhood and a plateau thereafter. The model further specifies a positive asymptotic cohort gradient; i.e., successively smaller increments in performance for successive generations. Finally the model specifies increasingly favorable environmental impact. The reason for calling this alternative the "great society" model should be readily apparent. The model implies (a) that maturity is an irreversible condition of the organism, (b) that the rapid development of our people is reaching the plateau of a mature society, and (c) that any further advance would now be a function of continually enriching the environment for us all. Note that the cross-sectional study of groups of different age at this time in our history will still conform to the textbook cross-sectional gradients. Their longitudinal replication, however, would result in a gradient which would be steep during childhood, which would level off during adulthood, but which would show continued growth until the demise of the organism.

Obviously, it is still possible that the straightforward decrement model might hold equally well for the classical gra-

dients. The information we have on longitudinal studies such as those of Owens (1953) and Bayley and Oden (1955) and the more recent sequential studies by Schaie and Strother (1964 II; 1964 III) let it appear that any one of the above alternatives may be a more plausible one.

It is hoped that the examples just given have alerted the reader to some of the flaws in the traditional designs used for the studies of aging phenomena. Caution is in order at this time lest the premature conclusion be reached that the increase in sophistication of our methods has indeed led to a better understanding of how and why organisms age. Thus far it seems just as likely that all which has been investigated refers to differences among generations and thus in a changing society to differences whch may be as transient as any phase of that society. Only when we have been successful in differentiating between age changes and age differences can we hope therefore that the exciting advances and methods in the more appropriate studies now in progress will truly assist us in understanding the nature of the aging process.

SUMMARY

The concepts of age change and age difference were differentiated by introducing a three-dimentional model for the study of developmental change involving the notions of differences in maturational level (age), differences among generations (cohorts), and differential environmental impact (time of measurement). It was shown that age differences as measured by cross-sectional methods confound age and cohort differences while age changes as measured by the longitudinal method confound age and time of measurement differences. Conceptual unconfounding permits specification of alternate models for the prediction of age changes from age differences and resolution of the meaning of discrepancies in the findings yielded by cross-sectional and longitudinal studies. Examples of alternative models for aging phenomena were provided.

KLAUS F. RIEGEL, RUTH M. RIEGEL, and GÜNTHER MEYER

A STUDY OF THE DROPOUT RATES IN LONGITUDINAL RESEARCH ON AGING AND THE PREDICTION OF DEATH

Intelligence, verbal abilities, attitudes, interests, and social conditions of 380 Ss above 55 years of age were measured. Five years later Ss were retested. Some refused to cooperate again, and others had died or become ill. Retested Ss differed significantly from the total group, but in particular from the other subgroups. The prediction of death on the basis of sociopsychological variables was more successful for Ss below than above 65 years of age. It was concluded that developmental trends are based on increasingly biased samples, that previous studies have underestimated the amount of attrition, and that nonsurvivors under 65 years form a sociopsychological subgroup of different characteristics than survivors.

During recent years, an increasing number of longitudinal studies of adult and aged subjects have been reported in the psychological literature. Most of these studies are based on special subsamples of the population and have applied restricted sets of psychological measures only. Owens (1953) retested the intelligence of a group of superior adults, and Bayley and Olen (1955) reported on the longitudinal analysis of Terman's subjects. At the other end of the continuum, Kaplan (1943, 1956) and Bell and Zubek (1960) retested mentally inferior persons. In both cases it would be inappropriate to generalize the reported findings since there is, most likely, an interaction between the rate of change and the original level of functioning. This has been emphasized by Foster and Taylor (1920), Jones and Conrad (1933), and Miles (1933).

More recently, Jarvik, Kallman, and Falek (1962), Jarvik, Kallman, Falek, and Klaber (1957), Jarvik and Falek (1963),

and Falek, Kallman, Lorge, and Jarvik (1960), in a number of joint publications, reported on a longitudinal investigation of intellectual functioning and longevity of senescent twins. Kleemeier (1962) and Kaplan, Rumbaugh, Mitchell, and Thomas (1963) retested the intelligence of residents in a home for the aged after various time intervals, and observed sudden and marked preformance decrements preceding the death of the subjects. Among the best-matched samples of the aging population were those by Berkowitz and Green (1963), Eisdorfer (1963), and by Schaie and Strother (1964 III). The former two studies were restricted to the measurement of intelligence, while the latter also included some attitudinal scales applied to stratified samples ranging from 20 to 70 years of age.

In most of these studies, developmental psychologists have never questioned the superiority of the longitudinal over the cross-sectional design. Only very recently has the complementary nature of both strategies been recognized. In particular, Schaie (1959 II, 1965) and Schaie and Strother (1964 III) have provided a thor-

Adapted from the *Journal of Personality and Social Psychology*, vol. 5 (1967), no. 3. Copyright 1967 by the American Psychological Association and reproduced by permission.

ough discussion of the experimental strategies in gerontological research, in emphasizing more general designs in comparison with which the two traditional approaches are merely specialized and incomplete cases.

In a more concrete sense, the limitations of the traditional research strategies have long been recognized. In their cross-sectional study, Jones, Conrad, and Horn (1928) analyzed the performance of subjects who had originally refused to participate in their study, thus biasing the sample. More recently, Sussman (1964), Damon (1965), and Rose (1965) discussed the representativeness of samples

TABLE 1

FATE OF SUBJECTS FROM THE ORIGINAL
SAMPLES AT THE TIME OF
THE SECOND TESTING

	55–59	60–64	65–69	70–74	75+	Sum
Retested....	51	48	44	34	25	202
Deceased....	2	8	12	17	23	62
Too ill......	4	2	6	11	9	32
Refusals....	19	18	14	14	19	84

in longitudinal research primarily concerned with the health of the subjects.

Because of systematic factors, of which sickness and death are the most obvious, the problem of sample bias is equally important for longitudinal and cross-sectional studies in psychological gerontology. Indeed, if systematic selection by dropout factors (such as selective death rates) can be detected, the concept of psychological development based on observed trends would itself be seriously challenged, because then cross-sectional or longitudinal research would represent averages for sets of systematically biased age samples only; therefore any inferences about general developmental trends would be questionable.

The present analysis has been undertaken primarily to determine the psychological characteristics of subjects who either did not survive the time period be-

tween the two testings, were too ill, or refused to be retested. Since significant differences between the subgroups were detected, attempts have also been made to predict the ensuing death of the subjects on the basis of sociopsychological factors. The present analysis is restricted to major comparisons between the four subgroups mentioned. (In a supplementary technical report—Riegel, Riegel, & Meyer, 1967—statistical details on the 43 variables and five age groups at both testings have been provided, and differences in the distributions of test scores and the effect of multiple testing have been discussed.)

METHOD AND PROCEDURE

SUBJECTS

The present analysis is based on the results of the first testing of a study on sociopsychological factors of aging, conducted in Germany in 1956–57 and a retest study in 1961–62.

The original sample consisted of 190 females and 190 males. These cases were drawn from a group of about 500 subjects, and were subdivided into five age levels of 38 females and 38 males each. The five age levels were 55–59, 60–64, 65–69, 70–74, and over 75 years (average age = 79.0 years). Aside from controlling for age and sex, each age level was matched against census statistics on the following criteria: occupation, source of income, marital status, refugees versus nonrefugees, and religious affiliation. The samples can be regarded as representative for the population of northern Germany. Fuller descriptions of the samples and the procedures are given elsewhere (Riegel & Riegel, 1959; Riegel, Riegel, & Skiba, 1962).

At the time of the second testing all subjects had moved into the next higher age levels. Of the 380 persons originally tested, 202 participated in the second testing, 62 had died during the intervening 5 years, 32 were too ill to be retested (were in hospitals or had to remain in bed during the weeks of the testing), and 84 refused to be retested. A comparison of these four categories of subjects by age levels is given in Table 1 and shows that the number of subjects retested decreased rather regularly with age, whereas the number of deceased subjects increased. The number of sick subjects increased irregularly. No systematic differences in the number of noncooperative subjects existed between the age levels.

METHOD

The following measures were used:

1. Short forms of the Hamburg Wechsler Intelligence Test for Adults. These scales were administered to all subjects and the full test to a random subsample of 128 (see K. F. Riegel & R. M. Riegel, 1962; R. M. Riegel, 1960; R. M. Riegel & K. F. Riegel, 1959, 1962).

2. Five multiple-choice verbal tests (synonyms, antonyms, selections, classifications, analogies) as described by Riegel (1959, 1967). Though subjects were under no time stress, the duration of the test performances were recorded. Half of the items of the antonyms, selections, and classifications tests were mixed (m); the others were presented each in separate forms (s).

3. Four attitude and interest scales of the Likert type (rigidity, dogmatism, attitude toward life, interests) as described by Riegel and Riegel (1960).

4. A general questionnaire on the social and living conditions of the subjects, including inquiries on the following topics: education, financial status, health, physical activities, leisure-time activities, social activities, itemized activities, expressions of well-being, comparisons of situations, as well as many single items dealing with the conditions and habits of daily life (see Riegel et al., 1962).

TREATMENT OF THE DATA

DEVELOPMENTAL TRENDS OF SUBSAMPLES

The main problems to be analyzed can be outlined in reference to Figures 1 and 2, which represent the average scores of the various subgroups on the scale of behavioral rigidity (see Riegel & Riegel, 1960). According to Figure 1, which includes the data from the first testing only, rigidity increased rather steadily with age. Subjects who were later retested were less rigid than the total group, but the rate of increase was about the same for both. Subjects who died during the

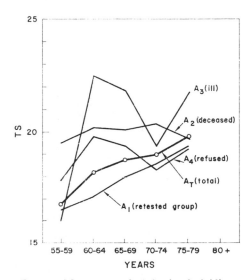

FIG. 1.—Mean scores in behavioral rigidity at the first testing for five age levels and four subgroups of subjects.

following 5 years were much more rigid than both the total group and the subjects to be retested. Age differences were small for nonsurvivors. The scores of subjects who were ill at the time of the second testing varied rather markedly between the age levels, but generally were far above those of the other groups. The same held for the subjects who later refused to be retested. However, this group did not deviate as much from the general trend as did the ill subjects.

Figure 2 compares the mean scores obtained at the second testing with mean scores for the total sample at the first testing. Again the rigidity of the retested subjects increased with age. The trend of the means was closely parallel to that of the first testing, though the means were significantly higher (p < .01). Of greater importance, however, was the fact that the means for the retested group were still below the averages of the total group at the first testing. This may be attributed to the absence of those subjects who died, became ill, or refused to be retested. If one reinstated these subjects by averaging their scores from the first testing with the

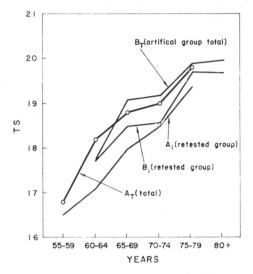

FIG. 2.—Mean scores in behavioral rigidity for five age levels of the total group and the group of retested subjects at the first (A) and second (B) testing.

second scores from the restested group, artificially complete samples would be created on the rather disadvantageous assumption that the scores of the subjects not retested would have remained unchanged during the intervening 5 years. The means of these artificial groups were comparable to those of the total group at the time of the first testing. As Figure 2 shows, they were above those of the first testing as well as above all other subgroups; that is, rigidity was higher during the later years than estimated in any of the other analyses. Of major concern in our discussion below will be the question of which of the various curves of Figure

2 would represent most appropriately the developmental trend.

COMPARISON OF SUBSAMPLES AT FIRST TESTING

We return now to the data obtained from the first testing. Since at the younger age levels some of the four subgroups did not include enough cases to allow for reliable estimates, the five consecutive age samples were pooled using the retirement age of 65 years as the cutting point. The significance of the retirement age for changes in behavior has been strongly suggested by the authors' as well as by earlier investigations. But aside from any such considerations, the age of 65 years subdivided the group of retested subjects in nearly equal sections of 99 and 103 subjects, respectively, and was selected primarily for this reason.

In the following analysis, the 43 variables tested are being regarded as a sample of measures not all of which are independent of one another but whose interdependencies—though slightly increasing with age—do not yield different correlation matrices at the two age levels. The variability in scores did not change markedly with age even though the dropout of subjects at the earlier age levels seemed to depend on systematic rather than random factors. These results justify the following comparisons in the numbers of significant differences between the subgroups.

For each variable the differences between the means of the four subgroups at the two age levels have been tested for significance by analyses of variances. Subsequently, the most important t-test comparisons between the subgroups have been made and are explained in the footnote to Table 2. Signs are given whenever the differences are significant at or beyond the .05 level. In particular, positive signs indicate that the direction of differences in the first group of comparisons leaned toward greater intelligence, superiority in verbal abilities, more rigidity, more negativism in their attitude toward life, less interested, better education and financial support, poorer health, greater activity, feeling of well-being, and a favorable comparison of their present situation with the past.

It was evident that the subsamples deviated from one another in the older age group. Below 65 years there were 35 significant differences, whereas for those over 65 there were 63 significant signs. This difference was particularly marked for the three intelligence measures, where the ratio of the signs for the two age groups was 3:12, as well as for the battery of verbal tests (ratio of 8:19) and the questionnaire scales (ratio of 5:13). An equal number of significant signs occurred for the two age groups on the various attitude scales (ratio of 19:19). Similar results were obtained by comparing the retested and nonretested subjects $(1 - N)$. Eleven of the 32 variables listed in Table 1

TABLE 2

SIGNIFICANCE OF DIFFERENCE IN MEAN SCORES BETWEEN VARIOUS
SUBGROUPS AT FIRST TESTING[a]

ITEM	AGE GROUPS 55–64						AGE GROUP OVER 65					
	1–2	1–3	1–4	2–3	A–2	1–N	1–2	1–3	1–4	2–3	A–2	1–N
Age							−		−			−
Intelligence		+				+	+	+	+			+
Verbal		+				+		+	+	+		+
Performance							+	+	+			
Verbal tests	+	+		+			+	+	+			+
Synonyms							+	+	+	+		+
Antonyms	+	+			+	+		+	+			+
Selections								+	+			+
Classifications												+
Analogies					+			+	+			+
Rigidity		−				−	−	−				−
General	−					−		−				−
Personal		−		−			−	−	−			−
Dogmatism		−	−			−						−
Anxiety		−				−						−
Intolerance	−					−						−
General				+			−		+		−	−
Attitude toward life	−					−						
Proretrospect												−
Contemporary	−					−						+
Interests												+
Receptive activity												
Productive activity								+	+	+		+
Physical activity												
Education					+			+		+		
Financial status												
Health	−				−	−						
Physical activity							+					+
Social activity												
Leisure-time activity				−			+		+			+
Itemized activity							+		+			+
Well-Being									+			
Competitive situations							+				−	
Σ signs	7	8	2	1	6	11	12	13	14	5	1	18

[a] The subgroups are denoted by the numbers and letters in the heading of the table in the following way: 1 = retested subjects. 2 = deceased subjects, 3 = subjects too ill. 4 = subjects refusing to be retested. A = alive subjects (retested + ill + refusing subjects). N = not retested subjects (deceased + ill + refusing subjects). Thus, the denotation 1 − 2 indicates the differences between subgroup 1 and 2, etc. If any of the differences was significant ($p < .05$) and positive, a positive sign (+) was used; if negative, a negative sign (−) was given.

were significant for the younger, but 18 for the older age group.

In particular, both the deceased and the sick subjects deviated on a rather large number of variables from the retested subjects. Below 65 years, seven and eight variables, respectively, differed significantly. Above 65 years, the corresponding figures were 12 and 13. For variables discriminating between noncooperative and

TABLE 3

RANKS AND *F* LEVELS FOR THE PREDICTION OF DEATH AT TWO AGE LEVELS

VARIABLE	55–64		OVER 65	
	Rank	F	Rank	F
Personal rigidity....	11	4.51*	.....	....
General rigidity....	10	3.10*	.....	....
General dogmatism.	2	6.91	2	9.48
Productive activities	4	5.48	4	3.13*
Classifications m...	.....	....	5	3.74*
Antonyms T.......	3	9.37	.....	....
Classifications T....	5	4.42	.....	....
Total testing time m	7	4.48	.....	....
Financial status....	9	3.01*	.....	....
Health...........	1	11.94	.....	....
Physical activity...	.....	....	1	8.80
Free time..........	8	3.16*	.....	....
Yrs. married.......	.....	....	3	4.81
No. acquaintances..	12	3.57*	.....	....
Itemized activities..	6	3.91	.....	....
Widow(er) or not...	13	2.76*	.....	....

*p = .10.

retested subjects there was also a rather marked age difference. Below 65 years these two groups differed only on two scales (dogmatism and leisure-time activity). Above 65 years, however, 14 variables were significantly different. For both age groups, there were few significant differences between deceased and sick subjects. Only one variable was significant for subjects below 65, and five for subjects above 65 years of age.

Undoubtedly of greatest importance was the finding that in the younger group the deceased subjects differed from all the survivors (including those retested or not retested) on six variables, whereas there was only one significant difference at the higher age level. This finding encouraged

a search for systematic differences that might have allowed the prediction of the subjects' death on the basis of their sociopsychological functioning at the time of the first testing.

PREDICTION OF DEATH

Multiple-regression predictions of death were calculated on an IBM 7090 computer. Age and sex were excluded from the predictions since both of them—being known as good predictors—could have covered up the more interesting psychological variables, even though their elimination would necessarily reduce the overall degree of correlation.

The predictions were made by successively reducing the *F* level at which variables would enter into the equations. The *F* levels were set at .05 and .10, but for each variable the *F* values were also empirically determined. This was necessary because under the more lenient conditions of $p = .10$ the *F* values for some of the variables already entered could have changed, depending on their correlations with the newly entering measures. Indeed, in some cases, high-ranking predictor variables have been dropped altogether from the equations. Generally, in a new field of investigation it seems reasonable to go somewhat beyond the conventional level of $p = .05$ because additional variables will pick up unaccounted portions of the variance. Even though they will increase the likelihood of Type 2 errors, it seems more appropriate to retain hypotheses initially, which after sufficient further research turn out to be false, rather than to reject hypotheses too early that may turn out to be true.

As shown in Table 3, 13 variables entered into the equation for the 55- to 64-year-old subjects at an *F* level of .10, but only five for the subjects above 65 years. Moreover, one of these five variables correlated highly with age, namely, the number of years married, and may have been excluded for the same reason for which age has been eliminated. Only two of the five variables were also predictors for the younger age group, namely, general dogmatism and productive activities (interests). The remaining variables were different for both groups. Even though the best single predictors were health for the younger, and the amount of physical activity for the older group, both the attitude and the intellectual measures entered strongly into the regression equations. Because the various intercorrelations were taken into account, the variables selected and shown in Table 3 were not necessarily identical with those significantly different in means between deceased and live subjects (see Table 2).

The point-biserial multiple correlations at the F level of .05 were .47 for the seven variables selected into the equation of the younger, and .31 for the three variables of the older subjects. When the F level was lowered to .10, the multiple correlations were raised to .60 and .35, respectively. In further lowering the F level to .50, the correlations could have been increased to .68 and .46, respectively, but at the same time the errors of estimate would have grown considerably so that this gain would not have been beneficial.

DISCUSSION

The present analysis was based on five cross-sectional samples of consecutive age groups above 55 years. Five years after the first testing, attempts were made to retest all subjects. However, success was not possible in these attempts because, in numbers increasing with age, some subjects had died or had become sick. Others refused to be retested, but their numbers seemed to be independent of age. If the biological determinants of death and disease interact with psychological or sociological factors—as has been shown in the present study—a number of far-reaching conclusions can be drawn.

First, a concept of development as represented by curves of growth and decline is questionable, regardless of whether these curves are based on longitudinal or cross-sectional data.

Development as reflected by trends of average test or rating scores would be a meaningful concept only if the dropout of subjects in consecutive age groups is strictly a random process. However, biologically weak subjects will die earlier or will become increasingly unable to participate in the testings. A particular occupational, financial, educational and/or social status may increase the risks and may decrease the chances of survival. According to the present study, groups of dropouts (particularly the younger ones) are also psychologically different in their abilities and attitudes.

Age samples drawn for cross-sectional studies or followed up in longitudinal studies become increasingly biased, the further one moves upward in the age scale, and thus the generalized trend will be confounded by the increasing degree of sample bias.

Second, older reports on the decline of intelligence have been received with shock or suspicion. Relief was felt when some longitudinal studies (Bayley & Oden, 1955; Owens, 1953) reported higher stabilities than originally observed, even though these studies were restricted to subjects with superior capacities. According to the present findings and aside from other psychological factors, less able persons die earlier or are more likely to become seriously ill. Thus, the samples are increasingly loaded with highly able persons. If it had been possible to retest all of the subjects originally involved in the study, the decline would have been more marked than either cross-sectional or longitudinal studies have revealed.

A third conclusion can be added concerning the determinants of death. Even though the groups of dropouts differed on an increasing number of variables, prediction of death was more successful at the earlier than at the later age levels. This should be attributed to slightly lower intercorrelations between the predictor variables, and to the larger differences in average scores between the groups of subjects who were either sick, refused to be retested, or had died. The differences in accuracy of predictions indicate that at lower age levels nonsurvivors can be described as a subgroup which differs sociopsychologically from the rest in almost the same sense as victims of cancer or heart attacks may differ from healthy persons. At the higher age levels, however, death seems to strike at random, and psychological predictions become less valid. Using again the biological analogy, nonsurvivors resemble persons with general syndromes of aging rather than specific diseases which cause their death.

CONTRIBUTORS

C. KNIGHT ALDRICH, Professor of Psychiatry, University of Chicago

LOUISE SHEDD BARKER, Research Assistant, Midwest Field Station, University of Kansas

ROGER G. BARKER, Professor of Psychology and Director, Midwest Field Station, University of Kansas

HOWARD S. BECKER, Professor of Sociology, Northwestern University

EUNICE BELBIN, Director, Industrial Training Research Unit, University College, University of London

R. M. BELBIN, Consultant, Industrial Training Research Unit, University College, University of London

GRETE L. BIBRING, Research Consultant, Psychoanalyst, Radcliffe College

JAMES E. BIRREN, Professor of Psychology and Director, Gerontology Center, University of Southern California

ROBERT BLAUNER, Associate Professor of Sociology, University of California, Berkeley

LEE G. BURCHINAL, Director, Division of Information Technology and Dissemination, Bureau of Research, Office of Education, Washington, D.C.

ROBERT N. BUTLER, Research Psychiatrist, Washington School of Psychiatry, Washington, D.C.

FRANCES M. CARP, Director, Human Development Research Program, American Institutes for Research, Palo Alto, California

M. MARGARET CLARK, Director, Subcultural Studies, Adult Development Program, Langley Porter Neuropsychiatric Institute, San Francisco

WAYNE DENNIS, Professor of Psychology, Brooklyn College

IRWIN DEUTSCHER, Director, Youth Development Center, Syracuse University

LENORE A. EPSTEIN (BIXBY), Deputy Assistant Commissioner for Research and Statistics, Social Security Administration, Washington, D.C.

ERIK H. ERIKSON, Professor of Human Development, Harvard University

KENNETH FEIGENBAUM, Associate Professor of Psychology, Antioch College

ELSE FRENKEL-BRUNSWIK (deceased), formerly Associate Research Psychologist, Institute of Industrial Relations, University of California, Berkeley

HENNIG FRIIS, Director, The Danish National Institute of Social Research, Copenhagen

BARNEY G. GLASER, Associate Professor of Sociology, University of California Medical Center, San Francisco

LEONARD R. GREEN, Executive Secretary, Medical Research Study Section, Social and Rehabilitation Service, Department of Health, Education, and Welfare, Washington, D.C.

DAVID L. GUTMANN, Associate Professor of Psychology, University of Michigan

WILLIAM H. HARLAN, Professor of Sociology, Ohio University

CLAYTON HAVEN, Research Assistant, Adult Development Program, Langley Porter Neuropsychiatric Institute, San Francisco

ROBERT J. HAVIGHURST, Professor of Education and Human Development, University of Chicago

REUBEN HILL, Professor of Sociology and Director, Minnesota Family Study Center, University of Minnesota

VIRGINIA E. JOHNSON, Research Associate, The Reproductive Biology Research Foundation, St. Louis

RUTH J. KRAINES, Lecturer in Human Development, University of Chicago

RAYMOND G. KUHLEN (deceased), formerly Professor of Psychology, Syracuse University

HARVEY C. LEHMAN (deceased), formerly Professor of Psychology, Ohio University

MORTON A. LIEBERMAN, Associate Professor of Psychiatry and Human Development, University of Chicago

FLORINE LIVSON, Clinical Associate, California Medical Center for Psychotherapy, San Francisco

MARTIN B. LOEB, Professor and Director of School of Social Work, University of Wisconsin

BARBARA LOOMIS, Assistant Professor, Curriculum Coordinator of Occupational Therapy, School of Associated Medical Sciences, College of Medicine, University of Illinois

JOHN C. LOWE, graduate student, University of Chicago

MARJORIE FISKE LOWENTHAL, Professor in Residence, Department of Psychiatry, University of California Medical School, San Francisco

GEORGE MADDOX, Professor of Sociology, Duke University

MARTIN U. MARTEL, Associate Professor of Sociology, Brown University

WILLIAM H. MASTERS, Research Director of the Reproductive Biology Research Foundation, St. Louis

ETHEL MENDKOFF, Illinois Department of Mental Health, Charles F. Read Zone Center, Chicago, Illinois

GÜNTHER MEYER, Diplome Psychologist, Hamburg, Germany

POUL MILHØJ, Professor of Economics, Copenhagen School of Economics and Business Administration, Copenhagen

STEPHEN J. MILLER, Associate Professor of Medical Sociology, Florence Heller Graduate School for Advanced Studies in Social Welfare, Brandeis University

DAVID O. MOBERG, Professor of Sociology and Chairman of Department of Sociology and Anthropology, Marquette University

JOAN W. MOORE, Associate Professor of Sociology, University of California, Riverside

JANET H. MURRAY, Consultant, Office of Research and Statistics, Social Security Administration, Washington, D.C.

BERNICE L. NEUGARTEN, Professor of Human Development, University of Chicago

ROBERT F. PECK, Director, Research and Development Center for Teacher Education, Austin, Texas

PAUL G. PETERSEN, Associate Professor of Psychology, California State College at Long Beach

PETER C. PINEO, Professor of Sociology, Carleton University, Canada

SUZANNE REICHARD (deceased), formerly Associate Research Psychologist, Institute of Industrial Relations and Human Development, University of California, Berkeley

KLAUS F. RIEGEL, Professor of Psychology, University of Michigan

RUTH M. RIEGEL, Research Associate, Department of Psychology, University of Michigan

ARNOLD M. ROSE (deceased), formerly Professor of Sociology, University of Minnesota

JACQUELINE L. ROSEN, Research Associate, Bank Street College of Education

IRVING ROSOW, Professor, School of Applied Social Sciences, Case Western Reserve University

K. WARNER SCHAIE, Professor and Chairman, Department of Psychology, West Virginia University

ETHEL SHANAS, Professor of Sociology, University of Illinois at Chicago Circle

JAN STEHOUWER, Lecturer and Head of the Department of Sociology, Institute of Political Science, University of Aarhus, Denmark

ANSELM L. STRAUSS, Professor of Sociology, University of California Medical Center, San Francisco

GORDON F. STREIB, Professor and Chairman, Department of Sociology, Cornell University

MARVIN B. SUSSMAN, Professor and Chairman, Department of Sociology, Case Western Reserve University

YONINA TALMON(-GARBER), (deceased), formerly Associate Professor of Sociology, The Hebrew University of Jerusalem

SHELDON S. TOBIN, Assistant Professor Social Service Administration and Human Development, University of Chicago

PETER TOWNSEND, Professor and Chairman, Department of Sociology, University of Essex, England

MICHAEL A. WALLACH, Professor of Psychology, Duke University

HOWARD WEBBER, Author

DOROTHY WEDDERBURN, Lecturer in Industrial Sociology, Imperial College of Science and Technology, University of London

KAROL K. WEINSTEIN, Consulting Psychologist, Headstart Program, Worthington and Hunt & Associates, Chicago

HAROLD L. WILENSKY, Professor of Sociology, University of California, Berkeley

RICHARD H. WILLIAMS, Assistant to the Director for Special Projects, National Institute of Mental Health

VIVIAN WOOD, Assistant Professor of Social Work, University of Wisconsin

REFERENCES

NOTE. In this volume the figures in parentheses
refer to the pages on which the reference appears.

Abraham, Karl. 1913. Some Remarks on the Role
of Grandparent in the Psychology of Neurosis. In *Clinical Papers and Essays in Psychoanalysis*, vol. 1. New York: Basic Books, 1955.
(280)

Adland, Marvin L. 1947. Review, Case Studies,
Therapy and Interpretation of Acute Exhaustive Psychoses. *Psychiatric Quarterly* 21:38–
69. (488)

"Aging and the Aged." 1961. *The University
of Chicago Reports* 12, no. 2 (November).
(113)

"Aging in General." 1962. *The Gerontologist*
2:104–5. (17)

Albrecht, Milton. 1956. Does Literature Reflect
Common Values? *American Sociological Review* 21:722–29. (49)

Albrecht, Ruth. 1954. The Parental Responsibilities of Grandparents. *Marriage and Family
Living* 16:201–4. (280)

Aldrich, C. Knight, and Mendkoff, Ethel. 1963.
Relocation of the Aged and Disabled: A Mortality Study. Appears in this book as chapter
44.

Aldridge, G. J. 1956. The Role of Older People
in a Florida Retirement Community. *Geriat-
trics* 11:223–26. (500)

———. 1959. Informal Social Relationships in a
Retirement Community. *Marriage and Family
Living* 21:70–73 (30)

Allport, Floyd H. 1924. *Social Psychology*. Boston: Houghton Mifflin Co. (27)

Allport, Gordon W. 1937. *Personality, A Psychological Interpretation*. New York: Henry
Holt. (435)

Angyal, Andras. 1965. *Neurosis and Treatment:
A Holistic Theory*. New York: John Wiley
and Sons, Inc. (391, 400)

*Annals of the American Academy of Political
and Social Science*. 1961. "Teen-Age Culture."
Vol. 338 (November). (20)

Anonymous. 1946. Ageing in Man and Other
Animals. *Nature* 158:276–80. (103)

Anonymous. 1952. Do Americans Believe in
God? *Catholic Digest* 17:1–5. (500)

Apple, Dorrian. 1954. "Grandparents and Grandchildren: A Sociological and Psychological
Study of Their Relationship." Unpublished
Ph.D. dissertation, Radcliffe College, 1954.
(280)

———. 1956. The Social Structure of Grandparenthood. *American Anthropologist* 58:656–
63. (280)

Ariès, Philippe. 1962. *Centuries of Childhood:
A Social History of Family Life*. Translated
by Robert Bladick. New York: Alfred A.
Knopf. (532)

Arth, Malcolm. 1962. American Culture and the
Phenomenon of Friendship in the Aged. In
Social and Psychological Aspects of Aging,
edited by Clark Tibbitts and Wilma Donahue.
New York: Columbia University Press. (391,
398)

———. 1965. "The Role of the Aged in a West
African Village." Paper read at the annual
meeting of the Gerontological Society, Los
Angeles, November, 1965. (434)

Atkin, S. 1940. Discussion of the Paper by M. R.
Kaufman, Old Age and Aging. *American
Journal of Orthopsychiatry* 10:79–83. (125)

August, H. E. 1956. Psychological Aspects of
Personal Adjustment. In *Potentialities of
Women in the Middle Years*, edited by Irma
F. Gross. East Lansing, Michigan: Michigan
State University Press. (195)

Axelrod, Morris. 1956. Urban Structure and Social Participation. *American Sociological Review*, 21:13–18. (252)

Axelson, Leland J. 1960. Personal Adjustments
in the Postparental Period. *Marriage and Family Living* 22:66–70. (268)

Babkin, B. P. 1951. *Pavlov: A Biography*. London: Gollancz. (112)

Bakke, E. W. 1934. *The Unemployed Man*. New
York: E. P. Dutton & Co. (322)

———. 1940. *Citizens Without Work*. New Haven: Yale University Press. (322)

Balint, Michael. 1951. The Psychological Problems of Growing Old. In *Problems in Human
Pleasure and Behavior*. London: Hogarth.
(494)

Barber, Bernard. 1961. Family Status, Local-
Community Status, and Social Stratification:
Three Types of Social Ranking. *Pacific Socio-
logical Review* 4, no. 1:3–10. (252)

Barker, Roger G. 1960. Ecology and Motivation.
In *Nebraska Symposium on Motivation*, edited

by M. R. Jones. Lincoln: University of Nebraska Press. (453, 460)

——. 1968. *Ecological Psychology: Concepts and Methods for Studying the Environment of Human Behavior.* Stanford: Stanford University Press. (453)

Barker, Roger G., and Barker, Louise S. 1961 I. The Psychological Ecology of Old People in Midwest, Kansas and Yoredale, Yorkshire. Appears in this book as chapter 50. (123)

——. 1961 II. Units for the Comparative Study of Culture. In *Studying Personality Cross Culturally*, edited by B. Kaplan. New York: Harper and Row, Publishers, Inc. (453–60)

Barker, Roger G., and Wright, H. F. 1955. *Midwest and its Children.* New York: Harper and Row Publishers, Inc. (453, 454)

Barnacle, C. H. 1949. Psychiatric Implications of the Climacteric. *American Practitioner* 4:154–57. (195)

Barnouw, V. 1963. *Culture and Personality.* Homewood, Ill.: Dorsey Press. (435)

Barron, Milton L. 1953. Minority Group Characteristics of the Aged in American Society. *Journal of Gerontology* 8:477–82. (34)

——. 1954. Attacking Prejudices against the Aged. In *Growing with the Years.* New York State Legislative Committee on Problems of Aging, Legislative Document, no. 32. (36)

——. 1961. *The Aging American: An Introduction to Social Gerontology and Geriatrics.* New York: Thomas Y. Crowell Co. (36, 43, 44, 124, 500, 502, 502, 507)

Bayley, Nancy, and Oden, M. H. 1955. The Maintenance of Intellectual Ability in Gifted Adults. *Journal of Gerontology:* 10:91–107. (553, 562, 563, 569)

Beals, A. R. 1963. *Gopalpur, A South Indian Village.* New York: Holt, Rinehart & Winston, Co., Inc. (470)

Beauvoir, Simone de. 1953. *The Second Sex.* New York: Alfred A. Knopf. (36)

Becker, Howard S. 1951. The Professional Dance Musician and his Audience. *American Journal of Sociology* 58:136–44 (315)

——. 1952. The Career of the Chicago Public Schoolteacher. *American Journal of Sociology* 57:470–77. (316)

——. 1960. Notes on the Concepts of Commitment. *American Journal of Sociology* 66:32–40. 153, 154)

——. 1964. Personal Change in Adult Life. Appears in this book as Chapter 15. (363, 436)

Becker, Howard S., and Carper, James. 1956. The Development of Identification with an Occupation. *American Journal of Sociology* 61:289–98. (313)

Becker, Howard S., and Geer, Blanche. 1957. Participant Observation and Interviewing: A Comparison. *Human Organization* 16:28–32. (520)

——. 1960. Latent Culture: A Note on the Theory of Latent Social Roles. *Administrative Science Quarterly* 5:304–13. (152)

Becker, Howard S., and Strauss, Anselm L. 1956. Careers, Personality, and Adult Socialization. Appears in this book as Chapter 34. (152, 324)

Becker, Howard S.; Geer, Blanche; Hughes, Everett G.; and Strauss, Anselm L. 1961. *Boys in White: Student Culture in Medical School.* Chicago: University of Chicago Press. (150, 152, 155)

Beigler, Jerome S. 1957. Anxiety as an Aid in the Prognostication of Impending Death. A.M.A. *Archives of Neurology and Psychiatry* 77:171–77. (509)

Belbin, Eunice, and Belbin, R. M. 1966. New Careers in Middle Age. Appears in this book as chapter 36.

Bell, A., and Zubek, J. P. 1960. The Effect of Age on the Intellectual Performance of Mental Defectives. *Journal of Gerontology* 15:285–95. (563)

Bell, E. T. 1937. *Men of Mathematics.* New York: Simon & Schuster, Inc. (108)

Bell, Wendell, and Boat, M. D. 1957. Urban Neighborhoods and Informal Social Relations. *American Journal of Sociology* 43:381–98. (252)

Bell, Wendell, and Force, Maryanne T. 1956. Urban Neighborhood Types and Participation in Formal Associations. *American Sociological Review* 21 (February). (45)

Bellak, L. 1952. *Psychology of Physical Fitness.* New York: Grune & Stratton, Inc. (202)

Bellak, L., and Haselkorn, F. 1956. Psychological Aspects of Cardiac Illness and Rehabilitation. *Social Casework* 37:483 (202)

Bellin, Seymour S. 1960. *Family and Kinship in Later Years.* New York State Department of Mental Hygiene, Mental Health Research Unit Publication. (252)

——. 1961. "Relations Among Kindred in Later Years of Life: Parents, their Siblings and Adult Children." Paper read at American Sociology Association meeting, September 1, 1961, St. Louis, Mo. (220)

Bender, I. I. 1958. Changes in Religious Interest: A Retest after 15 Years. *Journal of Abnormal Social Psychology* 57:41–46. (552, 555)

Bender, Loretta. 1938. A Visual Motor Gestalt Test and its Clinical Use. *Research Monograph*, no. 3. New York: American Orthopsychiatry Association. (510)

Bendig, A. W. 1960. Age Differences in the Interscale Factor Structure of the Guilford-Zimmerman Temperament Survey. *Journal of Consulting Psychology* 24:134–38. (120)

Benedek, Therese. 1952. *Psychosexual Functions in Women.* New York: The Ronald Press Co. (195)

Benedict, Ruth. 1938. Continuities and Discontinuities in Culture Conditioning. *Psychiatry* I: 161–67. (22, 442)

Berelson, Bernard R.; Lazarsfeld, Paul F.; and McPhee, William N. 1954. *Voting: A Study of Opinion Formation in a Presidential Campaign.* Chicago: The University of Chicago Press. (42)

Berelson, Bernard R., and Salter, Patricia J. 1946. Majority and Minority Americans: An Analysis of Magazine Fiction. *Public Opinion Quarterly* 10:168–97. (47)

Berezin, Martin A. 1963. Some Intrapsychic Aspects of Aging. In *Normal Psychology of the Aging Process,* edited by N. A. Zinberg and I. Kaufman. New York: International Universities Press, Inc. (201)

Berger, Bennett M. 1960. How Long is a Generation? *British Journal of Sociology* 11:10–23. (22)

Berkman, Paul. 1964. *Deprivation and Mental Illness among the Community Aged.* Publication Pending. (226)

Berkowitz, B., and Green, R. F. 1963. Changes in Intellect with Age: I. Longitudinal Study of Wechsler-Bellevue Scores. *Journal of Genetic Psychology* 103:3–21. (563)

Bibring, E. 1953. The Mechanism of Depression. In *Affective Disorders,* edited by P. Greenacre. New York: International Universities Press, Inc. (208)

Bibring, Grete L. 1956. Psychiatry and Medical Practice in a General Hospital. *New England Journal of Medicine* 254:366. (202)

Birren, James E., ed. 1959. *Handbook on Aging and the Individual.* Chicago: University of Chicago Press. A selection appears in this book as Appendix A:545–51.

Birren, James E., and Botwinick, Jack. 1955. Speed of Response as a Function of Perceptual Difficulty and Age. *Journal of Gerontology* 10:433–36. (237)

Birren, James E.; Butler, Robert N.; Greenhouse, Samuel W.; Sokoloff, L.; and Yarrow, Marian, eds. 1963. *Human Aging: A Biological and Behavioral Study.* National Institute of Mental Health, PHS Publication #986. Washington, D.C.: U.S. Government Printing Office. (194, 236, 238)

Blau, Zena Smith. 1956. Changes in Status and Age Identification. *American Sociological Review* 21:198–203. (463)

———. 1961. Structural Constraints on Friendship in Old Age. *American Sociological Review* 26: 429–39. (220, 364, 391, 398, 399)

Blauner, Robert. 1966. Death and Social Structure. Appears in this book as chapter 58.

Blood, Robert O., Jr., and Wolfe, Donald M. 1960. *Husbands and Wives.* New York: Free Press of Glencoe, Inc. (290)

Bogdanoff, Earl, and Glass, Arnold. 1954. "The Sociology of the Public Case Worker in an Urban Area." Unpublished A.M. report, The University of Chicago. (313, 315)

Borkenau, Franz. 1955. The Concept of Death.

The Twentieth Century 157: 313–29. Reprinted in Fulton 1965. (536)

Bott, Elizabeth. 1957. *Family and Social Network.* London: Tavistock Publications, Ltd. (26, 252)

Bottenberg, R. A. and Ward, J. H., Jr. 1963. *Applied Multiple Linear Regression.* Unclassified technical documentary report, 6570th Personnel Research Laboratory, Aerospace Medical Division, Air Force Systems Command, Lackland Air Force Base, Texas. (412)

Botwinick, Jack. 1959. Drives, Expectancies, and Emotions. In Birren 1959. (274)

Botwinick, Jack, and Birren, James E. 1963. Mental Abilities and Psychomotor Responses in Healthy Aged Men. In Birren *et al.* 1963. (238)

Bowlby, John. 1958. The Nature of the Child's Tie to His Mother. *International Journal of Psychoanalysis* 39: 350–73 (391)

Braun, Rudolph. 1960. *Industrialisierung und Volksleben,* Erlenbach-Zurich: Reutsch. (250)

Breen, Leonard Z. 1960. The Aging Individual. In Tibbitts 1960. (36)

Breen, Leonard Z. *et al.* 1951. *The Adult Years.* Lafayette, Ind.: Department of Sociology, Purdue University. (38, 39, 45)

Brim, Orville G., Jr. 1960. Personality as Role-learning. In *Personality Development in Children,* edited by Irs Iscoe and Harold Stevenson. Austin: University of Texas Press. (148)

Britten, J., and Boulger, G. S. 1931. *A Biographical Index of Deceased British and Irish Botanists.* 2d ed. London: Taylor and France. (108)

Britten, R. H. 1931. Sex Differences in Physical Impairment in Adult Life. *American Journal of Hygiene* 13: 741–70. (129)

Brown, James S.; Mangalam, Joseph J.; and Schwarzweller, Harry K. 1961. "Kentucky Mountain Migration and the Stem Family: An American Variation on a Theme by LePlay." Paper given at meetings of the American Sociological Association, September 1, 1961. (252)

Brozek, Josef M. 1952. Personality of Young and Middle-Aged Normal Men: Item Analysis of A Psychosomatic Inventory. *Journal of Gerontology* 7: 410–18. (127)

Buber, Martin. 1957. Guilt and Guilt Feelings. *Psychiatry* 20: 114–29. (493)

Buhler, Charlotte. 1933. *Der Menschliche Lesbenslauf als psychologishes Problem.* Leipzig: Verlag von S. Hirzel. (77, 134, 138)

———. 1935. The Curve of Life as Studied in Biographies. *Journal of Applied Psychology* 19: 405–9. (138)

———. 1951. Maturation and Motivation. *Personality* 1: 184–211. (119)

———. 1957. Zur Psychologie des menscrlichen

Lenebslaufes. *Psychologische Rundschau* 8:
1–15. (119, 135)

———. 1961 I. Meaningful Living in the Mature
Years. In Kleemeier (ed.) 1961. (121, 368)

———. 1961 II. Old Age and Fulfillment of Life
with Consideration of the Use of Time in Old
Age. *Vita Humana* 4: 129–33. (135)

———. 1962. Genetics Aspects of the Self. *Annals
of New York Academy of Science* 96: 730–64.
(126, 135, 138)

Burchinal, Lee G. 1959 I. Comparisons of Factors Related to Adjustment in Pregnancy-
Provoked and Non-Pregnancy Provoked
Youthful Marriages. *Midwest Sociologist* 21:
92–96. (250)

———. 1959 II. How Successful Are School-age
Marriages? *Iowa Farm Science* 13: 7–10. (250)

Burgess, Ernest W. 1926. The Romantic Impulse
and Family Disorganization. *Survey* 57 (December): 290–295. (258)

———. 1950. Personal and Social Adjustment in
Old Age. In *The Aged and Society*, edited by
M. Derber. Champaign, Ill.: Industrial Rela-
tions Research Assn. (184)

———. 1960. Family Structure and Relationships.
In *Aging and Western Culture*, edited by Ernest W. Burgess. Chicago: University of Chicago Press. (469)

———. 1963. The Transition from Extended
Families to Nuclear Families. In Williams,
Tibbits, and Donahue 1963, vol. 2. (469)

Burgess, Ernest W. and Wallin, Paul. 1953. *Engagement and Marriage*. Philadelphia: J. P.
Lippincott Co. (258, 259)

Busse, Ewald W. 1959. Psychopathology. In Birren 1959. (493)

———. 1961. Psychoneurotic Reactions and Defense Mechanisms in the Aged. In *Psychopathology of Aging*, edited by Paul H. Hoch
and Joseph Zubin. New York: Grune & Stratton, Inc. (219)

Butler, Robert N. 1960. Intensive Psychotherapy
for the Hospitalized Aged. *Geriatrics* 15: 644–
53. (242, 486)

———. 1961. Re-awakening interests. *Nursing
Homes: Journal of American Nursing Home
Association* 10: 8–19. (486)

———. 1963. The Life Review: An Interpretation
of Reminiscence in the Aged. Appears in this
book as Chapter 54. (141, 242, 534)

———. February 1963. The Façade of Chronological Age. Appears in this book as chapter
25.

Butler, Robert N. and Perlin S. 1957. "Depressive
Reactions in the Aged: The Function of Denial, Awareness and Insight." 113th annual
meeting. American Psychiatric Association.
Chicago, May, 1957. (239)

Butler, Robert N. *et al.* 1965. Relationships of
Senile Manifestations and Chronic Brain Syndromes to Cerebral Circulation and Metabolism. *Journal of Psychiatric Research* 3: 229–
38. (241)

Cain, Leonard D., Jr. 1963. *Age Status and Social Structure*. New York: Holt, Rinehart &
Winston, Inc. (19)

Cajori, F. 1937. *A History of Mathematics*, 2d
ed. New York: The Macmillan Co. (108)

Camargo, O. and Preston, G. H. 1945. What
Happens to Patients Who Are Hospitalized
for the First Time When Over 65? *American
Journal of Psychiatry* 102: 168–73. (401, 407)

Campbell, Angus. 1962. Social and Psychological
Determinants of Voting Behavior. In Donahue
and Tibbitts 1962. (17, 33, 361)

Campbell, Angus, and others. 1960. *The American Voter*. New York: John Wiley and Sons,
Inc. (17)

Cannon, Walter B. 1942. "Voodoo" Death.
American Anthropologist 44: 169–81. (488)

Caplow, T., and McGee R. J. P. 1958. *The Academic Market Place*. New York: Basic Books,
Inc. (104)

Carmichael, H. T., and Noonan, W. J. 1941. The
Effects of Testosterone Propionate in Impotence. *American Journal of Psychiatry* 97:
919–43. (275)

Carp, Frances M. 1965. Effects of Improved
Housing on the Lives of Older People. Appears in this book as chapter 45.

———. 1961. *A Future for the Aged: The Residents of Victoria Plaza*. Austin: University of
Texas Press. (410)

Carp, Frances M., and Carp, A. 1961. "Demographic and Psychological Characteristics of
Applicants for Public Housing for the Aged
in San Antonio, Texas." Mimeograph. Austin:
University of Texas Press. (409, 411)

Cattell, R. B. 1963. The Theory of Fluid and
Crystallized Intelligence: A Critical Experiment. *Journal of Educational Psychology*. 54:
1–22. (557)

Cavan, Ruth S. 1959. Unemployment—Crisis of
the Common Man. *Marriage and Family Living* 21 (May 1959): 139–46. (248)

———. 1962. Self and Role in Adjustment during
Old Age. In *Human Behavior and Social
Processes*, edited by Arnold M. Rose. Boston,
Mass.: Houghton Mifflin Co. (184, 280, 284,
366)

———. 1963. *The American Family*. 3d ed. New
York: Thomas Y. Crowell Co. (248, 263)

Cavan, Ruth S.; Burgess, Ernest W.; Havighurst,
R. W.; and Goldhammer, H. 1949. *Personal
Adjustment in Old Age*. Chicago: Science Re-
search Associates. (124, 125, 503, 507)

Chalke, H. D. 1957. Patients without Relatives.
University of Leeds Medical Journal, June,
1957. (221)

Christ, E. 1965. The Retired Stamp Collector:
Economic and Other Functions of Systema-

tized Leisure Activity. In Rose and Peterson. 1965. (188)

Christe, Richard, and Merton, Robert K. 1958. Procedures for the Sociological Study of the Values Climate of Medical Schools. *Journal of Medical Education* 33, part 2: 125–53. (149)

Clague, Ewan. 1962. Demographic Trends and Their Significance. In *The Changing American Population. A Report of the Arden House Conference*, edited by Hoke S. Simpson. New York: Institute of Life Insurance. (21)

Clark, Lincoln H., ed. 1955 vol. 51. *The Life Cycle and Consumer Behavior. Consumer Behavior*, New York: New York University Press. (290)

Clark, Margaret. 1967. The Anthropology of Aging: A New Area for Studies of Culture and Personality. Appears in this book as Chapter 48.

Clark, Margaret, and Anderson, B. G. 1967. *Culture and Aging: An Anthropological Study of Older Americans*. Springfield, Ill.: Charles C Thomas. (442)

Cleveland, S. E. and Johnson, D. L. 1962. Personality Patterns in Young Males with Coronary Disease. *Psychosomatic Medicine* 24: 600. (202)

Cloward, Richard A., and Ohlin, Lloyd E. 1960. *Delinquency and Opportunity: A Theory of Delinquent Gangs*. New York: Free Press of Glencoe. (152)

Cloward, Richard A., et al. 1960. *Theoretical Studies in Social Organization of the Prison*. New York: Social Science Research Council. (151)

Cobbett, W. W. 1929, 1930. *Cobbett's Cyclopedia Survey of Chamber Music*. London: Oxford University Press. (108)

Cohen, Albert K. 1955. *Delinquent Boys: The Culture of a Gang*. New York: Free Press of Glencoe. (152)

Coleman, James. 1961. *The Adolescent Society*. New York: Free Press of Glencoe. (20)

Collins, Orvis. 1946. Ethnic Behavior in Industry: Sponsorship and Rejection in a New England Factory. *American Journal of Sociology* 51: 293–98. (313)

Colvin, H. M. 1954. *Biographical Dictionary of British Architects, 1660–1840*. London: J. Murray. (108)

Comfort, A. 1956. *The Biology of Senescence*. London: Routledge & Kegan Paul. (551)

Connolly, J. 1962. The Social and Medical Circumstances of Old People Admitted to a Psychiatric Hospital. *The Medical Officer*, August 1962: 95–100. (221)

Corey, L. 1935. *The Crisis of the Middle Class*. New York: Covici-Friede (325)

Corson, John J., and McConnell, John W. 1956. *Economic Needs of Older People*. New York: The Twentieth Century Fund. (43)

Covalt, Nila K. 1958. The Meaning of Religion to Older People—The Medical Perspective. In *Organized Religion and the Older Person*, edited by D. L. Scudder. Gainesville, Florida: University of Florida Press. (505)

———. 1960. The Meaning of Religion to Older People. *Geriatrics* 15: 658–64. (498)

Cowgill, Donald O. 1965. "Social Life of the Aging in Thailand." Paper read at the annual meeting of the Gerontological Society, Los Angeles, November 13, 1965. (434)

Cressey, Paul G. 1932. *The Taxi-Dance Hall*. Chicago: University of Chicago Press. (315)

Cressey, Donald R., ed. 1961. *The Prison: Studies in Institutional Organization*. New York: Holt, Rinehart and Winston, Inc. (151)

Crittenden, John. 1963. Aging and Political Participation. *Western Political Quarterly* 16: 323–31.

Culver, E. T. 1961. *New Church Programs with the Aging*. New York: Association Press. (507)

Cumming, Elaine. 1963. Further Thoughts on the Theory of Disengagement. *UNESCO International Social Science Bulletin* 15: 377–93. (159, 173, 184–89, 363, 534)

Cumming, Elaine and Henry, William H. 1961. *Growing Old: The Process of Disengagement*. New York: Basic Books, Inc. (33, 39, 45, 123, 124, 159, 161, 163, 173, 181, 184–89, 201, 207, 221, 363, 502, 534)

Cumming, Elaine, and Parlegreco, Mary Lou. 1961. The Very Old. In Cumming and Henry 1961. (218)

Cumming, Elaine, and Schneider, David M. 1961. Sibling Solidarity: A Property of American Kinship. *American Anthropologist* 63: 498–507. (252, 301)

Cumming, Elaine; Dean, Lois R.; Newell, David S.; and McCaffrey, Isabel. 1960. Disengagement: A Tentative Theory of Aging. *Sociometry* 23: 23–35. (33, 45, 123, 159, 184)

Daedalus. 1962. Youth, Change and Challenge. *Journal of the American Academy of Arts and Sciences*, Winter 1962. (20)

Dalton, Melville 1951. Informal Factors in Career Achievement. *American Journal of Sociology* 56: 407–15. (313)

Damon, A. 1965. Discrepancies between Findings of Longitudinal and Cross-sectional Studies in Adult Life: Physique and Physiology. *Human Development* 8: 16–22. (564)

Dana, R. H. 1957. A Comparison of Four Verbal Subtests on the Wechsler-Bellevue, Form I, and the WAIS. *Journal of Clinical Psychology* 13: 70–71. (482)

Dastur, D. K., et al. 1963. Effects of Aging on Cerebral Circulation and Metabolism in Man. In *Human Aging: A Biological and Behavioral Study*, edited by James E. Birren. PHS publication #986. Washington, D.C.: U.S. Government Printing Office. (238)

Davidson, P. E. and Anderson, H. D. 1937. *Occupational Mobility in an American Community.* Stanford: Stanford University Press. (323)

Davis, Fred. 1960. Uncertainty in Medical Prognosis. *American Journal of Sociology*, July 1960: 41–47. (526)

Davis, Kingsley. 1940. The Sociology of Parent-Youth Conflict. *American Sociological Review* 5: 523–35. (22)

Davis, Kingsley and Coombs, J. W. 1950. The Sociology of an Aging Population. In *The Social and Biological Challenge of Our Aging Population,* edited by I. Galdston. New York: Columbia University Press. (469)

Davis, M. E. 1965. Estrogen and the Aging Process. In *Yearbook of Obstetrics and Gynecology, 1964–65.* Chicago: Year Book Medical Publishers. (269)

Dean, Dwight G. 1961. Alienation: Its Meaning and Measurement. *American Sociological Review* 26: 753–58. (220, 227)

Dean, Lois R. 1960. Aging and the Decline of Instrumentality. *Journal of Gerontology* 15: 440–46. (123)

de Charms, R., and Moeller, G. H. 1962. Values Expressed in American Children's Readers: 1800–1950. *Journal of Abnormal Social Psychology* 64: 136–42. (554)

de Grazia, Sebastian. 1962. *Of Time, Work, and Leisure.* New York: The Twentieth Century Fund. (361)

Demming, J. A., and Pressey, S. L. 1957. Tests "Indigenous" to the Adult and Older Years. *Journal of Consulting Psychology* 4: 144–48. (557)

Dennis, Wayne. 1956. Age and Achievement: A Critique. *Journal of Gerontology* 11: 331–33. (114)

———. 1966. Creative Productivity between the Ages of 20 and 80 Years. Appears in this book as Chapter 12.

Dentler, Robert A., and Pineo, Peter C. 1960. Marriage Adjustment, Sexual Adjustment and Personal Growth of Husbands: A Panel Study. *Marriage and Family Living* 22: 45–48. (259)

Deutsch, Helene. 1945. *The Psychology of Women. Vol. 2, Motherhood.* New York: Grune & Stratton, Inc. (195, 200, 270)

Deutscher, Irwin. 1962. Socialization for Postparental Life. In *Human Behavior and Social Process,* edited by Arnold M. Rose. Boston: Houghton Mifflin Co. (268).

———. 1964. The Quality of Postparental Life. Appears in this book as Chapter 29.

Donahue, Wilma, ed. 1955. *Earning Opportunities for Older Workers.* Ann Arbor: University of Michigan: Division of Gerontology. (359)

Donahue, Wilma; Orbach, Harold L.; and Pollak, Otto. 1960. Retirement: The Emerging Pattern. In Tibbitts 1960. (357, 360)

Donahue, Wilma, and Tibbitts, Clark, eds. 1962. *Politics of Age.* Ann Arbor: University of Michigan: Division of Gerontology. (17)

Dotson, F. 1951. Patterns of Voluntary Association among Urban Working Class Families. *American Sociological Review* 16: 689–93. (252)

Dovenmuehle, R. H., and Verwoerdt, A. 1962. Physical Illness and Depressive Symptomatology. I: Incidence of Depressive Symptoms in Hospitalized Cardiac Patients. *Journal of Gerontology* 9: 932.

———. 1963. Physical Illness and Depressive Symptomatology. II: Factors of Length and Severity of Illness and Frequency of Hospitalization. *Journal of Gerontology* 18: 260. (202)

Dube, S. C. 1955. *Indian Village.* London: Routledge & Kegan Paul. (470, 474)

Dubin, Robert. 1956. Industrial Workers' Worlds. *Social Problems* 3: 131–42. (360)

———. 1958. *The World of Work.* Englewood Cliffs, N.J.: Prentice-Hall, Inc. (324)

Dulles, Rhea Foster. 1950. *America Learns to Play.* New York: Appleton-Century-Crofts, Inc. (367)

Dunham, H. W. 1945. Sociological Aspects of Mental Disorders in Later Life. In *Mental Disorders in Later Life,* edited by O. J. Kaplan. Stanford: Stanford University Press. (469)

Durkheim, Emile. 1947. Some Notes on Occupational Groups. In *The Division of Labor in Society,* translated by George Simpson. New York: Free Press of Glencoe. (322)

———. 1960. *Suicide.* New York: Free Press of Glencoe. (220, 491)

Duvall, Evelyn M. 1962. *Family Development.* Philadelphia: J. P. Lippincott Co. (287)

Dykman, R. A.; Heimann, E. K.; and Kerr, W. A. 1952. Lifetime Worry Patterns of Three Diverse Adult Cultural Groups. *Journal of Social Psychology* 35: 91–100. (131)

Eisdorfer, C. 1963. The WAIS Performance of the Aged: A Retest Evaluation. *Journal of Gerontology* 18: 169–72. (563)

Eisenberg, P., and Lazarsfeld, P. 1938. The Psychological Effect of Unemployment. *Psychological Bulletin* 35: 358–90. (322)

Eisenstadt, S. N. 1956. *From Generation to Generation: Age Groups and the Social Structure.* New York: Free Press of Glencoe. (22, 322)

Eissler, Kurt R. 1955. *The Psychiatrist and the Dying Patient.* New York: International Universities Press. (538)

———. 1959. On Isolation. In *The Psychoanalytic Study of the Child.* New York: International Universities Press, Inc. (220)

England, Ralph W., Jr. 1960. Images of Love and Courtship in Family Magazine Fiction.

578

Epstein, A. 1931. Facing Old Age. In *The Care of the Aged*, edited by I. M. Rubinow. Chicago: University of Chicago Press. (469)

Epstein, Lenore A., and Murray, Janet H. 1967. The Aged Population of the U.S.: The 1963 Social Security Survey of the Aged. Dept. HEW, Research Report no. 19, U.S. Gov. Printing Office. A selection appears in this book as chapter 38.

Erikson, Erik H. 1950. *Childhood and Society*. New York: W. W. Norton & Co., Inc. (86, 320)

———. 1953. Growth and Crisis of the "Health Personality." In *Personality in Nature, Society and Culture*, edited by C. Kluckhohn. H. A. Murray, and D. M. Schneider. New York: Knopf. (86)

———. 1956. The Problem of Ego Identity. *Journal of American Psychoanalysts Association* 4: 56–121. (86)

———. 1959. Identity and the Life-cycle. *Psychological Issues*, Monograph I. New York: International Universities Press, Inc. (86, 126, 130, 391, 496)

———. 1963. *Childhood and Society*, 2d ed. New York: W. W. Norton, & Co., Inc. A selection appears in this book as Chapter 8. (86, 137)

Eron, Leonard D. 1955. Effect of Medical Education on Medical Students. *Journal of Medical Education* 10: 559–66. (149)

Ewalt, J. R.; Strecker, E. A.; and Erbaugh, F. G. 1957. *Practical Clinical Psychiatry*. New York: McGraw-Hill Book Co., Inc. (207)

Falek, A.; Kallman, F. J.; Lorge, I.; and Jarvik, L. F. 1960. Longevity and Intellectual Variation in a Senescent Twin Population. *Journal of Gerontology* 15: 305–9. (563)

Faris, Robert E. L. 1947. Interactions of Generations and Family Stability. *American Sociological Review* 12: 159–64. (248)

Faris, Robert E. L., and Dunham, H. Warren. 1960. *Mental Disorders in Urban Areas*. New York: Hafner Pub. Co., Inc. (220)

Feifel, Herman. 1956. Older Persons Look at Death. *Geriatrics* 11: 127–30. (505)

———. 1957. Judgment of Time in Younger and Older Persons. *Journal of Gerontology* 12: 71–74. (510)

Ferenczi, Sandor. 1913. The Grandfather Complex. In *Further Contributions to the Theory and Techniques of Psychoanalysis*. New York: Basic Books, Inc. (280)

Ferreira, A. J. 1964. The Intimacy Need in Psychotherapy. *American Journal of Psychoanalysis* 24: 190–94. (391)

Fessler, L. 1950. Psychopathology of Climacteric Depression. *Psychoanalytic Quarterly* 19: 28–42. (195)

Fichter, J. H. 1954. *Social Relations in the Urban Parish*. Chicago: University of Chicago Press. (501)

Filer, R. N., and O'Connell, D. D. 1962. A Useful Contribution for the Aging. *Journal of Gerontology* 17: 51–57. (123, 135)

Finkle, A. L. *et al.* 1959. Sexual Potence in Aging Males. *Journal of the American Medical Association* 170: 113–15. (273)

Fisher, R. A. 1950. *Statistical Methods for Research Workers*. New York: Hafner Publishing Company, Inc. (515)

Fiske (Lowenthal), Marjorie. 1960. *Some Social Dimensions of Psychiatric Disorders in Old Age*. San Francisco: Langley Porter Neuropsychiatric Institute. (508)

———. 1961. Geriatric Mental Illness: Methodologic and Social Aspects. *Geriatrics* 16: 306–10. (501)

Form, W. H., and Miller, D. C. 1949. Occupational Career Pattern as a Sociological Instrument. *American Journal of Sociology* 54: 317–29. (323)

Foster, G. M. 1965. Peasant Society and the Image of Limited Good. *American Anthropologist* 67: 293–315. (442)

Foster, J. C., and Taylor, G. A. 1920. The Application of Mental Tests to Persons over 50. *Journal of Applied Psychology* 4: 39–58. (563)

Fox, H. M.; Rizzo, N. D.; and Gifford, S. 1954. Psychological Observations of Patients Undergoing Mitral Surgery. *American Heart Journal* 48: 645. (202)

Frank, L. K. 1943. The Older Person in the Changing Social Scene. In *New Goals for Old Age*, edited by G. Lawton. New York: Columbia University Press (469)

Frazer, James G. 1933, 1934, 1936. *The Fear of the Dead in Primitive Religion*, 3 vols. London: The Macmillan Co. (533)

Frazier, E. Franklin. 1957. The Impact of Urban Civilization upon Negro Family Life. In *Cities and Society*, edited by P. K. Hatt and H. S. Reiss, Jr. New York: Free Press of Glencoe. (252)

Freeman, H., and Pincus, G. 1963. Endocrine Agents Other than the Adrenal Forms. In *Clinical Principles and Drugs in Aging*, edited by J. T. Freeman. Springfield, Ill.: Charles C Thomas. (269)

Freidson, Eliot. *Patients' Views of Medical Practice*. New York: Russell Sage Foundation. (149)

Frenkel-Brunswik, Else 1963. Adjustments and Reorientation in the Course of the Life Span. Appears in this book as Chapter 7.

Freud, Sigmund. 1959. Inhibitions, Symptoms and Anxiety. In *The Complete Works of Sigmund Freud*, vol. 22, translated by J. Strachey. London: Hogarth Press and the Institute for Psychoanalysis. (208)

Friedberg, C. J. 1956. *Disease of the Heart.* Philadelphia: W. B. Saunders Co. (202)

Friedmann, E. A., and Havighurst, Robert J. 1954. *The Meaning of Work and Retirement.* Chicago: University of Chicago Press. (360, 362, 363, 463)

Friedmann, Georges. 1961. *The Anatomy of Work.* New York: Free Press. (359)

Friis, Hennig, and Manniche, Erik. 1961. Old People in a Low-Income Area in Copenhagen. In *Socialforskningsinst.* Copenhagen: Technisk Forlag. (220)

Froimovich, J., *et al.* 1962. *Estrogenic Response of the Vagina in Geriatric Patients.* In *Medical and Clinical Aspects of Aging,* edited by H. Blumenthal. New York: Columbia University Press. (269)

Fromm, E. 1941. *Escape from Freedom.* New York: Holt, Rinehart & Winston, Inc. (138)

Fromm-Reichmann, Frieda. 1950. *Principles of Intensive Psychotherapy.* Chicago: University of Chicago Press. (220, 434)

———. 1959. Loneliness. *Psychiatry* 22: 1–15. Also in *Psychoanalysis and Psychotherapy,* edited by Dexter M. Bullard. Chicago: University of Chicago Press. (488)

———. 1960. Psychiatric Aspects of Anxiety. In *Identity and Anxiety,* edited by M. Stein, A. J. Vidich, and D. M. White. New York: Free Press of Glencoe. (208)

Fulton, Robert L. 1961. Symposium: Death Attitudes. *Journal of Gerontology* 16: 63–65. (505)

———. 1965. *Death and Identity.* New York: John Wiley & Sons, Inc. (534)

Gass, Gertrude Zemon. 1959. Counseling Implications of Woman's Changing Role. *Personnel and Guidance Journal* 37: 482–87. (267)

Getzels, Jacob W., and Walsh, J. J. 1958. The Method of Paired Direct and Projective Questionnaires in the Study of Attitude Structure and Socialization. *Psychological Monographs,* 77, whole no. 454. (26)

Glaser, Barney G., and Strauss, Anselm L. 1964. Awareness Contexts and Social Interaction. *American Sociological Review* 29. 669–78. (526)

———. 1965. *Awareness of Dying.* Chicago: Aldine Press. (535, 536)

———. 1965. Temporal Aspects of Dying as a Non-scheduled Status Passage. Appears in this book as chapter 57.

Glasstone, S. 1958. *Sourcebook on Atomic Energy.* 2d ed. Princeton, N.J.: D. Van Nostrand Co., Inc. (101)

Glick, Paul C. 1955. Life Cycle of the Family. *Marriage and Family Relations* 17: 3–9. (6, 188)

Glick, Paul C.; Heer, David M.; and Beresford, John C. 1963. Family Formation and Family Composition: Trends and Prospects. In Sussman, 1963. (12)

Glock, C. Y. 1962. On the Study of Religious Commitment. *Religious Education* 57: S-98–S-110. (498)

Gluckman, M. 1955. *Custom and Conflict in Africa.* Oxford: Basil Blackwell. (463)

Goffman, Erving. 1952. On Cooling the Mark Out: Some Aspects of Adaptation to Failure. *Psychiatry* 15: 451–63. (315, 324, 371, 373)

———. 1955. On Face-Work. *Psychiatry* 18: 213–31. (371)

———. 1956. Embarrassment and Social Organization. *American Journal of Sociology* 62: 264–71. (371)

———. 1961. *Asylums: Essays on the Social Situation of Mental Patients and Other Inmates.* Garden City: Doubleday & Co., Inc. (152)

Goldberg, David. 1960. Some Recent Developments in Fertility Research. In Reprint #7, *Demographic and Economic Change in Developed Countries.* Princeton, N.J.: Princeton University Press. (253)

Goldfarb, Alvin. 1956. The Rationale for Psychotherapy with Older Persons. *American Journal Medical Science* 232: 181–85. (494)

———. 1965. Psychodynamics and the Three-generation Family. In Shanas and Streib 1965. (391)

Goldstein, Rhoda. 1954. "The Professional Nurse in the Hospital Bureaucracy." Unpublished Ph.D. thesis, University of Chicago. (314)

Goode, William J. 1963. Industrialization and Family Change. In *Industrialization and Society,* edited by Bert F. Hoselitz and Wilbert E. Moore. Paris: Unesco-Mouton. (296)

Goody, Jack. 1962. *Death, Property and the Ancestors.* Stanford: Stanford University Press. (532, 533, 537)

Gordon, Margaret S. 1960. Aging and Income Security. In Tibbitts 1960. (43)

———. 1961. Work and Patterns of Retirement. In Kleemeier (ed.) 1961. (360)

Gorer, G. 1948. *The American People, A Study in National Character.* New York: W. W. Norton & Co., Inc. (440)

Gray, R. M. and Moberg, David O. 1962. *The Church and the Older Person.* Grand Rapids: Wm. B. Eerdmans Publishing Co. (500, 506)

Greenberg, Clement. 1953. Work and Leisure under Industrialism. *Commentary* 16: 58. (367)

Greenfield, Sidney M. 1961. Industrialization and the Family in Sociological Theory. *American Journal of Sociology* 76: 312–22. (250)

Greer, Scott. 1956. Urbanism Reconsidered. *American Sociological Review* 21: 22–25. (252)

Gregory, Francis W. and Neu, Irene D. 1952. The American Industrial Elite in the 1870's. In *Men in Business,* edited by William Miller. Cambridge, Mass.: Harvard University Press. (14)

Gross, Edward. 1958. *Work and Society*. New York: Thomas Y. Crowell Co. (324)

———. 1961. A Functional Approach to Leisure Analysis. *Social Problems* 9: 2. (366, 368)

Gross, Edward, and Stone, Gregory P. (no date). "Embarrassment and the Analysis of Role Requirements." Paper read at the meetings of the Midwest Sociology Society, Milwaukee, Wisconsin. (371, 373)

Grotjahn, Martin. 1940. Psychoanalytic Investigation of a Seventy-One-Year-Old Man with Senile Dementia. *Psychoanalytic Quarterly* 9: 80–97. (488)

———. 1951. Some Analytic Observations about the Process of Growing Old. In *Psychoanalysis and Social Science*, vol. 3, edited by G. Roheim. New York: International Universities Press, Inc. (494)

Gruenberg, Ernest M. 1954. Community Conditions and Psychoses of the Elderly. *The American Journal of Psychiatry* 110: 888–96. (221)

Gurin, G.; Veroff, J.; and Feld, Sheila 1960. *Americans View Their Mental Health*. Joint Commission on Mental Illness and Health, Monograph Series, no. 4. New York: Basic Books, Inc. (122, 125, 129, 130, 207, 210)

Gurwell, John K. 1941. Governors of the States. In *State Government* 14, July. (17)

Gutmann, David L. 1964. An Exploration of Ego Configurations in Middle and Later Life. In Neugarten and Associates 1964. (167, 207)

———. 1966. Mayan Aging—A Comparative TAT Study. *Psychiatry* 29: 246–59. (452)

———. 1967. Aging among the Highland Maya: A Comparative Study. Appears in this book as chapter 49. (168)

Gutmann, David L.; Henry, William E.; and Neugarten, Bernice L. 1959. "Personality Development in Middle-Aged Men." Unpublished paper read at American Psychological Association meeting, Cincinnati, September, 1959. (207)

Habenstein, Robert U. 1968. The Social Organization of Death. In *International Encyclopedia of the Social Sciences*. Edited by David L. Sills. New York: The Macmillan Company and The Free Press. (536)

Haber, Lawrence D. 1962. Age and Integration Setting: A Re-appraisal of the Changing American Parent. *American Sociological Review* 27: 682–89. (9)

Hacker, Helen Mayer. 1951. Women as a Minority Group. *Social Forces* 30, October. (36)

Hall, E. T. 1959. *The Silent Language*. New York: Doubleday & Co., Inc. (481)

Hall, G. Stanley. 1923. *Senescence: The Last Half of Life*. New York: Appleton-Century-Crofts, Inc. (42)

Hall, Oswald. 1948. The Stages in a Medical Career. *American Journal of Sociology* 53: 332. (312, 313, 319)

Haller, A. O. 1961. The Urban Family. *American Journal of Sociology* 66: 621–22. (250)

Hamilton, G. V. 1942. Changes in Personality and Psychosexual Phenomena with Age. In *Problems of Aging*, 2d ed., edited by E. V. Cowdry. Baltimore: The Williams and Wilkins Co. (129)

Harlan, William H. 1964. Social Status of the Aged in Three Indian Villages. Appears in this book as Chapter 52.

Harlow, Harry F., and Zimmermann, Robert R. 1959. Affectional Responses in the Infant Monkey. *Science* 130: 421–32. (391)

Hart, Hornell. 1933. Changing Attitudes and Interests. In *Recent Social Trends*. Report of the President's Committee on Social Trends. 2 vols. New York: McGraw-Hill Book Co., Inc. (47)

Hartmann, H. 1951. Ego Psychology and the Problem of Adaptation. In *Organization and Pathology of Thought*, translated by D. Rapport. New York: Columbia University Press. (510)

Hastings, D. W. 1963. *Impotence and Frigidity*. Boston: Little, Brown & Co., Inc. (278)

Havighurst, Robert J. 1954. Flexibility and the Social Roles of the Retired. *American Journal of Sociology* 59: 309. (467)

———. 1957. I. The Social Competence of Middle-aged People. *Genetic Psychology Monographs* 56: 297–395. (45, 347)

———. 1957. II. The Leisure Activities of the Middle Class. *American Journal of Sociology* 53: 152–62. (137)

Havighurst, Robert J., and Albrecht, Ruth. 1953. *Older People*. New York: Longmans, Green & Co., Inc. (126, 131, 502)

Havighurst, Robert J.; Bowman, Paul H.; Liddle, Gordon P.; Matthews, C. V.; and Pierce, J. V. 1962. *Growing Up in River City*. New York: John Wiley & Sons, Inc. (137)

Havighurst, Robert J., and Feigenbaum, Kenneth 1959. Leisure and Life Style. Appears in this book as Chapter 37.

Havighurst, Robert J.; Neugarten, Bernice L.; and Tobin, Sheldon S. 1963. Disengagement and Patterns of Aging. Appears in this book as Chapter 16. (186, 363)

Heller, C. G., and Maddock, W. O. 1947. The Clinical Use of Testosterone in the Male. *Vitamins Hormones* 5: 393–423. (278)

Hendin, Herbert. 1964. *Suicide and Scandinavia*. New York and London: Grune & Stratton, Inc. (219)

Henry, J. 1956. *Culture against Man*. New York: Random House, Inc. (434)

Henry, William E. 1963. "The Theory of Intrinsic Disengagement." Paper presented at the International Gerontological Research

Seminar, Markaryd, Sweden. (159, 173, 184, 186, 363)

Hertz, Robert. 1960. The Collective Representation of Death. In *Death and the Right Hand*, translated by Rodney and Claudia Needham. Aberdeen: Cohen and West. (532, 533)

Hess, Robert D. 1962. "High School Antecedents of Young Adults' Performance." Mimeograph. The Committee on Human Development, University of Chicago. (137)

Hilditch, T. P. 1911. *A Concise History of Chemistry*. New York: D. Van Nostrand Co., Inc. (108)

Hill, Reuben. 1961. Patterns of Decision Making and the Accumulation of Family Assets. In *Household Decision Making*, edited by Nelson Foote. New York: New York University Press. (287)

———. 1964. Methodological Issues in Family Development Research. *Family Process* 3, no. 1: 186–206. (290)

———. 1965. Decision Making and the Family Life Cycle. Appears in this book as Chapter 32.

Hoagland, H. 1943. The Chemistry of Time. *Scientific Monthly* 56: 56–61. (485)

Hobart, Charles W. 1958. Disillusionment in Marriage and Romanticism. *Marriage and Family Living* 20: 156–62. (258)

Hollingshead, August B., and Redlich, Frederick C. 1958. *Social Class and Mental Illness: A Community Study*. New York: John Wiley & Sons, Inc. (210, 220)

Honigmann, J. J. 1954. *Culture and Personality*. New York: Harper & Row Publishers, Inc. (435)

Honzik, Marjorie P. 1966. "A 30-year Study of Personality Consistency and Change." Unpublished paper read at meetings of the American Psychological Association, New York, September, 1966. (137)

Hoskins, R. G. 1944. Psychological Treatment of the Menopause. *Journal of Clinical Endocrinology* 4: 605–10. (195)

Hoyt, D. P. 1965. The Relationship between College Grades and Adult Achievement: A Review of the Literature. *ACT Research Reports*, September 1965, no. 7. Iowa City, Iowa: American College Testing Program. (139)

Hoyt, G. C. 1954. The Life of the Retired in a Trailer Park. *American Journal of Sociology* 59: 361–70. (30, 32)

Hsu, F. L. K. ed. 1961. *Psychological Anthropology: Approaches to Culture and Personality*. Homewood, Ill.: Dorsey Press. (435, 440)

Hughes, Everett C. 1943. *French Canada in Transition*. Chicago: University of Chicago Press. (313)

———. 1951. *Social Psychology at the Crossroads*. New York: Harper & Row Publishers, Inc. (367)

———. 1958. *Men and Their Work*. New York: Free Press. (324)

Hunt, J. M. 1961. *Intelligence and Experience*. New York: The Ronald Press Co. (557)

Hunt, Raymond G. 1959. Socio-Cultural Factors in Mental Disorder. *Behavioral Science* 4: 96–106. (221)

Hunter, Floyd. 1953. *Community Power Structure*. Chapel Hill, N.C.: University of North Carolina Press. (41)

Hunter, W. W., and Maurice, H. 1953. *Older People Tell Their Story*. Ann Arbor: University of Michigan Press. (502)

Indra, R. K. 1963. "The Problems of Old Women, a Village Study in Rattan Garh, Punjab." Unpublished master's thesis, Punjab University. (471, 473)

Inglis, Ruth. 1938. An Objective Study of the Relationship between Fiction and Society. *American Sociological Review* 3: 526–31. (47)

Irwin, John, and Cressey, Donald R. 1962. Thieves, Convicts and the Inmate Culture. *Social Problems* 10: 142–55. (152)

Jaco, E. Gartly. 1954. The Social Isolation Hypothesis and Schizophrenia. *American Sociological Review* 19: 567–77. (220)

Jaffe, A. J. 1963. Population Needs, Production, and Older Manpower Requirements. In Orbach and Tibbitts 1963. (358)

Jaffe, A. J., and Carleton, R. O. 1954. *Occupational Mobility in the United States 1930–1960*. New York: Kings Crown Press. (323)

Janowitz, Morris, ed. 1961. *Community Political Systems*. New York: Free Press of Glencoe. (41)

Jarvik, Lissy F., and Falek, A. 1963. Intellectual Stability and Survival in the Aged. *Journal of Gerontology* 18:173–76. (509, 563)

Jarvik, Lissy F.; Kallman, F. J.; and Falek, A. 1962. Intellectual Changes in Aged Twins. *Journal of Gerontology* 17:289–94. (557, 563)

Jarvik, Lissy F.; Kallman, F. J.; Falek, A.; and Klaber, M. M. 1957. Changing Intellectual Functions in Senescent Twins. *Acta Genetica et Statistica Medica* 7:421–30. (563)

Jeffers, F. C., and Nichols, C. R. 1961. The Relationship of Activities and Attitudes to Physical Well-being in Older People. *Journal of Gerontology* 16:67–70. (499, 507)

Jeffers, F. C.; Nichols, C. R.; and Eisdorfer, Carl. 1961. Attitudes of Older Persons toward Death: A Preliminary Study. *Journal of Gerontology* 16:53–56. (505, 508)

Johns-Heine, Patrick, and Gerth, Hans. 1949. Values in Mass Periodical Fiction, 1921–40. *Public Opinion Quarterly* 13:105–13. (47)

Johnson, G. H. 1951. "Differences in the Job Satisfaction of Urban Teachers as Related to Age and Other Factors." Unpublished Ph.D. dissertation, Syracuse University. (117)

Johnson, Virginia E., and Masters, William H. 1964. I. A Team Approach to the Rapid Diagnosis and Treatment of Sexual Incompatibility. *Pacific Medical and Surgical Journal* 72: 371–75. (275)

———. 1964. II. Sexual Incompatibility: Diagnosis and Treatment. In *Human Reproduction and Sexual Behavior*, edited by C. W. Lloyd. Philadelphia: Lea & Febiger. (275)

Jones, Ernest. 1913. The Fantasy of Reversal of Generations *and* Significance of the Grandfather for the Fate of the Individual. In *Papers on Psychoanalysis*. New York: William Wood. (280)

Jones, H. E. 1958. Problems of Method in Longitudinal Research. *Vita Humana* 1:93–99. (549)

Jones, H. E., and Conrad, H. S. 1933. The Growth and Decline of Intelligence: A Study of a Homogeneous Group between the Ages of Ten and Sixty. *Genetic Psychology Monographs* 13, no. 3:223–98. (558, 560, 563)

Jones, H. E.; Conrad, H. S.; and Horn, A. 1928. Psychological Studies of Motion Pictures. II: Observation and Recall as a Function of Age. *University of California Publications in Psychology* 3:225–43. (564)

Josselyn, I. M. 1952. *The Adolescent and his World*. New York: Family Service Association of America. (207)

Jung, C. G. 1933. *Modern Man in Search of a Soul*. New York: Harcourt, Brace & World, Inc. (137)

Kagan, Jerome, and Moss, H. A. 1962. *Birth to Maturity*. New York: John Wiley and Sons, Inc. (137)

Kahl, J. A.. 1957. *The American Class Structure*. New York: Holt, Rinehart and Winston, Inc. (210)

Kaplan, Oscar J. 1943. Mental Decline in Older Morons. *American Journal of Mental Deficiency* 47:227–85. (563)

———. 1956. *Mental Disorders in Later Life*. Stanford: Stanford University Press. (563)

Kaplan, Oscar J.. Rumbaugh, D. M.; Mitchell, D. C.; and Thomas, E. D. 1963. Effects of Level of Surviving Abilities, Time of Day, and Test-Retest upon Psychological Performance in Seniles. *Journal of Gerontology* 18: 55–59. (563)

Kaplan, S. M. 1956. Psychological Aspects of Cardiac Disease. A Study of Patients Experiencing Mitral Commissurotomy. *Psychosomatic Medicine* 18:221. (202)

Kaufman, M. R. 1940. Old Age and Aging; the Psychoanalytic Point of View. *American Journal of Orthopsychiatry* 10:73–79. (125)

Kay, D. W. and Roth, Martin. 1961. Physical Illness and Social Factors in the Psychiatric Disorders of Old Age. *Third World Congress of Psychiatry, Proceedings*, vol. 1. Montreal: McGill University Press. (214, 217)

———. July, 1961. Environmental and Hereditary Factors in the Schizophrenias of Old Age (Late Paraphrenia) and Their Bearing on the General Problem of Causation in Schizophrenia. *Journal of Mental Science* 107:649–86. (221, 226)

Kay, D. W. K.; Norris, V.; and Post, F. 1956. Prognosis in Psychiatric Disorders of the Elderly. *Journal of Mental Science* 102:129–40. (401)

Kelly, E. C. 1948. *Encyclopedia of Medical Sources*. Baltimore: The Williams and Wilkins Company. (102)

Kelly, E. L. 1955. Consistency of the Adult Personality. *American Psychologist* 10:659–81. (552)

Kephart, William K. 1950. Status after Death. *American Sociological Review* 15:635–43. (535)

Kerckhoff, Alan C. 1964. Husband-Wife Expectations and Reactions to Retirement. *Journal of Gerontology* 19:510–16. (363)

———. 1965. Nuclear and Extended Family Relationships: a Normative and Behavioral Analysis. In Shanas and Streib 1965. (304)

Kerr, W. A.; Newman, H. L.; and Sadewic, A. R. 1949. Lifetime Worry Patterns of American Psychologists. *Journal of Consulting Psychology* 13:377–80. (131)

Kesson, W., and Kuhlman, C. 1962. Thought in the Young Child. *Monograph of Social Research and Child Development* 17, no. 2. (557)

Key, William H. 1961. Rural-Urban Differences and the Family. *Sociological Quarterly* 2:49–56. (252)

King, Stanley H. 1963. Social Psychological Factors in Illness. In *Handbook of Medical Sociology*, edited by Howard E. Freeman, Sol Levine, and Leo G. Reeder. Englewood Cliffs, New Jersey: Prentice-Hall, Inc. (216)

Kinsey, A. C.; Pomeroy, W. B.; and Martin, C. E. (1948). *Sexual Behavior in the Human Male*. Philadelphia: W. B. Saunders Company. (32, 273, 274)

Kinsey, A. C.; Pomeroy, W. B.; Martin, C. E.; and Gebhard, P. H. 1953. *Sexual Behavior in the Human Female*. Philadelphia: W. B. Saunders Company. (32, 271)

Kirkpatrick, Clifford, and Hobart, Charles. 1954. Disagreement, Disagreement Estimate and Non-empathic Imputations for Intimacy Groups Varying from Favorite Date to Married. *American Sociological Review* 19:10–19. (258)

Kleemeier, Robert W. 1954. Moosehaven: Congregate Living in a Community of the Retired. *American Journal of Sociology* 59:347–51. (32)

———. 1961. "Intellectual Changes in the Senium or Death and the IQ." Presidential Address,

Division 20 of the American Psychological Association, New York, September, 1961. (509)

———. 1962. Intellectual Changes in the Senium. In *Proceedings, Social Statistics Section, American Statistical Association,* Washington, D.C.: American Statistical Association. (563)

Kleemeier, Robert W., ed. 1961. *Aging and Leisure.* New York: Oxford University Press, Inc. (252, 434)

Kluckhohn, C., and Kluckhohn, Florence R. 1947. American Culture: Generalized Orientations and Class Patterns. In *Conflicts of Power in Modern Culture.* Symposium of Conference in Science, Philosophy and Religion, New York, 1947. (440)

Kluckhohn, Florence R. 1954. Dominant and Variant Value Orientations. In *Personality in Nature, Society, and Culture,* edited by C. Kluckhohn, H. A. Murray and D. M. Schneider. New York: Alfred A. Knopf, Inc. (461, 481)

Knapp, R. H., and Garbutt, J. T. 1958. Time Imagery and the Achievement Motive. *Journal of Personality* 26:426–34. (481, 482)

Kogan, Nathan, and Wallach, Michael A. 1961. Age Changes in Values and Attitudes. *Journal of Gerontology* 16: 272–80. (126, 128)

Kohn, Melvin L. 1964. Social Class and Parent-Child Relationships: an Interpretation. In *Mental Health of the Poor,* edited by F. Riessman, J. Cohen, and A. Pearl. London: Collier-Macmillan. (210)

Kohn, Melvin L., and Clausen, John A. 1955. Social Isolation and Schizophrenia. *American Sociological Review* 20:265–73. (220, 226)

Komarovsky, Mirra. 1940. *The Unemployed Man and His Family.* New York: Dryden. (322)

Koos, Earl L. 1946. *Families in Trouble.* New York: Columbia University Press. (252)

Kornhauser, W. 1959. *The Politics of Mass Society.* New York: The Free Press of Glencoe. (322)

Kosa, John; Rachiele, Leo D.; and Schommer, Cyril O., S. J. 1960. Sharing the Home with Relatives. *Marriage and Family Living* 22:129–31. (252)

Krapf, E. Eduardo. 1953. *On Aging.* Proceedings of the Royal Society of Medicine (London) 46:957–64. (493–94)

Kreps, Juanita. 1966. Employment Policy and Income Maintenance for the Aged. In *Aging and Social Policy,* edited by John C. McKinney and Frank T. de Vyver. New York: Appleton-Century-Crofts, Inc. (358)

Krzywicki, Ludwik. 1934. *Primitive Society and Its Vital Statistics.* London: The Macmillan Company. (531)

Kuhlen, Raymond G. 1940. Social Change: a Neglected Factor in Psychological Studies of the Life Span. *School Sociology* 52:14–16. (552)

———. 1948. "Age Trends in Adjustment during the Adult Years as Reflected in Happiness Ratings." Paper read at a meeting of the American Psychological Association, Boston, 1948. (125)

———. 1951 I. "Expansion and Constriction of Activities during the Adult Years as Reflected in Organizational, Civic and Political Participation." Paper read at Second International Gerontological Congress, St. Louis, 1951. (121, 122)

———. 1951 II. Nervous Symptoms Among Military Personnel as Related to Age, Combat Experience and Marital Status. *Journal of Consulting Psychology* 15:320–24. (130)

———. 1962. Trends in Religious Behavior during the Adult Years. In *Wider Horizons in Christian Adult Education,* edited by L. C. Little. Pittsburgh: University of Pittsburgh Press. (508)

———. 1963. Age and Intelligence: The Significance of Cultural Change in Longitudinal versus cross-sectional findings. Appears in this book as Appendix B.

———. 1964. Personality Change with Age. In *Personality Change,* edited by P. Worchel and D. Byrne. New York: John Wiley and Sons, Inc. (137)

———. 1964. Developmental Changes in Motivation during the Adult Years. Appears in this book as chapter 13.

Kuhlen, Raymond G., and Johnson, G. H. 1952. Changes in Goals with Increasing Adult Age. *Journal of Consulting Psychology* 16:1–4. (119, 120, 121)

Kutner, Bernard; Fanshel, D.; Togo, Alice M.; and Langer, T. S. 1956. *Five Hundred over Sixty: a Community Survey on Aging.* New York: Russell Sage Foundation. (123, 124, 126, 234)

LaBarre, Maureen B.; Jessner, Lucie; and Ussery, Lon. 1960. The Significance of Grandmothers in the Psychopathology of Children. *American Journal of Orthopsychiatry* 30:175–85. (280)

Landis, J. T. 1942. What is the Happiest Period of Life? *School Sociology* 55:643–45. (125)

Landsberger, Henry A., and Hulin, Charles L. 1961. A Problem for Union Democracy: Officers' Attitudes Toward Union Members. Industrial and Labor Relations Review 14:419–31. (39)

Lane, Robert E. 1959. *Political Life.* New York: The Free Press of Glencoe. (17)

Larrabee, Eric, and Meyersohn, Rolf, eds. 1960. *Mass Leisure.* New York: The Free Press of Glencoe. (366)

Lasagna, L., and Von Felsinger, J. M. 1954. *Science* 20:359. (239)

Lazerwitz, B. 1962. Membership in Voluntary Associations and Frequency of Church Attendance. *Journal of the Scientific Study of Religion* 2:74–84. (504)

Lehman, Harvey C. 1947. The Age of Eminent Leaders: Then and Now. *American Journal of Sociology* 52, January. (17)

———. 1953. *Age and Achievement*. Princeton, N.J.: Princeton University Press. (42, 99, 100, 104, 113, 124)

———. 1962. The Creative Production Rates of Present versus Past Generations of Scientists. Appears in this book as chapter 11.

Lehner, G. F. J. and Gunderson, E. K. 1953. Height Relationships on the Draw-a-Person Test. *Journal of Personality* 21:392–99. (126)

Leichter, Hope J. 1958. "Life Cycle Changes and Temporal Sequence in a Bilateral Kinship System." Paper read at Annual Meetings of the American Anthropological Association, Washington, D.C., 1958. (252)

———. 1959 I. "Kinship and Casework." Paper read at meetings of Groves Conference, Chapel Hill, North Carolina. (252)

———. 1959 II. "Normative Intervention in an Urban Bilateral Kinship System." Paper read at meetings of the American Anthropological Association. (252)

LeMasters, E. E. 1959. Holy Deadlock: a Study of Unsuccessful Marriages. *Midwest Sociologist* 21:86–91. (258)

Leninger, C. A. 1963. Some Aspects of the Economic Situation of the Aged: Recent Survey Findings. In Orbach and Tibbitts, 1963. (358)

LeVine, Robert A. 1965. Intergenerational Tensions and Extended Family Structures in Africa. In Shanas and Streib. (433)

Levy-Bruhl, Lucien. 1928. *The "Soul" of the Primitive*. London: Allen and Unwin. (533)

Lewin, K. 1939. Field Theory and Experiment in Social Psychology. *American Journal of Sociology* 44:868–96. (117)

Lewis, O. 1958. *Village Life in Northern India*. Urbana: University of Illinois Press. (470, 472)

Lieberman, Morton A. 1961. Relationship of Mortality Rates to Entrance to a Home for the Aged. *Geriatrics* 16:515–19. (401)

———. 1962. "Excessive Response Variability: a Problem for Research with Aged Subjects." Paper presented at the American Psychological Association meeting, August 31, 1962, St. Louis, Missouri. (513)

———. 1965. Psychological Correlates of Impending Death: Some Preliminary Observations. Appears in this book as Chapter 56. (141)

Life. 1959. Old Age: Part 4. August 3, 1959:67–74. (490)

Lifton, Robert J. 1963. Psychological Effects of the Atomic Bomb in Hiroshima: the Theme of Death. *Daedalus* 92:462–97. (534)

Linton, Ralph. 1959. The Natural History of the Family. In *The Family: Its Function and Destiny*, edited by Ruth N. Anshen, New York: Harper and Row Publishers, Inc. (247)

———. 1936. *The Study of Man*. New York: Appleton-Century-Crofts, Inc. (22)

Lipset, Seymour Martin. 1960. *Political Man: the Social Bases of Politics*. New York: Doubleday and Company. (17)

Lipset, Seymour Martin and Bendix, R. 1952. Social Mobility and Occupational Career Patterns. *American Journal of Sociology* 57:336–374, 494–504. (323)

Litwak, Eugene 1959–60. The Use of Extended Family Groups in the Achievement of Social Goals: Some Policy Implications. *Social Problems* 7:177–87. (253)

———. 1960 I. Geographical Mobility and Extended Family Cohesion. *American Sociological Review* 25:385–94. (247, 249, 253, 466)

———. 1960 II. Occupational Mobility and Extended Family Cohesion. *American Sociological Review* 25:10. (249, 253)

———. 1965. Extended Kin Relations in an Industrial Democratic Society. In Shanas and Streib, 1965. (305)

Lloyd, R. G. 1955. Social and Personal Adjustment of Retired Persons. *Sociology and Social Research* 39:312–316. (499)

Locke, Ben Z.; Kramer, M.; and Pasamanick, Benjamin. (1960. Mental Diseases of the Senium at Mid-Century: First Admissions to Ohio State Public Mental Hospitals. *American Journal of Public Health* July 1960:998–1012. (221)

Locy, W. A. 1925. *The Story of Biology*. New York: Henry Holt and Company. (107)

Loewenberg, A. 1955. *Annals of Opera, 1597–1940*, 2d ed. 2 vols. Geneva: Societas Bibliographica. (108)

Lowenthal, Marjorie Fiske. 1964 I. *Lives in Distress*. New York: Basic Books, Inc. (217)

———. 1964 II. Social Isolation and Mental Illness in Old Age. Appears in this book as Chapter 24. (390, 391, 395)

———. 1965. Antecedents of Isolation and Mental Illness in Old Age. *Archives of General Psychiatry* 12:245–54. (390)

Lowenthal, Marjorie Fiske, and Berkman, Paul L. 1962. The Problem of Rating Psychiatric Disability in a Study of Normal and Abnormal Aging. *Journal of Health and Human Behavior*, n.d. (226)

Lowenthal, Marjorie Fiske; Berkman, Paul L.; and Associates. 1967. *Aging and Mental Disorder in San Francisco: a Social Psychiatric Study*. San Francisco: Jossey-Bass, Inc. (393, 394, 398, 400)

Lowenthal, Marjorie Fiske, and Boler, Deetje. 1965. Voluntary Versus Involuntary Social

Withdrawal. *Journal of Gerontology* 20:363–71. (390)

Lowenthal, Marjorie Fiske, and Haven, Clayton. 1968. Interaction and Adaptation: Intimacy as a Critical Variable. Appears in this book as Chapter 43.

Lowie, Robert H. 1920. *Primitive Society*. New York: Harper and Row Publishers, Inc. (22)

Lubin, M. I. 1964. Ego Functions in the Middle and Later Years: Addendum. In *Personality in Middle and Late Life*, edited by Bernice L. Neugarten *et al.* New York: Atherton Press. (207)

Maddox, George L. 1963. Activity and Morale: A Longitudinal Study of Selected Elderly Subjects. *Social Forces* 42, no. 2:195–204. (181, 182)

———. 1964 I. Self-Assessment of Health Status, A Longitudinal Study of Selected Elderly Subjects. *Journal of Chronic Diseases* 17:449–60. (213)

———. 1964 II. Disengagement Theory: A Critical Evaluation. *The Gerontologist* 4:80–83. (363)

———. 1965. Fact and Artifact: Evidence Bearing on Disengagement Theory from the Duke Geriatric Project. *Human Development* 8, no. 2/3:117. (181)

———. 1966. Persistence of Life Style Among the Elderly: A Longitudinal Study of Patterns of Social Activity in Relation to Life Satisfaction. Appears in this book as Chapter 19.

———. 1966. Retirement as a Social Event in the United States. Appears in this book as Chapter 39.

Malzberg, Benjamin. 1956. A Statistical Review of Mental Disorders in Later Life. In *Mental Disorders in Later Life*, edited by Oscar J. Kaplan. Stanford: Stanford University Press. (220)

Mandelbaum, D. G. 1949. The Family in India. In *The Family, its Function and Destiny*, edited by Ruth N. Anshen. New York: Harper and Row, Publishers, Inc. (470, 471)

———. 1959. Social Uses of Funeral Rites. In *The Meaning of Death*, edited by Herman Feifel. New York: McGraw-Hill Book Co., Inc. (537)

Mannheim, Karl. 1940. *Man and Society in an Age of Reconstruction*, translated by E. A. Shils. New York: Harcourt, Brace & World, Inc. (323)

———. 1952. The Problem of Generations. In *Essays on the Sociology of Knowledge*. New York: Oxford University Press, Inc. (22)

———. 1953. *Essays on the Sociology of Knowledge*, edited by Paul Kecskemeti. New York: Oxford University Press, Inc. (311)

Marriott, McKim, ed. 1955. *Village India*. Chicago: University of Chicago Press. Also in American Anthropological Association, memoir 83, June, 1955. (470)

Marris, Peter. 1958. *Widows and their Families*. London: Routledge and Kegan Paul. (538)

Marshall, H., and Oden, M. H. 1962. The Status of the Mature Gifted Individual as a Basis for Evaluation of the Aging Process. *Gerontologist* 2:201–6. (499)

Martel, Martin U. 1963, rev. 1968. Age-Sex Roles in American Magazine Fiction 1890–1955. Appears in this book as Chapter 5.

———. 1964. Reality Orientation and the Pleasure Principle: A Study of American Magazine Fiction (1890–1955). In *People, Society and Mass Communications*, edited by L. Dexter and D. White. New York: Free Press of Glencoe. (49)

Martel, Martin U. and Morris, W. W. 1961. *Life After Sixty in Iowa*. Iowa City: Iowa State University Press. (38, 43, 44)

Martin, N. H., and Strauss, Anselm L. 1956. Patterns of Mobility within Industrial Organizations. *Journal of Business* 29:101–10. (316, 324)

Maslow, Abraham B.. 1943. A Theory of Human Motivation. *Psychological Review* 50:370–96. (116)

———. 1954. *Motivation and Personality*. New York: Harper & Row Publishers, Inc. (138)

Mason, Evelyn P. 1954. Some Correlates of Self-judgments of the Aged. *Journal of Gerontology* 9:324–37. (126)

Masters William H. 1953. "Long-range Sex Steroid Replacement: Target Organ Regeneration." *Journal of Gerontology* 8:33–39. (269)

———. 1957. Sex Steroid Influence on the Aging Process. *American Journal of Obstetrics and Gynecology* 74:733–46. (269, 270, 278)

Masters, William H., and Ballew, J. W. 1965. The Third Sex. In *Problems of the Middle Aged*, edited by C. G. Vedder. Springfield, Ill.: Charles C Thomas. (270)

Masters, William H., and Johnson, Virginia E. 1960. The Human Female: Anatomy of Sexual Response. *Minnesota Medicine* 43:31–36. (272)

———. 1961. Treatment of the Sexually Incompatible Family Unit. *Minnesota Medicine* 44:466–71. (275)

———. 1964. Sexual Response: Part II. Anatomy and Physiology. In *Human Reproduction and Sexual Behavior*, edited by C. W. Lloyd. Philadelphia: Lea & Febiger. (272)

———. 1965. Counseling with Sexually Incompatible Marriage Partners. In *Counseling in Marital and Sexual Problems (A Physician's Handbook)*, edited by R. H. Clemer. Baltimore: The Williams & Wilkins Co. (275)

Matthews, Donald R. 1954. *The Social Background of Political Decision-Makers*. New York: Doubleday & Co., Inc. (42)

Maves, Paul B. 1960. Aging, Religion, and the Church. In Tibbitts 1960. (500, 506)

Mayo, S. C. 1951. Social Participation Among the Older Population in Rural Areas of Wake

County, North Carolina. *Social Forces* 30:53–59. (501)

McCann, C. W. 1955. *Long Beach Senior Citizens' Survey*. Long Beach: Community Welfare Council. (502)

McClelland, D. C. 1953. *The Achievement Motive*. New York: Appleton-Century-Crofts, Inc. (119)

McCrary, Jack S. 1956. "The Role, Status, and Participation of the Aged in a Small Community." Ph.D. dissertation, Washington University, St. Louis.

McCulloch, T. L. 1957. The Retarded Child Grows Up: Psychological Aspects of Aging. *American Journal of Mental Deficiency* 62: 201–8. (553)

McKinney, John; Simpson, Ida Harper; and Back, Kurt 1966. *Social Aspects of Aging*. Durham, N.C.: Duke University Press. (362, 363)

McMahan, C. F. and Ford, T. R. 1955. Surviving the First Five Years of Retirement. *Journal of Gerontology* 10:212–15. (401)

McNemar, Q. 1962. *Psychological Statistics*, 3d ed. New York and London: John Wiley & Sons, Inc. (412)

Mead, Margaret. 1943. *And Keep Your Powder Dry: An Anthropologist Looks at America*. New York: William Morrow & Co., Inc. (440)

———. 1957. The Patterns of Leisure in Contemporary American Culture. *Annals of the American Academy of Political and Social Science* 313:11–15. (351, 369)

Menken, Adah I. 1888. *Infelicia*. London: Chatto and Windus. (491)

Mering, O. and Weniger, F. L. 1959. Social-cultural Background of the Aging Individual. In Birren, ed. 1959. (272)

Merton, Robert K. 1949. *Social Theory and Social Structure*. Glencoe, Ill.: Free Press. (220, 227, 228)

———. 1957. *Social Theory and Social Structure*, 2d ed. New York: Free Press of Glencoe. (22, 26)

———. 1959. Social Conformity, Deviation, and Opportunity Structures: A Comment on the Contributions of Dublin and Cloward. *American Sociological Review* 24:177–89. (26)

Meyers, Jerome K., and Roberts, Bertram H. 1959. *Family and Class Dynamics in Mental Illness*. New York: John Wiley & Sons, Inc. (220)

Michelen, L. C. 1954. The New Leisure Class. *American Journal of Sociology* 59:371–78. (466)

Miles, C. C. 1934. Influence of Speed and Age on Intelligence Scores of Adults. *Journal of Genetic Psychology* 10:208–10.

Miles, C. C. and Miles, W. R. 1932. The Correlation of Intelligence Scores and Chronological Age from Early to Late Maturity. *American Journal of Psychology* 44:44–78. (554)

Miles, W. R. 1933. Age and Human Ability. *Psychological Review* 40:99–123. (558, 563)

Miller, D. R., and Swanson, G. E. 1958. *The Changing American Parent*. New York: John Wiley & Sons, Inc. (325)

Miller, Stephen J. 1965. The Social Dilemma of the Aging Leisure Participant. Appears in this book as Chapter 40.

Mills, C. Wright. 1951. *White Collar*. New York: Oxford University Press, Inc. (325)

Mills, C. Wright; Senior, Clarence; and Goldsen, Rose K. 1950. *Puerto Rican Journey*. New York: Harper & Row Publishers, Inc. (252)

Mitchell, William E. 1961 I. Descent Groups Among New York City Jews. *The Jewish Journal of Sociology* 3:121–28. (252)

———. 1961 II. "Lineality and Laterability in Urban Jewish Ambilineages." Paper read at 60th Annual meeting of American Anthropological Association, Philadelphia, Pa. (252, 254)

Mitchell, William E., and Leichter, Hope J., n.d. Unpublished paper from project "Studies in Family Interaction" sponsored jointly by the Jewish Family Service of New York City and the Russell Sage Foundation. (252)

Moberg, David O. 1951. "Religion and Personal Adjustment in Old Age." Ph.D. dissertation, University of Minnesota. (507)

———. 1953 I. Church Membership and Personal Adjustment in Old Age. *Journal of Gerontology* 8:207–11. (506)

———. 1953 II. Leadership in the Church and Personal Adjustment in Old Age. *Sociology and Social Research* 37:312–16. (506)

———. 1956. Religious Activities and Personal Adjustment in Old Age. *Journal of Social Psychology* 43:261–67. (506)

———. 1958. Christian Beliefs and Personal Adjustment in Old Age. *J. Amer. Sci. Affil.* 10: 8–12. (506)

———. 1962. *The Church as a Social Institution*. Englewood Cliffs, New Jersey: Prentice-Hall, Inc. (504)

———. 1965 I. The Integration of Older Members in the Church Congregation. In Rose and Peterson 1965. (502)

———. 1965 II. Religiosity in Old Age. Appears in this book as Chapter 55.

Moberg, David O. and Taves, M. J. 1965. Church Participation and Adjustment in Old Age. In Rose and Peterson 1965. (506)

Modell, H. H. 1951. Changes in Human Figure Drawings by Patients Who Recover from Regressed States. *American Journal of Orthopsychiatry* 21:584–96. (510)

Moore, Wilbert E. 1950. The Aged in Industrial Societies. In *The Aged and Society*, edited by

M. Derber. Champaign, Ill.: Industrial Relations Research Association. (469)

———. 1963. *Man, Time, and Society*. New York: John Wiley & Sons, Inc. (361, 529)

Moreno, J. 1960. The Social Atom and Death. In *The Sociometry Reader*, edited by J. Moreno. New York: Free Press. (537)

Morgan, Christine F. 1937. The Attitudes and Adjustments of Recipients of Old Age Assistance in Upstate and Metropolitan New York. *Archives of Psychology*, no. 214. (125, 131)

Morgan, James; Martin, David; Cohen, Wilbur; and Brazer, Harvey 1962. *Income and Welfare in the United States*. New York: McGraw-Hill Book Co. (358, 359)

Munnichs, J. M. A. 1964. "Loneliness, Isolation and Social Relations in Old Age." Paper given at the Sixth International Congress, International Association of Gerontology, Copenhagen, 1964. (216)

Myrdal, Gunnar 1944. *An American Dilemma*. New York: Harper & Row Publishers, Inc. (36)

Nadel, S. F. 1952. Witchcraft in Four African Societies: An Essay in Comparison. *American Anthropologist* 54:18–29. (442)

———. 1953. *The Foundations of Social Anthropology*. New York: Free Press of Glencoe. (280)

Nardini, J. E. 1952. Survival Factors in American Prisoners of War of the Japanese. *American Journal of Psychiatry* 109:241–45. (401)

National Opinion Research Center. 1953. Jobs and Occupations: A Popular Evaluation. In *Class, Status and Power*, edited by Reinhard Bendix and Seymour M. Lipset. New York: Free Press of Glencoe. (39)

Nelson, E. N. P. 1954. Persistence of Attitudes of College Students Fourteen Years Later. *Psychological Monographs* 68, no. 2. (552, 555)

Nelson, H 1928. The Creative Years. *American Journal of Psychology* 40:303–11. (99)

Netter, L. G. 1962. "The Use of Housing Authority Criteria in Tenant Selection for Victoria Plaza, an Apartment Building for the Elderly." Thesis, Trinity University, San Antonio, Texas. (410)

Neugarten, Bernice L. 1966. Adult Personality: A Developmental View. *Human Development* 9:61–73. (435)

———. 1967. The Awareness of Middle Age. Appears in this book as Chapter 10.

——— 1968. Adult Personality: Toward a Psychology of the Life Cycle. Appears in this book as Chapter 14.

Neugarten, Bernice L., and Associates. 1964. *Personality in Middle and Late Life*. New York: Atherton Press (58, 140, 173)

Neugarten, Bernice L., and Gutmann, David L. 1958. Age-Sex Roles and Personality in Mid-

dle Age: A Thematic Apperception Study. Appears in this book as Chapter 6. (119, 207)

Neugarten, Bernice L.; Havighurst, Robert J.; and Tobin, Sheldon S. 1961. The Measurement of Life Satisfaction. *Journal of Gerontology* 16:134–43. (168, 174)

———. 1965. Personality and Patterns of Aging. Appears in this book as Chapter 17.

Neugarten, Bernice L., and Moore, Joan. 1968. The Changing Age-Status System. Appears in this book as Chapter 1. (143)

Neugarten, Bernice L.; Moore, Joan; and Lowe, John C. 1965. Age Norms, Age Constraints, and Adult Socialization. Appears in this book as Chapter 2. (145, 146)

Neugarten, Bernice L., and Peterson, Warren A. 1957. A Study of the American Age-grade System. *Proceedings of the Fourth Congress of the International Association of Gerontology*, vol. 3:497–502. (144)

Neugarten, Bernice L., and Weinstein, Karol K. 1964. The Changing American Grandparent. Appears in this book as Chapter 31.

Neugarten, Bernice L.; Wood, Vivian; Kraines, Ruth; and Loomis, Barbara. 1963. Women's Attitudes toward the Menopause. Appears in this book as Chapter 21.

Newman, G., and Nichols, C. R. 1960. Sexual Activities and Attitudes in Older Persons. *J.A.M.A.* 173:33–35. (272, 273)

Nickles, J. M. 1923–24. *The Geological Literature of North America, 1785–1918*, 2 vols. Washington, D.C.: U.S. Gov. Printing Office. (108)

Nicoll, A. 1952–59. *A History of English Drama, 1660–1900*, 6 vols. Cambridge, England: Cambridge University Press. (108)

Nimkoff, M. F. 1961. Changing Family Relationships of Older People in the United States during the Last Fifty Years. *The Gerontologist* 1:92–97. (280)

Norbeck, E. 1953. Age-grading in Japan. *American Anthropologist* 55:373–83. (434)

Nordenskiöd, E. 1935. *The History of Biology*. New York: Alfred A. Knopf. (107)

Norman, R. D. 1949. Concealment of Age Among Psychologists: Evidence for a Popular Stereotype. *Journal of Psychology* 30:127–35. (126)

Nosow, Sigmund, and Form, William H. 1962. *Man, Work, and Society*. New York: Basic Books, Inc. (359)

Nye, R. B. 1944. *George Bancroft: Brahman Rebel*. New York: Alfred A. Knopf. (111, 112)

Obrist, Walter C.; Henry, C. E.; and Justiss, W. A. 1961. "Longitudinal Study of EEG in Old Age." Paper read at the Fifth International Congress of Electroencephalography and Clinical Neurophysiology. Rome, Italy, September, 1961. (509)

Ogburn, William F. 1934. The Family and its Functions. In *Recent Social Trends, Report of the President's Research Committee on Social Trends.*. New York: McGraw-Hill Book Co., Inc. (296)

Oles, E. S. 1949. "Religion and Old Age, A Study of the Possible Influence of Religious Adherence on Adjustment." Thesis, Bucknell University. Lewisburg, Pa. Reviewed in *Journal of Gerontology* 5:187. (507)

Olsen, I. A., and Elder, J. H. 1958. A Word-association Test of Emotional Disturbance in Older Women. *Journal of Gerontology* 13:305–8. (130)

Olsen, Kenneth M., and Neugarten, Bernice L. 1959. "Social Class and Age-graded Behavior in Adulthood: An Empirical Study." Paper read at American Sociological Associations meetings, Chicago, September, 1959. (7)

Orbach, Harold L. 1961. Aging and Religion: Church Attendance in the Detroit Metropolitan Area.. *Geriatrics* 16:530–40. (502–3)

Orbach, Harold L., and Tibbitts, Clark, eds. 1963. *Aging and the Economy*. Ann Arbor: University of Michigan Press.

O'Reilly, C. T., and Pembroke, M. M., n.d. "Older People in a Chicago Community." Chicago: Loyola University Survey, 1956. (499, 501, 505)

Orenstein, Henry 1961. The Recent History of the Extended Family in India. *Social Problems* 8:341–50. (250)

Owens, William A., Jr. 1953. Age and Mental Abilities: A Longitudinal Study. *Genetic Psychology Monographs* 48:2–54. (553, 563, 569)

———. 1962. Age and Mental Abilities: A Second Phase of a Longitudinal Study. Abstract. *Journal of Gerontology* 17:472. (557)

———. 1966. Age and Mental Abilities: A Second Adult Follow-up. *Journal of Educational Psychology* 57, no. 6:311–25. (553)

Pagani, Angelo. 1962. Social Isolation in Destitution. In *Social and Psychological Aspects of Aging*, edited by Clark Tibbitts and Wilma Donahue. New York: Columbia University Press. (220)

Palmer, G. L. 1954. *Labor Mobility in Six Cities*. New York: Social Science Research Council. (323)

Palmore, Erdman. 1964. Retirement Patterns among Men: Findings of the 1963 Survey of the Aged. *Social Security Bulletin* 27:3–10. (358, 359)

Pan, J. J. 1954. Institutional and Personal Adjustment in Old Age. *Journal of Genetic Psychology* 85:155–58. (501)

Parke, Robert J., and Glick, Paul C. 1967. Prospective Changes in Marriage and the Family. *Journal of Marriage and the Family*, May, 1967: 249–56. (6)

Parsons, Talcott. 1942. Age and Sex in the Social Structure of the United States. *American Sociological Review* 7:604–16. (22, 188, 220)

———. 1943. The Kinship System of the Contemporary United States. *American Anthropologist* 45:22–38. (247, 296)

———. 1953. Revised Analytical Approach to the Theory of Social Stratification. In *Class. Status, and Power,* edited by R. Bendix and S. M. Lipset. New York: Free Press of Glencoe. (247)

———. 1958. Definitions of Health and Illness in the Light of American Values and Social Structure. In *Patients, Physicians, and Illness,* edited by E. Garley Jaco. New York: The Free Press of Glencoe. (216)

———. 1959. The Social Structure of the Family. In *The Family: Its Function and Destiny*. 2d ed., edited by Ruth Anshen. New York: Harper & Row Publishers, Inc. (247, 296)

———. 1963. Old Age as a Consummatory Phase. *Gerontologist* 3:35–43. (184, 186)

Parsons, Talcott, and Bales, Robert F. 1955. *Family Socialization and Process*. New York: Free Press of Glencoe. (247)

Pascal, G. R., and Suttell, B. J. 1951. *The Bender-Gestalt Test*. New York: Grune & Stratton, Inc. (510)

Peck, Robert 1956. Psychological Developments in the Second Half of Life. Appears in this book as Chapter 9. (138, 218)

Peck, Robert, and Berkowitz, H. 1964. Personality and Adjustment in Middle Age. In *Personality in Middle and Late Life*, edited by Bernice L. Neugarten, *et al.* New York: Atherton Press. (207)

Perlin, S. and Butler, Robert N. 1963. Psychiatric Aspects of Adaptation to the Aging Experience. In *Human Aging: A Biological and Behavioral Study*, by James E. Birren *et al.* PHS publication #986. Washington, D.C.: U.S. Gov. Printing Office. (239, 489)

Perlin, S. *et al.* 1958. *American Medical Association Archives of Neurological Psychiatry* 80:65. (239)

Perrier, F. 1955. The Meaning of Transference in Schizophrenia. *Acta Psychotherapy* (Basel) 3, Supplement: 266–72, translated by M. A. Woodbury. (495)

Peterson, Robert L., n.d. The Effectiveness of Older Office and Managerial Personnel. *Business Management Aids* (BMA 10). College of Commerce and Business Administration, University of Illinois. (38)

———. 3,000 Older Workers and Their Job Effectiveness. *Business Management Aids* (BMA 15). College of Commerce and Business Administration, University of Illinois. (38)

———. 1953. The Effectiveness of Older Personnel in Retailing. *University of Illinois Bulletin* 50, no. 67 (38)

Peterson, Robert L. 1954. The Effectiveness of Older Personnel in Industry. *University of Illinois Bulletin* 52, no. 3 (38)

Philips, Bernard S. 1957. A Role Theory Approach to Adjustment in Old Age. *American Sociological Review* 22:212–17. (123, 124, 126, 220, 463)

———. 1961. Role Change, Subjective Age and Adjustment: A Correlational Analysis. *Journal of Gerontology* 16:347–52. (220)

Pinner, Frank A.; Jacobs, Paul; and Selznick, Philip. 1959. *Old Age and Political Behavior.* Berkeley: University of California Press. (33, 40, 361)

Pineo, Peter C. 1961. Disenchantment in the Later Years of Marriage. Appears in this book as Chapter 28.

Powell, M., and Ferraro, C. D. 1960. Sources of Tension in Married and Single Women Teachers of Different Ages. *Journal of Educational Psychology* 51:92–101. (130, 132)

Pressey, Sidney L., and Kuhlen, Raymond G. 1957. *Psychological Development through the Life Cycle.* New York: Harper & Row Publishers, Inc. (75)

Prins, A. H. J. 1953. *East African Age-Class Systems.* Groningen: J. B. Wolters. (22)

Radcliffe-Brown, A. R. 1950. *African Systems of Kinship and Marriage.* London: Oxford University Press. (280)

Rappaport, Ernest. 1958. The Grandparent Syndrome. *Psychoanalytic Quarterly* 27:518–37. (280)

Raskin, A. H. 1964. Automation: Road to Lifetime Jobs? *Saturday Review,* November 28, 1964:14. (359)

Raskin, E. 1936. A Comparison of Literary and Scientific Ability. *Journal of Abnormal Psychology* 31:20–40. (111)

Rechtschaffen, Allan. 1959. Psychotherapy with Geriatric Patients: A Review of the Literature. *Journal of Gerontology* 14: 73–84. (486)

Reichard, Suzanne; Livson, Florine; and Petersen, Paul G. 1962. *Aging and Personality.* New York: John Wiley & Sons, Inc. A selection appears in this book as Chapter 18. (159, 186)

Reiser, M. F. 1951. Emotional Aspects of Cardiac Disease. *American Journal of Psychiatry* 107:781–95. (202)

Reiser, M. F., and Bakst, H. 1959. Psychology of Cardiovascular Disorders. In *American Handbook of Psychiatry,* vol. 1, edited by S. Arieti. New York: Basic Books, Inc. (202)

Reiser, M. F.; Ferris, E. B.; and Levine, M. 1954. Cardiovascular Disorders, Heart Disease, and Hypertension. In *Recent Developments in Psychosomatic Medicine,* edited by E. D. Wittkower and R. A. Cleghorn. Philadelphia: J. P. Lippincott Co. (202)

Reiss, A. J., Jr. 1955. Occupational Mobility of Professional Workers. *American Sociological Review* 20:693–700. (323)

Reiss, Paul J. 1959. "The Extended Kinship System of the Urban Middle Class." Unpublished Ph.D. dissertation. Harvard University. (252)

Reissman, L. 1953. Levels of Aspiration and Social Class. *American Sociological Review* 18: 233–42. (119)

Richter, Curt P. 1957. On the Phenomena of Sudden Death in Animals and Man. *Psychosomatic Medicine* 19:191–98. (488)

Riegel, Klaus F. 1959. A Study on Verbal Achievements of Older Persons. *Journal of Gerontology* 14:453–56. (551, 565)

———. 1967. Changes in Psycholinguistic Performance with Age. In *Human Behavior and Aging: Recent Studies in Research and Theory.* New York: Academic Press, Inc. (565)

Riegel, Klaus F., and Riegel. Ruth M. 1960. A Study on Changes of Attitudes and Interest during the Later Years of Life. *Vita Humana* 3:177–206. (565)

———. 1962. Analysis of Differences in Test Performance and Item Difficulty between Young and Old Adults. *Journal of Gerontology* 17: 96–105. (565)

Riegel, Ruth M. 1960. Faktoreanalysen des Hamburg-Wechsler-Intelligentztests für Erwachsene (HAWIE) für die Altersstufen 20–34, 35–49, 50–64 und 65 Jahre und älter. *Diagnostica* 6:41–66. (565)

Riegel, Ruth M., and Riegel, Klaus F. 1959. Standardisierung des Hamburg-Wechsler-Intelligentztests für Erwachsene (HAWIE) für die Altersstufen über 50 Jahre. *Diagnostica* 5: 97–128. (564, 565)

———. 1962. A Comparison and Reinterpretation of Factorial Structures of the W-B, the WAIS, and the HAWIE on the Aged Persons. *Journal of Consulting Psychology* 26:31–37. (565)

Riegel, Klaus F.; Riegel, Ruth M.; and Meyer, Gunther. 1967. Socio-psychological Factors of Aging: A Cohort-sequential Analysis. *Human Development* 10, no. 1:27–56. (564)

———. 1967. A Study of the Dropout Rates in Longitudinal Research on Aging and the Prediction of Death. Appears in this book as Appendix D. (553)

Riegel, Klaus F.; Riegel, Ruth M.; and Skiba, G. 1962. Untersuchung der Lebensbedingungen, Gewohnheiten und Anpassung älterer Menschen in Norddeutschland. *Vita Humana* 5: 204–47. (564, 565)

Riesman, David. 1950. *The Lonely Crowd: A Study of the Changing American Character.* New Haven: Yale University Press. (366)

———. 1954. *Individualism Reconsidered.* New York: Free Press of Glencoe. (440)

———. 1957. The Suburban Dislocation. *Annals of the American Academy of Political and Social Science* 314. 123–46. (351)

———. 1960. Leisure and Work in Post-Industrial

Society. In Larrabee and Meyersohn 1960. (368)

Riesman, David, and Bloomberg, Warner, Jr. 1962. Work and Leisure: Fusion or Polarity? In Nosow and Form 1962. (360)

Riezler, K. 1960. The Social Psychology of Fear. In *Identity and Anxiety*, edited by M. Stein, A. J. Vidich, and D. M. White. New York: Free Press of Glencoe. (208)

Rokeach, Milton. 1960. *The Open and Closed Mind*. New York: Basic Books, Inc. (26)

Roethlisberger, F. J., and Dickson, W. J. 1939. *Management and the Worker*. Cambridge: Harvard University Press. (416)

Rollins, James M. 1963. Two Empirical Tests of a Parsonian Theory of Family Authority Patterns. *The Family Life Coordinator* 12, January–April, 1963. (289)

Rose, Arnold M. 1949. *The Negro's Morale*. Minneapolis: University of Minnesota Press. (30)

———. 1956. *Sociology*. New York: Alfred A. Knopf. (368)

———. 1961. The Mental Health of Normal Older Persons. *Geriatrics* 16:459–64. (33, 184)

———. 1962. The Subculture of the Aging, A Topic for Sociological Research. Appears in this book as Chapter 3. (21, 187)

———. 1962. Organizations for the Elderly: Political Implications. In Donahue and Tibbitts, 1962. (16)

———. 1964. A Current Theoretical Issue in Social Gerontology. *The Gerontologist* 4. 46–50. Appears in this book as Chapter 20. (184, 363, 364)

———. 1965. Group Consciousness among the Aging. In Rose and Peterson 1965. (187, 372)

Rose, Arnold M., and Peterson, Warren A., ed. 1965. Older People and Their Social World. Philadelphia: F. A. Davis Co.

Rose, C. H. 1965. Representatives of Volunteer Subjects in a Longitudinal Aging Study. *Human Development* 8:152–56. (564)

Rosen, Jacqueline L., and Bibring, Grete L. 1966. Psychological Reactions of Hospitalized Male Patients to a Heart Attack: Age and Social Class Differences. Appears in this book as Chapter 22.

Rosen, Jacqueline L., and Neugarten, Bernice L. 1960. Ego Functions in the Middle and Later Years: A Thematic Apperception Study of Normal Adults. *Journal of Gerontology* 15: 62. (122, 166, 207)

Rosenmayer, Leopold 1958. Der Alte Mensch in der socialen Umwelt von Heute. *Kölner Zeitschrift*, 4:642–57. (465)

Rosenmayer, Leopold, and Köckeis, Eva. 1963. Propositions for a Sociological Theory of Aging and the Family. *International Social Science Journal* 15, no. 3. (300)

Rosenzweig, S. 1943. Psychology of the Menstrual Cycle. *Journal of Clinical Endocrinology* 3:296–300. (270)

Rosow, Irving. 1961. Retirement Housing and Social Integration. *The Gerontologist* 1:85–91. (33)

———. 1965. Housing and Local Ties of the Aged. Appears in this book as Chapter 42.

———. 1967. *Social Integration of the Aged*. New York: Free Press of Glencoe. (382, 391, 399)

Ross, M. 1951. Psychosomatic Approach to the Climacterium. *California Medicine* 74:240–42. (195)

Rossi, Peter H. 1955. *Why Families Move*. New York: Free Press of Glencoe. (252)

Roy, Donald. 1952. Quota Restriction and Goldbricking in a Machine Shop. *American Journal of Sociology* 57. 427–42. (152, 314)

———. 1954. Efficiency and the "Fix": Informal Intergroup Relations in a Piecework Machine Shop. *American Journal of Sociology*. 60:255–66. (315)

Rubin, A. and Babbott, D. 1958. Impotence and Diabetes Mellitus. *J.A.M.A.* 168:498–500. (278)

Rudfeld, Kirsten. 1962. Suicides in Denmark 1956. *Acta Sociologica* 6, no. 3. (219)

Russell, J. C. 1958. Late Ancient and Medieval Population. *Transactions of the American Philosophical Society* 48, part 3:25–29. (532)

Sachuk, N. N. 1963. "Some General Studies of the State of Health of the Aged." In World Health Organization *Seminar on the Health Protection of the Elderly and the Aged and on the Prevention of Premature Aging*, Kiev, May 14–22, 1963. Copenhagen: World Health Organization, Mimeographed. (213)

San Antonio Housing Authority. 1959 I. "A Discussion of Admission Criteria, Apartments for the Elderly." San Antonio, Texas: San Antonio Housing Authority, Mimeographed. (410)

———. 1959 II. "Supplement to Application and CO's for Elderly Persons." *Ibid*. (410)

Sarell, M. 1961. Continuity and Change—the Second Generation in Collective Settlements. *Megamoth* 11: 32–123. (462)

Saunders, L. 1954. *Cultural Difference and Medical Care: the Case of the Spanish-Speaking People of the Southwest*. New York: Russell Sage Foundation. (443)

Schaie, K. Warner. 1959 I. The Effect of Age on a Scale of Social Responsibility. *Journal of Social Psychology* 5:221–24. (123)

———. 1959 II. Cross-sectional Methods in the Study of Psychological Aspects of Aging. *Journal of Gerontology* 14:208–15. (563)

———. 1965. A General Model for the Study of Developmental Problems. *Psychological Bulletin* 64: 92–107. (559, 563)

Schaie, K. Warner. 1967. Age Changes and Age Differences. Appears in this book as Appendix C.

Schaie, K. Warner, and Strother, C. R. 1964 I. "Models for the Prediction of Age Changes in Cognitive Behavior." Unpublished mimeographed paper, West Virginia University. Abstract in *Gerontologist* 4:14. (561)

———. 1964 II. "A Cross-sequential Study of Age Changes in Cognitive Behavior." Paper presented at the Midwestern Psychological Association, St. Louis. Unpublished mimeographed paper, University of Nebraska. (562)

———. 1964 III. "The Effect of Time and Cohort Differences upon Age Changes in Cognitive Behavior." Unpublished multilith paper, West Virginia University. Abstract in *American Psychologist* 19:546. (562, 563)

Schatzman, L., and Strauss, Anselm. 1955. Social Class and Modes of Communication. *American Journal of Sociology* 60:329. (210)

Schmale, A. H. 1958. Relationship of Separation and Depression to Disease. I. A Report on a Hospitalized Medical Population. *Psychosomatic Medicine* 20:259–67. (41, 401)

Schmidhauser, John R. 1958. The Political Behavior of Older Persons: a Discussion of Some Frontiers in Research. *The Western Political Quarterly* 11, March. (41, 42)

———. 1962. Age and Judicial Behavior: American Higher Appellate Judges. In Donahue and Tibbitts, 1962. (17)

Schorr, Alvin L. 1960. *Filial Responsibility in a Modern American Family*. Washington, D.C.: Social Security Administration, U.S. Department of Health, Education and Welfare. (252, 296, 304)

Schultz, Clarence. Personal communication to Robert N. Butler. (495)

Schwartz, Arthur N., and Kleemeier, Robert W. 1965. The Effects of Illness and Age upon Some Aspects of Personality. *Journal of Gerontology* 20:85–91. (217)

Scott, J. P.; Fredericson, E.; and Fuller, J. L. 1951. Experimental Exploration of the Critical Period Hypothesis. *Personality* 1:162–83. (118)

Scudder, H. E. 1895. Noah Webster. Boston: Houghton Mifflin Co. (113)

Seeman, Melvin. 1959. On the Meaning of Alienation. *American Sociological Review* 24:783–91. (220, 227)

Shanas, Ethel. No. 16, 1960. *Medical Care among Those Aged 65 and Over*. New York: Health Information Foundation, Research Series. (43)

———. No. 17, 1960. *Meeting Medical Care Costs among the Aging. Ibid.* (38)

———. May 1960. The "Very Sick" in the Older Population. *The Journal, Michigan State Medical Society* 58. (42)

———. 1961. *Family Relationships of Older People*. New York: Health Information Foundation. (252)

———. 1962. *The Health of Older People: a Social Survey*. Cambridge, Massachusetts: Harvard University Press. (298)

———. 1967. Family Help Patterns and Social Class in Three Countries. Appears in this book as Chapter 33.

Shanas, Ethel, and Streib, Gordon F., eds. 1965. *Social Structure and the Family: Generational Relations*. Englewood Cliffs, N.J.: Prentice-Hall, Inc.

Shanas, Ethel; Townsend, Peter; Wedderburn, D.; Friis, H.; Milhoj, P.; and Stehouwer, J. 1968. *Older People in Three Industrial Societies*. New York and London: Atherton Press. A selection appears in this book as Chapter 23. (255, 304)

Sharp, Harry, and Axelrod, Morris. 1956. Mutual Aid among Relatives in an Urban Population. In *Principals of Sociology*, edited by Ronald Freedman and Associates. New York: Holt, Rinehart and Winston, Inc. (250, 252)

Shelton, A. J. 1965. Ibo Aging and Eldership; Notes for Gerontologists and Others. *Gerontologist* 5:20–23. (434)

Shorr, E. 1938. Problems of Mental Adjustment at the Climacteric. In *Mental Health and Later Maturity*. Suppl. 168, Public Health Reports. Washington, D.C.: United States Public Health Service. (270)

Sicher, L. 1949. Change of Life; a Psychosomatic Problem. *American Journal of Psychotherapy* 3:399–409. (195)

Siegel, S. 1956. *Nonparametric Statistics for the Behavioral Sciences*. New York: McGraw-Hill Book Company, Inc. (207)

Simenon, Georges. 1958. *The Man Who Watched the Trains Go By*. New York: Berkley Publishing Corporation. (495)

Simmons, Leo W. 1945. *The Role of the Aged in Primitive Society*. New Haven: Yale University Press. (433, 446, 532)

———. 1946. Attitudes toward Aging and the Aged: Primitive Societies. *Journal of Gerontology* 1:72–95. (124)

———. 1952. Social Participation of the Aged in Different Cultures. *Annals of the American Academy of Political and Social Science* 279:43–51. (469)

———. 1960. Aging in Preindustrial Societies. In Tibbitts 1960. (469)

Simon, Alexander; Lowenthal, Marjorie Fiske; and Epstein, Leon J. (Publication pending). *Crisis and Intervention* (working title). New York: Basic Books, Inc. (393)

Singer, Margaret T. 1963. Personality Measurements in the Aged. In Birren *et al.*, eds. 1963. (68)

Singh, J. 1962. "Problems of the Old Men in Burail." Unpublished Master's Thesis, Punjab University. (470)

Slavick, Fred, and Wolfbein, Seymour L. 1960. The Evolving Work-Life Pattern. In Tibbitts 1960. (38, 358)

Smith, D. E. 1929. *A Source Book in Mathematics*. New York: McGraw-Hill Book Company, Inc. (108)

Smith, M. Brewster. 1959. Research Strategies toward a Conception of Positive Mental Health. *American Psychologist* 14:673–81. (141)

Smith, M. Brewster; Haan, Norma; and Block, Jeanne 1968. Activism and Apathy in Contemporary Adolescents. In *Contributions to the Understanding of Adolescence*, edited by J. F. Adams. Boston: Allyn and Bacon, Inc. (16)

Smith, T. L. 1950. The Aged in Rural Society. In *The Aged and Society*, edited by M. Derber. Champaign, Illinois: Industrial Relations Research Association. (469)

Smith, William M. Jr.; Britton, Joseph H.; and Britton, Jean O. 1958. *Relations within Three Generation Families*. Pennsylvania State University College of Home Economics Research Publication 155. (280)

Solomon, David. 1952. "Career Contingencies of Chicago Physicians." Unpublished Ph.D. dissertation, University of Chicago. (313)

Spencer, P. 1965. *The Samburu; a Study of Gerontology in a Nomadic Tribe*. Berkeley and Los Angeles: University of California Press. (433)

Spiro, Melford E. 1956. *Kibbutz: Venture in Utopia*. Cambridge: Harvard University Press. (462)

Spitz, René A., and Wolf, Katherine M. 1946. Anaclitic Depression. *Psychoanalytic Study of the Child* 22:313–42. New York: International Universities Press, Inc. (391)

Srinivas, M. N., ed. 1960. *India's Villages*. Bombay: Asia Publishing House. (470)

Starbuck, E. D. 1911. *The Psychology of Religion*, (3d ed.) New York: Walter Scott. (500)

Stecker, Margaret L. 1955. Why Do Beneficiaries Retire? Who among Them Return to Work? *Social Security Bulletin* 18:3–12. (358, 359)

Stehouwer, Jan. 1963. "Urban-rural Differences in the Contact between the Aged and Their Children in Denmark." Unpublished paper given at the International Social Science Seminar in Gerontology, Markaryd, Sweden, 1963. (302)

———. 1965. Relations between Generations and the Three-Generation Household in Denmark. In Shanas and Streib 1965. (305)

Steiner, Peter O., and Dorfman, Robert. 1957. *The Economic Status of the Aged*. Berkeley and Los Angeles: University of California Press. (43, 356)

Stern, K., and Prados, M. 1946. Personality Studies in Menopausal Women. *American Journal of Psychiatry* 103:358–68. (270)

Stieglitz, E. J. 1954. *Geriatric Medicine, Medical Care of Later Maturity*. Philadelphia: J. B. Lippincott Company. (202)

Stine, L. A. 1958. The Medical Patient. In *The Psychology of Medical Practice*, edited by M. H. Hollender. Philadelphia: W. B. Saunders Co. (202)

Stokes, W. R. 1951. Sexual Functioning in the Aging Male. *Geriatrics* 6:304–8. (273)

———. 1963. Personal communication. (273)

Strauss, Anselm L. 1959. *Mirrors and Masks: the Search for Identity*. New York: Free Press of Glencoe. (152, 520, 522)

Streib, Gordon F. 1955–56. Morale of the Retired. *Social Problems* 3:271–80. (463)

———. 1958. Family Patterns in Retirement. *Journal of Social Issues* 14, no. 2. 46–60. (252, 280)

———. 1965. Are the Aged a Minority Group? Appears in this book as Chapter 4.

Streib, Gordon F., and Thompson, Wayne E. 1960. The Older Person in a Family Context. In Tibbitts 1960. (44)

Strong, E. K., Jr. 1943. *Vocational Interests of Men and Women*. Stanford: Stanford University Press. (120)

Sudnow, David N. 1965. "Passing On: the Social Organization of Dying in the County Hospital." Unpublished Ph.D. dissertation, University of California, Berkeley. (535, 536)

Sumner, William Graham. 1907. *Folkways*. Boston: Ginn and Company. (152)

Sussman, Marvin B. 1953 I. The Help Pattern in the Middle Class Family. *American Sociological Review* 18: 22–28. (250, 252)

———. 1953 II. Parental Participation in Mate Selection and its Effect upon Family Continuity. *Social Forces* 32:76–81. (250)

———. 1954. Family Continuity: Selective Factors which Affect Relationships between Families at Generational Levels. *Marriage and Family Living* 16: 112–20. (250, 252)

———. 1955. Activity Patterns of Post Parental Couples and Their Relationship to Family Continuity. *Marriage and Family Living* 27: 338–41. (250)

———. 1959. The Isolated Nuclear Family: Fact or Fiction. *Social Problems* 6:338. (250)

———. 1960. Intergenerational Family Relationships and Social Role Changes in Middle Age. *Journal of Gerontology* 15:71–75. (250)

———. 1962. Parental Aid to Married Children: Implications for Family Functioning. *Marriage and Family Living* 24, November. (251)

———. 1964. Use of Longitudinal Designs in Studies of Long-term Illness, Some Advantages and Limitations. *Gerontologist* 4:25–29. (564)

———. 1965. Relationships of Adult Children with Their Parents in the United States. In Shanas and Streib 1965. (296, 298)

Sussman, Marvin B., ed. 1963. *Sourcebook in*

Marriage and the Family, 2d ed. New York: Houghton Mifflin Co. (6)

Sussman, Marvin B., and Burchinal, Lee. 1962. Kin Family Network: Unheralded Structure in Current Conceptualizations of Family Functioning. Appears in this book as Chapter 26.

Sussman, Marvin B., and White, R. Clyde 1959. *Hough: A Study of Social Life and Change.* Cleveland: Western Reserve University Press. (252)

Sward, K. 1945. Age and Mental Ability in Superior Men. *American Journal of Psychology* 58:443–70. (126)

Swenson, C. 1957. Empirical Evaluation of Human Figure Drawings. *Psychological Bulletin* 54:431–66. (510)

Swenson, Wendell M. 1961. Attitudes toward Death in an Aged Population. *Journal of Gerontology* 16:49–52. (505)

Taietz, Philip, and Larson, Olaf F. 1956. Social Participation and Old Age. *Rural Sociology* 21:229–38. (501)

———. No date. "Social Integration of the Older Person in the Rural Community." Unpublished manuscript, Ithaca, N.Y.: Department of Rural Sociology, Cornell University. (44)

Talmon-Garber, Yonina. 1956. The Family in Collective Settlements. *Transactions of the Third World Congress of Sociology.* Amsterdam: International Sociological Association 4: 116–26. (464)

———. 1957. Occupational Placement of the Second Generation. *Megamoth* 8. 369–92. In Hebrew. (461)

———. 1958. Social Structure and Family Size. *Human Relations* 12:121–46. (461, 462)

———. 1959. "Sex-role Differentiation in an Equalitarian Society." Mimeographed. (467)

———. 1961. Aging in Israel, a Planned Society. Appears in this book as Chapter 51.

———. 1963. "Dimensions of Disengagement: Aging in Collective Settlements." Unpublished paper read at the International Gerontological Research Seminar, Markaryd, Sweden. (188)

Tamplin, A. R. 1959. Quantitative Aspects of the Relationship of Biological Measurements to Aging Processes. *Journal of Gerontology* 14:134–55. (547)

Taves, Marvin J., and Hansen, G. D. 1963. Seventeen Hundred Elderly Citizens. In *Aging in Minnesota*, edited by Arnold M. Rose. Minneapolis: University of Minnesota Press. (499)

Terman, L. M., and Miles, C. C. 1936. *Sex and Personality: Studies in Masculinity and Femininity.* New York: McGraw-Hill Book Co., Inc. (552)

Theisen, S. P. 1962. "A Social Survey of Aged Catholics in the Deanery of Fort Wayne, Indiana." Ph.D. dissertation, University of Notre Dame. (501)

Thompson, Prescott W. 1966. Personal communication. (400)

Thompson, Prescott W., and Chen, Ronald. 1966. Experiences with Older Psychiatric Patients and Spouses Together in a Residential Treatment Setting. *Bulletin of the Menninger Clinic* 30:23–31. (400)

Thompson, Wayne E., and Streib, Gordon F. 1958. Situational Determinants: Health and Economic Deprivation in Retirement. *Journal of Social Issues* 14:18–34. (43, 401)

Thurston, Elsie.. 1941. Grandparents in the Three Generation Home: A Study of Their Influence in Children. *Smith College Studies in Social Work* 12:172–73. (280)

Thurstone, L. L. 1947. *Multiple Factor Analysis.* Chicago: University of Chicago Press. (484)

Tibbitts, Clark 1953. Retirement Problems in American Society. *American Journal of Sociology* 59:301. (463)

———. 1961. A Regional Approach to Social Gerontology. In *Aging, A Regional Appraisal*, edited by Carter A. Asterbind. Gainesville, Fla.: Institute of Gerontology Series, 10. (45)

Tibbitts, Clark, ed. 1960. *Handbook of Social Gerontology.* Chicago: University of Chicago Press. (358, 360, 543)

Tilgher, Adriano. 1962. Work through the Ages. In Nosow and Form, 1962. (359, 360)

Tilton, J. W. 1949. A Measure of Improvement in American Education over a Twenty-five-year Period. *School Sociology* 69:25–26. (555)

Tobin, Sheldon S., and Neugarten, Bernice L. 1961. Life Satisfaction and Social Interaction in the Aging. *Journal of Gerontology* 16:344–46. (123)

Toch, Hans. 1953. Attitudes of the "fifty plus" Age Group; Preliminary Considerations toward a Longitudinal Study. *Public Opinion Quarterly* 17:391–94. (501, 554)

Townsend, Peter. 1957. *The Family Life of Old People.* New York: Free Press of Glencoe. A selection appears in this book as Chapter 46. (44, 220, 252, 280, 298, 465, 467)

Treanton, Jean R. 1961. Symposium: Death Attitudes. In "Comments," *Journal of Gerontology* 16:63. (505)

Tryon, Robert C. 1955. *Identification of Social Areas by Cluster Analysis.* Berkeley: University of California Press. (225)

Tuckman, Jacob, and Lorge, Irving 1952. The Best Years in Life: A Study in Ranking. *Journal of Psychology* 34:137–49. (126)

———. 1953. When Does Old Age Begin and a Worker Become Old? *Journal of Gerontology* 8:483–88. (39)

United Nations. 1961. *Demographic Yearbook, 1961*, 13th ed. New York: Department of Economic and Social Affairs. (531)

United States, 87th Congress. 1961. Health and Economic Conditions of the American Aged.

Committee Print of the Special Committee of Aging, United States Senate, 1st Session. Washington, D.C.: U.S. Gov. Printing Office. (38)

U.S. Public Health Service. 1959. *Menopause Health Information Series*, Publication no. 179. Washington, D.C.: U.S. Gov. Printing Office. (196)

Van Gennep, Arnold. 1908. *The Rites of Passage.* Chicago: The University of Chicago Press, 1960. (22, 536)

Veroff, J.; Atkinson, J. W.; Feld, Sheila; and Gurin, G. 1962. Dimensions of Subjective Adjustment. *Journal of Abnormal and Social Psychology* 64: 192–205. (119, 125)

Videbeck, R., and Knox, Alan B. 1965. Alternative Participatory Responses to Aging. In Rose and Peterson 1965. (186)

Volkart, Edmund. 1957. Bereavement and Mental Health. In *Explorations in Social Psychiatry,* edited by Alexander H. Leighton, John A. Clausen, and Robert N. Wilson. New York: Basic Books, Inc. (538)

Von Hentig, Hans 1946. The Social Function of the Grandmother. *Social Forces* 24:389–92. (280)

von Mering, O. 1966. "Growing Old the Outpatient Way." Paper read at meeting of Society for Applied Anthropology, Milwaukee, May 6, 1966. (434)

Wahlke, John C.; Heinz, Eulau; Buchanan, William; and Ferguson, Leroy C. 1962. *The Legislative System.* New York: John Wiley & Sons, Inc. (17)

Walker, Helen M. and Lev, J. 1953. *Statistical Inference.* New York: Holt, Rinehart & Winston, Inc. (484)

Walker, K. and Strauss, E. B. 1939. *Sexual Disorders in the Male.* Baltimore: The Williams & Wilkins Co. (275)

Wallach, Michael A., and Kogan, Nathan. 1961. Aspects of Judgment and Decision Making: Interrelationships and Changes with Age. *Behavioral Science* 6:23–36. (127)

Waller, Willard W., and Hill, Reuben 1951. *The Family: A Dynamic Interpretation.* New York: Dryden Press, 1951. (258)

Warner, W. Lloyd. 1958. *A Black Civilization: A Social Study of an Australian Tribe,* rev. ed. New York: Harper & Row Publishers, Inc.; 1st ed. 1937. (433)

———. 1959. *The Living and the Dead.* New Haven: Yale University Press. (536)

Warner, W. Lloyd, and Abegglen, James C. 1955. *Occupational Mobility in American Business and Industry, 1928–1952.* Minneapolis: University of Minnesota Press. (14, 323)

Warner, W. Lloyd and Lunt, Paul S. 1941. The Social Life in a Modern Community. New Haven, Conn.: Yale University Press. (248)

Warren, R. L. 1952. Old Age in a Rural Township. In *Old Age Is No Barrier,* Albany, N.Y.: N.Y. State Joint Legislative Committee on Problems of Aging. (499)

Webber, Howard. 1963. Games. *The New Yorker,* March 30. Appears in this book as Chapter 47.

Wechsler, D. 1939. *The Measurement of Adult Intelligence,* 1st ed. Baltimore: Williams & Wilkins Co. (554)

———. 1944. *The Measurement of Adult Intelligence,* 2d ed. *Ibid.* (482, 558, 560)

———. 1955. *Manual for the Wechsler Adult Intelligence Scale.* New York: Psychological Corporation. (551, 554)

———. 1956. *Die Messung der Intelligenz Erwachsener.* Stuttgart: Hans Huber. (551)

———. 1958. *The Measurement of and Appraisal of Adult Intelligence,* 4th ed. Baltimore: Williams & Wilkins Co. (554)

Wehr, M. R., and Richards, J. A. 1960. *Physics of the Atom.* Reading, Mass.: Addison-Wesley Pub. Co., Inc. (100)

Weinberg, S. Kirson. 1955. A Sociological Analysis of a Schizophrenic Type. In *Mental Health and Mental Disorder,* edited by Arnold M. Rose. New York: W. W. Norton & Co., Inc. (220)

Weiss, E.; Blin, J. B.; Rolin, H. R.; Fisher, H. K; and Epler, C. R. 1957. Emotional Factors in Coronary Occlusion: Introduction and General Summary. *Archives of Internal Medicine* 99:628. (202)

Welford, A. G. 1951. *Skill and Age.* London: Oxford University Press. (130)

Welford, Alan T. 1963. Social-psychological and Physiological Gerontology—An Experimental Psychologist's Approach. In Williams, Tibbitts and Donahue 1963, vol. 1. (358)

Werner, Martha M.; Perlin, Seymour; Butler, Robert N.; and Pollin, William. 1961. Self-perceived Changes in Community-resident Aged. *Archives of General Psychiatry* 4:501–8. (239, 495)

West, James. 1945. *Plainville, U.S.A.* New York: Columbia University Press. (41)

Wheeler, Stanton 1961. Socialization in Correctional Communities. *American Sociological Review* 26: 697–712. (151)

White House Conference on Aging: The Nation and its Older People. 1961. Washington, D.C.: U.S. Department of Health, Education, and Welfare. (469)

White, R. W. 1963. Ego and Reality in Psychoanalytic Theory. *Psychological Issues* 3:3. (138)

Whittier, J. R., and Williams, D. 1956. The Coincidence and Constancy of Mortality Figures for Aged Psychotic Patients Admitted to State

Hospitals. *Journal of Nervous and Mental Disorders* 124:618–20. (401, 407)

Whyte, W. H. Jr. 1956. *The Organization Man.* Garden City, N.Y.: Doubleday & Co., Inc. (440)

Wilensky, Harold L. 1960. Work, Careers, and Social Integration. *International Social Science Journal* 12:543–60. (321, 323)

———. 1961. Life Cycle, Work Situation, and Participation in Formal Associations. In Kleemeier 1961. (221, 322, 362)

———. August 1961. Orderly Careers and Social Participation: The Impact of Work History on Social Integration in the Middle Mass. Appears in this book as Chapter 35.

Wilensky, Harold L., and Edwards, H. 1959. The Skidder: Ideological Adjustments of Downward Mobile Workers. *American Sociological Review* 24:215–31. (323)

Will, Otto Allen, Jr. 1959. Human Relatedness and the Schizophrenic Reaction. *Psychiatry* 22:205–23. (488)

Williams, H., *et al.* 1942. Studies in Senile and Arteriosclerotic Psychoses. *American Journal of Psychiatry* March, 1942:712–15. (221)

Williams, Richard H., and Loeb, Martin 1956. The Adults' Social Life Space and Successful Aging: Some Suggestons for a Conceptual Framework. Appears in this book as Chapter 41.

Williams, Richard H.; Tibbits, Clark; and Donahue, Wilma. 1963. *Processes of Aging.* 2 vols. New York: Atherton Press.

Williams, Richard H., and Wirths, Claudine. 1963. "Styles of Life and Successful Aging." Unpublished paper read at the International Gerontological Research Seminar, Markaryd, Sweden. (186)

Williams, Robin M. 1951; 2d ed. 1963. *American Society: A Sociological Interpretation.* New York: Alfred A. Knopf. (469)

Wilmott, Peter, and Young, Michael. 1960. *Family and Class in a London Suburb.* London: Routledge and Kegan Paul. (304)

Wirth, Louis. 1938. Urbanism as a Way of Life. *American Journal of Sociology* 44:1–24. (247)

———. 1945. The Problem of Minority Groups. In *The Science of Man in the World Crisis.* New York: Columbia University Press. (35)

Wolfenstein, Martha. 1955. Fun, Morality: An Analysis of Recent American Child-Training Literature. In *Childhood in Contemporary Cultures,* edited by Margaret Mead and Martha Wolfenstein, Chicago: University of Chicago Press. (284)

Wolff, K. 1959 I. Group Psychotherapy with Geriatric Patients in a State Hospital Setting: Results of a Three Year Study. *Group Psychotherapy* 12:218–22. (504)

———. 1959 II. *The Biological, Sociological, and Psychological Aspects of Aging.* Springfield, ill.: Charles C Thomas. (505)

———. 1961. A Co-ordinated Approach to the Geriatric Problem. *Journal of American Geriatric Society* 9:573–580. (499)

Woodworth, Robert S. 1921. *Psychology: A Study of Mental Life.* New York: Henry Holt and Company. (99)

Worchel, P. and Byrne, D. 1964. *Personality Change.* New York: John Wiley & Sons. (138)

Wuarantelli, Enrico L. 1960. A Note on the Protective Function of the Family in Disasters. *Marriage and Family Living* 22:263–264. (252)

Yarrow, Marian Radke 1963. Appraising Environment. In Williams, Tibbitts and Donahue 1963. (217)

Yarrow, Marian R. *et al.* 1963. Social Psychological Characteristics of Old Age. In Birren *et al.* 1963.

Yi-Chuang Lu 1952. Marital Roles and Marital Adjustments. *Sociology and Social Research* 36:365–68. (259)

Youmans, E. G. 1963. Aging Patterns in a Rural and an Urban Area of Kentucky. *University of Kentucky Agriculture Experimental Station Bulletin* 681:45. (500)

Young, Michael, and Willmott, Peter. 1957. *Kinship and Family in East London.* New York: Free Press of Glencoe. (252, 298)

Zawadski, B., and Lazarsfeld, P. 1935. The Psychological Consequences of Unemployment. *Journal of Social Psychology* 6:224–51. (322)

Zelditch, Morris, Jr. 1962. Some Methodological Problems of Field Studies. *American Journal of Sociology* 67:567–569, 575. (520)